FREE MOVEMENT OF PERSONS IN EUROPE
LEGAL PROBLEMS AND EXPERIENCES

ASSER INSTITUTE COLLOQUIUM ON EUROPEAN LAW
SESSION XXI
1991

T.M.C. ASSER INSTITUUT

THE HAGUE

Free Movement of Persons in Europe

Legal Problems and Experiences

edited by

Henry G. Schermers
University of Leiden

Cees Flinterman
University of Limburg

Alfred E. Kellermann
T.M.C. Asser Instituut

Johan C. van Haersolte
T.M.C. Asser Instituut

Gert-Wim A. van de Meent
Erasmus University Rotterdam

MARTINUS NIJHOFF PUBLISHERS

DORDRECHT/BOSTON/LONDON

T.M.C. Asser Instituut — Institute for Private and Public International Law, International Commercial Arbitration and European Law
22 Alexanderstraat, 2514 JM The Hague, The Netherlands — tel. (0)70-3420300 — telex: 34273 asser nl, telefax: (0)70-3420359

Director: C.C.A. Voskuil

The T.M.C. Asser Instituut was founded in 1965 by the Dutch universities offering courses in international law to promote education and research in the fields of law covered by the departments of the Institute: Private International Law, Public International Law, including the Law of International Organisations, Law of the European Communities and International Commercial Arbitration. The Institute discharges this task by the establishment and management of documentation and research projects, in some instances in co-operation with non-Dutch or international organisations, by the dissemination of information deriving therefrom and by publication of monographs and series. In addition, the Institute participates in the editing of the Yearbook Commercial Arbitration and in the editing and publishing of, *inter alia*, the Netherlands International Law Review and the Netherlands Yearbook of International Law.

The Institute provides the nine university law faculties in the Netherlands with a research assistant's post-graduate course in international and European law, and assistance to *Asser College Europe*, a partnership venture with eastern and central European countries which offers a framework for the organisation and implementation of research and educational projects.

Library of Congress Cataloging-in-Publication Data

Free movement of persons in Europe : legal problems and experiences /
    edited by Henry G. Schermers . . . [et al.].
        p. cm.
    At head of title: T.M.C. Asser Instituut, The Hague.
    Papers from the Asser Institute Colloquium on European Law,
Session XXI, 1991.
    Includes index.
    ISBN 0-7923-1479-4 (acid-free paper)
    1. Freedom of movement--Europe--Congresses.   I. Schermers, Henry
G.   II. T.M.C. Asser Instituut.   III. Asser Instituut Colloquium
Europees Recht (21st : 1991 : Hague, Netherlands)
KJC5171. A8   1991
342. 73'082--dc20
[347. 30282]   92-34731

Linguistic editing by Eugene D. Cross, St. Louis/Leiden.

ISBN 0-7923-1479-4

Published by Martinus Nijhoff Publishers, P.O.Box 163, 3300 AD Dordrecht, The Netherlands. Kluwer Academic Publishers incorporates the publishing programmes of Martinus Nijhoff Publishers.

Distributors
_____

for the United States and Canada: Kluwer Academic Publishers, 101 Philip Drive, Norwell, MA 02061, U.S.A.
for all other countries: Kluwer Academic Publishers Group, P.O.Box 322, 3300 AH Dordrecht, The Netherlands.

V

FOREWORD

The present collection of studies on the free movement of persons is the result of a Conference organized in 1991 to celebrate the 25th anniversary of the T.M.C. Asser Instituut at The Hague.

Apart from being highly topical, the subject selected for the Conference has an additional quality which made it particularly suitable for the occasion: it covers a wide range of legal issues relevant to the areas of both European and international law on which a large section of the Institute's research, documentation and training programmes are focused. Moreover, it allowed us to include among those who prepared the studies and those who were invited to join in the discussions, a broad selection of the legal scholars and practitioners with whom, through the years, the T.M.C. Asser Instituut has developed most valuable and close ties.

There was yet another feature which emerged very clearly in the Conference and is so well reflected in the present publication: the cooperation between the nine Dutch Law Faculties, which, since its foundation, has supported the Institute and which in the Netherlands has so uniquely served to enhance the conditions for advanced training and academic research in international and European law. To that feature, more than to anything else, the festive celebration of our 25th anniversary was dedicated.

It is a privilege to introduce this publication and to express our sincere gratitude to all those, including the members of the editorial board, who contributed to it with such scholarly expertise and dedication.

C.C.A. Voskuil

The Hague, January 1993

ACKNOWLEDGEMENTS

The T.M.C. Asser Instituut gratefully acknowledges the generous support it received in the organization and/or financing of the Colloquium on 'Free Movement of Persons in Europe', 12-13 September 1991 in The Hague, from the following Institutions:

EUROPEAN CULTURAL FOUNDATION
FONDATION EUROPÉENNE DE LA CULTURE

The Ministry of Justice of The Netherlands
The Hague

Justitie

The Municipality of The Hague

The Commission of the European Communities
Brussels

---

advocaten notarissen
Barents & Krans

VIII

TABLE OF CONTENTS

Foreword   V

Acknowledgements   VII

List of Abbreviations   XIII

Introduction   XVII

REPORTS AND COMMENTS

Abolition of Border Controls   3

Abolition of Border Controls
  J.P.H. Donner   5

Abolition of Border Controls, Some comments on Mr. Donner's paper
  A. Fortescue   27

Benelux Experiences in the Abolition of Border Controls
  E.D.J. Kruijtbosch   31

Schengen Information System, Privacy and Legal Protection   41

The Schengen Information System: Privacy and Legal Protection
  B. Schattenberg   43

Data Exchange, Privacy and Legal Protection; Especially regarding aliens
  P. Boeles   52

**Cooperation in the Field of Criminal Law, Police and Other Law
Enforcement Agencies**   59

Cooperation on Law Enforcement, Criminal Justice and Legislation
in Europe; Nordic experience
  H. Fode   61

Cooperation in the Field of Criminal Law, Police and Other Law
Enforcement Agencies
    J.H. Grosheide   70

The 'Communitization' of Police Cooperation in Western Europe
    C.J.C.F. Fijnaut   75

Criminal Law and the European Community
    J.J.E. Schutte   93

Cooperation between Fiscal and Customs Authorities   97

The Single Market after 1992 and Customs Cooperation in the EC
    M. Brown   99

Fiscal Barriers on the Free Movement of Persons
    C. Garbarino   115

Cooperation in the Field of Aliens Law   123

Issues and Problems in the Greek Law of Aliens
    Th. Antoniou   125

The Last Frontier: Free Movement of Persons in Greater Europe
The role of the Council of Europe
    F.W. Hondius   154

Fortress Europe and (Extra-Communitarian) Refugees: Cooperation
in Sealing Off the External Borders
    H.U. Jessurun d'Oliveira   166

Cooperation in the Field of Aliens Law; The granting of visas,
passports and asylum and refugee status
    C.D. de Jong   183

Cooperation in the Field of Aliens Law in the United Kingdom
and Ireland
    J.P. Gardner   199

Spanish Viewpoints and Problems with the Schengen Agreement,
Free Movement of Persons and Aliens Law
    I. Lirola Delgado   216

Cooperation in Aliens Law: The Implications for Individual Rights
Enforcement
    Chr. Vincenzi   227

Human Rights and Free Movement of Persons   233

Human Rights and Free Movement of Persons: The Role of the European
Commission and Court of Human Rights
    H.G. Schermers   235

Thou Shalt Not Oppress a Stranger (Ex. 23:9): On the Judicial Protection
of the Human Rights of Non-EC Nationals - A critique
    J.H.H. Weiler   248

Applying the Common Rules on the Free Movement of Persons;
The role of the national judiciary in the light of the jurisprudence of
the European Court of Justice
    A. Arnull and *F.G. Jacobs*   272

The Free Movement of Persons in Europe - The Role of the National
Judiciary
    R. Plender   286

Human Rights and the Free Movement of Persons in Europe
- The role of the national judiciary in the Netherlands
    P. van Dijk and *M. Schreuder-Vlasblom*   298

Free Movement of Persons, Human Rights and Judicial Policy:
Assessment and Prospects - French law and practice
    R. Errera   319

Institutional Problems and Free Movement of Persons   333

Institutional Problems and Free Movement of Persons; The legal and political
framework for cooperation
    J.W. de Zwaan   335

Free Movement of Persons and the Division of Powers between
the Community and Its Member States — Why do it
the intergovernmental way?
    C.W.A. Timmermans   352

Free Movement of Persons — Democratic Control
  J.P. van Iersel   369

Democratic Control without Frontiers? The European parliament and
free movement of persons
  M.M. van den Brink and *R.M.S. Vierhout*   379

Three Questions about Free Movement of Persons and Democracy
in Europe
  C.A. Groenendijk   391

Free Movement of Various Categories of Persons   403

Freedom of Movement and Equal Treatment for Students in Europe:
An Emerging Principle?
  W. van Gerven and *P. van den Bossche*   405

Free Movement of Students, Retired Persons and Other European
Citizens - A difficult legislative process
  H.C. Taschner   427

The Free Movement of Professionals in the European Community
  F. Capelli   437

Free Movement of Legal Persons
  I.G.F. Cath   450

Free Movement of Workers and Freedom to Provide Services
Considerations on the employees of the provider of services with
specific references to France
  A. Desmazières de Séchelles   472

Free Movement of Non-EC Nationals; A review of the case-law of the
Court of Justice
  W. Alexander   485

Free Movement and Integration of Non-EC Nationals and the Logic of
the Internal Market
  T. Hoogenboom   497

General Remarks on the Free Movement of Various Categories of Persons
   M.R. Mok   512

Comments on the Free Movement of Various Categories of Persons
   D. O'Keeffe   515

REPORT OF THE CONFERENCE ON
FREE MOVEMENT OF PERSONS IN EUROPE
12 AND 13 SEPTEMBER 1992   521

DOCUMENTATION

The Schengen Agreement of 14 June 1985   547

The Schengen Convention of 19 June 1990   552

Treaty on European Union   606

Agreement on the European Economic Area   614

INDICES

Table of International Legislation   619

Table of Cases of the Court of Justice of the European Communities   624

General Index   632

List of participants   637

ABBREVIATIONS

AB	Administratiefrechterlijke beslissingen
AB Kort	Administratiefrechterlijke beslissingen Kort
ACP States	Africa-Caribbean-Pacific States
AE	Agence Europe
AJDA	Actualité Juridique Droit Administratif
AJIL	American Journal of International Law
All ER	All England Law Reports
AP	Areios Pagos (Supreme Court of Greece)
Ar.	Recopilación Aranzadi (Spain)
Arm.	Armenopoulos (legal journal of the Greek Council of State)
ASIL	American Society of International Law
Bay. VerwBl	Bayerisches Verwaltungsblatt
Benelux	Belgium, Netherlands and Luxemburg
BOE	Boletín Oficial del Estado (Spain)
Bull. EC	Bulletin of the European Communities
BVerfGE	Entscheidung(en) des Bundesverfassungsgerichtes
BVerwE	Entscheidung(en) des Bundesverwaltungsgerichtes
CAHAR	Ad Hoc Committee of experts on the legal aspects of territorial asylum, refugees and stateless persons
CCC	Customs Cooperation Council
CDCJ	European Committee on Legal Cooperation
CDE	Cahiers de Droit Européen
CDMG	European Committee on Migration
CE	Constitución Española (Spanish Constitution)
CELAD	Comité Européen pour la Lutte Anti-Drogue
CIRC	Circulaire
CMLR	Common Market Law Reports
CML Rev	Common Market Law Review
COM	Commission Document
Com.	Commission Document
Cornell ILJ	Cornell International Law Journal
CRE	Commission for Racial Equality
CSCE	Conference on Security and Cooperation in Europe
CSIS	Central Service Computer on behalf of SIS
D	Dalloz
D & R	Decisions and Reports
DEA	Drug Enforcement Administration
DIKI	Greek legal journal ('The Trial')
DOEV	Die Öffentliche Verwaltung
DR	Decisions and Reports
DVBl	Deutsches Verwaltungsblatt
EAEC	European Atomic Energy Community
EC	European Community
ECHR	European Convention for the Protection of Human Rights and Fundamental Freedoms

ECHR A/B	European Court of Human Rights Series A/B
ECJ	European Court of Justice
ECOFIN	EC Council for Economic and Financial Affairs
ECR	European Court Reports
ECSC	European Coal and Steel Community
EDDD	Epitheorissi Demossiou kai Dioikitikou Dikaiou (Greek legal journal: 'Review of Public and Administrative Law')
EDIU	European Drugs Intelligence Unit
EEC	European Economic Community
EEN	Ephemeris Ellinon Nomikon, Greek legal journal
EKMR	Europäische Kommission für Menschenrechte
EllD	Elleniki Dikaiossyni (Greek legal journal: 'Greek Justice')
ELR	European Law Review
EPC	European Political Cooperation
EPU	European Political Union
ETA	Euskadi Ta Askatasuna (= Baskenland en Vrijheid)
ETS	European Treaty Series
EuGRZ	Europäische Grundrechte Zeitschrift
Europol	Central European Investigation Bureau
GAFI	Groupe d'Action Financière
GATT	General Agreement on Tariffs and Trade
GISTI	Groupe d'Information et de Soutien des Travailleurs Immigrés
Giur.Cost.	Giurisprudenza Costituzionale
Hand. I	Proceedings of the First Chamber of the Dutch parliament
Hand. II	Proceedings of the Second Chamber of the Dutch parliament
HC	House of Commons
HL	House of Lords
HMSO	Her Britannic Majesty's Stationery Office
HR	Hoge Raad der Nederlanden (Supreme Court of the Netherlands)
HRLJ	Human Rights Law Journal
IBW-Heft	Internationales Bildungswesen Heft
ICAO	International Civil Aviation
ICLQ	International and Comparative law Quarterly
IGC	Intergovernmental Conference
ILM	International Legal Materials
ILO	International Labour Organisation
ILRM	Irish Law Reports Monthly
Imm.AR	Immigration Appeal Reports
IR	Irish Report
IRA	Irish Republican Army
IRIRC	International Refugee Integration Resource Center
IRO	International Refugee Organization
Ir.Soc.Eur.L.	Irish Society for European Law
ICLQ	International Comparative Law Quarterly
JCP	Juris-Classeur Périodique
JDI	Journal de droit international (Clunet)
JO	Journal Officiel
JORF	Journal Officiel de la République Française

JZ	Juristenzeitung
KLM	Koninklijke Luchtvaart Maatschappij
LD	Legislative Decree (Greece)
LR	Law Reports
MAG	Mutual Assistance Group
MALP	Mutual Assistance Liaison Point
MLR	Modern Law Review
MoU	Memorandum of Understanding
MP	Member of Parliament
NATO	North Atlantic Treaty Organization
NILR	Netherlands International Law Review
NJ	Nederlandse Jurisprudentie
NJB	Nederlands Juristenblad
NJCM	Nederlands Juristen Comité voor de Mensenrechten (Netherlands Committee of Lawyers for Human Rights)
NJW	Neue Juristische Wochenschrift
NoB	Nomikon Bema
NSIS	Decentralized data files of the SIS countries
NVwvZ	Neue Zeitung für Verwaltungsrecht
OECD	Organisation for Economic Cooperation and Development
OEEC	Organisation for European Economic Cooperation
OJ	Official Journal of the European Communities
Pas.	Pasicrisie
PD	Presidential Decree (Greece)
PIN	Personal Identification Number
QB	Law Reports Queen's Bench Division
RA	Revue Administrative
RCDIP	Revue critique de droit international privé
RD	Real Decreto (Royal Decree, Spain)
RDP	Revue du droit public et de la science politique
Rec.Cons.d'Etat	Recueil des arrets du Conseil d'Etat
RFDA	Revue Française de Droit Administratif
RJF	Revue de Jurisprudence Fiscale
RMC	Revue du marché Commun
RTDE	Revue Trimestrielle de droit européen
RV	Rechtspraak Vreemdelingenrecht
RvdW	Rechtspraak van de Week
SAN	Sentencia de la Audiencia Nacional (Spain)
SEA	Single European Act
SEC	Document of the Secretariat of the Commission of the EC
SEW	Sociaal Economische Wetgeving
SI/S.I.	Statutory Instrument
SIS	Schengen Information System
STAR	Standige Arbeitsgruppe Rauschgift
Stb.	Staatsblad (Netherlands)
StE	Council of State of Greece
STS	Sentencia del Tribunal Supremo (Spain)
ToS	To Syntagma (Greek legal journal: 'The Constitution')
Trb.	Tractatenblad

TREVI	(Groupe de Travail sur) Terrorisme, Radicalisme, Extremisme, Violence
UCLAF	Unité pour la coordination de la lutte anfifraudes
UN	United Nations
UNESCO	United Nations Educational, Social and Cultural Organisation
UNHCR	United Nations High Commissioner for the Refugees
UNTS	United Nations Treaty Series
VAT ·	Value Added Tax
Wiss.R	Wissenschaftsrecht
WLR	Weekly Law Reports
YEL	Yearbook of European Law
ZaöRV	Zeitschrift für ausländisches öffentlichtes Recht und Völkerrecht

INTRODUCTION

One of the many activities of the TMC Asser Instituut is the organization of an annual colloquium on current issues of European Community law. The first Colloquium of this sort took place in 1972. Since then the Colloquia have developed into a regular major event for all those who are interested in or concerned with European Community law, whether it be from an academic or a practitioner's point of view.

The 1991 Colloquium possessed a special character. It was designed to mark the 25th anniversary of the TMC Asser Instituut and the 20th anniversary of the colloquium itself and for that reason a special two-day international conference was held on a subject which is regarded as being of central importance for the realization of one of the objectives of an internal market, to be achieved in 1992: the free movement of persons within Europe.

For the benefit of the participants in the Colloquium a Reader was produced containing relevant texts relating to the freedom of movement of persons, such as the Schengen Agreement of 1985, the Convention of 19 June 1990 applying the 1985 Schengen Agreement, the Geneva Convention on the Status of Refugees (1951) as amended by the New York Protocol of 1967, Articles 3c, 8a, 48-66, 100a of the EEC Treaty and various other international agreements. This Reader facilitated an in-depth discussion of the various aspects of the concept of freedom of movement of persons within Europe.

The Colloquium took place on 12-13 September 1991. Since then a number of important developments have taken place which will be briefly noted here.

On 22 October 1991 the European Economic Community, its Member States and the Member States of the EFTA (Iceland, Norway, Sweden, Finland, Switzerland, Austria and Liechtenstein) concluded an agreement on the European Economic Area (the 'EEA'). The EFTA States have agreed to adopt the existing regulatory framework of the EC concerning freedom of movement. According to the Agreement of 22 October 1991 the freedom of movement of persons should in principle be implemented on 1 January 1993. On 14 December 1991 the Court of Justice of the EC delivered an opinion (Opinion 1/91) on the Agreement. The twelve Member States of the EC subsequently signed the Agreement on 2 May 1992 in Oporto. The European Parliament assented to this Agreement on 28 October 1992.

Another most significant development was the adoption by the European Council in Maastricht in December 1991 of the Treaty on the European Union. This Treaty was signed by the Member States of the EC on 17 February 1992. Various articles of this Treaty refer to matters discussed at the Colloquium, among others the citizenship of the Union (articles 8-8e) and measures concerning the entry and movement of persons within the internal market (article 3d et seq.). For that reason it was deemed useful to include the relevant articles of the 'Treaty of Maastricht' in the Documentation section of this book.

Both the Agreement on the EEA and the Maastricht Treaty on the European Union are still subject to ratification by the Member States of the EC. This might still take a long time in light of the majority no-vote in the referendum which was held in Denmark in June 1992 and the no-vote in the referendum which was held in Switserland in December 1992. It is nevertheless clear that the Maastricht Treaty on the European Union and the Agreement on the EEA will have an impact on the freedom of movement of persons within Europe. The inclusion of the texts of these international agreements may, therefore, contribute to a better understanding of the future development of the free movement of persons witin Europe.

It is also of interest to note that in May 1992 the Commission of the EC in a Communication to the Council and Parliament[1] gave an extensive interpretation of Article 8A of the Treaty. The phrase 'free movement of persons' refers to all persons, whether or not they are economically active and irrespective of nationality. The Commission considered that the internal market could not operate under conditions equivalent to those in a national market if the movement of individuals within this market were hindered by controls at the internal frontiers.

The Reports and Comments in the present book have been written by experts from various Member States of the EC. The Reports and Comments together present a comprehensive survey of the various aspects of the freedom of movement of persons within Europe. The first section is devoted to the abolition of border controls, which is so essential in the creation of an internal market and eventually of a political union. The next item is the Schengen Information System and its implications for the protection of privacy. The freedom of movement has important consequences also for the issues of law enforcement: these are discussed in the section on cooperation in the field of criminal law, police and other law enforcement agencies.

The focus then shifts to cooperation between fiscal and customs authorities, followed by various papers on cooperation in the field of aliens law. A special section has been devoted to the issue of human rights and free movement of persons. Institutional problems in this field, such as the division of powers between the Community and its Member States, are discussed in the penultimate section. In the final section of this book the freedom of movement of various categories of persons, such as students,[2] retired persons, legal persons, non-EC nationals and professionals is addressed in a number of papers.

The numerous reports and comments were the basis of a lively, in-depth discussion during the Colloquium. An attempt has been made to summarize these

---

1. Commission Communication to the Council and the Parliament (SEC(92)877 fin.), p. 10.

2. In Case C-295/90 of 7 July 1992 the Court of Justice annulled Council Directive 90/366/EEC of 28 June 1990 on the right of residence for students. The case concerned an action by the European Parliament for annulment of a Council Directive. It was supported by the Commission (Agent, *inter alia*, C.W.A. Timmermans). The action was against the Council of the European Communities which was supported by the Kingdom of the Netherlands (Agent, *inter alia*, J.W. de Zwaan). The view of the European Parliament was not only supported by the Commission (C.W.A. Timmermans), but also by the Advocate-General (F.G. Jacobs) and finally, on 7 July 1992, by the Court. One may perhaps consider this judgment to be a follow-up to the discussion during the Colloquium that it might be Article 7 second paragraph EEC that is the correct legal basis for the Directive on the right of residence for students and not Article 235 EEC.

discussions analytically in the Proceedings of the Conference which follow the sections containing the Reports and Comments. The Proceedings of the Conference certainly do not do justice to all participants in the discussions, but the editors hope that they provide a better understanding of the many, sometimes thorny, questions and issues raised by the authors of the substantive papers in this book.

The Asser Colloquium of 1991 has already had some impact. Papers presented to the Colloquium have been published elsewhere (e.g., European Journal of International Law) or have been used for other publications in this field, such as the Netherlands Reports to the XVth FIDE Conference as well as the General Report of that Conference held in September 1992. Since September 1991 many conferences on the freedom of movement of persons in Europe have been organized during which various aspects of Schengen, the EEA and the Maastricht Treaty have been discussed. From the debates during the 1991 Asser Colloquium and during other conferences that took place one may deduce that there are two principal approaches of the freedom of movement of persons in Europe: a Community approach and an intergovernmental approach. These opposing approaches are clearly visible in the various papers contained in this book. A clear plea for a Community approach was made in a speech given on behalf of Piet Dankert, State Secretary for Foreign Affairs of the Netherlands, during the Colloquium dinner hosted by the TMC Asser Instituut on 12 September 1991. It is fitting to close this Introduction by quoting extensively from that speech:

'The issue of the free movement of persons and the internal borders which it affects can be approached from various angles. One approach is to look at what you lose if those borders are abolished. Another is to look at what you gain.

There are a great many parties with an interest in borders: the judicial authorities, the police, the customs service and even national statisticians. All of them care very much about our borders, no matter how leaky they may already be. The Ministry of Foreign Affairs' interest in the national borders is not quite what it once was; since the Federal Republic of Germany became a member of NATO it is the borders of the NATO area and especially of our neighbour to the East which have been of interest from a security point of view, and even they have become less important since 1989. In economic terms it is the EC borders which are of significance, though we say that we do not find even those borders all that important when we are talking in the context of GATT and UNCTAD, for example. Any meaning still attached to national borders in the economic context will itself diminish further with the Single Market, EMU and EPU. To be brief, it is our contention that our job will be one of moving borders.

The question of the movement of persons is an obstacle in this context and article 8A of the EEC Treaty can be used to remove it.

Unfortunately not all EC Member States share our interpretation of Article 8A. In particular those countries which acceded to the EC for essentially non-political reasons hold the view that EC law can be applied only to EC citizens.

One can see the logic of their argument, but it militates against the free movement of EC citizens, because non-EC citizens, more and more of whom are now travelling within the Community, can be distinguished only by means of identity card or passport checks. The Netherlands has traditionally had few problems with border control. Grotius was in favour of free movement, we have been a transit country for centuries and we have had nothing but good experiences with the Benelux Union. On the latter subject I should perhaps add one observation which could well be relevant in the context of Schengen and the EC: when the Belgian border was opened as a result of the Benelux Union, we believed that the Belgian-French border was less well controlled than the Dutch-German border. Since the Belgians held exactly the opposite view we never really had a problem!

Leaving border control to the Spanish, the Germans or the English is of course a different kind of problem. Madame Cresson, who worked with us on Schengen, responded to our plea for harmonisation of the material aspects of asylum law with the remark that asylum-seekers had better chances of success in France. In terms of the numbers of admissions per 1,000 inhabitants she was certainly not wrong. The Dutch, the Germans, the Danish, the French . . . we all have the best asylum policy, no matter what the figures say. Thus national borders will not disappear with the abolition of internal frontiers. That is the direction we must move in, however.

Does this mean that we are the ayatollahs of the Community approach, as I recently heard us described? I do not think so. If the real significance of a national border can be removed — and thanks to the security situation and the development of the European Community it can — then we must use the opportunity to our advantage. This is what we did in Schengen, in a manner that was acceptable to the various Ministries of Justice. Some compensation for the removal of borders within the EC has been made by shifting border control activities to the external borders, with part of the remaining problems to be dealt with through the Schengen Information System. I still hear mutterings of discontent, however. In essence Schengen dates from before the great "Aufbruch" in Eastern Europe, i.e., from the era of an hermetically-sealed eastern border. I have gained the impression recently that a supplementary agreement concluded this year would have looked very different and that we would have kept internal border controls in addition to the strengthened external ones and the Schengen Information System. From the Community angle I am tempted to say that though negotiations took too long they were, fortunately, concluded just in time.

Because negotiations took so long Schengen could not become what the Benelux Union is — an experimental forum for the free movement of persons that the Single Market will bring in its wake and thus an intergovernmental forerunner to a solution which must eventually be a Community one. Unfortunately it looks as if Article 8A of the Treaty will only be accepted in intergovernmental form and even then it is likely to apply primarily only to the continental part of the EC.

The twelve of us are now negotiating twelve laborious steps towards article 8A. Proceedings so far do not set my mind at rest: it is not only a question of different interpretations of article 8A but also because I am concerned about the "accidents de parcours" which can happen inside or outside a national parliament. After all, because of the method chosen by the Twelve, ratification of a great many treaty texts will be required if Article 8A is to be implemented. Partly on account of the like it or lump it situation in which the parliaments concerned find themselves, obstacles can easily arise. I am also concerned about the complexity of, the lack of coordination among and the relatively limited political — I do not say parliamentary — control over the labyrinth of intergovernmental consultative structures which exist: the ad hoc group on immigration, Trevi, the various EPC working groups and the Groupe d'Assistance Mutuelle. In such a situation it is hard to achieve anything coherent, and even more anything attractive.

This can only be achieved by a closer interpretation of article 8A, something we will have to arrive at during the further revision of the EC Treaty. The barometer readings over the last few months have at least been more favourable in this regard. During the recent European Council in Luxembourg, Chancellor Kohl made a significant first move towards the necessary EPU discussion, though I personally consider his comments to have been somewhat oversimplified.

In the Netherlands it is generally agreed that a number of subjects which are essential for the realisation of article 8A could soon be dealt with on a Community basis. These include visa policy, provisions governing how external border controls are to be organised, the law on circulation and provisions on asylum policy. As far as the latter are concerned, the provisions are not likely to be finalised all that soon, let alone implemented and enforced. Immigration policy might also be communitarised, but, I fear, not by the date mentioned by Chancellor Kohl.

Many of the subjects on the Chancellor's list — political and judicial cooperation, drugs trafficking, terrorism — will remain areas of national competence and thus of intergovernmental cooperation for a long time yet. It will be difficult to keep Community competence in these areas separate — drugs trafficking and terrorism, for example, plus the movement of persons, services and capital, including the problem of money laundering — and to prevent these Community competences from coming into conflict with another.'

This speech by Piet Dankert found wide support during the Conference.

The editors of this book hope that the Reports, which, where necessary, have been up-dated, and Comments discussed at the 1991 TMC Asser Instituut Colloquium will contribute to the realisation of the objective of the freedom of movement of persons within Europe.

December 1992

REPORTS AND COMMENTS

Abolition of Border Controls

ABOLITION OF BORDER CONTROLS

J.P.H. Donner[*]

1.   INTRODUCTION

Why abolish border controls?[1] By the time this Colloquium has been held almost a fifth of the European population will have crossed one or more national frontiers in one of its annual fits of travel mania, called summer holidays. Controls during these border crossings will have undoubtably been perfunctory and caused less trouble and delay than passing a tollbooth on an Italian or French motorway. Much of the thrill of going abroad has been taken away, with children asking for miles on end when they will get to the border. If the Ministers for Cultural Affairs or the tourist boards had their way, bordercontrol posts might even be protected as objects of European cultural heritage and the controls subsidized to restore the feeling of 'doing' Europe for the benefit of American and Japanese tourists.

But then again: why not abolish border controls if nobody takes them seriously? The idea is not new. Controls at several European frontiers have disappeared or been reduced. Most of the smaller sovereign entities in Europe (Andorra, Liechtenstein) have hardly any controls at their borders. The countries of the Nordic Union and the three members of Benelux abolished controls at their mutual borders in the early 1960s, while the Republic of Ireland and the United Kingdom have limited controls at their mutual borders with regard to their own citizens. These precedents prove that the abolition of border controls is not a Trojan horse, which irrevocably commits Member States to progressive integration and a steady loss of sovereignty.

The idea of abolishing border controls at the frontiers between the Member States of the European Communities has been on the agenda since the Tindemans report of 1972.[2] This report proposed abolition as one of the measures to make the Communities more of a reality for its citizens. It initially met with a lukewarm reception, and has not since led to anything more tangible than a uniform border signpost at the frontiers of Member States. The adoption of the realisation of an internal market by the end of 1992 as an aim of the Community has, however, prompted a renewed debate on the subject. This debate also has not yet made much progress. It seems to

---

* Member of the Scientific Council for Government Policy
1. This report only considers border controls on the movement of persons.
2. Report by the Belgian Prime Minister Tindemans to the Conference of heads of state and prime ministers on the further development of the Communities.

H.G. Schermers et al., eds., Free Movement of Persons in Europe

be bogged down in a multitude of technical groups in different fora, each dealing with separate aspects of the problem.

Though the problem of abolishing border controls is a complex one, it is not the only reason for the absence of results. Under the Schengen Convention of 19 June 1990, which implements the Schengen Agreement of 1985, Belgium, Germany, France, Luxembourg and the Netherlands reached agreement on the terms for abolishing border controls at their mutual frontiers. This Convention was subsequently accepted by Italy in December 1990, and by Portugal and Spain in June 1991. The scope and implications of the Schengen Convention for such diverse subjects as immigration, police and judicial cooperation — subjects that so far have been held to fall outside the scope of Community competence — reveals the fundamental issues raised by the discussions on border controls and the free movement of persons, and explains the reluctance on the part of some Member States of the Community to commit themselves to such a course. Abolishing border control is therefore not merely a technical problem.

2.   THE ISSUES RAISED BY THE ABOLITION OF BORDER CONTROLS

At first sight, the problem of abolishing border controls appears to be no different from many other problems which the Community has faced in the past thirty years. Border controls are but an instrument for enforcing compliance with national law, the need for which can be eliminated by harmonizing national legislation. National border controls at the mutual frontiers arguably could be replaced by equivalent controls on the basis of uniform conditions of entry at the external frontiers, thereby affording Member States a protection similar to their former national controls. This solution initially seems satisfactory when one considers that economic and social integration and the resulting intensification of transborder flows of persons have forced most European countries during the past decades to reduce the intensity and efficacy of their controls without any compensation.

However, harmonization of national law in this field raises practical and fundamental issues. The need for border controls erroneously tends to be identified with the enforcement of immigration and customs legislation. Border controls have, however, a more general function with regard to the protection of internal order and the enforcement of national law, not just by ensuring compliance, but as an expression of the power of the State, preventing some persons from entering the national territory and apprehending others who are about to leave. Their operation at the limits of the jurisdictional reach of the State provides a measure of physical protection to the national society, the efficacy of which is enhanced by the fact that a bordercrossing is one of the few situations in which a person is required to identify himself in the absence of any criminal suspicion. Even though border controls and surveillance may be relaxed in practice, their mere existence continues to have a preventive effect. States are unlikely to waive this power of control, unless they can be provided with an equivalent protection with regard to both persons arriving at the external frontiers and those admitted in one of the countries concerned.

Uniform conditions of entry and the harmonization of national legislation in function of which border controls are operated would require the harmonization of immigration laws, criminal laws, the laws of criminal procedure and police and safety legislation. Completion of this harmonization would take the abolition of border controls far into the next century. But even if harmonization were to be practical, it raises fundamental questions with regard to the further course of European integration. The relevant legislation is closely connected with the identity of Member States in such politically sensitive areas as humanitarian relief and the protection of rights, and it affects the performance of national governments in the field of public order and security. Harmonization of legislation in these areas would therefore take the Community beyond the current discussion on its intergovernmental or federal destiny, and would put it on a course towards a centralized European State.

Moreover, harmonization by itself would not be sufficient. The relevant legislation which seeks to protect and order the national society, is, by its very object, inherently national in character. Obstacles resulting from differences in human health and safety requirements can be eliminated through harmonization, because human health is roughly similar from one end of the Community to the other. Such is not the case with regard to the interests protected by border controls. Complete uniformity of national immigration laws, even if it could be achieved, would not alter the fact that if a Member State admits a non-EC national because of a shortage on the national labour market for his skills, such shortage exists in that Member State only. Likewise criminal law is primarily concerned with criminal acts committed on the national territory. Harmonization would not alter the fact, that, with a few exceptions, a person who commits a crime in one Member State cannot be arrested and prosecuted in any of the others for that crime. This situation could only be changed by the transformation of separate national societies into one encompassing social and legal order.

Although abolishing border controls at the internal frontiers requires a certain measure of harmonization (e.g., conditions of entry, visa policy, the level of controls and frontier-surveillance), these jurisdictional problems can only be solved by accepting the idea that national powers of enforcement can be used, both at the external frontiers and within the national territory, in the interest of enforcing foreign law. This idea is not wholly alien to national law. Judicial assistance, extradition and police cooperation are currently practised, but they stand apart from the mainstream of law enforcement practices, and are characterized by heavy controls and procedures as well as a number of national exceptions. The disappearance of border controls requires such cooperation and assistance to become a normal aspect of law enforcement, with a minimum of special procedures and controls. As an efficient exchange of relevant information is an initial requirement for any cooperation in this field, the establishment of an efficient system for the exchange of information with a minimum of formal and practical obstacles, is an essential condition for the abolition of border controls.

The practical improvement of judicial and police cooperation raises another issue. Most European countries are party to one or more bilateral or multilateral agreements and conventions on border controls and to police and judicial cooperation. The establishment of new rules in the framework of the abolition of border controls runs the risk of creating new impediments with regard to the cooperation in these areas with other European countries. By deciding on future police and judicial cooperation Member States are therefore deciding at the same time on the pattern of future relations with other non-participating European States. Either the necessary rules on uniform controls and cooperation have to be inserted into the already existing network of relations with non-participating countries, or the abolition of border controls at the internal frontiers implies a progressive seclusion from the rest of Europe.

Most of these problems and questions relating to the abolition of border controls present themselves in a technical guise. It should, however, be kept in mind that almost all are of a political nature. The abolition of border controls is theoretically possible without any compensation in the form of uniform controls at the external frontiers and with a minimum of police and judicial cooperation. Member States could continue their current policy of steadily decreasing the intensity and effectiveness of their border controls, at the price of a diminished capacity to protect essential public interests (immigration, public order) or at the price of increased controls inside their own territory (which are in general more costly and less efficacious). The introduction of uniform controls and cooperation in the framework of the abolition of border controls is therefore in part compensation for controls that had already lost some or most of their effectiveness in the past. The need to compensate for the abolition of border controls by establishing uniform controls at the external frontiers and by a close cooperation of police and the judiciary, has, on the other hand, its price in limiting the autonomy of each of the countries concerned in a field (law enforcement and public order) that has traditionally been considered as the hard core of national sovereignty, reflecting national values and traditions. This need must therefore be balanced against political demands of national identity and freedom of action of the Member States with regard to their own territory and the situation at their own external frontiers. The balance struck between the competing claims of uniformity and national diversity, between cooperation and national autonomy and between the needs of closer relations between the cooperating countries and their relations with other countries, are ultimately political choices. For this reason it is impossible to present a generally valid blueprint of measures as a necessary corollary to the abolition of border controls. In each individual case, decisions are taken in the light of the specific situation, circumstances and problems, that face the cooperating countries. The problem of abolishing border controls and its solution should therefore be studied in the context of a specific example, even though it may have limited value as a precedent for other countries trying to agree on the abolition of controls at their mutual frontiers.

3.   ABOLITION OF BORDER CONTROLS IN THE FRAMEWORK OF 'SCHENGEN'

3.1   Background

The Schengen Agreement of 1985 between Belgium, France, the Federal Republic of Germany, Luxembourg and the Netherlands grew out of the earlier Saarbrücken Agreement of 1984 between France and the Federal Republic of Germany to abolish controls at their mutual borders. In the Schengen Agreement five EC Member States agreed to abolish controls if a number of subjects, spelled out in the Agreement, could satisfactorily be dealt with in further negotiations. Despite a clear objective, centralized negotiations, and a recognition of the different problems that had to be solved, it nevertheless took almost five years of further discussions to reach agreement on the terms that would enable the Parties to waive the right of control on the movement of persons across their mutual borders. Moreover, the result of that process, namely the Schengen Convention, does not contain all the necessary rules and regulations. On many points the Schengen Convention requires the elaboration of further implementing rules that have to be established by the Committee of Ministers created by the Convention. Finally, in the annexes to the final act of the Convention, the Parties have listed a number of subjects on which negotiations should continue.

Thus the Schengen Agreement and Schengen Convention are not limited to the abolition of border controls at the internal frontiers, but rather, constitute the framework for a further process of harmonization and cooperation. This process has grown in the meantime through the accession of Italy in December 1990 (Italy, like the European Commission, had been an observer to the negotiations on the Schengen Convention) and the accession by Portugal and Spain in June 1991. The approach reflected in the Schengen Convention has gained momentum as an alternative to the abolition of border controls at the internal frontiers in the Community, even though the Schengen Convention has not yet been ratified by any of the original parties to the Schengen Agreement and has run into fierce opposition from the Council of State[3] in the Netherlands.

---

3. The Council of State took the unprecedented step of attempting to dissuade the Netherlands Government from submitting the Schengen Convention to the States-General for its consent. At the same time, however, the Council of State stated that it supposed the Netherlands Government would not follow this advice. (Hand. II, 1990-1991, 22 140 and 22 142).

3.2   The Schengen Convention

3.2.1   *The organisation of the Schengen Convention*

The organization of the content of the Schengen Convention should be seen in the light of one of the major obstacles to reaching an adequate and balanced solution to the many problems posed by the abolition of border controls. This obstacle is the departmental organization of national governments. Responsibility for immigration, police, judicial assistance, criminal law, visa policy and customs is, in most countries, distributed among as many different departmental services and responsible politicians. National bureaucracies have a natural inclination to project these same divisions into the organization of international negotiations, thereby separating aspects that in practice constitute an integrated whole. The negotiations on the Schengen Convention enjoyed a major advantage in that the coordination and final responsibility for the texts was concentrated, at the administrative level, in the hands of a central group of negotiators who were responsible to one group of Ministers and State-Secretaries. This organization stands in marked contrast to the present discussions on the abolition of border controls among the Member States of the Community. It was a decisive factor in bringing about the Schengen Convention as an integrated set of rules and regulations, even though national divisions between immigration services and police are still reflected in the division of subjects between Titles II and III, and in some differences between these titles.[4]

Article 2, paragraph 1, is the central dispositive provision of the Schengen Convention. It establishes the freedom for any person to cross the internal borders of the Parties to the Convention. Except for Title V, which deals with border controls regarding transport and goods, the Convention deals almost exclusively with the consequences of this single paragraph. The main elements of the Convention are as follows: the institution of uniform controls and surveillance at the external frontiers, both in the interest of immigration and public safety and security (Title II, Chapters 2, 3 and 6); the measures with regard to the internal circulation of aliens,[5] in particular with regard to refugees (Title II, Chapters 4, 5 and 7); police cooperation, with special attention to hot pursuit and surreptitions surveillance of persons (Title III, Chapter 1); judicial cooperation and assistance (Title III, Chapters 2 to 5); harmonization and cooperation with regard to narcotic drugs and firearms (Title III, Chapters 6 and 7); the institution of a system of computerized information exchange (Title IV) and the protection of privacy, both with regard to the automated exchange of information exchange and with regard to other forms of information exchange (Title IV, Chapter 3, and Title VI). Finally, Titles VII and VIII contain general procedural and final clauses.

---

4. One can wonder, for example, at the difference between the detailed disposition on the exchange of liaison officers in Article 47 and the summary disposition on the same subject in Article 7.

5. The term 'alien' as used in this report, and as defined in the Schengen Convention, means 'any person other than a national of a Member State of the European Communities.' Convention, Art. 1. The terms 'alien' and 'non-EC national' are used interchangeably, with preference given to the latter.

3.2.2 *Uniformity at the outside*

As a first condition to compensate for the effects of the elimination of border controls at the internal frontiers, the Schengen Convention establishes a uniform level of control and uniform conditions of entry at the external frontiers. The relevant dispositions are conceived on the basis of the principle that the actual and juridical conditions of entry at the external frontiers should be uniform, but that the aim of uniformity should be subordinated to imperative needs of national policy. Thus, a Party can derogate from the uniform conditions of entry (Art. 5, para. 2) and admit, for reasons of international obligation, national interests or humanitarian relief, persons who do not meet these conditions. In addition, the inadmissibility of an alien national in one Member State does not permanently prevent his admission to residence in one of the others (Art. 25). Similarly, the uniform criteria for control and surveillance at the external frontiers (Art. 6) allow for a temporary shift in priorities (Art. 6, para. 2, sub e), and the principles of a uniform visa policy allow for the possibility of a departure from the common visa requirements in exceptional circumstances. Although the effects of deviations from the rule of uniformity do not bind the other Parties,[6] they will not be immune from some consequences, owing to the lack of controls at the internal frontiers.

With regard to aliens who envisage a short stay (less than three months) the Convention does not grant a right of entry if the conditions of entry are met. Parties have a discretion to admit them. Holders of residence permits, return visas (Art. 5, para. 3) or visas for a stay longer than three months (Art. 18), on the other hand, have a right to enter unless they appear on a national list of inadmissibles. Some commentaries on the Schengen Convention have objected that the conditions of entry are but the sum of national conditions.[7] It is correct that the uniform conditions of entry apply only to aliens entering for a short stay (up to three months). This corresponds with the distinction made in most continental immigration laws between the admission of aliens entering for a stay of less than three months and a longer stay. Admission for a short visit is dependent on the visitor meeting a set of legal requirements; a visitor entering for a longer period has to obtain a residence permit before entry.[8] Because of this difference border controls with regard to persons entering for a visit of more than three months can be limited to a check on their holding a residence permit issued by one of the Parties, while the conditions for issuing these permits need not be harmonized. On the other hand, the legal require-

---

6. Thus the admission of a person who does not meet the conditions of entry is limited to the admitting State: Art. 5, para. 2, and deviations from the uniform visa policy should be decided with an eye to the interests of other parties: Art. 9, para. 2.

7. See Prof. Dr H. Meyers, 'Schengen: Inleiding' in the issue of the 66 NJB (1991) pp. 161-164, which is devoted entirely to the Schengen Convention.

8. English and Irish immigration law differs in this respect, in that it requires all aliens to apply for a residence permit, which is granted at the frontier in the case of persons visiting the country for a period less than six months. The fact that residence permits are issued at the frontier in these countries, requires a continuation of controls at all ports of entry.

ments for the admission of persons entering for a short visit have to be harmonized in order to achieve uniformity.

On one point uniformity cannot be achieved, i.e., the condition that a person should not constitute a danger to public safety and security of any of the Parties. As has been argued in the preceding paragraph, uniformity on this account can not be obtained, due to the national character of the concept of public safety and security itself; even a uniform definition would not achieve uniformity. The difficulty in applying this condition is solved to a large extent by the establishment of a common list of inadmissible persons, to whom entry has to be refused. Persons can only be added to this list if they have been declared inadmissible by one of the Parties in accordance with its national law (Art. 96). It could be argued that this process constitutes an addition of national criteria, but that is inevitable. The common list of inadmissable persons is part of the Schengen Information System, and will be available at all border control posts and to visa authorities (Art. 101, para. 2). But even if the name of a person is not included on the common list, he nevertheless must be refused admission if it is established that he will endanger public order and security in one of the other Schengen countries. In other words, if he plans some act of violence elsewhere (which would not constitute a danger to the public order of the admitting country) then the border authorities must refuse entry. The border authorities will, however, apply their own national concept of public order and security, even though the relevant facts fall outside their national jurisdiction.

Because visa requirements are now one of the main instruments of border control, their uniformity is essential at the external frontiers. Differences in visa policy could easily lead to a diversion of the flow of travellers to countries with the least rigorous requirements. Article 9, paragraph 1, establishes the principle of a common policy with regard to aliens and especially with regard to visas. The use of the term 'common' instead of 'uniform' indicates that complete uniformity is not required. In fact the mechanism provided for in Article 9, paragraph 2, parts from the assumption that uniformity will not be achieved at the outset, but will only be brought about by funnelling national policies into a common policy. Once the Schengen countries have agreed on a common policy towards a third country (which can either be a decision to establish a visa requirement or to grant visa freedom), it can only be amended by common agreement, except in extraordinary situations (Art. 9).[9] It should be noted that the Schengen Convention does not require decisions on visa policy to be taken by the Committee of Ministers, but instead refers to consultations among the Parties, which allows for decisions to be taken in the framework of the Council of the Community. The Schengen countries will also adopt a common visa that will be valid for all of them, unless its validity is expressly limited; awaiting this common visa they will mutually recognize their national visas (Art. 10). Both the recognition of national visas in the interim period and the common

---

9. At the time of signature of the Convention such a decision had been taken with regard to some 140 countries. The provision in Art. 9, para. 2, with respect to the retroactive effect of the common visa list, avoids the risk of a growing divergence during the period of ratification of the Convention.

visa, relieve non-EC nationals from the burden of obtaining a visa in each country they visit. Although the term 'common visa' suggests an international kind of decision, it will be no more than a common form, while the decision to grant it remains a national one, which has to be taken by the authorities of the country of primary destination (Art. 12, para. 2).

Most of these elements of the Schengen Convention can also be found in the Benelux Convention. There are, however, some novelties. A major one is the definition of the external frontiers. In excluding flights and ferry-services[10] between two or more Schengen countries from border controls at the port of destination, the Schengen Convention differs from both the Benelux and Nordic Union schemes. This definition of the external frontiers implies that persons who change at an airport from an international flight to an internal Schengen-flight, will have to be controlled at that airport, but will then be able to fly to any other Schengen country without further controls.

The provisions on a uniform treatment of carriers and on aiding illegal entry and residence (Arts. 26 and 27) are another novelty. Both are a response to the modern phenomenon of the commercial organisation and exploitation of illegal entry on a massive scale.

3.2.3   *Freedom of circulation*

The agreement grants an alien, once he has been admitted in accordance with the conditions of entry, the right to move freely within the territories of the Schengen countries for a period up to three months (Arts. 19 and 20) provided that he continues to fulfil the conditions of entry. His visa will, in principle, be valid for all the Schengen countries although he can be required to declare his entry, either at the border or with local authorities (Art. 22). For obvious reasons this right does not apply to persons who are admitted on the basis of the exception clause of Article 5, paragraph 2, or who hold a visa with a limited validity. The absence of controls at the internal frontiers could, of course, tempt some aliens to disregard this restriction, but they would then risk immediate expulsion to a third country if they are found in any of the other Schengen countries (Art. 23, para. 1). In order to limit the risks of illegal residence, aliens who no longer meet the conditions of entry are to be expelled directly to a third country, unless they are granted residence (para. 3) or unless it has been otherwise agreed with another Schengen country (para. 4). As this obligation could lead to disproportionate costs of expulsion for some countries, Article 24 envisages the possibility of a reimbursement by the others.

Aliens holding a residence permit in one of the Schengen countries also have the same right of free movement discussed above, except in those countries where their name appears on a national list of inadmissible aliens (Art. 21). This right to free

---

10. The exception of ferry services has value only with respect to future accessions to the Convention, because only one regular ferry service between the original Schengen countries (between the island of Borkum (Germany) and the port of Delfzijl (The Netherlands)).

movement can also be applied to asylum applicants if they are granted a temporary residence permit or a return visa (Art. 21, para. 2). None of these persons needs a visa for the other Schengen countries and if they are found to be illegally in another Schengen country, they have to be expelled to the country of residence (Art. 24, para. 2). In view of this right, special provision has been made for the situations in which one Schengen country wants to add the name of the holder of a residence permit to the common list of inadmissibles, or in which a country wants to grant a residence permit to a person whose name appears on that list (Art. 25). In these situations the decision not to withdraw or to grant the residence permit, prevails in the end over the decision to put a person on the common list.

3.2.4   *The examination of asylum applications*

One of the most controversial features of the Schengen Convention (at least in the Netherlands) is the chapter concerning the responsibility for the examination of asylum applications (Title II, Chapter 7). The need for some rules on this subject has been felt for some time and is not strictly related to the effects of the abolition of border controls. For years proposals for such rules were discussed in the framework of CAHAR. In 1990 the Member States of the Community signed a convention on the same subject in Dublin;[11] many other European States have since expressed an interest in joining the Dublin Asylum Convention. The increased likelihood, in the absence of controls at the internal frontiers, of asylum applicants being sent from one country to the other on the basis of the argument that they have to introduce their application somewhere else, or of the reverse situation of an asylum applicant introducing an application in one country after the other, requires a regulation dealing with such situations in the framework of the abolition of border controls.

The criteria established by the Schengen Convention for the determination of the State responsible for the examination of an asylum application are in accordance with the principles concerning entry and the right to free movement. In combination, these principles imply that a person who does not comply with the conditions of entry can be admitted, but remains the responsibility of the country of entry, unless he holds a visa or a residence permit from one of the other Parties. Likewise the State responsible for the examination is, in the following order, the State that has granted a residence permit, a visa or has admitted the applicant at the external frontier (Art. 30), unless another country has granted asylum to one of his immediate family members (Art. 35). If none of these rules applies, the country where he has introduced his application is responsible. Responsibility for the examination of an application includes the obligation to determine the refugee status of the applicant in accordance with national law and in observance of the Geneva Convention on Refugees, as amended by the New York Protocol of 31 January 1967 (Arts. 29 and 32). The designated State has to readmit the applicant if he is found to be illegally

---

11. Convention of 15 June 1990, determining the State responsible for examining an application for asylum lodged in one of the Member States of the European Communities (Dublin Asylum Convention).

present in one of the other States and has to expel the applicant if he is not admitted to residence (Arts. 33 and 34).

The main objection to these rules is that in the absence of harmonized rules on the recognition of refugees, their application could amount to a contravention of the Geneva Convention. For example, differences in national asylum laws could lead to a situation where an applicant is turned over by one State where he might have been admitted as a refugee to another State where his application will certainly be refused; this could be considered as an indirect 'refoulement' by the first State.[12]

This objection is however unfounded for two reasons. On the one hand, the Schengen Convention explicitly defers to the Geneva Convention; Article 135 stipulates that the Schengen Convention cannot be applied in conflict with the Geneva Convention. On the other hand, the Schengen Convention establishes common rules on asylum law in Article 28, in which the Parties reaffirm their commitment to the application of the Geneva Convention. This commitment implies that no Party will expel an asylum applicant in conflict with the rules of the Geneva Convention. Thus, even in the above example, returning the applicant to another State would not raise a conflict with the Geneva Convention, unless it is assumed that some Parties will nevertheless depart from their obligations under both the Geneva and Schengen Convention. But if such an assumption is valid, no measure of harmonization of asylum law would be able to achieve compatibility with the Geneva Convention; if it has to be assumed that one of the Parties would willingly ignore some of its obligations under international law, it is likely to ignore others as well. Finally, the Schengen Convention agreement does not bind any Party to apply for readmission of an applicant under the rules of responsibility. Article 29, paragraph 4, leaves it up to each country to decide whether to treat an application itself or to ask for readmission in another country.

This is not to deny the existence of differences between the asylum laws of the Parties. However, these differences arise from differences in policy and in the appreciation of circumstances in the country of origin of refugees. In the final act to the Schengen Convention the Parties have agreed to take an inventory of these differences in view of their future harmonization. Moreover, the Parties have bound themselves to mutually inform each other about changes in practice and in law, and to work for a common appreciation of the circumstances in the countries of origin of refugees (Art. 37). In this way, the Schengen Convention provides a basis for the practical harmonization of national asylum practices, which seems to be a more sensible approach than the establishment of further international binding rules that would give rise to new divergences in interpretation under the pressure of increasing flows of refugees.

12. See the advice of the Dutch Council of State, *supra*, n. 3, on the proposal to ratify the Schengen Agreement (Hand. II, 1990-1991, 22 140, bijlage B).

3.2.5   *Police and judicial cooperation and assistance*

It has been stressed that cooperation by police and the judiciary, rather than harmonization should be considered as an essential condition to compensate for the effects of the disappearance of controls at the internal frontiers. As most of these aspects of the Schengen Agreement will be dealt with in the context of other reports, a summary discussion seems to be in order. Yet, these aspects are not a separate side issue in relation to the abolition of border controls; they are one of the main issues to be addressed.

With regard to police cooperation the Schengen Convention establishes three basic principles. (1) cooperation functions within the limits of national police powers; (2) assistance cannot lead to the application of police force; and (3) police cooperation does not replace judicial assistance (Art. 39, para. 1). Within these limitations the substance of police cooperation rests upon the exchange of information, both on request and unrequested, the improvement of communications and the exchange of liaison officers. Information obtained from another country can, however, not be used in court as evidence without the consent of the judicial authorities (Art. 39, para. 2). It may be assumed that even in the absence of such provisions, some exchanges of information will take place. The importance of these provisions, therefore, lies in the fact that they provide a basic set of rules with regard to such exchanges and by regulating both the use that can be made of the information and the protection of privacy, substantially enlarge the scope for the exchange of information.

A specific form of cooperation and information exchange is provided for through the institution of the Schengen Information System. The introduction of information into this system is for purposes of distribution, but at the same time it is also a request for executive assistance. The system consists of a number of separate lists, each with a specific purpose, for which the Schengen Convention spells out the action that has to be taken by the authorities in the other Schengen countries. Thus, the insertion of a name on the list of inadmissibles, implies the obligation, by virtue of Article 5, paragraph 1, to refuse entry to the person concerned. In the same way the insertion of a name on the extradition list implies a request to notify the authorities in the country where the information originated if the person concerned is found to be in one of the other States and to hold him provisionally pending an extradition request (Art. 64 jo. 95).[13] With regard to each list the Schengen Convention specifies its purpose, and the rules concerning the addition or deletion of information, the use that can be made of the information, the measures a receiving country is obliged to take and the rights of persons to whom the data pertain. One major advantage of this system of lists is that it overcomes the normal problems of translation, as each receiver can deduce all the relevant information from the location of the data in the system.

---

13. Art. 95, para. 3, however provides for the possibility that a receiving State indicates that a person cannot be held by its police.

The Schengen Convention provides for two other forms of executive police cooperation, to wit surreptitious surveillance and the 'hot' pursuit of criminals. The necessity to deal with these two forms of cooperation arises from the fact that the disappearance of border controls implies the disappearance of frontier police who can block the road or take over the surveillance or the pursuit. The political sensitivity of permitting police officers to cross borders should be self-evident. It lies at the root of the complicated provisions of both Articles 40 and 41. In fact these Articles contain only the basic rules that apply in these situations and provide for a menu of alternatives from which each country has to choose, leaving it to bilateral agreements to provide for more elaborate cooperation.

With regard to judicial assistance and cooperation, the main thrust of the Schengen Convention is not to introduce an entirely new set of rules, but to harmonize, improve and supplement a number of already existing treaty obligations concerning the mutual relations between the Parties. The techniques used by the Schengen Convention vary. The provisions relating to judicial assistance in criminal matters and to extradition are an addition to existing treaty obligations. In contrast, the provisions relating to the application of the principle of *ne bis in idem* are copied from the relevant text of the Convention between the Member States of the European Communities on double jeopardy[14] of 25 May 1987, which has not yet been ratified by any of the Member States. In most cases the improvements and additions either relate to the scope of the existing treaties (Arts. 49, 50 and 61), to procedural simplifications (Arts. 53 and 65) or to deficiencies that could prove to be a problem with the disappearance of border controls (Art. 68). Thus the need to adopt provisions with regard to the transfer of sentence arises from the fact that the existing treaty does not cover the situation in which a subject of one country escapes prison in another and returns home. The need to agree on the application of the principle of *ne bis in idem* arises on the contrary from the actual situation that a number of German citizens, who have been convicted for drug-related crimes in the Netherlands, remain indefinitely in the Netherlands for fear of being prosecuted a second time in Germany in connection with the same facts.

In most cases the movement of persons across national borders is controlled separately from the flow of goods. This is different with regard to narcotic drugs and firearms, because the illegal importation of both frequently goes by way of individual persons. In both instances existing differences in national policy or legislation could, in combination with the disappearance of border controls, thwart national control policies. For these reasons the Schengen Convention establishes in respect of both fields, in contrast with other areas, certain minimum standards of internal policy and legislation (Title III, Chapters 6 and 7). In relation to drugs the Schengen Convention requires the Parties to adopt the necessary legislation to allow confiscation of all financial profit from illegal drug trafficking (Art. 72) and to allow police-controlled sales of drugs (Art. 73). Furthermore, the Schengen Convention provides for harmonization and cooperation with regard to controls on the legal trade

14. Trb. 1987, No. 167.

and transportation of drugs (Arts. 74 and 75) and with regard to measures against illegal drug trafficking. The provisions concerning firearms must be set against the fact that both Belgium and France have so far refused to ratify the European Convention on firearms[15] or to adopt more restrictive legislation on the sale and possession of certain firearms. The Schengen Convention does not only oblige the Parties to apply the European Convention on firearms in their mutual relations (Art. 91),[16] but attempts a first step towards harmonization of firearms legislation, which, though modest in scope, nevertheless constitutes an improvement on the existing situation.

3.2.6   *The protection of personal data*

Because the application of the Schengen Convention will give rise to an extensive exchange of information, which in many cases will relate to private individuals, the Convention provides specifically for the protection and the proper use of personal data. The relevant provisions are found in three different places. Title VI contains general rules regarding he exchange of personal data. A distinction is made between exchange to or from automated or non-automated personal registers (Arts. 126 and 127, para. 1) and other exchanges of personal data (Art. 127, para. 2). Additional rules are applicable to the exchange of data in the framework of police cooperation (Art. 129). The Schengen Convention does not allow any exchange of personal data, unless the necessary legislation to implement these rules has been adopted and entered into force (Art. 126, para. 2) and unless the control on its application has been organized (Art. 128, para. 1). This condition is of specific significance for Belgium, which still has to introduce national legislation addressing automated treatment of personal data.

In addition to these general rules the Schengen Convention deals separately with the exchange of data concerning refugees (Art. 38) and with regard to the operation of the Schengen Information System (Title IV, Chapter 3). The need for special rules in relation to this information system is obvious. It will consist of identical registers, one in each of the Parties and a central register that will be located in France. Each of the registers will be subject to the law of the country in which it is located, while the central register will be subject to French law. Differences between national legislation could therefore result in differences between the separate registers. To avoid such discrepancies the Schengen Convention provides for a comprehensive set of rules with respect to the different relevant aspects (use, access, deletion, etc.) and to the rights of individuals regarding information that concerns their person. These rules do not replace national law entirely; if the Schengen Convention does not contain specific rules, national law remains applicable (Art.

---

15. European Convention of 28 June 1978, concerning the acquisition and possession of firearms by private citizens.

16. This means that the Parties, i.e., Belgium and France, are not bound to ratify the European Convention on firearms, but only to apply it in their relations with the other Parties.

104). The application of the uniform rules is left to the national judiciary in each of the countries; a judicial decision has to be applied throughout the system, while the country that has supplied incorrect or illegal personal data has to indemnify another country if that country is condemned to pay damages (Art. 116).

The need for special rules in relation to the exchange of personal data on refugees (Art. 38) appears to be have been more of a political nature. In practice there are only small discrepancies between the general rules and these specific rules. As their formulation closely follows the formulations used in Article 15 of the Dublin Asylum Convention, their adoption seems to be inspired more by the wish to avoid even the shadow of a difference with the Dublin Asylum Convention than by any other justification.

3.3   The Schengen Convention and community law

As should be apparent from the preceding paragraph, among others, particular attention has been paid in the Schengen Convention to the way in which it relates to the network of existing treaties and conventions. This careful approach was necessary in order to avoid the introduction of new rules when existing ones are sufficient, but to improve on them when it appears to be required. Special attention has been paid to the relationship with Community law. Article 134 establishes as a general rule that the Schengen Convention can be applied only insofar as it is compatible with Community law. As a further precaution against conflicts with Community Law, the Schengen Convention excludes EC-nationals from the definition of aliens. Finally, the Schengen Convention considers the possible impact of the current negotiations among the Member States on the abolition of border controls. Any such agreements between the Member States are excluded from the requirement of information and consent that is established in Article 136 relating to agreements on border controls that a Party may want to conclude with other countries. Moreover, Article 142 establishes the principle that in the case of agreements between the Member States of the Community relating to subjects that are covered by the Schengen Convention, the adaption to such an agreement must be considered by the Parties and is required if any incompatibilities exist.

4.   ABOLITION OF BORDER CONTROLS IN THE COMMUNITY

4.1   An ambiguous objective

Compared to the development of the Schengen system, the work on the abolition of border controls throughout the Community is in its early infancy. The only tangible result so far has been the adoption of the Dublin Convention on the examination of applications for asylum. In the rules established in the Dublin Asylum Convention, the continued existence of border controls at the internal frontiers is assumed. The lack of results is due in part to a confusion about the aims of the Community in this area, which is further complicated by a question of competence.

The present discussion has been initiated by the Community's adoption of the concept of the internal market: 'an area without internal frontiers in which the free movement of persons, goods, services and capital is ensured in accordance with the provisions of the Treaty.' This concept is less unambiguous than it appears at first sight because of the use of the phrase 'free movement of persons' in addition to the requirement that the internal market has to be realized on the basis of the powers granted by the Treaty. The traditional interpretation that the phrase 'free movement of persons', as used in the original EEC Treaty, applies only to nationals of the Member States, and the lack of an explicit amendment of this interpretation by the Single European Act, both suggest, in the opinion of some Member States, that border controls should be abolished with regard to EC nationals only. This interpretation seems to be strengthened by the conclusions of the European Council of Dublin on the European Political Union, which deals with the free movement of persons in the context of the proposals for an 'EC citizenship'. However, this interpretation is unrealistic; abolishing border controls only for EC nationals is impossible. As long as some categories of persons are subject to full controls, all persons must be subject to some controls, systematic or at random, in order to ascertain whether or not they belong to the privileged categories. If the abolition is meant to apply to EC nationals only (or even to all legal residents of the Community) but not to aliens travelling in the Community, border controls will remain necessary and even EC nationals will have to be controlled from time to time. This situation would hardly differ from the existing one, in which border controls are primarily directed at non-EC nationals and do not really hamper the movement of EC-nationals, given the restrictions Community law imposes in this respect.[17]

Therefore, the question remains as to how to interpret the concepts of the internal market and 'EC citizenship'. These concepts could require either a complete abolition of all border controls with regard to both EC nationals and non-EC nationals, or only a reduction of controls insofar as that would be compatible with the continued control of non-EC nationals. This question has to be answered by the Council of Ministers, as the internal market will be realized by implementing decisions and will not be brought about by the entry into force of a set of Treaty obligations with direct effect, which would allow the Court of Justice to decide the question.

4.2   A question of Community competence

This question on the interpretation of the concept of the internal market coincides with the problem of Community competence with regard to the immigration of non-EC nationals. The Single European Act did not explicitly extend the powers of the Community in this respect. It is true that the Council of Ministers has so far inter-

---

17. Relevant Community directives require the Member States to allow entry to holders of passports. Moreover, the interpretation by the Court of Justice of the notion of rendering and obtaining services covers almost any EC national who has sufficient means of subsistence.

preted the concept of 'free movement of persons' as applying to EC nationals and their dependants. However, assumption that the original Treaty of Rome did not grant any powers with regard to non-EC nationals could be questioned. This latter interpretation is only partially supported by the text of the Treaty. Of the three main Treaty Articles dealing with the free movement of persons only the text of Article 52 is strictly limited to EC nationals. Although Article 59 uses the same formulation in its first paragraph, its second paragraph empowers the Council to extend the applicability to non-EC nationals. Finally, Article 48(2) uses the phrase 'workers of the Member States', which has been interpreted by the Council in Regulation 1612/68 as applying to EC nationals only. Although it is unlikely that the Court of Justice will correct this interpretation, this does not exclude the possibility that the Council will reconsider this interpretation in view of the number of non-EC nationals admitted on the national labour market and the objective of creating a common labour market.

But even if these Treaty provisions dealing with the free movement of persons do not provide for the necessary powers, the Community could avail itself of the power of Article 235, provided that the Council decides that the realization of the objective of Article 8A requires a complete elimination of controls at the internal borders. The adoption of the concept of the internal market as an aim of the Community has broadened the scope of Article 235 to include the necessary powers (as the Council already assumed in Regulation 1612/68 with regard the foreign relatives of EC nationals).

The same logic would apply to the necessary rules concerning police cooperation and judicial assistance, although this would appear to be more controversial.[18] But in this context, as with the immigration of non-EC nationals, the fact that the powers of the Community do not cover criminal law and policy as such, does not prevent the Community from regulating this subject in an ancillary manner in relation to the abolition of border controls[19].

The interpretation of the concept of the internal market with regard to controls of non-EC nationals is therefore essentially a political one. There are however sufficient reasons why the European Commission should not try to force the issue by submitting pertinent proposals to the Council. As will be argued below these reasons favour an initial approach to the issues and problems relating to the abolition of border controls by way of international conventions instead of Community law.

4.3   And other problems

Controversies over the aim of the Community with regard to border controls and over Community competence are not the only existing obstacles. Another major problem is the baffling variety and impressive array of technical working groups and

---

18. See Y. Buruma: 'Het naderend einde van het souvereine strafrecht: een tendens in het zicht van 1992' in *Grensoverschrijdend strafrecht* (Gouda Quint, 1990), p. 31.

19. Cf., Case 68/88 *Commission* v. *Greece* [1989] ECR, p. 2965.

fora among which the discussion of relevant issues has been parcelled out. There are at least four main venues for the discussion: the TREVI sub-group 'Europe 1992' (aspects of police cooperation and police controls at the frontier); the Ad Hoc Group on Immigration (immigration, asylum, alien law and immigration controls); the '*cooperation juridique*' (judicial assistance), and finally the Council of Ministers (directive-proposals on firearms and ammunition and the protection of privacy). This is by no means a complete picture. A whole range of related problems is dealt with in other fora: drug-trafficking, the position and free movement of non-EC nationals resident in the Community (Ministers for Social Affairs), visa policy (European Political Cooperation) and custom controls ('Gam 1992' and Ministers of Finance). To provide some organizational infrastructure and coordination in the work of all these groups, the European Council instituted a group of national coordinators in 1988.[20] This coordination is sorely needed if any satisfactory results are to be obtained. At the border custom controls, security controls and passport controls are integrated. And yet the discussion on each of these aspects takes place in completely unrelated fora that are hardly aware of each others existence.

The geographical situation of Europe and of its separate Member States is another complicating factor. Because of the peninsular nature of Europe only a few Member States will have to shoulder the burdens of control at the external land frontiers. At the same time the southern Member States carry the burden of controlling the Mediterranean approaches to the Community. Moreover, the relevance of free movement of persons with regard to Greece, the United Kingdom and the Republic of Ireland turns on the question whether air and sea-traffic between Member States is to be considered as internal circulation or not. Together these problems imply that even the definition of the external frontiers of the Community is a choice with important financial and political implications. This choice is further complicated by the issue of existing relations of Member States with territories or states outside the Community. In the Schengen Convention the Netherlands and France limited the application of the Convention to their European territories (disregarding their mutual border on the Caribbean island of St. Maarten). This solution is apparently less acceptable to Denmark with regard to the relations between its European territories and Greenland, or to the United Kingdom with regard to its relations with the Crown dependencies. Finally, Denmark is a member of both the Community and of the Nordic Passport Union, which implies that it has to choose between these two unless an seperate agreement resolving the problem is reached between the Community and the Nordic Passport Union.

---

20. In 1989 the coordinators established a list of all the relevant issues and aspects that should be dealt with in respect of the abolition of border controls: the Palma Document.

5.   ABOLITION OF BORDER CONTROLS AND THE DEVELOPMENT
        OF THE COMMUNITY

The abolition of border controls at the mutual borders in the Community is likely to
remain on the political agenda. This is not because of any major economic or social
benefits that can be obtained from their disappearance, but because it involves issues
the Community has to face if it is to develop beyond a framework restricted to
economic cooperation.

5.1.   Immigration

Europe as a whole is faced with an already strong but still increasing immigration
pressure, both from regions just over its eastern and southern frontiers and from
regions further away. Member States have tried to cope with this flow on a national
basis with diminishing returns. At best, Member States can temporarily shift the
burden to some other Member State, but this still leaves the total influx of immigrants into Europe unaffected. The mounting financial and social costs of uncontrolled immigration into Europe require a more effective control over these movements. Member States are faced with a growing population of unemployed immigrants in the inner cities who, because of their illegal status, often cannot apply for
social assistance. In the past year three Member States (Italy, France and Belgium)
have been faced with social unrest and an explosive growth in this population. As
economic and social integration within the Community continues to erode the
effectiveness of controls at the internal frontiers, Member States can no longer hope
to keep themselves apart from such developments, while the embryonic emergence
of a common foreign policy requires an increasing solidarity with Member States
that are faced with a sudden explosive increase of refugees from neighbouring
countries (such as the influx of Albanian refugees in 1990).

    Confronted with these problems, most Member States seem to agree on the need
for stricter and more effective uniform controls at the external frontiers. Since
December 1989 the European Council has repeatedly stressed the importance of
reaching agreement on a convention concerning controls at the external frontiers.
Stricter controls at the external borders of Member States, while necessary, do not
provide a sufficient answer. Member States cannot isolate themselves from neighbouring non-Member States and thereby try to shift the burdens of immigration onto
them. Existing relations with neighbouring States and the obligations of the Geneva
convention on Refugees limit the possibility of restricting controls. Moreover,
Member States, after having denounced travel limitations in eastern Europe for
years, cannot react to their abolition by introducing equally strict controls of their
own.

    Uniform controls at the external frontiers and the integration of immigration
policies will therefore create a need for closer cooperation and coordination with
neighbouring non-Member States. Existing economic and social relations with these
countries, or the need to develop such relations, are incompatible with strict and
effective border controls. The resulting loss of efficacy will therefore have to be

compensated by the coordination of visa policy and border controls and by agreements on readmission to these States. This type of cooperation is both in the interest of the Member States and of these neighbouring countries, as they face the risk of being excluded from easy access to the internal market and from the benefits of a more effective control over immigration. In this light it is hardly surprising that some neighbouring non-Member States have expressed their interest in joining the results of the current discussions among the Member States (the Dublin Convention or even the Schengen Convention). In this way the development towards free movement of persons and the abolition of border controls will require not only extensive regulation of relations between Member States, but also require a more comprehensive ordering of relations between European States generally.

5.2. Social integration of Non-EC nationals

The need to obtain effective control over the flow of new immigrants is one aspect that will push Member States into closer cooperation. The growing discrepancy in the Community between the freedom of movement of EC nationals and of non-EC nationals, is another. At present non-EC nationals legally settled in one of the Member States, are excluded from the benefits of free movement. This exclusion will increasingly prove to be an obstacle to both their social integration and to the proper functioning of the internal market. In order to secure social stability most Member States are now actively pursuing a policy of social integration with regard to non-EC nationals permanently established within their borders. This policy requires the elimination of differences in legal status between nationals and foreigners. At the same time these non-EC nationals are fast becoming second-rate residents of the Community, as the rights and opportunities of EC nationals to free movement and establishment are increasing. Moreover, the internal market will not be able to function properly as long as a substantial and potentially mobile part of the labour force is tied to the territory of one Member State. A first step towards the solution of this aspect of the problem would be the abolition of controls at the internal borders and the concomitant abolition of visa-obligations with regard to non-EC nationals residing in a Member State. In the end the scope of the right of free movement and establishment will probably have to be extended to include all or certain categories of third country nationals residing in the Community. In turn, this will require harmonizing national immigration and asylum policies to prevent Member States with relatively lax immigration policies from becoming clearing-houses for non-EC nationals eager to settle elsewhere in the Community.

In solving the problems Member States presently face with regard to immigration, the abolition of controls at the internal borders and the installation of uniform controls at the external borders are essential first steps towards a more comprehensive solution of which the harmonization of immigration and asylum law will be an element. As most Member States dread the possibility of massive migratory movements resulting from sudden changes in their immigration rules, this harmonization will probably not be achieved by the initial establishment of a set of harmonized rules. The more likely development is a gradual convergence of national policies in the framework of the cooperation required by the abolition of controls at the mutual borders. In the framework of the Community this cooperation will create its own dynamic. Thus the establishment of uniform controls at the external borders will put the burdens of control and surveillance almost exclusively on the shoulders of four or five Member States. In reaction to this increased responsibility, some of them will ask for financial assistance as a condition for their cooperation. Financial burden-sharing could in turn lead to demands from the other Member States for a measure of Community control over the way these border controls are performed. Similarly harmonization of asylum policies will probably engender the need for a common asylum policy and its integrated application, given that disparities that distort the even distribution of burdens will not be generated by fundamental differences in the applicable rules,[21] but by the separate national application of these rules. Thus the abolition of border controls combined with the pressures of immigration and the need to extend the scope of free movement to non-EC nationals, could in the end lead to the executive integration of border controls and application of immigration policy.

5.3   Police cooperation and judicial assistance

The problems of immigration are not the only reason that will keep the abolition of border controls on the political agenda; police cooperation and judicial assistance are an equally important motive. The discussion on the abolition of border controls has been the first occasion for a comprehensive debate on these subjects. The need for such a debate, is however, not limited to the consequences of abolishing border controls. The growing integration of national markets and society within the internal market stands in marked contrast to the predominantly national character of the instruments of enforcement and of criminal law. Member States increasingly find themselves in a situation where European-wide activities and social phenomena can no longer be adequately controlled by police forces and a judiciary operating on a national basis.[22] Even without the specific issue of border controls, Member States would sooner or later find themselves faced with the necessity of integrating their efforts in the area of enforcement. Whether this should be achieved by the harmonization national law and policy or by the creation a distinct and separate system of enforcement is a major constitutional question that still has to be answered.

5.4   Community-law or international cooperation

The importance of the discussion on the abolition of border controls should not be measured by the social and economic benefits of their disappearance at the internal

21. The application by all Member States of the Geneva Convention on Refugees goes a long way to unifying the main rules of asylum law.
22. In this respect, the German request at the recent European Council meeting in Luxembourg for a study on the possibilities of a European police force is significant (see conclusions of the European Council in Luxembourg, June 1991).

frontiers, but by its general relevance for the development of European integration. This argument would seem to reinforce the demand for the formal integration of these discussions into the process of Community decisions and Community law.

It is almost certain that, in the end, Member States will turn to the use of Community law and its advantages; both because of the need for simple procedures and because of the need for uniform interpretation and legal protection. This need for simple procedures instead of multilateral negotiations followed by the ratification of the results by each of the participants is becoming clear already; in the Dublin Convention the application of the exception clause (Art. 18, para. 3) required the acceptance of a procedure of majority voting.

While uniformity of Community law and its pre-emptive effect on national laws may ultimately be an advantage where a uniform application of rules is required, it will, however, prove to be a disadvantage in the short term. In the first stage of integration of these policy areas, there is a need for coordination of national rules and regulations and a general equivalence of national systems rather than the uniform application of rules. As has been argued in respect of national immigration and asylum law, the problems of immigration and social integration of non-EC nationals will probably, by their own dynamic, result in an almost complete unification of law and the transfer of executive power to a common authority, which will probably have to be the Community. But this will have to be the outcome of a process that at the outset has to start with practical cooperation and coordination of national policy in the framework of national law. To adopt rules of Community law at this stage, with regard to a few aspects of immigration and asylum policy only, would result in isolating these aspects from their natural context of national law and in giving their application overriding priority because of the pre-emptive effect of Community law, thereby diminishing effective overall control over these problems.

With regard to police cooperation and criminal law in general, these considerations are of an even more fundamental nature. National legislation on these subjects constitutes a self-contained, organic whole, of which the internal consistency is a fundamental aspect. The introduction of rules of Community law with regard to certain aspects would breach this internal consistency. Moreover the adoption of uniform rules in this area would imply a fundamental decision concerning to the future development of the Community. As has been indicated earlier, one of the major remaining constitutional issues in the Community is the question whether the Community, in respect of criminal law, should proceed towards a unified system or develop along lines similar to those adopted in the United States. As long as this constitutional issue has not been decided, it should not be pre-empted by the incidental adoption of rules of Community law on the abolition of border controls. Neither is it possible to distinguish in the meantime between immigration and police aspects of border controls, integrating the first aspect into Community law and leaving the other to international law, as this would give immigration aspects a pre-emptive effect over police aspects.

ABOLITION OF BORDER CONTROLS
Some comments on Mr Donner's paper

Adrian Fortescue*

1. Anyone who has worked with Mr Donner could be sure that a report by him on a subject which he knows backwards would be rigorous, readable and complete. His report on the 'Abolition of border controls', entirely matches up to expectations, except, curiously, in its title which could more accurately be worded 'Abolition of controls on *people* crossing *internal* frontiers within Europe', since it is clear that the subject which his report addresses is that of internal or common frontiers (hence his long and interesting chapter on the maintenance, indeed the strengthening, of the *external* frontier) and of controls at frontiers on *individuals rather than of traded goods* in the traditional customs and excise sense. The distinction is worth making, because the shorter title can give the impression of much more far reaching aspiration, open to the charge of irresponsibility, not to say anarchy — indeed critics of the enterprise have been known deliberately to blur the distinction precisely in order to create this misleading impression.

2. That small quibble apart, the report is excellent. In particular, its Chapter 3 is as complete and clear account as I have read anywhere of the purpose and content of the Schengen Convention of 1990. As such, it deserves to become a standard work on the subject. I would quarrel with only one detail, which itself is only to be found in a bracket in the second paragraph of page 9 where he mentions the observer status enjoyed by the European Commission and Italy at the Schengen negotiations. This status in each case was very different in form, in timing and in purpose. In the case of Italy (and later of Spain and Portugal) it was with a view to future membership. In the case of the Commission, the status was accorded from the beginning and had a different and very precise purpose, duly achieved as is explained in Chapter 3.3 of the report, of ensuring that the Schengen 'implementation-agreement' would be compatible with current and evolving community law and aspirations.

3. Since it could serve no useful purpose for the commenter simply to endorse and eulogise the wisdom of the rapporteur, I will permit myself the luxury — even the risk — of posing some questions, not about the detail and certainly not about the

---

* Director, Commission of the European Communities.

H.G. Schermers et al., eds., Free Movement of Persons in Europe

legal soundness, but about the general approach underlying Mr Donner's report. My comments should not be seen as criticism except insofar as perfectionism can be open to criticism.

4. In a word, I attach a higher value than he does to the abolition of controls on people at the European Community's internal frontiers as an end in itself and am, therefore, more inclined than he to contemplate, for the sake of advancing toward the objective, what he would regard as less than perfect solutions. The freedom of movement of people is after all a major objective of the Treaty and one of the famous 'four freedoms', arguably the freedom which has the most direct bearing on the lives of individual citizens. Of course, I accept his long-term view that such abolition raises important and interesting questions about such weighty matters as common asylum and immigration policies; about the extension of Community competence into new but important areas; and about the rights of third country nationals. But I see dangers in establishing any linkage between the immediate objective of removing the frontier controls within the European Community on the one hand and the solving of these other long term issues on the other. Such linkage could lead to the conclusion that the infrastructure of internal frontier apparatus needs after all to be maintained a very long time, thus ensuring that there will not be a genuinely frontier-free Europe after 1992.

5. To stimulate reflexion, I would suggest that there are three possible approaches to the frontier issue, in the sense intended in this session. For shorthand's sake, I will call them the 'Donner approach', the 'Yeltsin approach' and the 'Palma approach'. Declaring my interest from the start, I will not conceal from you that my preference goes to the 'Palma approach' — and I am comforted in this by the fact that it is the one to which the European Council committed itself in Madrid in June 1989 and therefore has a certain political momentum behind it.

6. The 'Donner approach' I would characterise as intellectual and legal perfectionism — and therefore inevitably in danger of so overloading the aircraft that it may never be able to take off. As far as some of the legal issues are concerned, Mr Donner's fascinating second section 'The issues raised by the abolition of border controls' is both dazzling and disheartening. As he himself admits, the amount of legislative harmonisation theoretically involved to achieve the level of internal free movement such as the United States enjoy would 'take the abolition of border controls far into the next century.' And, in his powerful intellectual and political honesty, he goes further still and points out that even such a long term prospect would not deal with the problems of relations with Eastern Europe and other immediately neighbouring countries. In other words, for the truly rigorous and exhaustive thinker, it is virtually inconceivable that the conditions will ever, let alone by the end of 1992, be met which would allow people to move freely and unhampered across the frontiers of the European Community which we are attempting to construct. Goods, services and capital, yes. People, no. For all the respect and admiration what I have for Mr Donner's contribution to the European cause, I

wonder whether he would ever have allowed such an incomplete document as the Treaty of Rome to be signed, given how much secondary legislation and even treaty revisions have turned out subsequently to be necessary!

7. At the other extreme I would put what I call, for shorthand's sake and with frankly admitted ignorance about the innermost thoughts of the gentleman in question, the 'Yeltsin approach'. Under this approach, one simply declares a radical and politically exciting objective and announces that this is the way of the future, preferably throwing in a clearly indicated starting date in the not too distant future. For example, one might simply declare that from 1 January 1993 frontier controls of any kind between Member States of the European Community will be illegal. One would leave to the national governments concerned the task of adapting their laws and practices to this accounced reality. This method has its attractions, particularly in the fiscal area and it *might* have the effect of concentrating minds wonderfully. The Danes might look again at their VAT rates; the Germans might wonder whether they could afford to leave untouched there constitutional obligations on asylum; the French might take a fresh view of their visa requirements; the Dutch might wonder whether their particular approach to the narcotics problem really made sense in the new context; the British might have to think hard about whether their traditional certainty that islands are different stood up to examination in the age of the aeroplane. I am not saying that any of them would necessarily change their opinions, but they would know that the application of their existing rules and practices could be less easy in a genuinely frontier-free Community. If no adjustments were made in advance of D-day, they might have to be in somewhat frantic circumstances on D-day plus one. But the likelihood, alas, is that each government in turn would declare the whole enterprise too difficult and irresponsible — and the frontier controls would firmly remain.

8. In between these two extremes lies the 'Palma approach'. If I have a single quarrel with the Donner report, it is the relegation to the footnote on page 22 of what I regard to be the realistic middle way, as worked out after six intensive months of negotiation by the group of coordinators set up by the December 1988 Rhodos European Council. Faced with the bewildering spread of subject matter and fora related in one way or another to frontier control abolition, this group drew up a programme of measures that would need to be adopted if the conditions could be said to have been met for the frontier controls on people to be dismantled. They examined each chapter of measures with great care and divided them into those which should be considered 'essential' (i.e., virtually the *sine qua non* for frontier abolition) and those which should be considered 'desirable' (i.e., valuable objectives in their own right but not preconditions for the removal of frontier controls — a very similar approach to the one underlying the Schengen Convention). With twelve governments and the European Commission represented around the table, I need hardly tell you that agreement was not immediate on which measurers should be put in which category. As always in the Community, compromises were necessary. But the result was a comprehensive and responsible programme which, if completed on

schedule, should make it possible to confront governments with this stark but essential question: since the programme you agreed to be necessary in Madrid is now complete, how can you any longer justify the maintenance of controls at the frontiers between you? The advantage of this approach was and remains that it is not open to the accusation of throwing the baby in at the deep end to see whether it can swim (the 'Yeltsin approach'); nor to the charge that — to adjust the metaphor — by overloading the boat, you ensure that it has no chance of sailing. My quarrel with Mr Donner is that he has done such a thorough job of outthinking the coordinators and pointing out what he perceives to be gaps in their programme, that those who wish to exploit his admirable report will try to argue that the Palma programme was actually not enough and that a whole lot of new preconditions for frontier abolition will have to be added. For me, that could imperil any chance of achieving on time the one freedom of the four listed on the Treaty of Rome which most affects the lives of the Community's citizens — a possible result of his brilliance which, I hope, he never intended when he picked up his pen to write his admirable report.

BENELUX EXPERIENCES IN THE ABOLITION OF BORDER CONTROLS

E.D.J. Kruijtbosch[*]

1.   INTRODUCTION

The various aspects of the economic integration, and limited political integration, of the Benelux Economic Union, like the abolition of border controls for persons, cannot be fully understood without a brief description of its history, its achievements and its decision-making process. Section 2 of this report sketches this broader framework.

Section 3 describes in some detail the Benelux Convention of 1960 which abolished internal border controls and shifted them to the external borders of the Benelux territory.

Section 4 focuses on the Benelux Court of Justice, which has been entrusted with the interpretation of the Benelux common rules of law, the rules of the Benelux Convention, and subsequent protocols or ministerial decisions executing common policy in this field.

Certain problems have arisen in the course of more than thirty years of experience with the execution of the Benelux Convention, problems which will be dealt with briefly in Section 5.

Section 6 makes a rough comparison between the Benelux Convention and the more recent Schengen Convention, which was signed in 1990 by the Governments of the Benelux Economic Union, France and Germany, and subsequently by several other Member States of the European Communities.

Finally, section 7 addresses an important question about the continued need for the Benelux Convention in the light of the Schengen Convention.

2.   BENELUX

In 1944, in the hotel suite 'Patience' at the Savoy in London, the Governments in exile of Belgium, the Netherlands and Luxembourg signed a treaty forming a customs union between the three countries. This treaty came into effect on 1 January 1948 after the adoption of the necessary rules to reflect the damages of World War II

---

[*] Former Secretary-General of the Benelux Economic Union.

H.G. Schermers et al., eds., Free Movement of Persons in Europe
© 1993, T.M.C. Asser Instituut, The Hague.

and the general disruption during the early postwar years. Customs tariffs between the three countries were abolished and a common external tariff was introduced. Most quantitative restrictions were gradually removed in the 1950s. In order to establish free movement of goods within the Benelux territory, a common trade policy took shape through the conclusion of approximately twenty Benelux bilateral trade agreements with third countries. To comply with OEEC[1] liberalisation rules, Benelux presented itself as a unified entity with common liberalisation percentages.

Even though the economic union had not been perfected by 1958 the time was ripe to sign and later ratify a Benelux treaty of economic union, which would guarantee freedom of movement of goods, services, labour and capital. The Benelux Governments, which sought to broaden European economic integration by pushing for the conference of Messina and other conferences which finally led to the Treaty of Rome in 1957, did not want to throw their old shoes away before being certain that the new shoes suited. Their hesitation is reflected in Article 233 of the Treaty of Rome, which provides that the Benelux countries could continue their regional integration. This Treaty provision has remained to the present day as the basis of all kinds of exploratory work by Benelux in the processes of integration. An example is the free movement of persons, the main theme of this report, which was enacted in the Benelux Convention on the free movement of persons of 1960.

The Convention of 1960 is of particular interest because it goes beyond the objectives of an economic union. It can be regarded as a cautious step towards political integration. This is reflected by agreements between the Benelux Governments relating to a common policy towards governments of third countries and their citizens, which is primarily a matter of foreign policy.

With regard to the decision-making process of Benelux, it is worth noting that the governmental administration of the three partners have played a major role. The cautious but continuous effort of civil servants have marked Benelux. Every decision in Benelux is carefully prepared by civil servants who participate in working parties and commissions and polish draft decisions with a view to mitigating the whims of temporary politicians.

Before addressing the other topics of this report, it is useful to draw some general conclusions about the character of Benelux economic integration. These characteristics are:

1. The highest priority has always been given to freedom of movement.
2. The Benelux Governments have accepted the need for a common policy with regard to third countries on the matter of freedom of movement.
3. Harmonisation of policies except where absolutely necessary has been limited to a bare minimum.
4. The Benelux approach has always been pragmatic.
5. The unification of Benelux has never been a goal in itself. The Benelux efforts have always served a broader European ideal; they can be regarded as intermediate

---

1. The Organisation for European Economic Co-operation (OEEC) was the predecessor to the Organisation for Economic Co-operation and Development (OECD).

steps or as experiments which show that something can be done between independent, sovereign nations.

6. Benelux progress has been slow but continuous; not forged by political force, but realized by gentle persuasion at all levels of the society.

3.   FREE MOVEMENT OF PERSONS

The Benelux Convention of 11 April 1960, which abolished internal border controls and shifted them to the external borders of the Benelux territory, came into effect on 1 July 1960, even before the treaty of economic union, which was signed in 1958 and ratified in November 1960. In Benelux history this was a political speed record. It marked the common political desire to proceed with the elimination of burdensome border formalities.[2]

The Benelux Convention is very brief, containing only 18 articles, which describe its main principles, and leave the formulation of more detailed rules to ministerial working parties. The main principles of the Benelux Convention are as follows:

Article 1 provides definitions, including the definition of a ministerial working party. The working parties consist of the competent ministers, such as the ministers of foreign affairs and of justice and, for the Netherlands, the minister of internal affairs. The Committee of Ministers of the Benelux Economic Union, which was the only decision-making power in the Economic Union, delegated its decision-making power from the outset to the ministerial working party with regard to the execution of the Benelux Convention.

Article 2 abolishes the border controls for persons at the internal borders of Benelux.

Article 3 obliges the three countries to pursue a common policy with regard to the entry of aliens.

Article 4 institutes a common visa that allows persons to circulate freely within the Benelux territory.

Article 7 requires aliens to report their presence to the authorities.

Article 12 is an escape clause that allows reintroduction of internal border controls for reasons of public order or national security.

Article 13 provides a very broad mandate to the ministerial working party to execute the Benelux Convention.

Article 15 entrusts a special commission to prepare draft decisions of the ministerial working party and subsequently to execute them.

In 1982 the Benelux Convention was amended for the first and only time. Article 3 was broadened to require harmonization of the national policies which permitted aliens to stay longer than three months. These policies of granting longer stays had

---

2. The complete text of the Benelux Convention and related ministerial decisions are available at the Secretariat-General of the Benelux Economic Union (39, Rue de la Régence, 1000 Brussels).

created problems because the Benelux Convention originally only dealt with permission to enter for a three-month period and not for longer periods.

Ratification of this amendment took longer than expected. Beginning in 1984, attention was focused on the negotiation of the Schengen Agreement, which sought to apply the principle of free movement of persons within the territory of Benelux, France and Germany. In these negotiations, the Benelux Convention served as an example.

Because the Benelux Convention only defined the main principles, and left further detailed regulations to be fixed by the ministerial working party, a number of important decisions were made through the working party process. Between 1960 and 1982, the following subjects were addressed:

1960 : registration of aliens

1961 : rights of working refugees

1967 : removal of persons

1967 : undesirable aliens

1969 : conditions for entry of aliens

1971 : procedure relative to reintroduction of internal border controls

1978 : external border controls

1982 : circulation of aliens replacing a decision of 1967.

On the basis of the Benelux Convention and the above-mentioned ministerial decisions, an instruction manual was developed and maintained for the border officials in order to guarantee uniform application of the existing regulations.

4.   BENELUX COURT OF JUSTICE

The Treaty establishing the Benelux Court of Justice was signed in 1965. The Benelux Court of Justice is designed to ensure uniform and fair interpretation of the common Benelux rules of law. It consists of judges of the highest courts of the three member countries. These judges are designated by the Benelux Committee of Ministers. Its seat is in Brussels. The Benelux Court of Justice has two tasks: to administer justice and to advise on common rules of law upon proper request.

In contrast with the Treaty of Rome, which can be regarded as a treaty, Benelux common rules of law grew steadily in time. Benelux consists not only of a treaty on economic union, but also a very long list of treaties, conventions and protocols signed and usually ratified in the course of time. Therefore, the need arose to state explicitly the common rules of law that the Benelux Court of Justice would be competent to interpret.

In 1969 and 1974, protocols to the Treaty establishing the Benelux Court of Justice were signed and later ratified. These protocols define the common Benelux rules of law for which the Court is competent. The common rules of law of the

Benelux include the Benelux Convention and all subsequent ministerial decisions taken by the ministerial working party for the free movement of persons.[3]
As far as I could discover the Court judged only in one case in 1988, concerning visa policy. It goes without saying, that the Benelux Court dealt with a great number of other cases related to other common Benelux rules of law, for which it is competent. The greatest number of cases are related to the common Benelux legislation on marks and models dating from 1966.

5.   THIRTY YEARS OF EXPERIENCE

Although the drafters of treaties try to anticipate everything, a treaty is always a product of its time and will require adaptation or interpretation by an authority that monitors its execution. The Benelux Convention was well-drafted in this respect. It laid down the general principles and left room for competent authorities (the ministerial working party and the special commission) to execute and adapt the rules to changing circumstances.

The execution of the Benelux Convention has worked well. Freedom of movement has never been halted; the escape clause in Article 12 has never been formally invoked, although one of the partners once threatened to do so. When changes in the common visa policy have been needed, unanimity has always been reached albeit sometimes slowly.

The history of these thirty-plus years of the Benelux Convention can be found in the yearly reports of the three Governments to the Advisory Interparliamentary Benelux Council. This 'Benelux Parliament' was founded by treaty in 1957. It has 49 members (21 + 21 + 7), delegated by the respective parliaments of each member country. The obligatory yearly report of the Governments on the state of the economic union covering a period from 1 July to 30 June of the following year, which is submitted in September or October, forms the basis of a yearly debate. The Benelux Council cannot bind governments, but rather, can only recommend certain policies. Although the members are not satisfied with their current lack of power, they have nevertheless certainly influenced the policies of the Benelux Governments.

Reading through the hundreds of pages of dull reporting[4] one can derive some main lines of development and problems arising in a rapidly changing world. In my view, three periods can be distinguished: (1) the founding and liberalisation period of the 1960s; (2) the period of confrontation with a less friendly and more troublesome world in the 1970s and early 1980s, and (3) the period following the signing of the Schengen Agreement in 1985 to the present.

---

3. The complete list of treaties, conventions, protocols, ministerial decisions and recommendations is published regularly by the registry of the Benelux Court of Justice (39, Rue de la Régence, 1000 Brussels).
4. The reports are available in the office of the Secretary-General of the Council in the Belgian Senate in Brussels.

In the first period the common policy and procedure were laid down. A great number of former colonies became independent and, following the establishment of diplomatic relations, visa arrangements were concluded. The obligation of a visa was abolished with respect to many countries. Because of the rapid economic growth during this period, there was a need for immigrant labour. This, in turn, resulted in liberal admission policies.

The second period featured a recession in economic growth, increased unemployment, budgetary constraints and rising international terrorism and criminality. A more stringent immigration policy was needed. Visa requirements were reintroduced with respect to some countries which featured substantial emigration for economic reasons. This was the case for instance with Turkey and Surinam. For other countries, such as Iran and South Africa, visa requirements were reestablished because of specific political problems.

One major problem that seriously endangered the free movement of persons was a leak in the Southern border between Belgium and France. Many citizens of Surinam, for example, were able to fly to Paris, hire a minibus and cross the Belgian border unnoticed in order to join friends and relatives in the Netherlands. The Dutch Government became nervous and, although not invoking the escape clause of Article 12, reinstalled some internal border controls by making use of a mobile police brigade and increased controls in the trains between Roosendaal and Rotterdam. Finally, in 1983, the Belgian Government decided to re-enforce its controls on the southern border. This enabled the Dutch police slowly to eliminate their internal controls. The common inspection teams reported that the controls at the Southern border were substantially improved. The method of common inspection thereby proved its usefulness.

This period also involved some painful incidents unrelated to immigration from third countries. Some Dutchmen were fined in Belgium because they did not have an identity card, which is obligatory in Belgium. The Netherlands has always been reluctant to reintroduce an obligatory identity card because of reminiscences of the horrors of the German occupation. After 1975 a very cheap identity card was introduced in the Dutch border provinces in order to avoid difficulties in Belgium. However, little use has been made of this card.

Another incident was the arrival of a group of gypsies, who were able to enter the Netherlands from Germany and, after being pursued by Dutch police, tried to escape to Belgium. Belgium police officials stopped them at the border and refused entry because of lack of sufficient means of subsistence (Art. 5). The gypsies stayed there for a few wintery nights as a symbol of the problems connected with a free border. They were finally directed to temporary camping sites in the Netherlands. During this incident I paid a visit to gipsy King Petalo, not having expected this kind of trouble as Secretary-General of an economic union.

After this darker period, in which the Benelux Convention could not be maintained without major difficulties, the economic sky started to clear up and the Benelux Governments thought the time ripe for another important European initiative. European unification had been stagnating and disintegration threatened. Rather, the years of 1984 and 1985 were full of new initiatives: the Agreement of Mitterrand

and Kohl of Saarbrücken, the introduction of the one and only document (Benelux 50) within Benelux substantially to simplify the border controls on goods, the Cockfield report, the Single European Act, and the start of the 'Schengen' negotiations with a Benelux memorandum agreed on 12 December 1984 by the Committee of Ministers and submitted to the Governments of France and Germany.

The Schengen Agreement was negotiated and concluded in four months, from mid-February to mid-June 1985. Its final objective was the complete abolition of border controls on persons, goods and transport.

One of the aims of the agreement was to harmonize the visa policy of the three contracting parties (Benelux, France and Germany). A converging programme was set up. France had the longest list, Germany the shortest and Benelux in between. Benelux acted accordingly and reintroduced visa obligations with regard to some countries.

France and Germany studied very carefully all Benelux acts on free movement of persons, visa policy, freedom of transport, transborder pursuit and other relevant matters to benefit from this experience. The Schengen Convention, officially known as the Convention applying the Schengen Agreement of 14 June 1985, was signed in June 1990 again on the Mosel in the village of Schengen in Luxemburg, very near to the borders of France and Germany.

6.   THE BENELUX CONVENTION OF 1960 AND THE SCHENGEN CONVENTION OF 1990.

It is not my task to describe the Schengen Convention. Other reporters will deal with it in detail. Nevertheless you cannot avoid the temptation, having participated in both, to sketch a rough comparison, the 1960 Benelux Convention being a source of inspiration for the Schengen Convention of 1990.

Without trying to be complete, let me mention a few interesting points.

1. The Benelux Convention is part and parcel of a broader framework, the Benelux Economic Union, with its institutions, general legal framework, and well-known procedures. The Schengen Convention is loose in this respect. It is a separate convention without an institutional link to the European Community and a rather informal link with the secretariat of Benelux, performing up to the present time all administrative, logistic and coordinating tasks. Only three articles of the Schengen Convention out of a total of 142 relate to the Executive Committee, entrusted with the execution of the Convention.

2. The Schengen Convention covers much more than the Benelux Convention. Only Title II of the Schengen Convention, dealing with free movement of persons, external controls, visa policy, etc. is comparable to the Benelux Convention. Title II alone comprises 37 articles compared to a total of 18 for the entire Benelux Convention. Moreover Article 4 of the Benelux Convention regarding a common visa policy is more stringent than Article 9 of the Schengen Convention. In this title 'Schengen', however, deals also with problems relating to a longer stay (more than three months)

and requests for asylum. These 'asylum' articles have given rise already to the present heated public debate.

3. From the outset the Schengen Agreement was aiming at the abolition of all border controls. As the internal market programme of the European Community took shape the focus on other than persons-control lost its importance. Only six articles (Arts. 120-125) deal with goods and transport. The Benelux Convention being part and parcel of the Economic Union depended greatly on the progress made within the Benelux Economic Union with regard to the abolition of border controls on goods and transport.

4. The Schengen Convention deals at length with police and security (Arts. 39 to 91). The Benelux Convention does not address this aspect of free movement. Nevertheless, Benelux was aware of these problems and dealt with them separately. Examples are the Treaty of 1962 regarding extradition and help in penal cases, an arrangement on hot pursuit and the never-ratified convention on arms and munition. In 1960 the computer was still in a stage of infancy. Nobody thought about a computerized information system. In contrast, the Schengen Convention provides for such a system, which will certainly facilitate the effective application of the Convention. This part of the Schengen Convention is entirely different from the Benelux Convention.

5. In my opinion, the greatest difference between the two conventions is the absence from the Schengen Convention of any reference to a court of appeal. Although the Benelux Court of Justice was created five years after the Benelux Convention and only had to deal seriously with one case, it nevertheless remains important as a guarantee for legal security. We all know how important the Court of Justice of the European Communities is in the framework of European integration. In fact, we should not draft a treaty with such significant consequences for private persons without giving some legal security against administrative procedures.

7.   A FINAL QUESTION

During the fifteen years I worked for the Benelux I was often asked the same question: 'Do you still need Benelux within a free European market?' My answer was always: 'On the basis of Article 233 of the Treaty of Rome, Benelux is pursuing objectives that have not yet been realized by the European Community.' I quoted as examples free movement of persons, common physical planning, and transborder cooperation.

Now the question will be asked after the Schengen Convention is ratified: 'Do we still need a separate Benelux Convention?' My answer will be in the affirmative. The Benelux countries signed the Schengen Agreement and the Schengen Convention as members of the Benelux Economic Union. The internal borders addressed in the Schengen Convention are the borders between Benelux, France and Germany and the other Member States which are recent signatories. The freedom of movement within Benelux remains a matter dealt with in the Benelux Convention. In particular Article 9 of the Schengen Convention regarding a common visa policy is less stringent than Article 4 of the Benelux Convention. Benelux should therefore participate as an entity in the shaping of Schengen external policy and controls. The Benelux Convention of 1960 should thus remain in force.

Schengen Information System
Privacy and Legal Protection

THE SCHENGEN INFORMATION SYSTEM: PRIVACY AND LEGAL PROTECTION

Bernd Schattenberg[*]

1. INTRODUCTION

A crucial event in the European integration process — the creation of the European internal market by 31 December 1992 — is approaching. The Treaty establishing the European Communities, as supplemented by the Single European Act, provides — in the interpretation of most Member States — that border controls are to be abolished at the Community's internal borders. Article 8A of the Treaty stipulates the adoption by this date of all Community measures required to create the internal market, an area without internal borders where free movement of goods, persons, services and capital is guaranteed.

2. THE SCHENGEN AGREEMENT

On 13 July 1984, France and the Federal Republic of Germany signed an intergovernmental agreement containing the first thoughts on the gradual abolition of border controls. Using this agreement as a basis, the Governments of France, the Netherlands, Belgium, Luxembourg and the Federal Republic of Germany signed the Schengen Agreement on 14 June 1985, concerning the gradual abolition of controls at common borders. Article 17 of the Schengen Agreement states:

> 'In regard to the movement of persons, the Parties shall endeavour to abolish, the controls at the common frontiers and transfer them to their external frontiers. To that end, they shall first endeavour to harmonize, where necessary, the laws and administrative provisions concerning prohibitions and restrictions which form the basis for the controls and to take complementary measures to safeguard security and combat illegal immigration by nationals of States that are not members of the European Communities.'

---

[*] First Director of the Bundeskriminalamt, Bonn.

H.G. Schermers et al., eds., Free Movement of Persons in Europe
© 1993 T.M.C. Asser Instituut, The Hague.

3.   THE SCHENGEN CONVENTION

In pursuance of the above goals, the parties to the Schengen Agreement negotiated a series of compensatory measures in order to fill any security gaps resulting from the abolition of border controls. These compensatory measures, which were to be stipulated in an international treaty and adopted in national legislation, include:
— improved cooperation in the fields of international legal assistance and extradition,
— harmonization of legal provisions in the field of narcotics, movement of arms and explosives, registration of hotel guests,
— harmonization of visa policies and conditions for entry,
— improved cooperation and harmonization regarding the law of asylum,
— regulations on pursuit and cross-border surveillance, and
— the creation of an automated Schengen Information System for improved cooperation in the search for wanted persons and objects.

The date originally fixed for the abolition of border-controls, 1 January 1990, could not be met since it was not possible to conclude the negotiations on the Schengen Convention in due time. One important reason for the delay was the developments taking place in Germany. After the inner-German border was opened on 9 November 1989, the signing of the Schengen Convention originally planned for December 1989 was cancelled.

The negotiations were continued under special consideration of the political developments in Germany. The key issues were:
— extension of the Schengen Convention to include the territory of former German Democratic Republic following unification,
— exemption of the former eastern German population from visa requirements when entering the territories of the signatory countries, and
— guaranteed implementation of effective border controls at the eastern German border by the Federal Republic of Germany.

In addition, it was laid down that the Schengen Convention would only take effect after the requirements for its implemention in the signatory countries have been fulfilled and the controls planned are actually conducted at the external borders. Hence, the Convention's ratification does not automatically signify that it is actually in force. The Schengen Convention was finally signed at Schengen on 19 June 1990.

The Schengen Convention was subsequently accepted by Italy on 27 November 1990, and by Spain and Portugal on 25 June 1991.

3.1   **Border controls as filters**

Border police controls are extremely important in the search for wanted persons and objects. Arrest and seizure figures provide evidence for this observation. Experts state that approximately 60 per cent of all arrests and seizures by the police occur at borders. In 1990, for example, 35,000 arrests and seizures were made at Germany's borders. When compared to the roughly 300,000 persons and 4.5 million objects sought by police in Germany the arrest and seizure figures show clearly that border controls serve as significant filters. One reason is that borders offer the only possibility to effect controls even in cases where no grounds for suspecting criminal activity exist. As a result, the planned abolition of border controls between the parties to the Schengen Convention can only be tolerated from a police standpoint if the expected deficits are more or less compensated.

4.   THE SCHENGEN INFORMATION SYSTEM (SIS)

The Schengen Information System, often called the 'heart' of the compensatory measures, is designed to play a key role in minimizing these deficits, especially with regard to wanted persons and objects. The Schengen Convention prescribes the creation of a joint information system that provides the law enforcement authorities of all signatory countries access to search information on persons and objects circulated as wanted for the purposes of police controls and checks at external borders or within the country in accordance with national law.

4.1   Contents

The following data will be included in the Information System with regard to *wanted persons*:
— arrest for the purpose of extradition to the country seeking extradition,
— refusal of entry and deportation,
— custody in order to prevent danger or harm (e.g., prevention or crimes or protection of helpless persons, missing minors),
— establishment of whereabouts,
— discreet registration (without the knowledge of the relevant person, data on the person's discovery and on any discreet observations made on the circumstances of the person's discovery, e.g., companions with or without motor vehicle, objects carried, etc., are transmitted to the authority circulating the wanted person), and
— specific checks on persons and motor vehicles, for example, in cases of suspected arms and drugs smuggling or distribution of counterfeit currency.
      Any information indicating that a person is violent or armed may also be included in the personal datafiles.
      Data on refusal of entry can be used not only for police checks, but also when granting visas. The Schengen Information System is therefore more than just a pure police search facility.
      The *categories for wanted objects* will include:
— motor vehicles in excess of 50 cc,
— trailers and caravans with an unladen weight in excess of 750 kg,
— firearms,
— blank documents,

— identification documents issued (restricted to passport, identity card, driving licence), and

— bank notes (registered notes).

Any information on persons or objects must be of sufficient importance to justify inclusion in the enlarged search area. In other words, not every wanted person or object listed in national search indices will be incorporated in the Schengen Information System.

4.2   Technical aspects

The Schengen Information System will be composed of a central service computer located in Strasbourg (CSIS) and decentralized data files in the signatory countries (NSIS). Each signatory country is required to maintain, parallel to the entire system, materially identical files based on the ownership principle. Data input and updating are conducted by the reporting country (data owner) on-line via the service computer, which transmits the data required to the national data collections in real time. The national data files are maintained separately and are accessible for requests by the other signatory countries. The average response time for a request will be less than five seconds maximum.

The ownership principle means that only the country that entered a data file is allowed to amend or delete it. The following rules ensure that the national data files are identical:

— No country can amend its national file directly. The central facility carries out all data entry.

— Each data file must contain a deletion and review deadline. The data owner is notified one month prior to termination of the review period only in the case of wanted person reports. The data owner can ask for extension of the data retention period if desired; otherwise the data will be deleted after the one-month notice period. Upon termination of the deletion period, which is generally a maximum of ten years for property, five years for identity documents, and three years for motor vehicles, the system automatically deletes the data without prior notice.

4.3   Volume of data and data protection

Based on the data categories given, an estimated 800,000 personal data files and 6.7 million object data files are expected. The transmitted data will be coded for security reasons. Encoding is achieved by means of a so-called 'hardware encoding system' located at both ends of every data transfer line and conducted by special units independent of the type of computer used.

Regardless of the security concepts employed for the national data files, the central service computer will be equipped with a data transmission logger in order to reconstruct files in the event any data are lost.

4.4   Data file features

The data files will be created along the following lines: the categories persons, motor vehicles, firearms, blank documents, and identity documents issued will each have its own distinct form. Most of the information will be coded and inserted in tables in order to avoid language problems and limit file length and amendment details. Inclusion of free text is not planned.

These tables include, among other things, details on the reporting country, nationality, personal characteristics and, most importantly, the reason for the report and requested measures (e.g., notification of reporting country, collection of further information, seizure of objects, identification of owner, etc.).

4.5   Legal problems

This form of computerized cooperation — a novelty in the international field — of course entails a series of unfamiliar legal and organisational problems. In addition, it has now become necessary to harmonize differing national rules, e.g., in the field of extradition and data protection. This situation led to long and difficult negotiations in preparing the Schengen Information System. Let me give you some examples.

4.5.1   *Prior check of circulars on persons wanted for arrest with a view to extradition*

International requests for arrest are directed presently to the relevant National Central Bureau via Interpol. Before including the request in its national wanted index, the National Central Bureau examines whether the case described offers sufficient grounds according to its national law to allow the wanted person's arrest and subsequent extradition.

During the negotiations, opinions were divided whether such a prior check could be omitted when including international arrest data in the Schengen Information System. The majority of the signatory countries favoured this solution since the wanted circulars would have to be included without delay in a search situation if they wanted to be an effective compensatory measure. Otherwise the advantages obtained through a computerized search facility, i.e., searching authorities' access to larger amounts of data within shorter periods of time, would not be fully utilized.

In order to avoid unjustified arrests caused by wanted data in the Schengen Information System, most signatory countries believed it to be sufficient that the Treaty include a provision prescribing that all signatory countries check whether the desired arrest and extradition are authorised by the other States. The legal examination is hence shifted forward from the addressee of the request to the submitting State. In cases of doubt, the other signatory countries must be consulted in advance. Furthermore, in the event of an arrest, the country seeking arrest must immediately ask for details on the circumstances of the case. This additional transmission of information was included so that the country where the arrest was effected can itself examine whether the arrest is justified. In order to ensure that this additional information can be communicated, the signatory countries are required to operate a 24-hour information service.

These provisions, which are all included in the Schengen Convention, were regarded as insufficient by the French Government. France demanded that the requested country have the opportunity to conduct a prior check. The reason given for this objection was that the concept of sovereignty included in the French Constitution does not allow French search authorities to comply with international arrest requests without prior examination by the French judicial authorities.

After lengthy negotiation and extensive technical review, the French Government's wishes were met with the following solution.

Through a technical procedure, it is ensured that a requested contracting party may add a special note to the data file in its national section prohibiting arrest in connection with the report until such time as the note is deleted. The requested contracting party then has 24 hours to conduct the legal examination discussed above. This time limit can be extended to one week maximum. Alternative measures are defined in the Schengen Convention for the duration of the legal examination. If the examination by the requested contracting party does not result in a refusal within this time limit, the special note is deleted and the search request becomes valid. In addition, a search request may include a note indicating that the action requested cannot be carried out in general. The other contracting parties which also have the search request in their national files may execute the requested arrest within the first 24 hours.

4.5.2 *Legal data protection supervision including right to disclosure of personal data and right of court action by the individual concerned*

Reaching a mutually acceptable solution on these issues also proved to be extremely difficult. The reason was that the French Data Protection Commission has different and, in some sectors, more extensive powers than the Data Protection Commissioners for example in the Federal Republic of Germany. According to French data protection law, it is not the data-collecting entity that is responsible for disclosing personal data to a requesting individual, but rather, the National Data Protection Commission alone. The latter has quasi-judicial authority and can, for example, order a data-collecting entity to delete data. In comparison, the Data Protection Commissioner in the Federal Republic of Germany only has advisory powers or may submit complaints to the data-collecting entity. An individual wishing to enforce disclosure or deletion of personal data by the data-collecting entity can only do so by undertaking court action.

The original solution whereby legal data protection supervision, right to disclosure of personal data and right of court action were to be generally placed under the national law of the national data file concerned was first not carried by France on account of the legal differences portrayed above. France's position was that any French national reported and included in the national SIS files of the other signatory countries should be covered by French data protection law.

In the end, a compromise was found. According to this final solution, data supervision by a data protection authority is governed by the law of the country where the supervision is conducted. However, if the data concerned relate to a person and have been included by another contracting party, the data check must be carried out in close co-ordination with that contracting party's data protection authority. Regarding the right to disclosure of personal data and the right of court action, the original solution was accepted whereby these rights are exercised in accordance with the law of the contracting party before which they are invoked

5. NATIONAL DATA PROTECTION LEGISLATION OBLIGATORY

Protracted negotiations were also necessary in order to solve other legal issues on data protection which in some fields even required political decisions. Problems arose not only because of contrasting data protection regulations, as exemplified above, but also because no data protection law exists in Belgium, for example, or in Italy and Spain.

Eventually, a provision was included in the Schengen Convention prescribing that each contracting party shall, not later than when the Convention enters into force, make the national arrangements necessary to achieve a level of protection of personal data at least equal to that resulting from the principles of the Council of Europe Convention of 28 January 1981 for the Protection of Individuals with regard to the Automatic Processing of Personal Data. In addition recommendation R (87) 15 of 17 December 1987 of the Committee of Ministers of the Council of Europe regulating the use of personal data in the police sector must also be respected.

As, in particular, the European Data Protection Convention of 1981 merely contains an obligation to achieve a certain level of data protection through corresponding national regulations, accession to the European Data Protection Convention is alone not sufficient. The Schengen Convention therefore prescribes that the transmission of personal data in connection with the Schengen Information System may only begin after the required data protection provisions for attaining the standards indicated above have entered into force in the territory of the contracting parties participating in the data transmission.

6. LEGAL PRINCIPLES OF DATA PROTECTION

The Schengen Convention also contains the following legal principles regarding data protection:
— The responsibility/ownership principle whereby the contracting party supplying data is responsible for data accuracy and lawfulness of data inclusion, and, as indicated above, is the only body authorised to amend or delete data.
— The principle of strictly defined purpose; i.e., the data transmitted may only be used for the defined purpose of the relevant category. Exceptions are only allowed following prior consent by the reporting country as well as in the prevention of a

serious threat or serious offences. Use of data for administrative purposes — except in connection with visa applications — is not permitted. Inclusion of data in other data collections is also prohibited.

— Log records on data transmissions in order to monitor the admissibility of data requests, spot checks are prescribed, and central storage of deleted data in order to check the accuracy and lawfulness of earlier data inclusions if necessary.

— Review and deletion time limits which, as mentioned above, prescribe, independent of any shorter national limits, review of personal data within five years at the latest. An absolute deletion limit is not given. The data retention principles are very much in accord with the regulations of the new German Federal Data Protection Act. Thus, the operators of the CSIS as well as the NSIS are required to take the necessary measures to avoid unauthorized data access, amendment, storage, transmission and reading.

In order to carry out data protection controls of the NSIS, each contracting party is required to set up a supervisory authority in compliance with national data protection regulations.

The CSIS is controlled by a joint supervisory authority consisting of two representatives of each national supervisory authority. The joint supervisory authority is governed by the provisions of the Schengen Convention, the aforementioned European Data Protection Convention of 1981 and the Council of Europe Recommendation regulating the use of personal data in the police sector. Further, the national law of the contracting party operating the CSIS, namely, the French data protection law, also applies. The joint supervisory authority is also competent to examine any difficulties of application or interpretation which may arise during the operation of the Schengen Information System, to study problems which may arise with the exercise of independent supervision by the national supervisory authorities or in the exercise of the right of access to the system, and to draw up harmonized proposals for the purpose of finding joint solutions to problems.

7.   PROSPECTS

Once the goal of free movement of persons in Europe is reached, the parties to the Schengen Convention and, soon afterwards, all EC countries will form not only a single economic market but also a uniform region from a criminological point of view. Especially those types of organized crime specialising in the illicit transport of and trafficking in goods and people will in the future hardly have any reason to fear being hindered by border controls. Stricter enforcement of controls at the external borders will have no impact on 'domestic' European crime.

The following security deficits can be expected:
— a drop in the number of persons apprehended and amount of evidence seized;
— the lack of drug transport controls (and a concomitant in so-called 'ant trafficking', i.e., trafficking in small amounts of drugs);

— reduced control of growing organised crime, such as illicit trafficking in stolen motor vehicles, counterfeit currency offences, illegal arms trade, prostitution and trafficking in human beings;

— reduced possibilities for compilation of intelligence on the movements of drug dealers and couriers or members or terrorist circles through police observation;

— reduced possibilities to counter forms of abuse directed against social systems (clandestine labour and illicit collection of welfare payments) due to expected migrations among the illegal aliens population;

— reduced possibilities for border interception of hooligans travelling to and from certain events (refusal of entry no longer possible), and

— the use of other preventive measures by the police, such as the refusal of entry for vehicles not meeting traffic security standards.

These prospects urgently require the implementation of the compensatory measures mentioned and laid down in the Schengen Convention.

The Schengen Information System is of special importance in connection with the above as it allows data inquiries not only at external borders but also within the territory of the signatory countries.

The Schengen Convention and the Schengen Agreement are generally seen as the motor for attaining the goals sought by the entire European Community. They therefore provide for accession by all EC countries. The Schengen Information System is technically devised also to allow inclusion of all EC countries.

Unfortunately, the European Parliament — in contrast to the positive appraisal by the EC Commission — has spoken against the Schengen Convention, arguing that the negotiations were lacking in transparency and the compensatory measures are exaggerated. The United Kingdom, Ireland, Denmark and Greece have not shown any signs of acceding to the Schengen Convention for various reasons.

We can only hope that the Schengen Convention will be ratified by the legislative bodies of the contracting parties by 1992 as planned and that the remaining legal, organizational and technical requirements for the implementation of the compen-satory measures are also met by this date.

The Federal Republic of Germany has never left any doubt that a complete removal of border controls would be irresponsible before most compensatory measures — including, for certain, the Schengen Information System — are actually implemented. 'Free movement of citizens' is a slogan which security authorities can only support if everything is done to avoid that the abolition of border controls does not entail 'free movement of criminals'.

DATA EXCHANGE, PRIVACY AND LEGAL PROTECTION
Especially regarding aliens

Pieter Boeles[*]

1. DATA EXCHANGE THROUGH THE SIS

The Schengen Information System (SIS) will become a huge reservoir of private information. Mr B. Schattenberg in his presentation to this colloquium mentions an estimated 800,000 personal data files. He seems to be satisfied that the Convention of 19 June 1990 applying the Schengen Agreement of 14 June 1985 contains enough safeguards for the legal protection of privacy.

Others, at least in the Netherlands, have, however, expressed considerable doubts. The Netherlands Council of State, for instance, in its official advice to the Dutch Government, criticised the wide range of possibilities created in Article 99 of the Convention to report people for the purpose of 'discrete surveillance or specific checks.' Such a report may be made for the purpose of preventing threats to public safety, 'where an overall assessment of the person concerned, particularly on the basis of offences committed hitherto, gives sufficient reason to suppose that he will also commit extremely serious offences in future.' The persons concerned are not supposed to know that they are reported (Art. 109 sec. 2). The Council fears that application of Article 99 'could lead to very fundamental infringements of privacy.' These and other objections led the Netherlands Council of State to the opinion that the Convention should not be ratified.

Equally worried is Mr Luc F.M. Verhey, who in his contribution to the recently published book on Schengen by H. Meijers et.al.,[1] surveys the privacy aspects of the Convention. He is particularly concerned with, *inter alia*, the very general grounds on which reporting in the SIS is sometimes based, the derogation from the 'purpose limitation principle', the lack of clear arrangements on the supply of data, the potentially long period of retention, the obscure dispute settlement arrangements and the general grounds for the limitation of access. Verhey notes that there are a number of 'important provisions of interest' in the Convention. To give substance to these provisions it might be necessary, he suggests, to require that the Contracting

---

[*] Member of the Netherlands Bar Amsterdam; Immigration Lawyer.
1. *Schengen, Internationalisation of central chapters of the law on aliens, refugees, privacy, security and the police*, Tjeenk Willink/Kluwer, Deventer, 1991.

H.G. Schermers et al., eds., Free Movement of Persons in Europe

Parties respect mutual decisions. On the other hand too much latitude remains with the Contracting Parties for the application of domestic law.

2.   DATA EXCHANGE OUTSIDE THE SIS

It would be a mistake, though, to focus all attention on the SIS when privacy protection in the Schengen Convention is at stake. The Convention contains many other possibilities for transborder flow of data than those provided in the SIS. An example is Article 46 which permits each Contracting Party to give information on its own initiative to any other Contracting Party which may be important, *inter alia*, in the fight against criminal offences, avoidance of criminal offences, or averting danger to public order and security. Minimum guarantees for proper use of the information supplied and with regard to the protection of privacy are lacking in the Convention, as the Dutch Council of State sadly establishes in its official advice.

Verhey again points out that, although the Schengen Convention of 1990 obliges the Contracting Parties to strive towards harmonisation of the domestic legislation on privacy protection to the level of the Data Protection Convention of the Council of Europe and in certain cases obliges them to take supplementary measures above the level of the Data Protection Convention, too many gaps have been left open. Certain forms of data exchange have been exempted to a greater or lesser extent from the provisions on harmonisation. These deal with exchange of data for mutual assistance in criminal cases, the application of the *non bis in idem* principle, extradition and transfer of execution of a criminal sentence. In addition, a special arrangement for exchange of data on asylum seekers was made.

3.   TWO THEMES

In this presentation I shall elaborate on two themes connected with transborder flow of data concerning aliens; two themes characteristic for the Schengen Convention of 1990. The first theme is the subordination of the legal position of asylum seekers compared to any other category of persons covered by the Convention. The second is the accumulation of (unilaterally modifiable) national provisions, which have to be applied by each national authority, and which are subject to differing national interpretations of the protection of their own public order and national security.[2]

2. See the Opinion of 11 July 1991 of the Dutch 'Standing Committee of experts on international immigration, refugees and criminal law.'

4.   ASYLUM SEEKERS

Asylum seekers especially have a vital interest in the protection of their personal data. They fled from a country where they claim to risk persecution. The guarantees for data protection in Article 38 are, however, less effective when compared to those in the general title IV (protection of personal data) of the Schengen Convention. Article 126 section 3d, which states that a Contracting Party may not, in order to avoid its liability under its national legislation *vis-à-vis* an injured party, plead that another Contracting Party had transmitted inaccurate data, is not applicable here. Also inapplicable is the provision in Article 128 that the transmission of personal data may not take place until the Contracting Parties involved in that transmission have instructed a national supervisory authority to monitor independently the examination of personal data in data files. Article 38(11), which resembles the latter, is non-committal.

The asylum seeker is not expressly guaranteed a right to an appropriate legal remedy. An applicant for asylum is entitled, *inter alia*, to be made aware of information exchanged regarding him, ascertain whether this information is incorrect, and require its correction or deletion. It is not, however, indicated by what means he may ensure compliance with these provisions.

It is only at the stage where information is being automated that one may be able to fall back on the Convention of Strasbourg (Convention for the Protection of Individuals with regard to automatic processing of personal data, 28 January 1981). The said Convention specifically makes provision for the right to a legal remedy in cases where no definite answer is given to a request for information, or, as circumstances may require, communication, correction or deletion of personal data. It also regards as being 'data of special category': information on race, political or religious inclination or other, as well as those which refer to a person's health or his sexual propensities. This personal information may not be processed in an automated system unless provision is made in national law for appropriate guarantees. The same applies to personal information on criminal sentences. Here we see a clash between the Data Protection Convention and the Schengen Convention of 1990. It is quite obvious that the 'other particulars necessary for establishing the applicant's identity' indicated in Article 38(2)c of the Schengen Convention can, with regard to asylum seekers, fall under the special category of the Strasbourg Convention. The Schengen Convention of 1990 does not seem to care much about this. Such information may, one should even say *must*, according to Article 38(1), be exchanged without the consent of the asylum seeker.

5.   ALIENS AND PUBLIC ORDER IN SCHENGEN STATES

5.1.   Reporting for the purpose of being refused entry

It will be fairly easy for each Contracting State to ban aliens (i.e., non-EC nationals) from the joint territories. Article 96 of the Schengen Convention of 1990 says that reporting may be based upon 'a threat to public order or national security and safety which the presence of an alien in national territory may pose.' Such may in particular be the case with:

1. an alien who has been sentenced for an offence carrying a sentence of at least one year. (Evidently it is not decisive whether the alien has in reality been so sentenced. He could — provided the offence fits the description of this article — even be reported for having been fined.)

2. an alien who upon ample evidence has committed serious offences, or against whom there is genuine evidence of an intention to commit such offences in the territory of a Contracting Party. (In spite of the words 'serious' and 'genuine' the given opportunity could be abused by less serious and less genuine suspicion).

Decisions to report aliens may also be based on the fact that the alien has been the subject of a deportation, removal or expulsion order which has not been rescinded or suspended, included or accompanied by a prohibition on entry or, where appropriate, residence, based on non-compliance with national regulations on the entry or residence of aliens.

In short, aliens may be reported in the case of unimportant convictions, unproven suspicions and non-compliance with domestic immigration regulations. The criteria for reporting being so liberal, it is hardly a consolation that Article 111 of the Convention gives the right to any person to proceed before the courts or the authority competent under national law to seek to correct, delete or provide information or obtain compensation in connection with a report concerning him. According to Article 110 any person may have 'factually inaccurate data' relating to him corrected, or 'legally inaccurate data' relating to him deleted. The Contracting Parties shall undertake among themselves to execute final decisions of these courts or authorities. According to Article 116 each party shall be responsible, in accordance with its national law, for the injury caused to a person through the use of the national data file of the Schengen Information System.

But there is in the provisions of this Convention no way to challenge the report for being disproportionate. This is a grave deficiency. When I come to speak hereafter on the subject of refusal or withdrawal of residence permits as a consequence of reporting, it will be seen that the decision to report an alien for the purpose of being refused entry may affect his rights under the European Convention on Human Rights, particularly the right to family life and private life or the right not to be exposed to inhumane treatment. So aliens might certainly bring *arguable claims* that reporting decisions are in breach of one or more rights enshrined in the European Convention on Human Rights. Will there be an effective remedy as Article 13 European Convention on Human Rights requires for such cases? The formal system as laid down in Articles 110, 111 and 116 of the Schengen Convention of 1990 come close to an 'effective remedy' within the meaning of Article 13 of the European Convention on Human Rights, provided that a judge or an authority within the meaning of Article 111 is available under domestic legislation, and — if no judge but only an 'authority' is available — that such an authority will be sufficiently independent and competent. But as I have already noted, there is still the serious problem that the given remedy is doomed to be fully ineffective if it comes to challenging the proportionality of the reporting decision.

5.2. Refusal of residence permits and withdrawal of residence permits as a consequence of reporting

As already indicated, entry to the common territory of the Schengen Countries must be denied to an alien who has been reported by any Contracting State for the purpose of being refused entry (Art. 5). What are the consequences of a report on the acquisition of residence permits? This is what Article 25 of the Schengen Convention of 1990 is about. It contains basic rules for inter-State bargaining over the heads of the aliens involved.

Where a Contracting Party considers issuing a residence permit to an alien who has been reported as a person not to be permitted entry, it shall first consult the reporting Contracting Party and shall take account of its interests. The residence permit shall be issued only on serious grounds, in particular of a humanitarian nature or pursuant to international obligations. If a residence permit is issued the reporting Contracting Party shall withdraw the report but may put the alien concerned on its national reporting list of persons not to be permitted entry.

Where it emerges that an alien holding a valid residence permit issued by one of the Contracting Parties has been reported as a person not to be permitted entry, the reporting Contracting State shall consult the Party which issued the residence permit in order to determine whether there are sufficient grounds for the withdrawal of the residence permit. If the residence permit is not withdrawn the reporting Contracting Party shall withdraw the report but may put the alien in question on its national reporting list.

Will the alien, if the bargain results in denial or withdrawal of the residence permit, have a reasonable chance to challenge the decision effectively? The domestic legal remedy available will probably enable the competent judge or authority to consider the responsibility of the State where the alien resides. But will the responsibility of the other Contracting State — the one that made the report — also fall within its competence? I have my doubts. There is a real risk that the national judge or authority will not be competent to weigh the outcome of the bargain fully because the other State will remain out of reach. In this regard the remedy will not be effective. What is striking is the fact that with regard to injury caused to a person through the use of the national data file of the Schengen Information System, the Schengen States did discern this sort of problem and made arrangements in Article 116. This Article could be read as being applicable to the above-mentioned problem, but it is more likely that it was only provided to cover the case of financial damages caused by legally or factually inaccurate data.

Moreover, the chances of success in an appeal against the negative result of the inter-State bargain are impeded by the fact that, after a report for the purpose of being refused entry, residence may only be granted 'on serious grounds'. This seems to mean: 'serious in the eyes of the bargaining States'. It is to be expected that judges will limit themselves to answering the marginal question whether the conclusion of the bargaining States was not 'a result that no reasonable State could reach.' It is highly questionable whether such marginal and incomplete examination might be considered to be effective in the sense of Article 13 European Convention on Human Rights if, for instance, the right to family life or protection against inhumane treatment of the alien concerned were to be at stake.

Here we see that under the Schengen Convention of 1990 the rights to residence of the alien will be affected by the cumulative public orders and national securities of all Schengen States, instead of (as it used to be) just the public order and national security of the State where he resides. Not only his privacy but in a wider sense his private life will be in danger once the Schengen States start to report aliens in the SIS 'for the purpose of being refused entry.' This Convention not only lacks sufficient protection for personal data, but also sufficient clarity on the common concept of 'public order and national security.'

Cooperation in the Field of Criminal Law
Police and Other Law
Enforcement Agencies

COOPERATION ON LAW ENFORCEMENT, CRIMINAL JUSTICE AND LEGISLATION IN EUROPE
Nordic experience

Henning Fode[*]

1.   INTRODUCTION

In recent years the development of the European cooperation on combating terrorism, drug crime and other types of organized cross-border crime has been marked by the perspectives presented to police and security services by the scheduled introduction of the EC internal market as from 1 January 1993, a situation which will involve freedom of movement within the European Community. The linkage to this appointed date, which at times has loomed large as a somewhat overwhelming and almost awe-inspiring guiding principle, has had the primary effect of infusing into this field a considerable extent of dynamics, which I personally would rather not have missed.

Every aspect of the cooperation between the EC Member States within this sphere has been thoroughly scrutinized, especially within the TREVI framework. The main reason for this scrutiny is directly connected with the objective of improving efforts on the European and international levels. Irrespective of the extent to which the primary objective will actually be achieved, the process itself will provide a kind of extra benefit. It automatically, as it were, compels each Member State to take a step backwards in order to re-assess in a different light its own national structures, functions and policies.

Apart from the strongly increased dynamics, the development of the European cooperation on policing and security has been characterized by increasing formalization such that a growing proportion of the activities, within TREVI, for instance, consists of an actual production of regulations in the form of somewhat convention-like texts. This trend can hardly be said to have surprised anyone. The establishment of common regulations within other areas is, as such, far from being unfamiliar to the EC Member States.

Another essential element that may be added is the experiences and traditions that the five original Schengen countries have gained and developed by virtue of the leading role they have taken in the efforts towards the implementation of freedom of

* Deputy Permanent Secretary, Ministry of Justice, Denmark.

H.G. Schermers et al., eds., Free Movement of Persons in Europe
© 1993, T.M.C. Asser Instituut, The Hague

movement. The mere fact that five, six or perhaps eight out of twelve Member States from the very outset of a negotiation process can present a complete common draft will, inevitably, have an impact on negotiation positions even within such fora which, like TREVI, are based upon the principle of consensus.

Beyond this, we must not underestimate the importance of the 'mental advantage' which negotiators and decision-makers from the Schengen Group bring as extremely useful ballast when entering into negotiations. This applies, for instance, to talks within TREVI on issues on which a settlement has been reached by Schengen, possibly as a result of a long period of discussion.

Therefore, it is indeed not surprising — and indeed not unfortunate either — that developments within the field of immigration, as well as within TREVI, have been so extensively influenced by the results of the Schengen cooperation.

Similarly, there is nothing strange in the fact that the Schengen cooperation has been able to benefit from, *inter alia*, the experiences with freedom of movement gained by three of the original Schengen countries within the Benelux cooperation.[1] In a sense, the connection is well evidenced by the fact that the special Benelux secretariat in Brussels provides support services to the Schengen organization.

Once in a while, however, there may be reason to call to mind the fact that experiences with free movement of persons across national boundaries have been made by others than the parties of Benelux and Schengen. This applies, not least, to the framework of the Nordic Passport Control Agreement [*Den Nordiske Paskontroloverenskomst*], within which Denmark has participated since 1957. As a matter of fact, this could provide a basis for an in-depth comparative analysis of differences and similarities in the approaches applied in various regions where free movement of persons across national borders has been introduced without a simultaneous creation of a federal state as such.

Such an analysis would, however, fall outside the scope of the present paper. I shall instead confine myself to a brief presentation of the Nordic Passport Control Agreement and attempt to describe the framework within which the Nordic cooperation on policing is conducted. I shall provide some examples which may illustrate certain differences and similarities between the Nordic cooperation and developments within the Schengen organization as well as within TREVI. In this context I shall set out some quite personal — and rather unscientific — views relating to the possible historical, political and juridical reasons for differences in the approaches to the 'compensatory measures'.

2.   THE NORDIC PASSPORT CONTROL AGREEMENT

The history of the Nordic countries is characterized by a number of common features, and this holds true of the judicial sphere as well. This applies to Denmark

---

1. See E.D.J. Kruijtbosch, 'Benelux Experiences in the Abolition of Border Control', elsewhere in this volume.

and Norway, which were a united kingdom until the Congress of Vienna in 1814. It also applies to the relations between Norway and Sweden, which formed a union until Norway obtained its independence in 1905. Prior to the latest Finnish independence in 1917, Finland had been subordinate to the Swedish Crown for a considerable period until 1809. Similarly, until 1918, Iceland was under the rule of Denmark, and from 1918 to the summer of 1944 it had the status of an independent kingdom in a personal union with Denmark.

In addition, since the end of the last century, considerable political and cultural endeavours have been directed towards developing the judicial uniformity existing among the Nordic countries — especially Denmark, Norway and Sweden. Efforts have included cooperation on the actual drafting of bills, concerning essential parts of civil law.

These efforts increased after World War II. It is true that early attempts to create a Nordic defence union failed, as well as subsequent moves towards introducing a close and binding Nordic 'internal market'. At the same time, however, the post-war era has seen a number of important initiatives directed towards a substantially close Nordic cooperation on, inter alia, political and legal issues.

Thus, a Nordic interparliamentary body, the Nordic Council was established in 1952. The Nordic Council, whose members are appointed by and from among members of the national parliaments, is charged with the task of 'discussing matters of common interest to the countries concerned and to make recommendations to the governments on such matters.' The work of the Nordic Council has covered a wide range of issues with the main emphasis on matters relating to culture, education, traffic, communications, the labour market, health and environment. This choice of topics reflects the general acceptance that matters such as security policy, for instance, does not fall within the purview of the Nordic Council.

In continuation of the establishment of the Nordic Council, cooperation was strengthened on a governmental level with the establishment of the Nordic Council of Ministers. The cooperation activities were provided with a rather fixed framework through the adoption of the Nordic Cooperation Agreement [Den Nordiske Samarbejdsoverenskomst] of 1962, which emphasizes, inter alia, a strengthening of judicial cooperation, including that within the field of criminal justice.

Already in June 1957, however, Denmark, Finland, Norway and Sweden had signed the agreement on the abolition of passport controls at the common Nordic borders, the Nordic Passport Control Agreement to which Iceland acceded in September 1965. The Agreement was amended in April 1973 in order to enable Denmark to meet its obligations as a new member of the European Community.

The Passport Control Agreement abolished passport controls at the common Nordic borders. Accordingly, a Nordic external border crossing functions as a point of passport and entry control for the entire Nordic region. Pursuant to Article 1 of the Agreement the Nordic international airports are considered as constituting external frontiers, and Article 8 provides that the contracting parties have a right to carry out spot checks of third country nationals at the internal frontiers.

Further, Article 6 of the Passport Control Agreement includes a regulation on a 'joint negative list' of third country nationals who, should occasion arise, are to be refused entry at the common Nordic external borders, and Articles 9 and 10 include rules on the taking back of third country nationals.

The Nordic Aliens Commission, established in accordance with Article 13 of the Passport Control Agreement, aims at introducing a common visa policy and uniform practices with respect to the granting of visas, just as the Commission provides a framework for the exchange of general information on these issues.

Almost simultaneously with the signing of the Passport Control Agreement, the Nordic countries entered into certain other agreements which provide, *inter alia*, that Nordic nationals shall be exempt from holding a passport and a residence permit while staying, or residing, in another Nordic State. By virtue of another such agreement the Nordic countries will constitute a single labour market.

These agreements entitle Nordic nationals to establish themselves or take up residence and employment within the Nordic region, and they confer on Nordic nationals, in particular, an extensive degree of freedom of movement within the area. Hence, there exist within the individual countries no specific aliens controls directed at nationals from other Nordic countries. However, inasmuch as Norway and Sweden impose considerably higher consumption taxes on luxury goods than does Denmark, the two countries have found it necessary to retain fairly systematic customs controls on their own nationals, especially on arrival from Denmark.

3.   THE NORDIC COOPERATION ON POLICING AND CRIMINAL
          JUSTICE

3.1   General

During the post-war era the Nordic cooperation on policing and criminal justice has been developed and intensified considerably. This has come about, I believe, as a natural element of the Nordic cooperation process in general, rather than as a result of deliberate attempts to introduce 'compensatory measures'in order to remedy the negative consequences for policing and security of the implementation of free movement of persons within the Nordic region.

Formalized cooperation procedures have been especially developed within the area of criminal justice. This has been effected by the adoption of various agreements and conventions as well as by the introduction of uniform legislation on a number of matters including the extradition of offenders, the carrying out of sentences (including the transfer of sentenced persons), the transfer of proceedings and the development of mutual legal aid. It is worthwhile to note that the uniform legislation on inter-Nordic extradition procedures opens the possibility that, under specific conditions, nationals may be extradited by their home country for criminal proceedings in another Nordic country.

In many ways, this level of Nordic cooperation exceeds that which has been established under the auspices of the Council of Europe, which includes the Scandinavian countries among its full members. It also exceeds that which the EC Member

States, parallel with the work in the Council of Europe, have established within the framework of the European Political Cooperation.

Nordic cooperation on criminal justice has been developed even to the point of a formal commitment towards an extremely intensive cooperation. In contrast, the process of cooperation on policing has taken a somewhat different direction. Although Nordic police cooperation has been intensified significantly, the extent to which such cooperation is based on formal agreements is limited. Thus, the Nordic police agencies still cooperate without a statutory basis such as is provided by the rules on police cooperation laid down in Chapter III of the Schengen Convention. This lack of, and the fact that it is probably not felt as a problem within the Nordic countries is, I believe, due to a number of factors. In the following I shall attempt to give a brief outline of the apparently most influential ones.

In connection with their own mutual cooperation and with the European integration process, the Nordic States have belonged to the group of countries, that, in the tightrope walk between a 'functional' and a 'federal' approach, have been traditionally inclined to attach the greatest importance to the functional side. In the debate over European integration, the 'federalists'generally seem to have been too eager to explain the preference for the functional approach to the integration process as being solely due to a lack of political will to enter into a close and binding cooperation. It is my opinion, however, that the close and yet quite informal Nordic police cooperation should predominantly be viewed as a consequence of the close linguistic, cultural and historical affinities between the countries concerned, as a consequence of which basing close cooperation upon mutual trust rather than upon a detailed statutory basis in the shape of conventions or the like is not politically unobjectionable.

It is obvious that the existing extensive juridical uniformity amongst the Nordic countries, which is an outcome of history as well as of conscious efforts throughout this century, has contributed towards clearing the path for the Nordic cooperation. Something quite similar applies to the substantial uniformity of administrative structures, including the organizational structure of the police and prosecution services. Undoubtedly, this uniformity enables the individual official to comprehend, practically offhand, the basic structures of the administrative and judicial hierarchies of another Nordic country. This has contributed greatly towards creating the conditions of a profound trust in the legal and administrative steps which might be taken by the authorities of another Nordic country. At the same time, a certain scepticism cannot be excluded, especially within those Nordic countries that won their independence fairly recently against taking formal steps that might be interpreted as a cession of sovereignty.

In the following sections I shall attempt to provide some examples that illustrate some of the differences between the Nordic cooperation on policing and the corresponding cooperation under the auspices of Schengen and TREVI.

3.2   **The Nordic judicial and police cooperation in a number of specific fields of activity**

3.2.1   *Direct contacts*

As indicated above, the Nordic cooperation within certain spheres is characterized by an extensive range of direct contacts between authorities and officials. Thus, in actual practice it has been approved that all of the 54 police districts, into which the Danish national police service is divided, are in direct communication with their opposite numbers in the other Nordic countries. Direct contacts usually occur without any registration of the communication with central authorities such as the central National Interpol Bureau (NCB), which acts a national service unit (without independent executive powers) placed under the National Commissioner's Office.

In contrast, communication between the Danish police and police agencies in countries other than the Nordic ones will usually be transmitted via the Danish Interpol Bureau. Excluded are matters to which further formal regulations on the prescribed procedure apply, such as, for instance, extradition cases.

With the adoption of the Schengen Convention in June 1990, the signatory States have taken steps to simplify procedures in a number of cases for which the conventions of the Council of Europe prescribe particular formal requirements. This applies, for example, to extradition proceedings, on which Title III, Chapter 4 of the Schengen Convention contains a number of provisions intended to supplement the European Convention of 13 September 1957 on Extradition. The Schengen Convention still requires, however, that requests for extradition 'shall be sent by the relevant Ministry of the requesting Contracting Party to the relevant Ministry of the requested Contracting Party.'[2]

By way of comparison, it should be noted that the Nordic countries have acceded to a special agreement on extradition and have adopted separate legislation on the implementation of the said agreement, which permits extradition without requiring the involvement or even the notification of the respective Ministries of Justice.

3.2.2   *Drug liaison officers*

At an early stage the Nordic countries established a network of drug liaison officers on secondment to third countries. This was done as part of a quite extensive Nordic police and customs cooperation scheme on combating drug crimes. It entailed a substantially improved utilization of the fairly limited resources available to each of the participating agencies, including resources allocated to the secondment of liaison officers.

In recent years, the EC Member States have established a similar cooperation on the secondment of drug liaison officers within the TREVI framework of cooperation

---

2. Art. 65 the Schengen Convention.

on policing and security — partly modelled on the Nordic construction. From Denmark's point of view, however, it is significant that the cooperation within TREVI has not been developed to the same extent as applies within the Nordic countries. Among the latter, there exists a widespread acceptance of the fact that a drug liaison officer on secondment from one Nordic country communicates directly with police or customs authorities in another Nordic country without notifying the central authorities of his own country. The wording of the facultative provision in Article 47(4) of the Schengen Convention seems to indicate that within this field the Schengen States have been unable to proceed further than the 12 EC Member States within TREVI.

3.2.3   Liaison officers in the EC Member States

Inter-Nordic secondment of police officers has occurred on a quite limited scale. In contrast, the secondment of liaison officers among the EC Member States, and the conditions for such secondment, seems to have attracted much greater attention.[3] Amongst the Schengen countries also there seems to exist a correspondingly greater interest in seconding liaison officers to other contracting States.[4]

Several elements appear to be involved in the explanation for this difference in the attention given to the secondment of 'internal' liaison officers. As is emphasized by Article 47(2)(a) and (b) of the Schengen Convention, two of the main objectives of the secondment of internal liaison officers are the promotion of the 'exchange of information for the purposes of fighting crime by means both of prevention and of punishment' and the facilitation of 'mutual police assistance and legal assistance in criminal matters'. As far as the Nordic countries are concerned, however, I believe that the mutual exchange of information and mutual legal assistance are being performed in such a non-frictional and unproblematic manner that the costs of an increase in secondments of internal liaison officers would be disproportionate to the consequential modest improvement, at best, of the Nordic police cooperation.

It may be expressed in this way: the linguistic, cultural and political barriers which liaison officers are often required to confront are too minimal in the Nordic countries to present any noticeable obstacles to police cooperation within the region.

3.2.4   Surveillance and cross-border pursuits

Articles 40 and 41 of the Schengen Convention permit police officers from one Contracting State to cross the borders of another Contracting State and to operate within its territory without prior authorization. This can be done under certain exceptional circumstances only, and is subject to a number of scrupulously listed conditions. The mere dimensions of the Articles concerned indicate that the negotiation process relating to surveillance and pursuits across borders has not been quite

---

3. Para. 9 of the TREVI Ministers Programme of Action.
4. Art. 47 (1-3) the Schengen Convention.

painless. Moreover, the declarations made by the Contracting States in accordance with Article 41(9) of the Schengen Convention more than indicate that at least the majority of the Contracting States consider the right to perform a 'hot pursuit' as constituting a rather considerable encroachment on the basic conceptions of sovereignty.

Notwithstanding the fact that for more than 35 years the region has provided free movement of persons, the Nordic States have not drawn up convention texts on 'hot pursuit' and the like. It stands to reason that the geography of Denmark, which does not have a common Nordic-Danish land border, makes the question of academic interest from a Danish point of view. With respect to the other Nordic countries, their extensive borders make efficient surveillance almost impracticable. Hence, I cannot exclude the possibility that incidents might have occurred in which it has been impossible for police to obtain prior authorization to perform cross-border pursuits. I assume, however, that such incidents have been managed in an informal, pragmatic and sensible way. Likewise, I assume that the same applies to incidents in the Schengen countries prior to their signing of the Convention, which has not yet come into force.

Therefore, there may be occasion to consider whether and to what extent, at the present stage of the European integration process, the Schengen cooperation on policing has been bolstered by the introduction of stipulated, formalized provisions on 'hot pursuit'. The possibility cannot be excluded that the insistence on formalizing the basis will contain the risk, in certain politically sensitive areas, of actually hampering police cooperation.

3.2.5 *Joint computer-based information systems*

Within the field of immigration control and within TREVI the EC Member States recently took the initiative to set up computer-based information systems. By and large, these will contain the same types of information which will be included in the Schengen Information System that is currently being established in Strasbourg in accordance with Title IV of the Schengen Convention.

Thus, the Draft Convention of the Member States of the European Communities on the crossing of their external borders, which Ministers responsible for immigration control are expected to sign shortly, contains a provision on the establishment of a common data file of persons reported for the purpose of refusal of entry into one EC Member State and who should not, accordingly, be afforded the opportunity to contravene the proscription by entering into the Community via another Member State.

As stated in section 2 above, the Nordic Passport Control Agreement operates with a corresponding 'negative list' in accordance with Article 6 of the Agreement. The list has not been computerized, which must be ascribed mainly to the fact that the Nordic Passport Control Agreement came into existence at a time when modern information technology was still in its infancy.

During the next few years, however, the Nordic countries will undoubtedly become more closely linked as far as police information technology is concerned. In this regard, one should also consider the ever increasing traffic across the Nordic common borders, which will be significantly effected, for one thing, by the construction of a combined road and rail bridge across the Sound between Sweden and Denmark.

The coming years will show whether developments in this field will occur within the framework of an enlarged European Community which will include the Nordic countries or whether they will occur within a separate Nordic context.

4.   CONCLUSIONS

In the foregoing sections I have been inclined to focus on a number of areas marked by a range of dissimilarities, perhaps even by incompatibilities, between on one hand, the police and judicial cooperation that is currently being developed in the European Community within TREVI and European Political Cooperation as well as the concurrent efforts related to the Schengen Convention and, on the other hand, the Nordic cooperation.

By applying such a bias one runs the risk of forgetting that there exist quite as many similarities in the cooperation process within the two 'families' to which Denmark belongs. However, I believe it to be a generally accepted educational idiom that 'exaggeration promotes understanding'. It is a greater intellectual challenge to concentrate on the differences rather than on the similarities in the cooperation structures. Therefore, by emphasizing a number of differences found in the development of judicial and police cooperation I hope to have contributed towards enabling others to benefit from some of the experiences — be they positive or negative — that have been gained within the Nordic countries.

COOPERATION IN THE FIELD OF CRIMINAL LAW, POLICE AND OTHER LAW ENFORCEMENT AGENCIES

J.H. Grosheide[*]

1. The principal tasks of the modern constitutional State include safeguarding the rights and freedoms of its citizens and protecting them against the actions of others and, more generally, the preservation of order and enforcement of the law. In performing these tasks the State makes use of legislation which prescribes or prohibits all kinds of behaviour under threat of punishment. The authorities also maintain bodies which are responsible for the enforcement of these rules: the police and other investigation services, the public prosecutions department, the judiciary, etc. Since the State also wishes the activities of its organs to be bound by the law, it regulates the powers of the various agencies in great detail and specifies the procedural rules which must be observed with regard to the investigation, prosecution and adjudication of offences. So in each of the present West European States a system of national criminal law and procedural law has arisen, which is enforced in the first instance by national police forces and other investigation services with nationally regulated powers.

Borders, whether they are controlled or not, indicate where national sovereignty begins and ends and symbolise, as it were, national sovereignty. Those who cross a border enter another judicial area or the domain of another legal system; they are then in the territory of another sovereign State with its own national law for the maintenance of internal security. Even the fact that some States have introduced the principle of universality for certain offences does not undermine the national character of criminal law. Borders are shifted for certain purposes but are not abolished.

2. The pre-eminently national character of criminal law and methods of enforcement does not mean, however, that no international aspects are involved. This in itself is nothing new. Criminal offences are also committed by citizens of other States, suspects are sometimes found to be in another country, and crimes are committed by people with different nationalities and sometimes in more than one State. To overcome the problems of investigation and adjudication in such cases, a number of instruments have been developed in the course of time. The police began to exchange data via Interpol, extradition conventions were signed and international legal assistance arose. In the framework of the Council of Europe in particular, a number of important conventions

---

[*] Director-General for European Affairs and Immigration, Ministry of Justice, The Hague.

H.G. Schermers et al., eds., Free Movement of Persons in Europe

on cooperation in criminal justice have been drawn up in recent decades. Although all these forms of cooperation were based on sovereign, national decisions and were therefore of a purely intergovernmental nature, the strictly national character of criminal and procedural law has nevertheless been reduced somewhat. A telling example is that a country such as the Netherlands, which until recently never extradited its own citizens, has now removed the legal and constitutional obstacles to such action. The first decision to extradite a Dutch citizen was taken very recently.

3. A certain degree of harmonisation of national criminal and, more particularly, procedural systems has also been caused by the European Convention on Human Rights and the case-law of the European Court of Human Rights. Many people may not have expected such a development. As far as the Netherlands is concerned, for example, I would point to the period during which a person may be deprived of his/her liberty without recourse to a judge. This period had been shortened in response to a judgement of the European Court. It is noteworthy that experts in continental criminal law state that it seems as if only Anglo-Saxon lawyers have a seat in the European Court, while a British colleague recently assured me that the case-law of the Court suggests that it no longer has any judges trained in Anglo-Saxon law.

In this connection I wondered in a more general sense whether the influence of the literature and case-law concerning other legal systems is not much greater than several decades ago. Again taking the Netherlands as an example, I would mention the gradual development of the doctrine of unlawfully obtained evidence, which is not being introduced as a matter of course in the moderately inquisitorial structure of criminal procedure in this country.

4. There are several reasons for considering whether the existing pattern of national criminal law, enriched by international cooperation in the form of agreements, conventions or scholarship and case-law, is still sufficient.

Encouraged by modern means of communication and greater prosperity, people are now crossing borders in huge numbers. In the European Community this will soon take place without any controls. The scope for transboundary crime will therefore continue to increase. The enormous sums of money involved in organised crime make complicated transactions in numerous countries attractive and feasible. This requires coordinated action by police and judicial authorities, extending across borders.

Although the necessary measures can be achieved by means of intergovernmental agreements or conventions, the process is sometimes very laborious. For example, during the drafting of convention provisions on the Schengen Information System, highly diverse national data protection regulations had to be taken into account. It took a great deal of effort to find a solution which did not render the exchange of data completely impossible. Just imagine how difficult it would be for the twelve Member States to regulate something similar. Genuine international crime is also making its appearance, such as fraud against the European Communities. Is existing national legislation sufficient to deal with this problem properly?

5. It is not surprising that in recent years various proposals have been made to put international cooperation against transboundary crime on a new footing. Without making any attempt to be comprehensive, I would mention the following. After all manner of practical subjects had been tackled for many years in the framework of police cooperation within TREVI, the responsible ministers adopted a programme of action in Dublin in June 1990, to deal with the consequences of the disappearance of border controls within the EC on 1 January 1993. One of the most striking points in this programme of action is the establishment of a European Drugs Intelligence Unit (EDIU), the preparations for which are now well under way.

It has been concluded, first by the Schengen Group and then by the twelve Member States of the EC, that there is a need for a Schengen or European Information System, containing data on persons not to be admitted, wanted and missing persons, suspects to be arrested, stolen property, etc. The question of whether transboundary surveillance by the police must be made possible is under discussion, and the issue of hot pursuit is also being considered in the framework of Schengen.

The most far-reaching proposal, however, was submitted by Chancellor Kohl during the European Council in Luxembourg. He proposed the establishment of Europol, a European police service regulated in the treaty (whether that on EPU or the EEC treaty is not clear) for tackling drug trafficking and organised crime, both at institutional level and — in anticipation of this — on a more practical level. To start with, this service would merely exchange information, but at a later stage it would also acquire the executive power of investigation. The European Council has accepted the objectives underlying the German proposal and has asked the responsible ministers (TREVI) to produce a report for the European Council in Maastricht. Part of the German proposal is that the secretariat of the Council of Ministers and the European Commission should play a coordinating role during the elaboration of the plans.

The wording of the decision of the European Council does not make clear what the exact scope of the decision is and what role Community institutions will play. As far as substantive criminal law is concerned, I would mention, again by way of example, the activities that have been developed in the framework of the group of seven industrialised countries (G7) to tackle drug trafficking. First it was decided to establish a Financial Action Task Force, with the task of drafting recommendations for tackling the phenomenon of money laundering, and then it was agreed that a Chemical Action Task Force should be formed for the purpose of drafting proposals for controls on trade in precursors, in order to prevent them being used for the illegal production of drugs. These activities were developed relatively soon after the signing of the 1988 Vienna Convention against the illicit traffic in psychotropic and other drugs, in which these matters are dealt with.

Also noteworthy is the fact that detailed consultations were held in the framework of Schengen on tackling drug trafficking and the problem of firearms possession. The observation that a country which has a reputation for being tolerant of the one can be very strict with regard to the other is interesting but does not make it any easier to find a solution.

6. The implementation of the measures and proposals discussed in point 5 and other similar measures will require some considerable thought. If an investigating officer acquires the power to take action in another country, by which regulations is he then bound? One must presume that it will be those in force in the country where he takes action. It makes no difference whether the action involves hot pursuit or is undertaken by officers of different nationality as part of a European police force. If the rules of criminal procedure in the country where the action is taken apply, are the officers familiar with them? If not, to what sort of problems involving unlawfully obtained evidence, etc. could this give rise? I am deliberately passing over the question of how local people might react to foreign police officers taking action in their country.

A convention on data protection would probably be sufficient for the operation of an EDIU, but much more would need to be regulated for executive police activities. One question, for example, leaving aside the matter of costs and management, is what authority would be responsible for the activities of the police on a European scale and who would exercise the necessary democratic control.

The relationship between the national agencies and the proposed international police service is also an interesting question. It is not impossible, for instance, that the latter may be able to exercise executive powers only if a number of essential matters relating to criminal procedure are regulated in the same way in all the States concerned: stopping suspects, arrest, searches of the person, seizure, house searches, tapping of telephone calls, etc. This might lead to a situation where international procedural law might develop alongside national law, or indeed even take its place. Similar questions could arise as far as substantive criminal law is concerned. Should definitions of criminal offences be harmonised? Should sentencing be the same, and therefore the proportion of a sentence which must be served before release on licence is possible? If the increase in the free movement of persons and the abolition of border controls necessitates such harmonisation, a complicated process of consultation, negotiation and amendment of legislation lies ahead of us.

7. The question, however, is whether such internationalisation of criminal law is necessary or desirable as far as the free movement of persons is concerned. Another scenario is also quite conceivable, which would look something like this. Investigation agencies exchange data on organised and transboundary crime in a regular and systematic manner. Via a joint service, they then analyse the material and draw up profiles of offenders, etc. The various forensic laboratories cooperate closely on technical matters. Undesirable behaviour, even if it is of an international character, such as fraud against the EC, is punished in accordance with national legislation. The powers of investigating officers, public prosecutors, examining magistrates, etc., are also regulated nationally. Intensive consultations are held between EC Member States on matters relating to criminal law, procedural law and investigation. These consultations may lead to the harmonisation of criminal law provisions and powers, etc. In this way a process of growth will be initiated which may eventually lead to a decision to regulate certain matters or carry out certain responsibilities jointly.

8. It seems strange — and frustrating for those concerned — that everyone is allowed to cross borders freely, except the police and other officers who enforce the law. But the police in particular are bound by the law in the performance of their duties and at present the power they have to act on behalf of the State (in so far as it is not explicitly legitimised by international law) stops at the border, beyond which the same power is exercised by others on behalf of a different State.

The home country of the people who are allowed to move freely is the State whose nationality they possess. States have cultural and other traditions, which exert a strong influence on the manner in which criminal behaviour and offenders are dealt with. The free movement of persons can and will contribute to a better understanding of cultural differences, but also to the gradual coordination and harmonisation of sometimes highly divergent legal systems. This process can be granted the necessary time without there being any need for immediate concern about a serious threat to the national legal order, provided we follow with conviction the path of consultation, cooperation and the exchange and analysis of information.

THE 'COMMUNITIZATION' OF POLICE COOPERATION IN WESTERN EUROPE

C.J.C.F. Fijnaut[*]

1.   INTRODUCTION

At present we are experiencing exciting developments in the field of police cooperation in western Europe, both inside and outside the European Community (EC). In this report I aim not so much at the rapidly changing cooperation between the European Commission and national regulatory agencies with a view to the enforcement of Community law — interesting though it is[1] — but rather at the actual efforts of the German Government within the framework of the European Council to bring about, at least to some degree, what could be called a 'Communitization' of the cooperation between the regular police forces in the Member States of the EC. Or, to state it yet more clearly: the focus is on the efforts to establish a regular Community police institution, named Europol. It is the struggle concerning this political issue that is the subject of my contribution to this colloquium.

The report is divided into three main parts. To catch the significance of the German proposal it is first necessary to sketch the historical background and the actual organization of the (regular) police cooperation between the Member States. The main point I want to stress here, however, is that this form of cooperation has always been organized in a particular — not to say special and unusual — way, that is outside the general structures of political cooperation. To illustrate this point I just want to describe in broad outline the way Interpol and TREVI are organized at this moment.

Second, against this background it is useful to sketch the German position during the past few decades concerning the structuring of international police cooperation. The first part of this description is related to the more or less loose proposals that

---

* Professor of Criminology and Criminal Law at the Catholic University of Leuven and Erasmus University Rotterdam.
1. Commission of the European Communities, Legal Protection of the Financial Interests of the Community; Proceedings of the Seminar organized by the Directorate-General for Financial Control and the Legal Service of the Commission of the European Communities on 27, 28 and 29 November 1989 in Brussels (Brussels, 1990); H. de Doelder, ed., *Bestrijding van EEG-fraude* (Arnhem-Antwerpen, 1990); C.J.C.F. Fijnaut and F.G.A. Lely, eds., *Economisch strafrecht en justitieel politieoptreden* (Lochem, 1990).

H.G. Schermers et al., eds., Free Movement of Persons in Europe
© 1993, T.M.C. Asser Instituut, The Hague

76   C.J.C.F. FIJNAUT

were put forward in the beginning of the 1970s and 1980s by German police
officers, senior officials and politicians. The second part concerns the Schengen
Agreement and the Schengen Convention in relation to the 'Communitization' of
police cooperation. And, of course, within this context it is necessary to reflect upon
the resistance to the 'Schengenization' of police cooperation in western Europe.

Finally, I will give my opinion on the above-mentioned German proposal to
institutionalize the police cooperation concerned within the framework of the EC.
How does it relate to the earlier German proposals and the Schengen Treaties? What
does it mean in respect to the existing EEC Treaty and, in particular, the Single
European Act? What is its connection with the suggestions of the Luxemburg
Chairmanship of the European Council made in April 1991 regarding the establishment of a European Political Union (EPU)?

2.   THE EXISTING FRAMEWORK FOR INTERNATIONAL POLICE
        COOPERATION

An examination of police history in (western) Europe quickly reveals that for many
centuries international police cooperation has existed, in the form of exchange of
arrest warrants, the organization of cross-border round-ups of tramps and other
similar actions.[2] But it is only during the nineteenth century that we can descry the
tracks of the efforts made to organize this form of cooperation on a regular basis, to
institutionalize it, so to speak. This took place particularly with respect to the fight
against political crime and political opposition. Among these efforts were the secret
Police Association (*Polizeiverein*) of the member states of the German Confederation, the confidential activities of the Russian Okranha in western Europe, and the
diplomatic European conference of senior officials and high-ranking police officers
in Rome in 1898, which aimed at the international control of violent anarchism.[3]
With a view to what follows it is important to note that these forms of cooperation
were not only hidden from public view but also were very informal, unofficial and
not based on formal agreements or conventions.

These features are still very characteristic of both of the two main mechanisms
and structures of multinational police cooperation in western Europe: namely,
Interpol and TREVI. The organization, mission, duties and activities of both
institutions are not based on unambiguous international treaties. And their operations
are still more or less concealed from the general public, let alone the subject of

2. F. Egmond, *Banditisme in de Franse Tijd; Profiel van de Grote Nederlandse Bende, 1790-1799*
(Amsterdam, 1986); C. Küther, *Raüber und Gauner in Deutschland; das organisierte Bandewesen im 18.
und frühen 19. Jahrhundert* (Göttingen, 1987).
    3. R.B. Jensen, 'The international anti-anarchist conference of 1898 and the origins of Interpol', 16
Journal of Contemporary History (1981) p. 323-347; W. Siemann, Deutschlands Ruhe, Sicherheit und
Ordnung; die Anfänge der politischen Polizei, 1806-1866 (Tübingen, 1985), p. 242-304; F. S. Zucker-
man, The Russian Political Police at Home and Abroad (1880-1917): its Structure, Functions, and
Methods and its Struggle with the Organized Opposition (New York University, 1973).

anything resembling independent, external, democratic review, control or accountability. Moreover, these two institutions can be qualified as examples of intergovernmental cooperation. They have this characteristic in common too! Nevertheless, the current position of Interpol is very different from the position of TREVI. And it is important in this context to pay attention to differences between them.

2.1 The ambiguous structuring of Interpol

It is well-known that from the end of the nineteenth century until World War I efforts to organize police cooperation in western Europe in the criminal field were made in a more or less formal, official, institutional way. Ideas were put forward during that period to create not only an international centre for the exchange of information, but also a real international detective force that would have disposed of executive powers to investigate transnational crime.[4] This debate culminated in 1923 with the establishment of Interpol. Although many interesting questions can be asked about the real background and intentions of the creation of Interpol, and also about its history in the 1930s and 1940s, it is the actual juridical foundation and appearance of Interpol which are its significant features for the purposes of this report.

Although Interpol is not based on an international treaty, it can be characterized as an international public institution. This characterization is founded not only on its aims and tasks, as described in its Constitution of 1956, but also on (1) the role Interpol has been assigned in several treaties relating to legal assistance (e.g., the European Convention on Mutual Assistance in Criminal Matters 1959), (2) its agreements with the French Government concerning, *inter alia*, the immunity of its personnel, the controls on the information stored and the ownership of its buildings, and (3) the fact that the States which are involved in the activities of Interpol, at least in theory, pay allowances, send delegates to meetings and otherwise treat it as an institution.[5] Nevertheless, it still retains important characteristics of the more or less private international association of chiefs of police that was set up in 1923. For example, the lack of clarity in the Statutes of Interpol can lead one to ask whether its real members are the States or the police chiefs concerned. And, more importantly, unlike other international, intergovernmental, (public) institutions, Interpol not only lacks a formal participatory role in global, or at least international political structures

4. C.J.C.F. Fijnaut, 'Naar een Europees FBI', in G.N.M. Blonk, C.J.C.F. Fijnaut and E.L.A.M. de Kerf, eds., *Grensverleggende recherche; congres aan de rechercheschool* (Lochem, 1990), p. 131, at pp. 135-138. Concerning the pre-war history of Interpol, see P. Marabuto, *La collaboration policière internationale en vue de la prévention et de la répression de la criminalité; les institutions internationales de police* (Nice, 1935).

5. M. Anderson, Policing the World; Interpol and the Politics of International Police Cooperation (Oxford, 1989) p. 57-73; A. Goldenberg, La Commission Internationale de Police Criminelle, (Université de Paris, 1953); H. Möllemann, Internationale Polizei - Polizei des Völkerrechts? Zur Problematik der Abgrenzung öffentlicher und privater internationaler Organisationen am Beispiel der Internationalen Kriminalpolizeilichen Organisation (IKPO-Interpol) (Würzburg, 1969); B. Napombejra, L'évolution de la cooperation internationale de police (Université de Strasbourg, 1975).

like the United Nations, the Council of Europe, let alone the European Community, but also lacks, at least at the level of high officials, a representative structure emanating from the States concerned that would govern the management and operations of Interpol. In addition, there is still much current resistance to any evolution of Interpol in such a direction: that would mean the 'politization' of Interpol.[6]

However, these characteristics do not alter the fact that the ambiguous position of Interpol clearly shows the marks of the history of (political) police cooperation in Europe: it still functions more or less as an international police association. And although its structures are much more formalized than those of the German *Polizei-verein* and its activity is much more familiar, the fraternal appearance of Interpol has always been a source of negative criticism, insinuations and so on.[7]

To illustrate the ambiguous character of Interpol it is interesting to compare it with the Drug Enforcement Administration (DEA) of the United States federal government. Of course, making such a comparison is a venturesome undertaking. The DEA is in no way an international public police institution, but 'only' an American, federal police service. And the tasks of the DEA are very different too: its field of operation is much more limited (to the illegal drug trade), on the one hand, and much more operational, on the other. But the point I wish to make in this context is that the DEA, while operating worldwide as an executive international police service, is clearly embedded in the federal government of the United States.[8] In relation to the foregoing analysis of Interpol's position the lesson that can be drawn from this example is that in an international democratic community where the rule of law plays a vital role, an operational, and even more an executive police service, can only be organized if — in terms of political and official control — some fundamental conditions are fulfilled.

2.2   The exceptional structuring of TREVI

Besides Interpol only TREVI can be seen as a full-fledged institutional mechanism of police cooperation in western Europe.[9] It is not necessary to elaborate upon the origins of TREVI here. However, with a view to its relationship with Interpol, it is

6. A very good example of this strong opposition is the report of the Home Affairs Committee, House of Commons, Session 1989-90, Practical Police Cooperation in the European Community, Vol. I (London, 1990) pp. XIX-XXI.

7. See e.g., M. Fooner, *Interpol; Issues in World Crime and International Criminal Justice* (New York, 1989) pp. 35-60; O.V. Garrison, *The Secret World of Interpol* (New York, s.d.); L. Greilsamer, *Interpol; le siège du soupçon* (Paris, 1986); B. Schwitters, *Dossier Interpol; de verborgen wereld van Interpol* (Amsterdam, 1978).

8. E.A. Nadelmann, *Cops across Borders: Transnational Crime and International Law Enforcement* (Harvard University, 1987); D.A. Torres, *Handbook of Federal Police and Investigative Services* (Westport, Connecticut, 1985) pp. 126-131; J.Q. Wilson, *The Investigators; Managing FBI and Narcotics Agents* (New York, 1978).

9. A general overview of international police cooperation in western Europe is presented by J. Benyon et al., *Police Cooperation in Europe; a Preliminary Investigation* (University of Leicester, 1990).

important to note that in the 1960s much criticism was directed at Interpol, especially for being much too bureaucratic and much too inoperational to be adequate for efficient and effective police cooperation in western Europe. The clearest sign of the general discontent was that totally without any involvement of Interpol, even without tuning in with Interpol, many new and very divergent forms of police cooperation were established in the 1960s and 1970s — some of them aimed at cooperation in common border areas, others aimed at cooperation concerning specific issues like the safety of airports.[10] And it took Interpol many years before it conceded this development by organizing regional conferences in Europe and by creating a European Secretariat.[11]

The bureaucratic, global, ineffective organization of Interpol, however, was only one of the important factors in the decision-making process that ultimately led to the foundation of TREVI. The second important factor was that Interpol, even if it had been a smoothly and effectively run intelligence centre for the police in western Europe, was not at all an appropriate mechanism for coping with the major problem that confronted many Member States of the EC at the beginning of the 1970s: terrorist activities of groups and movements from European and non-European origins. Interpol was not a suitable vehicle for the police to tackle this international problem for two reasons. The first is related to the task of Interpol and notably to the rule in its Statutes (Art. 3) that Interpol may not become involved in political, military, religious and racial matters. For this means that if Interpol had been used for the coordination of police efforts to contain the action of the IRA, the ETA and other such groups, it would inevitably have been deeply implicated in political issues too.[12] The second reason is related to the ambiguous position of Interpol: the grip of the States concerned on this institution is not strong enough to enable them to use it as their own instrument to steer international police cooperation in such a sensitive matter as (the fight against) terrorism. In short, at that time, in 1975-1976, the political leaders in Europe, and notably the responsible Ministers of Interior and Justice had to look for a different solution than the mobilization of Interpol. They hit upon the idea of creating a radically new consultation and cooperation mechanism for the Member States: TREVI.[13]

10. C.J.C.F. Fijnaut, 'The Internationalization of Criminal Investigation in Western Europe', in C.J.C.F. Fijnaut and R. Hermans, eds., *Police Cooperation in Europe* (Lochem, 1987) p. 32 at pp. 37-39.

11. A. Baum, 'An Interesting Development within Interpol : the Technical Committee on Cooperation in Europe', 42 *International Criminal Police Review* (1987) pp. 24-25; R. Schmidt-Nothen, 'Europäisches Verbindungsbüro wird endlich war', *Kriminalistik* (1989) pp. 73-75.

12. Meanwhile the position of Interpol in this question has changed to some degree, notably as a result of the signing of the European Convention on the Suppression of Terrorism 1977 by the Member States of the European Community.

13. C.J.C.F. Fijnaut, loc. cit., n. 12 at pp. 39-40; Ph. de Schoutheete, *La coopération politique européenne* (Paris, 1980) pp. 131-146; H. Busch, 'Von Interpol zu TREVI; polizeiliche Zusammenarbeit in Europa', *Bürgerrechte und Polizei* (1988) pp. 38-55.

Presently everybody who is really interested in the general workings of TREVI has many sources at one's disposal.[14] In summing up its most important aspects in the context of this report I would like, however, to briefly discuss three points.

First, TREVI is extraneous not only to the European Community but also to the European Political Cooperation (EPC). It is, indeed, an intergovernmental mechanism in itself, not at all based on a treaty or the like. Moreover, it is a very confidential and secretive organization; much more secretive than Interpol. TREVI's meetings are inaccessible to outsiders, its reports are not distributed outside the inner circle, and, usually the only direct 'open' source of information about its decisions are the press releases made in the wake of the official meetings of the Ministers involved.

Second, the hierarchical structure within TREVI, makes clear its real intergovernmental character and, in this way, its institutional differences with Interpol. At the top of TREVI are the Ministers of Interior and Justice concerned. They meet at least twice a year under the chairmanship of the Minister of the Member State that chairs the European Council. The former chairman, the present chairman and the future chairman form more or less the presidium of TREVI, the so-called Troika. At the second level are the committee of senior officials (from the Ministries concerned) who prepare the meetings of the Troika and direct the working parties at the third level. These working parties consist of lower officials and police officers. At this moment the four regular working parties are concerned with (1) terrorism; (2) equipment, public order, training, etc., (3) drugs and serious crime and (4) '1992'.

Third, TREVI not only duplicates, in some respects, the work of Interpol, but also is, to some degree, much more operational than Interpol, on matters such as the exchange of information (on terrorism in any case) and the training and equipment of anti-terrorism units. Therefore, rivalry between Interpol and TREVI is understandable.

More important, however, is the institutional difference between Interpol and TREVI. Whereas TREVI clearly constitutes an international governmental institution, Interpol only consists of a rather peculiar international police organization. And this difference justifies the conclusion that the foundation of TREVI increased the level of police cooperation in western Europe to an extent which surpasses anything that has been accomplished or pleaded for during the past hundred years in this part of the world. Furthermore, its establishment extended political cooperation namely outside the formal structures of the European Political Cooperation between the Member States of the EC to the domain of interior politics.

---

14. See the report of the House of Commons, *supra*, n. 6, at pp. XX - XXIV, and the report of J. Benyon et al., *supra*, n. 9, at pp. 97-106. Further can be refered to e.g., F. Geysels, 'Europe from the inside', 6 *Policing* (1990) pp. 348-351.

3.   THE GERMAN POSITION IN THE DEBATE ON THE REFORM OF
      POLICE COOPERATION IN WESTERN EUROPE

As stated in the introduction to this report it is useful to provide an overview of the German position during the past few decades concerning the organization of police cooperation or, in general terms, of policing in Europe. In order to do so, I will first discuss the opinions and proposals of individual German police officers, senior officials and politicians in the last twenty years or so. Second, I want to draw attention to some important German aspects of the Schengen Treaties, notably in their relation to the 'Communitization' of police cooperation in Europe. And it goes without saying within this context that it is necessary indeed to reflect briefly on the resistance to the 'Schengenization' of police cooperation in Europe.

3.1.   The debate in Germany since the 1970s and its international response

One has to give the Germans credit for advancing, during the last twenty years, the debate in Europe concerning the future of police cooperation on this continent. But it evidently is not accidental that they always have shown much interest in this topic. First of all, one should not lose sight of Germany's central geographical position on the European continent; this position means that Germany — much more than any other State in western Europe — takes part in the problems of (international) crime and crime-fighting of many western, eastern, Nordic and southern European States. Second, one should not forget that since the 19th century, criminal investigation in Germany has always been put into practice on a relatively high professional level; and this also explains why the German police dislike amateurism in their international relations.[15] Third, based on my reading of the German police literature, I believe that most Germans consider an effective and efficient, but also a formal or, in any case, official and clear regulation of these relations to be necessary given the barbarian role that the German SS-police apparatus played in the occupied countries of Europe during the Second World War and the distrust this has created towards the German police in the neighbouring countries.[16] And, lastly, I may note the well-known German tendency — some people call it a virtue, others a vice — to lock up the conduct of daily life in laws. Overdoing things it could be said: what has not been regulated does not exist, even cannot exist . . .

Anyway, from the 1970s the Germans have pressed for the reorganization of police cooperation in western Europe. There is no doubt about that. It is clear, however, that their opinions have always been divided on the way such reorganiz-

15. C.J.C.F. Fijnaut, *De reguliere recherche in Nederland; enkele algemene beschouwingen over haar opbouw rond de voorbije eeuwwisseling* (Lochem, 1985); A. Mergen, *Die BKA Story* (München, 1987); B. Wehner, *Dem Täter auf die Spur; die Geschichte der Deutschen Kriminalpolizei* (Bergisch Gladbach, 1983).

16. Some important recent publications are: J. v. Lang, *Die Gestapo; Instrument des Terrors* (Hamburg, 1990); J. Tuchel and R. Schattenfroh, *Zentrale des Terrors* (Berlin, 1987); G. Werle, *Justiz — Strafrecht und polizeiliche Verbrechensbekämpfung im Dritten Reich* (Berlin, 1989).

ation should be put into effect. In any case, the ideas of some of their commentators and leaders differed greatly concerning the role of Interpol in a new arrangement of police cooperation in western Europe. And, in addition, it often was and still is unclear in the statements of German officials and politicians what the future role of the European Communities and, particularly, of the European Commission should be in this context.

In 1974, this division of opinion appeared immediately when for the first time the Germans organized a major conference regarding the question whether the EC would have some significance for criminal investigation, judicial policing and *Kriminalpolizei*.[17] R. Grunert, the President of the Association of German Detectives (*Bund Deutscher Kriminalbeamter*), pleaded on this occasion for (1) the establishment of an Europol, a European police authority, consisting of a centre for the coordination of international requests for police assistance, also manned by public prosecutors; (2) an operational division directed at the investigation of violations of 'European' criminal laws and at the support of international investigations started by national police forces; (3) an information centre in relation to inter-european investigations; (4) a legal aid bureau for the police services that also had to be charged with the development of proposals for the harmonization of criminal law and criminal procedure in the Community; and (5) — in the long term — a forensic science department and a training centre. Grunert was undoubtedly of the opinion that this Europol should be founded by the Ministers of the Member States of the EC. However, he neither made clear, whether this Europol would be part of the EC (e.g., established within the European Commission), nor did he explain the relationship between such a new European police authority and Interpol.

This relationship, however, occupied a very central place in the contribution of the then director of the *Bundeskriminalamt*, H. Herold. He too took the position that police cooperation in Europe should be improved considerably. But he was very opposed to the creation or foundation of an operational police service within the EC and even to the establishment of a special police information and communication centre at this level, named Europol or otherwise. His two main arguments for rejection of the Europol idea were first that effective policing, which includes criminal investigation, is only possible in a decentralized, local context where much information is available concerning the population, the administration, etc. and, second , that the EC did not constitute a unity, an entity from a criminal-geographical viewpoint: most international crime transgresses the borders of the Community. Accordingly, he urged the policy of improving European police cooperation within the framework of Interpol. Did he award the EC no role at all in this context? Certainly not! His view called for two types of Member State involvement. First, the Member States should invest more money in Interpol to enable it to enlarge its services for the police in (western) Europe. Second, the Member States should make

---

17. *Bund Deutscher Kriminalbeamter, Europäische Gemeinschaft - auch für die Kriminalpolizei* (Düsseldorf, 1974). See also the report of W. Sielaff on this conference, 'Interpol-Europol?', *Kriminalistik* (1974) pp. 302-306.

provision for a better legal assistance system among themselves, both at the police level and the level of the judiciary.

These contrasting viewpoints proved to be unchanged at the 1980 conference, concerning cross-border criminal investigation, organized by the above-mentioned Association of German Detectives.[18] The president of the Association at the time stuck to the idea that a Europol should be founded, although he commented that European States outside the EC, such as Switzerland, should also have the possibility to participate in such an initiative. Herold, however, again emphasized that the improvement of police cooperation should be realized by adaptation of Interpol. And he gained support for this idea from H. Boge, at that moment an important senior official in the Federal Ministry of Interior but some years later his successor as director of the *Bundeskriminalamt*.

Also in the 1980s leading policemen and officials uttered different, and most of the time, somewhat unclear opinions concerning this issue. For instance, M. Klink, a subsequent director of the *Bundeskriminalamt*, stated in 1987 that in the long run the foundation of a European Criminal Investigation Authority would be necessary, and that such an Authority should not be disconnected from Interpol but, on the contrary, should be integrated into it. [19] He did not advocate a central role to the EC. In his view only the Member States should make agreements on the conditions under which cross-border police operations can take place.

In the light of this discussion in professional circles, but notably with a view to the long-standing and outspoken preference of the top management of the *Bundeskriminalamt* for a reorganization of European police cooperation within the framework of Interpol, it is very interesting and important to examine the views taken by of the German politicians on this issue. A review of statements made during the 1970s judicates that leading politicians did not share the opinions of the successive heads of the *Bundeskriminalamt*. Already at the beginning of the 1970s Minister Schwarz, the President of the Federal Commission of the Ministers of Interior of the different states, took the position that the establishment of a special Europol was needed.[20] And some ten years later B. Vogel, at that time President of Rheinland-Pfalz, repeated this view: a Europol within the EC would be a better solution for the problems of European crime fighting than the individual efforts of the police forces within the Member States.[21]

During the 1980s this political position has been increasingly accepted as the official policy of the German Government. For example, in 1987, F. Zimmermann, the then Federal Minister of Interior, declared at the Interpol conference of the European region that Interpol was an institution of great merits for police cooperation in Europe, but at the same time, that the German Government reserved the

18. *Bund Deutscher Kriminalbeamter, Grenzüberschreitende Verbrechensbekämpfung im Spiegelbild zwischenstaatlicher Verträge und gesetzlicher Regelungen* (Berlin, 1980).
19. M. Klink, 'Die Zusammenarbeit Europäischer Polizeien in Sicherheitsfragen', 78 *Die Polizei* (1987) pp. 183-189.
20. See the booklet, cited *supra*, n. 18, p. 16.
21. See the booklet, cited *supra*, n. 19, p. 3.

right to organize close police cooperation with individual States or groups of States outside of Interpol.[22] The arguments he developed in support of this position were notably that in some areas Interpol could not take any responsibility for police cooperation, and that the legal, organizational and other differences between its member States were too great for easy-going and intensive cooperation arrangements. One year later this Minister and his Secretary, C. Spranger, substantially clarified these arguments. Refering to the discussion in TREVI about the containment of the drug trade, they expressed the opinion that police cooperation among the Member States of the EC should be enlarged and accelerated by the creation of a new European police authority.[23] In 1989 and 1990 the same Secretary and his new Minister, W. Schaüble, explained the eventual features and powers of such an institution.[24] It should be part of the EC and could be held responsible for, *inter alia*, the gathering and analysis of information, the development of crime-fighting methods and strategies, the training of police officers and the administration of common forensic facilities. Both policymakers, however, left aside the question whether the personnel of this European Authority should be given executive police powers and/or be empowered to investigate international crime. And in this important respect their views greatly differed from that of the Federal Chancellor, H. Kohl, who already in 1988 and again in 1989 argued in favour of the establishment — following the American model — of an European FBI (Federal Bureau of Investigation).[25]

Interesting though it is to relate these findings to the role of Germany in the Schengen Agreement and the Schengen Convention and the recent initiative of the German Government to 'Communitize' police cooperation between the Member States, it is now above all important to point to the reactions outside Germany to these professional and political lines of policy. First, it can be stated that the provocative positions concerned never received much attention in western Europe. In any case, they did not bring about in the Member States anything like a continuing public debate on the way the problem of police cooperation should be settled. And this means that it is very difficult to record the significance and bearing of the scanty reactions that have been recorded.

Looking at the reactions from the police in western Europe it will be no surprise that leading French police officers also took the position that Interpol should remain the framework for police cooperation in Europe: they have for a very long time dominated this organization.[26] But they were not the only police officers in Europe

22. The speech he has given on that occasion has been published in: *Innere Sicherheit* (1987) No. 3, pp. 14-16.

23. See the text of some of their addresses in: *Innere Sicherheit* (1988) No. 5, pp. 2-5, and *Innere Sicherheit* (1990) No. 4, pp. 8-11.

24. For the text of the important address given by W. Schäuble in The Hague on this issue, see: *Innere Sicherheit* (1989) No. 5, pp. 10-14.

25. A condensed summary of his addresses has been published in: *Europa-Bericht* (1988) No. 131, p. 9 and *Europa van Morgen* (1988) p. 599.

26. See the address of S. Langlais, published in the report referred to in n. 17, at pp. 50-57.

who defended the traditional position of Interpol in this part of the world. Recently, in an important memorandum to the Home Affairs Committee of the House of Commons, the representative associations of senior police officers in the United Kingdom also defended Interpol as the most appropriate police cooperation mechanism inside and outside western Europe. This position implicitly showed their rejection of some 'Communitization' of this form of cooperation.[27] Their arguments are, in general, not very clear, but they remind us of the arguments once put forward by Herold: international crime crosses the geographical boundaries of the EC. Therefore, Interpol — modernized as it is at this moment — is the most practical way to bring about effective cooperation in specific cases because its organization guarantees sufficiently a lawful handling of requests for help from police services in other countries. And one should not lose sight of the fact that senior police officers in the Nordic countries, certainly in Denmark, seem to subscribe to the ideas of their British colleagues.[28]

This, however, does not alter the fact that the major European police confederations for many years have advocated the foundation of a Europol. More specifically I refer to the Eurofedop proposals and the repeated claims of the International Union of Police Associations. Although their ideas also suffer from the defect that they are unclear in relation to issues like the institutional framework of such a police service, the control of its functioning, the powers of its members and so on, they nevertheless show that not only on a German level but also on an European level the debate in professional circles concerning the reorganization of police cooperation is an ambiguous one and contains divergent opinions about which road to follow. Consequently, it is not surprising at all that even well-informed police officers sometimes have much difficulty in making a choice between the different options.

As far as the reactions of foreign politicians to the German debate are concerned it is even more difficult to draw a picture of the situation in western Europe because of the real lack of public debate on the German proposals up to the present time. For this reason, I want only to indicate the opinion of the present Dutch Minister of Justice, E. Hirsch Ballin, on the idea of Europol. Being the chairman of TREVI at this moment it is important to know how he regards this idea. In a nutshell: very negatively! In April 1990 at least he clearly stated in a lecture to the Dutch Society of Public Administration that the conditions for the development of an Europol are not at all realized at this moment: there is no system of federal rules, no framework for the governance of policing and no democratic control system concerning its governance. Europol, so the Minister explained, can only be the outcome of very important developments in western Europe but never their starting point.[29] In other words: if E. Hirsch Ballin sticks to his opinion he is at loggerheads with his German counterparts at this moment . . .

27. See the report, cited in n. 3.
28. K. Peterson, 'International Police Cooperation in Scandinavia', in *Report of the European Police Summer Course 1989* (Zutphen - Apeldoorn, 1990) pp. 21-26.
29. This address has been published in the *Staatscourant* (1990) No. 69, pp. 1, 15.

3.2. Some German aspects of the Schengen Agreement and Schengen Convention

Germany not only occupies a leading position in the European debate concerning the (re-)organization of police cooperation in Europe, it is also the country that has concluded by far the most treaties and agreements with western, eastern and southern European States in this field. In an effort to define the position of Germany in respect of the Schengen Treaties and to elucidate also in this way its recent proposal to 'Communitize' the cooperation of the regular police forces in western Europe, it is important therefore to go back to the direct source of these treaties: the French-German Agreement on police cooperation in the Saar region from 1977.

We do not have the opportunity now to analyze the French-German Agreement in detail. And such an analysis is not necessary at this moment either. The most important thing in this context, however, is that the French-German Agreement was the first clear sign that the German Government was indeed willing to modernize its police cooperation with neighbouring countries in western Europe outside of Interpol. Interpol was not radically put out of action in this Agreement, but it lost its status as the centre of police cooperation in the area concerned.[30] And it is just as much important to point to the fact that the German Government at the time was of the opinion not only that the scope of this Agreement with France should be enlarged to the whole territory of both countries, but also that similar agreements had to be concluded with other western European countries such as the Benelux countries.[31] This showed that the German Government was willing to establish something like a parallel system of police cooperation in Europe.

It should also be emphasized that the content of the French-German Agreement completely fits the pattern of the traditional European arrangements concerning police cooperation in border areas. In other words, this Agreement contains no explicit rules relating to cross-border operations such as hot pursuit or international surveillance. However, it compels police authorities to accept mutual exchanges of information and mutual assistance in specific investigations, etc. Besides, it is remarkable that the French-German Agreement grants no explicit role to judicial authorities with respect to the supervision of police action. International police cooperation, in other words, is predominantly seen as an affair for the police themselves, at least in the first resort.[32]

The German Government's abandonment of this line of policy in the mid 1980s was evidenced in 1984 with the Treaty of Saarbrücken with France, which in turn led to the Schengen Agreement of 1985. The change in policy must be understood in the light of the 1984 Decision of the European Council in Fontainebleau to abolish

30. *Bundesgesetzblatt* (1978) T. II, pp. 1402 - 1404.
31. See the reaction of the Federal Secretary of State Fröhlich to a parliamentary question on this issue, published in *Innere Sicherheit* (1984) No. 76, p. 19.
32. C.J.C.F. Fijnaut, 'De Overeenkomst van Schengen: een doorbraak van de formele regeling van de internationale politiesamenwerking ?', in J. D'Haenens, B. de Ruyver, eds., *Schengen en de praktijk* (Gent 1992) pp. 47-66.

the internal borders within the EC. Notably for the Germans such a Decision could not be implemented unless simultaneous measures were taken to counteract what they considered to be the more or less negative effects of such a policy, including the negative effect on internal safety and crime-fighting in the countries concerned. Nevertheless, I want to venture the thesis that the German Government was also rather happy with this opportunity to reorder police cooperation in western Europe because its efforts to conclude agreements similar to the French-German Agreement with other countries had been unsuccessful up to then.

In any event, if one looks at the Schengen Agreement and the Schengen Convention against the background of the debate in Germany with respect to international police cooperation in Europe, it is clear that these two treaties embody fully the line of policy preferred by leading German politicians since the 1970s. There are several reasons for this conclusion. First, these treaties compel (some of) the Member States of the EC to improve international police cooperation by developing formal rules for the exchange of information, the regulation of cross-border operations and so on. And in the second place, these treaties pose a serious threat to Interpol's role as the central information centre for the police in western Europe by establishing the Schengen Information System totally outside Interpol and by urging the Parties concerned to found — unrelated to Interpol — a common central bureau for the exchange of information concerning the drug trade in Europe. The only thing that remains unclear within this context is the institutional relationship, at least in the long run, between these initiatives and the EC, at the level of the EEC Treaty as well as at the level of the European Commission or the European Council.

Important though it is to make a detailed analysis of the content of these treaties with respect to police cooperation, with a view to the actual evolution of the German policy in this field, it is much more important to point out the criticism that the Schengen treaties received within police circles.[33] The general feeling within the German police is that Schengen is only a first step towards the needed organization of police cooperation in Europe. The German critics estimate that not only are the measures that have been taken too minor and too restrictive, but also that criminal investigation in western Europe, within the EC, badly needs central steering and central support.[34] In the United Kingdom in contrast — as could be expected — senior police officers and senior officials, attending the Senior Command Course at the Police Staff College in June 1991, told me that they are afraid of the 'Schengen-

---

33. C.J.C.F. Fijnaut, 'Police cooperation within Western Europe', in F. Heidensohn and M. Farrell, eds., *Crime in Europe* (London, 1991) pp. 103-120.

34. See e.g., P. Ingenerf, 'Das Schengener Abkommen; eine kritische Betrachtung aus der Sicht einer Polizeibehörde im Grensraum', 43 *Kriminalistik* (1989) pp. 341-344, 361-362; R. Rupprecht, 'Wettlauf der Schnecken; Probleme und Konsequenzen des Abbaus von Grenzkontrollen', 43 *Kriminalistik* (1989) pp. 263-270; W. Schreiber, 'Polizeiliche Zusammenarbeit in einem Europa ohne Grenzen; Realität und Perspektiven', 45 *Kriminalistik* (1991) pp. 369-376; A. Stümper, 'Sicherheit in Europa; ein Aufruf zur Besinnung', 44 *Kriminalistik* (1990) pp. 2-8; B. Walter, 'Europäischer Enthusiasmus; grenzüberschreitende Kriminalität im Spannungsfeld zwischen Kontrolle und Liberalisierung des Grenzverkehrs', 43 *Kriminalistik* (1989) pp. 66-71.

ization' of police cooperation in western Europe and took the position that the role of Interpol should be strengthened. And to preclude any misunderstanding: 'Schengenization' means in this context: needless political and judicial control of the police, too many formalities in daily police work and so on.[35] All in all it consequently goes without saying that the Schengen treaties really have made a hot issue of the 'Communitization' of police cooperation by the establishment of an Europol within the EC. Police officers, senior officials and politicians, at least in some countries concerned, hold very different opinions concerning the opportunity of such a development.

4.   THE SIGNIFICANCE OF THE GERMAN INITIATIVE TOWARDS THE EUROPEAN COMMUNITIES

These remarks in respect of the Schengen treaties evidently relate to the proposal the German Government made in Luxemburg in June 1991 to establish a Europol within the framework of the EC. More precisely this proposal reads as follows: no later than 31 December 1993 the commitment will be inserted into the Treaty to establish a Central European Investigation Bureau (Europol) with respect to the fight against the international drug trade and organized crime; the details of this undertaking will be settled by common consent of the European Council; the tasks of this Bureau will be developed step-by-step: in the first resort a bureau will be founded for the exchange of information and experience (up to 31 December 1992); thereafter, in the second phase, executive powers will be assigned, also within the Member States; the Commission as well as the individual Member States dispose of the right to submit proposals. A very important note is that this proposition is set forth only in the annexes of the general conclusions of the Luxemburg Chairmanship. For in these conclusions themselves it has been stated that the European Council agrees upon the aims which lie at the root of the proposal of the German delegation . . . In other words, the Council disassociates itself somewhat from the German initiative.[36]

In a discussion about this proposal one should draw a distinction between several questions. The most interesting and important questions in my opinion are: how does this proposal relate to the ideas that have been put forward earlier in the German debate concerning police cooperation in Europe? Why has the European Council accepted, to some degree at least, the German proposal? And is there any connection between this relatively positive answer and the suggestions of the Luxembourg Chairmanship of the European Council in April 1991, in relation to the establishment of a European Political Union? What does this proposal mean in relation to the existing arrangements of police cooperation in western Europe?

35. See also the comment of R. Birch, 'Policing Perspectives of the Single Market without Interior Border-Controls; the Schengen Convention: a Model for the Europe of 12 in 1993? Views and Expectations within the British Police', in *No Border Controls any more within the EEC? Policing Perspectives of the Single Market of 1993*; Report on an IPA-Seminar (Marienheide, 1990) pp. 16-25.

36. See *Europa van Morgen* (1991) pp. 324-332.

In addressing the first question one has to stress above all that the proposal concerned completely fits into the line of policy the German Government has already pursued for a long time. It embodies a clear choice for the establishment of a specific, peculiar criminal investigation bureau in western Europe — independent of and in addition to Interpol. And in this way it also clearly shows that the German Government rejects the policy that the *Bundeskriminalamt* has always defended, notably: to establish a European bureau within the framework of or, in any case, in close connection with Interpol. In the second place one should not lose sight of the fact that this proposal reflects the core of the ideas and suggestions that the successive Federal Ministers of Interior and the Federal Chancellor have brought to the fore in the past few years. They have pointed out that it is necessary to establish within the EC a police authority, service or bureau with, on the one hand, coordinating powers and, on the other, executive powers. It is only somewhat surprising that no mention has been made of more secundary aspects of the named authority such as its potential technical and forensic support function and its eventual contribution to police training and police research in Europe.

The second question set forth above is much more complicated. To start with I would like to emphasize, referring to what has been said above, that the German proposal in itself might not have been a surprise for the participants in the gathering of the European Council in Luxemburg: it is the more or less logical outcome of a long term process of political pressure, inside and outside Germany. At the very most only the timing of the German Government's proposal in the official discussions of the European Council might have been somewhat surprising, but only for outsiders. Insiders could have expected that Germany would grasp the summit in Luxembourg as the opportunity to go on the offensive for the establishment of a Europol. Why?

There are several reasons. During the past years conditions have been created within the intergovernmental structure of TREVI wherein such a proposal can flourish. I note in particular the establishment in 1985-1986 of Working Group III concerning the fight against the drug trade and serious crime. Furthermore, one should not lose sight of the second important step in this context, notably the 'programme of action' that the Working Group '1992' elaborated in 1990 in relation to the reinforcement of police cooperation. This programme of action for the first time not only put forward proposals in very different ways and at very different levels to enlarge, to intensify and, to some degree, to regularize the (up to then mostly secretive) cooperation of the Member States on many related questions, but also reflected the tendency to centralize that cooperation in western Europe by building strong similar national information centres and coordination structures, by establishing European collections of objects, substances, products and documents, and by enlarging and accelerating the international exchange of information. And lastly, it is well-known that in the wake of this programme the European Council in Dublin, in June 1990, decided upon the foundation of a European Narcotics Bureau.

A further major development was the revival in 1990-1991 of the public debate on the monetary and political union of western Europe, and the fact that the Luxembourg Chairmanship introduced in April 1991 a comprehensive paper concerning these and other issues.[37] This is important because this paper, especially within its section concerning the (intergovernmental) cooperation between the Member States in the areas of internal affairs and justice, not only underlines the necessity for close mutual (police) cooperation with respect to internal security in general and the fight against illegal activities in particular, but also makes room for the foundation of central (police) authorities to lead and to coordinate cross-border police operations within the territory of the Community. In any event, this paper offered a more or less clear view of an institutional framework for the implementation and realization of the recent ideas and plans developed within the framework of TREVI.

And within this general situation it is, in my opinion, not at all surprising that the German Government pushed the foundation of a Community Europol in Luxembourg in June 1991. The German delegation may have thought it was a last and unique opportunity to present a Community alternative for the intergovernmental solution. And it is no more surprising that the other delegations at that moment more or less went along with the German initiative. This is because the content of this proposal not only fits very well with the desire within TREVI to institutionalize police cooperation in western Europe, but also matches very well the desire to forge a political union from the Member States of the EC.

However, although the German proposal looks like the most rational and legitimate answer to the present political developments and to the ongoing evolution within European police cooperation, it is now not at all definite that the British, the Dutch and the Danish representatives, for example, have swallowed their objections to the German approach and let things go. On the contrary, it goes without saying that the debate concerning the realization of Europol, in line with the Community model, will be a very difficult one because the Member States that have always opposed its foundation will try to restructure this initiative in the direction of their own intergovernmental preference.

Following these considerations with respect to the 'adoption' of the German proposal with respect to Europol in Luxembourg in June 1991, I now want to tackle the third and last question: what does this proposal mean in relation to the existing arrangements of police cooperation in western Europe. Although the way in which the idea of Europe shall be elaborated in the future is not yet clear, and there is also uncertainty as to whether the implementation of this idea will result in a modification of the EC Treaty, one can nevertheless come to the present conclusion that its realization would be a third real breakthrough in this field, the first one being the foundation of Interpol and the second one being the establishment of TREVI. Why such an event can be characterized as a 'breakthrough' is a somewhat complicated matter. In any case from two perspectives, it is convenient to make use of this tense word.

The first perspective is based upon the existing arrangements for police cooperation. As discussed in the first part of this report, the existing arangements can be

---

37. See the Non-Paper : Projet d'articles de Traité, en vue de la mise en place d'une union politique (Luxemburg, 1991).

described as having a special, exceptional, more or less informal, secretive character. If a Europol is realized within a Community conception of the European Political Union, it would be for the first time in the western European police history that police cooperation is to some degree made part of the general political structures and institutions in this area. Evidently, the implications of such a radical change, in terms of (democratic) political control, of criminal law and criminal procedure, of relations with national police services, are yet far from clear, but this takes nothing away from its eventual historical significance.

The second perspective is based upon the EEC Treaty. The experts on the Treaty know very well that several of its Articles (e.g., Arts. 5, 85, 86) allow the European Commission in some respects to function as a regulatory agency and that the Commission with a view to the enforcement of EC law is increasingly involved in the foundation and training of national regulatory agencies and in the coordination of their operations. The establishment of UCLAF in 1988 is the clearest example of this development.[38] In the field of regular, general police matters, however, the Treaty does not give any footing to the Commission or any other Community institution for specific action. And although the Declarations added to the Single European Act, and notably the Declaration with respect to Articles 13 to 19 of the Single European Act clearly give some room for action in this field to the European Commission and the Council, they have yet to grasp this opportunity to intervene in the ongoing processes with respect to this form of cooperation. Apparently they have taken the view that cooperation between the regular police forces and the intelligence services is within the reach of TREVI. In any case, neither the famous White Paper of the Commission nor its report of 1989 concerning the abolition of border controls within the Community nor the Palma Document the same year contain any proposal for the organization of police cooperation within the EC itself, let alone its Commission.[39] And all this makes very clear that the decision to establish an Europol within their reach really would be a drastic innovation.

5.   CONCLUSION

The story, the exciting story of police cooperation in western Europe will continue. The recent German initiative really has opened up a new chapter. Many unknown events and developments lie ahead. We may think of the relationship between Europol, Interpol and TREVI. The relationship between Europol and the national

38. See the report *Fraude in de Europese Gemeenschappen* (The Hague, 1990) and J.A.E. Vervaele, *EEG-fraude en Europees economisch strafrecht* (Deventer, 1991).

39. See Commissie van de Europese Gemeenschappen, De voltooiing van de interne markt; Witboek van de Commissie voor de Europese Raad (Com (85) 310 def); Commissie van de Europese Gemeenschappen, Rapport van de Commissie betreffende de opheffing van de personencontroles aan de binnengrenzen van de Gemeenschap (Com (88) 640 def.); Groep Coördinatoren voor het Vrije Verkeer van Personen, Overzicht van de in diverse instanties aan te nemen maatregelen inzake het vrije verkeer van personen en tijdschema voor de toepassing ervan (CIRC 3625/89).

police forces is important. Many questions can be put forward in relation to the control and management of Europol. What kind of relationship has to be developed with respect to the Prosecution Services? What will the position of the European Commission look like? And the European Parliament: will it fill up the democratic gap in this area in an effective and rational way? By asking these questions I clearly want to demonstrate my own view on this issue of Europol too. And this view amounts to the conclusion that from a democratic and constitutional viewpoint the establishment of an Europol has to be welcomed. The most important things to do now are, on the one hand, to institutionalize Europol as far as possible in a democratic and constitutional way and, on the other, to elaborate on this idea on the basis of firm knowledge of the developments in the field of international (organized) crime.

CRIMINAL LAW AND THE EUROPEAN COMMUNITY

J.J.E. Schutte[*]

There is currently a discussion in Europe regarding the extent to which matters related to criminal law enforcement should be placed within the ambit of Community law. In other words, the issue is whether these matters should be dealt with in the future at a Community level through procedures provided by Community law. This discussion is held from different perspectives; I will talk about three of them.

The first one, which is very much the focus of this particular Colloquium, addresses the inevitable or desirable consequences of the realization of a system of free movement of persons within a Community without internal border controls. The discussion here is spurred onward by the continuing efforts to realize the internal market and by the proposals for the creation of a European Political Union.

The second perspective is that the Community has an increasing need, given the ever-growing scope of Community law, to develop instruments of penal or at least punitive law enforcement. In order to meet such needs it has been suggested that the Community be provided with its own sanctioning powers as well as the power to compel the Member-states to use their criminal justice systems for the enforcement of Community law, preferably on the basis of harmonized rules and policies.

The third perspective is based on an assessment of the growing internationalization of crime, frequently internationally organized crime, which individual Member States cannot control on their own and in respect of which, as is the case with other matters transcending the capacities and capabilities of individual Member States, the Community would present the only viable alternative.

Let me present you with some observations on each of these three perspectives. The Schengen Convention of 1990 is frequently perceived as the best available model of an all-embracing regulation of the abolition of internal border controls and the consequential compensatory provisions. However, it would be inaccurate to read the Convention's provisions on police and security as a complete picture of the necessary consequences of abolition of frontier controls. With the exception of the establishment of the Schengen Information System (which has never had a comparable counterpart in the Benelux) and the provisions on 'trans-frontier' hot-pursuit (which does have a precedent in the Benelux), all provisions inserted in the

---

* Ministry of Justice, The Hague.

H.G. Schermers et al., eds., Free Movement of Persons in Europe
© 1993, T.M.C. Asser Instituut, The Hague

Convention deal with matters which would also be of relevance if internal frontier controls had been maintained. I refer to the cooperation among national police services of Member States which presently exists on a largely customary basis (but is now being codified).

I refer also to judicial cooperation where Schengen provisions are building on existing conventional intergovernmental arrangements of the Council of Europe and the Benelux. I refer also to the selection of matters addressed in the Schengen Convention, which happen to have been a rather arbitrary one and based on a priority list drawn up by the negotiators. Issues that were supported by more than two countries received priority, and discussion about the other subjects was postponed. But this adheres to the usual pattern of existing multilateral intergovernmental agreements.

The relationship with the free movement of persons is also quite arbitrary with respect to the substantive issues that have been addressed in the Schengen Convention, such as narcotic drugs and the control of firearms. Their regulation is not an absolutely inevitable consequence of abolition of border controls on persons. And their choice — a balanced choice I would say — is a result of the particular preoccupations of the five original countries. If Italy had participated from the beginning, I am sure that the matter of stolen art objects would have been on the list, and if Spain had participated early on, the subject of terrorism might have been included.

In any event, my conclusion on this particular perspective is that one cannot deduce from the inclusion of certain matters in the Schengen Convention that all those matters are equally closely related to the free movement of persons, and that they should therefore be regulated on behalf of the Twelve Member States by Community law and by Community law only.

With regard to the second perspective, there was until recently a general consensus that Community law is and should be completely separate from criminal law, and that criminal law is and should remain within the domain of the Member States. The explicit creation of Community competence in the area of criminal law would require amendment of the Treaties, to be approved by Member States through their constitutional procedures. The general consensus as to strict separation is wearing thin, particularly as a result of developments stimulated by the Community institutions themselves, in particular the Court of Justice and the Commission.

One of these developments concerns the matter of attributing sanctioning powers to the Community itself, not *vis-à-vis* the Member States but *vis-à-vis* individual persons and organizations and the second development is the matter of imposing the obligation on Member States to introduce and apply punitive sanctions. Moreover, the Community has acquired and continues to acquire controlling powers over the law enforcement efforts including powers effected through the use of criminal procedures of the Member States.

If the developments in Community law continue in this piecemeal and somewhat unstructured way, confusion and uneasiness about the limits of Community competence in this area are likely to increase. This has recently resulted in a 'mandate' provided by the Ministers of Justice of the Member States to conduct a general study of the situation to be presented for discussion and, if possible, to reach a common position. Although this study, which is presently being undertaken by legal experts of the governments of the Member States together with the Commission, has not yet been completed, it appears that views vary quite substantially, and that the differences can probably only be solved through Treaty amendments. In any event, the view that there is little or no room for regulation by Community law of subjects of criminal law still seems to be held by a substantial number of Member States.

The third perspective: those who contend that international or transnational crime in Europe can be countered more effectively through a Community law approach rather than an intergovernmental approach have the burden of proof. This burden seems to me particularly heavy after having been informed in the report of Mr Fode how the harmonization of criminal law and cooperation in criminal matters has been organized and is functioning well in Scandinavia. Mr Grosheide has indicated in his report the gigantic institutional and constitutional problems which are emerging if one were seriously to propose that the detection and investigation of certain forms of international crime should be entrusted to a Community institution. The argument is that investigation cannot be isolated from prosecution or prosecution from trial, trial from criminal procedure nor criminal procedure from the organization of the judiciary, nor can the organization of the judiciary be isolated from the relationship between the judiciary and the other branches of government which exercise legislative and executive functions. These points are so overwhelming and legitimate that I find it hard to take seriously those who propose to simply begin working on the establishment of a European police with its own executive powers.

The Community, although a bureaucratic entity par excellence, has nevertheless some human features. It can be characterized as having an irresistible attraction to popular subjects with much sex appeal, such as the fight against drugs, money laundering, insider trading in securities, theft of art and terrorism. In all these areas the Community considers itself competent, sometimes challenged by Member States, sometimes without fear to be misunderstood by public opinion.

From the point of view of legitimacy, those developments should not remain unquestioned. I fully recognize that there should be ample room for a creative and progressive development of Community law. However, where this development affects principles of the rule of law, which are fundamental when it comes to the exercise of authority under public law − as is the case with criminal law − the Community must not risk following a path on which it would jeopardize its own reputation.

Let me conclude by making a plea based on the consideration that, contrary to what many people may believe, the existing decision-making procedures under Community law are not necessarily more democratic than procedures of inter-state cooperation. I would suggest that in the area of the development of European criminal law and of European cooperation in criminal matters there should be a liberal interpretation of the so-called principle of subsidiarity. This principle implies as you may know, that in areas in which there is no exclusive competence for the Community there should be regulation at the level of the Community only when such regulation cannot be established better or equally well by the individual Member States. This principle should also imply, I contend, that there should only be regulation at the level of the Community when the same purpose cannot be achieved better or equally well by way of arrangements between and among Member States, subject to each of their constitutional requirements.

Cooperation between Fiscal and Customs Authorities

THE SINGLE MARKET AFTER 1992 AND CUSTOMS COOPERATION IN THE EC

Martin Brown[*]

1. INTRODUCTION

The purpose of this paper is to outline Customs' current functions at the frontier, to look at areas where change will be necessary in the Single Market after 1992. The paper describes the developments already taking place in the United Kingdom to streamline customs checks and explains why there will still be a need to keep certain essential checks even after 1992. It also describes the development of customs cooperation, particularly in the forum of the EC's Customs Mutual Assistance Group 1992 (MAG '92).

2. CUSTOMS FUNCTIONS AT THE FRONTIER

Customs' primary interest is in goods in any shape or form, whether as freight consignments or as passengers' baggage. However, goods are, for all practical purposes, inextricably linked to the people who own or handle them. This applies equally to the commercial importer, the freight forwarder, the carrier and the holiday-maker. But it is this link with *people* — with travellers — that catches the attention of the public and makes the Customs area such a sensitive one in the whole 1992 debate.

The Commission has sometimes taken a rather narrow view of customs work, as in their original 1985 White Paper on the Single Market:

'the Customs authorities' primary role at internal frontier posts . . . is to ensure that the indirect taxation system of the member state in question . . . continues to operate. It therefore follows that, from the Customs viewpoint, the problem of removing physical controls is largely related to that of removing fiscal barriers.'

(Commission white paper on completing the Internal Market: 1985).

* CD Division 4 (anti-smuggling controls), HM Customs and Excise, London.

H.G. Schermers et al., eds., Free Movement of Persons in Europe

In some EC countries, the Customs authorities do have a more restricted role than in the UK, and are often split between a fiscal bureaucracy collecting duty and tax on imported goods, and a border guard service on the lines of the Italian Guardia di Finanze. But in the UK we have a Customs and Excise whose functions are broad and deep. We collect duties and VAT not only on imports, but also on domestic transactions; we regulate the trade in a wide variety of prohibited and restricted goods; and with smuggling offences — drugs in particular — we perform our own investigations and conduct our own prosecutions. Other EC countries organise law enforcement differently. When some EC Customs services encounter a drugs smuggler, they must hand them straight over to the police to conduct the investigation, and in most countries public prosecutors are responsible for bringing offenders to court.

2.1   Fiscal frontier control

Fiscal frontier controls, which the Commission correctly say must be removed to create a Single Market, are therefore only one facet of our work. Fiscal controls apply to both goods and people. As far as *freight* consignments are concerned, Customs collect VAT, excise duty, Community customs duty and trade statistics by way of frontier documentation — a written declaration is presented for each consignment at import or export. For *people*, fiscal control takes the form of travellers' allowances — the limits on the amount of goods passengers can bring into the country without being required to pay duty and taxes.

2.2   Regulatory control

Regulatory controls are part of the system of authorisation, monitoring and rationing that applies for many reasons across a wide field of prohibited or restricted goods. These range from works of art and antiques to defence and strategic goods, from fish and plant material to products made from endangered species. Taking heritage goods as an example, at present an export licence is required for certain works of art and antiques, which must be presented to Customs for check and endorsement before the goods can be released for export.

2.3   Anti-smuggling control

Anti-smuggling controls provide a system of checking both goods and people to enforce the fiscal and regulatory controls. Customs are looking for illicit transactions: undeclared goods on which revenue is due; goods that need a licence but have not got one; and illegal importations of prohibited items. Most work in this area, of course, concentrates on the fight against drugs smuggling.

3.   UK CUSTOMS' INTERNAL ORGANISATION OF THE ENFORCEMENT EFFORT

Within Customs, anti-smuggling work is divided between the uniformed preventive staff at ports and airports and Customs' specialist national forces, such as the cutter fleet and the Investigation Division. In the drugs smuggling field, there is a broad spectrum of activity. Major, long-term operations by the specialist forces rely heavily on specific intelligence, while the more routine seizures made by frontier staff at the ports and airports depend on a combination of factors: the analysis of current smuggling trends; the development of local risk profiles; background information and intelligence; and, not least, the knowledge and experience of the officer on the ground. It is a mistake to assume, as many in the European Commission often do, that most drugs seizures come from intelligence tip-offs. In 1990, many large seizures did indeed result from intelligence leads from our overseas Drugs Liaison Officers, target information from within the UK or other specific pointers. But a vast quantity of drugs is seized either *'cold'* (with officers relying on no more than a hunch) or by reference to broad intelligence *'profiles'*. Cold or profiled seizures in 1990 gave rise to 77% by weight of our cocaine seizures and 41% of heroin. These are the seizures that depend critically on the presence *at the frontier* of customs officers, and if '1992' resulted in all border controls being swept away, these seizures would not be made.

4.   POLICE / CUSTOMS LIAISON

In the field of anti-smuggling control, Customs and the Police in the UK perform complementary roles. As laid out in the Government's strategic document 'Tackling Drugs Misuse', Customs have the 'primary responsibility for preventing and detecting the illegal import and export of controlled drugs, the investigation of organisations and individuals engaged in international drugs smuggling, their prosecution and the identification of any proceeds of such crime.' We operate under the Customs and Excise Management Act 1979. The primary task of the Police, operating under the Misuse of Drugs Act 1971, is 'dealing with offences of manufacture, supply and possession within the UK.' There is a recognised overlap where organised criminal activity runs both importation and distribution networks, and our staff co-operate closely with the Police.

This is shown by *joint* operations to conduct *controlled deliveries*, under which drugs are allowed to move under surveillance from the port to detect the organisers of the smuggling run inland (controlled delivery is at least a weekly occurrence for us). Police and Customs also cooperate closely in the National Drugs Intelligence Unit operating out of Scotland Yard, which has 18 Customs investigators seconded to it. The UK intends that Customs staff will also participate in the emerging European Drugs Intelligence Unit (EDIU), plans for which are being made by the TREVI committees at the request of EC Interior and Justice Ministers.

Looking to the longer term, interest is currently being stimulated again in the German idea of a European-wide criminal investigation organisation — a Euro-FBI or

Europol. There are obvious legal, constitutional and political obstacles to a *supra-national* enforcement agency, but it is important for those involved in the negotiations at the 'Union' inter-governmental conference to be aware of the clear *practical* need to tap into Customs' expertise : Europol *cannot* be seen as merely a police concern. The UK believes that the EDIU should be the first stage of the Europol development, which will ensure that Customs staff are included from the start.

5. INTERNATIONAL CUSTOMS COOPERATION

The primary forum for international Customs cooperation is provided by the Customs Cooperation Council (CCC), which has a membership of some 111 customs authorities worldwide. The CCC coordinates action to improve the effectiveness of customs authorities in the prevention and detection of movements of illicit goods through greater international cooperation, while at the same time facilitating the free movement of innocent goods and people. For example, the recent G7 summit in London declared its support for the CCC's carrier cooperation initiative. This has the aim of extending and enhancing cooperation between customs authorities, private carriers and the international trade community to the mutual benefit of all parties. By cultivating information from trade sources, Customs can increase the effectiveness of the fight against drugs trafficking, with a knock-on effect of faster processing for low-risk cargo if Customs have been assisted in highlighting higher risk movements for check.

6. PUBLIC EXPECTATIONS FOR FREEDOM OF MOVEMENT IN THE SINGLE MARKET

There is a belief among certain sections of the press and travelling public that there will be no Customs checks for intra-community travellers after 1992. On a superficial view, this seems to be confirmed by the Single European Act:

> 'The Community shall adopt measures with the aim of progressively establishing the internal market over a period expiring on 31 December 1992 . . . The internal market shall comprise an area without internal frontiers in which the free movement of goods, persons, services and capital is ensured in accordance with the provisions of this Treaty.'

> (Treaty of Rome Article 8A, added by Article 13 of the Single European Act).

This would appear to mean that, in future, travel between London and The Hague will be as simple as travelling from Amsterdam to The Hague. However, as usual it is not quite so simple. Of the 'four freedoms' — movement of goods, persons, services and capital — it is the movement of persons which attracts most attention. The man in the street may have no interest in Community proposals on company law, but he knows all about queuing to get through Customs on return from his holiday. The free movement of persons sounds like a great idea to him, but it causes great concern to Customs officers. Why? Because people smuggle. That leaves Customs officers with a very simple but awkward problem. On the one hand travellers will expect to be allowed to travel freely across the continent as citizens of the new Europe: on the other those same citizens of Europe will expect the Customs officer still to protect society from drugs, firearms, diseased plants and animals and similar threats.

There is no easy solution to this dilemma, just as there is no clear view in Europe about the threats that face us, for example the different cultural and bureaucratic attitudes to drug usage, pornography, control over 'heritage' items, etc. Customs services — and their Governments — may take differing views of the changes ahead.

7.   FISCAL CHANGES

On the fiscal side there will be a number of major changes affecting freight movements. For a start the whole conceptual basis will change: the terms 'import' and 'export' within the Community will be replaced for fiscal purposes by the concepts of 'acquisition' and 'dispatch', thus removing at a stroke the *fiscal* significance of the line drawn on a map or the striped pole across a road. After 1992, there will be no *fiscal* intervention at the frontier, so the multi-copy, 54 box import entry document known as the Single Administrative Document will be abolished. Liability to tax for movements within the Community will be shown on businesses' normal VAT and excise duty accounts and periodic tax returns, and will be checked by audit visits rather than at transaction level each time a consignment comes into the country. This is a major change which will be good for business, and coupled with harmonisation of product standards, should encourage greater economic activity within the internal market of 320 million consumers.

The issue of tax rate harmonisation or approximation is seen by the European Commission and several Member States as a logical consequence of the removal of fiscal frontiers. In theory, goods should pay VAT, for example, in the Community country of purchase, irrespective of where they are used or consumed. However, because of rate differences (the standard rate varies from 12-22% among EC countries), there would be a risk of either severe revenue leakage or the need for complex adjustment mechanisms. The Member States have therefore agreed that, until the end of 1996 at least, *businesses* will still account for tax in the country of destination rather than sale. The UK Government has made quite clear its view that forced rate approximation is unnecessary for the completion of the single market: the fiscal frontier can be dismantled without it. But the EC Finance Ministers Council of 24 June 1991 did reach agreement on a compromise proposal for a 15% minimum standard rate of VAT within the EC.

Exciseable goods will also pay tax in the country of destination, and commercial movements will be facilitated by a new post-1992 control system. Bonded excise movements between warehouses throughout the Community will take place without any frontier declaration. The goods will travel in a duty-suspended state, the duty becoming payable only when the goods are released from the warehouse system for final consumption.

With excise duties, the extreme divergence in rates within the Community is even more of a problem than with VAT. The excise duty on a litre of alcohol in Denmark is over 100 times greater than in Greece, and five Member States have no duty whatsoever on wine. This presents particular problems for *personal* shopping. The EC Council of Ministers has decided that *personal* cross-border shopping should pay duty and tax in the country of *purchase*, not destination. In theory this means removing all limits on travellers' allowances for goods bought *tax paid* in other Community countries. Proposals for transitional increases in the allowance limits were tabled in 1989, but so far, because of excise rate disparities the Council has been able to agree no increases whatsoever in the limits for tobacco and alcohol. For goods liable only to VAT, agreement was only recently reached on an increased value limit of 600 ECU (420), which took effect on 1 July 1991.

It is, however, certain that the Community will set 'indicative limits' for the main tobacco and alcohol products, to guard against abuse by private individuals importing products bought cheaply in one Member State only to resell them in another. Limits have not yet been finalised, but the principle will be that if an individual imports more than the specified quantities, they will be treated as a commercial transaction — thus dutiable in the country of destination — unless *proof* of personal use is provided.

The future of duty-free shopping, so popular with travellers, has also been called into question by the Single Market. The Commission felt, with some justification, that duty-frees for intra-community travellers should be abolished with effect from 1 January 1993. But the duty-free industry is a very important sector of the Community economy and some Member States, including the UK, believed that a longer transitional period would give affected companies time to re-organise and seek alternative sources of revenue. The ECOFIN (Economic and Finance Ministers') Council of 11 November 1991 finally agreed that duty-free shopping would be retained for intra-EC travel until 1 July 1999. But it is essential that the control mechanisms needed to ensure that travellers are able to get only 200 cigarettes, 1 litre of spirits, etc., should not require the re-erection of fiscal barriers at the frontier. The ECOFIN agreement requires Member States to take the necessary measures to prevent abuse, and it is likely that the best available system will be one of vendor control, under which the seller limits what people can buy.

8.   NEW OPPORTUNITIES FOR FISCAL CRIME

The removal of fiscal frontier controls on intra-EC trade risks the creation of new opportunities for fraud. The abolition of a formal written frontier declaration for freight imports and exports, and fiscal collection by periodic returns, will make it impossible for Customs to identify and verify all importations made by individual traders. Suppression of records of high-value imported goods subject to VAT, and fictitious exports (free of tax) hiding off-record sales within the UK, could be seen as easy routes to increased profits by the more unscrupulous members of the business community.

New opportunities for crime inevitably require new forms of control to ensure that legitimate businesses, EC-wide, are able to complete on level terms. The post-1992 control of traders will be based largely on retrospective audit-based checks on transactions and on greatly increased cooperation to exchange information between Member States. A uniform approach to such administrative cooperation will be needed throughout the Community to avoid the creation of loopholes.

To achieve this, the Commission has proposed a new Regulation building upon existing arrangements for mutual assistance. Under the proposals each Member State will answer queries from other Member States to ensure compliance with indirect tax law. Each Member State would set up a central office to be known as the Mutual Assistance Liaison Point (MALP), to coordinate all enquiries and liaise with other Member States and the Commission. Basic information about exports to other Member States would be stored on a database which could be accessed by other Member States' authorities if the information was required for their checks. This information would be gathered from quarterly aggregate sales lists to be prepared by all EC VAT-registered traders, summarising the total transactions in the quarter with each taxable customer in the EC. Member States would not be bound to provide information where there was a likelihood of prejudice to 'public policy', but they would have to give reasons for refusing assistance. A standing committee of the Commission and Member States would oversee the satisfactory operation of the cooperation arrangements, paying particular attention to the pooling of experience on new methods of tax evasion or avoidance.

There will also be cooperation in the investigation of fiscal fraud. UK Customs' Investigation Division is already taking a systematic approach to forging new links between fraud investigation specialists in each Member State. The UK has long recognised that the best way to obtain results in the fight against fraud is to direct resources into intelligence gathering in high-risk areas. To this end, the UK has had a specialist team of investigators, the VAT Intelligence and Research Team, in operation since 1976. New VAT fraud posts have been created to meet the specific challenge posed by the Single Market; and the UK has suggested that, in parallel with the new mutual assistance arrangements, a number of Fiscal Fraud Liaison Officers should be located in other Member States. The overall aim is to develop a rapid and effective exchange of fraud information, leading to joint anti-fraud operations involving a number of Member States.

On a different level, the commercial exploitation of 'personal' tax-paid travellers' allowances could also become a problem. As explained earlier, the EC intends to abolish all limits on personal cross-border shopping, but this would lay a number of Member States open to fiscal leakage in favour of neighbours with lower VAT and excise duty rates. Therefore, at a meeting of the ECOFIN Council on 24 June 1991, Ministers agreed that rules would be required to differentiate between genuine personal importations and illicit commercial activity. As explained, ECOFIN is expected to adopt *indicative* quantities of liquor and tobacco, above which (in the absence of proof to the contrary) importations would be assumed to be commercial, hence taxable in the country of arrival. But there will be some scope for abuse even so, and we are planning for enhanced intelligence gathering and some inland checks, to guard against bootlegging.

9.   REGULATORY CONTROL CHANGES

In the regulatory field, control of prohibited and restricted goods, the main change with the advent of the Single Market will be the removal of the requirement for licensable goods to be declared at the internal frontier. The Community is moving towards *inland* licensing schemes as a replacement for intrusive frontier controls. At present, for example, all commercial transactions in firearms require a licence: private importations into the UK need a British Visitor's Permit, and all importations must be declared to Customs on entry for check of the documentation. Under a new EC Weapons Directive, systematic border formalities will cease. Licences of some form, possibly a new 'European Firearms Passport' will still be required, but consideration is currently being given to how these documents can be verified by inland checking. Similar solutions are in sight for animal and plant licensing regimes.

As with fiscal crime, the need after 1992 will be to develop better mutual assistance, and particularly intelligence, to detect concerted attempts to breach licensing regimes. The abolition of routine frontier documentation after 1992 is perhaps less of a problem than it might seem: even now we are highly dependent on intelligence collection, collation and enhancement to detect those intent on avoiding a licensing regime.

Several problems do remain, however, with regulatory work. To give one example, how can the UK enforce breaches of Italian restrictions on the exportation of *their* works of art, if the goods have been imported into the UK in accordance with UK law? Heritage goods are a particular source of concern for the UK, as London is one of the world's most important art markets. Recently, the UK was able to restore to the Soviet Union a number of icons illegally exported from that country. But the only reason UK Customs were able to seize the consignment at importation was that it had not been declared: the icons were smuggled inside other goods. Remove the need for a declaration intra-EC, and a similar export from Italy involving a Fra Angelico panel could not be treated similarly on arrival in the UK.

10.   ANTI-SMUGGLING CONTROL CHANGES

Assuming that internal frontier fiscal controls, on both freight and passengers, can be abolished, and that regulatory controls on licensable goods can be moved inland, what remains is anti-smuggling checks on trafficking in sensitive goods. For the UK this means primarily drugs, firearms and the instruments of terrorism, pornographic material involving children, animals susceptible to rabies and strategic exports.

The Treaty of Rome recognises the right of Member States to retain:

'. . . prohibitions or restrictions on imports, exports or goods in transit justified on grounds of public morality, public policy or public security . . .'

(Treaty of Rome: Article 36)

And at the passing of the Single European Act in 1985, the EC Governments made a Declaration saying:

> 'Nothing in these provisions shall affect the right of Member States to take such measures as they consider necessary for the purpose of controlling immigration from third countries, and to combat terrorism, crime, the traffic in drugs and illicit trading in works of art and antiques.'

(Declaration on Articles 13-19 of the Single European Act)

The British Government has maintained consistently that a minimum level of such essential frontier checks will continue beyond 1992 to protect society. However, such measures will be subject to certain qualifications: they must be objectively justified, proportionate to the threat involved and must not cause distortions in intra-Community trade. UK Customs recognise the need to make anti-smuggling controls at the internal frontier far less obtrusive than at present; and to minimise their impact on legitimate trade and innocent travellers.

11.   THE NEED FOR FRONTIER-BASED DRUGS CHECKS

Drugs are currently the most high-profile problem area in smuggling terms, though similar considerations apply to illicit trafficking in other sensitive goods. Some figures may help to demonstrate the objective justification of the checks.

In 1990, UK Customs seized a total of just over 26 tonnes of illicit drugs, with a combined street value of £ 245 million.

Customs drugs seizures 1990

	Kg	% change over
Heroin	576	+71%
Cocaine	561	+37%
Cannabis (all types)	24896	-51%*
Amphetamines	81	+252%

(* NB 1989 included single seizure of 17400 kg)

Customs authorities in other EC countries make similar large seizures every year.

EC drugs seizures 1990 (Kg)

	France	Germany	Spain
Heroin	254	645	256
Cocaine	1409	514	969
Cannabis (all types)	19262	3465	25789
Amphetamines	10	29	0

The statistics also show that frontier checks are a much more efficient and effective way of catching drugs smugglers than by tackling the problem inland. By far the majority *by number* of drugs seizures in the UK are made by the police, acting mainly inland. But *by weight*, 79% of all UK seizures are attributable to Customs checks at frontiers. The conclusion must be that the most effective method of catching drugs when they are moving in bulk is to do so as they cross national boundaries, before consignments are broken up for distribution and use inland.

Unfortunately, the bulk of UK Customs' drug seizures do not come direct from the source areas of the Golden Triangle, the Golden Crescent and South America. Instead, they come from or through other Community countries. The following table shows that this phenomenon is not unique to the UK:

Drugs seizures from or via the EC 1990 (%)

	UK	France
Heroin	58	49
Cocaine	3	3
Cannabis (resin)	60	37
Cannabis (herbal)	67	13

In total, 61% of *all* drugs seized by UK Customs in 1990 had come from, or via, another Community country. Indeed some Member States act as major storage warehouses for bulk supplies of drugs and have to be viewed in a similar manner to the primary drug production countries. With the UK making such significant proportions of its total drugs seizures at the internal frontier, it would be nonsensical to abolish all customs presence there from the end of 1992.

This argument is reinforced for the UK by consideration of specific national advantages. Because of the UK's island geography, any traffic is likely to enter the country in bulk and to enter through the natural pinch-points at the major ports and airports. This provides the ideal situation for frontier checks: goods in bulk entering the country at easily identifiable points. Some other Member States have long land frontiers, which are naturally difficult to police. Here there is some logic in relaxing checks at the frontier and relying more on internal controls. Indeed, the UK will be moving in this direction for controlling smuggling across our only current land frontier, the Northern Ireland Land Boundary. But where we have natural advantages of geography it would be pointless not to use them to the best effect.

12. SCHENGEN: A MODEL FOR THE COMMUNITY?

Even where there is considerable political commitment to abolishing frontiers, the practicalities of enforcement are a major stumbling block. Five countries in Europe (France, Germany and the Benelux nations) signed the original Schengen Agreement in 1985 to abolish frontier controls between each other by 1 January 1990. The slow progress of negotiations on a more detailed supplementary Convention applying the 1985 agreement demonstrates the difficulty of *compensating* for the withdrawal of frontier controls. A land frontier may be an artificial line drawn for political purposes centuries ago, but it serves to separate different judicial systems, cultural identities and civil rights. The Schengen States had severe problems in reaching a common position on vital issues such as hot pursuit by enforcement agencies across internal borders and the establishment of a common, computer-based suspect index.

The supplementary Schengen Convention was finally signed on 19 June 1990, six months after the initial deadline for implementation, which is now due on 1 January 1993. However, before this the Convention has to be ratified by the eight Schengen States and other measures such as the common Schengen Information System computerised database must be in place. It is still by no means certain that all this action will be complete in time: recent reports of difficulties the Netherlands is having with Parliamentary approval suggest that ratification of the Convention is more difficult than signature! But there is no doubt that the 8-State Schengen grouping is a formidable force in the Community politics.

Even within Schengen countries, however, internal border checks still prove effective. Two press cuttings tell their stories. On 24 May 1991 the Daily Mail reported:

'Two Britons were arrested for alleged drugs trafficking on the Belgium-Holland border yesterday. Andrew Charnock, 31, and Michael Wright, 45, from Liverpool, were held at Vise. Nearly 50 kilos of cannabis resin, worth £ 330,000 was found in their car.'

And more curiously, on 6 June 1991 The Guardian carried a story showing that EC Customs colleagues are vigilant in enforcing the provisions of the Washington Convention on international trade in endangered species:

'Fifty tiger penises, destined to be sold in sex shops as aphrodisiacs, were seized from a Chinese man at the French-Luxembourg border yesterday. "I'm told you grate them on your food like cheese", a customs spokesman said.'

13. THE BAGGAGE REGULATION

An area in which we have recently seen Schengenisation, and experienced occasional differences of view between EC administrations, airport operators and airlines, is the proposed EC Baggage Regulation, tabled by the Commission in August 1990. As drafted, this would have abolished *all* checks on the baggage of passengers travelling by air or sea within the Community. The only exceptions were for transit and transfer passengers from outside the EC whose journey involved an intra-community leg. This draft Regulation cut directly across the need, recognised by Article 36 of the Treaty of Rome, to carry out essential frontier checks on intra-community travellers. The UK is not alone in its desire to retain such checks: only *one* Member State is content to lose all right to check passengers arriving from another EC country. By implication the draft Regulation would also have had an impact on immigration and police checks carried out at the frontier, and would have involved enormous infrastructural expenditure on the re-organisation of airports to cope with a vastly expanded redefinition of 'domestic' traffic.

Several EC countries have already agreed to similar arrangements in the Schengen Convention, and they are clearly content to spend large amounts of money on airport reorganisation: rebuilding is in progress or planned at Zaventem, Schiphol and other EC airports. Indeed, some transport ministries woke up rather belatedly to the implications of what their Governments had agreed in the Schengen accord. Schengen airports' control authorities must also be ready to cope with the complaints of a transfer passenger from New York who may find it annoying to be required (as is the case also with the EC Regulation) to go through immigration and *hand* baggage control in one country, only to have to present their *hold* baggage for customs check in the country of final destination.

During the EC negotiations the UK, along with some other countries, foresaw problems with both the principles and the practical implementation of the draft Baggage Regulation, though for broader reasons many administrations preferred to sweep the difficulties under the carpet in the interests of free movement. But in the area of drugs control, an important change was accepted during the negotiations: the 'common position' reached at the Internal Market Council in July 1991 protects the position of essential anti-smuggling checks. However, the expensive practical problems of airport re-organisation have only been reduced, not eliminated.

14.   ANTI-SMUGGLING CONTROLS IN THE SINGLE MARKET

But the need to keep essential checks does not mean that *nothing* will change at the UK's internal EC frontiers after 1992. The Single Market has developed its own momentum and the public expects visible changes. Luckily, freer movement is coming about anyway in the UK as a result of an internal review of our anti-smuggling work, which highlighted the benefits of better targeted, more selective and overall more flexible controls. The Single Market provides an opportunity to challenge both conventional methods of working and entrenched attitudes to the travelling and trading public. The last thing we want to be accused of is what the Commission once called 'routine mindless interference with the great mass of ordinary innocent travellers going about their legitimate business.' The UK is actively working to make checks more selective on EC passengers and freight, to improve the level of intelligence information and profiling techniques and to be more accurate in selecting cars, freight consignments and people for check. The aim is to check fewer people and consignments and to make our selections in advance based on better information.

Already this greater selectivity has had an effect at the ferry ports. Last year Customs introduced a system called Freeway. The practice of stopping all cars for a few quick questions before deciding whether to do an in-depth examination has ceased. Most cars now drive straight through with only a few pulled out for check. This is creating for cars what happens already for passengers at airports, where more than 95% of travellers walk straight through the green channel without being stopped.

The reduced importance of revenue collection after 1992 is encouraging experimentation with the current red and green channel system. We have already trialled the concept of a 'red point', where passengers with goods to declare call at an advanced cash till to pay any duty or taxes (possibly by credit card) and then leave through a single spot check area. Later this year, Customs hope to extend the experiment even further by removing completely all the barriers and frosted partitions that make up red and green channels, to create a truly *open plan* spot check area.

At Dover, Customs and the Immigration Service are working together to create a new system of coach controls at the UK's largest coach traffic port. Instead of requiring all passengers to leave their coaches and walk through immigration controls and then customs checks with their hand baggage, we are currently introducing a new system in which over 70% of coach passengers will be able to remain on board their coach. These procedures were trialled successfully in 1990 and will apply on a permanent basis from the summer of 1991.

The intention of *all* these changes is to make a difference even *before* 1993. Innocent travellers will be shown that they are welcome to the UK; that they can pass through Customs checks quickly and with a minimum of disruption; but that the UK law enforcement agencies remain vigilant in their role of protecting society.

15.   ENLISTING TRADE SUPPORT FOR ANTI-SMUGGLING WORK

In pursuit of the objective of enlisting trade support for Customs in the fight against drugs, a number of Memoranda of Understanding (MoU) have been signed with trade associations. These MoU derive from the Customs Cooperation Council initiative mentioned earlier. Their main aims are to:

— make trade members more aware of the drug trafficking problem and its effects;
— encourage trade members to review and, where necessary, to increase their security to prevent illegal access to and use of their facilities by drug smugglers;
— encourage the trade to meet customs' requests for access to commercial information; and
— facilitate the trade as far as possible, as a result of better targeting of customs controls.

So far, UK Customs have signed MoU with the:
— Freight Transport Association;
— British International Freight Association;
— General Council of British Shipping;
— Road Haulage Association;

— Association of International Courier and Express Service; and
— Institute of Chartered Shipbrokers.

The information obtained by *voluntary* cooperation from traders after 1992 is essential for Customs' anti-smuggling work. It will go some way towards replacing — from access to commercial records — the information contained at present in compulsory frontier declarations which will be abolished after the removal of fiscal frontiers.

16.   EUROPEAN COMMUNITY CUSTOMS COOPERATION — MUTUAL
        ASSISTANCE GROUP 1992

A key feature of the Single Market will be increased *cooperation*, both nationally with the Police (as described above) and with EC Customs partners.

Enforcement cooperation within the Community is being actively pursued in a wide variety of Community bodies. The Rhodos group of frontier Coordinators set up by the EC Heads of Government in 1988 has drawn up an inventory of the action still needed to bring about free movement — including the compensatory measures that must be set in place at the external frontier. The CELAD group of Coordinators — named after the French acronym for the European Committee for the Fight against Drugs, was specifically set up to coordinate the Community's action on drugs, involving elements of enforcement, health and education policy.

At the sharper end of cooperation there are the Trevi network of committees looking at issues of police cooperation; the ad-hoc group on Immigration, which has drawn up a Convention on immigration procedures at the external frontier; and in Customs the Mutual Assistance Group and its 1992 counterpart MAG '92.

For many years EC customs authorities have assisted each other under the provisions of the Naples Convention 1967. This was superseded for matters within EC competence by Council Regulation 1468/81, but is still in force for cooperation in trafficking of sensitive goods such as drugs. The Naples Convention provides, *inter alia* for:
(a) general assistance to prevent, investigate and prosecute offences;
(b) surveillance of persons, places, goods and means of transport at the request of EC partners;
(c) supply of reports, documents and evidence to other EC services;
(d) appearance as witnesses in other States' courts; and
(e) initiating inquiries on request, with officers of the requesting party being present.

MAG '92 is a new committee of EC customs experts looking specifically at 1992 issues in the area of smuggling of sensitive goods. It was set up in 1989 at the initiative of the Chairman of UK Customs, and the UK chairs the group. Areas of work include:
(a) the adoption of a political declaration by EC Customs Ministers in October 1990, which recognised the important role of customs authorities within the Community and endorsed the intention to increase mutual cooperation;
(b) the drafting of a new protocol to update the 1967 Naples Convention on Customs Mutual Assistance. This envisages the enhancement of cooperation through joint control teams and posting of customs liaison officers, provides for bilateral agreements

on cross-border surveillance and pursuit, and encourages international controlled deliveries of drugs (unfortunately we offer far more controlled deliveries to other countries than we receive: cooperation should be a two-way process!);

(c) the creation of an enforcement strategy for the Community's external frontier, initially through a risk evaluation of smuggling trends and results to identify main trafficking groups and entry points into the Community. This work has just started, and will be followed by the harder task of deciding how to plug the gaps at the external fence, what improved technical equipment is needed, what common training is required for enforcement officers, and finally what will be the most appropriate funding mechanism for the strategy; and

(d) a common computerised information system for customs services. A user requirement has already been defined, and a decision to proceed with development was taken by Directors-General of EC Customs in October 1991. A simple system based on standard formats, automatically translated into the appropriate language on despatch and receipt, should be in place early in 1992 for direct contact between airports and ports across the Community.

The computerised messaging system will allow certain basic data about goods, means of transport, persons and freight consignments to be transmitted, and phase 2 of the system, which could be ready by 1 January 1993, would attach a central database to provide a historical record and lookup index. As with the TREVI and Immigration plans for databases, everything could get stranded on the rocks of data protection and privacy standards on which EC practice is hopelessly varied. Several countries have not yet signed the Council of Europe Convention on Data Protection, and a Commission package of draft Directives and Resolutions on the subject is most unlikely to reach the EC statute book by 1993. A special coordinating group of TREVI, Immigration and Customs MAG '92 experts is at present looking into 'horizontal' issues common to all proposed systems, with a view to defining common solutions.

17. EFFECTIVE CURRENT EC COOPERATION

Community Customs cooperation is in fact already pointing the way ahead to a strong coordinated approach to control of the external EC frontier and close liaison within it. A good example is maritime surveillance cooperation in the Eastern Atlantic and Channel. In 1985 the UK signed a formal surveillance cooperative agreement with French Customs, and this has been reinforced by further agreements with Spain and the Channel Islands. Customs vessels, aircraft and coordination centres of these countries, together with Portugal and the Netherlands, cooperate on a daily basis and in specific exercises to monitor yacht and small vessel movements around the Community's external frontier. In 1990, eight vessels involved in smuggling were detected as a result of this cooperation, carrying a total of 9.2 tonnes of drugs.

Under a more recent initiative funded by the European Commission, the Community Customs services have initiated a programme of staff exchanges, known as the Matthaeus project. This is designed to offer Customs officers from ports and airports secondments of up to one month to observe, and participate in, similar work in another Member State. The UK will send approximately 120 officers on such secondments in 1991. Cross Channel ports have already built up very close relations with their French, Belgian and Dutch counterparts through these and other bilateral exchanges. Similar exchanges of officers responsible for indirect taxation work are now being set up under the 'Interfisc' programme.

18.   CONCLUSION

This paper has attempted to demonstrate that UK Customs are making real changes in the style and methods of all forms of control. Fiscal checks will disappear, but inevitably some essential checks will remain on intra-Community travellers after 1992. These checks will *occasionally* inconvenience innocent travellers and traders, but they are needed. The public expect protection as well as freedom of movement: protection from drugs, from terrorists, from child pornography and (for islands like the UK and the Republic of Ireland) from the threat of rabies. It is the responsibility of Customs, as a control agency, to provide that protection. Our strategy is to work with the grain of the Single Market, cooperating with EC colleagues to strengthen the external frontier, transfer expertise, exchange intelligence and provide mutual assistance. At the internal frontiers, more selective, light-touch but sharply focussed checks will be in place. For most travellers and businesses, the Single Market will be a reality. For drugs smugglers and other criminals, it will not.

FISCAL BARRIERS ON THE FREE MOVEMENT OF PERSONS

Carlo Garbarino[*]

1.   INTRODUCTION

It is generally expected that by the end of 1992 the European Community will establish a single integrated market without internal frontiers in which the free movement of goods, services, persons and capital is ensured in accordance with the Treaty. The Community has launched a comprehensive programme to remove physical, technical and fiscal barriers to the internal market.

The goal of the Colloquium is to highlight the legal problems relating to the free movement of persons in Europe.

The focus of this report is on the fiscal barriers to the free movement of persons within the territory of the Community. This report will analyse fiscal barriers encountered by individuals, rather than business enterprises, with particular attention to the taxation of income resulting from migrant labour. The goal of this report is also to shed light on the structure and extent of fiscal barriers to the movement of individuals and to identify workable policies for the elimination of such barriers.

The process toward the full application of the free movement of goods, services, persons and capital within the Community can be divided into several stages. Initially, the 1957 Treaty of Rome laid down basic legal rules to achieve, *inter alia*, the elimination, between Member States, of customs duties and of quantitative restrictions on the import and export of goods, and of all measures having equivalent effect, as well as the abolition, between Member States, of barriers to freedom of movement for persons, services and capital.

During the 1960s numerous policies of economic integration provided for by the Treaty were adopted. In particular, the common customs tariff was fully established in 1968 ahead of schedule. However, during the 1970s not all the developments which might have taken place did occur.

Finally, by the mid-1980s slow European growth, high unemployment, internal barriers, and policy conflicts resulted in something of a paralysis for the European Community.

In 1985 the Commission issued a White Paper entitled 'Completing the Internal Market', putting forward proposals to expedite the full integration of the European

[*] Associate Professor, University of Siena, Italy; Studio Legale Bisconti, Milano, Italy.

H.G. Schermers et al., eds., Free Movement of Persons in Europe

market. The White Paper analysed the existing barriers to the 'four freedoms', and listed almost 300 legislative proposals to promote the internal market. The critical step in implementing the White Paper proposals was the adoption of the Single European Act, which revised the Treaty. The Single European Act, which took effect on 1 July 1987, requires qualified majority voting to most internal market issues, so that unanimity is now required only in certain areas such as taxation, the movement of persons, the rights of employees, and the environment. The movement of persons is the focus of this Colloquium, and the tax issues related to them are the particular concern of this paper.

In summary, from the development of EEC policy toward full integration it is possible to single out, on the one hand, four goals, that is, the achievement of the four freedoms of movement (of goods, services, persons and capital), and, on the other , three types of obstacles or barriers to these freedoms (physical, technical and fiscal barriers).

Thus, the completion of the internal market must also be intended as the result of the most extensive implementation of the basic freedoms of movement; the Colloquium and this paper are aimed to an in-depth analysis of the extent of such freedom for persons to the extent that such is possible of assessment at this time and as it can develop in the near future.

2.   THE FREEDOM OF MOVEMENT FOR PERSONS

The Treaty provisions relating to the free movement of persons include rules on rights of nationals of the Member States to move throughout the Community in order to exercise their profession or to look for job positions. Article 48 of the Treaty applies to employed persons and Article 52 applies to self-employed persons. In certain cases, the person is also entitled to remain in the host country after he has ceased working or carrying on his economic activity.

The freedom of movement within the Community for employed persons has a non-discriminatory effect to the extent that it bars any disparity of treatment based on nationality between workers of the Member States as regards employment, remuneration and other conditions of work and employment. Member States must grant EC nationals the right to enter and leave their territory in order to take up activities as employed persons and to pursue such activities in another Member State.

Another form of free movement, the freedom of establishment, includes the right to pursue activities as self-employed persons and to set up and manage companies and firms. Generally, the right of establishment applies to all economic activities, with the exception of activities involving the exercise of official authority. Some restrictions, however, can be imposed by the Member States on the grounds of public security or public health. Community directives relating to mutual recognition of diplomas, certificates and other evidence of formal qualifications also facilitate the exercise of freedom of movement and establishment.

3.   BARRIERS TO THE FREEDOM OF MOVEMENT OF PERSONS

The 1985 White Paper, entitled 'Completing the Internal Market', classified existing barriers to the free movement of persons under three categories: physical, technical and fiscal. Of these, the most obvious obstacles to free movement of persons are physical barriers such as customs controls and immigration restrictions. These barriers are related to the technical and fiscal divisions between Member States, but they also serve as a means of state control over matters such as immigration and illegal drugs. Thus, the elimination of technical and fiscal barriers is a process that is necessarily connected with the issue of how to maintain such forms of control. The White Paper addressed the issues of arms legislation, drug control, immigration, right of asylum and the status of refugees, national visa policies and extradition.

However, there are various other reasons for border controls within the Community: differing value added tax (VAT) rates and excise duties, reporting needs of public authorities, adjustments of prices in order to offset currency fluctuations, and checks to safeguard residual national quotas aimed at non-EC suppliers. The White Paper estimated the costs of border delays alone at about $ 10 billion annually (not considering the relevant costs resulting from the segmentation of the markets). This estimate is supported by the fact that the introduction of the Single Administration Document in January 1988 has reduced the paperwork on EC cross-border trade.

Technical barriers to free movement also cause a wide range of problems for the achievement of the internal market. Technical barriers take numerous and complex forms, such as the national requirements imposed by health, safety, environmental or consumer protection regulations, or by government procurement standards that discriminate against foreign competitors.

Although these impediments to the internal market are usually considered to be 'physical' or 'technical' barriers, they have also a clear fiscal nature, in so far as they are implemented to ensure the application of tax rules concerning the movement of goods or persons. Thus, these obstacles can also be viewed as fiscal barriers in the wider sense.

Traditional fiscal barriers can be found in the rules concerning indirect taxation (particularly value added taxes and excise taxes) and direct taxation of intra EEC transnational transactions. These fiscal barriers play an important role in restricting the freedom of movement of persons, and their effects should be evaluated in conjunction with the effects of physical and technical barriers.

Member States fear that large national differences in VAT and excise tax rates could result in a form of 'tax competition' in which high-tax jurisdictions would lose revenue to low-tax jurisdictions. In addition, Member States fear that producers located in high-tax jurisdictions would be at a disadvantage *vis-à-vis* their competitors located in low-tax jurisdictions.

In addressing the problems raised by fiscal barriers, the White Paper proposed a set of combined policies related to indirect taxation: the harmonization of VAT and excise tax rates, the imposition of indirect taxes only by the country of origin, and the establishment of a clearing-house among Member States to separate tax receipts to ensure that it is eventually collected by the country of destination.

The White Paper, did not address the issue of harmonization of the national income tax rules of Member States. Yet the very effect of fiscal barriers is found in the distortions to economic choices of individuals (i.e., freedom of movement), determined by income tax rules. The notion of fiscal barriers and the understanding of the complex issues related to the process of European tax integration, requires a brief description of a few theoretical assumptions.

4.   FISCAL BARRIERS TO THE FREE MOVEMENT OF PERSONS:
        METHODOLOGICAL CRITERIA

Briefly, the concept of fiscal barriers requires the definition of the following terms: national transaction, transnational transaction, and tax neutrality.

National transactions occur exclusively within the territory of a Member State ('source country') and are therefore subject to the taxing power of the Member State. Transnational transactions can be affected by two or more national tax schemes. Member States attempt to locate transnational transactions inside their national territories by establishing criteria that can be used to establish a territorial nexus between a person or a transaction and a Member State. These criteria are, therefore, particularly important because they provide a Member State with the legal basis for its power to tax a person or transaction. A 'residence country' levies taxes on the basis of the location or residence of the taxpayer, and a 'source country' on the basis of a territorial location of the transaction. If both of these bases for taxation apply, the transaction may be subject to double taxation.

When a person receives income from either domestic or foreign activities, national tax authorities will attempt to tax that income by establishing that the person is located within the national territory. When the person resides in a foreign county, the national tax authorities will try to source the person within the territory on some other basis.

With respect to a simple movement of goods between two Member States (A and B), if both Member States adopt a country of destination principle the transaction is taxable in the receiving country B. If both Member States adopt a country of origin principle the transaction is taxable in country A. The harmonized European VAT system uses the criterion of the country of destination.

The model that considers only exports of goods and services is related to the fiscal barriers to free movement of persons in the form of indirect taxes. This model, however, must be extended to cover also other types of transactions, especially factor remuneration transactions (e.g., income derived from labour and capital) in order to understand the effects of fiscal barriers in the form of direct taxes.

In the basic model, the transactions considered represent intra-EEC transfers of goods and services, and the tax directly affects these goods and services transactions. In the field of direct taxes (e.g., income taxes, corporate taxes) what is taxed is not the export or import of factor services, but the *flows* of effectively received or imputed incomes, profits, interests, rents, royalties, salaries, etc., on the basis of these factor remuneration transactions.

Another difference between taxing goods transactions and income transactions is that the tax base for direct taxes of income is not the value of any single transaction. Income transactions are summed up for a certain period (normally one year) and tax rates are applied to these yearly income flows less allowed deductions. Consequently, when a person resident in one country receives income from different domestic and foreign sources, the country of residence will have a tax claim on his worldwide income.

Thus, the choice of location of investment and the movement of labour and persons are affected by tax rules concerning such flows of income. A full understanding of this effect requires a clarification of the notions of tax neutrality and tax efficiency.

5.   TAX NEUTRALITY AND FREE MOVEMENT OF PERSONS

The notion of tax neutrality efficiency is rooted in classic economic theory. Efficiency refers to an allocation of economic resources that maximizes production or economic growth. In a hypothetical world in which all investors are profit maximisers and perfect competition exists throughout the world's economy, the resulting international allocation of capital would be economically 'efficient'. In a tax efficient economy, domestic investors would either invest capital or locate their labour abroad where it can yield the greatest returns. Foreign investment by domestic investors would increase to the point at which world productivity is maximized. At this point, the marginal productivity of capital or labour at home and abroad would be equal.

This theoretical model can be applied fully to the Community scenario and to the achievement of free movement of persons. The differential tax rates of various Member States play a key role in determining both the allocation of capital and/or labour and the distribution of income and tax revenues between the Member States.

The first standard for tax neutrality is capital-export neutrality, This refers to a situation in which the taxpayer's choice between investing or working at home or abroad is not affected by the pattern of taxation. Assuming perfect competition, the capital-export neutrality standard would serve as a standard for perfect freedom of movement of persons. It would result in the most efficient allocation of capital and labour within the Community, since tax factors would not affect the movement of persons. Capital-export neutrality is also equitable in an international sense, because taxpayers with the same worldwide or pan-european income would pay the same taxes overall.

A second standard is national neutrality. This is a situation in which total domestic returns on capital or labour, which are shared between the domestic taxpayer and the public revenue of his country of residence, are the same whether the capital is invested or labour is carried out at home or abroad. Under this neutrality standard, domestic taxpayers compare net foreign income after payment of foreign taxes with gross domestic income before payment of the tax of their country of residence. Under this standard, domestic capital or labour is invested or located abroad up to the point at which pre-tax profits at home equal after-tax profits abroad, thereby promoting the most efficient allocation of resources from the viewpoint of the capital-exporting country. This results in what has been termed 'national efficiency'.

The third neutrality standard, capital-neutrality, is achieved when an individual carrying out his activities in a foreign country is taxed by such source country at the same ultimate rate regardless of the taxpayer's nationality. Capital-import neutrality does not promote national or world efficiency, but rather, it encourages at best only the most efficient use of resources within the capital-importing country.

In conclusion, fiscal barriers to the free movement of persons, in particular migrant workers, are not direct obstacles to such freedom, but may have relevant indirect effects in so far as they consist of forms of taxation that modify the investment choices of individuals and, therefore, interfere with an optimal tax neutrality situation. Thus, in order to ensure free movement of persons at its fullest extent the most desirable tax policies are those which eliminate distortions to the economic choices of taxpayers and ensure tax neutrality in one of the forms described above. This standard can be adopted to evaluate the EEC action toward the elimination of fiscal barriers to the free movement of persons.

Notwithstanding the applicable bilateral tax Treaty provisions, the current tax systems of the Member States distinguish between resident and non-resident workers and apply different rates of taxation to their income. These income tax disparities impede the attainment of tax neutralities and result in tax barriers to the free movement of workers.

6.   STEPS TOWARDS THE ELIMINATION OF FISCAL BARRIERS TO THE FREE MOVEMENT OF PERSONS

In the White Paper, the Commission stated that one of its goals is to abolish the obstacles to the free movement of workers and rights of residence. Two Community directives have been proposed to deal with the taxation of migrant workers and their families. These directives are designed to help eliminate the influence of tax factors in the choice of location of the place of work. They also deal with the simplification of the procedures requested for residence permits.

The first proposed directive concerns the harmonization of income tax provisions with respect to freedom of movement for workers within the Community. This proposal addresses national tax measures concerning the taxation of the income of 'frontier workers' and of other non-resident employed persons and also the national taxation treatment of certain other payments. Under this proposed directive, the term resident would be interpreted according to national tax provisions and relevant double taxation treaties. The proposed directive defines a 'frontier worker' as an individual deriving income from employment in a Member State where he is not resident, and who is resident in another Member State to which he returns every day. Under the proposed directive, a frontier worker who is assigned by his employer to a place of work located in another Member State so that he is prevented from returning daily to the place where he resides would not lose his status as a frontier worker, provided that the assignment did not exceed in aggregate one third of the days in the calendar year for which he has the status of a frontier worker.

Under the proposed directive, the income of the frontier worker would be subject to tax in the country of residence. If the country of source levied a withholding tax on that income, it would be credited against the tax due in the country of residence. The excess of the withholding tax would be returned and the Member States would agree upon the apportionment between them of the tax receipts and the amounts of refund.

Other rules apply to individuals, who are resident in one Member State and taxed in another on income from independent personal services and pensions and other similar remunerations. This income would not be subjected in the country of source to any more burdensome taxation than if the taxpayer were resident in that State so that domestic tax rules would apply. Under the proposal the source of country could restrict the allowances, exemptions, deductions and other general tax reliefs reserved for resident taxpayers within certain limits.

Existing directives are also concerned with other tax barriers to free movement of persons such as personal allowances in international travel, small private consignments, the final importation of vehicles, and imports of personal property, and also allow for tax-free and duty-free allowances on movement within the internal market. These factors, although they relate primarily to goods, may also create tax barriers to the free movement of persons, and should be gradually eliminated. Directives 85/348/EEC[1] and 87/198/EEC[2] amended the previous allowances provided by Directive 69/169/EEC,[3] and a further proposal for increases has been made by the Commission. The existing allowances should be abolished by the end of 1992, so that there will be no fiscal obstacle to the movement of persons connected with the frontier controls. The duty-free goods covered by Directive 69/169/EEC may be imported only within the limits set by that directive for travel between Member States. Those limits shall be reduced except in the case of tobacco products.

The elimination of tax factors affecting the freedom of movement has been achieved for certain other transactions, such as intra-Community consignments of non-commercial goods, temporary importation of means of transports, and final importation of other goods. Pursuant to Directive 74/651/EEC,[4] non-commercial goods consigned by a private person intended for another private person in another Member State are not subject to taxes or duties on importation into this Member State. These goods must have been fully taxed in the Community at the moment of purchase, must not have a commercial use, must be sent free of charge and must not exceed a certain value.

1. Council Directive 85/348/EEC of 8.7.1985 OJ No. L 183/24 of 16.7.1985.
2. Council Directive 87/198/EEC of 16.3.1987 OJ No. L 78/53 of 20.3.1987.
3. Council Directive 69/169/EEC of 28.5.1969 OJ No. L 133/6 of 4.6.1969.
4. Council Directive 74/561/EEC of 19.12.1974 OJ No. L 354/57 of 30.12.1974.

Temporary importation of a vehicle is exempt from turnover taxes and excise duty if it was taxed at the time of acquisition or import. The exemption is granted for a period of not more than six months if the individual importing the vehicle has his normal residence in another Member State and uses the vehicle for his private use. The vehicle may not be disposed of or hired out in the Member State of temporary importation to a resident of that State. A private vehicle imported temporarily for business use is exempt from tax if the individual importing the vehicle has his normal residence in another Member State and does not use the vehicle within the Member State of temporary importation in order to carry passengers for hire, or for the industrial or commercial transport of goods, whether for reward or not. In the case of a student, exemption from tax applies when the vehicle is used in another Member State where the student is residing for the sole purpose of pursuing his studies. In either case, the vehicle may not be disposed of, hired out or lent in the Member State of temporary importation.

To ensure full freedom of movement, value-added-tax and excise duties should not be levied on the final importation of certain goods into a Member State. Some of the rules governing this exemption, which are set out in Directive 83/181/EEC,[5] apply only to importation of goods from outside the Community. Others apply also to imports from another Member State. Only the latter are relevant in the context of the completion of the internal market.

Directive 83/183/EEC[6] also exempts imports of personal property from turnover taxes and excise duties. Certain amendents to this directive have been proposed in order to harmonize and relax certain formalities necessary for the grant of the exemption.

Finally, exemption from tax and other formalities is granted in respect of personal property imported by a private individual when transferring his normal residence.

---

5. Council Directive 83/181/EEC of 28.3.1983 OJ No. L 105/38 of 23.4.1983.
6. Council Directive 83/183/EEC of 28.3.1983 OJ No. L 105/64 of 23.4.1983.

Cooperation in the Field of
Aliens Law

ISSUES AND PROBLEMS IN THE GREEK LAW OF ALIENS

Theodora Antoniou[*]

1. THE NOTION OF ALIEN

According to Article 4(3)(1) of the Greek Constitution, a Greek citizen is one who possesses the qualification of citizenship as specified by law. Some conditions are regulated by the Constitution itself, as, for example, by Article 105(3)(3), according to which all persons leading a monastic life on Mount Athos acquire Greek citizenship without further formality upon admission as novices or monks. Other conditions are determined by the Code of Greek Citizenship of the year 1955,[1] as amended by law 1438/84. A person who does not satisfy these requirements must therefore be an alien or a stateless person.

There is, however, a special category of aliens, who enjoy special treatment under the Greek Constitution. These are aliens belonging to the Greek nation, i.e., persons of Greek descent or origin (homogenes) who are not Greek citizens.[2] Typical in this respect is the provision of Article 108 of the Constitution, according to which the Greek State is under an obligation to care for the welfare of people of Greek national origin living abroad and to preserve the ties of these people to the motherland. The notion of a nation possesses a particular legal significance which is determined in Articles 1(3) and 51(2) of the Constitution. According to the first of these provisions, all powers exist on behalf of the people and the nation; the second provision refers to members of Parliament, specifying that they represent the nation. But the Code of Greek Citizenship, in Article 5, also contains specific provisions about persons of Greek descent, regulating the issue of the acquisition of Greek citizenship by stateless persons of Greek descent resident abroad. To become a Greek citizen, a stateless alien of Greek descent residing abroad must file a petition with the competent Greek consular authority of the place of his residence; a special report is then prepared and

---

* Dr.iur.utr. Lecturer of Constitutional Law at the University of Athens.
1. Legislative Decree [hereafter LD] 3370/1955.
2. At this point it should be mentioned that for the distinction between persons of Greek descent and persons not of Greek descent, the criteria of race and national consciousness are particularly important. See the decision of the Greek Council of the State [hereafter StE] 2756/1983; see also Triantafyllos Karagiannis, *The Code of Greek Nationality* (Athens, 1988), pp. 10-11 [in Greek]. The new Bill for police control of the country's frontiers, the entry, residence, work and expulsion of aliens and the process of granting refugee status to aliens and more precisely in Art. 1(b) thereof, as persons of Greek descent are defined the persons of Greek origin who accept this capacity and behave as Greeks.

H.G. Schermers et al., eds., Free Movement of Persons in Europe
© 1993, T.M.C. Asser Instituut, The Hague.

the petition must be granted by the Minister of the Interior who enjoys full discretion to grant or deny it. This is a case of naturalisation *sui generis*.[3] Finally, aliens of Greek descent may acquire Greek citizenship by entering a military academy or enlisting in the Greek army in time of war or mobilization pursuant to a petition to the Prefect or even without it, provided that, in the latter case, they reach the rank of officer or petty officer.[4] Issues concerning citizenship are also dealt with in some bilateral treaties signed by Greece, such as the bilateral treaties with Albania.[5]

Finally, special treatment is reserved to aliens of Greek descent wish to be naturalized and become Greek citizens. In this case the Administration's discretion in examining the case is narrower, while a refusal has to be reasoned and is subject to judicial review as far as its conformity with the law is concerned.[6] Generally speaking, the Greek State possesses a sovereign right to naturalize or refuse to naturalize an alien, and this right may be exercised freely. According to Article 3(3) of Law 1438/84, a decision rejecting a naturalization petition need not to be reasoned. The Council of the State has, of course, interpreted this provision narrowly: according to this Court, a ministerial decision rejecting a naturalization petition does not need to provide a reason or justification thereto, but if the same or any other document to which this explicitly refers mentions specific reasons as the basis on which the Administration turned down the naturalization petition, these reasons must be legal and are open to review by the court.[7] The status of stateless aliens, i.e., aliens who possess no nationality status at all, is governed by the Convention relating to the Status of Stateless Persons of 28 September 1954, ratified by Greece by virtue of Law 139/1975. Further, the status of stateless persons is governed by the Convention on the Reduction of Statelessness of 13 September 1973, ratified by Greece by virtue of the Law 535/1977. This latter

---

3. See Elias Krispis, *Private International Law* (Athens-Komotini, 1979), p. 276 [in Greek]; Zoe Papasiopi-Passia, *The Law of Citizenship* (Thessaloniki, 1987), p. 33 et seq. [in Greek].

4. Arts. 12 and 13 of the Code of Greek Nationality.

5. See the Treaty on Nationality of 2/13 Oktober 1928 between Greece and Albania, ratified by Law 3655/28. See also the decision of the Greek Supreme Court [*Areios Pagos*: hereafter AP] 569/1980 in 28 *Nomikon Bema* (1958)[Greek legal journal, hereafter NoB] .

6. See Velissarios Karakostas, 'Note to StE 2279/1990' in 22 DIKI [The Trial; Greek legal journal; hereafter DIKI] at p. 531 [in Greek].

7. See StE 2279/1990, 22 DIKI p. 527 et seq. This judgment had three interesting dissenting opinions. According to the first, the ministerial decision which denies a naturalization petition constitutes an act of State and may not be reviewed by the Courts. According to the second dissenting opinion, the true meaning of Art. 3(3) of Law 1438/1984 is that the decision which denies a naturalization petition may not contain a reasoning, but that this reasoning, which may become apparent by facts contained in the file of the case with the administration, need not refer to reasons pertaining to a broader category of persons including the interested person, nor express a broader political commitment. Finally, according to the third dissenting opinion, the legality of the reasoning of a negative decision is reviewable by the Courts, not only when this reasoning is contained in the said decision or in a document to which it explicitly refers, but also when this reasoning can be clearly derived from other sources included in the file of the case with the administration. See also Panos Lazaratos, 'The justification provided for turning down an alien's petition for citizenship, In view of Decision 22791/1990', *Armenopoulos* (1991) [Greek StE legal journal, hereafter: Arm], p. 749 et seq.

Convention was particularly taken into account in the revision of the Code of Greek Citizenship in 1984.[8]

Further, the Greek Constitution contains two other articles that have a direct impact on the status of aliens: these are Article 5(2)(c), according to which the extradition of an alien persecuted because of his activities in furtherance of the cause of freedom is prohibited, and Article 28(1), according to which international conventions prevail over any contrary provision of the law. By virtue of this last provision, a number of international treaties have become absorbed into domestic Greek law and will be mentioned herein below at the appropriate places; one should already notice, however, that the addition of a reciprocity clause to this constitutional provision is unfortunate.[9]

2. ENTRY AND RESIDENCE

2.1 Entry

The fundamental statutory text that regulates entry and residence of aliens in Greece is Law 4130/1929; this law is noticeably liberal and favourable in its treatment of aliens.

According to Law 4310/1929, the granting of a permit of entry to the country depends on the following conditions:

— a valid passport or other identification document on the basis of existing bilateral treaties. Passengers of private vessels and cruisers are exempted;

— a visa issued by a Consulate of Greece, unless the obligation to obtain one has been removed by virtue of a bilateral treaty.

On extraordinary occasions, entry may even be allowed without the above formalities pursuant to the directions of the Minister of the Interior (Art. 3(3) of Law 4310/29). Of course, there also exists a category of privileged aliens, e.g., diplomats and consuls,[10] representatives of and to international organizations, members of the

---

8. Law 1438/1984. Cf., P.Dagtoglou, 'Faktische und rechtliche Grundlagen des Ausländerwesens' in J. Frowein and T. Stein, eds., *Die Rechtsstellung von Ausländern nach staatlichem Recht und Völkerrecht* (Berlin, 1987), p. 529 at p. 538.

9. See Krateros Ioannou, *The Expulsion of a Citizen of a Member-State of the EEC* (Athens, 1981) p. 33 et seq. [in Greek].

10. Cf., the verbal note exchanged between the Ministers of Foreign Affairs of Greece and Bulgaria No. F.834-5/AS 1154, according to which the visa regime for the holders of diplomatic and service passports issued by the Foreign Ministries of the two countries was abolished from 1 April 1991. Also, on 26 May 1988, discussions took place in Athens about the mutual abolition of the visa regime for the holders of diplomatic and service passports between Greece and Turkey; the implementation of this agreement has not, however, begun. See also Law 217/1975, Art. 23(1)(2), ratifying the consular Convention signed in Athens on 17 December 1974 between the Hellenic Republic and the Federal Socialist Republic of Yugoslavia, according to which members of the consular authorities and their dependents are not subject to the laws and the regulations of the country of residence concerning residence permits and the duty to report to the authorities.

armed forces assigned for local duty under international agreements[11] and traders, investors and others whose migration is protected by treaty and who are exempted from the formalities concerning possession of a valid passport and visa in order to enter and leave the country.

Finally, no visa or other equivalent formality is required for citizens of Member States of the European Communities, who have the right to travel and reside freely in Greece in order to work as employees[12] or to establish an independent business.[13]

The entry of an alien is forbidden if:
1. He is mentally disturbed or has a contagious disease.
2. He has been convicted abroad for a crime listed in the relevant treaty of judicial assistance.
3. He has previously been deported from Greece.
4. He does not possess the necessary means for maintaining himself and his family, as defined occasionally by orders of the Minister of the Interior.
5. Whilst possessing a transit visa in order to travel through Greece: (a) he does not possess the necessary visas to enter the country and to travel through the intermediate countries and (b) he does not possess the sum of money necessary to cover his expenses until he reaches the country of his destination.
6. Whilst arriving in Greece in order to work, he has a visa that does not mention the number and the date of the special work permit as provided by the law (Art. 4 of Law 4310/29).

A pending Bill concerning the status of aliens includes in Article 11 an innovation, which consist of the drafting of a catalogue of unwanted aliens. The criteria and the process whereby an alien's name may be included in or excluded from this list of unwanted aliens are to be determined by a joint decision of the Ministers of Foreign Affairs, Justice and Public Order. According to Article 6 of the Bill, one of the reasons why an alien may be prohibited from entering the country, is the inclusion of his name in this list of unwanted aliens. The Bill expressly provides that this decision will not be published in the Government's Gazette. An initial critical appraisal of this provision should certainly begin by underlining the following: it is clear that what we have here is a regulatory act of the Administration, since the latter is thereby enacting general and impersonal rules. The existing constitutional order mandates that all regulatory acts be

11. See Art. 3 of Law 2799/1954 ratifying the Treaty signed in London on 19 June 1951 between the NATO Member States, concerning the legal status of such forces, as well as the Protocol signed in Paris on 28 August 1952 and concerning the legal status of the international military headquarters established pursuant to the NATO Treaty; this provision relieves the members of the land, naval or air forces who are on duty in Greece from the obligation to submit to passport and visa formalities in their entry or exit from Greece, as well as from reporting to the immigration authorities their entry or exit from the territory of the Country of residence. See also Art. III of Law 1403/1983, ratifying the Agreement on Defence and Economic Cooperation between the Governments of the Hellenic Republic and the USA, which refers to the above mentioned Agreement between NATO members, so far as the status of US forces, their military personnel, their civil personnel and their dependents is concerned.

12. See Art. 2 of Presidential Decree [hereafter: PD] 525/1983.

13. See Art. 3 of PD 499/1987.

published. Thus, the legislature may not exclude a certain category of regulatory acts from all publicity. However, the jurisprudence of the Council of State has pronounced that a law providing that regulatory acts (in their entirety or parts thereof) may not be published if such publication would prejudice the security of the Country — as is the case with regulations referring to the structure, composition and ammunition of the armed forces[14] — is not by this fact alone unconstitutional.

Also, so far as the provisions under consideration are concerned, another doubt should be expressed: since by this provision the power to issue regulatory decrees is deferred to the Administration and not to the President of the Republic, in order for it to conform with the provisions of Article 43(2)of the Constitution, it must visualize the regulation of specific issues, or issues of a local interest, or issues technical and detailed as compared to the fundamental disposition included in the provision in question.

'Specific issues' are issues which in their content and in their relationship to the disposition included in the statutory text constitute a partial case of a certain issue which happens to be the object of the statutory provision in question. A 'detailed issue' is an issue which constitutes the minor and non-important part of a broader provision.[15] Issues which are not regulated in themselves, even in outline within the provision deferring legislative authority, but which are nevertheless specific, may be deferred only to the Chief of the Administrative Power.[16] In the case at hand, the manner in which the list is to be compiled is not determined in the pending draft, not even in outline, and may not be considered as a technical and specific issue as compared to the fundamental disposition of the statute, which reads as follows: 'The competent Service of the Ministry of Public Order prepares and keeps a catalogue of unwanted aliens.' Therefore, the statutory provision concerning the preparation of the said list should further delegate regulatory power to the President of the Republic alone. Regulation by means of presidential decrees contains a further guarantee, i.e., the constitutional guarantee which provides for the preparation of these decrees by the Council of the State.[17]

2.2   Residence

An entry permit normally allows residence for up to 30 days. If the consular visa determines a residence period of less than a month, the Minister of the Interior may extend the residence permit further.[18] The positive and negative conditions that must

14. Cf., Ep. Spiliotopoulos, *Manual of Administrative Law I* (Athens-Komotine, 1988), p. 101 et seq.; p. 162 [in Greek].

15. See the working documents of the committee on the preparation of the draft of decree 51/87, *To Syntagma* (1987) [*The Constitution*; Greek legal journal; hereafter: ToS], p. 158 et seq.

16. See StE 2764/1981, ToS (1982) pp. 292-93.

17. See the working documents of the committee on the preparation of the draft of decree 51/87, loc. cit. n. 15, at p. 159. Argument *a contrario* from the dissenting opinion to StE 2075/1978, ToS (1979) p. 87, at p. 89.

18. See Art. 6(1)(4) of Law 4310/1929.

obtain for the issue of an entry permit also apply to the permission to reside. The law contains special conditions only in these cases where the purpose of the trip to Greece is to work, in which case the alien must have previously obtained a work-permit from the competent Greek Consulate, and which appears on his passport.[19] If the alien intends to stay in Greece for a period exceeding 30 days, he must file a declaration of arrival and obtain a residence permit for up to three months; the permit's duration may be further extended.[20] The residence permit does not of itself include the freedom to travel in the country, nor the freedom to chose the location of one's residence. By means of presidential decrees issued pursuant to a proposal of the Minister of the Interior acting in concert with the Ministers of Foreign Affairs and Defence, aliens may be prohibited from permanently or temporarily residing in certain districts or cities of the country. Moreover, for reasons of public or social interest, the Minister of the Interior may impose on specific aliens further restrictions that he deems necessary (e.g., a prohibition on entering or residing in Greece or in a specific part thereof, an obligation to appear before the police, to move, to exercise only a specific trade, etc.).[21] The acts of the Minister of the Interior issued pursuant to the above statutory provision need not include a reason, not mention those facts which were considered and which led to the conclusion that reasons of public or social interest necessitated the taking of such onerous measures against the alien. However, the Council of the State has underlined that these facts must be apparent from the evidence upon which the ministerial decision was based, so as to make judicial review of the correct application of the law possible by the courts.[22]

Greece has not, on this point, assumed any international obligations, for it has not signed the 4th Protocol of the European Convention of Human Rights, which protects freedom of movement and choice of domicile. The Convention does not, however, prevent States imposing statutory restrictions which are justified by reasons of public interest. In addition, each country is free to determine when and under what conditions the residence of an alien is lawful; each country may issue a residence permit with geographical restrictions. Article 2 of the 4th Protocol does not create, nor does it broaden, any right of residence of the alien.[23] Moreover, so far as the free movement of refugees as opposed to other aliens is concerned, Greece is among the six countries which have expressed reservations to this right of refugees, which is included in the Convention of 1951 and more specifically in Article 26, reserving for herself the right to determine the location of residence either on general or on national security, public order or public interest grounds.[24] The effect of the above-mentioned provisions is

19. See Art. 4(1)(6) of Law 4310/1929.

20. See Art. 6 of Law 4310/1929.

21. See Art. 14 of Law 4310/1929.

22. See StE 2397/1966, *Epitheorissi Demossiou kai Dioikitikou Dikaiou* (1966) p. 400 et seq. [*Review of Public and Administrative Law*; Greek legal journal; hereafter: EDDD].

23. See Europäische Kommisssion für Menschenrechte (EKMR) Strassburg Entsch. 1 Dezember 1986 - Beschw. No. 11825/85 - Fall Sivakumaran gegen Bundesrepublik Deutschland, EuGRZ (1987) p. 335 et seq.

24. See Goodwin-Gill, *The Refugee in International Law* (Oxford, 1983) p. 53, n. 24.

that further residence in the country may be denied to an alien to whom entry and residence in Greece has been permitted; this denial must, however, be dictated by reasons of public or social interest, the sufficiency of which may always be reviewed by the courts.[25] Such reasons may be either general or specific and may refer either to the person directly or to the broader category of persons to which he belongs. Therefore, it would not, e.g., be possible to give as a valid reason for not extending an alien's residence permit in Greece the fact that he intends to stay in the country for a long period of time.[26] Of course, the Greek legal order does not recognize any right on the part of an alien who enters the country to permanent residence. There are cases however, where, because of a series of lawful extensions of the initial residence permit, a situation has *de facto* ensued which may justify a right to permanent residence.[27]

One thing that could be accomplished by means of an interpretation of the existing laws, which would be concordant with the Constitution, would be the application of a stricter standard of proof for a refusal to renew an alien's residence permit.[28]

2.3   Citizens of the Common Market

Contrary to other provisions of international law, according to which one might at most suggest that a State has a duty to admit aliens if they pose no serious threat to its public safety, security, general welfare or institutions,[29] European community law recognizes for every citizen of the Common Market a right to enter and reside in another Member State's territory. This right is also guaranteed by domestic Greek legislation, and more precisely by a network of provisions included in Presidential Decree 499/87 which regulates the movement and residence in Greece of citizens of other EEC Member States (and their families) who work in the country. These provisions have been enacted to comply with the EEC Council's Directives Nos. 64/221/EEC of 25 February 1964, 68/360 EEC of 15 October 1968 and 72/194/EEC of 18 May 1972 as well as in the application of the EEC Regulations 1612/68 of the Council of 15 October 1968 and 1251/70 of the Commission of 29 June 1970. The right of entry and the claim to be issued with a residence permit are now grounded on the following provisions: Article 3(1) of Presidential Decree 499/77, according to which entry to Greece is allowed by the mere presentation of a valid passport or an identification document issued by one

25. See StE 2879/89. The refusal to renew an alien's residence permit must not by law contain a reasoning, but it may be reviewed to determine whether it was in fact premissed on lawful grounds and whether the facts on the basis of which the Administration reached its judgment do indeed constitute the notion of public or social interest. See StE 1947/1960.

26. See StE 218/1987, 28 *Elleniki Dikaiossyni* (1987) p. 936 et seq. [*Greek Justice*; Greek legal journal; hereafter: EllD].

27. See StE 665/1990, which refers the case to a seven member session because of the importance of the issue. See also the decision of the seven member session 1101/1991, EDDD (1992), 103.

28. See Dagtoglou, op. cit. n. 8, at p. 540.

29. See James Nafziger, 'The General Admission of Alien Under International Law' 77 AJIL (1983) p. 804 at p. 847. In a later piece (International Law bearing on the entry of aliens regardless of refugee status in: *Thesaurus Acroasium* Vol. XIII (Thessaloniki, 1987) p. 517 et seq. the same author is unsure wether the duty of the States not to deny entry to all aliens has yet ripened into custom.

of the Member States; Article 5 (2)(a), according to which for the issue of an initial work permit an applicant need only submit the documents with which he entered Greece, an employment statement by the employer and a medical certificate proving that he does not suffer from one of the diseases or handicaps mentioned in the same Presidential Decree as being susceptible of endangering public health; Article 5(3), according to which the finalisation of the formalities necessary to obtain the residence permit may not in any way impede the performance of the employment contract entered into by the petitioner; and Article 11(3), according to which the expiration of the formal identification document or the passport used by the person concerned to enter Greece and to obtain a residence permit may not constitute a reason for his expulsion from the country.[30] Finally, geographical restrictions on the right of residence within the national territory may not be imposed against citizens of the other EC Member States, unless they also apply in the same measure to the citizens of the country imposing the restrictions.[31]

2.4   Legal protection by the courts

The right of aliens to enjoy legal protection by the courts in conjunction with the issues discussed above is laid down in a number of legal provisions, including the Constitution. According to Article 20(1) of the Constitution, 'every person shall be entitled to receive legal protection by the courts and may plead before them his views concerning his rights or interests, as specified by law.' Further, in Article 95(1)(a), it is stated that 'the jurisdiction of the Council of State pertains mainly to the annulment upon petition of executive acts of administrative authorities for abuse of power or violation of the law.'

3.   THE RESIDENT ALIEN'S DEPENDENTS

The Greek law of aliens does not contain any specific provision concerning the fate of the aliens' family. Article 9 simply provides that the head of the family (either the father or the mother) or if such does not exist, the person providing domicile, notify the authorities of the presence of minor aliens, i.e., aliens under 18 years of age. During the month of January of the year in which these minors reach the age of 18 years, they must file a petition to obtain a residence permit and a passport. The law does not distinguish between aliens who have a family in Greece or whose spouse is a Greek

---

30. For the grounding of this right, as well for the non-constitutive nature of the residence permit - which means that its absence cannot in any way impair the person's right of free movement in the EEC, see Jürgen Kranz, 'Die Freizuegigkeit nach dem EWG-Vertrag und das nationale Ausländer - und Melderecht', DOEV (1977) p. 111, at p. 113.

31. See St. Vallas, 'Entry, Residence and Movement of the Citizens of the Member-States Inside the EEC. Freedom of Establishment - Free Movement of Workers', 28 NoB (1958) p. 9, at p. 18.

citizen, even when the residence permit of the same is curtailed or not renewed and the alien has to leave the country.[32]

On the basis of Article 21 of the Greek Constitution, which protects marriage, the family and minority, one is tempted to ask a number of questions about an alien's right to marry and have a family. Initially, of course, an alien has the right to seek his personal and professional development in his country of origin.[33] However, on the basis of the above-mentioned constitutional provision, read in conjunction with several rules of international law which are binding on Greece, one could ground a duty on Greece, as a country of reception, to facilitate the entry of the alien's family. These international law rules include:

— Article 19(6) of the European Social Charter, ratified by Greece by virtue of the Law 1426/1984. The Charter obliges the Contracting Parties to facilitate so far as possible the reunion of the immigrant worker's family whom they have allowed to reside in their territory. Of course, the duties imposed by the Social Charter need further specification by internal legislation of the Contracting Parties. However, they can be used as guidelines of interpretation in favour of aliens, to be taken into consideration by the competent authorities when exercising their discretionary powers.[34]

— Article 8(1) of the European Convention on Human Rights. This article provides that in the taking of administrative measures leading to the interruption of an alien's residence permit special consideration should be given to existing family obligations. However, this provision cannot be considered either as 'special' or as more binding than the constitutional provision mentioned above.[35]

— Articles 17(1) and 23(1) of the International Covenant on Civil and Political Rights of 19 December 1966, not ratified by Greece, according to which arbitrary interventions in a persons's family life are prohibited. These provisions do not, however, preclude the introduction of statutory restrictions so far as the residence of aliens is concerned, unless these restrictions are overtly arbitrary, i.e., there is no substantive justification for imposing them or they discriminate on the basis of arbitrary criteria.[36] The new Bill, in Article 14, takes a stand vis-à-vis the problem of the residence of the alien's family members. According to this article, an alien who has been granted a residence permit may demand that the other members of his family are allowed to come and reside with him, provided that the conditions specified by a joint decision of

32. See Art. 6(6) of Law 4310/29. The alien's family status must, of course, be taken into consideration in the exercise of his discretionary powers by the Minister of the Interior, in view of the constitutional provision of Art. 21(1) of the Constitution, which places marriage, maternity and young age under the protection of the State. See Dagtoglou, op.cit. n. 8, at pp. 546-547.

33. See the similar thoughts for an analogous German provision of Art. 6 of the Fundamental Law of the Federal Republic of Germany [Grundgesetz] in Kay Heilbronner, 'Der Nachzug ausländischer Familienangehörigen und die Schutzpflicht fuer Ehe und Familie', JZ (1983) p. 574 et seq.

34. See Heilbronner, loc. cit. n. 33, at p. 576.

35. For arguments concerning the obligation to admit aliens for purposes of family unification on the basis of other clauses of the Convention, as for example those contained in Arts. 12 and 14 and for a critical appraisal on the issue of grounding aliens' rights see Bertold Huber, 'Europäische Menschenrechtskonvention und Familiennachzug', NJW (1985) p. 1247 et seq.

36. See Heilbronner, loc. cit. n. 33, at p. 576.

the Ministers of Foreign Affairs, Employment and Public Order are met. To these members of the alien's family a special residence permit is issued, which follows the fate of the residence permit of the person who initially invited them. According to paragraph 4 of the same article, these family members may, when they reach the age of 18, obtain an independent residence permit, provided of course that they have the necessary means for their own maintenance. It can be seen from the above that the most important issues concerning the alien's right to invite and unite the members of his family are left to the discretion of the Administration, which is to determine the specific conditions concerning the establishment of the alien's family members by means of ministerial decisions.[37] Further, the Bill in question does not deal with the serious practical problems posed by the contraction of bogus marriages whose only aim is to facilitate the alien's stay in Greece; nor does it deal with the problems posed by marriages between Greek citizens and aliens in general, where all regulation must begin with the need to protect the Greek spouse.[38]

4.   IDENTITY AND TRAVEL DOCUMENTS

Linked to the subject of free movement of people is the issue of possession of a passport. One speaks today of the individual's right to a passport but in reality one means the individuals's right to leave the country.[39] The right to leave any country, including one's own, and to return to one's country is embodied in a number of different international conventions ratified by Greece.[40] The passport is an aid to establishing the right to reenter the issuing State. Passports are public documents. Passports issued by the Prefecture and the Greek Consular authorities are divided into personal, family and group passports.[41] Passports are valid for all countries of the world and for multiple return-trips, with the exception of group passports which are valid for all countries of the world but for one return trip only.[42] In order to travel to other EC countries, Greeks may use as a travel document not only their passport, but their valid, national identification document as well.[43] The Ministry of Foreign Affairs is competent to issue diplomatic and other special official passports.[44] In extraordi-

37. In other legal systems legislation is particularly detailed on these issues. On Art. 17 of the German AuslG see B. Huber, 'Das neue Ausländerrecht', NVwvZ (1990) p. 1113 et seq.; p. 1115 et seq.
38. See Heilbronner, loc. cit. n. 33, at p. 577 et seq.
39. S. Daniel Turack, *The Passport in International Law* (1972) pp. 14, 19.
40. See Art. 1 (1) of the International Convention on the Elimination of all Forms of Racial Discrimination, ratified by Legislative Decree 494/1970. See also Art.1 of the European Convention of Establishment ratified by Law 4429/64 which introduces the right to travel. Under Part II of the European Social Charter and especially in Arts. 18 and 19 ratified by Law 1426/84, the Contracting parties undertook to recognize the right of their nationals to leave the country to engage in a gainful occupation.
41. See Art. 1(1) of Law 1004/1980.
42. See Art. 1 of PD 938/1980 'on the regulations of the formalities, the geographical and temporal validity and the necessary documents for the issue of passports.'
43. See Art. 2(1) of PD 308/1991 (Government Gazette A 106/10/7/91).
44. See Art. 1(2)(áf) of Law 419/1976 'on the Organization of the Ministry of Foreign Affairs.'

nary cases, where the issue of a common passport is not possible, the administration may issue a temporary travel document with a limited duration. Today, temporarily limited travel documents may be of the following kinds:

1. Temporary passport (*passeport provisoire*): this is issued by the Greek Consular Authorities outside Greece to Greeks residing abroad and lacking a passport because of loss or because the passport was taken away from them for other reasons. This passport takes the form of a piece of paper with certain specified qualifications; it is valid only for the bearer's return to Greece and may not be used for the issue of an ordinary passport.[45]

2. Travel document (*titre de voyage*) of the Geneva Convention of 28 July 1951. This document is issued by the Ministry of Public Order to refugees who arrive in Greece and who are not of Greek origin; it is independent of the granting of asylum. Details concerning the duration and geographical restrictions of this travel document are contained in the Regulatory Order of the Ministry of Public Order No. 23/1976.

3. Travel document (*titre de voyage*) of the New York Convention of 28 September 1954. This document is issued by the Ministry of Public Order to stateless aliens legally resident in Greece. Details of the duration and geographical restrictions of this travel document are also contained in the Regulatory Order of the Ministry of Public Order No. 23/1976.

Travel documents for refugees and stateless persons also fulfil the function of providing evidence of identity and status, as Article 27, common to the International Convention relating to the status of Stateless Persons 1954, demands.[46]

People of Greek descent from Northern Epirus and Turkey are issued with special passports according to the Decision No. 22/1 March 1976 of the Council of Ministers and the joint decision of the Ministers of the Interior, of Foreign Affairs and of Public Order, dated 26 February 1977. It should be noted that the bearer of such a passport does not thereby acquire Greek citizenship.

It is possible for a national passport not to indicate the nationality of the bearer in the document.[47] All these documents entitle the bearer to return to Greece, as returnability as essential to the validity of a travel document is dictated by a rule of customary international law. But it is his status and not the possession of a passport which places the States under an obligation to protect the bearer.[48]

The identification of aliens above 14 years of age is exclusively proved a. by their passport; and b. their resident permit in Greece, issued by the Aliens' Service.[49] If the alien is granted a long period of residence in Greece, the alien is issued with a regular identification document. [50] Greece has signed the European Agreement on Travel by young persons on collective passports between the member countries of the Council of Europe and therefore admits upon its territory parties of young persons from the

45. See Art. 1(2) of Law 1004/1980.
46. S.G. Goodwin-Gill, *International Law and the movement of persons between States* (1978) pp. 43-44.
47. Turack, op. cit. n. 39, at p. 225.
48. Goodwin-Gill, op. cit. n. 46, at pp. 46-47. See also Turack, loc. cit. n. 39, p. 18 et seq.
49. See Art. 5(3) of LD 127/1969.
50. See Art. 7 of Law 4310/1929.

territory of the other Contracting Parties on a collective travel document. According to Article 12, these people must be able to prove their identity in some other way, if requested to do so.

5.   EXPULSION – DEPORTATION[51]

5.1   Expulsion

Law 4310/29, Article 26(7), contains a general clause, according to which, notwithstanding criminal prosecution, an alien who breaches the law is subject to deportation from the Greek territory. Thus the Administration may order the deportation of aliens who enter Greece without having been subjected to the necessary control by the police or without a duly certified passport, of aliens who are mentally disturbed or suffer from a contagious disease, aliens who have been condemned abroad for crimes specified in the existing extradition treaties, aliens lacking the necessary means for their own maintenance, aliens lacking the necessary work permit to undertake employment in Greece, aliens who are considered dangerous to the safety of the State, aliens who do not obtain an extension of their 30 days residence permit and aliens who do not report to the police an intervening change in their status (change of citizenship, name, profession, occupation, marriage or birth of child). The tendency now is to prefer the administrative process to expel an alien, instead of seeking his criminal prosecution, which is also possible according to the existing legislation on the status of aliens. We might mention here Article 19(3)(2) of Law 4310/29 as amended by Law 1943/91, which gives to the Public Prosecutor the right to interrupt the prosecution of an alien who has illegally entered or left the country and refer him to the competent administrative authorities for deportation. Even an alien who has secured his residence permit may be subsequently deported after extension of his permit has been denied. Such deportation must be grounded on reasons of public or social interest. The latter must in turn be justified on the basis of the overall behaviour or of a single action of the alien, which has, however, broader ramifications and social significance and offends public opinion. In the absence of such offence, the sanction of deportation may not be employed. The deportation of an unwanted alien does not absolutely depend upon the unfettered discretion of the Administration. Their decision to deport an alien is normally subject to an appeal before the Courts, with the exception of cases where the act of deportation has the character of an act of State.[52]

In respect of the valid grounds and the conditions under which an alien may be deported, Greece is bound by the European Convention on Establishment signed in Paris on 13 December 1955 and ratified by Greece by virtue of Law 4429/1964. Article

---

51. For the meaning of these terms see Adrienne Masters, 'Statutory and constitutional limitation on the indefinite detention of excluded aliens', 62 *Boston University Law Review* (1982) p. 557 et seq., fn. 36.

52. Bendermacher-Gerousis, 'The Judicial Control of Discretionary Power in Expulsion of Aliens', NoB (1985) p.1827 et seq. [in Greek].

3(3) of this Convention provides that 'nationals of any Contracting Party who have been lawfully residing for more than ten years in the territory of any other Party may only be expelled for reasons of national security or if the offence against ordre public or morality are of a particularly serious nature.'[52a] This provision does not seem, however, to add anything new to the Greek legislation, as has been explained above. The jurisprudence of the Greek courts uses the notion of the 'common sentiment' as the standard for judging 'offence against ordre public or morality'.[53] Otherwise, this particular provision of the European Convention on Establishment has been criticized as representing a 'triumph of national resistance', given the fact that it does not allow the alien an unconditional right of appeal against the deportation decision.[54]

5.2   Immediate refoulement exclusion

Article 6(4) of Law 4310/29 provides for an alien's duty to leave the country after his residence permit has expired, i.e., even before deportation takes place. There is one case of rejection of aliens, which refers to transit visitors who do not leave the country on time.[55] The new Bill also provides for a procedure of immediate refoulement. Thus, Article 4(4) provides that, irrespective of any criminal acts committed, aliens illegally entering Greek territory are to be immediately and by the fastest possible means expelled to the country from which they originate, pursuant to a decision of the chief of the public authority which discovered the illegal entry in the first place. Paragraph (2) of the same Article provides that if the immediate expulsion of the alien is not possible, the alien is to be referred to the competent administrative authority which then sets in motion the process of his deportation. Article 10 of the pending Bill contains similar provisions and places a number of duties on the owners of the means of public transportation. Prima facie the provision of Article 4(4) of the new Bill is contrary to Article 33 of the 1951 Convention. This Article is applicable also to measures such as rejection at the frontier without investigation whether the country of origin will cease further action once retaliatory measures against a person so rejected have been discontinued, in cases where the alternative is a clear risk of persecution.[56] Further, because of the provision about carrier sanctions in the pending Bill Greece will also be in breach of its Conventional obligation under Article 31. This new piece of legislation on carrier sanctions includes the following three elements which are common to the laws in question:[57]

52a. See also Act. 19(8) of the Social Charter (Law 1426/84) and Art. 1(2) of the Seventh Protocol to the European Convention on Human Rights ratified in Greece by Law 1705/84.

53. See StE 2438/1966.

54. See Aug. Macheret, *L'immigration etrangère en Suisse a l'heure de l'intégration européenne* (1969) p. 205.

55. See Art. 16(2) of Law 4310/1929.

56. S.G. Goodwin-Gill, 'Non-refoulement and the new asylum seekers', in D. Martin, *The New Asylum Seekers: Refugee Law in the 1980s. The Ninth Sokol Colloquium on International Law*, p. 105. See also Atle Grahl-Madsen, *Territorial Asylum* (London, 1980) pp. 53-54.

57. S. Erika Feller, 'Carrier Sanctions and International Law', *International Journal of Refugee Law* (1989) p. 48 et seq. (50-51).

1. A duty on a carrier to remove from the country any passenger without proper documentation (Art. 10 of the new Bill).

2. An obligation on a carrier to pay the costs of detaining such a passenger (Art. 10).

3. Fines or other penalties on a carrier for bringing in an undocumented non-national (Art. 33(1) of the new Bill).

This legislation is also designed to prevent the illegal entry and access to asylum procedures of persons who would otherwise seek asylum and not simply to inhibit migration flow, because it does not discriminate between asylum seekers and other aliens. This limitation of the access of refugees to status determination procedures and to the rights of the 1951 Convention results in an infringement of Article 31 of the 1951 Convention since this last provision does provide for certain instances of illegal entry.[58]

Nor does the proposed legislation penalizing airlines for bringing in improperly documented passengers find support in the 1944 Chicago Convention on Civil Aviation.[59] Article 4(4) of the proposed legislation needs to incorporate special regulations to deal with asylum seekers.

Article 25(6) of the same Bill further provides for the possibility of the Minister of Public Order granting temporary refuge to asylum seekers and not returning them to a country in which their lives or freedom may be endangered. Greece will therefore in future afford protection to *de facto* refugees, i.e., to non-Convention refugees with B-Status.[60] If Article 4(4) of the pending Bill is not changed, many problems of implementation will arise.

The above-mentioned measures of expulsion refer to aliens who have already 'entered', while those who have not entered are subject to exclusion. According to Article 6(5)(d) of the new Bill, an alien may be prohibited from entering the country if his name is included in a list of unwanted aliens. There will therefore be a category of aliens who will be immediately rejected without having even the possibility of applying for recognition as refugees. This point is the central foundation for a restrictive legal structure which various legal orders have introduced in order radically to avoid to solve the aliens problem. Here also, the possibility of allowing temporary refuge to asylum seekers who have been refused refugee-status will be seriously restricted because of Article 6(5) of the new Bill.

---

58. S. Feller, loc. cit. n. 57, at p. 57 et seq.

59. Ratified by Greece with Law 211/1947. See about this question in Feller, loc. cit. n. 57, at p.53 et seq.

60. S.G. Goodwin-Gill, ASIL Proceeding 80 (1986) p. 98. This right to *de facto* asylum could arise from the European Convention, as the jurisprudence under Arts. 3,8 and 13 shows. Thus the temporary protection against deportation incompatible with strong humanitarian concerns, the right to temporary residence for family members of a non-national who enjoys national or international protection against deportation and the right to an effective remedy, provide an important basis for *de facto* asylum under ECHR. S. Terje Einarsen, 'The European Convention on Human Rights and the Notion of an Implied Right to *de facto* Asylum', *International Journal of Refugee Law* (1990) p. 361 et seq.

5.3 Detention of aliens

If, after the issue of a ministerial decision concerning the deportation of an alien, the alien does not leave the country of his own volition, administrative agents must take all measures necessary for the implementation of the decision. Thus, the police may arrest, search and detain the alien. Detention functions here as a means of facilitating deportation and cannot constitute punishment.[61] The law does not provide for a maximum time of detention; however, the interpretation of Article 23 of Law 4310/29 which provides that the alien should be deported by force as soon as this is feasible, leads one to the conclusion that the alien's detention should be of the shortest possible duration;[62] this interpretation also finds constitutional support. Thus, some scholars support the view that Article 6(4) of the Greek Constitution, which places a limit on the maximum time for pre-trial detention, intends, as a matter of fact, to place a limit on all stages and kinds of restriction of personal freedom by the administrative authorities and even by the judges themselves.[63] We should here note, that despite the problems created by the existing provisions, Article 27(6) of the pending Bill does not determine a maximum time for the detention of aliens prior to deportation. As a part of the deportation process detention cannot be justified if the alien is undeportable or the deportation is not being sought in good faith.[64]

Finally, all administrative action undertaken with the aim of forcibly implementing the deportation decision, such as arrest, search or detention, must be accompanied by an official police report; this is not provided for by Law 4310/29, but is warranted by the importance of the measures taken, i.e., measures which touch upon fundamental human rights, as well as by the overarching principles of administrative law, namely the principle of administrative benevolence and the principle of the protection of citizens.[65]

6. THE GRANTING OF REFUGEE STATUS

6.1 The process whereby refugee status is recognized

We should begin by defining the notion of a 'refugee', for that will dictate the solution to other problems, such as the obligations of the State in matters such as non-refoule-

---

61. Masters, loc. cit. n. 51, at p. 584.

62. See also conclusion No. 5 (e) on International Protection, adopted by the Executive Committee of the High Commissioner's Programme at its 2th Session, Annex to Goodwin-Gill, 'Entry and Exclusion of Refugees', Transnational Legal Problems of Refugees, *Michigan Yearbook of International Legal Studies* (1982) p. 291 et seq., p.322 et seq. (325), according to which it is: 'Recommended that an expulsion order should only be combined with custody or detention if absolutely necessary for reasons of national security or public order and that such custody or detention should not be unduly prolonged.

63. See Ar. Manessis, *Constitutional Rights* (Thessaloniki, 1982), p. 190 [in Greek]. See also Masters, loc. cit. n. 51, at p. 580.

64. Masters, loc. cit. n. 51, at p. 586 et seq.

65. See the Opinion of the Acting Prosecutor S. Alexopoulos No. 13/1984, 33 NoB p. 875 et seq.

ment, non-rejection at the frontier, the period of entry of the temporary refugee and the treatment of refugees after entry.[66]

The only Greek regulation concerning refugees is contained in two joint ministerial decisions signed in 1977[67] by the Ministers of the Interior and of Public Order. These decisions concern the process whereby refugee status is recognized and other similar matters which relate to the 28 July 1951 Geneva Convention relating to the status of refugees[68] and to the 31 January 1967 Protocol of the same name.[69] Thus, the Greek legal order has adopted the term 'refugee' as it is understood by the Geneva Convention and considers as refugees those who:

1. are outside their country of origin (as far as this point is concerned, the jurisprudence of Greek courts has made it clear that the person who arrives in Greece and asks to be recognized as a refugee, need not have come directly from the country whose citizenship he has);

2. are unable or unwilling to avail themselves of the protection of that country, or to return there; and,

3. such inability or unwillingness is attributable to a well-founded fear of being persecuted;[70] and

4. the persecution feared is based on reasons of race, religion, nationality, membership of a particular social group or political opinion.

This definition has served as the basis of a number of other regional agreements, most of which Greece has not ratified by law. Most important among them are the European Agreement on the Abolition of Visas for Refugees,[71] the 1972 European Convention on Social Security,[72] and the 1980 European Arrangement on Transfer of Responsibility for Refugees.[73] These internationally-binding commitments of Greece acquire an added importance in view of Article 28(1) of the Greek Constitution, which provides that international treaties ratified by law enjoy a status that places them above common statutory laws. Indeed, the infringement of these international treaties may lead to the annulment of administrative acts, the reversal of judicial decisions and result in civil liability on the part of the Greek State as per Article 105 of the Introductory Law to the Civil Code.[74]

The competent authorities and the process whereby the Greek State determines whether to grant or deny a petition to qualify as a refugee are described in detail in the above-mentioned ministerial decisions. According to these decisions, an alien who has

66. Goodwin-Gill, loc. cit. n. 62, at p. 18.

67. These are decisions Nos. 5401/1-166958 (Government Gazette B 500/28/5/77) and 5401/1-374659 (Government Gazette B 1113/8-11-1977) which replaces the first paragraph of Art. 4 of the former Intra-Ministerial decision. See on these decisions Paroula Naskou-Perrakis, *The Legal Status of Refugees in the International and the Greek Legal Order* (Athens-Komotine, 1991) p. 184 et seq.

68. LD 3989/1959.

69. Compulsory Law 389/1968.

70. StE 830/1985.

71. Not signed by Greece.

72. Not signed by Greece.

73. Not signed by Greece.

74. See Dagtoglou, op. cit. n. 8, at p. 536 et seq.

arrived in the country in any way may demand from the Greek authorities recognition as a refugee. In such a case, the competent authorities are under an obligation to notify the UN High Commissioner for Refugees, who has the right to visit the alien in question; the latter is also informed of the existence of this international authority. Subsequently, the competent and duly authorized security personnel investigate and determine whether the conditions for the alien in question to qualify as a refugee are indeed met; their decision must be reasoned and brought to the knowledge of both the alien involved and the representative of the High Commissioner for Refugees. If the determination is negative, the alien may appeal to the Minister of Public Order within a thirty day period. The Minister makes his decision after having solicited the opinion of a Committee composed of three members. If pursuant to a negative initial determination of the competent Greek authorities the alien submits to the Minister new evidence, the latter may remand the case for examination by these authorities.

Ministerial decision No. 5401/1-166958 provides a number of guarantees, to the alien, including:

— The advisory committee of the Ministry of Public Order must be composed of one high-ranking diplomatic servant of the Ministry of Foreign Affairs, one high-ranking officer of the Security Corps and one judge of the Council of the State.

— In the procedure before the advisory Committee may be present the alien, who also has the right to submit memoranda, and the representative of the High Commissioner, who may express his opinions orally or in writing. Finally, the alien may appeal to the Council of the State against an adverse decision of the Minister of Public Order.

6.2   The proposed provisions of the pending Bill

One should note, however, that the above-mentioned Ministerial decision regulating the process of determination of refugee status was not issued pursuant to any statutory authorization and thus lacks a secure legal foundation. It was the outcome of the need to apply in Greece the Geneva Convention, which, incidentally, says nothing with regard to the establishment of procedures for the determination of refugee status or for otherwise ascertaining and identifying those who are to benefit from the substantive provisions included therein. The pending Bill on the status of aliens represents the first comprehensive attempt by Greece to place the issue of refugee status on a statutory basis. Article 24 of the Bill gives the necessary authorization for the issue of decrees to regulate the process of examination of an alien's petition to qualify as a refugee, and regulates the way in which cooperation with and notification to the UN High Commission for Refugees will take place. The novel aspects of the pending Bill refer to the limitations imposed on an alien's right to petition for the recognition of refugee status. More precisely, according to Article 25(1) of the Bill, such a petition is not acceptable if:

1. the petition is not filed immediately upon arrival at the border or, in case of illegal entry, at the nearest public authority to which the alien presents himself;

2. the alien does not arrive directly from the country which threatens his life or liberty in the sense of Article 1 of the Geneva Convention.[75]

The international law notion of persecution is somewhat wider and includes measures such as the imposition of serious economic disadvantage, denial of access to employment, to the professions, or to education, or other restrictions on the freedoms traditionally guaranteed in a democratic society, such as speech, assembly, worship, or freedom of movement.[76] The new Greek Bill, in para. 3 of Article 25, explicitly rules out petitions which aim at the facilitation of immigration or at frustrating a duly ordered deportation of the alien from the country.

Finally, the new Bill contains provisions regulating the so-called 'small asylum'. Thus, according to Article 25(6), the Minister of Public Order may in extraordinary cases and especially for humanitarian reasons, allow an alien whose petition for refugee status has been denied, to stay in the country until his departure becomes possible. This provision is important for a number of aliens who are victims of civil strife and are endangered in their life or liberty but not by the State from which they fled (which in fact has done everything to stop their persecution), as well as for victims of uprisings and human rights violations occurring without political motive, and, finally, for aliens who live under totalitarian regimes and suffer from famine and poverty.[77] Paragraph 7, however, makes it clear that the so-called 'small asylum' is a temporary situation which does not give rise to any rights whatsoever. This could mean that judicial protection is not available in this case,[78] although Article 20 of the Greek Constitution quite clearly applies to all persons. Finally, the provisions of paragraph 7 of Article 25 of the new Bill seem to imply the possibility of granting temporary asylum, until the country of destination decides whether or not it will grant permanent asylum (residence in view of the examination for the recognition of an alien's refugee status).

Certainly, according to the Geneva Convention, the recognition of refugee status does not constitute a prerequisite to the granting of asylum; asylum may be granted

75. Because this country is normally the country of origin, the Bill chooses a solution which is in contrast with the jurisprudence of the Council of the State today; see StE 830/85 *supra*. However, because in essence it simply repeats the provision of Article 31 of the Geneva Convention, it might be useful to refer to the interpretation of this provision. The critical fragment is the one referring to [refugees] 'coming directly from a territory where their life or freedom was threatened,' which has been given a temporal and not a geographic interpretation, i.e., in the sense that the refugee arrives without delay even if he is obliged to travel through a third country. See Naskou-Perrakis, op. cit. n. 67, at p. 140 et seq.

76. Goodwin-Gill, loc. cit. n. 62, at p. 39.

77. See G. Renner, 'Grenzfragen des Asylrechts und des allgemeinen Ausländerrechts' NVwZ (1983) p. 649, at p. 657. See also J.Frowein, 'Asylrecht aus rechtsvergleichender Sicht', Aus Politik und Zeitgeschichte Beilage zur *Wochenzeitung Das Parlament* (1987) B26. The temporary refuge of asylum seekers has acquired the character of a general principle of international law. Nevertheless, this principle leads often the states to undermine the principle of non refoulement and to avoid granting durable asylum S.Goodwin-Gill, Note 62, p.291 et seq. (306, 320).

78. Renner, loc. cit. n. 77, at p. 657.

even if the 'politically persecuted' persons do not fully qualify as 'political refugees'.[79] Between the time a refugee flees and the time a permanent solution is found for him and after the recognition of refugee status, a number of stages and problems arise which are closely connected to the above issues and refer to the notions of asylum and non-refoulement.[80]

7. THE RIGHT TO ASYLUM

7.1 Activities in furtherance of the cause of freedom

The 1951 Refugee Convention does not regulate matters of asylum, although it makes reference to asylum in the Preamble and in the Final Act. The term asylum has no universally accepted definition. More particularly the right of asylum must be understood in the sense of a permanent right to settle. Theoretically, an individual, who qualifies as a refugee, but who is not given asylum, could be sent back, because recognition as a refugee does not entail entitlement to asylum.[81] Nearly all those who have been recognised as refugees have also been given asylum status. But the State has the right to grant asylum at will. That the granting of asylum status usually bestows upon the person the same benefits with regard to juridical status, gainful employment and welfare, as Articles 12 through 24 of the 1951 Convention does not mean that the mere recognition of refugee status in itself renders that person's presence lawful.[82] The provisions of Articles 31, 32 and 33 of the 1951 Convention do not give to refugees a right to enter another country and do not provide[83] a durable solution and full protection for them. Because of the incorporation of the 1951 Convention in the Greek legal order, we cannot speak of a right to asylum even for the refugees under the definition of Article 1(a) of the Convention, and certainly not for all persons fearing persecution. Asylum is a positive concept which entails protection, residence and admission. The Greek Constitution in Article 5(2)(c), does not refer directly to asylum, but talks of the non-extradition of aliens persecuted because of their activities in

---

79. Cf., BVerfGE 9, p. 174 at p. 181. The Convention had in any case a side-effect in State practice regarding the criteria for granting asylum. E.W. Vierdag, '"Asylum" and "Refugee" in international law', 24 NILR (1977), p. 297.

80. See Goodwin-Gill, loc. cit. n. 62, at p. 103.

81. E.W. Vierdag, 'The country of "first asylum" some European aspects', in D. Martin, *The New Asylum Seekers: Refugee Law in the 1980s — The ninth Sokol Colloquium on International Law*, p. 75.

82. S. Thomas Alexander Aleinikoff and David A. Martin, *Immigration Process and Police* (1985) pp. 647-649.

83. S.P. Hyndmann, 'Refugees under International Law with a reference to the conception of asylum', 60 *The Australian Law Journal* (1986) pp. 152-153, Goodwin-Gill, ASIL Proceedings 80 (1986) p. 97 et seq., G. Gornig, *Das Refoulement-Verbot im Völkerrecht* (Wien 1987) p. 94 et seq. One may also find contrary opinions in the literature: Grahl-Madsen, op. cit. n. 56, at p. 42 et seq.

furthering the cause of freedom. Non-extradition does not, of course, coincide with asylum.[84] Asylum may be the consequence of non-extradition. In substance though, extradition is connected to legal assistance in penal matters.[85]

The above-mentioned constitutional provision poses a number of problems of interpretation. To begin with, legal scholarship strongly contested the view that Article 5(3)(c) only provides for protection in cases of extradition. The argument is that the constitutional lawgiver did not use the term 'political crime' but the notion of 'activities in furtherance of the cause of freedom'.[86] The notion of 'activities in furtherance of the cause of freedom' may alternatively have a broader or a narrower scope than the notion of political crime.[87] The criteria applied by the judge in order to determine the boundaries of the notion of 'activities in furtherance of the cause of freedom' must be located in the meeting point between constitutional freedoms and human rights — as these are guaranteed in international documents.[88] However, one should not at this point forget that in discharging his duties, the judge may be influenced by the status of the international relationships of his country at that particular historical moment.[89] Despite the weighty arguments outlined above, the language of Article 5(2)(c) of the Constitution, speaking of non-extradition of the alien, does not leave much room to draw from it a right of asylum.[90] Apart from the fact that extradition is only one of the different aspects comprising the right of asylum, the guarantee under domestic law of non-extradition of political refugees is particularly important, given that the text of the Convention Relating to the Status of Refugees does not prohibit extradition of political refugees, but only introduces, in Article 33(1), the principle of non-refoulement. Further, there is no customary law to the effect that States are duty-bound to refuse

84. The connection between asylum and non-extradition was made by older legal scholarship. S.F. Krenz, 'The refugee as a subject of international law', 15 JCLQ (1966) p. 101 et seq., who thought that states are normally only in the position to grant asylum if the offence in question is not listed in the relevant text as an extraditable offence, if the principle of 'double criminality' is not satisfied, or if the treaty excludes political offenders from extradition. The same author qualifies his thesis by accepting the gradual widening of the scope of asylum through its exemption of the 'illegality' of any act with which the asylum seeker may have been connected in his country of origin (102).

85. Cf., P. Weis, 'The Present State of International Law on Territorial Asylum', *Schweizerisches Jahrbuch für internationales Recht* (1975) p. 71 at p. 79.

86. See An. Loverdos, 'Constitutional Guarantee of Political Asylum. A Contribution to the Interpretation of article 5 (2) (c) of the Constitution of 1976/1986' 36 NoB p. 38 at pp. 46 and 54.

87. At the international law level, we observe a tendency to move from political to humanitarian asylum, which might occasionally mean offering asylum to common criminals and not to political criminals. See Chr. Van den Wijngaert, *The political offence exception to extradition* (1980) p. 70 et seq.

88. See Loverdos, loc. cit. n. 86. at p. 47. See also I. Katras, 'A Contribution to the Interpretation of Article 5(2)(c) of the Constitution' *Ephemeris Ellinon Nomikon* (1981) p. 239 at p. 243 [*Journal of Greek Lawyers*; Greek legal journal; hereafter EEN].

89. See Loverdos, loc. cit. n. 86, p. 47.

90. See Dagtoglou, op. cit. n. 8, at p. 536; I. Voulgaris, *The Constitutional Protection of the Alien in Five Years of Application of the Constitution of 1975* (Komotine, 1981) pp. 132, 133 [in Greek]; A. Bredimas, 'The Principle of non-Refoulement; Theoretical Aspects and Greek Practice' 38 NoB (1990) p. 561 at p. 572 [in Greek].

the extradition of political victims of political persecution.[91] Thus, political refugees may be effectively protected if and only if it is expressly provided that:

a. extradition can be justified; and

b. the execution of any decision to extradite must remain pending until the issue of refugee status is decided.[92]

The first of the above conditions is satisfied in Greek law by virtue of Article 5(2)(c) of the Constitution and also by Article 3(2) of the 1957 Paris European Convention on Extradition, which has been ratified in Greece by virtue of Law 4165/61. This last Convention provides that if the requested party has substantial grounds for believing that a request for extradition for an ordinary criminal offence has been made for the purpose of prosecuting or punishing a person on account of his race, religion, nationality or political opinion, or that the person's position may be prejudiced for any of these reasons, then it should not extradite the alien. The above provisions intend to regulate the conceivable case of a refugee who has committed a political crime in his country, but his country of origin, in order to make his extradition possible, redefines by virtue of a legislative change his act as a common crime. In such a case, the language providing for 'activity in the cause of freedom' employed by the Greek Constitution may prove extremely helpful to the alien concerned. The second condition, i.e., the one providing for the non-extradition while the petition for the grant of refugee status is still pending, is now guaranteed by virtue of Article 25(7) of the new Bill on the status of aliens, which provides for temporary residence in view of the examination of a petition for refugee status by the alien.

Further, if one begins by noting that the political offence exception protects all political offenders and the principle of non-refoulement only protects political offenders who are recognized as political refugees, one can see that the constitutional provision acquires — so far as the law of extradition is concerned — an additional meaning, in the sense that the defence to extradition is extended from the perpetrators of political crimes and the political refugees to broader categories of people, following in this respect the provision of Article 3(2) of the European Convention on Extradition.[93]

Thus, so far as the constitutional provision is concerned, the protection of political refugees and political offenders become indistinguishable. This does not, however, mean that their legal status is identical.[94] What is common between these two categories — and is also a common feature of the granting of asylum status and non-extradition — is a well-founded fear of persecution.[95] In any case, the Greek Constitution presupposes the fact of 'offender'; by contrast, a constitutional provision that explicitly guarantees the right of asylum, is that of Article 16(2)(2) of the Fundamental Law of the Federal Republic of Germany? (*Grundgesetz*), which refers to the 'political-

---

91. Grahl-Madsen, op. cit. n. 56, at p.39.

92. See Van den Wijngaert, op. cit. n. 87, at pp. 79-80.

93. See Bredimas, loc. cit. n. 90, at p. 570.

94. See Van den Wijngaert, op. cit. n. 87, at pp. 27-28.

95. See O. Kimminich, 'Der Schutz politisch Verfolgter im Auslieferungsverfahren', EuGRZ (1986) p. 317 at p. 323.

ly persecuted' alien, irrespective of whether a punishable act is imputed to him.[96] In other words, the right of asylum in a positive sense is directed mainly at the protection of the perpetrator from political persecution, irrespective of the nature of the act committed, while the defence of non-extradition centres around the political content of the act and the nature of the legal right infringed.[97]

Moreover, the derivation of a right of asylum from the provision of Article 5(2)(c) of the Greek Constitution would mean for the refugee concerned a right to remain in the country and also a guarantee of the ability to exercise a profession and pursue his personal development and well-being.[98] Such a positive content may be difficult to attribute to the provision of the Greek Constitution as it is now phrased. First, we must distinguish between the refugees' admission to the territory of the receiving State, and the question of his status once admitted. The admission of an asylum seeker in Greek law is the result of the recognition of his refugee quality, which is — as we have seen above — a matter not of the Constitution, but of the two ministerial Decisions. If the Greek provision had sought to protect the person persecuted for his activity in furtherance of the cause of freedom to that extent, it would have preferred the phrasing of the Preamble of the French Constitution of 1946, which became part of the French Constitution of 1958 by virtue of the latter's Preamble, and which reads as follows: 'Every person who is persecuted because of his activity in furtherance of the cause of freedom, has a right of asylum in the territory of the Republic.'[99]

7.2   The political offence

Reference to the institution of extradition according to Greek law should help clarify the workings of the above-mentioned Constitutional provision. We shall refer particularly to judicial precedents which approach the issue of the common border existing between the concept of political crime and activity in furtherance of the cause of freedom. Apart from the Constitution, we should also mention the provisions of Article 438 (c) of the Code of Criminal Procedure, which state that extradition is precluded if the crime perpetrated is characterised under Greek law as political, military, tax-related or a crime of the press. Additionally, Article 3 of the European Convention on Extradition states that extradition shall not be granted if the offence in respect of which it is

96. See BVerfGE 60, p. 348 at p. 359. But see in Greek legal scholarship Ev. Apostolopoulos, 'Limitations in the Law of Extradition for Political Reasons' NoB (1982) p. 1543 et seq. at p. 1547, who argues that the Constitution raises to the status of a legally protected right such action - passive or aggressive irrespective - and irrespective of possible criminal consequences.

97. See Kimminich, loc. cit. n. 95, at p. 321.

98. See A. Randelzhofer, 'Asylrecht' in J. Isensee and P. Kirchhof, *Handbuch des Staatsrechts* (Heidelberg, 1989) p. 185 at p. 205.

99. This right was severely curtailed by the jurisprudence of the Conseil d'Etat (France Terre d'Asile, 27 September 1985, Recueil Lebon, p. 263), according to which the right to asylum status may be a constitutional principle; it does not however find an area of application in the French legal order, because it has not been concretized by a law and by international treaty. In other words, in France too the right to asylum boils down to the application of the Geneva Convention. See e.g., Frederic Tiberghien, *La protection des refugees en France*, 2nd. edn., (Paris, 1988) p. 60 et. seq.

requested is regarded by the requested party as a political offence or as an offence connected to a political offence. Similar provisions are also included in bilateral treaties for the extradition of criminals which Greece has occasionally signed with other countries.

Greek legal scholarship has developed three different theories relating to the issue of what may constitute a political crime:[100] according to the so-called 'objective' theory,[101] political crimes are those crimes which constitute an affront to the existence or the organisation of the State as well as those which constitute an affront to civil rights; according to the so-called 'subjective' theory,[102] political crimes also include those crimes which may not constitute an affront to the State, but result nevertheless from socially motivated aspirations of a particular social class; finally, according to the so-called 'intermediate' theory,[103] in order to characterize a crime as political, one should consider both the nature of the object or right attacked and the motives of the perpetrator.

Finally, according to the true meaning of Article 438(c) of the Code of Criminal Procedure, a demand for extradition should be considered as politically motivated when the Government of the State demanding the extradition is thereby seeking to avenge itself or to silence its political rivals who have sought refuge abroad because of their opposition to that Government.[104]

We may now turn to examine two precedents in which Greek courts refused to characterize particular crimes as political crimes, whilst also avoiding an examination of whether these acts could fall under the category of 'activities undertaken to promote the cause of freedom' in the sense of Article 5(2)(c) of the Constitution.

In its decision 1741/1984 the *Areios Pagos* [Supreme Court of Greece][105] was faced with the following facts: Palestinians had thrown grenades and fired shots into a Synagogue in Italy; as a consequence one person had died and many more had been injured. The *Areios Pagos* decided that these acts could not be characterised as political crimes, but were instead to be considered as common crimes, because they were not aimed against the political organisation of the Italian Republic and were not directed at the overthrow or modification of the status quo and the existing Italian constitution,

---

100. See generally for the definition of political crime by Greek courts A. Loverdos, *On Terrorism and Political Crime* (Athens, 1987), pp. 189-197 [in Greek]; see also Catherine Manolopoulos-Varvitsiotis, 'Terrorism and the International Measures for its Prevention' 35 *Poinika Chronika [Criminal Chronicles;* Greek legal journal]* p. 513 at p. 518 et seq. [in Greek].

101. See for example AP 1260/1987 (Decision in Council), 35 NoB p.1452 et seq.

102. AP 288/22 *Themis [Justice;* Greek legal journal]* (1922- 23) p. 377.

103. See the decisions of the Court of Appeals of Athens 12-13/1976 in 26 *Poinika Chronika* p. 659 et seq. and the decision of the *Areios Pagos* 890/1976 in 27 *Poinika Chronika* p. 317 et seq. (in council) which dealt with the extradition of the German citizen R. Pohle.

104. See AP 2047/1985 (in council) in 26 *Poinika Chronika* p. 371 et seq.; AP 1338/1983 (in council) in 34 *Poinika Chronika* p. 276 et seq. See also the comments about this decision in: M.S. Perrakis, *Les tendances recentes de l'evolution des legislations et des pratiques nationales dans le domaine de l'asile et des refugees.* Actes du seizième Colloque de droit européen, Lund, 15-17 septembre 1986 (Strasbourg, 1987) p. 61 et seq. (65-66).

105. 35 *Poinika Chronika* p. 552 et seq.

nor otherwise connected to such crimes. In the case in question, the defendant argued that his action could fall under Article 5(2)(c) of the Greek Constitution, since it had been committed with the purpose of fostering the cause of self-determination of the Palestinian people. The *Areios Pagos* circumvented this argument by holding that even if one conceded that the action in question took place for the purpose alleged, it could not lead to non-extradition, since it ran counter to the fundamental provisions of Article 2(1) of the Greek Constitution guaranteeing the protection of human dignity, and also because of the overall circumstances of the action, the victims it created and the place at which it took place.

In the other case, the above-mentioned constitutional provision was not even mentioned.[106] This case concerned the extradition of the German citizen R. Pohle, a member of the well-known Baader-Mainhof group. The criminal acts for which extradition was demanded were the following: participation in a criminal gang aiming at the perpetration of forgery, fraud, theft, blackmailing, armed resistance to the police and other crimes relating to the possession and use of explosives. The *Areios Pagos* held[107] that the determinations contained in the dicta of the relevant judgment of the German court (which referred to the constitution of armed units undertaking broad anarchic activities in the fashion of Palestinian and South-American organizations structured according to the instructions of a Brazilian leader of armed rebels and contained in a manual published by him with guidelines for the perpetration of acts of terrorism against the existing order with a view to the preparation of an armed insurrection of the masses in the entire world aimed at changing the existing social system of the western countries), could not suffice to give the above crimes the character of political crimes or politically-related crimes, because these constituted mere incentives and were distant objectives of the person whose extradition was demanded, lacking all legal significance. It is worth noting that the Greek Court of Appeals[108] had previously held, on the basis of the reasoning contained in the German judgment, that the crimes of the person whose extradition was demanded were immediately and directly connected to the political aims of the organization to which he belonged. Certainly, in the case under consideration the additional factor of terrorism also enters; but this does not initially preclude arguments centred around the notion of 'activities furthering the cause of freedom'.[109]

8.   APPENDIX

The new statute 'on the entrance, departure, residence, work and deportation of aliens, the process for recognizing refugee status and other provisions' has been given the number 1975/1991; it was published in the Government Gazette on 4 December 1991

---

106. See Loverdos, op. cit. n. 100, at p. 48.
107. See AP 890/1976 (in council) in 27 *Poinika Chronika* p. 371 et seq.
108. Court of Appeals of Athens 12-13/1976 (in Council), 25 NoB p. 107 et seq.
109. See Art. 5 of the European Convention for the Prevention of Terrorism which has been ratified by Greece.

(Issue A', No. 184). According to its ultimate provision, the statute enters in force six months after its publication in the Government Gazette. The new statute abolishes the old Law 4310/1929 which formed the basis of the above discussion. However, because the new statute provides for a number of delegations for the issue of presidential decrees and ministerial decisions, Article 36 provides that until the pertinent presidential decrees and ministerial decisions are issued, the provisions of the older law continue to apply where appropriate, provided of course that they do not run contrary to the new legislation.

For this reason, reference to the old law is still important and it seems appropriate to deal with the new piece of legislation in an appendix.

On the occasion of the discussion of the new law in parliament, a number of hard to find statistical data were cited.

The speaker for the Party in Office, D. Stamatis,[110] said that at the present time approximately 250,000 aliens live in Greece, of which only 70,000 are known and have been reported to the authorities. Of these, 25,000 have a work permit and 5,000 are political refugees. The need to avoid a wave of economic immigrants was repeatedly underlined. Greece attracts illegal emigrants mostly from South Asia and the Far East. These arrive in the country as part of the slave-trade. Greece also attracts illegal emigrants from the countries of central and eastern Europe, Russia and the Russian Pontus — some of whom have Greek roots — and finally Albanian fugitives, who may or may not be of Greek descent. They all fall under the category of economic immigrants.[111] In order to stop this wave of economic immigrants, the country has tried better policing of its borders, which unfortunately are extremely long, consisting of 33,000 kilometres of water-borders and 1,170 kilometres of land-borders; the Government has also tried to neutralize the incentives that normally propel illegal immigration.[112] In the new Law 1975/1991, and more specifically in Article 1, the effort initially undertaken to provide a definition of the term 'homogenes' [i.e., person of Greek descent] was abandoned. The Minister of Public Order explained that the determination of the notion of 'homogenes' was best left to the Courts to fashion; this choice, he reasoned, was justified in view of the great indeterminacy of this notion and of the great importance this notion might play in particular cases.[113]

The new law deals with people of Greek descent (homogenes) in Article 17; this article pertains to the residence permit of people of Greek descent, but of course it cannot avoid involving issues of definition of the notion or the quality of homogenes. This time, according to Article 17(2), if doubt or controversy arises as to whether someone falls under the category of 'persons of Greek descent', it is the Minister of Foreign Affairs who is called upon to decide pursuant to an opinion of the Minister of

110. S.D. Stamatis, Debates of Parliament, Sitting of 10 October 1992, at p. 36.
111. S. K. Rigas, Debates of Parliament, Sitting of 15 October 1991, at p. 191. See also a recent article in the daily newspaper *Kathimerinh*, which mentions 6000 refugees coming from Iraq, Iran, Ethiopian, Somalia and Sri Lanka and who, according to this article, are the first victims of racist feelings in Greece.
112. S. Pahtas, Debates of Parliament, Sitting Z of 16 October 1991, at p. 255.
113. See the Debates of Parliament, Sitting Z of 16 October 1991 and more specifically the speech of Anagnostopoulos, at p. 266.

Public Order; the entire process may be initiated either *ex officio* or pursuant to a petition by the interested party. This provision has been criticized, because it entails giving to the Minister of Foreign Affairs power to bestow upon an alien Greek nationality without the stipulation of specific criteria.[114] The provision included in the original draft at least mentioned the criteria of Greek descent, of acceptance of this capacity by the alien himself and the criterion of 'behaving like a Greek'. Beyond this, the Members of Parliament appealed to decision No. 2756/1983 of the Greek *Conseil d'Etat*,[115] which contains some guidelines on the construction of the notion of 'person of Greek descent'.

As far as the entry of aliens, the termination of the residence of aliens (which may occur either because the alien's residence permit has expired, or by deportation or extradition of the alien) and the alien's freedom of movement in the country are concerned, the new statute contained a number of controversial provisions, which attracted fierce criticism during the debates in Parliament; some of these hotly contested provisions were finally struck out.

Thus, the obscure phrase 'reasons of social interest'[116] was omitted from among the various grounds for deportation; also omitted was a provision which prohibited the publication of the list of unwanted aliens.[117]

But besides this 'list', the new statute on aliens leaves too much room to the Administration further to preclude the entry of aliens into the country, even where they possess the necessary travel documents.

Typical in this respect are the provisions of para. 7 and Article 6, which give to the competent Greek authorities the power to refuse entry to aliens, even when the latter have a visa. In answering the criticism that this provision indirectly introduces additional lists of unwanted aliens — i.e., over and above the list envisaged in Article 11[118] — the Minister of Public Order responded that this provision is concerned with people who may harm Greece, such as spies and drug dealers.[119]

The provisions of Article 14 regarding the reunion of families, was finally voted through in its originally proposed form with only one amendment: the age of 21 years for unmarried children to be considered as members of the family entitled to apply for residence in Greece was lowered to 18 years.

114. S. G. Papandreou, Debates of Parliament, Sitting Z of 16 October 1991, at p. 265. See also Kotsonis, Sitting H of 17 October 1991, at p. 291.

115. S. Sevastakis, Debates of Parliament Sitting H of 17 October 1991, at p. 300. See also Papadopoulos, at p. 301.

116. See the Debates of Parliament, Sitting IA of 22 October 1991 and more specifically the speeches of Kotsonis and Anagnostopoulos, at p. 424.

117. See the speech of the Minister of Public Order Th. Anagnostopoulos, Debates of Parliament, Sitting Z of 16 October 1991 and the opposite opinion of Stamatis, Debates of Parliament, Sitting H of 17 October 1991, at p. 292.

118. See the speech of Sevastakis, Debates of Parliament, Sitting H of 17 October 1991, at p. 300.

119. See the speech of Anagnostopoulos, Debates of Parliament, Sitting H of 17 October 1991, at p. 302.

This provision was criticized on the following grounds:
— When an alien's residence permit expires, deportation is not stayed even if the alien in the meantime has entered into a marriage with a Greek citizen; this effectively results in the citizen's spouse being 'deported' as well[120]
— It should explicitly provide that family members may also be granted a work permit.[121]
Criticism centred around the issue of the time of the reunification of the family.

An alien has the right to petition for the arrival and residence with him of the members of his family, if he has been granted a two-year residence permit after having previously resided in the country for a period of five years. During the debates in parliament, this period of time was criticised as too long.[122] Generally speaking, given the determinations of Article 21 of the Hellenic Constitution which specifically provides for the protection of the family, one might judge this provision unconstitutional,[123] as hostile to marriage and the family, both because of the great length of the time that has to elapse before reunification of the family is possible and because of the lowering of the age for unmarried children.

On the other hand, it should be remembered that the Greek law does not introduce any additional conditions that might preclude entry into the country of family members as defined therein, and further, that it expressly protects some members of the alien's family from deportation.[124] One should mention in this respect Article 28 of the law, according to which it is expressly forbidden to deport an alien minor whose parental family resides in Greece, an alien mother of a minor who is a Greek citizen and who resides with her, or the parent of a minor who is a Greek citizen if the parent has custody of the minor. The provision regarding refugees was the subject of a special discussion.

The new law dedicates a chapter to refugees: this is chapter F, Articles 24 et seq. However, it was noticed that provisions regarding refugees may be found scattered throughout the entire statute; they refer mainly to issues of entry and residence of refugees.[125]

One should mention in particular Article 4(4) of the Draft, which was finally voted through unchanged; this provision, which deals with the issue of the repulsion of an alien illegally entering Greece from his country of origin or descent, has been subjected to severe and extensive criticism in the foregoing discussion.

---

120. See the Debates of Parliament, Sitting C of 10 October 1991 and more specifically the speech of Lendakis, at p. 45.

121. See Kotsonis, Debates of Parliament, Sitting H of 17 October 1991, at pp. 290, 304.

122. See Debates of Parliament, Sitting H of 17 October 1991 and more specifically the speech of Sevastakis, at p. 292 and Korakas at p. 294.

123. Compare the similar issues raised under the German law in Fritz Franz, 'Der Nachzug ausländischer Familienangehöriger im Lichte der Verfassung', NJW (1984) p. 530 et seq., at p. 533.

124. There is a parallel set of problems faced by the American and the French legal orders but answered in a different direction. See John Gündelsberger, 'The Right to Family Unification in French and United States Immigration Law', Cornell ILJ 21 (1988) p. 1, at p. 90 et seq.

125. See the Debates of Parliament, Sitting H of 17 October 1991 and more specifically the speeches of Sevastakis at p. 291, Korakas, at p. 293, Sideris at p. 294 and Anagnostopoulos, at p. 297.

During the debates on the Bill, this provision was connected with the overall question regarding refugees. It was urged that an additional clarificatory paragraph be added concerning refugees, so that petition for the granting of refugee status[126] by the latter is facilitated by the authorities. The response of the Minister of Justice, that this provision only visualizes cases of massive arrivals, does not seem, at first sight, to be satisfactory.[127]

Immediate repulsion without a prior examination of the particular case in hand does not significantly differ from exclusion of the alien at the border. This latter case is visualized in Article 11 of the law, which provides that the Ministry of Public Order keep a list of unwanted aliens. Thus, the law creates a category of aliens who will be denied the opportunity even to file a petition for asylum. This provision is all the more problematic because the criteria whereby an alien may be included in this list are not mentioned in the law, but must be determined by a joint decision of the Ministers of the Interior, of Justice and of Public Order. This is one of many unconstitutional delegations of legislative authority; the new law contains a total of 48 delegations of legislative authority for the issue of ministerial decisions and 7 for the issue of presidential decrees, all of which were fiercely criticized during the debates as leading to the virtual abolition of Parliament.[128]

Article 8 of the new law contains another provision which relates to the alien's repulsion and his ability to petition for refugee status. According to this provision, an alien's stay in the transit zone of a port or an airport of the country in view of the continuation of his trip aboard the same or another plane, does not constitute an entry to the Greek territory. Thus, the provision of Article 25(1)(a) of the law, which visualizes a process for the recognition of refugee status to aliens who arrive at an outpost at the border, does not apply to an alien who files a petition while in the transit area.[129]

For this reason, during the debates on the Bill, a proposal was submitted to consider transit areas in ports and airports as Greek territory, so that immediate repulsion be precluded.[130]

On the other hand, the provisions of the new law concerning refugees do follow the practice established at the international level. Thus, the determinations of the Geneva Convention on refugees are followed inasmuch as the issues concerning the process of the examination of an alien's petition for the recognition of refugee status and the revocation of the same are concerned.

126. See the Debates of Parliament, Sitting Z of 16/10/91 and more specifically the speech of Kotsonis Sevastakis, at p. 262 and Korakas at p. 263 and Vounatsos, at p. 264.
127. See the Debates of Parliament, Sitting Z of 16 October 1991 and more specifically the speech of Anagnostopoulos at p. 267.
128. See the Debates of Parliament, Sitting C of 10 October 1991 and more specifically the speech of Kotsonis at p. 37, Korakas at p. 42 and Lendakis at p. 44. See also Sitting Z of 16 October 1991 and more specifically the speech of Androulakis at p. 241. See also the paper of the Scientific Service of the Parliament of 9 October 1991, written by Achilleas Skordas.
129. See Skordas, loc. cit. n. 128.
130. See the Debates of Parliament, Sitting Z of 16 October 1991 and more specifically the speech of Pahtas at p. 266.

Besides the innovations regarding the so-called small and temporary asylum already mentioned above, one more innovation should be mentioned here: it pertains to Article 25(2) which provides for refugees *sur place*. The provisions of the Greek law, however, only accepts the reasons which arise at a time prior to the alien's entry and subsequently lead the alien to file a petition for the recognition of refugee status. Despite the fact that the Convention of 1951, in Article 1 A[2], does not seem to preclude subjective reasons, such as the refugee's political activity in the host country, the provisions of the Greek law recognise as the only valid reason for the submission of the petition a fear of persecution which is grounded on facts which must have in all cases taken place in the country of origin of the refugee.[131]

---

131. See Stefan Richter, 'Selbstgeschaffene Nachfluchtgründe und die Rechtsstellung von Konventions-flüchtlingen nach der Rechtsprechung des Bundesverfassungsgerichts zum Grundrecht auf Asyl und dem Gesetz zur Neuregelung des Ausländerrechts', ZaöRV (1991) p. 1 et seq (18-19).

154

THE LAST FRONTIER: FREE MOVEMENT OF PERSONS IN GREATER EUROPE
The role of the Council of Europe

Frits W. Hondius[*]

1.   INTRODUCTION

The freedom to move, and to stop and establish residence, have been enduring human characteristics since prehistoric times. For practically all people who inhabit the Earth, including those of Europe, it can be proved that their ancestors came from somewhere else. From these broad historical, biological and anthropological perspectives, therefore, any pronouncements about freedom of movement and settlement are statements of the obvious.

Yet there is a need for such statements because organised human societies have placed two types of restrictions upon movement and settlement of humans. The first is the frontier, the Great Wall, the *limes*, the pale, and other devices erected with the aim of keeping some people out of a territory and of protecting those within the enclosure. But the wall can also be used for the opposite purpose; i.e., for keeping people inside an area and preventing them from leaving it, as was the case with the former Berlin Wall. A second type of restriction is one that forcibly binds a person to a place or a territory and prevents him from leaving it of his own free will. This type of restriction may take many forms: slavery, serfdom, forced or compulsory labour (*corvée*), debenture, military duty are a few examples. There are even peoples in certain parts of Europe whose ancestors were specifically implanted there to guard frontiers, such as the Serbian *granicari* in South Croatia, who were defenders against the Ottoman Empire. These historical situations can become a source of armed conflict centuries later.

The freedom of movement is inherent in human nature and needs no confirmation other than by way of a human right, which is *jus cogens* in international law. This right is proclaimed by Article 13 of the Universal Declaration of Human Rights of 1948, Article 12 of the International Covenant on Civil and Political Rights of 1966 and the 4th Protocol to the European Convention on Human Rights adopted in 1963. These documents also forbid slavery, servitude, and forced labour.

   [*] Deputy Director of Legal Affairs, Council of Europe, Strasbourg. Visiting Fellow to St. Cross College, Oxford. Opinions expressed in this paper are strictly personal.

H.G. Schermers et al., eds., Free Movement of Persons in Europe
© 1993, T.M.C. Asser Instituut, The Hague

It is the limitations on the freedom of movement that require justification under the law. Detention and extradition are examples of two such limitations. The former is covered by Article 5 of the European Convention on Human Rights , and the latter by the European Convention on Extradition (ETS No. 24) signed in Paris on 13 December 1957, which fully respects the safeguards required by the European Convention on Human Rights.

Human rights instruments do not dwell on the notion of frontiers. The Universal Declaration of Human rights addresses the 'freedom of movement and residence within the borders of each State', and the Fourth Protocol to the European Convention on Human Rights refers to such a freedom belonging to persons 'lawfully within the territory of a State' (Art. 2(1)). The most specific reference to frontiers appears in Article 10(1) of the European Convention of Human Rights concerning the freedom of information 'regardless of frontiers'.

Similarly, the CSCE Charter of Paris for a New Europe of 21 November 1990, which can be viewed as the proto-constitution of greater Europe, reaffirms that 'free movement and contacts among our citizens . . . are crucial for the maintenance and development of free societies and flourishing cultures'. Moreover, it declares that 'every individual has the right to . . . freedom of movement' and that the protection and promotion of such human rights is the first responsibility of government for 'human rights are the birthright of all human beings'. However, rather than referring to frontiers directly, the Charter of Paris for a New Europe addresses the broader notion of territorial integrity of the participating States.

National and international rules in Europe relating to the movement and settlement of persons must establish a balance between three elements: personality, nationality (citizenship) and territoriality. In many central and eastern European countries, there is a further, intermediate category between personality and nationality; i.e., ethnic national allegiance.

2.   THE ROLE OF THE COUNCIL OF EUROPE

The Council of Europe, founded in May 1949, is the oldest of European organisations, and has the widest mandate. The view may be held that anything that is good for the greater unity of its Member States is good for the Council of Europe. It also has the widest membership: 25 Member States in western, central and eastern Europe, plus eight eastern European non-Member States that enjoy 'special guest' status. Depending upon the territorial and political developments in the former Soviet Union and Yugoslavia, the total number of Member States of the Council of Europe at the end of 1992 will probably be 30 or more. The Council of Europe is therefore well-suited to search for equitable solutions to problems of movement of persons.

The Council functions at two levels; the parliamentary level, within the Parliamentary Assembly, and the intergovernmental level in the Committee of Ministers, which is composed of the various ministers of foreign affairs of the Member States. It is to be noted that the Council of Europe not only has regular conferences of European ministers responsible for migration affairs, but that it also sponsors special ministerial conferences such as that held in Vienna in January 1991, on the movement of persons coming from central and eastern European States. Another special ministerial conference on the movement of gypsies has been proposed by the Netherlands Secretary of State for Justice.

The question of regulations relating to the movement of persons has three distinct aspects: political, legal and technical. Efficient intergovernmental cooperation can be expected only if full attention is given to each of these aspects. All too often, the absence of willingness to face the political dimension can be hidden behind technical arguments and vice versa. The Council of Europe has become fully aware of these problems in intergovernmental cooperation throughout its forty plus years of existence, and has established modes of cooperation that take account of all three aspects.

At the political level, a number of constantly changing parameters must be taken into account. The first parameter concerns political borders, which may be changed only by mutual consent among the countries concerned. The question of political borders has taken on increased importance in the new architecture of Europe. It should be noted that, while the European Community aims to abolish internal borders, there is an opposite phenomenon in eastern and central Europe. The creation of new State borders, such as the union of the two parts of Germany in 1990 and those of several entities previously forming part of the Soviet Union and reestablished by the break-up of the Soviet Union and Yugoslavia, has given rise to considerable conflict.

3.   NATIONALITY

In matters of nationality and citizenship, the official doctrine has been that every person in Europe should be able to be a citizen of a nation, and that statelessness, as well as multiple nationality, should be avoided. These principles are reflected in the Convention on reduction of cases for multiple nationality and military obligations in cases of multiple nationality (ETS No. 43), signed in Strasbourg on 6 May 1963, and its Additional Protocol of 24 November 1977 (ETS No. 96). This Convention was based on the concept that a person who freely seeks and acquires another nationality, should automatically lose his former nationality.

This thesis has been overtaken by the realities of Europe in the late 20th century. Mixed marriages and the presence of first, second and third generations of migrants have led to new situations in which the possession of more than one citizenship by one person or within a couple or family is now considered by many States to be not only tolerable but in certain cases even commendable. For this reason the Council of Europe's committee of experts on multiple nationality has proposed the adoption of an additional protocol to the Convention No. 43, which would allow spouses of different nationalities and the children of such couples to possess more than one nationality. The political and social realities of Europe need to be acknowledged in order to maintain the credibility of the legal regime established by the Convention. Several countries have indicated that they would have to denounce the Convention unless the legal structure is brought into line with political and social realities. On 9 September 1991, the European Committee on Legal Cooperation (CDCJ) committee on family law was instructed to proceed to the preparation of the protocol on multiple nationality. The committee is expected to examine numerous new developments, including the consequences of the recognition of equality between women and men.

4. NATIONAL MINORITIES

The enlargement of the Council of Europe to include countries in central and eastern Europe as Member States (e.g., Hungary and the Czech and Slovak Federal Republic) or future Member States (e.g., Poland, Bulgaria, the Baltic States and parts of Yugoslavia) has confronted the Council of Europe with new political, legal, social and cultural challenges. In the past, the Council of Europe had studiously avoided national minorities. When the Council of Europe began to include central and eastern European States, those States urgently asked it for assistance in order to find an adequate solution to the problem of national minorities. Now that the lid of communism, which sublimated that problem, has been lifted, Pandora's box has been opened. The central and eastern European States have emphasised that a solution to this problem is an essential condition for the establishment of democracy, justice, stability and peace. This request has been made through two different channels: the governments of central and eastern European countries and those countries' local and regional representatives to the Standing Conference of Local and Regional Authorities in Europe. Both the Council of Europe and the CSCE are committed to helping these eastern European States find adequate solutions.

The Council of Europe has drafted two legal texts regarding this matter. The first is a proposal for a European Convention for the protection of minorities, which was submitted by the European Commission for Democracy through Law. The second is a draft treaty entitled European Charter for Regional or Minority Languages. These two texts are pending before the intergovernmental organs of the Council of Europe. Both have important implications for the movement of persons since members of national minorities are often separated by national borders. With regard to the draft Convention for the protection of minorities, it is interesting to note that, according to Article 2(1), the term 'minorities' applies to identifiable groups within the population of a State, whose members have certain distinct ethnical, religious or linguistic features and are *nationals* of the State. This cross-reference to nationality raises another debate that will have to be settled outside the framework of this draft Convention.

5. SUPREMACY OF INTERNATIONAL LAW

The western European Member States of the Council of Europe have consistently recognised the supremacy of international law over domestic law, and have accepted certain rules of international law, such as the dignity and equal worth of human beings, as *jus cogens*. The new Member States have also accepted the validity of these principles. Clearly then, it is the duty of States, separately and collectively, to protect human rights and to prohibit derogations from certain human rights, even in times of national emergency.

6. TRAVEL AND IDENTITY DOCUMENTS

Throughout its forty plus years of existence, the Council of Europe has dealt extensively with the movement of persons to, from, and within its Member States. The original emphasis was on the relocation of displaced persons in the wake of World War II. A closely related phenomenon was the repatriation, particularly in the 1960s, of persons leaving former colonies and emigrating to the UK, France, the Netherlands, Belgium and Portugal. The cold war in Europe and upheavals in other parts of the world have resulted in intermittent but constantly growing streams of political and economic refugees. The new prosperity and unity of Europe has led to an exponential growth of the numbers of tourists and persons travelling for professional or educational purposes, as well as persons seeking employment and improved economic conditions. Finally, the number of persons travelling with criminal intent (terrorists, drug traffickers, etc.) has also kept pace with this overall growth.

The first practical achievement of the Council of Europe in the field of movement of persons relates to travel and identity documents. All States require travellers, whatever the nature of their voyaging, to comply with certain formalities such as presentation of a passport or an identity document, border crossings at authorised points, and sometimes visas. The European Agreement on regulations governing the movement of persons between Member States of the Council of Europe (ETS No. 25) was signed in Paris on 13 December 1957. At present, 13 States are parties to this Agreement, including all Member States of the European Community except Ireland and the United Kingdom. However, other States that are not yet parties to the Agreement also cooperate under its framework. This Agreement embodies an appendix that lists travel and identity documents required by the parties. This list is updated regularly through notifications to the Secretary-General by States that accede to the Agreement and States that alter the list of their travel and identity documents.

The principal rule of this Agreement treaty is contained in Article 5, which stipulates that States should allow entry to any person holding the listed travel and identity documents, even if the holder's nationality is under dispute. States have reserved the option, on grounds of *ordre public*, security or public health to suspend the Agreement with respect to States that are parties to the Agreement. When a State suspends the Agreement, the Secretary-General of the Council of Europe must be notified.

The most useful part of the Agreement is its appendix, which lists the various identity and travel documents of the parties. A detailed survey carried out in 1990 by a Rapporteur to the Council of Europe, Mr P. Uiterlinden (Netherlands), has revealed that, in spite of the professed aim of keeping the number and categories of travel and identity documents within reasonable bounds, there exist some 150 such documents, which can be subdivided into 23 categories (national passport, business passport, diplomatic passport, Seaman's card, ID card for railway staff, etc.) and which are issued by some 15 different types of authorities (central, local, cantonal, diplomatic, etc.).

Nevertheless, the list is still not complete because not all European countries are parties, and those countries which are parties have not reported all such required documents.

Two other agreements relating to travel and identity documents have been accepted by certain Member States of the Council of Europe. These are the European Agreement on the abolition of visas for refugees (ETS No. 31), opened for signature on 20 April 1959, and the European Agreement on travel by Young Persons on Collective Passport between the Member States of the Council of Europe (ETS No. 37) of 16 December 1961. These Agreements were early afforts to facilitate the travel of persons between States in western Europe at a time when it needed a special effort. In the present situation, however, in which millions of Europeans are circulating within and outside the confines of Europe these Agreements relating to outdated frontier formalities are overshadowed by newer and more substantial obstacles to travel, such as air and road traffic congestion.

7.   POLITICAL AND TECHNICAL COOPERATION

The experience of the Council of Europe in the field of facilitation and control of the movement of persons has demonstrated that technical cooperation and legal harmonization are useful, but only when they are supported by political cooperation. The implementation of existing laws and international agreements, and the analysis of statistical and other data concerning the movement of persons, is normally entrusted to national authorities responsible for the control of movement of persons. However, it is unreasonable to expect that national authorities will go beyond their strict mandate and become involved in international policy-making.

After the conclusion of the 1957 Agreement, on the movement of persons in Europe, discussed above (ETS No. 25), a committee of experts on frontier formalities was formed. In the course of 35 years this committee has been reformed and renamed several times: Ad Hoc Committee of experts on identity documents (CAHID), Ad Hoc Committee on Movement of Persons (CAHCP) and, since 1990, the Committee of experts for the mobility of citizens (CJ-MC). While this Committee has functioned successfully in applying agreed European principles, it has been less effective in dealing with problems on which the governments of the Member States were divided. For example, when western European countries reintroduced visas for Turkish citizens, or when decisions regarding pseudo-tourists (*faux touristes*) were needed, solutions required the political cooperation of the Member States.

8.   MOVEMENT OF PERSONS AND NEW TECHNOLOGICAL
         DEVELOPMENTS

During the 1970s the Committee concentrated on problems connected with mass tourism, especially those related to air travel. The International Civil Aviation Organisation (ICAO) predicted correctly that traditional procedures of entry and exit control at the borders would be unable to cope with the numbers of passengers arriving by ever larger, ever faster and ever more frequent international carriers. The ICAO explored the use of computer technology and, in particular, the replacement of the traditional passport book by machine-readable passport cards. The technical experts soon got lost in detailed debates on technicalities and on competition between national industries (cardboard versus plastic, character recognition versus codable magnetic strips, etc.). However, a number of wider issues gradually became apparent.

First, emerging data protection laws, and the Council of Europe's data protection Convention of 1981, (ETS No. 108) placed restrictions on the presentation, volume and type of information that may be included in travel and identity documents. Magnetic encryption, for which the ICAO experts had initially shown great enthusiasm, but which cannot be read by the naked eye, was found inadmissible on data protection grounds.

Second, many European experts speculated that, at least inside Europe, in the longer term traditional passports would no longer be required for the crossing of borders, and that other documents which suffice for the proof of identity within States would become an increasingly acceptable alternative.

At this stage, a third issue emerged. While in some European countries the carrying of national identity cards is customary or even obligatory (e.g., Germany and Belgium), in other countries it is only a facility (e.g., France), and in a third group of countries there is neither a duty nor even a possibility for citizens to obtain such cards (e.g., The Netherlands).

A fourth, related, issue was that of personal identification numbers (PINs). These numbers have been advocated by many governments that have begun to rely on computer technology. PIN's greatly facilitate the automatic checking of passports and identity cards at the borders and enable border police and customs officers to check this information against that held in other computerised records. However, PINs are deeply distrusted by data protection activists. Significantly, the use of PINs was prohibited in Portugal after the Revolution of Carnations.

A fifth issue was the plurality of identity cards used in some countries: one for reduced travel on the railways, another for senior citizens, a third for admission to libraries, etc. A hidden motive behind this complex situation was often simply profit-making by the issuing bodies.

Finally, just at the time when Europe readied itself to facilitate border crossing, new problems arose, involving illegal entries and other, more serious crimes such as hijacking, drug trafficking and terrorism, particularly targetted against air traffic. These new phenomena demand more thorough controls, greater international cooperation and better safeguards against forgery and counterfeiting.

As a result of these partly contradictory factors, the Council of Europe decided not to venture into the terrain of passports, but instead, continued to rely on the 1957 Agreement (ETS No. 25). The Council of Europe believed, however, that there was a case for putting forward certain standards in the field of national identity cards and their international recognition. These standards have been laid down in Resolution (77) 26 on the establishment and harmonization of national identity cards, and in Recommendation No. R (83) 11 on international recognition of national identity cards.

While the Member States were not inclined to entrust the Council of Europe with any work relating to passports, which they view as being intimately connected with their sovereignty and *ordre public*, they were even less willing to consider a proposal put to them by the Austrian Secretary-General, Lujo Toncic-Sorinj (1969-1974). This was the proposal to introduce a unified 'European passport', which is an idea that was eventually taken up by the European Community.

The Council of Europe's experts have continued to carry out useful work at the technical level. In order to enhance the fight against illegal immigration and the movement of drug traffickers and terrorists, they produced, as a service to governments, a 'Fraud Information Note', signalling on a confidential basis forgeries of passports and visas. They also commissioned the inventory, mentioned above, of 'genuine identity and travel documents'. This work was closely coordinated with the European Community's work on European passports.

9.   MISSING PERSONS

In 1973, the Council of Europe's experts were asked to deal with a specific problem resulting from the growing international movement of persons. The Parliamentary Assembly, in its Recommendation 646, called attention to the problem of missing persons. It noted that every year, thousands of persons in Europe became lost for a variety of reasons: usually temporarily young persons leaving home, victims of accidents, persons unable to provide for their own needs because of their physical or mental state or their poverty, as well as persons who disappear in order to avoid a legal obligation. In 1979, the Committee of Ministers adopted Recommendation No. R (79) 6 on Search for missing persons. This Recommendation requests governments to cooperate in order to help relieve or resolve the psychological and material difficulties of these persons and their families while respecting their fundamental rights.

10.   GYPSIES

A special category of persons circulating in Europe are gypsies. These people distinguish themselves by their itinerant way of life and by lack of firm attachment to a particular place of residence and often also by unpredictable variations with regard to their nationality. In 1975, the Committee of Ministers in its Resolution (75) 13 on the social situation of nomads in Europe recommended measures to facilitate their settlement. This Resolution helped to improve the lot of those nomads who were prepared to settle and who were nationals of the States concerned. However, it also appeared that there still are large groups of nomads who prefer to continue their itinerant way of life, moving from one European country to another. This group often encounters difficulties because many of them are stateless or of undetermined nationality. They are also confronted with social and legal problems such as the inability to obtain drivers' licences, and, insufficient or irregular schooling of children. Several applications made by gypsies under the European Convention on Human Rights on grounds of discrimination were declared inadmissable because among other things, they lacked sufficient legal advice to bring a proper application.

In May 1982 some of the questions regarding gypsies were examined by the European Ministers of Justice at their 13th Conference in Athens. Using the neutral term 'nomad' to indicate people such as gypsies or romanies, the ministers noted that the inability of these people to adjust to modern society and the legal problems connected with their migrations were sources of concern. In 1983 the Committee of Ministers adopted Recommendation No. R (83) 1 on stateless nomads and nomads of undetermined nationality. This recommendation requests States to ensure that their laws and practices do not discriminate against nomads solely because of their nomadic way of life. States were also advised to help nomads to establish a link with a particular State in order to develop greater security for their legal situation, enable movement to and from the country of attachment, and facilitate the reunion of families.

The present extension of the Council of Europe to the countries of central and eastern Europe, where gypsies still face many problems of discrimination, has led to renewed vigilance on the part of the Council of Europe and will be the subject of a special ministerial conference. It is noted, for example, that in some eastern European countries the gypsy prison population exceeds ten times their percentage of the general population.

11.   MIGRANT WORKERS

Apart from its general work on movement of persons in Europe, the Council of Europe has focused on the problems connected with the movement of migrant workers and political refugees. These two categories, although quite distinct theoretically are often intermingled in practice because persons illegally entering European countries in search of work often justify their presence on the grounds that they are political, rather than economic, refugees. The basic legal text of the Council of Europe concerning migrant workers is the European Convention on the legal status of migrant workers of 24 November 1977, which has been ratified by seven countries and to which five others are signatories. This Convention contains a complete checklist of matters connected with migrant workers, such as recruitment, admission, work contracts, work permits, residence permits, family reunion, housing, transfer of savings, social security, medical assistance and taxation. It applies to migrant workers only, and does not apply to frontier workers and seasonal workers, artists, entertainers, sportsmen, seamen and trainees.

The situation with regard to migrant workers is constantly changing and therefore to be kept carefully under review. One phenomenon is that of 'new immigration countries.' These are countries that traditionally exported migrant labour but now encourage worker immigration. Another recent phenomenon is the arrival of migrant workers from central and eastern Europe. This will be examined in the last section of this report.

12.   REFUGEES

In matters of political refugees and asylum seekers, the Council of Europe is facing exponential growth. In the early 1970s the average annual number of requests for asylum in western Europe was 13,000. This figure increased rapidly and by 1989 reached 315,000. The Member States of the Council of Europe take as their point of departure the 1951 Geneva Convention of the United Nations on the status of refugees and its 1976 New York Protocol. At the European level, the impact of this convention has been reinforced by several initiatives by the Council of Europe which aim in particular at allaying fears that in the face of the constant swelling stream of refugees and asylum-seekers the Council of Europe's policy towards them might become less friendly. On 16 October 1980, the Council of Europe concluded the European Agreement for transfer of responsibility of refugees (ETS No. 107), which aims at facilitating the 1951 United Nations Convention in respect of refugees who change their state of residence. This instrument was prepared by the ad hoc Committee of Experts on the Legal Aspects of Territorial Asylum, Refugees and Stateless Persons (CAHAR).

13.   ASYLUM

A particular legal problem that refugees and asylum-seekers are facing is the absence of any explicit right to asylum in the European Convention on Human Rights. In order to make up for this absence, the Committee of Ministers adopted on 18 November 1977 the Declaration on Territorial Asylum, under which Member States, individually and collectively, reaffirmed their commitment to respect the right of asylum. The Member States also declared that the grant of asylum is a peaceful and humanitarian act not to be regarded as an act unfriendly to any other State.

In 1978, the CAHAR started work on the important question of the 'country of first asylum'. It prepared a draft agreement on responsibility for examining asylum requests, which has not yet been adopted by the Committee of Ministers. The main thesis contained in this draft is that the State in which an asylum-seeker arrives should take responsibility for examining his case. This proposal poses problems, however, to the frontline countries which, due to their geographic location, are likely to receive the first influx whenever refugees leave troubled areas. Turkey is one of the Member States of the Council of Europe which frequently finds itself in this situation. For example, in the first part of 1991, Turkey faced immigration by half a million Kurdish refugees from Iraq. Other countries may also find themselves unexpectedly in such situations. Italy witnessed the arrival of 20,000 refugees from Albania, and Hungary has received many refugees from combat zones in Yugoslavia.

While political agreement on this draft Agreement is lacking, the Committee of Ministers of the Council of Europe has approved a special procedure that enables countries facing unexpected refugee problems to consult and act in unison with other European countries. This procedure consists in the holding of extraordinary meetings of the CAHAR at the request of one or more governments. The Council of Europe takes the view that refugee problems can be solved only by a combination of short-term and long-term measures. In the short-term, European governments should cooperate to alleviate the burden of sudden, massive arrivals of refugees in one place, and should coordinate their efforts with humanitarian organisations. In the longer term, efforts should be made to establish a dialogue with the refugees' countries of origin in order to promote their possible return to their homes under sufficient guarantees for the respect of their human rights and democratic aspirations. This policy has been expressed in the final communique of the 88th Session of the Committee of Ministers in Strasbourg on 25 April 1991 on the situation of the Kurds, Shiites and other refugees from Iraq.

14.   MIGRATION FROM CENTRAL AND EASTERN EUROPE

The process of profound economic and political change in central and eastern Europe is expected to be the single most important cause of movement of the largest numbers of persons in Europe since the end of World War II. With regard to the Soviet Union alone, where a liberalisation of travel restrictions is pending, it is estimated that from 1.5 to 2 million persons will attempt to migrate westward in the period 1991-1993.

In March 1990 the Austrian Government took an initiative on this matter at a special meeting of the Committee of Ministers of the Council of Europe in Lisbon. The Austrian Government noted that western European States, which had campaigned for so long in favour of the freedom of movement of the citizens of eastern Europe, should not close the borders to persons migrating from those countries now that this freedom is finally being achieved. Following this initiative, a ministerial conference was held in Vienna on 24 and 25 January 1991 in which all States of western, central and eastern Europe participated as full members, with only Albania participating at the observer level. Australia, the United States of America, the European Community and several other European and international organizations also attended as observers. During the Conference, the Secretary-General of the Council of Europe, Mrs Lalumière, criticized the Schengen and Dublin Agreements concluded between certain EC Member States on the grounds that they tended to create a special regime for a privileged part of Europe rather than sharing the burden with the whole of Europe on the basis of solidarity.

In recognition of the need for solidarity and good neighborliness, the final communiqué of the Vienna Conference recommended harmonization of policies and rules concerning migration flows originating from or passing through central and eastern Europe. Such harmonization should include a fuller compliance with the Geneva Convention, exchange of information on conditions of the labour market, prevention of disorderly migration, measures against illegal employment of workers, economic cooperation in border regions and interstate arrangements for short-term employment, training, reintegration of persons returning voluntarily to their countries of origin and readmission of illegal migrants by their states of origin. The Conference also decided that any developments which could result in an uncontrolled influx of migrants should be jointly observed and evaluated, and that speedy mutual information should be exchanged on such developments. A group of senior officials is now following up the conclusions of this Conference.

15.   CONCLUSION

As the foregoing survey shows, the Council of Europe has served, as a political, legal and technical forum that deals with the most diverse aspects of movement of persons. These movements exhibit certain, steadily increasing, patterns with regard to the circulation of tourists, migrant workers and other regular travellers. However, there are also intervening irregular patterns caused by political, economic or even climatic upheavals in Europe and elsewhere. It is significant that the series of events leading to the fall of communism in central and eastern Europe began with East German holiday-makers in Czechoslovakia and Hungary who eventually became economic migrants to West Germany. Events outside Europe, such as the 1991 Gulf War, have also caused atypical fluctuations in the movement of persons.

Greater Europe is finally establishing its own identity and is recognized as a functioning entity, whose well-being can be monitored. The results of those observations must be taken into account by governments, individually and collectively within the framework of European and international organizations. Certain parts of Europe, such as the Member States of the European Community, function well and perform to the best of expectations, but the overall well-being of the continent cannot only depend on the satisfactory functioning of some of its parts. All efforts must therefore be made to secure the proper functioning of Europe as a whole.

FORTRESS EUROPE AND (EXTRA-COMMUNITARIAN) REFUGEES: COOPERATION IN SEALING OFF THE EXTERNAL BORDERS

Hans Ulrich Jessurun d'Oliveira[*]

1.   INTRODUCTION

Just as, in many ways, environmental law can be perceived as law to allow and legitimatize pollution, so there are reasons to define modern refugees law as law designed to keep refugees away. It might have been different immediately after World War II. The Geneva Convention relating to the Status of Refugees[1] (hereafter: the Geneva Convention), in existence now for forty years, has been a sign, concededly weak, that a large part of the world community was cautiously prepared to absorb refugees, especially those issued from the Cold War. Several national constitutions, including those of Italy and the former Federal Republic of Germany and its constituent Länder, provided an even more liberal approach.[2]

France had a tradition as a host country for refugees from many parts of the world to the extent that one would expect every second taxi driver in Paris to be a Russian prince. Many more countries could be mentioned here.

But the tide has turned. In many European countries new bills have been proposed or announced, and some have already been turned into legislation, all concerning aliens and refugees. Nearly all of these laws tend to curtail immigration, to make entry into the territory more difficult, and to reduce possibilities for asylum seekers to gain entrance and recognition as refugees. Similarly, judicial and administrative decisions in these countries' case-law and decisions of administrative bodies have tended to narrow earlier interpretations of definitions of terms of the Geneva Convention, to give

---

*   Professor at the European University Institute (Florence) and the University of Amsterdam.

1. 1951 Geneva Convention of the UN Relating to the Status of Refugees, with Protocol, New York, 16 December 1966 which lifted the time barrier of events occurring before 1 January 1951.

2. The Italian Constitution (Art. 10 s.3) declares: '*Lo straniero, al quale sia impedito nel suo paese l'effettivo esercizio delle libertà democratiche garantite dalla Costituzione italiana, ha diritto d'asilo nel territorio della Repubblica, secondo le condizioni stabilite dalla legge.*' Cf., Bruno Nascimbene, *Lo straniero nel diritto italiano* (1988) p. 111 et seq., with *Appendice di aggiornamento* (1991); the German *Grundgesetz* - still - contains the provision '*Politisch Verfolgten geniessen Asylrecht*' (Art. 16(2)), cf., Hart, *Rechtsprechungssammlung zum Asylrecht mit Erläuterungen* (1984) 4. For France, one finds a reference in the Preamble of the current constitution to the Declaration of human rights of 1789 and the preamble of the 1946 Constitution which includes 'le peuple français (. . .) donne asile aux étrangers bannis de leur patrie pour la cause de la liberté .' Cf., Norek and Doumic-Doublet, *Le droit d'asile en France* (1989) p. 35.

H.G. Schermers et al., eds., Free Movement of Persons in Europe
© 1993, T.M.C. Asser Instituut, The Hague

larger discretion to governmental and administrative bodies, to abolish or redefine categories of non-conventional refugees or asylum seekers (such as those persons who could be granted a residence permit on other humanitarian grounds), and to reduce the access to judicial control by streamlining the judicial control of administrative decisions and by withdrawing state-financed legal aid in the asylum procedure. Moreover, asylum seekers have been subjected to extremely disagreeable conditions amounting to detention and idleness while their applications are being handled. In a healthy spirit of humanitarian rivalry the European States seem to be competing in creating the worst possible image in the hope of inducing asylum seekers to find a country next door.

> '*Heiliger Sankt Florian*
> *verschon' mein Haus,*
> *zünd' andre an!*'

The social, economic and political causes that have led to this change of attitude in European countries need hardly be discussed here as they are well-known and obvious. I mention the oil crisis and ensuing economic recession which has decreased the potential of absorbing foreign cheap labour. This in turn has led to a change in policy concerning labour immigration, with the result that in many countries the labour market has become sealed off for foreign, extra-communitarian immigrants. Admissions have been allowed only for specific shortages in the labour market or for purposes of family reunification.

This policy puts the remaining grounds for admission under heavy pressure. Increasingly, people have couched their applications for residence permits in the terms of the legal slots of family reunification or asylum, and some of them brought themselves into a factual position which augured a better chance. *Mariages de raison*, for many centuries not uncommon in western cultures and still extant, are concluded to gain entrance or force a right to stay in European countries. One could call them 'humanitarian marriages' as well, although the comparison with medieval virgins saving the neck of hero-villains on the brink of being put unjustly to death is not appropriate in each and every case. In some countries, attempts have been made to pierce the veil of these marriages; in others with a more nominalistic philosophy, qualifications relating to the length of the association have been introduced with the ensuing effects of slavery and blackmail.

Asylum seekers have also resorted to other devices, such as becoming an undocumented person. In normal circumstances, it is unwise for a person, due to fear of persecution in his country, to avail himself of the assistance of his country's authorities in issuing himself the required travel documents. This is at least the point of view of the Geneva Convention,[3] and in several countries we find this reflected in related legislation. Thus, the Netherlands administrative practice does not require a refugee who voluntarily wants to acquire the Dutch nationality by naturalization to do his part in renouncing his original nationality as is normally required from persons who

---

3. See e.g., Arts. 25, 27, 28 and 31.

want to be naturalized,[4] because such a requirement would imply contacting the authorities of the country which he left as a refugee.

Asylum seekers' travel operators advise their clients on the best ways to behave in order to improve chances of being admitted in view of the prevailing legislation and policies in the various target countries. This in turn has led to additional legislative and practical countermeasures, which have tightened controls in order to parry the increased know-how of asylum seekers. One of the measures is criminalizing and/or penalizing carriers of passengers with insufficient documents. I will return to this device later (part 5).

It is not only the recession of the 1970s and 1980s which is responsible for the closing of the frontiers of European countries to labour immigration. It is also the process of change from fairly homogeneous nation-states into something which is still called a nation-state but which has acquired a multi-ethnic, multi-cultural flavour as the result of decolonization and the residence, which has become permanent, of the labour influx of the 1960s and 1970s. That these migrants were here to stay, and that they introduced their family members in Europe as well, has come as a shock to many quarters of the indigenous populations. This shock has given birth to an upsurge of nationalism with clearly racist and xenophobic overtones. This reaction has translated itself partly in extreme right-wing white parties, which have enjoyed considerable electoral successes with the result that more respectable political parties have tried to win back this part of the electorate by promising to introduce just those measures which the extremist parties have urged for so clamorously.[5]

2.   THE SINGLE EUROPEAN MARKET AND INTERGOVERNMENTAL INITIATIVES

There is still another factor which has its own impact on the policies concerning migrants at large, including asylum seekers. This is the European Community with its own legal order, its own purposes, aims, perspectives.

Let me first put on record that the administrations in the Member States try desperately to distinguish between migrants, on the one hand, and refugees, on the other. Of course, analytically speaking, the distinction holds good and is sensible. One must not forget, however, that asylum seekers form a part of migration movements that can be characterized by diminished voluntariness. Most of them are not tourists, but rather, are persons forced to move away because of fate or circumstances as civil or

---

4. Art. 8 Law on Nationality 1985.

5. A case in point is the declaration, early July 1991, by the newly appointed French Prime Minister, Ms Edith Cresson, that she would organize special, chartered, flights to expel illegal immigrants, just as the former right-wing Minister of the Interior, Mr Charles Pasqua, had done earlier on 18 October 1986, in putting 101 Malians on a chartered plane. The Front National and Mr Chirac, the former Prime Minister, expressed satisfaction. Mr Giscard d'Estaing, on 20 September 1991, urged for a rigourous return to the *ius sanguinis* principle in French nationality law and asked for a referendum on this issue! For some neighbouring States this climate smells definitely of xenophobia and racism.

international wars, famine, deforestation, inundations and desertification, upheavals and disintegration of existing States with mixed populations. Thus, the analytical distinction between refugees and other forced migrants, some of whom are ostracized as economic refugees, holds some truth only if one sticks scrupulously and narrowly to the legal definition of persons for whom the Geneva Convention was designed: originally freedom fighters in eastern European countries.[6]

In the second place, it seems useful to point out that it may not be welcome, but not unreasonable either, to state that 'events occurring in Europe', as the Geneva Convention declares, are an important factor in causing streams of refugees in other continents. Colonization, decolonization, and economic recolonization are a few of these important factors. This means that taking care of this category of forced migrants is not especially humanitarian, but primarily a matter of accepting responsibility for influence in other continents. The same argument can be made about those forced immigrants who, technically speaking, cannot easily be brought under the definition of the Geneva Convention but who have very few options left other than to rely on their luck and try to survive in better surroundings. The displacement of many persons from other parts of the world is related to activities emanating from the developed States.

The advent of the Single European Market and its implications for the abolishment of internal borders of the Member States has momentous consequences for non-EC nationals (extra-communitarians). I will not discuss at any length the meaning of Article 8A of the Single European Act, as this has been done in several of the other reports of this Colloquium. Suffice it to say, that there is no political agreement between the Member States as to the issue of which 'persons' are to be granted the right of free movement by 1993; does the right extend to nationals of Member States or also to non-EC nationals with a regular permit to stay in one of the Member States?[7]

This debate is a reflection of the unresolved issue of Community competence concerning migration (and nationality as the other side of the coin).[8] These differences of opinion have blocked for the time being the 1985 White Paper proposals for directives of the Commission in the area of freedom of movement of persons. There are

6. This, of course, is the background of the declaration which each of the Contracting States was supposed to make concerning the geographical scope according to Art. 1(B)(1): events occurring in Europe (before January 1951) or in Europe or elsewhere. Until the Legge Martelli (of 28 February 1990 No. 39), Italy stuck to the limitation to European events. The Legge Martelli is in this respect part of the price Italy was prepared to pay to join the Schengen area.

7. Cf., the *Sixth Report of the Commission to the Council and the European Parliament* concerning the implementation of the White Paper on the Completion of the Internal Market, Com (91)237 fin., 19 June 1991. As a matter of fact the Commission states (p. 2) that 'particularly in the area of free movement for individuals, progress has been very limited since the last report,' and that 'the convention on crossing external borders, which constitutes the key element, has still not been signed despite the repeatedly stated wishes of the European Council. The main difficulty lies in the interpretation of Art. 8A.' See also p. 11, where the Commission remarks that: 'it is in the area of the abolition of physical frontiers that the credibility of the aim pursued to complete the internal market as defined in Art. 8a of the Treaty is not assured because (...) there are still fundamental disagreements regarding the free movement of persons.'

8. Cf., Evans and d'Oliveira, 'Nationality and Citizenship', in: Cassese, Clapham and Weiler, eds, *Human Rights and the European Community: Methods of Protection* (1991) pp. 299-350, and d'Oliveira, European Community Refugee Policy, *Migrantenrecht* (1991) pp. 76-82.

signs that countries like Denmark, Greece and the United Kingdom, which have objected to Community competence, are gradually coming round to at least condoning Commission activities in the field.

For the time being, however, activities of the Member States are 'paracommunitarian'; i.e., independent intergovernmental cooperation between Member States, oriented on the Community legal order, but outside of the Community institutions which normally produce elements of the Community legal order. It is extremely difficult, for obvious practical reasons, to abolish internal frontiers between the Member States only for nationals of the Member States, but to keep them closed and under strict control for other persons within the territory of a Member State, be it legally or illegally. It would be easy if persons crossing such borders could be identified simply as Member State nationals, but this is not the case. Nevertheless, authorities in many countries allow themselves to rely on external characteristics and subject non-white persons to special checks, as though not an appreciable part of the nationals of European States are coloured.

Be this as it may, the inevitable consequence of opening the internal frontiers to all Member State nationals is that it cannot be achieved in a selective way; it has to include all other categories as well. One of the effects of the abolition of internal borders is the speeding up of the freedom of movement of workers, among others, from Spain and Portugal. This was decided by the Social Affairs Council on 25 June 1991 in Luxembourg. Although this would allow Spanish workers as from 1 January 1993 free access to the other Member States, Spain agreed hesitantly because this arrangement will also allow Portuguese workers to enter the Spanish labour market.[9] The way has been paved already for Spanish and Portuguese workers by a decision of the Court of Justice which gave priority to the freedom of services above restrictions to the freedom of movement of workers.[10]

Two different international instruments relevant for refugees have appeared on the European market, namely, the Schengen Convention and The Dublin Asylum Convention. These are discussed below.

2.1   The Schengen Agreement of 14 June 1985 with the implementing Convention of 19 June 1990

The Schengen Convention contains in Chapter 7 of Title 2 some 11 Articles on 'Responsibility for the processing of applications for asylum' (Arts. 28-38). It has a predecessor in the form of a 1987 draft Convention developed by a working party of the *Comité ad hoc sur les aspects juridiques de l' asile territorial et des réfugiés* (CAHAR), established by the Comité des Ministres of the Council of Europe.[11] In this draft a

9. See *Migration News Sheet*, July 1991.

10. Case C-113/89, ECR [1990] I-1417 *Rush Portuguesa* v. *Office National d'immigration*; see Verschueren, *Migrantenrecht* 1991, pp. 187-191.

11. For a discussion of this draft Convention, see e.g., Wollenschläger and Becker, 'Harmonisierung des Asylrechts in der EG und Art. 16 Abs. 2 GG', *EURKZ* (1990) pp. 1-10; see also R. Fernhout, *Erkenning en toelating als vluchteling in Nederland* (1990) Nos. 16, 84, 197.

central element of the Schengen Convention can be found, i.e., the appointment of a Member State which is responsible *vis-à-vis* the other States for handling requests for asylum. The Parties to the Schengen Agreement were originally the Benelux States (who already had extensive experience with abolition of internal borders and a coordinated visa policy), Germany and France. Italy was allowed to become a Party after the introduction of the Legge Martelli in 1990, and after changing its Declaration to the Geneva Convention. Italy had been the only Member State with the territorial restriction to European events and one out of six of the 102 Parties to the Geneva Convention. It acceded on 27 November 1990.

Recently, on 25 June 1991, Spain and Portugal signed both the Schengen Agreement and the Schengen Convention. Greece has been granted observer status as per June 1991. This implies that Greece is willing to accept the Schengen Convention and that the territories of the continental Member States will form one travel area, with the exception of the Danish-German border and the border between Spain and Gibraltar.[12] The Schengen Group contacted Denmark in June of 1991 to sound out its readiness to join. In July 1991, there was a first information meeting with the United Kingdom, which emphatically did not imply its willingness to accede to the Schengen Agreement and Convention.[13] Up to the present the United Kingdom considers its borders to be external borders of the Community, except for Irish nationals.

2.2 Convention Determining the State Responsible for Examining Applications for Asylum Lodged in one of the Member States of the EC, 15 June 1990 ('Dublin Asylum Convention')

This paracommunitarian Convention has in the meantime been signed by all twelve Member States.[14] Unlike the Schengen Convention, it deals exclusively with the topic of asylum. However, it cannot be understood without its counterpart on the crossing of borders. This connection is at the same time a reason why one may now expect that, although the Schengen Convention was signed a few days later than the Dublin Convention, the Schengen Convention may nevertheless be ratified and enter into force earlier.

A symptom of the energy, or the rush with which the Schengen partners are proceeding is an Agreement on re-admission of persons in an irregular position, Brussels, 29 March 1991.[15] This is an agreement between the parties to the Schengen Convention and Poland that changes the Schengen Convention in a very discrete manner. Under Article

---

12. The disputed status of Gibraltar is also the reason why the signing of the Convention on the crossing of the external borders of the Member States of the European Communities ('External Frontiers Convention') has been postponed on 19 July 1991 *sine die*, until the UK and Spain have found a bilateral solution.

13. To Heinrich Heine is attributed the verdict on the Netherlands that everything happens there thirty years later. In the United Kingdom only European developments happen a generation later.

14. Originally Denmark was not in a position to sign as it first had to adapt and modify municipal legislation; it is now the first to even ratify the Convention.

15. Trb. 1991 No. 65.

I(1) of this agreement with Poland each party (primarily Poland) will re-admit, on the request of any other party, without formalities, persons who do not, or no longer, fulfill the conditions for entry or residence prevailing on the territory of the requesting party in so far as it can be established or presumed that the persons involved possess the nationality of the requested state.

This may seem to be in line with international law. Article 2, however, in effect provides the same for persons who entered through the external borders of the requested State. Poland will take back any irregular migrant entering the Schengen area; be it a Pole, a Rumanian, a Russian citizen or whomever. Why would Poland agree to accept these obligations? The *quid pro quo* is to be found in one of the recitals of the preamble. It is the abolishment of the requirement of visas for Polish citizens which is connected with this agreement to take back any irregular migrant who enters the Schengen area through the German-Polish border.[16] The rush is hidden in Article 6(2): the agreement with Poland is already provisionally to be applied immediately after having been signed, which makes the formal entry into force a rather irrelevant moment. The machinery works as of 1 April 1991,[17] at least, according to a declaration concerning Articles 2 and 5(3), which one finds in a Protocol to the agreement, as to Polish nationals. Any 'irregular' Polish citizen, found in the Schengen area, will be taken back without ado by Poland. The effect of this agreement with Poland will doubtless be that, in addition to the reinforced *Grenzschutz* at the Oder-Neisse, the Polish police will try to prevent the mechanism of the agreement from being put into operation. Other (eastern European) States may be invited to join the arrangement (Art. 7) which in effect will establish a *cordon sanitaire* around Schengen, or represent a rebuilt Iron Curtain.[18]

As Schengen seems to be coming out ahead of the paracommunitarian Dublin Convention(s), I will deal primarily with the Schengen instrument(s).

3.   SCHENGEN AND ASYLUM

Chapter 7 of the Schengen Convention — called 'Responsibility for the processing of application for asylum' — which already smells of bureaucratic handling of data, not of persons, starts with 're-affirming' the obligations under the Geneva Convention,

16. '... aux fins de compenser, notamment la charge qu'une circulation des voyageurs en exemption du visa, ressortissants des Parties Contractantes du présent Accord, est susceptible de créer,' see Hand. II 1990-1991, 19326, No 48 (6 February 1991). The abolition of visa is part of the bilateral German-Polish agreements settling the after effects of World War II.

17. In answer to questions asked in the Dutch parliament the Minister for Foreign Affairs, Hans van den Broek, indulged in a dubious lecture about the differences between provisional application and execution of an agreement which entered into force. But for his arrogance he could have been aware of the fact that running ahead of the parliamentary debate leading to ratification (or rejection) of the Schengen instruments would hurt the sensitivity of the Dutch parliament which repeatedly complained about the lack of democratic control. See Hand. II 1990-1991, 19326, No. 50, 25 June 1991.

18. See the Commentary of the Dutch Standing Committee of experts on international immigration, refugee and criminal law.

without any geographical restriction,[19] and 'the commitment' to cooperate with the UNHCR (Art. 28). In Article 135 the contracting parties repeat that the Schengen Convention shall apply 'subject to the provisions of the Geneva Convention'.

We know, of course, that the UNHCR has only in a late phase of the negotiations been invited to comment on the drafts and that this constitutes a breach of the obligations laid down in Article 35 of the Geneva Convention to cooperate with the UNHCR and to furnish it with information about proposed legal measures concerning refugees. UNHCR has made this clear to the Member States. This violation of formal obligations, which may partly be mended by the promise for future cooperation in the putting into effect of the instruments, has had consequences for the substance of the measures.

The key provision is Article 30, which has the purpose of giving a watertight system of rules determining the order of priority of States called to 'process' an application for asylum in such a way that there is always one and only one State responsible (Art. 29(3)). Once a (negative) decision on the request for asylum has been taken by the Member State involved, this decision will be recognized by all other Member States, thus depriving asylum seekers from second chances in other Member States. The obligation to deal with a request falls in the first place on the party that has issued a visa or residence permit to the applicant expiring later than any other visa or residence permit (a and b); it then trickles down — in the case that no visa requirements exist — on the party across the borders of which the applicant has entered the territory of the contracting parties. This obligation is a kind of punishment for the party with slack border controls. And so on.

There are to be distinguished *two main policies* behind these rules. Apart from the policy of reduction of the problem of refugees in orbit — asylum seekers who are driven from pillar to post — there is a second policy, i.e., reduction of what is called 'asylum shopping'. This is the label given to multiple applications by asylum seekers to various countries in the hope that at least one country will recognize the applicant as a refugee under the Schengen Convention or to acquire another status on humanitarian grounds.

This policy of suppressing multiple requests is visible, for example, in Article 30(f), which does not allow a State to deal with a new application if there is already an application 'being processed' in another Schengen party, and Article 30(g), which makes it impossible for an asylum seeker present in the Schengen area to present a request elsewhere in the Schengen area if there is already a (negative) final decision from one of the parties. In other words, only the same asylum shop may deliver another refusal on a renewed request for asylum.

There is, however, one exception, which was adopted because of the constitutional requirements of some of the Schengen States and which declares, that:

---

19. This is why the 'Legge Martelli' of 28 February 1990 No. 39 has changed Art. 1 of the *decreto legge* 30 December 1989, No. 416 and withdrawn the geographical limitation; at the same time it lifted the restrictions concerning the Arts. 17 and 18 (exercise of gainful activities) of the Geneva Convention.

'every Contracting Party shall retain the right, for special reasons concerning national law in particular, to process an application for asylum, even if under this Convention the responsibility for doing so is that of another Country (Art. 29(4)).'

This provision, which could be extremely useful in two respects, is at the same time disruptive of the one State responsibility system. It is well-known that the Geneva Convention does primarily lead to the award of the status of refugee, but this in itself does not guarantee asylum. Germany guarantees, however, such a right to asylum to the politically persecuted. The current debate on the change of Article 16 of the *Grundgesetz* only occasionally mentions the European and Schengen context of the issue; i.e., that if Germany retains its Article 16 it has generally to resort to Article 29(4) of the Schengen agreement and thus becomes exquisitely attractive as a country of asylum among European States.[20]

In France, the *Cour Constitutionnel* has been requested to control the compatibility of the Schengen Convention, especially its Articles 29(4), 31, 32 with the Constitution, which guarantees a right to asylum for a larger category than those defined in the Geneva Convention.[21] The reference in Article 29(4) to national law includes the French Constitution, which is more liberal than the Geneva Convention in awarding a right to asylum. Thus, the constitutional provision is not covered by the regular re-affirmation of the obligations under the Geneva Convention. In effect, the Constitutional Court has expressed its view that Chapter 7 of the Schengen Convention is only compatible with its constitution if the faculty under Article 29(4) is used in conformity with the existing obligations under the French Constitution.[22] That this narrow exception could grow to be the soft underbelly of the whole scheme has been well-understood by the Dutch Government, which has proposed to introduce this exception into its municipal legislation in a section, added to the existing Article 15 of the Aliens law, stating in effect that:

'the alien will not be received in his request for admission (as refugee) if another country is responsible under a convention for processing the request, unless this request is grounded on relevant facts that could not have played a role in the decision of the authorities of that country.'[23]

This national implementation is much narrower even than the Schengen Convention requires. It allows the Netherlands the right to deal with the request only *after* a

---

20. Cf., *supra*, n. 11.

21. See *supra*, n. 2.

22. Decision of 25 July 1991. According to *Le Monde*, 27 July 1991, the *Cour Constitutionnel* stated that Art. 29(4) reserved the right of each Contracting Party *d'assurer le traitement d'une demande d'asile, même si la responsabilité incombe à une autre partie*. This right could in France be exercised '*au profit des personnes susceptibles de bénéficier du droit d'asile en vertu du quatrième alinéa du préambule de la Constitution de 1946.* (. . .)'

23. Tweede Kamer (Second Chamber of the Dutch Parliament) 1990-1991, 22.142, 4 June 1991 (translation by author).

negative decision has been handed down by the country responsible under the Schengen Convention. This is an unnecessary and unwanted restriction.[24]

In my opinion, and not in mine alone,[25] not only the restrictive implementation of an already narrow exception in the Convention but also this conventional exception itself are both products of a misconception of the obligations under the Geneva Convention. This is not a non-committal document with a platonic and hypothetical character. Each and every Party to the Geneva Convention has accepted *obligations*, and one of these is to take a decision on the status of the asylum seeker — is he a refugee under the definition of the Geneva Convention? — and to decide on his admission on the territory. Of course, these obligations do not concern all asylum seekers in the world — only those who have a certain link with the country involved. These links, can be territorial (i.e., the person is present on the territory) or subjective (i.e., the person has addressed his request to the authorities of a specific State) or personal (i.e., there are already members of his family resident in the country involved). These categories are not mutually exclusive, but overlapping. It is on the basis of these different categories of overlapping links, or connecting factors, that the problem of orbiting should be addressed, not by trying to make these links irrealistically exclusive and by ranking them in a fictitious order of priority.

This means, that States have not 'retained the *right*' to deal with the asylum requests, but have retained the *obligation* to do so if there are relevant links. Given the priority of the Geneva Convention over the regional arrangements of Schengen and Dublin, Article 29(4) of the Schengen Convention and Article 9 of the Dublin Convention are the central rules, and the attempts at indicating only one responsible State are the exceptions to these rules. Each State that has a sufficient link with the application and the asylum seeker remains responsible or co-responsible, not *vis-à-vis* the other Parties to the Schengen or Dublin Conventions, but under the Geneva Convention, and *vis-à-vis* the more than hundred parties thereto.

This is also the view of the Dutch Council of State, which is an important and official advisory body on all Dutch legislation. In its Advisory Opinion of 8 April 1991

---

24. One reads in the Explanatory Memorandum, p. 6-7: 'It is not the task of the Netherlands under the Schengen arrangement to hand down anticipatory interpretations concerning municipal aliens law of one of the other parties and to utilize on this basis a hypothetical negative decision by this responsible Party as legal grounds to draw the substantive decision on the request to the Netherlands.' This is indeed not the task of the Netherlands. It may take the decision to handle an application immediately, before any other country has disposed of the request, as it has '*retained* the right' to do so on grounds derived from its own municipal (humanitarian, constitutional) law or from other conventions, such as the Geneva Convention.

There is, furthermore, ambiguity about the use of the term 'aliens'. Under the Schengen and Dublin arrangements, 'alien' means 'any person other than a national of a Member State of the European Communities' (Art. 1 Schengen). In Art. 15(1) Dutch Aliens Act alien is used in the sense of Art. 1 Aliens Act, as 'any person not in possession of the Dutch nationality'. In Art. 15(2) (Draft) 'alien' is in effect used in the sense of the Schengen Convention. See Part 4.

25. See e.g., the excellent essay by J.J. Bolten, 'From Schengen to Dublin: the new frontiers of refugee law', in: H. Meyers, ed., *Schengen. Internationalization of Central Chapters of the Law on Aliens, Refugees, Security and the Police* (1991) pp. 8-36. The essays assembled in this book have previously been published in the *Nederlands Juristenblad* (1991) p. 5 et seq. (Special Issue). See also H. Meyers, ibid, p. 3.

on the acceptability of the Schengen Convention (which it denies),[26] it stated as follows:

'5. *Compatibility with the Convention on Refugees*
In Article 135 of the Implementing Agreement it is established that the 1951 Geneva Convention on Refugees (Convention concerning the status of refugees as amended by the New York Protocol of 31 January 1967 (Trb. (1951) No. 131 and Trb. (1967) No. 76), which will henceforth be referred to as the Convention on Refugees) has precedence over that contained in the agreement's regulation. On the basis of the intention expressed by those who drew up the agreement to endeavour to avoid conflicts with the Convention on Refugees, the Council is not convinced that the aim has been fully achieved. The precedence of the Convention on Refugees would, in the view of the Council, result in parts of the agreement not being able to be applied, which would seriously weaken the appropriateness and the effectiveness of the system envisaged.

The application of obligations essentially deriving from the Convention on Refugees, including the limitation on expulsion (Art. 32) and the prohibition on returning refugees to a country where they fear persecution (refoulement) (Art. 33), depends on whether the person is judged to be a refugee in the meaning of Article 1 of the Treaty. This assessment is reserved for national authorities, taking into consideration the Convention on Refugees, but for the remainder, applying their national law and national procedures. The system in the Convention on Refugees assumes that the obligations apply to each of the States which are signatories to the Treaty separately, when a foreigner seeks asylum. The prevailing Dutch asylum law starts from the view that the Netherlands has its own independent responsibility to determine whether people presenting themselves at its borders to seek asylum or who are on its territory are actually granted refugee status (for example HR 29 May, 1987, NJ 1988 No. 56).

This specific, independent responsibility means that each of the Treaty States makes its own judgement about the basis for a decision about refusal or deportation, without there being any mention of consistency with other Treaty states. The national law on asylum, and the national policy on the issue in the State to which the request is made, together with the Convention on Refugees, are always determinant for the question of whether the State complies with its obligations under the Convention on Refugees with respect to individual applicants for asylum. On the other hand, the State to which the application is made can, in case of refusal, expulsion or order for return to the country from which the refugee has fled, only justify its negative response to the question of whether it was guilty of refoulement, by claiming that a decision has been made, and then upheld, in accordance with its national law on asylum, by the competent authorities, judging that the person concerned was not a genuine refugee. The State cannot pass on to another State its responsibility towards an applicant for asylum, and accordingly it cannot hide behind another State's decision either (the Council refers to the above-mentioned decree HR 29 May 1987, NJ 1988 No. 56). Of course, a State can delegate the decision on refugee status wholly or partially to a body which is not a government body, for example to (a representative of) the United Nations High Commissioner for Refugees; however, this does not absolve the State of its responsibility. In the opinion of the Council, the system under the Implementing Agreement, in as far as it

---

26. In constitutional language the final part of its advice is extremely strong: '(. . .) opposed to parts of the agreement, and asks you to consider not sending the draft Bill to the Second Chamber of the States General.'

leads to the transfer of responsibility to another State, which then decides on refugee status according to its own law on asylum (Art. 32 of the Implementing Agreement), has no basis in the Convention on Refugees. It opens a possibility for treaty States to back out of the obligations arising from the Convention on Refugees, and thus according to Article 135 of the Implementing Agreement, it cannot be applied. Still, a treaty State may not transfer an applicant for asylum to another State, unless a reasonable guarantee exists beforehand that the transfer by that State, assessed under the criteria used in the first State to which application was made, will not lead to refoulement.'

The counterpart of these overlapping obligations of each and every party to the Geneva Convention is the right of each asylum seeker to try his luck in different countries. It is not an 'abuse' to lodge applications for asylum in different countries; on the contrary, branding this tactic as 'asylum shopping' is clearly abusive. Given the obligation under the Geneva Convention, and given the fact that the parties to the Schengen and Dublin Conventions not only have very different views on the substance of the definition and interpretation of the concept of refugees under the Geneva Convention, but also have widely different procedures in dealing with applications,[27] it is simply the right of every asylum seeker to apply in different countries.[28]

Logically, if a State considers its interpretation of the Geneva Convention as the right one — although aware of the fact that other States with different interpretations likewise view their administrative and court decisions as correct — recognition of other State's negative decisions followed by the probability of expulsion amounts to disregard for the obligation of non-refoulement.

4.   EUROPEAN ASYLUM SEEKERS: REVERSE DISCRIMINATION

If it is the professed aim of the European States that are parties to the Dublin and Schengen Conventions, to combat the evil of orbiting of asylum seekers by appointing at least one State responsible to deal with the request, there is something very quaint with the way in which this noble aim has been pursued. In an extravagant gush of generosity these efforts are bestowed on 'aliens', which are as we have seen only those persons who do not possess a nationality of one of the Member States. Extra-communitarians only may profit from this humanitarian strain. But what about asylum

---

27. One example is the following. The decision by the Dutch Hoge Raad (29 May 1987, NJ 1988 No. 56) cited in the opinion of the Council of State, distinguishes between the determination of refugee status under the Geneva Convention, and the award of asylum or residence. The right to stay may be denied, e.g., because there is a country of first asylum. On the other hand, Art. 1 s. 4 of the Legge Martelli refuses 'entry to the Italian territory whenever (. . .) it is proven that the applicant has already been granted refugee status in another State.' Thus, a refugee, recognized as such by a Netherlands Court, may not enter Italian territory, although this is considered by Dutch authorities to be the country of first asylum. Orbiting may be the result.

28. See generally d'Oliveira, 'European Community Refugee Policy' (in English), *Migrantenrecht*(1991) pp. 76-82.

seekers from the Member States themselves?[29] Are they not subject to the danger of orbiting? Do they not exist? Are there not two different regimes for the *mafiosi* on the one hand, and for the *Brigate rosse*, on the other, in Italy? Does the framing of accused IRA sympathizers such as the Birmingham Six[30] not amount to persecution? What about the masked expulsion or refoulement by France of members of the ETA to Spain? What about the political asylum request of former GDR spy Markus Wolf not in one of the Schengen States but in Austria;[31] and indeed one even notices in several States of the Schengen area situations where aliens, refugees and asylum seekers or others have a grounded fear of persecution or where outbursts of xenophobia are condoned by the authorities, especially where it concerns gypsies, blacks, 'beurs', Vietnamese and eastern Europeans. Additional examples could be cited to, but so much is already clear that the exclusion of nationals of the Member States from the blessings of the Schengen and Dublin arrangements raises grave doubts about the sincerity of this professed aim of reducing the number of refugees-in-orbit. This *reverse discrimination* of Schengen or Community nationals is a clear symptom that these arrangements really try to deal with the influx of immigrants and are to be considered as one of the walls of 'Castle Europe under Siege', to quote the title of a recent cover story of the American weekly Time.[32]

But there is more. If indeed the situation of asylum seekers is improved by the Schengen and Dublin Conventions, which I doubt, it is contrary to Article 3 of the Geneva Convention to differentiate on the basis of the country of origin between asylum seekers.[33] It is here that the repeated lip service in the Schengen Convention to the Geneva Convention is put to the test. Either the Member States consider the arrangement as an improvement of the situation of asylum seekers, but then they have acted contrary to Article 3 of the Geneva Convention, or they have to concede that it is indeed not an improvement, and find themselves again in a situation prohibited by Article 3 of the Geneva Convention. National parliaments should take this into consideration when deciding whether to ratify the Schengen Convention. It is furthermore incompatible with Article 1 of the Dutch Constitution which contains a non-discrimination clause, and with obligations deriving from other international instruments not to discriminate on the grounds of national origin. I see no grounds to justify a distinction between extra-communitarians and communitarian asylum seekers and refugees.

29. Cf., d'Oliveira, 'De EG discrimineert zijn eigen asielzoekers' [the EC discriminates against its own asylum seekers], *Nederlands Juristenblad* (1991) p. 442.

30. And the Guildford Four, the Maguire Seven and others, see e.g., Forder and Steyger, De Birmingham Six: een juridische horror story, NJB (1991) pp. 1050-1056.

31. See *Süddeutsche Zeitung* 17 September 1991.

32. August 16, 1991. See also *Der Spiegel* 9 September 1991 with a cover story on: 'Flüchtlinge-Aussiedler-Asylanten: Ansturm der Armen'.

33. Art. 3: 'The Contracting States shall apply the provisions of this Convention to refugees without discrimination as to race, religion or country of origin.'

5. CARRIERS' LIABILITY

One of the ways to prevent asylum seekers from making their requests on the territory of the Member States is to impede them from leaving their country of origin or transitional countries. A first check is being organized in the country of origin of asylum seekers by a flexible system of requiring visas for travel from asylum seekers producing countries.

A second landing net is being put into place at the check-in desks of airports where the carriers' personnel is supposed to control the existence of travel documents other than the tickets. To ensure that this control is carried out with the required rigour, Article 26 of the Schengen Convention contains two measures, both again 'subject to the obligations arising out of their accession to the Geneva Convention (. . .)':

(a) the imposition on carriers of the obligation 'to take all necessary measures to ensure that an alien carried by air or sea is in possession of the travel documents required for entry into the territory of the Contracting Parties'; and

(b) the undertaking 'to impose penalties on carriers who transport aliens who do not possess the necessary travel documents by air or sea from a Third State to their territories', to which applies the potential restriction 'in accordance with their constitutional law'.

Some countries have already resorted to the use of police personnel masquerading as air carriers' check-in personnel in asylum seeker producing countries. Recently the Dutch Ministry of Justice has declared that it would cooperate with the Dutch national air carrier, the KLM, in the control of documents at foreign airports by sending there members of the military police.[34] This device works on two sides. First, for the Ministry of Justice, it is cheaper to bear the costs of detachment of unemployed officers abroad than the expenses in handling asylum seekers and their requests once arrived in the Netherlands. Second, KLM will be liberated from returning the asylum seekers to their port of origin at their expense and will have to pay less or no penalties, because the company may depend on the judgment of the experts. I should think that permission of the State where the airport is situated is necessary as the military police is exercising State authority in checking the documents of the passengers and 'advising' the air carriers' personnel.

What does the condition that these measures must be carried out 'subject to the obligations arising from the Geneva Convention' mean in practice?[35] In the context of the Dublin Convention, the UNHCR expressed clear concern about the effects of carriers' liability,[36] in that the sanctions 'might operate in the individual case in effect to prevent persons in need of international protection either from leaving their country

---

34. See *De Volkskrant* 5 September 1991. (Many members of the military police have to be re-attached somewhere after the abolition of the internal borders.)

35. Cf., A. Cruz, 'Compatibility of carrier sanctions in four Community States with international civil aviation and human rights obligations', in H. Meijers et.al., *Schengen; Internationalization of central chapters of the Law on aliens, refugees, security and the police* (1991) pp. 37-56.

36. See the Document issued by UNHCR on the occasion of the meeting with the Group of Coordinators of the EC on the Free Circulation of Persons, Brussels, 11 October 1990, p. 2.

or from reaching another country where they have access to procedures for the determination of their status.' UNHCR proposed to introduce sanctions only *after* the final determination that the person involved was non-admissible. It is open to doubt whether this restricted sanction would give asylum seekers more of a chance to get away. An air carrier which wants to avoid financial sanctions will naturally play it safe and refuse any doubtful passenger.[37] This cautiousness will be stimulated by the open, rather discretionary terms with which the criminal offence of carriers is defined in, e.g., the Dutch draft Bill for the changes in the Aliens Act.[38]Are the States signatory to the Schengen Convention obliged to penalize carriers? The Dutch Government in its introductory memorandum states that it thinks that this is indeed the case.[39] The Dutch Council of State had contested that this obligation to introduce criminal sanctions existed, and this body repeated its point of view, that Article 26 of the Schengen Convention was inconsistent with Standard 3.37.1, Annex 9 to the Chicago Convention.[40]

It is true that Schengen does not necessarily require the introduction of criminal penalties. Administrative sanctions can also be envisaged. But there is more. Some framers of the Schengen Convention emphasize that Article 26 leaves everything to the Member States and that it does not oblige the Member States to introduce penalties because of the condition that this introduction should be 'in accordance with their constitutional law'.[41] There are indeed several court decisions in Germany since its introduction of criminal carriers' liability contesting the compatibility with the German *Grundgesetz*.[42] As stated earlier, the German *Grundgesetz* contains a provision concerning asylum. As it is, to say the least, doubtful whether (criminal) sanctions of carriers are consistent with the Geneva Convention, especially Article 27 ('the Contracting States shall issue identity papers to any refugee in their territory who does not possess a valid travel document'), which envisages the situation of undocumented

---

37. Most national air carriers are state-owned; in these cases the States in imposing fines are draining their own companies, and indirectly themselves, i.e., their taxpayers.

38. Art. 6 Aliens Act will contain, according to the draft, the carriers' obligations in these terms: 'The carrier (. . .) is obliged to take the necessary measures and to exercise the reasonably required control in order to prevent that (. . .) the alien does not fulfill the conditions of the first section of this article.' See Hand II 1990-1991, 22.142, Nos. 1 and 2, 4 June 1991, p. 2 and the astonishing explanatory statements on p. 10. Indeed, in this memorandum it is explained, that the legislative definition has to be construed on the background of the general system of criminal defences such as justifiable error or duress. To my mind it is utterly wrong to depend so heavily on rules for individual defences and escapes to a general penalization in the case of handling asylum seekers. If carriers are to be penalized for not thoroughly checking documents of aliens at large, the government should make a general exception as to those aliens who tell that they are asylum seekers. Check-in personnel are not the right persons to judge on the credibility of the '*vluchtrelaas*', the story about the reasons for leaving the country and may make the State responsible for refoulement.

39. Ibid. doc. B, p. 12, p. 15.

40. Trb. 1973 No. 109. Cf., A. Cruz, loc. cit. n. 35 and the discussion there.

41. Dr. Horst Glatzel, Chairman of the Member States of Schengen during the German Presidency, was very explicit in denying that there existed such an obligation at the meeting organized by the regional office of the UNHCR in Brussels under the auspices of Jacques Delors on the occasion of the 40th anniversary of UNHCR (20-21 June 1991).

42. See for a description Cruz, loc. cit. n. 35, p. 44.

refugees on the territory, Article 28 concerning travel documents, and Article 31 (refugees unlawfully in the country of refuge; States shall not impose penalties on account of their illegal entry or presence, etc.). It is furthermore doubtful whether a positive obligation to introduce penalties is in accordance with the Chicago Convention, and thus with, for example, Article 90 *et seq.* of the Dutch Constitution, especially Article 94. This would imply the necessity of a two-thirds majority in parliament, according to Article 91 S.3 of the Dutch Constitution if parliament really wanted to ratify the Schengen Convention, notwithstanding its many ugly aspects. Finally, the rather undefined and loose character of the incriminated behaviour makes it doubtful whether these municipal provisions comply with the *nullum crimen* principle as laid down in several criminal codes of the Member States, and in international instruments, such as Article 7 of the Rome Convention on Human Rights.[43]

6.   CONCLUSIONS

As I have tried to demonstrate, European governments are inspired by the fear that hordes from the South and the East, masquerading as asylum seekers, will invade the territory of the Member States of the European Community. Without sacrificing their positions concerning the competence of the EC concerning migration and asylum they have put into place overlapping and partly identical intergovernmental instruments to reduce the influx of these 'aliens'.

They eroded the strength of UNHCR by first diminishing their contributions to this United Nations agency[44] and then exploited its weakness by side-tracking it by not admitting it to the intergovernmental negotiations. The repeated vows in the Schengen Convention to uphold the Geneva Convention, and the obligations deriving from it, are considered as a magic wand to ward off all discrepancies. I have tried to demonstrate that there are several major deficiencies in the light of the Geneva Convention and other international instruments dealing with fundamental human rights.

These violations concern the obligation to cooperate with the UNHCR (Art. 31 Geneva Convention) which *vitium originis* put into motion a chain reaction of other violations: divesting themselves from the individual obligation to deal with asylum seekers and their requests, they risk violating the non-refoulement principle (Art. 33 of the Geneva Convention); in penalizing carriers of asylum seekers they frustrate the principle behind Article 3 Geneva Convention and the Universal Declaration on Human Rights; and by (seemingly?) advantaging extra-communitarian asylum seekers ('aliens') they are guilty of reverse discrimination of their own citizens, which is prohibited by Article 3 of the Geneva Convention.

43. Cf., Van Dijk-van Hoof, *De europese conventie in theorie en praktijk*, 1990, p. 389.
44. Cf., Jean-Luc Mathieu, *Migrants et Réfugiés* (1991) p. 101-102: 'En 1989, certains programmes ont dû être réduits, l'année s'étant néanmoins achevée sur un déficit de 40 million de dollars. Le Haut Commissaire a été conduit à démissioner. Des coupures, encore plus drastiques, dans ces programmes, ont été effectuées en 1990. Les difficultés financières, pour une institution presque intégralement financée grace à des contributions volontaires des Etats, sont l'expression d'une crise profonde.'

Add to these serious flaws the lack of democratic control and the lack of judicial control over decisions taken under the Schengen Convention, including the decisions to be taken by the intergovernmental Executive Committee, and the final conclusion should be clear: this is an unacceptable offer by despotic bureaucracies whose isolation has led to such positive feedbacks that they went off the rails. Parliaments should introduce a negative feedback and reject this monstrosity. If they lack imagination they may be impressed by the preview which the Italian Government staged in Bari, where many thousands of Albanian asylum seekers were dealt with in clear violation of Article 4 of the Fourth Protocol to the European Convention on Human Rights, which prohibits collective expulsion of aliens, and which, it is submitted, is a fundamental principle of Community law to which Italy has heretofore adhered.

COOPERATION IN THE FIELD OF ALIENS LAW
The granting of visas, passports and asylum and refugee status

C.D. de Jong[*]

1.   INTRODUCTORY REMARKS

Many features of the free movement of persons within Europe are bound up with the law on aliens, by which is meant here the system of rules regulating the entry and admission of aliens. In this contribution to the colloquium an attempt will be made to chart these features. The regulations will be discussed as these have evolved in the various existing frameworks, and the relationships outlined between the areas they govern. Section 2 addresses the measures which are to realise the free movement of persons, and Section 3 examines the question of which of these measures have already been taken, or are presently being formulated, and in which fora.

To translate the concept of the free movement of persons into actuality entails a complicated process of regulation rooted neither in the legal systems of the countries of Europe nor in their relations with one another. Its very essence being the crossing of national frontiers, this encapsulates the problem, since these frontiers are precisely the point at which the jurisdiction of one sovereign State ends and that of another begins. Crossing frontiers is anything but 'free'; on the contrary, in origin it is a fundamental step. With increasing mobility and closer ties developing between States it is a step that has become easier to take. Nevertheless, borders have remained something of an obstacle for human traffic, whether of a natural or artificial kind.

Other articles in this book deal at length with the political motives for introducing free movement for persons in Europe at this point in time, focusing on the political and social issues involved. The emphasis here is rather on the legal consequences of this political decision. It will become clear that what began as a mere formality — the gradual phasing out of checks on persons at frontier posts within Europe — will eventually constitute the basis for intensive cooperation between EC Member States, in the legal sphere as well as with regard to social issues.

Free movement of persons means that frontiers will no longer constitute a hindrance to people: they may remain intact, but as abstract, legal and cultural concepts rather than as tangible obstacles. To reach such a stage it is not enough to

* Head Aliens Affairs Department, Ministry of Justice, The Hague

H.G. Schermers et al., eds., Free Movement of Persons in Europe
© 1993, T.M.C. Asser Instituut, The Hague

dismantle the barriers and send the border officials home. As frontiers also mark the limits of legal systems, measures are needed to ensure that these systems do not run up against one another unshielded, as it were; where necessary the gaps between them must be bridged.

Given that the political decision to bring about the free movement of persons has already been taken, the measures required to accomplish this objective must be determined. I shall chiefly confine myself to the consequences of this choice for the law on aliens, and to the ways in which changes in the law on aliens will be reflected in other policy areas. This article will not deal with measures to be taken within the police and judiciary, however, nor with the problem of frontier controls, as these issues are discussed extensively by other contributors.

2.   THE FREE MOVEMENT OF PERSONS AND THE LAW ON ALIENS

In the first place, the free movement of persons originally means abolishing controls along Europe's internal frontiers. This does not imply automatically, however, that every person will have the right to cross each such unguarded border. For this to be the case, a further political decision is needed, namely the decision to grant the right of free circulation within Europe — a right which might theoretically be restricted to nationals of the countries concerned, or which might be extended to all aliens who are legally resident in one of these countries.

Simply abolishing internal frontier controls does mean, however, that the possibility of crossing a border without complying with the conditions of entry into the country concerned (referred to hereafter as 'illegal' entry) is subsequently unlimited. The quality of the border controls along the remaining, i.e., external, frontiers thus becomes a matter of common concern to all the Member States, as all will wish to prevent aliens from outside the Community from entering it illegally. Within the Community, it will no longer be possible to control the illegal crossing of borders, so that the internal monitoring of aliens will be the only way of countering the subsequent illegal residence of aliens in the countries concerned.

If the decision is made to grant the — restricted or unrestricted — right to free circulation within the area, the question of external border controls will become even more a matter of shared concern, as some of the conditions of entry — even along these external borders — will be dictated by the fact that nationals of the Member States may, in principle, circulate freely. It would make little sense to grant these persons the right of circulation within the area, whilst refusing them entry at the external borders.

The next step is the full harmonisation of the conditions of entry. This means that it will no longer matter at what border an alien enters the European area; the conditions of entry will be the same at each point. This will decrease the pressure on the internal monitoring of aliens, because there can then no longer be any question of aliens crossing an external border legally but subsequently crossing an external border of one of the other Member States illegally. Exceptions to this rule are not inconceivable, but the principle remains the same.

Having considered the conditions of entry, it is logical to turn next to policy on visas. Harmonisation is necessary in this connection, because for many aliens the possession of a valid visa is one of the conditions of entry. Complete harmonisation of these conditions would never, therefore, be possible, if it were easier to obtain a visa for one country than for another. If an unrestricted right of circulation were decided upon, it would even be necessary to develop a uniform visa for the entire territory, making it possible to travel freely between the countries concerned during a certain period of time without having to have a separate visa for each country. As a transitional measure, perhaps, countries might agree to recognise each other's visas.

The abolition of internal frontier controls has yet another consequence. It will be a fairly simple matter — physically at any rate — for an alien wishing to enter one of the countries concerned to try each one in turn until he or she is finally allowed to stay. Where asylum-seekers are concerned this is known as 'asylum-shopping'. The Member States will obviously want to come to some agreement to allocate responsibility in this respect. However, this will entail having confidence in each other's policy on admissions.

Equally, granting the right of circulation to aliens with residence permits in one of the Member States presupposes the same confidence. After all, it is by no means unlikely that aliens availing themselves of this right of circulation will subsequently try to remain — legally or illegally — in the country concerned.

This need for confidence automatically creates the desire to harmonise admission policy, at which point the whole gamut of policy on entry and admission will have become a Community matter.

This is not the end of the story, however. A common law on aliens may bring about a shift in the flow of immigrants between the Member States. If it no longer matters to which country one applies for admission, the alien may well choose the country with, for instance, the best social provisions. This means that in these fields too, closer cooperation will be required. Common policies on numerous social issues will thus come to be the rule.

Given the above it is not going too far to say that the abolition of internal border checks within Europe is one of the most radical steps towards a general process of social integration that might be undertaken. Each of these points in turn, with the exception of the external border controls, will be addressed in the following section.

2.1   Uniformity of conditions of entry and policy on visas

Each State imposes its own conditions subject to which aliens may be permitted to enter its territory. Once several States decide to abolish checks along their common borders, such differences can no longer be retained; an alien crossing the external border is at least physically admitted to the entire territory. One of the measures that must be taken is therefore ensuring uniformity of conditions of entry. This includes reaching agreement on the length of stay permitted. European States distinguish between 'short' and 'long' stays. The latter refers to the taking up of residence; this is subject to certain conditions and the person in question acquires the legal status of a resident of that country. Short stays are visits only. As residence is not involved, such stays are not fraught with drastic consequences for a State, so that conditions of entry for short stays are more lenient.

To achieve harmonisation of the conditions of entry for short stays, the following areas must be regulated:
— the recognition of travel documents;
— policy on visas;
— the safeguarding of public order and the protection of national security.

2.1.1   *Recognition of travel documents*

In the first place, an alien must possess travel documents which are appraised in the same way along the entire external border. Three requirements are made in this respect:
— is the document in question recognised on the basis of political considerations (a problem related to the recognition of States and governments)?
— does the document enable the identity of the bearer to be determined? and,
— does the document entitle the bearer to return to the State which issued it?

The first of these requirements may create problems when a list is being drawn up of travel documents recognised by all the countries concerned, as different issues are at stake here than in the case of the other two, recognition being an element of foreign policy with regard to a third State.

2.1.2   *Policy on visas*

The obligation to obtain a visa enables a State to monitor compliance with conditions of entry at an early stage, when the alien is still in a third country. A visa does not, however, confer the right to enter the issuing country; it is merely an extra check prior to arrival at that country's territory. Nevertheless it will smooth the control procedure at the external border. Although the possession of a valid visa, whenever necessary, is itself one of the conditions of entry (along with the possession of a valid travel document), a visa also represents compliance with all the other conditions of entry, as these are identical to the conditions which must be met to obtain a visa.

As in the case of border controls, a choice must be made between two different forms of harmonisation: the participating States may wish to set up a single joint authority to issue visas, or they may opt to cooperate with each other. The difference is both practical and formal. A visa issued by a national authority is a national visa; it is necessary that the other participating States recognise it as a visa which is valid, as indeed stated on the visa itself, within their territories as well. This is most important for the alien, who would otherwise have to obtain separate visas for each State.

The possession of a valid visa being one of the conditions of entry, the issue of visas should be conducted in a uniform fashion; in other words, a common policy on visas is needed. This means, firstly, reaching agreement on nationals of which countries should be required to obtain visas. No easy matter, as policy on visas is in the first place an element of foreign policy, and as such is influenced by factors such as the historical and political ties which have existed with the State in question. Once arrived at, this list could only be changed in consultation. In certain cases, particularly for humanitarian reasons, a State may decide to issue a visa to an alien who cannot, or cannot fully, comply with the conditions of entry. In this case, consideration might be given to restricting the geographical area to which such a visa would apply, so that the alien concerned would not have the right of circulation. It should be said, however, that a large-scale resort to this measure would undermine the whole system, since after internal frontier controls have been abolished, the risk of illegal entry into other Member States would once again raise its head.

As visas are to be valid for the entire territory of the participating States, or geographically restricted for certain particular reasons, this must be apparent to border officials. Visas must therefore be uniform in appearance. It must be clear by what process visas are to be issued, and which are the competent authorities in this field. This necessitates cooperation between the diplomatic and consular missions of the participating States which are responsible for issuing visas.

2.1.3   *Safeguarding public order and the protection of national security*

In principle, aliens whose presence constitutes a threat to public order or national security in one of the participating States will obviously not be eligible to enter its territory. This condition of entry is by nature more difficult to check than the possession of a valid travel document and a valid visa. As the absence of such threat is likewise a condition for obtaining a visa, this is checked twice, when the visa is issued and again when the alien enters the territory.

It is difficult to judge, when deciding on whether to issue a visa, that the person concerned does not constitute a threat to public order or national security in one of the participating States. In order to facilitate this assessment, the participating States will draw up a table listing categories of persons whose compliance with this condition should be checked prior to the issue of a visa.

In addition, each State has its own lists of individuals who pose a threat to public order or national security. These lists are also at the disposal of frontier control officials and the aliens department. The fact of an individual's name being on this list becomes important if this is given as the reason for entry being refused. A common list is needed of persons who should be refused entry, to be consulted by the authorities responsible for issuing visas and granting admission. Clearly, a fresh set of regulations will be needed with regard to this list, dealing with all aspects of the exchange of information, the storage of data and data protection.

2.2   The right of transit and circulation

Included in the provisions governing short stays but counted as a special category is transit through the participating States to the particular participating State in which the alien has been granted a long-stay permit. Closely connected with this is the right of aliens who have entered the territory of the participating States legally to circulate in that territory.

In the case of an alien who wishes to enter the territory merely in transit to a State in which he has the legal right of residence, the requirements exacted may be slacker than when deciding on whether to grant a random alien the right to a short stay. After all, an alien who has complied with the stricter conditions attached to a long stay in one State will be most likely to meet the lower requirements generally prevailing for short stay admittance in another. The only checks that are relevant are those on identity and residence permit, and in addition the check that the person poses no threat to public order or national security. Particularly for aliens who are presently obliged to obtain visas but who have been granted long-stay permits in one of the participating States, this will diminish the barriers they face, as they will no longer be obliged to furnish themselves with visas every time they cross a frontier.

The right of circulation will constitute another significant improvement upon aliens' travel options, and will be a direct consequence of the abolition of internal frontier controls. This highlights the role of the internal monitoring of aliens. All checks concerning an alien's stay in one of the participating countries will now be conducted internally rather than along the external borders. The conditions are simple, being no more than the conditions on which entry has been granted. As long as these conditions are met during the short stay, circulation constitutes no problem from the point of view of immigration. In order to retain some scope for the monitoring of aliens, measures may be considered such as the introduction of an obligation to register. This would ensure that records were kept of aliens who spend the night at hotels, boarding houses and so forth. In particular this would make it easier to check whether the total length of the short stay, as agreed by the countries concerned, is being exceeded.

2.3   Asylum seekers

A special regulation is needed for asylum seekers, i.e., people stating at the external border that they wish to be granted the right of residence with the status of recognised refugees in accordance with the Geneva Convention. This group differs from other categories of aliens in that the persons concerned cannot return to their country of origin; they are consequently requesting long rather than short stays. A special regulation is required because the flow of asylum seekers to Europe is still increasing, and only a small fraction of this group is ultimately accorded refugee status or admitted on other grounds.

The need for a shared set of regulations requires clarification. Each participating State would be happiest with an even distribution of asylum seekers, something difficult to achieve in a territory without internal border checks. After all, once having arrived in one of the participating countries, the asylum seeker will be able to travel to one of the other countries without any further checks and submit a fresh asylum application, in the event of the initial application having been, or threatening to be, dismissed by the first country.

To counter this process of 'asylum-shopping', a regulation may be drawn up to determine, on the basis of certain criteria, where the responsibility lies for dealing with each application for asylum. The intentions of the asylum seeker may continue to play a role, but responsibility should be allocated largely according to objective criteria such as the point of entry. An important basic principle is that each and every asylum application submitted on the territory of one of the countries concerned must be dealt with. This precludes the creation of what are known as 'refugees in orbit'.

Such agreements have attracted a good deal of criticism. The notion that one State should accept without question a negative decision arrived at by another — i.e., the State assigned responsibility in a given case — presupposes that countries have confidence in each other's policy. Formally, this confidence could be based on the fact that all the countries concerned have adopted, without geographical reservation, the Geneva Convention and the accompanying New York Protocol, given that this implies that they all comply with the obligations imposed by this Convention and Protocol.

On the other hand, it cannot be gainsaid that there are differences among the Twelve in respect of how the relevant provisions should be interpreted. The Handbook compiled by the UNHCR with a view to streamlining this interpretation to some extent is not always used in the same way. Explicit reservations have even been expressed concerning some of the points it makes. This means that it is currently possible for an asylum application to result in the granting of refugee status in one State and not in another. This fact has led various pressure groups to adopt a critical stance vis-à-vis such apportionment of responsibility. They feel that no such arrangement should be entered into unless proper guarantees exist that countries will pursue an identical policy concerning the interpretation of the Geneva Convention.

Such objections are often countered on two fronts. On the one hand, it is pointed out that allocations of responsibility should generally be seen as a preliminary step in the direction of further cooperation, in which better harmonisation of both formal and substantive asylum law will be achieved by the Member States. On the other hand, objections are parried by stressing that there will be nothing to prevent a State from dealing with a given application, even if responsibility has been allocated elsewhere. This will be particularly important if a State has reason to believe that it will attach different weight to the facts on which the application is based than would the State designated responsible. Another case in which a different State might assume responsibility is one in which hitherto unknown facts are put forward by an asylum seeker.

If there are frequent deviations from the allocation of responsibility, however, the system will obviously have limited effectiveness. In this case too, the only option is to bring about a better harmonisation of policy.

There are other considerations which make harmonisation of asylum policy unavoidable, once the decision has been made to allocate responsibility as outlined above. For an asylum seeker is already making a certain choice by presenting him/herself at a particular border, and this choice will be influenced in part by the criteria for allocating responsibility, if these are known to the person concerned. For instance, if the point of entry is the determining factor, asylum seekers will plan their route with care.

Many factors may determine the choice of a particular country. I should like to discuss a few of them here. If it is known that the chance of being admitted to a particular country is relatively high, the asylum seeker will be inclined to proceed directly to that country. Other reasons for adopting a selective approach are: if the material provisions for asylum seekers are of a relatively high standard in a particular country, or if there is a reasonably good chance of being able to eke out an existence in the informal sector; or if a country's policy on expulsions is such that there is a fairly good chance of asylum seekers being allowed to remain on a discretionary basis.

An allocation scheme might therefore mean States with an attractive reputation in this respect having to process a disproportionate number of requests, and perhaps even being obliged temporarily to withdraw from the allocation scheme.

Everything therefore points in the direction of further harmonisation of policy, not only on admitting asylum seekers, but also that on reception and expulsion. Ultimately collaboration will also be needed to equalise the extent and accessibility of social provisions. If no superfluous distinction is to be retained in this regard between legally resident aliens and the citizens of the country concerned, one of the strong principles underlying the burgeoning European policy on minorities, this amounts to nothing less than the harmonisation of the social security systems of the participating countries.

2.4   Harmonisation of policy on admission of aliens (excluding asylum)

Once the step of harmonising asylum policy has been taken, it will be equally necessary to harmonise general policy on permitting aliens to enter the country. If asylum seekers with a clearly ill-founded asylum application know that they have a poor chance of their application being granted in any of the participating countries, they will seek other ways of achieving their actual objective, which is immigration. For instance, if forming a family, gaining employment or setting up in business increase the chance of being permitted to stay in a particular country, these options will immediately be seized upon. Another phenomenon which has received less publicity but is no less important is the increasing number of applications for admission already being submitted on grounds other than a claim to refugee status. This will undoubtedly increase still further, if the only way for an asylum seeker refused asylum to stretch the length of his/her stay is to submit a fresh application for admission on other grounds. By illegally crossing internal borders (without checks) the former asylum seeker can submit such an application to the country which seems most promising, in order to evade any, national provisions making repeated applications on different grounds unacceptable. At the same time States will not (as yet) have at their disposal any scheme to allocate responsibility for dealing with cases unrelated to asylum, and in many States expulsion of an individual will be impossible before the application has been heard at least at first instance.

Subsequent to, or simultaneously with, the harmonisation of asylum policy, it will therefore also be necessary to harmonise other elements of admission policy. Some of the points concerned are already being aligned by the European Commission and the European Court of Human Rights, both of which have their seat in Strasbourg. This applies particularly to policy on family reunification, which has been elaborated by way of case-law on the basis of Article 8 of the European Convention for the Protection of Human Rights and Fundamental Freedoms (ECHR). On other points too, however, national variations in policy on expulsions are being increasingly curtailed on the basis of Article 3 of the ECHR.

With the harmonisation of these elements, too, of admission policy, a very high degree of social integration will follow. With regard to admission for the purposes of employment, for instance, policy in this area is directly linked to policy on the labour market, which has thus far been a largely domestic concern. It will now no longer be possible, however, for this to remain a domestic issue; this too will become a matter of shared concern for the participating countries. The same applies to the international aspects of cultural policy, once the admission of foreign artists and performers is no longer bound by national rules.

What began as a small technical adjustment — the removal of a few frontier barriers — proves to have the most far-reaching of consequences for social cooperation.

3.   ACTIVITIES BEING UNDERTAKEN WITHIN A EUROPEAN
        FRAMEWORK IN CONNECTION WITH THE FREE
        MOVEMENT OF PERSONS

Several of the measures geared to realising the free movement of persons in Europe, as enumerated above, have already been taken in the various European fora, which will be discussed here in the following order:
— Benelux;
— Schengen;
— European Communities;
— Council of Europe.

3.1   Benelux

The first cooperative step among European countries in the direction of the free movement of persons, abolishing internal border controls, was taken by the Benelux Economic Union, the economic cooperative framework in which Belgium, the Netherlands and Luxembourg work together. On 11 April 1960 the Agreement shifting border controls on persons to the external borders of the Benelux area was signed at Brussels. In Article 2 the countries concerned agree to scrap internal border controls:

> 'From such time as this Agreement enters into force each of the High Contracting Parties shall cease to exercise controls on persons along their common borders, and shall exercise controls at their external borders which shall apply to the Benelux area.'

It was upon this Agreement, and the orders made by the competent Benelux ministers on the basis of this Agreement, that the regulations formulated by the Schengen partners were modelled in the 1980s, added to which the Benelux countries' long years of experience in this respect was decidedly influential.

The Agreement provides for border controls — in particular checks on persons — at the external frontiers, the harmonisation of conditions of entry (including the regulation of transit and circulation by aliens) and policy on visas. There have never been any Benelux regulations, however, in the field of asylum law.

3.2   Schengen

On 14 June 1985, in the Luxembourg border town of Schengen, the Agreement between the Benelux countries, Germany and France concerning the gradual phasing out of controls along these countries' common borders, was signed. Articles 17 and 20 of this Agreement contain the following provisions:

> 'Where the movement of persons is concerned, the Parties shall strive to abolish controls at the shared frontiers, concentrating instead on the external frontiers. Prior to this and to this end they shall make every effort, where necessary, to harmonise statutory and administrative regulations relating to the prohibitions and restrictions on the basis of which these controls are conducted, and to take supplementary measures for the protection of security and for the prevention of illegal immigration on the part of subjects of non-Member States of the European Communities' (Art. 17).

> 'The Parties shall strive to achieve the harmonisation of their policies with regard to visas, and of the conditions of entry into their territory. As far as is possible they shall also prepare the harmonisation of their regulations governing certain aspects of the law relating to aliens with regard to nationals of non-Member States of the European Communities' (Art. 20).

On the basis of these obligations to take steps clearly aimed at creating a free zone without internal border controls, efforts were then made to devise the measures needed to compensate for the abolition of these controls. The Convention to implement the Schengen Agreement, signed — again at Schengen — on 19 June 1990, lays down the measures which are to be taken to accompany the abolition of internal border controls.

The first provision of this so called Schengen Convention stipulates that internal border controls on persons shall cease to exist and that these shall only be, temporarily, reinstated in highly exceptional circumstances. Regulations then follow concerning the practicalities of border crossings, and the principles are enunciated on the basis of which controls on persons will be conducted at the external borders.

The harmonisation of conditions of entry for short (three months) stays has likewise been incorporated into the Schengen Convention. Also included are specific regulations for the transit and circulation of aliens in the territory of the Schengen partners. In order to provide States with the scope, should they so desire, to admit aliens who do not comply with the conditions of entry, a provision to that effect is included, with regard to both conditions of entry and conditions to be met prior to the issue of a visa.

The harmonisation of policy on visas exhibits a phased structure. The Schengen partners have committed themselves to introducing a standardised visa, and to reaching agreement concerning the list of countries whose nationals are to be obliged to obtain visas. The remaining elements of visa policy (i.e., issue, cost, etc.) must likewise be harmonised. During the transitional stage before the introduction of a standard visa, while this common policy is being shaped and harmonised, the States concerned will recognise each other's visas, thus creating immediately tangible advantages for foreign nationals.

The Schengen partners also undertake in the Convention to introduce (national) statutory penalties that may be imposed on transport companies responsible for carrying aliens without the requisite travel documents or visas to the territory of these States. Likewise, the transportation of illegal aliens to the Schengen territory for the pursuit of gain is to be made a statutory offence in each of the countries concerned.

Although the Schengen partners have agreed to harmonise their policy on the granting of asylum, the Convention goes no further than to lay down a regulation determining which State shall bear responsibility for dealing with an asylum application submitted on the territory of the Schengen partners. This regulation largely corresponds with the one incorporated into the European Asylum Convention (see below in section 3.3.2) but deviates minimally from this on certain points because on the basis of the Schengen Convention a standardised form of control will be conducted at the external borders, internal frontier controls having altogether ceased to exist.

3.3   European Communities

The steps that have been taken in the framework of the EC may be distinguished according to whether they have or have not been taken through Community channels. This distinction is presently of some topical interest, as is the debate being thrashed out on the interpretation of Article 8A of the EEC Treaty, which sets the realisation of the single European market as an objective. Important questions raised in this debate are whether this internal market must be brought about by the Community institutions or whether this is not obligatory with regard to the movement of persons; this is related to the question of whether the abolition of internal frontier controls, including those on nationals of third countries, is in fact implicit in the intention expressed to create a single European market. This latter point is crucial to the realisation of the free movement of persons within Europe. The distinction between EC and third country nationals means in practice that the free movement of persons (in this case, of EC nationals) is impossible to achieve since it entails retaining internal frontier controls. EC nationals could not be exempted from checks in this situation, as they would at least have to produce proof of identity to determine whether they need be checked! Article 8A of the EEC Treaty should therefore be interpreted as implying that the free movement of persons requires the abolition of internal frontier checks. To date, however, reaching agreement on this interpretation has proved impossible.

The first question concerning the competence of the EC to devise the measures referred to in section 2 above will not now be examined in full. The Commission has been marking time in anticipation of the progress expected in intergovernmental bodies. At the time of the drafting of the Single European Act, however, the Commission did adopt the stand that it was competent to draw up the Community legislation that would bring into effect the free movement of persons, including the compensatory measures that would be needed. According to the White Paper it presented to the European Council in June 1985, the Commission's intentions were as follows:

'As a first step, the Commission will propose in 1988 at the latest coordination of the rules on residence, entry and access to employment, applicable to nationals of non-Community countries. Measures will be proposed also in 1988 at the latest on the right of asylum and the position of refugees. [...] It will therefore be necessary to go further than the existing collaboration in the context of political cooperation and develop a Community policy on visas.'

The Commission did not, however, take these steps, and the measures were subsequently discussed in an intergovernmental framework.

The questions referred to above have also been raised in the European Political Union (EPU) negotiations. These negotiations are not yet at a sufficiently advanced stage to enable any pronouncement to be made concerning the ultimate form EPU will take, but the movement of persons will certainly be discussed, as one of the issues requiring the Twelve to reach new agreements.

3.3.1   Community channels

Various measures have already been taken in a Community framework to realise the free movement of persons. It is characteristic of these regulations, however, that their main concern is (and indeed, some believe that it can only be) EC nationals, and is in many ways even further limited to those EC nationals engaged in economic activity, the 'favoured EC nationals', as they are referred to. On the basis of Article 3c of the EEC Treaty, Regulation 1612/68/EEC and Directive 68/360/EEC have been adopted by the Council, implementation measures concerning the free movement of employees and their families. Measures have been taken for this category of persons in the area of standardising conditions of entry, as well as more far-reaching measures concerning long-term residence, in particular with regard to the access to social provisions. These EC nationals are granted short-stay permits if they do not constitute a burden to public funds. This regulation is being extended by Directives

90/364/EEC, 90/365/EEC and 90/366/EEC to effectively cover all EC nationals. If they possess sufficient resources and have taken out adequate health insurance, they may be admitted to another EC State.

It would appear impossible, therefore, to extend these Community measures without again becoming enmeshed in the problematic questions broached above. For any extension would either involve including non-EC nationals or ruling on points concerning which the EC's competence is a matter of controversy.

3.3.2   *Intergovernmental channels*

In the intergovernmental cooperation among EC States, many measures are presently under discussion and several have already been taken. Intergovernmental cooperation takes the form of consultations between ministers responsible for immigration affairs, these ministers being assisted by the offices of the Ad Hoc Group on Immigration, which prepares all the measures. Furthermore, the measures are enumerated in the Palma Document, which was compiled by the Coordinators Group dealing with the free movement of persons, a group of senior national officials who report to the European Council on the progress made towards achieving the free movement of persons. All measures concerning the shifting of the point at which frontier controls on persons are conducted, the harmonisation of the conditions of entry and the regulation of the rights of transit and circulation, as discussed in section 2 above, are currently under preparation. The difference in interpretations of Article 8A of the EEC Treaty also affects the preparation of these measures, particularly those related to the shifting of the point of control.

Where the harmonisation of asylum law is concerned, the EC States have now signed, in Dublin, the Convention determining the Member State responsible for examining requests for asylum submitted in one of the EC Member States (European Asylum Convention). The basic principle of this Convention is that such a request must be dealt with by one of the Member States. Therein lies the significance of this Convention, which rules out the possibility, in future, of there being 'refugees in orbit' among the EC States. To elaborate this basic principle the Convention lays down a number of criteria to determine where the responsibility for dealing with a particular request lies, criteria essentially relating to the procedure by which the asylum seeker was permitted to enter EC territory. It should be added that an important exceptional clause gives States the right to retain responsibility for a given case on the basis of their domestic law.

It has already been made clear, in section 2.3 above, that a document such as the European Asylum Convention will immediately lead to more intensive cooperation as regards policy on admission. The European Council at Luxembourg therefore decided recently that asylum law should be harmonised and that there should be close cooperation with a view to broadening the scope of this harmonisation to encompass immigration policy in general. This immediately places a heavy burden upon the Dutch Presidency, during which, at the very least, a concrete schedule must be agreed upon.

A sound step towards harmonising asylum policy throughout the EC would be to plan talks on various key points of this policy, to include, for instance:
— the devising of a procedure to deal with applications for asylum that are manifestly ill-founded;
— the concept of the 'country of first asylum';
— asylum policy in the narrow sense.
A definite need is felt in the Member States for a procedure to deal with requests for asylum that are manifestly ill-founded, now that it is clear that the majority of persons submitting applications in Europe are in fact economic migrants. At present many States already have such procedures, which do not differ greatly from each other in terms of content. This is why the short-term introduction of a uniform priority procedure may be considered. First and foremost, however, a clear definition of 'manifestly ill-founded' must be formulated. The next step would be to agree upon the length of time needed for the processing of an application, and — also of pressing concern — to align the provision made for the reception of asylum seekers whose requests are being dealt with. In addition, the legal safeguards furnished by the different States, and related matters, should at least be amenable to comparison.

Although the short-term introduction of a standard procedure to deal with manifestly ill-founded requests for asylum would appear likely, the difficulties involved should not be underestimated. It will be necessary to take account of significant differences between the procedures currently employed; some countries, for instance, require the initial decision to be made by an independent body. Changes made here all too easily verge on tampering with the essential organisational structure of a State, and with the balance between the executive and the judiciary.

The general rule employed by the Twelve is that of the 'country of first asylum'. This entails that if there is sufficient protection from the risk of refoulement in the country where an alien had stayed prior to entering the country in which he has submitted an application for asylum, the latter is entitled to send the individual back to the 'country of first asylum'.

This rule is not applied uniformly everywhere, however. Some Member States proceed on the assumption that the request should be dealt with anyway, in accordance with domestic case-law, even in cases involving a 'country of first asylum'. If the asylum seeker obtains the refugee status he or she can still be sent back to the country of first asylum but at least he or she enjoys the rights based on this refugee status. If the application is dismissed, the person concerned may be sent back to either the country of first asylum, or to the country of origin.

Other differences concern the interpretation of the concept of the country of first asylum itself. How long should an asylum seeker have stayed in the country concerned to justify the conclusion that he could have submitted his application there? Another point still in need of clarification is how the criterion of 'sufficient protection from refoulement' is applied in practice. If asylum seekers are to be expelled on the principle that there is a country of first asylum, guarantees must be given that the request for asylum will indeed be dealt with by that country.

'Asylum policy in the narrow sense' should be taken to refer to the set of criteria in the light of which a request for asylum is examined in order to decide whether to grant refugee status. What this comes down to is in effect the interpretation of the 1951 Geneva Convention. It is true that this 'asylum policy in the narrow sense' consists of a number of well-known, general tenets, but when an official is examining a particular application, his/her previous experience and knowledge of specific cases play at least as great a role. This makes harmonisation of asylum policy a good deal more complicated. Harmonisation will therefore have to be more in the nature of an abstract legal framework than a detailed European system of regulations.

In connection with this consideration could be given to drafting lists of indicators for each country of origin, for common use, facilitating the assessment of whether a particular request for asylum is well-founded. It is therefore essential to establish that the harmonisation of asylum policy is not the same thing as reaching agreement on a judicial framework. In practice what proves to be far more important is that there should be unanimity within the Community concerning the political assessment of the situation in the country of origin. This could be achieved by way of a system of pooled reports and by setting up a European database of 'hard' facts (possibly in collaboration with the UNHCR). A very different way to standardise the examination of requests for asylum would be to give the European Court of Justice a supervisory role, provided that the Court were to acquire the competence to answer preliminary questions posed by domestic courts in the area of asylum law.

3.4   Council of Europe

Since the Second World War, the Council of Europe has in many respects played a key role in cooperation between the democratic States of Europe. Although the movement of persons is not, according to its mandate, one of the Council's central concerns, this issue has nevertheless received a great deal of attention in recent times. In this connection reference should be made to the activities of existing committees within the Council, in particular the European Committee on Migration (CDMG) and the Ad hoc committee of experts on the legal aspects of territorial asylum, refugees and stateless persons (CAHAR).

The CDMG is the coordinating body of the Council of Europe in the areas of migration and the development of measures concerning the integration of aliens legally resident in the territory of the Member States. CAHAR was established in 1977 to work towards a convention on territorial asylum. This never materialised, partly because the Member States were reluctant to relinquish their sovereignty in regard to the admission of aliens. The groundwork needed before a convention could be drafted to determine the Member State responsible for dealing with requests for asylum consumed so much time that CAHAR, and therefore also the Council, was overtaken by the increased pace at which the Schengen partners and the Twelve (through intergovernmental channels) carried through their agreements. It is uncertain whether the present draft will ever develop into a convention, as the EC Member States presently have great reservations about becoming party to a convention that departs from the agreement already reached in the context of Schengen and the intergovernmental framework of the Twelve. It would appear more likely that the reverse process will occur, that is to say that non-EC members of the Council of Europe will become party to one or more of the instruments already agreed upon.

With the liberalisation of eastern Europe, the Council has received a fresh impulse as a forum for dialogue and a platform for the preparation of closer cooperation between western Europe and the previous eastern bloc States. This form of cooperation may develop in due course as something of an antechamber, as it were, to EC membership.

In January 1991 a conference was held in Vienna, on the initiative of Austria, concerning the implications of the changes in eastern Europe, in particular in the realm of migration. Agreements were reached on the form cooperation on migration should take, in relation to the movement of persons, social and economic development and the monitoring of developments in the States of eastern Europe. Three working groups are presently elaborating the details, and are due to make their next progress report in September 1991.

Finally, reference should be made to the most important work of the European Commission and the European Court for Human Rights. It may very well be that part of the harmonisation process of aliens law will be in the hands of these bodies, which have shown time and again the relevance of some articles of the European Convention on Human Rights in this respect.

COOPERATION IN THE FIELD OF ALIENS LAW IN THE UNITED KINGDOM AND IRELAND

J.P. Gardner[*]

1.   INTRODUCTION

According to statistics published by the Commission of the European Communities, out of every ten foreigners residing in a Community country, only four come from another Member State. It is in only four Member States (Belgium, Spain, Ireland and Luxembourg) that nationals from other Members States are more numerous than nationals from third countries. Although in four Community countries (Spain, Greece, Italy and Portugal) the total number of foreigners as a proportion of the population is less than one per cent, seven per cent of the population of Ireland and four per cent of the population of the United Kingdom are non-nationals and in the United Kingdom one-third of the latter are Community citizens, while the other two-thirds are from third States.

Against this background, this short report will summarise the legal machinery whereby the United Kingdom and Ireland respectively regulate aliens law.

This report will further be divided into the following constituent elements. Chapter 2 provides a review of the international instruments to which each country is a party and of the reservations which have been entered into, notably in relation to the United Nations Convention relative to the status of refugees and in respect of the United Kingdom's declaration as to the meaning of 'national' in the EC Treaties. Chapter 3 gives a description of the legislative framework adopted in each of the two countries, first relating to the establishment of nationality and citizenship affiliation in the United Kingdom and in Ireland respectively, and hence the definition provided of non-nationals and the scope and operation of that definition, and, secondly, the legislation relating to the control and regulation of immigration. In the case of the United Kingdom, both the treatment of nationality and immigration in the framework legislation makes particular provision for the treatment of nationals of Commonwealth countries, which will be summarised at this point. Chapter 4 will consider the nature of the delegated rules created in each of the United Kingdom and Ireland which provide the detailed regulation of immigration and will compare and contrast the nature of these rules with other forms of delegated legislation. This comparison is particularly important in the

* Director, The British Institute of International and Comparative Law, with S. Beckwith and A. Boadita-Cormican, Research Officers at The British Institute of International and Comparative Law.

H.G. Schermers et al., eds., Free Movement of Persons in Europe
© 1993, T.M.C. Asser Instituut, The Hague.

United Kingdom in the light of the *sui generis* nature of the immigration rules both as to form and interpretation.

Chapter 5 will briefly summarise the adjudication machinery which interprets the system of primary legislation and secondary rules described in chapters 2 and 3. It will also shortly illustrate examples of litigation in relevant areas where the exercise of discretionary powers afforded by the primary legislation (e.g., section 31 Immigration Act granting a generalised discretion to permit any alien person to enter the United Kingdom) as well as the compliance of the delegated rules with the doctrine of vires. Finally, chapter 6 will briefly illustrate the cooperation between the United Kingdom and Ireland through the common travel area, and illustrate by reference to the periodic adjustments made to access to the United Kingdom for Commonwealth subjects on the arrangements made for such persons to enter Ireland.

2.   INTERNATIONAL INSTRUMENTS

2.1   The 1951 Convention and the 1967 Protocol Relating to the Status of Refugees

The United Kingdom and Ireland are parties to the 1951 Convention (the Convention) and the 1967 Protocol (the Protocol) Relating to the Status of Refugees.[1] The Convention was signed by the UK on 28 July 1951 and ratified on 11 March 1954. Ireland acceded to the Convention on 29 November 1956.[2] Although bound by the Convention in international law, neither State has incorporated it into domestic law through legislation. Thus the Convention's provisions cannot be invoked directly in the Irish courts. The position in the United Kingdom is more complex since it appears that reliance may be placed on the Convention in certain circumstances and that the law in this area is evolving.[3]

Article 1 of the Convention defines 'refugee'. The definition could be applied to persons who became refugees within the meaning of the Convention by virtue of 'events occurring in Europe before 1 January 1951' (Art. 1(B)(a)) or 'events occurring in Europe or elsewhere before 1 January 1951' (Art. 1(B)(b)) at the option of the States party to the Convention. This option could be exercised by means of a declaration under Article 1, Section B(a) or Article 1, Section B(b) as appropriate. The UK and Ireland made declarations applying Section B(b) of Article 1.[4]

The strict wording of the Convention limited its application to persons who became refugees as a result of events occurring before 1951. The Protocol allowed States who became a party to it to apply Articles 2-34 of the Convention to refugees defined in Article 1 thereof without this limitation. The UK acceded to the Protocol on 4

---

1. 189 UNTS 150 and 606 UNTS 267 respectively.
2. Multilateral Treaties Deposited with the Secretary-General, Status as at 31 December 1988 ST/LEG/Ser.E/7 p.188.
3. See Chapter 3.3 *infra*.
4. *Supra*, n. 2, p. 189.

September 1968, Ireland acceded on 6 November 1968.[5] Apart, therefore, from the removal of the above-mentioned limitation, the obligations assumed under the Protocol are the same as those provided for in the Convention and, where relevant, these are dealt with below.

The UK made four reservations to the provisions of the Convention which were accompanied by a commentary,[6] Ireland also made four reservations.[7] No objections were made to these reservations.[8]

Both Governments made reservations to Article 17 of the Convention which calls for most-favoured-nation treatment of refugees lawfully staying in a Contracting State's territory as regards the right to engage in wage-earning employment. The permissible restrictions on this requirement, set out in paragraph 2 of Article 17, are not to be applied, *inter alia*, to a refugee who has completed three years' residence in the country or who has one or more children possessing the nationality of the country of residence. The UK reservation cuts down these immunities, omitting the latter exception relating to children and increasing the period of residence prescribed in the former case to four years but otherwise accepts paragraph 2 of Article 17. The Irish Government's reservation seems broader, effectively rejecting the application of most-favoured-nation treatment in stating that the Government does not undertake, pursuant to Article 17, to grant to refugees rights of wage-earning employment more favourable than those granted to aliens generally.

To Article 25 of the Convention, which provides for the granting of administrative assistance to a refugee by the authorities of the State in which he resides, reservations were made by the Governments of the UK and Ireland respectively. The UK Government states in its reservation that it could not undertake to give effect to the obligations contained in paragraphs 1 and 2 of Article 25 and that it undertook to apply paragraph 3 only so far as the law allows. Paragraph 1 requires the arrangement of administrative assistance from the national authority or an international authority for a refugee when the exercise of a right by that refugee would normally require the assistance of authorities of a foreign country to whom he cannot have recourse. Paragraph 2 requires the national or international authority concerned to ensure the delivery to refugees of documents or certifications which would normally be delivered to aliens by or through their national authorities. Paragraph 3 allows such documents to take the place of the official documents which would otherwise have been delivered by the refugee's national authorities. In its commentary, the UK Government stated that no arrangements exist in the UK for the provision of the assistance required by Article 25 and that no such arrangements had been found necessary in the case of refugees. It was stated that any need for the documents or certifications mentioned in paragraph 2 would be met by affidavits. The Government of Ireland undertook to give effect to

5. *Supra*, n. 2, p. 212.
6. *Supra*, n. 2, pp. 196-197.
7. *Supra*, n. 2, p. 192.
8. *Supra*, n. 2, p. 198.

Article 25 only insofar as may be practicable and permissible under the laws of Ireland but there was no accompanying commentary to indicate the possible effects of this.

The Convention, in Article 8, seeks to exempt refugees from the application of exceptional measures which might otherwise affect them by reason only of their nationality. Article 9 expressly preserves the right of States to take 'provisional measures' on grounds of national security against a person 'pending a determination by the Contracting State that that person is in fact a refugee and that the continuance of such measures is necessary in his case in the interests of national security.' The UK made a reservation concerning both of these provisions. It is stated that Article 8 will not prevent the exercise of rights by the Government over property acquired as an Allied or Associated Power under a Treaty of Peace concluded as a result of the Second World War. Property otherwise under the control of the Government as a result of the existence of a state of war at the date of commencement of the Convention is also to be considered beyond the scope of Article 8. The reservation thus appears to further entrench the powers reserved under Article 9.

The UK also made a reservation to Article 24 of the Convention which requires lawfully resident refugees to be afforded equal treatment with nationals in matters of labour legislation and social security. As regards the social security matters set out in paragraph 1 of the Article, the UK undertook to apply those which fell within the scope of the National Health Service only so far as the law allows. The UK commentary suggests that this reservation was intended to preserve the power existing under national legislation to make charges to persons not ordinarily resident in Great Britain (which would include refugees) who receive treatment under the service. The UK also undertook only to apply so far as the law allows the provisions of paragraph 2 of Article 24, which would require that any right to compensation for industrial injury or occupational disease due to the family of a refugee by reason of his death should not be affected by the fact that the beneficiary is resident outside the territory of the Contracting State. The commentary shows that this reservation was necessary because the scheme of Industrial Injuries Insurance in Great Britain did not, in general, meet the requirements of paragraph 2.

As regards reservations made by the Irish Government, there are two which have not already been mentioned. The first is an interpretive statement in relation to Article 32(1) which prohibits expulsion of a refugee lawfully in the territory 'save on grounds of national security or public order' and 'in accordance with due process of law.' The Irish Government stated that it would interpret the latter phrase as meaning 'in accordance with a procedure provided by law' and 'public order' as meaning 'public policy'. Finally, with respect to Article 29 which prohibits the imposition of various charges and taxes on refugees at a higher rate or other than those levied on nationals in similar situations, the Irish Government stated that it did not undertake to apply more favourable treatment to refugees in relation to income tax than that accorded to aliens generally.

2.2   Council of Europe Conventions

The European Agreement on the Abolition of Visas for Refugees 1959[9] (the Visa Agreement) seeks to facilitate travel for refugees residing in the parties' territories by granting such persons an exemption from the requirement of a visa for travel between the territories of parties to the Visa Agreement where, *inter alia*, they hold a travel document issued in accordance with the 1951 Convention on the Status of Refugees. The Visa Agreement was originally open to Council of Europe members but after its coming into force other States could be invited to accede to it by the Committee of Ministers. Ireland and the UK are both Council of Europe members and both have acceded to the Visa Agreement. The UK became a party on 26 August 1968 and Ireland became a party on 29 October 1969.[10]

The UK is also a party to the European Agreement on Transfer of Responsibility for Refugees 1980.[11] This Council of Europe Convention attempts to regulate in a uniform manner the question of transfer of responsibility for refugees between contracting States in order to facilitate the implementation of Article 28 of the 1951 Convention on the Status of Refugees. It is open to Council of Europe Members and to other States on the invitation of the Committee of Ministers. Article 1 of the 1980 Agreement expressly adopts the definition of 'refugee' set out in the Convention and Protocol. The UK was an original signatory to the Agreement which it ratified on 1 October 1986.[12]

2.3   The EC Treaties and the Final Act of the Treaty of Accession

By the Final Act and the terms of the Treaty of Accession of 22 January 1972 the United Kingdom and Ireland became parties to the Treaties. The treaties establish freedom of movement for workers within the meaning of EEC Articles 48 to 50, and the case-law of the European Court of Justice clearly illustrates that this term is a Community term, whose interpretation cannot be restricted by domestic law.[13] However, the United Kingdom annexed a Declaration to the Final Act on the definition of the term 'nationals'. This Declaration reflects the Declaration of the Federal Republic of Germany made on its accession to the Treaties establishing the European Communities. However, whereas the German Declaration set out the definition of Germans taken from the German Basic Law,[14] the United Kingdom Declaration created a class of 'nationals' for the purposes of the Treaties which did not correspond with an existing group identified by United Kingdom law. This selective definition was

---

9. 176 UNTS 85.

10. M.J. Bowman and D.J. Harris, *Multilateral Treaties, Index and Current Status* (1984) p. 238.

11. 20 ILM (1981) 1391.

12. Bowman and Harris, op. cit. n. 10, pp. 459-460; Seventh Supp. 1990 p. 172.

13. Case 75/63 *Hoekstra* v. *Bestuur der Bedrijfsvereniging voor Detailhandel en Ambachten* [1964] ECR 177.

14. The Declaration provides: 'All Germans as defined in the Basic Law for the Federal Republic of Germany shall be considered nationals of the Federal Republic of Germany.'

made necessary by the complex structure of the nationality arrangements which applied in the United Kingdom[15] and it has been suggested that the definition is not unreasonable as it:

> '. . . corresponds almost exactly to what the definition of a United Kingdom citizen would be if it had been decided to create such a citizenship on the basis of the same criteria as were adopted by other Commonwealth countries when they framed their citizenship laws.'[16]

That being so, it is to be noted that the Declaration cannot be supported in the face of a challenge that it must give way to the supremacy of Community law as to the scope of the term 'nationals' on the basis which supports the German Declaration, that the Declaration reflects the pre-established domestic legal order applied to individuals.

2.4   European Community 'Association Agreements'

Pursuant to its powers under Article 238 of the EEC Treaty, the European Community has entered into a number of agreements, known as 'Association Agreements', with non-EC countries. These agreements relate to various forms of cooperation between the Community and third States often including cooperation in the field of labour. Usually the Member States of the Community and the third State are required by a particular agreement to adopt reciprocal arrangements as regards matters such as social security and access to employment. The Agreement between the Community and Morocco is a typical example.[17] Article 40 of the EEC-Morocco Agreement states:

> 'The treatment accorded by each Member State to workers of Moroccan nationality employed in its territory shall be free from any discrimination based on nationality, as regards working conditions or remuneration, in relation to its own nationals. Morocco shall accord the same treatment to workers who are nationals of a Member State and employed in its territory.'

As members of the European Community, the UK and Ireland may be directly bound by provisions of such agreements according to the principle of 'direct applicability' in EEC law. In a recent case Article 41 of the EEC-Morocco Agreement was found by the European Court of Justice to be directly applicable in the Member States.[18] The relevant provision, which prohibited discrimination in matters of social security, was found to be sufficiently clear and precise and not subject, in its implementation or

---

15. See *infra*, Chapter 2.1.

16. T.C. Hartley, 'The International Scope of the Community Provisions Concerning Free Movement of Workers', in F.G. Jacobs ed., *European Law and the Individual* (1976) at p. 30. But see ibid., R. Plender, 'An Incipient Form of European Citizenship' and notes.

17. OJ 1978 L 264.

18. Case C-18/90 *Office Nationale de l'Emploi (ONEM)* v. *Bahia Kziber*, 31 January 1991, [1991] ECR I-199.

effects, to the adoption of any subsequent measure so it could be regarded as being directly applicable in Member States.[19]

2.5 Summary

It can be seen from the foregoing brief analysis of the international instruments which the UK and Ireland have undertaken to apply that the international obligations in relation to the treatment of refugees and other non-nationals which bind each State are broadly similar. Membership of the EEC has resulted in an inevitable convergence of obligations arising out of the agreements concluded by the Community. Membership of the Council of Europe has resulted in identical international obligations as required by the Visa Agreement although the UK alone of the two States has entered into the 1980 Agreement on the Transfer of Responsibility for refugees. As regards the 1951 Convention on the Status of Refugees the obligations assumed by each State are broadly of the same scope. Despite the different reservations made by each State there remain thirty substantive obligations to which neither party made a reservation.

3. THE LEGISLATIVE FRAMEWORK OF NATIONALITY AND IMMIGRATION LAW

3.1 Nationality and the definition of 'aliens'

In the case of the United Kingdom the British Nationality Act 1981 defines a British citizen. The first codification of the law on nationality and citizenship was the British Nationality and Status of Aliens Act 1914. The 1914 Act and subsequent legislation adhered to the traditional methods of acquisition of citizenship through birth, by descent and by naturalisation. However, the first two of these methods, known as the *jus soli* and the *jus sanguinis* respectively have been modified by the 1981 British Nationality Act.

Prior to the 1981 Act a complex concept of 'Citizenship of the United Kingdom and Colonies' was applicable in UK law.[20] The 1981 Act attempted to simplify this notion and to remove the anomalous situation relating to immigration law whereby the classification of persons who were not subject to immigration restrictions,[21] did not coincide with the definition of citizen of the UK and Colonies. The 1981 Act creates three separate citizenships in place of the previous definitions: viz., British citizenship, British Dependent Territories citizenship and British Overseas citizenship. In addition

---

19. For other examples of Association Agreements see European Community agreements with Algeria (OJ 1978 L 263); Egypt (OJ 1978 L 266); Jordan (OJ 1978 L 268); Lebanon (OJ 1978 L 267); Syria (OJ 1978 L 269); Tunisia (OJ 1978 L 265).

20. For the significance of this position for the definition of nationals under the EC Treaties see Chapter 2, section 3 above.

21. Immigration Act 1971, section 2.

to these categories of citizenship, other categories remain: British protected persons, Commonwealth citizens and citizens of Ireland — none of whom are aliens.[22]

The principal method of obtaining British citizenship under the 1981 Act is through birth in the UK to a parent who is a British citizen or who is settled in the UK. British citizenship can also be obtained by a person born outside the UK to a parent who is a British citizen by birth, adoption, registration or naturalisation. Adoption, registration, naturalisation or marriage to a British citizen are among the other means of acquiring citizenship under the 1981 Act.

In Ireland *Bunreacht na h'Eireann* (Constitution of 1937) provides, in Article 9, that the future acquisition and loss of Irish nationality and citizenship shall be determined in accordance with law and that no person may be excluded from Irish nationality and citizenship by reason of their sex. The law governing Irish citizenship is contained in the Irish Nationality and Citizenship Acts of 1956 and 1986. Unlike the current UK legislation, the Irish legislation retains the traditional notions of the *jus soli* and the *jus sanguinis* and there is no multi-form notion of Irish citizenship such as that outlined above in relation to citizenship in UK law. Irish citizenship can be acquired by birth in Ireland or by a person whose parent was an Irish citizen at the time of the person's birth. The legislation also provides for the acquisition of citizenship by, *inter alia*, adoption, registration, naturalisation, or marriage to an Irish citizen.

In the UK 'alien' is defined in the 1981 British Nationality Act section 50(1) as a 'person who is neither a Commonwealth citizen nor a British protected person nor a citizen of the Republic of Ireland.' As will be seen below, UK immigration controls no longer distinguish between the control of aliens and the control of Commonwealth citizens.

The principal Irish legislation relating to the definition of aliens is the 1935 Aliens Act which in section 2 defines an alien as 'a person who is not a citizen of *Saorstat Eireann*.' However, this definition has been amended, by statutory instrument under the Act, to exclude from the definition persons born in Great Britain (including the Channel Islands and the Isle of Man) or Northern Ireland. It is interesting to note that the category of persons 'born' in the aforementioned territories may include some persons who are not entitled to British citizenship under the provisions of the 1981 UK legislation and may exclude others who are entitled to citizenship under that legislation. There is thus a lack of symmetry between the Irish definition of 'alien' and the UK equivalent. Irish immigration control is exercised in relation to 'aliens'.

3.2   Immigration control

The control of immigration in the UK is regulated by the 1971 Immigration Act. This act ended the formal distinction which had previously existed between the control of aliens and the control of Commonwealth citizens. The 1971 Act replaces earlier legislation and substituted a single code on immigration control. The first part of the Act classifies those with right of abode in the UK as 'patrials' and those without as

---

22.   Section 50(1) 1981 Act.

'non-patrials'. Provisions for the regulation and control of non-patrials are also set out in this part. The Secretary of State is empowered to make rules of practice to be followed in the administration of the Act.[23] These rules of practice relate to such matters as leave to enter and remain in the UK along with conditions which may be attached to such leave. They must be laid before Parliament which can disapprove the rules by resolution within forty days. The power under the Act to give or refuse leave to enter the UK is exercised by immigration officers.[24] The power to give leave to remain in the UK or to vary such leave is to be exercised by the Secretary of State.[25]

Part II of the 1971 Act sets up a system of appeals. Appeal in general lies first to an adjudicator and subsequently to an Immigration Appeals Tribunal.[26] In some circumstances there may be an appeal directly to the Tribunal. Part III of the Act provides for criminal proceedings to be brought against illegal immigrants.

An interesting feature of UK immigration law is that control is exercised not only over aliens but also over Commonwealth citizens who, as already noted, are excluded from the definition of 'aliens'. The two classes are not completely assimilated. Commonwealth citizens are not required, for example, to register with the police while staying in the UK although aliens must do this. Moreover, the 1971 Act included a saving in section 15(5) preserving the statutory rights to enter and remain of any Commonwealth citizen 'settled' in the UK on 1 January 1973 and any wife or child of such a person who were themselves Commonwealth citizens.[27] Other distinctions existing between the position of Commonwealth citizens and the position of aliens include the fact that certain categories of entry are only available to Commonwealth citizens.

The position in Ireland is governed by the Aliens Act 1935 which is entitled 'An Act to Provide for the Control of Aliens and for Other Matters Relating to Aliens'. Essentially the administration of the Act is left to the Minister for Justice who is given power to control aliens by order pursuant to section 5. This power includes making such orders as to the administration of the relevant provisions by immigration officers or other persons such as the police, as may be determined by him as necessary. The Minister may also make regulations concerning matters such as fees and charges under section 11. The Aliens Orders and the Regulations made under the Act must be laid before the *Oireachtas* which may anull them by resolution within 21 days. The so-called 'Alien Orders' which section 5 of the Act authorises are classed as secondary legislation and, as will be seen below, this is substantially different from the position regarding the rules of practice which the UK Immigration Act empowers. Section 5 of the Act does not provide guidelines for the exercise by the Minister of his power to make orders under the Act and it has been suggested that the provision might therefore

23. Immigration Act 1971 section 3(2).
24. *Supra*, n. 23, section 4.
25. Ibid.
26. Set up under the Immigration Appeals Act 1969.
27. This provision was terminated by section 1 of the Immigration Act 1988, subjecting those within the provision to current statutory provisions and rules.

be unconstitutional for infringement of the exclusive legislative power of the *Oireachtas*.[28]

The 1935 Act also provides for powers of arrest without warrant of aliens. Various offences, including breach of an aliens order, are created by the Act and these may be prosecuted by, or at the suit of the Minister of Justice.[29] The Act makes no provision for appeals in relation to anything it authorises and no right of appeal against the determination of an immigration officer is prescribed in the relevant statutory instruments although judicial review would be available in the normal way under the general law.

3.3   Summary

In contrast with the position with regard to international instruments, the primary domestic rules employed by the UK and Ireland respectively are quite diverse. The UK system is more complex than the Irish system both in relation to the definition of nationality and the regulation of immigration. For the most part this complexity is peculiar to the historical basis of the relevant UK law which must deal with a more diverse range of claims to nationality and right of entry than are made in the Irish context. However, the Irish system lacks particular elements of regulation, such as a system of appeals in matters of immigration, which seem unrelated to the question of the number or diversity of claims.

4.   DELEGATED RULES

4.1   UK rules

An accurate description of the status of the rules in the UK is a point of some difficulty. They have been referred to merely as rules of practice, and are described as such in section 3(2) of the 1971 Act; as such they do not have the character of secondary legislation.[30] Lord Denning has described them as follows:

> 'They are not rules of law. They are rules of practice laid down for the guidance of immigration officers and tribunals who are entrusted with the administration of the Immigration Act 1971. They can be, and often are, prayed in aid by applicants before the courts in immigration cases. To some extent the courts must have regard to them because there are provisions in the Act itself . . . which show that in appeals to an adjudicator, if the immigration rules have not been complied with, then the appeal is to be allowed. In addition, the courts always have regard to those rules, not only in matters where there is a question

---

28. Costello, 'The Irish Deportation Power', 12 *Dublin University Law Journal* (1990) 89.

29. Aliens Act 1935 section 12.

30. *R. v. Chief Immigration Officer, London (Heathrow) Airport ex p Salamat Bibi*, [1976] 3 All ER 843; *Patel v. Chief Immigration Officer, London (Heathrow) Airport and the Secretary of State for the Home Department*, (Court of Appeal 7 July 1977).

whether the officers have acted fairly. But they are not rules in the nature of delegated legislation so as to amount to strict rules of law.'[31]

The rules, which are divided into two parts, control of entry and control after entry, make specific provision for refugees. Both parts are prefaced by the words:

'Where a person is a refugee full account is to be taken of the provisions of the Convention and Protocol relating to the Status of Refugees. Nothing in these rules is to be construed as requiring action contrary to the United Kingdom's obligations under these instruments.'[32]

In deciding whether to grant leave to enter or remain, the immigration officer or, where appropriate, the Secretary of State will determine all the relevant facts within their own discretion. As a result, that decision is only subject to review on the narrow grounds of judicial review for 'unreasonableness'.[33] Nevertheless, the courts have admitted scrutiny of the terms of the Convention itself, in particular in assessing the scope of the definition of a refugee and the meaning of a 'well founded fear of being persecuted . . .' To this extent the House of Lords held that the 'provisions (of the Convention and Protocol) have for all practical purposes been incorporated into United Kingdom law.'[34]

This special character of the UK immigration rules has important consequences. For example, the rules are to be construed more loosely than one might construe a statute or statutory instrument. The House of Lords so held in a case concerning the extent of a discretion conferred under the rules. It was held that the immigration rules were to be construed sensibly according to the natural meaning of the language which was employed and not with the strictness applicable to a statutory instrument. Thus the relevant discretion was found to be broader than might otherwise have been the case.[35]

It appears to remain the case nevertheless that the rules cannot confer rights in the way that legislation might. It was held in R. v. *Immigration Appeal Tribunal ex parte Dipak Kumar Nathwani*[36] that an individual could not insist on the application to his case of a particular set of rules which had been in force at the time of his application for permanent residence. The relevant rules had been superseded subsequently by new rules which were applied by the Secretary of State in refusing the application. The Court ruled that there was no right to dictate to the Secretary of State which rules he should apply. The rules were essentially rules of practice which had to be regarded at the time

31. Ibid. at 848.

32. Paras. 16 and 96, Statement of Changes of Immigration Rules (HC Paper (1982-83) No. 169).

33. Section 4(1) of the 1971 Act as applied in *Bugdayeay* v. *Secretary of State* [1987] 1 All ER 940 at 947d-e per Lord Bridge. The grounds of judicial review are those identified in *Associated Provincial Picture Houses* v. *Wednesbury Corporation* [1947] All ER 680, namely that an irrelevant matter has been considered, a relevant matter has been ignored, or that the decision is such that no reasonable person could reach it.

34. *R.* v. *Secretary of State ex p Sivakumaran and Others* [1988] 1 All ER 193 at 195b, per Lord Keith of Kuikel with whom Lords Bridge and Griffiths agreed.

35. *Alexander* v. *Immigration Appeal Tribunal* [1982] 2 All ER 766.

36. Queens Bench Division 23 Febuary 1979 [1979-80] Imm. AR. 9.

of a decision. The power given to the Secretary of State under section 2(1) was a matter entirely within his discretion and was thus not open to challenge.

4.2   Irish rules

By contrast the Aliens Orders which the Minister for Justice is empowered to make under the Irish legislation are not rules of practice but rather can be classed as secondary legislation. As such they must comply with the special constitutional rules which relate to delegated legislation in Ireland. Article 15.2 of the Constitution gives exclusive legislative power to the *Oireachtas* which therefore must not delegate power to make regulations which will go beyond the mere giving effect to the principles and policies in the parent Act.[37] Thus the principal Act must lay down the law with details only to be filled in by the secondary legislation. As already noted, at least one Irish author has suggested that the provision empowering the creation of Aliens Orders may fall foul of this constitutional requirement.

Questions of constitutionality aside, the Courts may also examine the validity of delegated legislation according to the principle of *vires* and the criteria of reasonableness. Interesting in this context, by comparison with the UK position illustrated in the *Dipak Kumar* case above[38] is the fact that, as delegated legislation, the Irish immigration rules will be subject to the presumption applied by the Courts that the *Oireachtas* did not intend to give retrospective effect to delegated legislation.[39]

4.3   Summary

The difference in legal nature of the rules which facilitate the administration of the law on immigration in the UK and Ireland, rules of practice and secondary legislation respectively, has important implications for the interpretation and justiciability of such rules in the courts. It is interesting that although at first sight it would appear that the rules in each jurisdiction are capable of being determined with reasonable certainty by a prospective immigrant due to the requirement of parliamentary scrutiny, in fact the UK rules may have a degree of retrospective effect, leading to uncertainty, which the Irish rules appear to avoid.

---

37. *City View Press Ltd.* v. *An Comhairle Oiliuna* [1980] IR 381.

38. *Supra*, n. 36.

39. See e.g., *Hamilton* v. *Hamilton* [1982] IR 466, and generally Hogan and Morgan, *Administrative Law* (1986, Irish Law Texts).

5. THE ADJUDICATION MACHINERY

5.1 The UK adjudication machinery

Part II of the 1971 Immigration Act envisages the possibility of appeal to an adjudicator with a further possible appeal to an Immigration Appeals Tribunal (although in some cases it will be possible to appeal directly to the Tribunal). In general there is a right of appeal to an adjudicator against refusal of leave to enter the UK and refusal of certificate of entitlement, entry certificate or visa, against certain conditions of entry, a deportation order made otherwise than on the recommendation of a court (a court recommended deportation may be appealed directly to the Tribunal), or the destination to which it is proposed to remove an individual. Appeals from the determination of an adjudicator to the Immigration Appeals Tribunal may be subject to a requirement of leave which may be obtained from the adjudicator or from the Tribunal itself.

The adjudicator must examine the relevant decision for compliance with both the law and the applicable rules of practice and must allow the appeal if no such compliance is found. On appeal, the Tribunal may affirm the determination of the adjudicator or make any other determination which the adjudicator could have made. For a time the Tribunal had expressed unwillingness to overturn the adjudicator's findings of fact except where these were considered to be unreasonable.[40] However, the Court of Appeal in R. v. *Immigration Appeals Tribunal ex parte Alam BI*[41] ruled that the Tribunal can hear appeals from the determination of an adjudicator on the facts and has the power and the duty to review and reverse such decisions and the determination based on them where it comes to the conclusion that the adjudicator's decisions on the facts were wrong.

The 1971 Act makes no provision for further appeal to the High Court but, pursuant to the general supervisory jurisdiction of the courts, decisions of immigration officials, tribunals and of the Secretary of State may be open to review by the Court on grounds, for example, of reasonableness, *vires* or natural justice.[42] Judicial review is thus more concerned with the manner in which a decision was reached than with its merits.

The leave of the Court is a pre-requisite to any application for judicial review[43] and the remedy is granted not as of right but at the discretion of the Court. The Court of Appeal has indicated that the discretion will not be exercised in favour of an applicant in an immigration case who has failed to avail of the statutory appeal procedures provided.[44] The Court ruled that because of the existence of a statutory appeal procedure it was only in exceptional circumstances that leave to apply for judicial review would be granted where the statutory procedure had not been followed.

40. See e.g., Grant and Martin, *Immigration Law and Practice*, (1982) p. 307.
41. [1979-80] Imm AR 146CA.
42. See generally O. Hood Phillips and Paul Jackson, *Constitutional and Administrative Law*, seventh edition (1987) Ch. 33 and n. 27 *supra*.
43. Order 53, Rules of the Supreme Court
44. R. v. *Secretary of State for the Home Department ex parte Swate* [1986] 1 WLR 477 CA; [1986] 1 All ER 717.

In the absence of such exceptional circumstances, the appeals procedure in the 1971 Act provided an alternative and appropriate remedy to judicial review.

The scope of judicial review is further limited by the fact that there are certain matters which the Court will refuse to review on the ground that they are matters solely within the discretion of the decision maker.[45] For example, the House of Lords in *Bugdacay* v. *Secretary for State Home Department*[46] held that the resolution of any issue of fact and the exercise of any discretion in relation to an application for asylum as a refugee were matters exclusively within the discretion of immigration officers and the Secretary of State within the terms of the 1971 Act. As such they were subject only to the Court's supervisory jurisdiction to ensure that the decision was not flawed in any way. The appellants were thus not entitled to judicial review of the Secretary of State's refusal to treat them as refugees.

5.2   The Irish adjudication machinery

It has already been noted that the Irish system provides no formal appeal procedure in relation to immigration decisions but that judicial review will be available in respect of decisions made by immigration officers. The Irish system of judicial review is broadly similar to the UK system insofar as it relates to questions of reasonableness, *vires*, etc., but an important difference between the two systems is that the Irish Courts can review administrative decisions and primary and secondary legislation for compliance with the constitution.[47]

Although the Irish Courts have the added dimension of the Constitution against which to judge the actions of immigration authorities, the Irish legislation does not provide aliens with procedural guarantees, such as the right to be given reasons for a decision, which the UK legislation requires.[48] Therefore the Courts have fewer legislative guidelines against which to judge the propriety of a particular decision. In the past the High Court has appeared reluctant to restrain immigration officers in the exercise of their powers tending only to review decisions thought to be perverse or unreasonable.[49] However, the Irish Courts have in recent times become quite liberal generally in applying the criterion of reasonableness.[50]

---

45. See Hood Phillips and Jackson, op. cit. n. 42, pp. 697-699.

46. [1987] All ER 940.

47. The potential importance of review on constitutional grounds was demonstrated in the recent Supreme Court case of *Fajujono* v. *Minister for Justice* [1990] ILRM 234, where it was held that the Irish deportation power was, in certain circumstances, subject to the Constitutional provisions on the protection of the family.

48. It appears, however, that the Courts may in future be willing to recognise a right to be given reasons for a decision in certain cases. See e.g., *State (Touray)* v. *Governor of Mountjoy Prison*, *Irish Times*, 14 December 1985; *Fajujono* v. *Minister for Justice, supra*, n. 47.

49. See Costello, *supra*, n. 28; Re Tharmanablan, *Irish Times*, 14 December 1984.

50. Hogan and Morgan, op. cit. n. 39, pp. 310-313; for an example in an immigration case see *State (Kugan)* v. *Station Sergeant, Fitzgibbon Street Garda Station* [1986] ILRM 95.

5.3 Summary

The Irish and UK systems of adjudication demonstrate similarities only at the level of judicial review due to the lack of any formal appeals system in the Irish legislation. However, even in relation to judicial review there is a divergence between the two systems due to the constitutional dimension to which the Irish Courts may have regard and the lack of legislative guidelines by which to judge administrative action in the Irish system. Thus, in substance, the adjudication procedures employed in each of the jurisdictions are quite different.

6. THE COMMON AREA OF TRAVEL

The United Kingdom, the Channel Islands, the Isle of Man and Ireland form a 'common area of travel' so that having legally entered one part of the area persons may travel within it without, in general, further restrictions by way of immigration control. The UK Immigration Act 1971 provides in section 1(3) that: 'Arrival in and departure from the United Kingdom on a local journey from or to any of the islands ... or the Republic of Ireland shall not be subject to control under this Act, nor shall a person require leave to enter the United Kingdom on so arriving, except insofar as any of those places is for any purpose excluded from this subsection under the powers conferred by this Act ...' Interestingly, this arrangement is not the result of any formal international agreement in the nature, for example, of the Schengen Agreement nor is there a provision in Irish primary legislation equivalent to section 1(3) above, designating the 'common area of travel' although, as will be seen, Irish secondary legislation contains the machinery for the operation of this area.

The smooth operation of the common area of travel depends very much on a certain degree of harmonisation of UK and Irish immigration rules concerning leave to enter the territory. The UK's fears in this regard were expressed in the parliamentary debates on the Commonwealth Immigrants Bill in 1961, when it was indicated that if UK attempts to stem the flow of Commonwealth immigrants into the country were in danger of being thwarted by the entry of such persons via the Republic of Ireland, the common area of travel would come to an end.[51] The Irish provisions regarding the definition of aliens were subsequently amended to take into account the UK changes relating to Commonwealth citizens.[52] Having lawfully entered the common area of travel, aliens may be subject to restrictions, such as registration with the police, which

---

51. See e.g., Parl. Deb. 5th Ser. Vol. 650 Cols. 1186-1187, 5 March 1961.

52. The Irish 'Aliens (Amendment) Order' 1962 S.I. No. 112 of 1962 in effect continued the exemption from control pursuant to the 1946 Aliens Order for persons born in the UK. Persons born in named States (Member States of the British Commonwealth) were no longer to be exempt from control but would be subject to special provisions, which effectively meant that such persons could now be refused leave to land or be subject to certain conditions in relation to leave to enter, and could also be liable to deportation.

may be imposed by the British[53] or Irish[54] authorities upon entry from another part of the common area of travel.

The machinery for the operation of the common area of travel envisages the application, at the place of original entry into the area, of the immigration policy applicable in the other parts of the area. The UK immigration rules provide that:

> 'A passenger arriving in the United Kingdom is to be refused leave to enter if there is reason to believe that he intends to enter any of the other parts of the common travel area and that he is not acceptable to the immigration authorities there.'[55]

Similarly in Ireland, the Aliens Order 1975 allows an immigration officer to refuse admission to an alien arriving in the State from outside the common travel area where the alien intends to travel to the UK and the officer is satisfied that the alien would not qualify for admission to the UK if he arrived there from another place.[56]

A recent Irish case illustrates a possibly unforeseen difficulty in the operation of this co-operative arrangement. In *State (Nsika)* v. *Officer in Charge of Fitzgibbon Street Garda Station*,[57] a Nigerian national challenged his arrest at Dublin airport. He had been on the way to the UK when arrested on grounds that he would not qualify for admission there. Egan J. released him on the ground that the Irish immigration officials had no jurisdiction to anticipate the decision of the immigration authorities of another State. This problem perhaps originates in the fairly informal nature of the arrangement between the two countries and the fact that Irish primary legislation makes no specific provision for its operation. Legislation directed specifically at the operation of the common area of travel could deal with the question of the jurisdiction of immigration officials and could eliminate the possibility of future challenge, on grounds of infringement of the exclusive legislative power of the *Oireachtas*, to what amounts to the enforcement in Ireland of UK provisions through secondary legislation.

Despite differences in the complexity and detail of immigration provisions in the UK and Ireland respectively and the possible difficulty mentioned in the preceding paragraph, the common area of travel between the UK and Ireland seems, in practice, to operate quite smoothly. This is facilitated by the fact that each country tends to impose immigration control on a similarly defined class of persons which, in general, excludes the nationals of the other country.[58] Theoretically therefore the immigration authorities in each State have the power to control the entry of an identical group of people. Given that, in relation to this group, the immigration officials at the place of entry to the common area of travel may take into account the provisions relating to

---

53. Immigration Act 1971, section 9.
54. S.I. No. 128 1975 Art. 597.
55. Statement of changes to the Immigration Rules, 23 March 1990, H.C. 251.
56. SI NO. 128 of 1975 Art. 5(2)(j).
57. *Irish Times* 20 April 1985.
58. Note that Irish nationals may be refused entry to the UK as security risks under the Prevention of Terrorism (Temporary Provisions) Act 1989.

entry to other parts of the area, the need for a complete harmonisation of the specific rules of entry to each jurisdiction seems unnecessary.

SPANISH VIEWPOINTS AND PROBLEMS WITH THE SCHENGEN CONVENTION, FREE MOVEMENT OF PERSONS AND ALIENS LAW

Isabel Lirola Delgado[*]

1. INTRODUCTION

An analysis of the free movement of persons within the territory of the European Community, from Spain's point of view, must consider a number of changing circumstances related to both the internal and external dimensions of the Community.

By 'internal dimension' we mean the free movement of nationals of the Member States within the area without internal frontiers, as declared in Article 8A EEC. In this respect, we refer to the end of the transitional period set in the Act of Accession of Spain and Portugal,[1] and the expiration date for the implementation of the directives granting residence to economically non-active persons.[2]

Within the framework of the Treaty on European Union, one should keep in mind the consequences that the creation of a 'European Citizenship' will have on the free movement of persons.

Outside the Community's institutions, in the external dimension, the enforcement of the Schengen Convention,[3] which provides for the abolition of internal border controls on persons, raises, problems related to the entry and circulation of nationals from non-Member States crossing Spanish borders that are, at the same time, external EEC borders.

---

[*] Assistant Lecturer in International Law, Faculty of Law, Santiago de Compostela University, Spain. Mrs. Isabel Lirola Delgado was not a reporter nor participant at the Colloquium. She was invited to write this article because the Spanish viewpoints were not represented.

1. Act concerning the conditions of accession of the Kingdom of Spain and the Portuguese Republic and the adjustments to the Treaties (hereinafter 'Act of Accession of Spain and Portugal') OJ 1985 L 302/23 of 15 November 1985, (Boletín Oficial del Estado, hereafter BOE, No. 1 of 1 January 1986).

2. Directives Nos. 90/365/EEC, 90/366/EEC and 90/364/EEC respectively granting rights of residence to pensioners, students and persons with economic means (OJ 1990 L 180 of 13 July 1990).

3. Schengen Convention 19 June 1990. Spanish and Portuguese Accession, 25 June 1991.

H.G. Schermers et al., eds., Free Movement of Persons in Europe

2.   FREE MOVEMENT OF COMMUNITY NATIONALS IN SPAIN

2.1   The adaptation of the Spanish legal order to Community law

As a consequence of its entry into the EEC, Spain had to adapt its legal order to the obligations set by the the founding Treaties and the acts of the Institutions according to the conditions foreseen by the Treaties and the Act of Accession.[4] To this end, Royal Decree (*Real Decreto*) 1099/86 (hereinafter RD 1099/86) was adopted.[5] This decree regulates the entry, stay and work of Community citizens in Spain. The term 'citizens' attracts our attention since it cannot be justified from a legal-technical viewpoint: in the Spanish legal order, nationality designates the link joining the individual to the State. The *raison d'être* for the expression 'citizen' might be found in a concept of 'European Citizenship',[6] but were it so, it would mean that this Spanish regulation goes beyond Community provisions.

Actually this is not the case for nationals of the other Member States, whose freedom of movement in Spain is related to economic aims. In this sense, RD 1099/86 does not recognize the right of free movement to all nationals of the Member States, but only to those who are exercising this right for the reasons foreseen by Articles 48, 52 and 59 EEC.[7] Nationals of the other Member States who do not fall within the scope of action just described, or who cannot prove the necessary prerequisites, are subject to the Aliens Law contained in Act (*Ley Orgánica*) 7/1985 (hereinafter 'Aliens Law') on the rights and liberties of foreigners in Spain.[8]

The differences between RD 1099/86 and those contained in the Aliens Law are particularly significant in relation to the measures concerning public policy, public security and public health. More specifically, persons within the scope of RD 1099/86 cannot be returned to the border because of illegal entry into Spanish territory.[9] Morover, under RD 1099/86, the failure to apply for a residence card or work permit can only be sanctioned with a fine, and cannot lead to expulsion.[10] In contrast, the Aliens Law sanctions illegal entry into Spanish territory with return to the border,[11] and illegal stay in Spain without the above-mentioned documents can be penalized, with expulsion.[12]

For these reasons, the determination of the method and timing of the enforcement of RD 1099/86, on the one hand, or the Aliens Law on the other, is of the highest

4. See Act of Accession of Spain and Portugal, *supra*, n. 2, Art. 2.
5. Real Decreto (hereinafter RD) 26.5.1986, No. 1099/86, BOE No. 139 of 11 June 1986, see *infra* n. 26a.
6. See J.L. Iglesias Buhigues, 'Entrada, permanencia y trabajo en España de los nacionales de los Estados Miembros de la Comunidad Europea', *La Ley* (31 December 1986) p. 2.
7. Art. 1, p. 1. RD 1099/86, *supra*, n. 5.
8. Ibid. Art. 3. See Ley Orgánica 1 July 1985, No. 7/85, (BOE No. 158 of 3 July 1985).
9. Ibid, Art. 23, p. 1.
10. Ibid. Art. 23, p. 2.
11. Art. 36, p. 2, Ley Orgánica, 1 July 1985.
12. Ibid. Art. 26, p. 1.

importance. RD 1099/86 does not refer explicitly to this point, although it does state the obligation of informing to the authorities, either at the moment of entry into Spain or within fifteen days, as to the activities and services that the foreign national intends to carry out.[13]

However, in our opinion, there are two reasons why this reporting obligation and its time limit should not be considered as determinants of the appropriate legal status. First, Article 4 of Directive No. 73/148/EEC and Article 8 of Directive No. 68/360/EEC refer solely to the obligation to report presence in the State's territory, which cannot be put on the same level as the obligation to report on the pursuit of activities.[14] Second, the Court of Justice of the European Communities has held that this reporting obligation is just a measure taken by the State for purposes of being apprised of movements of population within its own borders[15] without the police authorities being allowed to inquire, at the moment of entry, about the purposes of the trip or the economic means of the person concerned.[16] As a consequence, the enforcement of RD 1099/86 must conform to the presumption of a right of entry and stay of Community nationals. This right extends, except under the proviso foreseen by Directive No. 64/221/EEC,[17] over a period of three months for the development of the freedom of establishment and the provision of services,[18] and over a period of six months in the case of persons looking for a job.[19]

However, in the case of Spanish nationals, RD 1099/86 goes beyond present Community law. It extends Community regulations on the free movement of persons to family members of Spanish nationals from other Member States, *or even from non-EC countries*.[20] This application of Community law seems to be objectionable as contrary to the spirit of the principle of free movement. Under this principle, Community nationals can claim from their own State rights stemming from Community law only if they have previously exercised the freedom of movement contemplated by the EEC Treaty.[21]

2.2   The transitional period

The application to workers of the rules contained in RD 1099/86 was temporarily limited according to the transitional arrangements set by Articles 56, 57 and 58 of the Accession Act. This transitional period was designed to prevent the impairment of labour markets in older Member States due to anticipated waves of immigration

13. Art. 6, p. 5, RD 1099/86, *supra*, n. 5.

14. Directive No. 68/360, (OJ L 257 of 16 October 1968) Directive No. 73/148, (OJ L 172 of 28 June 1973).

15. Case 118/75 Lynn Watson and Alessandro Belmann ECR [1976] 1185 and Case 265/88, Lothar Messer ECR [1989] 4209.

16. See Case C-68/89, *E.C. Commission* v. *the Netherlands*, judgment of 30 May 1991, not yet reported.

17. Directive 64/221, (OJ L 56 of 4 April 1964).

18. Directive 73/148, *supra*, n. 14, Art. 4, p. 2.

19. Case C-292/89, Antonissen, judgment of 26 February 1991, not yet reported.

20. Art. 2, p. 2, RD 1099/86, *supra*, n. 5.

21. See Joined Cases 297/88 and C-197/89 *Massam Dzodi* v. *the Belgian State* ECR [1990] I-3763.

from the newer members. Accordingly, a distinction was made between Community workers who had already settled prior to the date of accession, to whom RD 1099/86 is directly applied,[22] and those demanding their first work or residence permit after that date. In the latter case, the Aliens Law was to be applied. Only after having been granted a first work or residence permit, according to the rules of Act 7/85, Community regulations were to be applied.[23]

The transitional period was originally established by the Act of Accession as being 1 January 1993. However, the Act of Accession also provided that as from 1 January 1991, the Council could pass regulations for the adjustment of such measures upon consideration of a report from the Commission and on the grounds of new data.[24] Making use of this proviso, the Council agreed to establish 31 December 1991 as the end of the transitional period for the free movement of workers between Spain and Portugal on the one side, and other Member States on the other.[25]

On this point one should keep in mind that since 1986, Spain has changed its traditional status from being a labour force exporter to being a receiver of foreign workers. In a written statement presented on the occasion of the Council Meeting when the agreement was reached, the Spanish Work Minister *(Ministro de Trabajo)* remarked '[i]n accepting an advance of the end to the transitional period, we show a solidarity with other Member States, particularly Portugal, that Spain did not receive when negotiating its accession.'[26]

Together with the end of the transitional period, one should also consider the implications of extending the principle of free movement and granting residence to economically non-active persons. Directives Nos. 90/364/EEC, 90/365/EEC and 90/366/EEC have 1 July 1992 as the deadline for implementation by the Member States. These directives are particularly important for Spain because of the high number of foreigners already living in tourist areas, and the likelihood of increased numbers of such persons in the future.[26a]

22. Art. 13(a), RD 1099/86, *supra*, n. 5.

23. Ibid. Art. 13(b) and p. 3.

24. Act of Accession of Spain and Portugal, *supra*, n. 2, Art. 56.

25. See Council Regulation No. 2194/91 of 25 June 1991. (OJ L 206 of 29 July 1991). In relation to the free movement of workers between Spain and Portugal, on the one hand, and Luxembourg, on the other, the date of reference is 31 December 1992.

26. See *El Pais* (26 June 1991).

26a. It should be noticed that RD 1099/86, *supra* n. 5, has been modified and replaced by RD 26.6.1992, No. 706/1992, BOE No. 156 of 30 June 1992, on the entry and stay in Spain of nationals of the Member States. The new norm aims at adapting Spanish legislation to the extension of the beneficiaries of the principle of the free movement that derives both from the end of the transitional period and the implementation of Directives 90/364, 365 and 366 (cf., M. Perez Gonzalez, 'Los nuevos aspectos de la libre circulación de personas en la perspectiva de une ciudadanía europea (una visión española)', Spanish report, XV FIDE Congress, Lisbon, 23-26 September, 1992, p. 201 at 221).

2.3	The reception by Spanish courts of Community law relating to the free movement of persons

Although the existence of a transitional period for workers has resulted in a restricted application by Spanish courts of Community law relating to the free movement of persons, a general examination of Spanish jurisprudence shows an evolution towards more European-like positions, thereby correcting an initially restrictive attitude on the Administration's side. The geographical distribution of the Spanish courts concerned reveals that Community nationals have not settled evenly within the Spanish territory, and are particularly concentrated in industrial and touristic regions.

As regards the questions faced by Spanish courts during the transitional period, these have been concentrated primarily on determining when the Aliens Law, on the one hand, or RD 1099/86 on the other, should apply in cases of expulsion from Spain decided by the administrative authorities.[27] This issue initially arose, in relation to Community nationals who had not regularized their situation, but who were already living or working in Spain prior to the date of accession. In these cases, the initial policy was to enforce the Aliens Law by ordering expulsion.[28] However, more recent jurisprudence tends towards the application of RD 1099/86, to nationals from Member States who were already working in Spain prior to the date of Spain's accession.[29]

However, with respect to Community nationals who requested a work permit *after* the date of accession, the courts have continued to apply the Aliens Law, and not the Community provisions. The Spanish Administration has therefore continued its policy of protecting the national labour market, and has refused to grant permits to such persons. Nevertheless, some pronouncements from the courts have led to a softening of that policy by forcing the Administration to justify its refusals.[30]

Reference must be made also to workers who had settled legally at the time of accession, and to the consequences derived from the freedom of establishment and provision of services, for which no time limit to the enforcement of Community regulations was set. These cases are the least conflictual, as the full application of RD 1099/86 is correct; the Courts' pronouncements have compelled the Administration to abide by Community Law.[31]

27. See the studies of C. Pico Lorenzo, 'Pronunciamientos jurisprudenciales españoles respecto al régimen transitorio de la libre circulación de los trabajadores', *Noticias CEE* (June 1991), p. 91 et seq, and D.J. Liñan Nogueras/J. Roldan Barbero, 'Crónica sobre la aplicación judicial del Derecho Comunitario en España (1986-1989)', 16 *Revista de Instituciones Europeas* (1989) p. 885 at p. 909.

28. Sentencia del Tribunal Supremo (hereafter STS) 5 June 1990, *Recopilación Aranzadi*, 4694 (hereafter Ar.).

29. Sentencia de la Audiencia Nacional (hereafter SAN), 9 February 1991, *La Ley* (18 September 1991) p. 1.

30. STS, 26 October 1987 (Ar. 6171), STS, 20 October 1989 (Ar. 7256), STS, 29 June 1990 (Ar. 4687).

31. STS 21 June 1990 (Ar. 5166), STS 21 June 1990 (Ar. 6145).

Finally we would like to comment on some very recent jurisprudence, not yet confirmed, that considers two different issues on the same level: the principle of free movement for the pursuit of economic activities (Community law) and the fundamental right of free movement in Spain as recognized by Article 19 of the Spanish Constitution (*Constitución Española*, hereinafter CE). From this consideration has come the existence of a fundamental right of free movement of Community nationals.[32]

In principle, this reasoning seems to be correct, since there is an effective identity of content between both rights, as far as physical mobility is concerned. In that respect, one should realize that Article 19 CE is not reserved to Spanish nationals, but also applies to foreigners residing legally in Spain.[33] If this right is recognized as fundamental to foreigners, then there is all the more reason to do so in the case of Community nationals who wish to exercise the right to free movement declared by the Treaty of Rome.

In our opinion, however, it is not correct for the national court to resort to this comparison in order to recognize the free movement of Community nationals in Spain. It would suffice to invoke Community provisions, by virtue of the supremacy and direct effect of Community law.[34]

3.   THE SPANISH PROPOSAL OF EUROPEAN CITIZENSHIP

Within the framework of the Interstate Conference for Political Union, initiated at the Rome Summit of 14–15 December 1990, the Spanish Government put forward a proposal for European citizenship, which essentially recognizes the full right of free movement and choice of residence for citizens of the Union.[35]

While this idea is not new the merit of the Spanish proposal lies in its timeliness, as shown by the consensus obtained for its discussion at the Interstate Conference,[36] and in the subsequent Spanish efforts to present a specific written text.[37]

---

32. SAN 26 October 1990, *La Ley* (29 May 1991) p. 3 et seq. and SAN 9 February 1991, *supra*, n. 29.

33. See also I. Borrajo Iniesta, 'El Status Constitucional de los Extranjeros en España', *Estudios sobre la Constitución Española. Homenaje al Prof. García de Enterría*, V.II (Madrid 1991) p. 719.

34. This jurisprudence might find an explanation in the National Court's determination to issue a ruling in spite of the fact that the defence chose procedures allowed by Act 62/1978, whose contents are limited to the protection of the Fundamental Rights of Art. 53, p. 2 of CE, and a mistaken choice in the reasons pleaded. See the commentaries by C. Calvo Sanchez, *La Ley* (3 July 1991) p. 1 and V. Escuin Palop, *La Ley* (18 September 1991) p. 1.

35. See the text in 18 *Revista de Instituciones Europeas* (1991) p. 405.

36. See P. Solbes Mira, 'La Citoyenneté Européenne', *Revue du Marché Commun et de l'Union Européenne*, No. 345 (1991).

37. The official proposal dates back to October 1990; a written text was presented by the Spanish Delegation to the Interstate Conference on Political Union in February 1991.

This text is evidence of a favourable Spanish position for the attainment of free movement of persons within the framework of Political Union.[38]

Nevertheless, it seems evident that the mere statement, 'Any citizen of the Union has the right to move and reside freely in the Union's territory without time limit' does not suffice by itself to achieve these rights.[39] At this point, two interesting problems have emerged in relation to the directives granting the right of residence to economically non-active persons: *the disposal of economic means*, and *the entitlement to medical insurance*.

In the project for Political Union, as fashioned under Luxembourg's Presidency, the development of free movement of persons and residence is subject to the Council's unanimous decision.[40] The risk arises that the above-mentioned problems may reappear, as it is not possible to assure that all Member States are ready to carry the additional economic burden on their social security or national assistance systems.

4. THE INCIDENCE OF THE SCHENGEN CONVENTION ON THE SPANISH ALIENS LAW

4.1 Spain as a country of immigration

Adherence to the Schengen Convention is further evidence of Spain's favourable position regarding achieving the free movement of persons within the Community through the abolition of police controls at the internal border of the Community. However, the enforcement of control measures on nationals from third States implies an adaptation of the Aliens Law, which does not fully correspond to Spain's present realities and needs. As mentioned above, since the 1980s, Spain is no longer a country of emigrants but, on the contrary, receives a surplus of immigrants.[41]

Several factors have contributed to this increased immigration. Spain's geographical peculiarities make it a weak point for maritime control because of its long coastline. More recently, Spain has become a crossroads for other European

38. The Spanish proposal provides for certain political rights, such as: participation in associations, enfranchisement at local and European Parliament elections, the right to stand for elective posts (Art. 7), common diplomatic protection to Community nationals abroad (Art. 8), as well the creation of an 'ombudsman' to assist Union citizens in the defence of rights recognized by the forthcoming Treaty (Art. 9).

39. Art. 6 in the Proposal.

40. Cf. D. Vignes, 'Le projet de la Présidence Luxembourgeoise d'un Traité sur l'Union Européenne', *Revue du Marché Commun et de l'Union Européenne*, No. 349 (1991) p. 504 at p. 509.

41. The number of foreigners legally settled in Spain has increased from 181,544 in 1980 to 399,377 in 1990. See *Situación de los extranjeros en España. Líneas básicas de la política española de extranjería* (Comunicación del Gobierno al Congreso) (Madrid, 1990) p. 2.

destinations, which adds to the existence of large illegal economic structures that favour clandestine immigration.[42]

Most non-EC nationals emigrate from two areas: Latin America and the Maghreb. Latin American emigration is based on the political and economic difficulties suffered by these countries. Spain is a preferential destination by virtue of its historical and cultural links to the region.[43] African emigration is caused by demographic and economic pressure in the Maghreb which is eased by crossing the Straits of Gibraltar to Spain.[44]

4.2   Consequences of a general character: entry and visa regulations

Generally speaking, the measures regulating the entry of foreigners into Spain[45] are strict enough to carry out controls in accordance with the Schengen Convention,[46] although some adaptation may be necessary to conform to the criteria contained therein, and, above all, to include unforeseen aspects, such as those derived from the Schengen Information System.[47]

An adaptation of Spain's visa policy is also necessary. In this regard, one should keep in mind that this policy heretofore has lacked general practical guidelines for its enforcement. This is because the interpretations given by embassies and consulates have lacked uniformity regarding scope, circumstances of issue, validity and concession. As a consequence, notable inequalities have been observed between various nationalities. These differences are not arbitrary; they conform to criteria based on an evaluation of the circumstances of each applicant not only of a personal character, but also, and very often, as regards nationality. Indeed, a number of countries have suffered restrictions on visa issuance, in accordance with directives from the Ministry of Foreign Affairs.[48]

Visa regulations will have to be adapted to the Schengen Convention, as well as to the rules developing it, within the framework of a common visa policy.[49] The requirement of a visa should become, despite its little practical demand up to now, *an essential instrument of border control by the Spanish authorities*. In this regard,

---

42. See R. Pastor Ridruejo, 'La desaparición de las fronteras en la Europa Comunitaria y los problemas demográficos e inmigratorios', *Información Comercial Española*, (July 1990) p. 12.

43. Latin Americans nationals constitute 19% of foreigners in Spain (44,392 in 1980; 77,678 in 1990), Situación de los extranjeros en España, loc. cit., n. 41, p. 2.

44. The percentage of African nationals in Spain has increased from 2.5% in 1980 to 6.5% in 1990, totalling 25,375 at present, Ibid. p. 3. See the study by J. Cazorla, 'CE-Magreb: Referentes demográficos, económicos y psicológicos', Estudios Regionales, No. 29 (1991) p. 31 at p. 40.

45. See Ley Orgánica 7/85, Arts. 11 and 12, RD 1119/86, 26 May 1986, (BOE No. 140 of 12 June 1986) Arts. 1 to 15, and Orden 22 February 1989, (BOE No. 55 of 6 March 1989).

46. Art. 3 in the Convention.

47. Ibid., Arts. 92 to 118. Spain has so far no legal system for the protection of individuals in respect of the automatic processing of personal data.

48. See R. Ferrer Peña, *Los Derechos de los Extranjeros en España* (Madrid, 1989) p. 112.

49. See Arts. 10, pp. 2 and 17 in the Convention. For example, the period of validity of transit visas should be reduced from 7 to 5 days.

favourable consequences could be derived from the possession of a visa, once the guidelines governing its issuance are clarified and standardized. For example, it could become a guarantee of entry and stay in the country, as well as an obstacle to the entry of persons posing a threat to public policy, public security and health. In the case of an extension to new countries, geographical reasons should play no role. Instead, only very concrete personal circumstances should be considered.[50]

4.3   Consequences for Latin American nationals

A distinction should be made between entry regulations, and regulations regarding residence and establishment.

With regard to entry regulations, Spain has signed agreements cancelling the visa requirement for short stays of up to ninety days. Spain's adherence to the Schengen Convention has affected only Cuba and the Dominican Republic, out of a list of 110 States for whose nationals a visa is required.[51] Attempts to include other Latin American countries in this list (Peru, Bolivia and Colombia) may fail because of the need for unanimous agreement among the members of the Executive Committee provided for in the Schengen Convention: Spain's vote to the contrary could possibly thwart these attempts to include these countries.[52]

Regulations relating to establishment and work permits, which provide preferential treatment to Latin Americans under the Aliens Law, will not be affected by the enforcement of the Schengen Convention since it refers solely to entries and stays for periods of up to three months.[53]

4.4   Consequences for nationals from the Maghreb

Nationals from the Maghreb are of special interest. Since Spain is a crossroads to other European destinations, it has become necessary to extend a visa requirement to nationals from Algeria, Morocco and Tunisia. Nevertheless, it is the intention of the Spanish Government to issue regulations that, while complying with the Schengen Convention, allow for the free circulation of persons between Spain and Northern Africa.[54] For example, nationals from Morocco, Algeria and Tunisia living in the Community or in possession of a visa from any Member State, will not be required to obtain a transit visa (normally valid up to four days).[55]

50. See Pastor Ridruejo, loc. cit., n. 42, p. 13.
51. Concerning the Dominican Republic, Spain has postponed this requirement until the Spanish Parliament ratifies the Additional Convention.
52. See *Diario ABC*, 26 June 1991. Besides, the Spanish Government has repeatedly stated its intention of not requiring visas from Latin American nationals, see *Situación de los extranjeros en España*, loc. cit., n. 41, p. 14.
53. See Art. 18, p. 3 of Act 7/85 and Arts. 38, 39, p. 3 of RD 1119/86. This preferential treatment extends also to Portuguese, Philippine, Andorran and Equato-Guinean nationals and to Sephardim.
54. For Spain's position on this point, see *Boletín del Congreso de los Diputados*, 28 January 1991, Serie D, No. 148, p. 43.
55. See Art. 5.3 of the Schengen Convention.

Also, border controls will be enforced at the point of entry into Spanish territory. In the cities of Ceuta and Melilla, travellers with destinations in Spain, or in transit, will have to be in possession of the corresponding visa. On the contrary, travellers with the destination Ceuta or Melilla may not need it, depending upon the length and purpose of the trip, as well as their nationality and province of residence.

These control mechanisms are designed to conform to Spain's own geographical characteristics and political needs.[56]

4.5   Consequences on the right of asylum and refugee status

The right of asylum is recognized under Spanish Law as a protection to political refugees. Abuse of this right has become a major source of illegal immigration.[57] Every applicant has the right to enter and stay in Spanish territory as long as his request is being examined.[58] In addition, asylum applicants may be entitled to a temporary identity card, as well as the provision of social and economic assistance in case of need.[59]

The guidelines are provided by the Schengen Convention for determining which State is responsible for dealing with the request of asylum. Among these guidelines is the rule placing responsibility on the State through whose borders the applicant has entered Community territory without the required documents.[60] This disposition is unfavourable to Spain since, as already mentioned, its long coastline is difficult to protect. In addition, some entries initially intended as tourist visits, are sometimes misused to request asylum.[61]

Given the increase in requests of asylum and refugee status, behind many of which hides the condition of economic immigrant, a reform of Spanish law in this area has become necessary in order to guarantee protection and assistance to persons in need of asylum, and rapidly to deny manifestly unfounded claims. This reform should focus on Bylaw (*reglamento*) 11/1985, which develops Act 5/1984, in order to adapt it to the Schengen Convention.[62] One should also consider the creation of a new specialized instructive organ linked to the Commission for Asylum and Refugees (*Comisión Interministerial de Asilo y Refugio*) and exclusively devoted to the examination of such requests. The opportunity to increase the participation of the United Nations High Commissioner for Refugees and other international, non-governmental organizations in that process should also be taken into account.

---

56. The recent signature (4 July 1991) of a Treaty of Friendship and Cooperation between Spain and Morocco allows for the possibility of cooperation in legal and consular areas.

57. See *Situacion de los extranjeros en España*, loc. cit., n. 41, p. 7.

58. Art. 1, p. 2 in Act 5/1984, 26 March 1984, (BOE No. 74 of 27 March 1984).

59. Arts. 6 and 8 in RD 511/1985, 20 February 1985, (BOE No. 94 of 19 April 1985).

60. Art. 31, p. 1, e) in the Schengen Convention.

61. See also D. Lopez Garrido, 'El hecho inmigratorio en Europa y la crisis del modelo de protección jurídica del asilo y del refugio', *Jueces para la democracia* (September, 1990) p. 57 at p. 62.

62. See *Situación de los extranjeros en España*, loc.cit., p. 24.

Finally, a unification and simplification of procedures would be desirable, in giving priority to the handling of abusive or manifestly unfounded claims.[63]

63. Spain has also signed the Dublin Convention relating to the determination of the State responsible for dealing with asylum requests presented within the Community, Dublin, 15 June 1990.

COOPERATION IN ALIENS LAW: THE IMPLICATIONS FOR INDIVIDUAL RIGHTS ENFORCEMENT

Christopher Vincenzi[*]

1.   ALIEN RIGHTS: A CONTRADICTION IN TERMS?

National constitutions generally confer rights only on citizens, and aliens, where they enjoy rights to do so as a concession, in some cases by a generous interpretation of the citizenship concept.[1] In the United Kingdom, one of the few industrialised States without a written constitution, aliens, although treated within the jurisdiction as 'local subjects' entitled to the protection of the law,[2] are subject to a number of specific disadvantages under statute, affecting their rights to enter and reside, to employment in the public service, to engage in industrial action and to vote in local and parliamentary elections.[3]

Even under the European Convention on Human Rights aliens have little protection in relation to entry and residence, although family connections may be of some benefit[4] and those claiming asylum have some procedural protection in relation to the processing of their claims for recognition.[5]

However, the last forty years in Europe have seen a substantial growth in the rights of non-citizens under local agreements in Europe, such as Benelux, the Nordic States, and the Common Travel Area of the United Kingdom and the Republic of Ireland. Most significantly, the right to work in other Member States is recognised, in the preamble to Regulation 1612/68, as a 'fundamental right'. It is not merely a device for securing the movement of labour. The Court has supported the idea that the Community worker is a human being and not a 'mere source of labour'.[6] However, as Judge Federico Mancini has said 'The Treaty does not safeguard the

---

* MA, PhD, Solicitor, Principal Lecturer in Law, Huddersfield Polytechnic, UK.

1. See for example, Art. 40. 4. 1. Constitution of the Irish Free State; *State (Mc Fadden)* v. *Governor of Mountjoy Prison* (1981) ILRM 113; *Osheku* v. *Ireland* [1987] ILRM 330.

2. *Johnson* v. *Pedlar* [1921] 2 AC 262; *Küchenmeister* v. *The Home Office* [1958] 1 QB 496.

3. Aliens (Restriction) Amendment Act 1919 Sec. 3 (2); Aliens Employment Act 1955; British Nationality Act 1981.

4. Case No. 31/1989/291 *Moustaquim* v. *Belgium, Times Law Report*, 8 May 1991.

5. *Vilvarajah* v. *Secretary of State* [1990] Imm AR 492, application to European Court of Human Rights pending. See also Art. 32 Geneva Convention Relating to the Status of Refugees 1951 and Art. 3 European Convention on Human Rights.

6. Case 7/75 *Fracas* v. *Belgian State* [1975] 2 CMLR 442, 450 and ECR 1975, p. 679 and following.

H.G. Schermers et al., eds., Free Movement of Persons in Europe
© 1993, T.M.C. Asser Instituut, The Hague.

228   CHR. VINCENZI

fundamental rights of the individuals affected by its application.'[7] Although the fundamental rights of Community nationals working abroad are not protected by the Treaty, the procedural and substantive protection afforded by Directive 64/221/EEC does go some way to making Community rights effective. In addition, the Treaty and the Cooperation Agreements even confer some rights in the social security and employment fields on nationals of third States which, the European Court of Justice has, this year, held are directly effective.[8]

These benefits have been secured by bi-lateral and multi-lateral agreements aimed as much at opening frontiers with a view to liberalising trade as at improving free movement facilities for individuals. That process of frontier-raising is, through the new Schengen Convention and the Single European Act, about to achieve a new impetus. Concerns about new immigration pressures on Western Europe and a pre-occupation with the administrative mechanics of the process of cooperation in immigration control, may mean that there is no improvement to existing rights, and that the new cooperation will result only in a major extension of power by States over individuals without a commensurate growth in rights and remedies. The papers in the first part of this Colloquium have tended to concentrate on these administrative changes, and on the development of Community law by the European Court of Justice and its application by national courts, rather than upon the impact that such changes have had on actual realisation of these rights by individuals.

As things stand at present, there are some minimal standards for rights enforcement under Directive 64/221/EEC in relation to exclusions and expulsions on public policy grounds on Community nationals, but not, for example where the host State has determined that an individual is not exercising a Treaty right. In relation to third State aliens there are no general standards of procedural protection, exception in relation to those claiming refugee status[9].

2.   COMMUNITY NATIONALS IN IRELAND AND
        THE UNITED KINGDOM

In addition to the rights which Community nationals enjoy under Community law, local agreements and *de facto* arrangement, such as those enjoyed by Danish nationals in relation to the other Nordic countries, rights to passport-free excursions under the Memorandum of Understanding 1971 between the United Kingdom and France, and the right to be treated as 'non-aliens' which Irish nationals have enjoyed since they left the Commonwealth in 1948[10] enlarge the rights of the citizens of the Member States who are parties to these agreements. They may even enlarge the rights of other Community nationals, since it is arguable, under Article 7 EEC

7. G. F. Mancini, 'The Making of a Constitution for Europe' (1989) CML Rev. 595, 596.
8. Case C-18/90 *ONEM* v. *Kziber*, [1991] ECR I-199.
9. Art. 32 Geneva Convention 1951.
10. British Nationality Act 1948 Sec. 32 (1); Ireland Act 1949 Secs. 1, 2; British Nationality Act 1981 Sec. 50.

Treaty that the immunity from deportation that resident Irish nationals enjoy,[11] should be equally applicable to other Community nationals. The same argument could be advanced in relation to the complete access to employment in the public service and to the franchise which Irish nationals enjoy and which has recently been extended to the British resident in Ireland.

Although, as Piers Gardner has indicated, there is no system of appeal in relation to immigration decisions in Ireland, the Aliens Orders do confer rights on Community nationals in Ireland which can be enforced through the judicial review process.[12] In the United Kingdom Community nationals are aliens who need leave to enter. That remains the case until Section 7 Immigration Act 1988 is brought into force, although under the Immigration Rules, which are directions to immigration officers, Community nationals should be admitted without being granted 'leave' following *R. v. Pieck*.[13] Under a strict construction of the Immigration Act 1971, although Community nationals have a right of appeal, it is only exercisable from abroad.[14] An English lawyer will say that, in practice, EEC nationals are allowed to remain for appeals, and will be permitted to appeal against a refusal to issue or extend a residence permit, although there is no right of appeal under British immigration law against decisions relating to residence permits.[15] These are concessions, however, and not rights under national law, although it is clearly arguable that they are directly enforceable rights under Directive 64/221/EEC. In addition, applying the principle of manifest conformity with Community law,[16] it seems unacceptable if national immigration rules do not state clearly which of such rules are, and which are not, applicable to Community nationals. A general disclaimer of the kind found in the British rules seems hardly sufficient.[17]

There is no legal aid available in relation to appeals before adjudicators or the Immigration Appeal Tribunal, who together hear the vast majority of immigration cases. In both Ireland and England legal aid is, however, available for judicial review proceedings. Preliminary advice on immigration matters is also legally aided in the United Kingdom, but the Government has announced an intention to terminate this facility.[18]

Discrimination on the grounds of nationality, which may affect Community nationals in a whole range of activities is not prohibited by Irish law, except to the extent prohibited by the EEC Treaty and the implementing legislation, and there is,

11. Immigration Act 1971 Sec. 7 (1) (b).

12. *State (Nsika)* v. *Officer in Charge of Fitzgibbon Street Garda Station, Irish Times* 20 April 1984. See J. P. Gardner et al., contribution to this Volume, p. 214.

13. Case 157/79 *R.* v. *Pieck* [1980] ECR 2171; [1980] 3 CMLR 220; Immigration Rules, para. 69, HC 251 (March 1990).

14. Sec. 13 (3) Immigration Act 1971.

15. *Rubruck* v. *Secretary of State for the Home Department* [1984] 2 CMLR 449, in which the immigration Appeal Tribunal recognised the existence of an informal system of extra-statutory review of such cases.

16. Case 29/84 *European Commission* v. *Germany (Re Nursing Directives)* [1986] 3 CMLR 579.

17. Paras. 68, 146 HC 251 (March 1990).

18. *The Daily Telegraph*, 2 July 1991.

consequently no agency equivalent to the Commission for Racial Equality (CRE) in the United Kingdom. The CRE in the UK appears to be limited to dealing with cases of discrimination which offend national law, and could not, therefore, deal with cases under which an EEC national was wrongly denied employment in the public service.[19]

Ireland and the United Kingdom are not in any sense unique in the way in which they do not fully implement Community law, and do not provide adequate remedies. They do, however, provide useful examples of what still needs to be done to make existing rights effective.

3.   THIRD COUNTRY NATIONALS

All the larger Member States who are ex-colonial powers have a history of non-EEC immigration. Some of those have also provided sanctuary for refugees from Eastern Europe and elsewhere. Many of these third State nationals have lived in Community countries for long periods without acquiring the nationality of the Host State. The practice of Member States in relation to them varies considerably. There is a strong case to be made for recognising their status at Community level,[20] but nothing has, as yet been done. In addition, there are third State nationals who have been granted refugee status, and other nationals who have more limited rights of residence. The Community has already reached agreement under the 1990 Dublin Convention on how asylum applicants will be dealt with, but there is no agreement on what, if any, rights they will have at Community level, and there is no standard of minimal procedural rights for them. On 2 July 1991 the British Government announced a new 'fast track' system for dealing with refugee cases, that does at least have the merit of allowing an 'in-state appeal' if a person cannot establish a *prima facie* claim to refugee status.[21] Refugees will still, however, have to overcome the initial hurdle of obtaining prior entry clearance for the United Kingdom from their country of departure, because airlines will refuse to carry them without such clearance documents.[22] Other States follow different procedures. It may, however, be possible to reach a common policy on visas, as Mr De Jong suggests,[23] but this is, unhappily, likely to be on the basis of the common denominator of the least generous criteria.

If such an objective is achieved, and information is exchanged about such applications following the Schengen model, then immigration control will have been largely 'Communitised'. The need, however, for Community-wide standards of

19. The Act only confers a role on the CRE in relation to 'unlawful discrimination' under the Act. Discrimination authorised by some other Act or Order will not be 'unlawful': Sec. 41 (1).

20. See T. Hoogenboom, contribution to this Volume at p. 511.

21. See *supra*, n 18.

22. Under the Immigration (Carriers Liability) Act 1987.

23. De Jong, contribution to this Volume at pp. 186-187; A limited degree of agreement has been achieved, although Britain is still insisting on questioning visa-holders on entry: *The Independent*, 5 July 1991.

appeal and judicial review of immigration cases, and for Community-wide remedies to secure information and rapid enforcement of judicial decisions will then become more pressing.

4. FREEDOM OF MOVEMENT AND THE SOCIAL ASSISTANCE BARRIER

The wealthy have never had much difficulty in securing rights of entry and residence in Europe. In the early stages of immigration control under the Aliens Act 1905 in the UK, passengers travelling First and Second Class were exempt from control.[24] Only those travelling steerage class were subject to examination. The rules have changed but the mentality remains. Both in Ireland and the United Kingdom even passengers who are Community nationals coming to exercise Treaty rights are subjected to detailed examination if they look 'down at heel'. The British Immigration Appeal Tribunal has upheld the legality of this practice,[25] although the European Court of Justice has recently refused to support it.[26] The fear of 'social tourism' has, however, remained a powerful factor, although based, it would seem, often on anecdotal evidence and press campaigns.[27]

The decision in *Antonissen*[28] has at last confirmed that the declaration of 1968, under which work seekers were allowed three months to find work and would have to leave if they claimed social assistance, is without legal effect. It had been acted upon in both Britain and Ireland.[29] The British Rules still deny a residence permit to a person who has drawn social assistance during his first six months of residence.[30] Although, of course, since *Lebon*,[31] a work seeker is not entitled to 'social advantages' under Article 71 Regulation 1612/68, he should not be denied a residence permit if he subsequently finds work. The decision in *Lebon* is a retrograde one, because indigenous nationals will be able to rely upon social assistance while they are looking for work. Community nationals from other Member States will be forced to rely on any benefits they can bring with them and upon their own resources. This seems hardly in line with the principle of non-discrimination enshrined in the Treaty.

---

24. Aliens Act 1905 Sec. 1 (3).
25. *Tisseyre* (6052) Unreported (1989).
26. Case C-68/89 *European Commission* v. *Netherlands*, Judgment of 30 May 1991, not yet reported.
27. See for example, *Daily Mail*, 8 October 1985 'Minister Praises Mail for Exposing Foreign Scroungers'; *Sunday Times*, 12 July 1986, 'Dole Racket is La Dolce Vita'.
28. *R.* v. *Secretary of State ex parte Antonissen*, [1989] 2 CMLR 957 (High Court QB); Case C-292/89, Judgment of 26 February 1991, [1991] 2 CMLR 373 (ECJ).
29. Sources within Irish Immigration Service (April 1991), and see Immigration Rules HC 251 paras. 69 (footnote) and 72.
30. Para. 148 HC 251.
31. Case 316/85 *Centre Public d'Aide Sociale de Courcelles* v. *Lebon* [1987] ECR 2811, [1989] 1 CMLR 337.

5.   A EUROPE WITHOUT FRONTIERS: A NEW APPROACH TO
      RIGHTS ENFORCEMENT?

For those who see freedom of movement as a right subject only to legitimate public
policy constraints, rather than simply a consequence of the creation of a trading area
without internal frontiers, there are serious risks in allowing free movement policy to
be determined according to 'managerial' criteria. If this were to be done, the
dominant ethic would be bureaucratic. The concerns would be about numbers,
record-keeping, information-exchanges and crime prevention, as they have in the
United Kingdom since the enactment of the Commonwealth Immigrants Act 1962.
Cooperation in the operation of immigration policy is to be welcomed, but not if the
price is a diminution in rights enforcement.

The Schengen Information System will be holding data on hundreds of thousands
of individuals. A community-wide system, feeding in to such national systems as the
British Suspects Index, is likely to contain information on even larger numbers. The
possibility of error will be considerable. Given the current inadequacy of national
remedies for protecting existing Community rights, any extension of rights and
obligations onto a Community level of inter-State cooperation will have to be
matched.

The Member States should not lose sight of the fact that all have benefited from
immigration in the past, not only materially, but in the enrichment of their national
cultures. Nor should they forget that birth rates are falling in Western Europe and
that the Community will be needing to recruit both skilled and unskilled workers in
non-EEC States. That process will not be helped if those individuals are treated as
third class citizens. For both Community and non-Community nationals living
abroad in the Community, the enforcement of such rights as they enjoy will be
crucial.

Consideration should be given, firstly, to a major revision of Directive 64/221/
EEC, to make the procedural provisions both more specific and applicable to all
types of decision affecting the entry and residence of Community nationals and
secondly, to the creation of a Community Ombudsman Service which would provide
advice and, if necessary, representation in each Member State. Such an Ombudsman
would have access to data, as in some national systems, and could provide a means
by which both existing rights conferred by Community law, and the new rights for
both Community nationals and third State nationals emerging with the Single
Market, could be made more effective. Such an Ombudsman would not operate
against the institutions of the Community (as proposed in the Luxembourg draft of
the new Treaty)[32] but against the national bodies which daily make administrative
decisions affecting the rights of entry and residence of Community and other
nationals living in the Member States.

32. Art. 137C.

Human Rights and
Free Movement of Persons

HUMAN RIGHTS AND FREE MOVEMENT OF PERSONS: THE ROLE OF THE EUROPEAN COMMISSION AND COURT OF HUMAN RIGHTS

Henry G. Schermers[*]

1. INTRODUCTION[**]

The free movement of persons in the European Community can be divided into three basic types: (1) movement within a particular Member State, (2) movement inside the Community between Member States, and (3) movement between Member States of the Community and third countries. For purposes of analysis of movement this latter type can be further subdivided into: a) movement out of the Community, and b) movement into the Community. All of these types of movement will be affected by the abolition of border controls inside the Community.

The free movement of persons within the territory of a Member State may be hampered somewhat if controls at the State borders are replaced by more controls inland. In practice, however, the movement of persons within State borders can hardly be influenced and cannot be prevented. It rarely causes problems.

Free movement of persons throughout the territory of the Community will in fact be possible when all border controls between the Member States of the Community are abolished. By exerting more controls within each Member State, law enforcement authorities may occasionally arrest people who moved illegally from one Member State to another. But it seems unlikely that these intrastate controls will actually prevent movement of persons between Member States. For these practical reasons, it will probably be impossible to prevent persons within the territory of the Community from moving freely inside that territory. The first question analysed in this report is the extent to which the European Convention on Human Rights grants them a fundamental human right to do so.

Free movement of persons from the Community to third countries offers no problems under Community law. The right to leave a country has been accepted by all

---

[*] Professor of Law, Leiden University, Member of the European Commission of Human Rights.

[**] Editor's note: All references to the 'Commission' and the 'Court' hereinafter made in this report shall mean the European Commission of Human Rights and the European Court of Human Rights, respectively. The Commission and the Court of Justice of the Europan Communities shall be referred to as the 'Court of Justice' and the 'EC Commission', respectively.

H.G. Schermers et al., eds., Free Movement of Persons in Europe
© 1993, T.M.C. Asser Instituut, The Hague.

Member States. Again, the question relevant to this report is whether the European Convention on Human Rights grants a fundamental human right to do so.

Most of the practical difficulties will arise with respect to movement of people into the Community. The questions presented are the extent to which the Community must grant a right of asylum, and the extent to which it is prohibited from expelling aliens. The European Convention on Human Rights is especially relevant to a determination of these issues.

2.   ARTICLE 2 OF THE FOURTH PROTOCOL

The European Convention on Human Rights does not contain any express provision on the free movement of persons. It also does not provide a right of asylum. In September 1963 the Fourth Protocol was added to the European Convention on Human Rights. Article 2 of that Protocol provides:

> 1. Everyone lawfully within the territory of a State shall, within that territory, have the right to liberty of movement and freedom to choose his residence.
> 2. Everyone shall be free to leave any country, including his own.
> 3. No restrictions shall be placed on the exercise of these rights other than such as are in accordance with law and are necessary in a democratic society in the interests of national security or public safety, for the maintenance of *ordre public*, for the prevention of crime, for the protection of health or morals, or for the protection of the rights and freedoms of others.
> 4. The rights set forth in paragraph 1 may also be subject, in particular areas, to restrictions imposed in accordance with law and justified by the public interest in a democratic society.

Most States that are parties to the European Convention on Human Rights are also parties to the Fourth Protocol.[1] In general, this means that movement of persons is guaranteed within the territory of each of the Member States of the Community under the European Convention of Human Rights. The three exceptions to this general statement are: (1) this guarantee does not apply to Greece, Spain and the United Kingdom, (2) France, Germany, Ireland, Italy and the Netherlands restricted the application of Article 2 of the Fourth Protocol by making certain reservations to it,[2] and (3) under paragraphs 3 and 4 of said Article, all participating States may make further restrictions. In practice, further restrictions permitted under paragraph 4 cannot be imposed by States that are also parties to the International Covenant on Civil and Political Rights (adopted by the General Assembly of the United Nations on 19 December 1966), which contains a similar Article (Art. 12) but without a qualification equivalent to paragraph 4 of Article 2. It is also important to note that,

---

1. Of the Member States of the Community, Greece, Spain and the United Kingdom are not parties to the Fourth Protocol (as of 15 April 1991).

2. See *European Convention on Human Rights*, collected Texts (1987) pp. 92-94.

regardless of whether further restrictions are imposed, the free movement of persons guaranteed by Article 2 of the Fourth Protocol only concerns movement *within* the Member States, not *between* them.

Paragraph 2 of Article 2 of the Fourth Protocol contains the fundamental human right to leave any country. We may, therefore, submit that the right to leave the Member States of the Community, and therefore also the Community itself, is a fundamental human right within the Community legal order, even though it has not been recognized by all Member States.

In April 1979 the Commission of the European Communities proposed that the Community should accede to the European Convention on Human Rights.[3] The EC Commission cited the anomaly between the fact that, on the one hand, all governmental acts of the Member States must comply with the European Convention on Human Rights and individuals have a right of petition if they do not, while on the other, acts of the Community are not subject to the same control. Both the increasing importance of international protection of human rights and the increasingly broad impact of Community legislation justify accession of the Community to the European Convention on Human Rights.

If the Community accepts the European Convention on Human Rights and its Fourth Protocol without making a reservation with respect to free movement, then all persons lawfully within the Community would have the fundamental human right of free movement within the entire territory of the Community. The question arises whether this fundamental right also exists without Community accession to the European Convention on Human Rights. In 1974 the Court of Justice of the European Communities held that:

'International treaties for the protection of human rights on which the Member States have collaborated or of which they are signatories can supply guidelines which should be followed within the framework of Community law.'[4]

This formula covers the Fourth Protocol because the Member States that have not ratified it, either collaborated on its drafting (Greece) or are signatories (Spain) or both (the UK). In practice, the Court of Justice applies the European Convention on Human Rights as much as possible.

The free movement of persons inside the Community is one of the aims of the Community. It is only a short step, therefore, to accept free movement of persons as a fundamental human right, even without the Community's formal accession to the European Convention on Human Rights.

3. Commission Memorandum 6724/79, Com. (79) 210, *Bulletin of the European Communities,* Supplement 2/79.

4. See e.g., Case 4/73, *J. Nold, Kohlen- und Baustoffgroßhandlung* v. *Commission of the European Communities [Second Nold Case],* [1974] ECR 491, at 507, para. 13.

3.   LAWFULLY WITHIN THE TERRITORY

In cases in which Article 2 of the Fourth Protocol is applicable, the main issue with respect to non-EC nationals is the lawfulness of their stay. When is a foreigner *lawfully* within the territory of the Community? The purpose of this provision is to restrict the right of free movement to those foreigners who have been expressly admitted to the State concerned. It is not necessary, however, that they have a residence permit. An early draft of the Fourth Protocol proposed: 'Everyone lawfully *residing* within the territory . . .' The word 'residing' was deleted in order to ensure that no residence permit would be needed.

The European Court of Human Rights has not yet ruled on the scope of the word 'lawfully' in the context of the Fourth Protocol. The case-law of the European Commission of Human Rights indicates that 'lawfully' means: 'in accordance with the law of the State concerned'. In the case of *Paramanathan* v. *Germany* the Commission held that the word 'lawfully' refers to the domestic law of the State concerned. Aliens admitted under certain conditions can only be regarded as 'lawfully within the territory' as long as they comply with those conditions.[5]

There may be cases involving aliens that have never been officially admitted to a State but who should nonetheless be considered as 'lawfully within the territory'. One should in particular consider the case where a foreigner is tolerated within the territory without express admission. In the Netherlands, for example, refugees from Iran, Iraq, Ethiopia, Sudan and Afghanistan are officially 'tolerated'. Certain refugees receive a letter stating that expulsion proceedings are pending against them, that they have no right to stay in the Netherlands, but that they would not be expelled for the time being because of the political situation in their State of origin. The letter also states that as soon as that political situation improves they could be expelled upon two weeks notice. This letter is accepted by the social services administration as sufficient basis for social security benefits but not for a right to take up employment. There may be other cases in which immigrants have not been officially accepted but are nonetheless tolerated in the country. For example, governmental toleration may be evidenced by the grant of a housing permit or the extension of social security benefits. The issue is whether the extension of such forms of governmental assistance establishes the recipient as being 'lawfully within the territory'. One should be careful in accepting this standard. For humanitarian reasons even illegal foreigners should be helped when their circumstances so require. A test for lawful stay that turns on a consideration of humanitarian aid would be undesirable because it would discourage such aid. However, a test for lawful stay should not discourage governmental authorities from delivering official documents to foreigners which they have accepted within the territory. If that were the case those foreigners would be deprived of their rights. If a State accepts a foreigner on its territory, it should also grant him the documents needed to legalise his stay. In the

---

5. *Paramanathan* v. *Federal Republic of Germany*, Application No. 12068/86, D & R 51, pp. 237-240.

Netherlands, a proposal has been made to grant a temporary residence permit to all aliens who have been in the country for eighteen months. This would mean that they are lawfully in the country during the term of validity of that permit.[6]

4. THE RIGHT OF ASYLUM

International law has never recognised a right to enter into the territory of a foreign State or a right not to be expelled or extradited once one is inside that territory. In fact, neither the Community, nor any State has ever recognised such rights. However, the Universal Declaration of Human Rights grants to everybody the right to seek and enjoy asylum from persecution in other countries. The right to enter into another State and to remain is limited to special cases. Even in these cases, however, the right is not accompanied by an obligation of any State to grant asylum. Furthermore, the right to seek asylum is not incorporated in the European Convention on Human Rights or in the Covenants of the United Nations.

In the Dublin Asylum Convention[7] of 15 June 1990 the EC Member States took a first step towards formulating a common policy for the admission of aliens. It is only a small step since each participating State has reserved the right to decide autonomously whether to admit any alien. The Dublin Asylum Convention is not part of Community law, which means that the Court of Justice has no competence to render preliminary rulings on its interpretation. Therefore, notwithstanding the large single territory of the Community, there is still no common authority or court responsible for immigration and asylum law and policy.

There is a need for a common authority in this field. Aliens prefer to appeal to an organ independent of the State that has refused them asylum. Increasingly, they appeal to the European Commission of Human Rights. By claiming that extradition or expulsion is inhuman treatment contrary to Article 3 of the European Convention on Human Rights or that it is an infringement of their right of family life guaranteed by Article 8, aliens try to persuade the Commission or the Court to prohibit their extradition or expulsion.

5. THE PROHIBITION OF INHUMAN TREATMENT

The European Convention on Human Rights does not cover States outside Europe. One cannot lodge a complaint to the Commission if a third country maltreats or threatens to maltreat its population. But under certain circumstances, expulsion or

---

6. The proposal of the 'Commissie Mulder' on this point was received sympathetically by the Netherlands Government. See Second Chamber Dutch Parliament [Tweede Kamer] 1990-1991, 21998, No. 2. See Hanneke Steenbergen 'Artikel 3 EVRM en de gedoogden', 16 NJCM Bulletin (June 1991) 296.

7. Convention determining the State responsible for examining application for asylum lodged in one of the Member States of the European Communities, done at Dublin, 15 June 1990, 30 ILM (1991) 425.

extradition to a third country engaged in such conduct may be contrary to the Convention. For example, the delivery of a person to a country where his life is in serious danger or where torture can be expected is inhuman treatment contrary to Article 3 of the Convention. This means that no person may be extradited or expelled to a country where he runs such risks, and that asylum must be granted to persons coming from such a country.

Does this mean that its high standards of human rights compel Europe to admit an unreasonably large number of refugees? Statistics show the contrary. Despite its strong financial capacities, Europe admits far fewer refugees than countries such as Thailand or Sierra Leone, which can hardly pay for its refugees.

The prohibition based on Article 3 against sending refugees to certain countries does not necessarily mean that they must be granted an unlimited freedom of movement. Article 5(1)(f) of the European Convention on Human Rights permits detention of a person either to prevent his unauthorised entry into the country or in preparation for deportation or extradition, provided, however, that any such detention is in accordance with a procedure prescribed by law. Furthermore, the Article 3 prohibition lasts only as long as the risk of torture or other danger to life exists in the third country. When circumstances change, extradition may become possible. The established case-law that no person may be expelled or extradited from a European country to a State where he may lose his life or be subjected to torture may result in the development of the European Commission on Human Rights into an institution of final appeal in expulsion and extradition matters in Europe, even though the right of asylum is not amongst the human rights incorporated in the European Convention of Human Rights. Before an applicant can bring a case before the European Commission of Human Rights, he must first exhaust all domestic remedies. However, after the exhaustion of those remedies, which is when the Commission becomes accessible, the expulsion may be effectuated. An opinion of the Commission or the Court that expulsion or extradition is in violation of the European Convention of Human Rights may then be too late to produce any practical effect.

The European Convention on Human Rights contains no provision for interim measures. To cope with the clear need for such measures, the Commission adopted Rule 36 in its rules of procedure:

'The Commission, or when it is not in session, the President may indicate to the parties any interim measure the adoption of which seems desirable in the interest of the Parties or the proper conduct of the proceedings before it.'[8]

When a case of imminent expulsion or extradition is brought before the Commission and it considers that there may be a serious risk of infringement of Article 3, the Commission will ask the State concerned to postpone expulsion or extradition until the Commission has had the opportunity to study the case. The Commission collects

---

8. For a discussion of this rule, see C.A. Nørgaard and H.C. Krüger, *Interim and Conservatory Measures under the European System of Protection of Human Rights*, Festschrift Ermacora, Engel Verlag (1988) pp. 108-117.

as much data as possible and may finally rule that expulsion of the alien, is in violation of Article 3.

The Commission has been reticent about applying Rule 36. The Commission requests postponement of expulsion or extradition only in serious cases accompanied by sufficient substantiation. As of the fall of 1989 Member States have always complied with Commission requests under Rule 36 in cases of expulsion. Requests to postpone extradition are also usually respected. In extradition cases a conflict of obligations may arise, when the government is obliged to extradite under an extradition treaty. The Government of the Netherlands once refused to postpone extradition on this basis.

The Commission is of the opinion that a request made under Rule 36 is legally binding on parties to the European Convention on Human Rights. The Commission bases its position on Article 25 of the Convention, which provides that States that have accepted the right of individual petition have undertaken not to hinder in any way the effective exercise of that right. Frustrating an application against expulsion by deporting the applicant before the Commission has had the opportunity to look at his case would be contrary to that Article 25.

In 1989 the Swedish Government refused to abide with two requests of the Commission under Rule 36 in cases of expulsion. The Commission declared both cases admissible. The Swedish Government subsequently reached a friendly settlement with one of the two applicants. He was permitted to return to Sweden and to reside there permanently. The Swedish Government offered to pay his costs and those of his lawyer and an additional 100,000 Swedish crowns as an *ex gratia* payment. The Commission, however, refused to accept the settlement offer unless the Swedish Government also admitted that it had erred by not following the Commission's request under Rule 36. Finally, the Swedish Government added a letter to its settlement offer in which it expressed its regret that the applicant was expelled after the indication under Rule 36 to the contrary. The Commission then accepted the friendly settlement.[9]

The Swedish Government did not want to settle the other case because it believed the expulsion had a less harmful effect. After studying the case, the Commission found no violation of Article 3. Nonetheless it sent the case to the European Court of Human Rights in order to obtain a Court decision on the binding effect of a request for interim measures. The Court ruled, by a majority of ten votes to nine, that no power to order interim measures could be inferred from either Article 25 or from any other source.[10] The judgment of the Court weakens the effect of Rule 36 and consequently, the position of aliens who are threatened with extradition.

Because the European Convention on Human Rights does not contain any right of asylum or prohibition of expulsion, aliens initially invoked it only rarely. Gradually, however, it was established that expulsion could constitute inhuman treatment contrary to Article 3. This caused a steady increase of applications to the Commis-

---

9. *Mansi* Case (15658/89), Report of the Commission of 9 March 1990.
10. Case of *Cruz Varas*, Judgment of 20 March 1991, Series A, no. 201.

sion against expulsion or extradition. Because there is no other international possibility of challenging their expulsion or extradition aliens now try to develop the Strasbourg procedures into a kind of judicial control over the European States' expulsion and extradition policies. The increase in cases demonstrates the need for such control. As most applications against expulsion or extradition are urgent, Rule 36 is increasingly invoked. The rule is applied only rarely to cases other than expulsion or extradition cases.

Until 1984 Rule 36 was invoked by applicants only about 50 times. About one third of these requests were accepted. After 1984 the number started growing. By the end of 1989 about 270 requests had been received. The percentage of cases in which the Commission or its President gave indications under Rule 36 decreased by fifty per cent during this period. Before 1985, one out of three cases were acted upon. By the end of 1989, only one of six cases were acted upon. The number of cases in which aliens invoke Rule 36 after an expulsion or extradition decision continues to increase rapidly. Between 1 January and 15 April 1991, about 300 requests to apply the Rule were received from applicants in the territory of France alone.

The Commission is not equipped to handle these large numbers of cases, especially as it is often impossible for applicants to provide the Commission with sufficient evidence. The Commission, therefore, leaves the final decision to the national authorities and applies Rule 36 only when an application is accompanied by documentary proof. This means that recently at least 95% of the requests had to be declared inadmissible.

From the human rights point of view the situation is unsatisfactory. Immigration officers usually consider their task to be the prevention of too large an influx of aliens. They are not charged with protecting human rights. Even though they must take human aspects into consideration, they may easily reach decisions that are unacceptable in terms of human rights. The national judiciaries do not, and will not, always have the means for proper control, particularly if future admission, expulsion and extradition decisions are taken (in whole or in part) by international institutions. The Schengen Agreement and the rules being developed between the Member States of the Community on the admission of aliens after 1992 have raised the fear that admission will be rendered more difficult and expulsion easier. Good international human rights supervision is desirable. Either the European Commission of Human Rights should be better equipped to handle these kinds of cases, or a special judicial organ should be established. Any such body should receive the fullest possible information about the situation in third countries in order to be able to assess the risk of harm resulting from deportation or extradition of aliens to such countries.

Apart from the *Cruz Varas* case, the role of the European Court of Human Rights in cases of expulsion or extradition of aliens has been limited. Claims that extradition or expulsion is contrary to Article 3 of the European Convention on Human Rights only rarely come before the Court. Normally when the Commission holds Article 3 applicable the State concerned will not expel.

The best example of a case in which extradition was considered to be in violation of Article 3 by the European Court of Human Rights is the *Soering* case. This case concerned the extradition by the United Kingdom of a 22 year old male charged with murder, which was allegedly committed in the Commonwealth of Virginia at the age of 18. As Mr Soering could be subject to the death penalty preceeded by a period on death row which lasts in Virginia an average period of seven years, it was submitted that extradition would be inhuman treatment contrary to Article 3 of the Convention. The Court held that the Convention does not require the Contracting States to impose Convention standards on other States. There is no general principle that a Contracting State may not surrender an individual unless it is satisfied that the conditions awaiting him in the country of destination are in full accord with each of the safeguards of the Convention. On the other hand, the Court held that a decision by a Contracting State to extradite a fugitive may give rise to an issue under Article 3, when there are substantial grounds to believe that the fugitive faces a real risk of being subjected to torture or to inhuman or degrading treatment or punishment in the requesting country. The Court concluded that extradition to Virginia would be contrary to Article 3 because of the real risk that Mr Soering would have to spend a very long period of time on death row under extreme conditions with the ever present and mounting anguish of anticipating the execution of the death penalty.[11]

6.   THE RIGHT OF FAMILY LIFE

In some cases in which family life could not otherwise have been enjoyed, the European Court of Human Rights has granted persons the right to join close relatives (spouses, parents) who were lawfully within the territory of a State that is party to the European Convention on Human Rights. The fundamental human right of family life requires admission to the State and prohibits subsequent expulsion.

The second paragraph of Article 8 of the Convention permits the participating governments to make certain exceptions to the right of family life. These exceptions must be based upon previous national legislation, and must be necessary in a democratic society for the protection of some important, and exhaustively enumerated, national interests. Among these possible national interests are the economic well-being of the country and the prevention of disorder. These interests permit a State to limit the admission of aliens. In order to establish whether an interference in the right to family life is necessary, the European Court of Human Rights requires that the relevant decisions must be justified by a pressing social need and, in particular, must be proportionate to the legitimate aim pursued. In practice both the Commission and the Court weigh the interests of the State against the interests of the individual.

Three examples may illustrate the cases where the Court will or will not accept that the right of family life will include the right to stay in a country.

---

11. *Soering* Case, judgment of 7 July 1989, series A, No. 161, pp. 33 and 44. After it became clear that the United Kingdom could not extradite Mr Soering without conditions, the United States accepted his extradition under the condition that the death penalty would not be imposed.

1. In the case of *Abdulaziz* the Court agreed with the Commission's established case-law: the right of a foreigner to enter or remain in a country is not as such guaranteed by the Convention, but immigration controls must be exercised consistently with Convention obligations, and the exclusion of a person from a State where members of his family are living may raise an issue under Article 8. The *Abdulaziz* case involved a number of foreign women who were lawfully established in the United Kingdom, but whose husbands were not permitted to have residence there. The Court accepted that in each case family life was at stake even if man and wife had not yet lived together. The Court held that the extent of a State's obligation to admit relatives of settled immigrants into its territory will vary according to the particular circumstances of the persons involved. It was not shown in the *Abdulaziz* case that there were obstacles to establishing family life in the home countries of either the wives or the husbands. Therefore, the Court did not find a lack of respect for the right of family life in the United Kingdom's refusal to admit the husbands to the country where the wives were lawfully living. However, when it was established that under similar circumstances a wive would be permitted to enter the United Kingdom in order to join her husband, the Court found an infringement of Article 14 which prohibits discrimination, *inter alia*, on the basis of sex.[12]

2. The case of *Berrehab* concerned the expulsion of a divorced husband whose child stayed with his former wife. In that case the Court held that cohabitation is not a necessary condition of family life between parents and minor children. The relationship created between the spouses by a lawful and genuine marriage has to be regarded as 'family life'. A child born of such a union is *ipso jure* part of that relationship. Subsequent events may break the tie, but that was not so in the case of Mr Berrehab who saw his daughter four times a week for several hours at the time. Because the Court accepted the existence of family life, the case turned on the applicability of the exception of Article 8 paragraph 2. The Court took into account that Mr Berrehab had lived for several years in the Netherlands, had a home and a job there, and that no complaint had ever been brought against him. In the light of these particular circumstances, the Court concluded that the interests of the individuals outweighted the interests of the State, and therefore, that the governmental means employed were disproportionate to the legitimate aim pursued. Because the measure taken was not considered necessary in a democratic society, the Court concluded that there was a violation of Article 8.[13]

3. The case of *Moustaquim* concerned an immigrant of the second generation. Abderrahman Moustaquim emigrated from Morocco to Belgium when he was one year old. For the rest of his life he lawfully lived in Belgium. Three of his seven brothers and sisters were born there. One of his elder brothers held Belgian national-

---

12. Case of *Abdulaziz, Cabales and Balkandali*, judgment of 28 May 1985, series A No. 94, p. 34, para. 67.

13. *Berrehab* Case, judgment of 21 June 1988, series A, No. 138, pp 15, 16, paras. 28 and 29.

ity. While Mr Moustaquim was still a minor (under eighteen years old), many charges of theft and five charges of robbery were brought against him. For several periods he was detained in a juvenile prison. After his 18th birthday he was again prosecuted and sentenced to two years imprisonment. After serving his prison sentence he was to be expelled from Belgium.

The question presented to the Court was whether the expulsion of a person from a country where he had virtually lived all of his life to a country where he knew neither the culture, nor the language, was an infringement of a fundamental human right. Two fundamental human rights, both recognized in Article 8 of the European Convention on Human Rights, were at stake: the right to respect for one's private life and the right to respect for one's family life. Private life is a vague notion. Any governmental order affecting a person can be viewed as an infringement of his private life. This would mean that no instructions can be given to persons unless the conditions of Article 8, paragraph 2 are fulfilled which means that the relevant governmental instructions must be in accordance with the law, and necessary in a democratic society in the interests of national security, public safety or the economic well-being of the country, or for the prevention of disorder or crime, the protection of health or morals, or the protection of the rights and freedoms of others. If the rights set forth in Article 8 are interpreted widely it may be possible to require the justifications set forth above for any governmental involvement with the private life of an individual. This may, however, stretch the scope of Article 8 too far.

Neither the Commission nor the Court considered it wise to base their decision on the notion of private life since they could find a sufficient basis in the notion of family life, which is more specific. Even though Abderrahman Moustaquim did not live with his parents and even though he was legally considered to be an adult, the Court held that there was an interference with the right to respect for family life. The Court pointed to the fact that he had never broken off relations with his parents and brothers and sisters and that the measure taken by Belgium resulted in his being separated from them for more than five years. Because the Court found that the family life of Abderrahman Moustaquim was affected, this case also depended on the applicability of the exception set forth in Article 8, paragraph 2 (which permit interference with family life). The Court accepted that the governmental interference was in accordance with the law and pursued at least one of the aims enumerated in Article 8, paragraph 2 (in particular 'the prevention of crime' and also 'the prevention of disorder'). The case turned on the question whether the deportation of Mr Moustaquim could be regarded as 'necessary in a democratic society'. Mainly because of the close ties of Mr Moustaquim with Belgium, the Court held that his interests were strong. On the other hand, the Court found the general interests of the Belgium Government less compelling in the light of the nature of the crimes committed and the relatively long interval between them and the deportation order. The Court held that a proper balance was not achieved between the interests involved, and therefore that the governmental means employed were disproportionate to the legitimate aim pursued. Accordingly, the Court found a violation of the applicant's right of respect for his family life.[14]

7.   CONCLUSION

The rapidly increasing number of cases brought by aliens who fear expulsion demonstrates the need for a legal framework for objective review of the expulsion decisions of the Member States. As it is also necessary to develop some kind of coordinated policy encompassing the Schengen Agreement and free movement of persons within the Community, it may be worthwhile to consider the establishment of a Community organ empowered to annul national decisions on expulsion and extradition. One of the main problems facing all decision-making authorities in this field is the difficulty of assessing the risks of harm resulting from the expulsion of aliens to a particular foreign country. These decision-makers must not only be informed about the actual political situation in foreign countries, but also should know how to identify members of prohibited opposition parties. A single central institution in Europe provided with all available information and expertise in this area would be better equipped to make decisions regarding the expulsion or extradition of aliens.

Of course, if one European organ is vested with this authority, the need will arise for judicial review of its expulsion and extradition orders. Article 1 of the Seventh Protocol to the European Convention on Human Rights provides:

1. An alien lawfully resident in the territory of a State shall not be expelled therefrom except in pursuance of a decision reached in accordance with law and shall be allowed:
   a. to submit reasons against his expulsion,
   b. to have his case reviewed, and
   c. to be represented for these purposes before the competent authority or a person or persons designated by that authority.

2. An alien may be expelled before the exercise of his rights under paragraph 1(a), (b) and (c) of this Article, when such expulsion is necessary in the interests of public order or is grounded on reasons of national security.

Not all of the Member States of the Community are party to the Seventh Protocol, but since it is an international treaty for the protection of human rights on which the Member States have collaborated, the Court of Justice of the European Communities could apply it as general principle of Community law.[15] Aliens lawfully within the territory of a Member State should, therefore, have some right of appeal, preferably to the Court of Justice. The Court of Justice could derive this right of appeal from the general principles of law, if it is not expressly provided elsewhere. Normally,

14. *Moustaquim* Case, judgment of 18 February 1991, series A, No. 193.
15. See *supra*, n. 4 and accompanying text.

Article 1 of the Seventh Protocol is not applicable to aliens who are seeking asylum or opposing their expulsion or extradition because these aliens are not lawfully within the territory of the State concerned. However, Article 60 of the European Convention on Human Rights permits the participating States to grant better protection of human rights than is provided for in the Convention. The European Community is a legal Community. It could play a leading role and set an example by granting legal review of all expulsion and extradition cases even when the person concerned is not lawfully within the territory of the Community.

THOU SHALT NOT OPPRESS A STRANGER (EX. 23 : 9): ON THE JUDICIAL PROTECTION OF THE HUMAN RIGHTS OF NON-EC NATIONALS
A Critique

J.H.H. Weiler[*]

1. INTRODUCTION

And I Charged Your Judges At That Time . . . Judge Righteously Between a Man and His Brother, and the Stranger That Is With Him. (Deu. 1: 16)

Frequently, the classical language of law, dispassionate, dry and technical conceals the dramatic social context to which it relates and masks the underlying ethical precepts and ideological prejudices on which it is premised. In the analytical and critical part of this essay I shall follow these hallowed cannons of our discipline.[1] But in this brief introduction I take the license to transgress the line. The treatment of aliens, in the Community and by the Community and its Member States, has become in my view a defining challenge to an important aspect of the moral identity of the emerging European polity and the process of European integration. Hermann Cohen (1842-1918), the great Kantian philosopher of religion, in an exquisite interpretation to the Mosaic law on this subject[2] captures its deep meaning in a way

---

[*] Professor of Law, Michigan Law School, Ann Arbor & Director, Academy of European Law, European University Institute, Florence. My thanks to Susanne Roggenbuck for her dedicated and skillful assistance.

1. The post-modernists among my readers can relax. The inability of a truly value free discourse is acknowledged and the possibility of exposing the contradiction of any normative language is always fun. It is a price I readily accept if the alternative is normatively empty critique. See Eagleton, *Literary Criticism* (1983) esp. pp. 144-150.

2. Ex. 22 : 20: And a stranger shalt thou not wrong, neither shalt thou oppress him; for ye were strangers in the land of Egypt. Ex. 23 : 9: And a stranger shalt thou not oppress; for ye know the heart of a stranger, seeing ye were strangers in the land of Egypt. Lev. 19 : 33,34: And if a stranger sojourn with thee in your land, ye shall not do him wrong. The stranger that sojourneth with you shall be unto you as the homeborn among you, and thou shalt love him as thyself; for ye were strangers in the land of Egypt: I am the Lord your God. Lev. 24 : 22: Ye shall have one manner of law, as well for the stranger as for the homeborn; for I am the Eternal your God. Num. 15 : 15,16: As for the congregation, there shall be one statute both for you, and for the stranger that sojourneth with you, a statute for ever throughout your generations; as ye are, so shall the stranger be before the Lord. One law and one ordinance shall be both for you, and for the stranger that sojourneth with you. Deu. 1 : 16: And I.

H.G. Schermers et al., eds., Free Movement of Persons in Europe

which seems ever more relevant in the 'European Ever Closer Union'. It has been usefully summarized as follows: 'This law of shielding the alien from all wrong is of vital significance . . . The alien was to be protected, not because he was a member of one's family, clan, religious community or people; but because he was a human being. In the alien, therefore, man discovered the idea of humanity.'[3]

It is this idea of humanity which the Community, or the Union, must safeguard. It is thus chilling, though not altogether unexpected, to watch the recent spate of ugly, at times murderous, racist, xenophobic and anti-semitic incidents sweeping through Europe, West and East.[4] There will, of course, always be those who perpetrate evil. They are few. There are those who avert their eyes, who pretend not to see, not to be involved. They are the many. It is the many who allow the few.[5] It is our reaction to the xenophobia which matters.

The reaction of European public authorities — representing 'the many' — has been complex. At one level, practically all public authorities have issued stern statements of disapproval regarding these events. Notably, the recent Maastricht Summit, at the very moment of making some first moves to the establishment of a European citizenship, issued a declaration on racism and xenophobia expressing its concern and revulsion '. . . that manifestations of racism and xenophobia are steadily growing in Europe . . .' especially towards third country nationals. But this principled reaction has not been without its own ambiguities. Electoral politics being what they are, politicians of all persuasions, at all levels in many Member States, have resorted to a new tough *'parlez vrai'* or even *'parlez cru'* type of discourse,

---

3. J.H. Hertz, *Commentary to the Pentateuch 313* 2nd edn. (1980) explicating H. Cohen, *Religion der Vernunft aus den Quellen des Judentums* [Religion of Reason, Out of the Sources of Judaism] Chs. 5, 8 and 9 esp. pp. 125 *et seq.* The early Teachers, all aliens in one sense or another, explicate the religious variant to this idea in their rendition of Leviticus 19.34 (But the stranger that dwelleth with you shall be unto you as one born among you, and thou shalt love him as thyself; for ye were strangers in the land of Egypt: I am the Lord your God).

4. This phenomenon has drawn attention world wide. It became notorious in the USA with the publication of a cover article in the Sunday Times Magazine of 15 September 1991 (Judith Miller).

5. Nowhere is this better expressed than in Richard von Weizsäcker's moving speech on 8 May 1985, one of the great speeches of this century:

'The perpetration of this crime [against Jews and other "aliens"] was in the hands of a few people. It was concealed from the eyes of the public, but every German was able to experience what [the victims] had to suffer, ranging from plain apathy and hidden intolerance to outright hatred.

. . .

The nature and scope of the destruction may have exceeded human imagination, but in reality there was apart from the crime itself, the attempt by too many people, including those of my generation, who were young and were not involved in planning the events and carrying them out, not to take note of what was happening. There were many ways of not burdening one's conscience, of shunning responsibility, looking away, keeping mum.'

I have addressed this issue more extensively in Weiler, 'The Patriarch Abraham, Law and Violence in the Modern Age', in *Rechtsstaat und Menschenwürde* — Festschrift für Werner Maihofer zum 70. Geburtstag (1988).

which while situated in the context of an inevitable debate on immigration policies, has had the effect of sanctioning or even inflaming, the excesses of the street.[6]

The very shaping of an external immigration policy — deciding who may come in and who will be left at the gate — involves a discourse which can easily pollute internal attitudes towards aliens within the polity. Two examples are sufficient to illustrate this point. Economic considerations such as weighing the utility of the migrant to the labour force and the costs of absorption to the host country are, perhaps, inevitable but they constitute a signal which feeds an attitude whereby aliens are regarded in utilitarian terms, like foreign investment or imported electrical energy. Concern for adequate cultural, linguistic and other adaptability may send a signal which accentuates both the otherness of the alien and an intolerance of the dominant culture towards such otherness.

So long as immigration policies are in place with their explosive social and political sensibilities they will continue to feed the internal xenophobic sentiments. This danger will persist, must be acknowledged and countered.

For the European Community there is a special responsibility — not only the legal responsibility under Community law (which I shall analyze below) towards non-Community nationals but also towards itself — its own identity, self-perception and ethos.[7]

Elsewhere I have argued[8] that one of the core ideas of the process of European integration has been to conceive of Europe as a community which does not only condition discourse among States but also spills over to the peoples of these States and thus seeks to influence relations among individuals. Take, for example, the classical provisions for free movement of workers. On the one hand they have a de-humanizing element in treating workers as 'factors of production' on par with goods, services and capital. But they are also part of a matrix which prohibits, for example, discrimination on grounds of nationality, and encourages generally a rich network of transnational social transactions. They may thus also be seen as intended not simply to create the optimal conditions for the free movement of factors of production in the common market. *They also as serve, echoing Hermann Cohen, to remove nationality and state affiliation of the individual, so divisive in the past, as the principal referent for transnational human intercourse.*

Here then is a dilemma and challenge of post-1992 Europe in this context. The successful elimination of internal frontiers will of course accentuate in a symbolic (and real sense too) the external frontiers of the Community. The privileges of Community membership for its Member States and of Community citizenship for

---

6. 'Social Parasites' (Haider, Austria); 'overdose of immigrants' (Chirac, France), etc. For more see, Miller, op. cit. n. 4.

7. *Sefer Hachinuch* [The Book of Education] published anonymously in Venice circa 1523 tries to explain the very deep meaning of Mosaic alien law. The very weakness of the alien acts as a temptation and the interdiction serves therefore to prevent us from abusing the power we have (over him or her). 'Each of us has the power to abuse the alien, and the Torah warns us to treat him as one of us, and through these interdictions we gain a precious soul, decorated and embellished with fine moral.'

8. Weiler, 'The Transformation of Europe', 100 *Yale Law Journal* (1991) pp. 2403 at 2478 *et seq.*

individuals are becoming increasingly pronounced. In one way, the more these external boundaries are accentuated the greater the sense of internal solidarity. (Thus, foregivably perhaps, the Community could not even resist the resort to statal symbols such as flag and anthem.[9] But in the very concept of citizenship a distinction is created between the native and stranger that tugs on their common humanity. The potential corrosive effect on the values of the community vision of European integration are self-evident. *Nationality as referent for interpersonal relations, and the human alienating effect of Us and Them are brought back again, simply transferred from their previous intra-Community context to the new inter-Community one. We have made little progress if the Us becomes European (instead of German or French or British) and the Them becomes those outside the Community.*

Thus, there is a delicate path to tread, one which is supportive of the process of European Union but acknowledges the dangers of feeding xenophobia towards non-Europeans and the even deeper danger towards one of the moral assets of European integration — its historical downplaying of nationality as a principal referent in transnational intercourse.

The task of traversing this path safely will not only fall on public authorities. There is an important role to be played by education (and educators), private groups, the Church and other 'non-statal' actors. But public authorities will be in the forefront.

I have already mentioned the ambivalence of holders of political office and the constraints of electoral politics. Similar doubts may be expressed as regards bureaucracies. Two factors may be mentioned, briefly, in this regard. First, their closeness to elected politicians and to the shaping and execution of immigration policies will tend to pull them to one side of the path. Second, bureaucracies tend to suffer from what may be called the banalization of suffering. Faced with large numbers of human problems, these become 'cases', the problems become 'categories', and the solutions become mechanical. We shall see examples of this even in the few Court 'cases' I shall discuss below.

Courts, especially high jurisdictions, are more removed from direct political pressures. They are also removed, one hopes, from the banalization effect. They will have thus a critical role to play in safeguarding the values of common humanity which must counter balance the exigencies of immigration policies.

In the sphere of application of Community law, the European Court must therefore approach its task of vindicating the rights of non-Community nationals with the full realization of the high stakes involved. Of course, the European Court, has to operate within a binding normative framework of rules and principles. But, like similar high jurisdictions, it also plays a role in shaping and developing the binding normative framework within which it operates. Likewise, its pronounce-

---

9. There has always been a flag waving over all manner of public villainy in Western history, and even Beethoven's Op. 125 stirring Ode to Joy was played to the victims of the greatest shame of Western civilization. Is it really necessary for the forging of a European consciousness to resort to those statal artifacts? Apparently yes.

ments not only resolve specific disputes but also constitute an important voice in the overall rethoric which is constitutive of the political culture of the polity.

Appreciation of these high stakes will impact, within the legitimate boundaries of judicial discretion, the way it shapes the normative framework.

2.   THE EUROPEAN COURT AND THE PROTECTION OF HUMAN
          RIGHTS OF NON-COMMUNITY NATIONALS

One critical dimension of the Court's charge[10] will be the extent to which it will be willing to review Community and Member State action for violation of fundamental human rights.

The strict legal question I shall pose is the following: 'What ought to be the jurisdictional limits of the European Court of Justice in protecting the Human Rights of non-EC nationals'?

Part of that answer is simple enough: The Court has stated and restated that it is its '. . . duty to ensure observance of fundamental rights in the field of Community law.' So, clearly and uncontroversially, all conduct by Community organs in this area, whether legislative, administrative or executive, is subject to review by the Court which must ensure observance of fundamental human rights by these organs. And one hardly needs reminding that the standard of review is not simply the European Convention of Human Rights (ECHR) — which must serve only as a base line — but all other norms of international law as well as Community norms deriving from the constitutional traditions of the Member States which might afford higher protection than the ECHR and other international guarantees.

Since, however, under the present stage of Community law most aspects of life of migrants within the Community are affected by Member State conduct, the delicate question is to enquire what in this area comes under the term 'in the field of Community law' and whether and how far should the European Court go in reviewing such conduct of the Member State authorities. As is well known the European Court has taken a prudent and self-limiting approach in this regard, but one that, nonetheless, has been expanding.[11]

In the field of non-Community nationals the Court has been, as we shall see, particularly prudent and has eschewed the boldness which characterizes some of its jurisprudence in other areas. It is understandable. This area is a political minefield in

10. This essay does not purport to cover the entire area of the treatment of non-Community nationals under Community law, but rather the very narrow topic of their rights to human rights protection by the European Court. Other aspects are dealt with extensively in other contributions in this volume.

11. Case C 159/90 *The Society for the protection of Unborn Children Ireland Limited* v. *Stephen Grogan and others*, Opinion of AG of 11 June 1991, OJ No. C 287/7 of 5.11.1991 and Case C 260/89 *Ellinik Radiophonia Tiléorassi* (ERT) v. *Dimotiki*. Judgment of 18 June 1991, OJ No. C 201/5 of 31.7.1991. See annotation by Slot, in 28 CML Rev. (1991) p. 964.

which governmental reaction to 'judicial meddling' may be particularly harsh.[12] It is also an area which in the past may have appeared less pressing in its social dimension and less critical to the evolving Community architecture and principles. As part of the phenomenology of judging, this is an area which may have appeared as not sufficiently important to 'spend judicial capital', measured in the coin of credibility and legitimacy, which is involved each time that a court breaks with the past and makes a new development.[13]

This, as I have been at pains to argue, has changed. The stakes now *are* high. The issue is critical. In other areas the Court has, in the face of a novel political, economic or social contexts, been willing to review its earlier jurisprudence and change course.[14] I am advocating a similar change here.

In the remainder of the article I shall try to show that this change is not only desirable but can be done well within the legitimate boundaries of judicial discretion and the classical cannons of legal construction and judicial interpretation practiced by the European Court.

It may of course be asked whether a more assertive role for the European Court, of expanding the type of case in which it would be willing to review alleged violation of human rights of aliens, is necessary. After all, in most Member States such migrants would enjoy protection under the national legal system by national courts. While in principle and in theory this is true, this solution is not always satisfactory. As Arnull and Jacobs argue, albeit in a slightly different context:

> 'Where national judges are called upon to apply those provisions, [protecting human rights] they should clearly give the same weight as the Court of Justice to the protection of fundamental rights. In practice, however, they may be influenced by the status accorded to such rights in their domestic law. Judges in the United Kingdom, for example, where there is no constitutional guarantee of fundamental rights and where the European Convention on Human Rights does not have direct effect may be less inclined to be swayed by arguments based on fundamental rights than judges in Member States where such rights are protected under their national constitutional law and where the European Convention is regularly applied by the national courts.'[15]

---

12. Note the caution whereby judicial review by the Court was excluded from the Maastricht Treaty provisions on Home Affairs, the code for immigration policy. See Article L, Title VII (Final Provisions) of Draft Maastricht Treaty.

13. See Kennedy, 'Toward a Critical Phenomenology of Judging', 36 *Journal of Legal Education* (1986) p. 518.

14. See for example the change of course in the Jurisprudence of the Court, conditioned, *inter alia*, by an appreciation of a new context: Case 302/87 *European Parliament* v. *Council* [1988] ECR 5615 ('*Comitology*'); Case 70/88 *European Parliament* v. *Council* [1990] I-2041 ECR ('*Chernobyl*'); Case 45/86 *Commission* v. *Council* [1987] ECR 1493 ('*General Tariff Preferences*'); Case 8/73 *Hauptzollamt Bremerhaven* v. *Massey-Ferguson GmbH* [1973] ECR 897.

15. Arnull and Jacobs, 'Applying the Common Rules on the free movement of persons - The Role of the National Judiciary in the light of the jurisprudence of the European Court of Justice ', paper submitted to the Asser Institute Colloquium on European Law, 12-13 September 1991 (hereinafter Asser Institute Colloquium), see p. 275 of this Volume.

One can think of other, political, reasons why national judges may not be as vigilant as the European Court and additionally, the Community standard of protection may, in certain instances, be higher than that prevailing in a particular Member State.

Further, if the scope of Community human rights law is extended to more situations covering non-EC nationals, also the Commission of the EC could play a role by bringing cases against Member State practices in situations where the non-EC national is unable to do so for either legal (e.g., lack of *locus standi* or direct effect) or practical (ignorance, poverty) reasons.

3.   THE PARADIGMATIC SITUATIONS

Most non-EC nationals enter Member States of the Community under the immigration rules of those States without any nexus to the Community and thus fall outside the scope of Community law. They are in the situation of a Member State national in his or her own country who, under the Court's doctrine of Reverse Discrimination, does not enjoy protection under Community law under the free movement provisions of the Treaty.

There are, however, two basic situations which bring non-EC migrants into the province of Community law:

a. Migrants falling under the umbrella of some international agreement between their country of origin and the Community bestowing 'direct rights' on migrants in the field of free movement; and

b. Migrants who enjoy 'derivative rights' by virtue of being family members of a Community national enjoying rights in another Member State.[16]

These situation concern the rights of residence itself. Of course, violation of human rights on non-EC Nationals might occur even if they are permitted residence in a Member State. Since the right of residence is politically the most explosive issue, and since all Member States accept that if a non-national is lawfully resident, his or her fundamental human rights may not be compromised, I shall focus only on the right of residence itself.

I have chosen to address some of the problems in this area by examining two typical cases representing the paradigmatic situation: the *Demirel* case[17] for the first category and the *Diatta* case[18] for the second.

---

16. This categorization is, of course, quite basic. One may identify other derivative rights such as employees of a firm providing services in another Member State. See Cases 62 & 63/81 *SECO SA and Desqueune & Giral SA* v. *Établissement d'Assurance contre la Vieillesse et l'Invalidité*, [1982] ECR 223 and discussion by W. Alexander, 'Free Movement of non-EC nationals. A review of the case-law of the Court of Justice', elsewhere in this Volume.

17. Case 12/86 *Meryem Demirel* v. *Stadt Schwäbisch Gmünd* [1987] ECR 3719.

18. Case 267/83 *Aissatou Diatta* v. *Land Berlin* [1985] ECR 567.

3.1   *Demirel* case

In its characteristically terse decision the Court tells us briefly that the action (an Art. 177 EEC reference) arose from an appeal against an order to leave the country issued by the German city of Schwabisch Gmund against Mrs Meryem Demirel, the wife of a Turkish national who had been lawfully living and working in Germany since 1979. Mrs Demirel did not come under the conditions of German law for family reunification which were tightened in 1982 and 1984 and which raised from three to eight years the period which a migrant in the situation of Mr Demirel had to live and work in Germany before his family could join him.[19]

There must be many cases such as this in many of the Member States. Was the order against Mrs Demirel a violation of his and her human rights? The reports by Errera, Schermers and others demonstrate how tricky interpretation and application of the rights to family life and others related rights is.[20] I leave, thus, that issue open.

Of interest to me then is not whether in this specific case Mrs Demirel's rights were infringed but, instead, whether and what role the European Court should have in determining that issue and whether it comes within the 'field of Community law'.

The Administrative Court in Stuttgart, to which Mrs Demirel appealed, made a preliminary reference to the Court, asking whether Article 12 of the Turkey EC Association Agreement and Article 36 of the Additional Protocol in conjunction with Article 7 of the Agreement lay down a prohibition, directly applicable in the Member States, on the introduction of further restrictions on freedom of movement applicable to Turkish workers. In other words whether these provisions created a standstill provision, which individuals could invoke before a national court, whereby under Community law Germany could not tighten the conditions for movement. The

---

19. Since we are dealing with human rights, it may be interesting to expand the narrative. The Report for the Hearing adds some human touch to this dry tale. When Mr Demirel arrived in Germany in September 1979 (himself under reunification law, joining his family) he would have had to wait only three years for reunification under the then existing law. He married in Turkey in August 1981 before the law was changed and when he would have had to wait only another 13 months for his bride to join him permanently. The Demirels had a son but the law changed and mother and son could not join husband and father; (son was conceived before the law changed.) On March 1984 Mrs Demirel entered with her son on a strict visitors visa. She violated her visa by not leaving Germany and her husband in June 1984 the visa expired. She also lied to the town authorities shortly before her visa expired saying she would leave. Instead she stayed. She was pregnant at the time and gave birth, in Germany, to another child. In May 1985 the City authorities issued the order to leave the country (threatening expulsion if she did not leave of her own volition) on the grounds that she had violated the conditions of her visa. They were not swayed by Mrs Demirel's plea of difficulty of establishing herself alone in Turkey, nor by the fact that again, she was pregnant with child. Her appeal to the Regional Administrative Authority in Stuttgart was also rejected. German authorities insisted that pregnant mother and children leave their country (and husband and father). Of course the option existed of her husband leaving his original family and his job in Germany and returning with his wife and children to Turkey; (meaning, of course, that he would be separated from his family).

20. See Schermers, 'Human rights and free movement of persons: the role of the European Commission and Court of Human Rights' at pp. 243-247 of this Volume.

Court also asked whether the expression 'freedom of movement' in the Association Agreement gave rights to workers resident in a Member State to bring children and spouse to join them. (Interestingly, the German Court, unlike the German administrative authorities, believed that the reply to both question was affirmative).

The European Court analyzed Articles 12 and 36 and concluded that they 'essentially serve to set out a programme and are not sufficiently precise and unconditional to be capable of governing directly the movement of workers.' As regards Article 7 (the functional equivalent of Art. 5 EEC) it concluded that '[t]hat provision does no more than impose on the Contracting Parties a general obligation to cooperate in order to achieve the aims of the Agreement and it cannot directly confer on individuals rights which are not already vested in them by other provisions of the Agreement.'

Consequently the European Court held that none of these Articles was directly applicable which obviated the need to answer the second question at all.[21]

That is a plausible interpretation of the provisions. Two other issues, which were not the subject of a specific question by the Stuttgart Administrative Court, were raised before the European Court which are of more direct concern to the jurisdictional issue at the centre of my enquiry.

The Government of the UK (forcefully) and that of Germany (ambivalently) challenged the jurisdiction of the Court to interpret those parts of the Association Agreement — a mixed agreement — dealing with Turkish migrant workers:

> 'The Agreement and Protocol constitute . . . a mixed agreement in which the Community has competence in relation to some matters and the Member States have competence in relation to others.'[22] 'The measures adopted by the Council approving those instruments in the name of the Community in accordance with Article 228 of the EEC Treaty as well as the Court of Justice's power of interpretation under Article 177 relate only to the provision which are within the powers of the Community. The EEC Treaty does not confer any powers on the Community either to legislate or to enter into external agree-

---

21. From a strict legal point of view this case does not resolve the substantive question of the referring Court. If the Commission had brought an action against Germany, the Court may have given a different reply on the substance. Imagine that in the Fisheries Case (Case 804/79 *Commission* v. *UK* [1981] ECR 1045) an individual would have brought an action rather then the Commission. Clearly, in that case too the Court would have held that the relevant provisions of Community law did not produce direct effect. And yet, since it was an action by the Commission the Court had to go into the merits and actually found against the UK.

22. It should not be assumed, as the German Government explicitly argued, that the 'mixed nature of the agreement proves that certain commitments entered into *vis-à-vis* Turkey could not and must not have been entered into by the Community.' (p. 3725) It is quite possible for the Community and its Member States to opt for a mixed agreement as a matter of internal political expediency even if the agreement actually covers matters falling entirely within putative Community competence. In Opinion 1/78 the financing of the Rubber Agreement could, according to the Court, have been done either by the Community or the Member states. The Court allowed the Community the option to go mixed or pure. Such an agreement would be clearly illegal only if the matters so covered fell within exclusive Community competence eg ex Article 113 EEC. On this issue see now also Case 192/89 *Sevince* v. *Staatssecretaris van Justitie* [1990] ECR I-3461.

ments with regard to the movement of workers from non-member countries.' (Submissions of the Parties, p. 3729).

It is important to follow the structure and content of the Court's reply with particular attention.

The Court first recasts the Member State challenge thus:

'[T]he German Government and the United Kingdom take the view that, in the case of "mixed" agreements . . . the Court's interpretative jurisdiction does not extend to provisions whereby Member States have entered into commitments with regard to Turkey *in the exercise of their own power which is the case of the provisions on freedom of movement for workers.'*[23]

'In that connection it is sufficient to state that that is precisely not the case in this instance.'

The recasting is subtle but significant. The UK (and Germany) in their submission contended that the Community had no power in this area and thus, *ipso facto* and *ipso jure*, the free movement provisions would be an exercise of Member State powers over which the Court has no interpretative jurisdiction. The Court could simply have refuted the absence of Community powers in this area. But that would have left open the possibility that this was an area of concurrent (Community and Member State) powers and that in relation to free movement the provisions in the Agreement were an expression of Member State rather than Community powers, even if the Community did have theoretical powers in this area.[24] So, to avoid this problem, the Court recasts the challenge to its jurisdiction. It asks not simply whether the Community had powers in this area but whether, in this agreement, the provisions in question were an *exercise of Member State powers*, a subtle but significant difference.

The Court than says: 'that is precisely not the case.' What is not the case? That the Community had no powers in this area? Not simply that, though that too of course. It is not the case that in relation to the Agreement with Turkey the provisions on free movement were an exercise of the Member States' own powers. The importance of this will transpire shortly.

The Court then interprets the Agreement with Turkey as creating 'special, privileged links' with a non-member country which must, at least to a certain extent partake in the Community system and thus, according to the Court, Article 238, the Visa of the Agreement:

'must necessarily empower the Community to guarantee commitments towards non-member countries in all the fields covered by the Treaty. Since freedom of movement for

---

23. Emphasis added.

24. One recalls that in the Opinion 1/78 (Rubber) [1978] ECR 2151 the Court held that both the Community and the Member States had jurisdiction over the financial provisions of the Agreement and that they could elect whose competence would be exercised. If they elected for the Member States, the Agreement would, as a result, be mixed.

workers is, by virtue of Article 48 et seq., . . . one of the fields covered by that Treaty, it follows that commitments regarding freedom of movement fall within the powers conferred on the Community by Article 238. Thus the question whether the Court has jurisdiction to rule on the interpretation of a provision in a mixed agreement containing a commitment which only the Member States could enter into in the sphere of their own powers does not arise.'[25]

It does not arise only if, indeed, in the Turkey Agreement the free movement provisions were an expression of Community powers and not that of the Member States.

An interim conclusion therefore is, that in establishing its jurisdiction to interpret the free movement provisions of the Agreement, the Court did not only assert the existence of Community competence in this area, but also actual exercise of such competence by the Community rather than by the Member States.

The Court ends this part of the decision by going on to state, that this conclusion is not affected by the fact that:

'in the field of free movement for workers, as Community law now stands, it is for the Member States to lay down the rules which are necessary to give effect in their territory to the provisions of the Agreement or the decisions to be adopted by the Association Council.'[26]

Recalling its decision in Kupferberg, the Court states that:

'in ensuring respect for commitments arising from an agreement concluded by the Community institutions the Member States fulfil, within the Community system, an obligation in relation to the Community which has assumed responsibility for the due performance of the agreement.'[27]

Kupferberg dealt, of course, with a pure rather than mixed agreement. But this fact is not material if we accept the logic of the Court whereby in the Turkey Agreement the free movement provisions were an exercise of Community powers.[28]

En route to establish its own jurisdiction the Court found thus, that:

a. the free movement provisions in the agreement are an exercise of Community rather than Member State powers;

---

25. Recital 9 of Decision.
26. Recital 10 of Decision.
27. Recital 11 of Decision.
28. In its judgment in the *Sevince* case, *supra* n. 22, 192/89 *Sevince*, the Court is even more forceful in asserting jurisdiction of a mixed agreement, without reference to the precise demarcation between Community and Member State competences: '. . . provisions of an agreement concluded by the Council under Articles 228 and 238 of the EEC Treaty form an integral part of the Community legal system' (Recital 8). In *Demirel* the Court qualified this statement by the inclusion of the words: '. . . as far as the Community is concerned' (Recital 7) thus alluding to the mixed nature of the Agreement, suggesting that this inclusion in the Community legal system will apply only to those areas for which the Community has competence. In *Sevince*, the qualifying phrase has been dropped.

b. the Community is the guarantor of the commitments in this field;

c. that the Member States in relation to these commitments act as executors of a Community responsibility.

In direct response to the questions posed by the preliminary reference the Court concluded that upon analysis of the relevant provisions,[29] the Agreement does not introduce a standstill as regards provisions for family reunification so that further restrictions in this matter are permissible under the terms of the Agreement and that in any event these provisions do not constitute rules of Community law which are directly applicable in the internal legal order of the Member States.

The Court examined Article 12 which provides that the Contracting Parties agree to be guided by Articles 48, 49 and 50 of the EEC Treaty for the purpose of progressively securing freedom of movement for workers between them. Article 36 of the Protocol to the Agreement provides that freedom of movement shall be secured by progressive stages in accordance with the principles set out in Article 12 of the Agreement between the end of the 12th and 22nd year of entry into force. Further, Article 36 charges the Council of Association with *exclusive* powers to lay down detailed rules for the progressive attainment of freedom of movement in accordance with political and economic conditions.

It is not surprising that in the face of these vague provisions, the Court concluded that these provisions:

'essentially serve to set out a programme and are not sufficiently precise and unconditional to be capable of governing directly the movement of workers.'[30]

But even assuming the Court to be correct, *neither of these responses disposes of the issue of Human Rights*. They miss the point.

It may be that the Agreement does not impose a standstill and that new restrictions on family unification may indeed be introduced. But it is a separate question whether one of the contracting parties to the Agreement, in introducing new restrictions, may violate the human rights of migrant workers in this connection. There is, after all, a large legal space between a conclusion which interprets the agreement as permitting the introduction of new restrictions on family unification and a conclusion which states that these new restrictions may violate human rights under the Agreement.

It may be that the correct interpretation of the Agreement is that new restrictions may be introduced, so long as these do not violate fundamental human rights.

The fact that the Court concluded that the provisions of the Agreement did not produce direct effect is also, from the perspective of protection of fundamental human rights, non-dispositive.

---

29. Articles 7 and 12 of the Agreement, Decision 1/80 adopted by the Council of Association pursuant to Article 36 of the Protocol to the Agreement.

30. Recital 23 of Decision.

First, even if individuals could not rely on provisions of the Agreement, this does not mean that, say, the Commission could not take the matter up. The Court has held that the GATT does not produce direct effect so that individuals cannot rely on it as against violations by Member States or the Community. But surely if the Commission could sue a Member State violating the GATT and a Member State could sue the Commission or Council for violation of the GATT. The holding of non-direct effect in this case is only procedural in nature: it establishes the inability of an individual to rely on a certain provision. It does not go to the merits.

But there is a deeper reason why the finding that Article 12 of the Agreement and Article 36 of the Protocol read in conjunction with Article 7 do not constitute rules of Community law which are directly applicable in the internal legal order of the Member States is not dispositive of the fundamental human rights issue.

In its famous line of cases starting with *Stauder* and going through *Nold, Hauer, Panasonic* and all the rest, the Court has held, and it is reaffirmed in the *Demirel* case as well, that 'it is the duty of the Court to ensure observance of fundamental rights in the field of Community law.' Provided the measure under attack is indeed in the field of Community law, (and this normally will be the case as regards a Community measure rather than a Member State measure,) the unwritten human right guarantees have always been held implicitly to produce direct effect, i.e., they were such that an individual could always rely on them. I do not recall any case where the Court has enquired whether the standards of Human Rights it applies to review measures in the field of Community law are themselves directly effective. It has always been assumed that they are in the sense of individuals being able to invoke them. How else could they afford protection to individuals? This is a juridically significant fact since it represents an important departure from the normal doctrine of direct effect which insists on measures being sufficiently clear precise and unconditional. Whereas the last condition is implicit in the human rights applied by the Court (unconditionality), the matter is more complex in relation to the first two conditions. Could it be said that the Human Rights which the Court applies — by a complex investigation into different international instruments and comparative constitutional law — are really 'clear' and 'precise'?

So, in this case, the fact that the substantive provisions of the Agreement are held not to have direct effect, does not mean that an individual cannot rely on human rights norms, provided these come within the jurisdictional province of the European Court of Justice. But whether they so come is not an issue which should turn on the separate issue of direct effect of this or that positive measure within the Agreement.

I want to stress this point further. Should the European Court of Justice receive under Article 177b a challenge to any internal measure of Community law on the grounds that it violates fundamental human rights, the Court will always give an answer to that preliminary reference. It would never decline an answer on the grounds that the challenged measure itself does not have direct effect. The individual is not relying on the challenged measure for his or her rights but on the human rights norm. In relation to this norm, it is always assumed that it has direct effect in the sense of allowing the individual to rely on it. If this were not so, the whole human rights protection would practically disappear since so many of the human rights which the Court asserts do not satisfy the trilogy of conditions for direct effect.

How does it deal with the issue of human rights in *Demirel*?

To its credit the Court, unlike one of the Member States intervening in the case, acknowledges that there is an issue of human rights here which is not simply disposed of by the direct effect issue. In dealing with this issue the Court makes the following moves:

The Court poses the question by asking whether Article 8 of the ECHR has any bearing on the issue.

The Court then repeats its Cinetheque formula:

'. . . although it is the duty of the Court to ensure observance of fundamental rights in the field of Community law, it has no power to examine the compatibility with the European Convention on Human Rights of national legislation lying outside the scope of Community law.'[31]

This formulation in itself is unexceptional; but the question becomes what is the scope of Community law in this area.

In this regard the Court states:

'In this case, however, as is apparent from the answer to the first question, there is at present no provision of Community law defining the conditions in which Member States must permit the family reunification of Turkish workers lawfully settled in the Community. It follows that the national rules at issue in the main proceedings did not have to implement a provision of Community law. In those circumstances, the Court does not have jurisdiction to determine whether national rules such as those at issue are compatible with the principles enshrined in Article 8 of the European Convention on Human Rights.'[32]

In my view this is a very problematic statement for a variety of reasons. First, and in passing, one should point out that putative review for violation of fundamental human rights should not only be conducted by reference to the ECHR but by reference to any internationally binding norm in this field, as well as any norm to be found as common to the constitutional traditions of the Member States. But this would be a moot point if, indeed, the Court were correct in stating that it had no power of review at all. This I believe is open to doubt.

It is correct that there is no positive provision of Community law defining the conditions in which Member States must permit the family reunification of Turkish workers lawfully settled in the Community. It is also true that the national rules at issue in this case did not have to implement directly a positive provision of Community law.

31. Recital 28 of Decision.
32. Recital 28 of Decision.

But it does not strictly follow from the absence of positive provisions of Community law defining the conditions in which Member States must permit family reunification and requiring implementation, that this field is totally 'outside the scope of Community law.' Nor does it follow that the Member States are totally free under the Agreement, and thus under Community law (*Kupferberg* and new *Sevince* formula) to do whatever they want, including the violation of the fundamental human rights of migrants from Turkey.

My contention is that even in the absence of positive Community law defining with precision many of the conditions of sojourn of migrants from Turkey, a situation which leaves much liberty to the individual Member States in setting such conditions, the European Court of Justice retains jurisdiction (and a duty) to ensure that the fundamental human rights of such migrants, in relation to their rights of residence, should not be violated either by the Community or by its Member States.

My reasoning is as follows: First I defend the proposition that by the mere fact that in a certain area there is no *positive* provision of Community law which the Member States must implement, the matter is not necessarily taken entirely outside the scope of Community law for the purposes of review by the Court of Justice in general, and review for violation of fundamental human rights in particular. I would like to argue, very cautiously, by analogy to similar provision from the Community internal system itself.

In *Rutili* the principal issue which the European Court had to answer concerned the conditions under which a limitation on the free-movement regime would be justified on grounds of public policy, a permitted derogation under Article 48 EEC.

Although the Court first confirmed that the Member States were '. . . *in principle*, free to determine the requirement of public policy in the light of their national needs' this determination would be subject to Community control.[33] Community control could of course derive from the substantive requirements of primary and secondary Community law. Thus, Directive 64/221/EEC requires, *inter alia*, consideration of the individual circumstances of the migrant.

Apart from specific secondary Community law, the freedom of the Member States to determine the scope of public policy as a ground for restricting the freedoms of the Community migrant worker is limited by more general, but explicit, provisions in the Treaty. Most important is the principle of non-discrimination on grounds of nationality articulated in Article 7 EEC. Thus, even if the definition of French public policy had not been at variance with specific provisions of Community law, some of which I outlined above, it could still fall foul of the Treaty regime if it involved a non-authorized discrimination between French nationals and Community migrants.

But what would be the situation if the state concept of public policy did not violate positive Community law? In other words, what if the national system

---

33. See the excellent discussion in Arnull and Jacobs: 'Applying the Common Rules on the free movement of persons - The role of the national judiciary in the light of the jurisprudence of the European Court of Justice ', at pp. 278-280 of this Volume.

permitted — in a *non-discriminatory way* — practices contrary to the standards of human rights accepted by the Court in its general jurisprudence of Human Rights?

Having earlier in the judgment asserted that the determination by Member States of public policy was subject to Community control, the Court then expanded on the explicit provisions of Community law on the subject, both general and specific, and in fact found the French practice in violation. Although in an *obiter dictum*, the Court went on to suggest, in language virtually identical to that in the human rights cases, that the explicit rules of Community law limiting the power of the Member States to control aliens (by devices such as public policy) *were a specific manifestation of the more general principle*, enshrined in Articles 8, 9, 10 and 11 of the Convention for the Protection of Human Rights and Fundamental Freedoms.[34]

If the Community law is but a specific manifestation of a general principle it should follow that the general principle forms part of the Community regime which controls the practices of the Member States under the derogation. It further follows, that a national practice which violated this general principle *without violating a specific rule of the Community regime*, would violate Community law and, by virtue of the principle of supremacy, be inapplicable.[35] The protection against violation of fundamental human rights accorded by EEC law to Community migrants, exists according to this logic, independently of the specific regulations and directives concretising the provisions in the Treaty.

We are of course aware that in the *Cinetheque* decision the Court refused to apply this reasoning in the field of free movement of goods, and indeed has relied on its *Cinetheque* formula in the *Demirel* case. But perhaps a distinction could, and should, be drawn, especially in relation to fundamental human rights, between provisions dealing with the situation of real living human beings and that dealing with goods?

---

34. Case 36/75 *Rutili* v. *Minister for the Interior* [1975] ECR 1219 esp. Recital 32.

35. At least two other cases are worth mentioning: in Case 222/84 *Marguerite* v. *Chief Constable Johnston of the Royal Ulster Constabulary* [1986] ECR 1651, in reviewing the compatibility of British administrative and legislative action with Directive 76/207/EEC (sex discrimination), the Court said:
'The requirement of judicial control stipulated by that article reflects a general principle of law which underlies the constitutional traditions common to the Member States. That principle is also laid down in Articles 6 and 13 [of the ECHR]. As the European Parliament, Council and Commission recognized in their Joint Declaration of 5 April 1977 . . . and as the Court has recognized in its decisions, the principles on which that Convention is based must be taken into consideration in Community law.'

In Case 118/75 *Watson and Belman* [1976] ECR 1185, Advocate-General Trabucchi was quite explicit:
'[R]espect for fundamental principles governing the protection of the rights of man... may, within the sphere of application of Community law, also be of importance in determining the legality of a State's conduct in relation to a freedom which the treaty accords to individuals . . . [W]ithout impinging upon the jurisdiction of other courts, this Court too, can look into an infringement of a fundamental right by a State body, if not to the same extent to which it could do so in reviewing the validity of Community acts, at least to the extent to which the fundamental right alleged to have been infringed may involve the protection of an economic right which is among the specific objects of the Treaty.'

In any event, *Rutili* has never, to my knowledge, been explicitly disapproved.[36] Arnull and Jacobs, particularly important commentators for obvious reasons, continue to cite Recital 32 in *Rutili* for the proposition that 'Fundamental rights are therefore capable of influencing the way in which the Community provisions on free movement of persons are interpreted and applied by the Court of Justice.'[37] They do not, of course, necessarily subscribe to my reading of that recital in the decision. The Decision of the Court in *Wachauf*,[38] the Opinion of the Advocate-General in the recent *Irish Abortion* case[39] and the Decision of the Court in *ERT*[40] suggest that the Court will review Member State action for violation of human rights in an *exception* to a positive provision of Community law, i.e., explicitly in an area in which the Member State *ipso facto* and *ipso jure* is not implementing a positive disposition of Community law.[41] It would seem that on this narrow issue *ERT* actually reverses the earlier decision in *Cinetheque*, or comes close to such reversal.[42]

It should be emphasized that I am not arguing here that *Rutili* and the other internal cases can be applied directly to the situation of the Turkish migrant. The scope of the Community Treaty and of the Association Agreement with Turkey are, after all, vastly different. I am, however, arguing for the narrower proposition, which I think these cases do prove, that the mere fact that the Member States are left a margin of action because of the absence of positive Community norms, does not *necessarily* mean that this area is totally outside the scope of Community law for the purpose of review by the Court.

One must still prove that similar protection must also derive from the Association Agreement and its Protocol. After all, Articles 48 EEC (in *Rutili*) or 56 and 66 (in *ERT*) produce direct effect whereas the Court found, correctly, that Article 12 of the Association Agreement and Article 36 of the Protocol did not produce such effect. There is a thesis which holds that the protection by the Court of fundamental human rights extends only to areas covered by directly applicable Community law capable

36. A very recent treatment of this topic suggests, cautiously, in an attempt to reconcile Rutili and Cinetheque that '. . . it might be said that [after Cinetheque the Rutili rationale] may be purely limited to questions concerning Article 48(3) EEC and not to Article 30.' A. Clapham, Human Rights and the European Community: A Critical Overview at page 38 (Nomos, 1991). Cf., too, Case 249/86 *Commission v. Germany* [1989] ECR 1263.

37. See *supra*, n. 18 and text thereto.

38. Case 5/88 *Wachauf* v. *Federal Republic of Germany* [1989] ECR 2609.

39. Case C 159/90 *The Society for the Protection of Unborn Children Ireland Limited* v. *Stephen Grogan and others*, opinion of AG of 11 June 1991, OJ No. C 287/7 of 5.11.1991. The Court in its Decision avoided the issue.

40. Case C 260/89 *ERT* of 18 June 1991, OJ No. C 201/5 of 31.7.1991.

41. See in particular Recital 43 or *ERT*.

42. I have dealt extensively with the problematic nature of Cinetheque in this regard in Weiler, 'The European Court at a Crossroads: Community Human Rights and Member State Action' in F. Capotorti et. al., eds., *Du droit international au droit de l'integration* – Liber Amicorum Pierre Pescatore (1987).

of producing direct effect. Additionally, in the Community situation, there were already implementing provisions to Article 48 EEC.[43]

Here, then, are my reasons to argue that also in the context of the Association Agreement with Turkey, despite the large margin of manoeuver accorded the Member State, this residual jurisdiction of the Court to review for violation of human rights should exist and that the Court may have erred in denying this in the *Demirel* decision.

It must first be noted that although Articles 12 and 36 lack the precision necessary to produce direct effect, the Association Agreement as a whole is directly applicable and capable of producing such effect. The references by the Court to its earlier *Haegeman* decision (Agreement with Greece) and *Kupferberg* (Agreement with Portugal) are evocative in this respect, and in subsequent decisions, the Court in fact found that some provisions under the Agreement did produce direct effect.[44]

It must also be noted, that although Articles 12 and 36 themselves do not produce direct effect, and also leave because of the vagueness of the obligations a large measure of discretion to the Member States, some other provisions are not quite in the same category. For example Article 37 of the Protocol prohibits any discrimination based on nationality between Turkish workers and Community workers as regards conditions of work and pay.

Could not then the principle announced by the Court in *Rutili* that the explicit rules of Community law limiting the power of the Member States to control aliens (by devices such as public policy) were a specific manifestation of the more general principles of human rights be applicable here? In other words that implicit in the Agreement is a prohibition on violation of Human Rights to which one adds, from time to time, specific positive duties setting explicit conditions.[45] Would it not be a strange construction of the Association Agreement and Protocol which forbade the Contracting Parties discrimination in working conditions and pay but allowed violation of the human rights in general? In other words, I think that it is a conservative interpretation of the Association Agreement with Turkey, to claim that whatever protection it gave migrants workers under specific disposition, there is an implicit prohibition on the parties to violate the fundamental human rights of migrant workers covered by the Agreement.

This argument is not nullified by the possible objection that Article 37 is addressed to the Member States. The Court held, in upholding its own jurisdiction to interpret the free movement part of the Agreement, that it was the Community which had overall responsibility and that the Member States were simply executing that

---

43. Quaere: Would the Court not protect the fundamental human rights of Community migrants even before the adoption of implementing legislation under Article 48? Note, too, as will be discussed below, that there is some implementing measures to the Turkey Agreement.

44. Judgment in the *Sevince* case, *supra*, n. 22, loc. cit., n. 22.

45. This has taken place already twice under the Association Council in its decisions 2/76 and 1/80. The later contains a very specific standstill provision as regards access to employment of migrants already legally in the Community.

general responsibility. As mentioned above, this construct is even further strengthened in the later *Sevince* case.

An additional argument derives from the general principles of pre-emption.

In the earlier part of its decision the Court held, it will be recalled, that it had jurisdiction over the free movement provisions of the Agreement since the Agreement in question creates special and privileged links with a third country which must, at least to a certain extent, take part in the Community system. It added that the Community must be empowered to guarantee commitments towards non-Member States in this field. What are these commitments? What exactly is the Community guaranteeing here? The objectives of the Agreement are, *inter alia*, the establishment '*des liens de plus en plus étroits entre le peuple turc et les peuples réunis au sein de la Communauté économique européenne*' (Preamble). It is towards, *inter alia*, this end that Article 36 of the Protocol affirms that the free circulation of workers will be secured by progressive stages in accordance with the principles set out in Article 12 of the Agreement and Article 12 of the Agreement provides that the Parties will be guided by Articles 48-50 of the Treaty.

Does this not mean, as a matter of pre-emption,[46] that whereas the Member States have not lost their competence in this field and retain a large margin of decision, they may, nevertheless, not adopt measures which actually obstruct the attainment of those provisions? And would not violations of human rights of migrant workers constitute such obstruction?

This legal duty may or may not be such that an individual could rely on it as a directly effective right, but surely in the existence of the Agreement, the Protocol, the Decisions of the Association Council we have sufficient 'elements of law'[47] to trigger such a duty on the Member States even absent a positive Community measure. If this is so, than the Court was wrong in its act of self-denial. At least the Commission, which is not subject to the requirements of direct effect as are individuals could bring suit should a Member State be found to be violating the fundamental human rights of Turkish migrants.

This of course does not mean that the German measure in this case would have necessarily been held to be such a violation. It does not mean that Member States would be faced with a legal obligation which they do not face now. After all the Member States themselves are subject to at least all the international law norms of human rights protecting migrants. It does mean that it would be the European Court of Justice which could, as a matter of Community law, ensure that these violations do not take place.

Finally, to take my position *does not mean that the gates of the Community will be opened or that Member States will have lost their competence in this regard*. It does mean that non-Community nationals who come into the Community under the umbrella of a Community Agreement (or a Mixed Agreement the free movement

---

46. See generally Waelbroeck, 'The Emergent Doctrine of Community Pre-Emption — Consent and Re-delegation', in Sandalow and Stein, *Courts and Free Markets* (1982) p. 548.
47. Case 804/79 *Commission* v. *UK* [1981] ECR 1045.

parts of which are held not to be the exercise of Member State powers) are entitled, even in relation to their, and their family, rights of residence, to protection of their fundamental human rights under Community law and with the vigilance of the European Court of Justice.

My position does not even entail that the European Court of Justice will be charged with the entire review. I subscribe fully to the analysis of Arnull and Jacobs[48] as regards the respective roles of European Court and national courts in adjudicating the tangled questions of fact and law in making specific determinations.

3.2   *Diatta* case

Ms Diatta, a Senegalese national, was the wife of a French national living in Berlin. She resided there since February 1978. The marriage did not work. She separated from her husband in August of that same year with the intention of divorcing him and lived in separate accommodation. Her residency permit having expired she sought to renew it. The Berlin Chief Commissioner of Police refused on the ground that she was no longer a member of family of a Community national and hence she no longer enjoyed the legal right to reside in Germany. The Berlin Administrative Court upheld the refusal though it held that formally she was still married.

On a preliminary reference the European Court of Justice was asked whether Article 10(1) of Reg. 1612/68 may be interpreted as meaning that the spouse of a worker who is a national of a Member State and who is employed in the territory of another Member State may be said to live 'with the worker' if she has in fact separated from her spouse permanently but none the less lives in her own accommodation in the same place as the worker. The Court was also asked whether Article 11 of the Regulation established for a spouse, who, though not a national of a Member State, is married to a national of a Member State in another Community country a right of residence which does not depend on the conditions set out in Article 10 if the spouse wishes to pursue an activity as an employed person in the territory of that Member State.

In replying to the first question the Court first held, that Article 10 'cannot be interpreted restrictively.' Consequently, '[a] requirement that the family must live under the same roof permanently cannot be implied.'[49]

The Court further held that 'the marital relationship cannot be regarded as dissolved so long as it has not been terminated by the competent authority. It is not dissolved merely because the spouses live separately, even where they intend to divorce at a later date.'[50]

---

48. Arnull and Jacobs, 'Applying the Common Rules on the free movement of persons - The role of the national judiciary in the light of the jurisprudence of the European Court of Justice', elsewhere in this Volume.

49. Recitals 17 and 18 of Decision.

50. Recital 20 of Decision

But, as regards Article 11, the Court stated that:

'it is clear from the terms of that provision that it does not confer on members of a migrant worker's family an independent right of residence, but solely a right to exercise any activity as employed persons throughout the territory of the state in question. Article 11 cannot therefore constitute the legal basis for a right of residence without reference to the condition laid down in Article 10.'[51]

Clearly the ruling implies that once the divorce was complete, and provided that Ms Diatta, or other ex-spouses in that situation, did not come under other positive provisions of Community law regulating family members (especially Commission Regulation 1251/70) she could be expelled.[52]

In reaching the implicit decision on this second point the Court was following its Advocate-General. It rejected the Commission which belatedly (only in the Oral Hearing and having earlier submitted in writing a contrary position) and half-heartedly ('in reply to a question posed by a Member of the Court, the Commission's representative candidly admitted that view was, or at least, might appear somewhat bold'[53]) argued that a spouse in this situation retained a right of residence. The sensitivity of the case is evident by the intervention of Germany, the UK and the Netherlands.

Since the decision of the Court is laconic it is worthwhile examining the reasoning of the Advocate-General. He argued:

a. That indeed the Commission position was bold (and wrong).

b. That '[w]hen the Community legislator wishes to transform a right which is initially consequential [derivative] into a personal right, it makes express provision to that effect.'[54]

c. Following a 'concern to provide a strict interpretation,'[55] the proper construction of Article 11 does not justify a conclusion that the Community legislator intended to transform the spouse's derivative right into a personal right.

The Court, as mentioned above, also adopted this strict approach, in holding that Article 11 '. . . does not establish a right of residence independent of that provided for in Article 10.'[56]

On a strict textual interpretation I agree with this conclusion, though I wonder about the criteria which prompt the Court and its Advocates-General to adopt in same cases a 'concern to provide a strict interpretation' and other cases to take a broader, purposeful or systemic view.

If I may be bold, I confess that either I did not understand the Advocate-General and the Court, or, if I did, that their reasoning is, in my view, a callosal non-sequitur.

---

51. Recital 21 of Decision.
52. See Oliver, 'Non-EC Nationals and the Treaty of Rome' (1985) *Yearbook of European Law* p. 66.
53. Thus put by the Advocate-General in para. 8 of his Opinion.
54. Para. 8 of the Opinion.
55. Para. 9 of Opinion.
56. Recital 22 of Decision.

Both Advocate-General and Court seemed to have avoided the central issue. This for two distinct lines of reasoning.

The first line of reasoning: fundamental human rights.

In the oral hearing the Commission argued that 'it would be contrary to fundamental rights if a migrant worker could remove, unilaterally and arbitrarily, the protection accorded by Community law to the members of his [or her] family.'[57]

The Commission thus argued (though, unfortunately, without the full legal apparatus of a written submission) that an interpretation of the Regulation (the one adopted by the Advocate-General and the Court) which allowed, nay empowered, a migrant worker to have such leverage over the life of his or her spouse by divorce (or even the threat of divorce) would violate the human rights which, let us not forget, it is the duty of the Court to protect in the field of Community law. In this case, unlike *Demirel*, there is no question that we are squarely in the field of Community law.

What kind of reply is it to this argument to try and construe, strictly or otherwise, the intention of the Community legislator and the proper meaning of the provisions of the Article *and do no more*? We can readily accept that indeed the Regulation means that once the divorce is complete (and provided no other measure of Community law may be pleaded)[58] the spouse loses the right of residence. But surely when a violation of fundamental human rights is at issue, a court cannot stop there, as do both the Advocate-General and the Court of Justice. It must first decide whether in fact there is a binding norm of human rights applicable in the context of the case. It may find that there is no such binding human rights norm or that a correct interpretation of that norm does not bring it into conflict with the Community measure as it did in the *Hauer* case and numerous others. But if there is a norm and it does appear to be in conflict with the Community measure, the Court has two, and only two, options: either to construe the Community measure in such as way that it does not conflict with human rights norm (as the Commission argued) or to strike the Community measure down.

Here, to drive the point home, is a *reductio ad absurdum*. Imagine that the Community Regulation had a provision which could be interpreted to mean that the police may enter a migrant's house and search it without an appropriate court warrant. Imagine further that this interpretation were challenged as violating fundamental human rights. Would it be an adequate judicial response simply to construe, strictly or otherwise, the measure and conclude that it indeed meant that the police could so enter? Or would the court have to determine if such an interpretation violated some fundamental human right.

---

57. [1985] ECR 585.

58. This point is what differentiates the Community spouse from the non-EC spouse. In similar circumstances the former will almost always have an independent personal right to stay *qua* Member State worker.

Thus, in the *Diatta* case simply to say that Article 11 does not itself give a right of residence, when that very interpretation is challenged as violating fundamental human rights, is no answer at all.

Note, that I am not arguing that the Commission was necessary right in saying that there was a violation of human rights. It would have been helpful if they were to show what kind of right and its source. There are several candidates: a construction of a Community measure which empowered say, a husband, to coerce his wife to do things under threat of divorce from which followed the consequence that she would be expelled, could potentially compromise the right to human dignity (encapsulated in Art. 1 of the European Parliament Declaration of Human Rights); or it could compromise the right to family life if the husband gained custody over the children and such expulsion would sever the relationship between mother and children (or vice versa). The Court should at least review the Regulation once a violation of human rights has been alleged and motivate its decision that the correct interpretation of Article 11 of the Regulation does not violate human rights.

One could try and explain the Opinion and the Decision on the grounds that the human rights basis was so specious that it did not even merit consideration. But that could hardly be the case, especially since both Ms Diatta and the Commission pleaded it. Even if the Advocate-General and the Court thought that the argument was specious, they should have addressed it.

I believe that they fell into a trap because of the way the Commission construed its argument. The Commission overstated their argument by stating that the right of the spouse to rest was automatic and absolute once she [or he] entered in conformity with the conditions set in Article 10 of the Regulation.

My view is that the correct construction would be to say that the spouse may not be expelled if such expulsion would compromise her or his fundamental human rights to be examined, according to the appropriate repartition of role by the European Court of Justice and national courts, under the standards of Community law. In some cases (fictious marriage, very short sojourn) the result may be that expulsion does not compromise fundamental human rights. But simply to construe the Regulation in accordance with the wishes of the Community legislator is not what judicial protection of human rights is all about.

There is a second line of reasoning which rests on the rationale of free movement of workers

Since this takes me out of the province of human rights I shall be extremely brief. The primary rationale and purpose of Article 48 EEC and the implementing legislation is to ensure free movement of workers as one of the factors of production in the Common Market. If a worker cannot be joined by his or her family, this reasoning goes, this worker's right to free movement will be affected negatively. It is probably still the case that most people like to live with their family and not being able to do so will affect their willingness and ability to move. The Court has gone a long way to give effect to this type of reasoning in order to ensure that the free movement provisions are truly effective.[59]

Let us assume a situation (still the more common) of the husband being the migrant worker wishing to move from one Member State to another. One can take of course the old fashioned view of family relations, that the women, especially if she does 'not work' (meaning of course that she toils in the home) will blindly follow her husband and that the only issue is whether he will have a right to bring her with him. I do not think that the Court of Justice in its jurisprudence should base its reasoning on that implicit assumption. The modern way which is becoming increasingly more realistic, is that the wife will have an autonomous and maybe even decisive say in this type of family decision. (The situation is even more evidently so in a situation where the woman is the putative primary migrant. In a better world the gender difference would not matter in this type of situation).

Will the spouse not be affected by the knowledge that if she agreed to move, relocate, reestablish herself, etc., and adopt, so to speak, a new country, she might nonetheless find herself expelled from her new country (unless she falls under some other Community measure) simply because her marriage broke down? To interpret Regulation 1612/68 in the 1990s as did the Court would defeat its primary purpose and that of the Treaty itself. It would act as an impediment to truly effective free movement.

If that is the case, were the Advocate-General and the Court justified in taking a strict approach to the interpretation of the Regulation? Usually, when an interpretation brings a measures into conflict with one of its objects and purpose one seeks another interpretation. The other interpretation would be that the rights of the spouse will be reviewed and that if she enjoys a right to remain based on consideration of fundamental freedoms, that right will not be compromised simply because the marriage dissolved. This is not only good human rights law, it is good free movement law.

3.3   Conclusion

Demirel and *Diatta* are paradigmatic. Similar situations are likely to come up again in a variety of situations. I think these cases should be carefully reviewed and not be followed in the future.

---

59. See e.g., case 9/74 *Casagrande* v. *Landeshauptstadt München* [1974] ECR 773 in which the Court, employing this principle, allowed the Community legislator to encroach on the education provisions of one of the Member States.

APPLYING THE COMMON RULES ON THE FREE MOVEMENT OF PERSONS – The role of the national judiciary in the light of the jurisprudence of the European Court of Justice

Anthony Arnull[*] and F.G. Jacobs[**]

1.   INTRODUCTION

In this report, we examine the role played by the courts of the Member States in applying the Community rules on the free movement of persons. The law is stated as at 15 May 1991, but some account has been taken of more recent developments in the footnotes.

The role of the national courts was emphasised in *Unectef* v. *Heylens*,[1] a case on Article 48 of the Treaty, where the Court of Justice stated: 'Since free access to employment is a fundamental right which the Treaty confers individually on each worker in the Community, the existence of a remedy of a judicial nature against any decision of a national authority refusing the benefit of that right is essential in order to secure for the individual effective protection for his right.' That requirement, the Court said, reflected a general principle of Community law which underlay the constitutional traditions of the Member States and which was enshrined in Articles 6 and 13 of the European Convention on Human Rights.

In more general terms, the importance of the role played by the courts of the Member States in giving effect to the Community rules on the free movement of persons derives from the fact that many of those rules are directly effective, that is they confer rights on individuals which the national courts are bound to protect. It would not be appropriate here to embark on a detailed examination of the cases in which the Court has found various provisions of Community law in this field to be directly effective, but it is worth mentioning the first paragraph of the operative part of the ruling in *Watson and Belmann*,[2] where the Court stated:

---

* Legal Secretary at the Court of Justice.
** Advocate General at the Court of Justice.
1. Case 222/86 [1987] ECR 4097, para. 14. See also Case C-340/89 *Vlassopoulou* v. *Ministerium für Justiz, Bundes- und Europaangelegenheiten Baden-Württemberg*, judgment of 7 May 1991, which concerned Art. 52 of the Treaty. The latter case is discussed in more detail at n. 26 below.
2. Case 118/75 [1976] ECR 1185.

H.G. Schermers et al., eds., Free Movement of Persons in Europe
© 1993, T.M.C. Asser Instituut, The Hague

'Articles 48 to 66 of the Treaty and the measures adopted by the Community in application thereof implement a fundamental principle of the Treaty, confer on persons whom they concern individual rights which the national courts must protect and take precedence over any national rule which might conflict with them.'

This statement is perhaps slightly misleading, in that some of the Community provisions concerning the free movement of persons are not apt to confer rights on individuals.[3] Nevertheless, it is clear that the provisions which are intended 'to regulate the situation of individuals and to ensure their protection'[4] may be invoked before the national courts. As is apparent from the Court's judgment in *Watson and Belmann*, this is true not only of articles of the Treaty, but also of the legislation adopted to give effect to them. In *Rutili* v. *Minister for the Interior*,[5] the Court ruled that Regulation No. 1612/68[6] and Directives 64/221/EEC[7] and 68/360/EEC[8] in particular were capable of producing direct effect and there is little doubt that the same is true of the other implementing measures which have been adopted.

One of the most striking developments in the Court's case-law in recent years has been the elevation of the first paragraph of Article 7 of the Treaty from a provision used to reinforce the effect of other provisions to a source of directly effective rights in itself. That paragraph provides: 'Within the scope of application of this Treaty, and without prejudice to any special provisions contained therein, any discrimination on grounds of nationality shall be prohibited.' Whilst the Court's case-law makes it clear that Article 7 'applies independently only to situations governed by Community law in regard to which the Treaty lays down no specific prohibition of discrimination,'[9] it is now well established that, where the applicability of Articles 48 to 66 of the Treaty is in doubt, Article 7 may be invoked in cases which fall within the general scope of the Treaty. Moreover, the Court does not take a strict view in such cases of the Treaty's ambit.[10]

The Court held in *Walrave* v. *Union Cycliste Internationale*[11] that the prohibition of discrimination on grounds of nationality laid down in Articles 7, 48 and 59 of the Treaty did not apply only to public authorities, but extended 'to rules of any other nature aimed at regulating in a collective manner gainful employment and the provision of services.' That ruling was reiterated in *Donà* v. *Mantero*,[12] where the Court said that it followed that the provisions in question, 'which are mandatory in nature, must

---

3. E.g., Art. 49 of the Treaty.
4. See case 36/75 *Rutili* v. *Minister for the Interior* [1975] ECR 1219, para. 17.
5. Ibid.
6. OJ Eng. Sp. Ed. 1968 (II), p. 475.
7. OJ Eng. Sp. Ed. 1963-64, p. 117.
8. OJ Eng. Sp. Ed. 1968 (II), p. 485.
9. See case 305/87 *Commission* v. *Greece* [1989] ECR 1461, para. 13; case C-10/90 *Masgio* v. *Bundesknappschaft*, judgment of 7 March 1991, para. 12.
10. See e.g., case 293/83 *Gravier* v. *City of Liège* [1985] ECR 593; case 24/86 *Blaizot* v. *University of Liège* [1988] ECR 379; case 186/87 *Cowan* v. *Trésor Public* [1989] ECR 195.
11. Case 36/74 [1974] ECR 1405.
12. Case 13/76 [1976] ECR 1333.

be taken into account by the national court . . .' In *Van Ameyde* v. *UCI*,[13] the Court added that the prohibition on discrimination laid down in Article 52 of the Treaty also extended to the acts of private parties and was not confined to the behaviour of public authorities. The result is that these provisions are capable of producing not only vertical but also horizontal direct effect. The same is undoubtedly true of the implementing legislation which takes the form of regulations (1612/68[14] and 1251/70[15]). Much of the legislation which has been adopted in this field, however, takes the form of directives and, as is well known, directives only bind the Member States to which they are addressed.[16] Nevertheless, it is submitted that this does not pose any serious problems in this context, as the directives in question are concerned principally (we hesitate to say exclusively) with the actions of public authorities.

The main responsibility for applying these provisions in particular cases lies with the competent national authorities and ultimately with the national courts. Although it is generally said that, in order for a provision of Community law to produce direct effect, it must be precise and unconditional, it is a striking feature of many of the provisions on the free movement of persons that, despite the fact that they enjoy this quality, their application in particular cases may involve the national courts in delicate balancing exercises. It is true that the assistance of the Court of Justice may be sought under the preliminary rulings procedure established by Article 177 of the Treaty, but recourse to that procedure is only compulsory for national courts of last resort. Even where the procedure is used, the application of the rulings of the Court of Justice is the task of the referring courts. The proper performance of this task requires the right balance to be struck between the interests of the Community and other interests which the national courts may be more accustomed to evaluating. Given the fundamental importance of the free movement of persons to the functioning of the common market, the heavy responsibility of the national courts is evident.

Where the national courts fail to discharge that responsibility correctly, not only are the rights of individuals prejudiced, but the uniform application of the Community rules is jeopardised. This danger is perhaps especially acute where fundamental rights are invoked before national courts. The Court of Justice has made it clear that 'fundamental rights form an integral part of the general principles of law, the observance of which it ensures.' In safeguarding those rights, the Court draws inspiration from the constitutional traditions of the Member States and from international treaties for the protection of human rights on which the Member States have collaborated or of which they are signatories.[17]

Fundamental rights are therefore capable of influencing the way in which the Community provisions on the free movement of persons are interpreted and applied by

13. Case 90/76 [1977] ECR 1091.

14. *Supra*, n. 6.

15. OJ Eng. Sp. Ed. 1970 (II), p. 402.

16. See case 152/84 *Marshall* v. *Southampton and S.W. Hampshire Area Health Authority* [1986] ECR 723.

17. See e.g., case 4/73 *Nold* v. *Commission* [1974] ECR 491; Case 44/79 *Hauer* v. *Land Rheinland-Pfalz* [1979] ECR 3727.

the Court of Justice.[18] Where national judges are called upon to apply those provisions, they should clearly give the same weight as the Court of Justice to the protection of fundamental rights. In practice, however, they may be influenced by the status accorded to such rights in their domestic law. Judges in the United Kingdom, for example, where there is no constitutional guarantee of fundamental rights and where the European Convention on Human Rights does not have direct effect may be less inclined to be swayed by arguments based on fundamental rights than judges in Member States where such rights are protected under their national constitutional law and where the European Convention is regularly applied by the national courts.

This problem is one aspect of the broader problem of ensuring the uniform application of the Community rules on the free movement of persons in the light of the extensive responsibility cast on the national courts by the case-law of the Court of Justice, a responsibility which derives mainly from the directly effective nature of many of the relevant provisions. In the following discussion, we comment briefly on some of the main areas where the correct application of the Community rules depends on the way in which the national courts carry out the responsibility conferred on them. We begin with the scope *ratione personae* of Article 48 of the Treaty. We then consider the recognition of qualifications and the circumstances in which Member States may derogate from the rights of free movement conferred by Community law.

2.   THE MEANING OF THE TERM 'WORKER'

The leading case on the meaning of the term 'worker' for the purposes of Article 48 of the EEC Treaty is *Levin* v. *Staatssecretaris van Justitie*.[19] There the Court explained that the term had a Community meaning and that, since it defined the scope of one of the fundamental freedoms guaranteed by the Treaty, it was not to be interpreted restrictively. It therefore extended to 'persons who pursue or wish to pursue an activity as an employed person on a part-time basis only and who, by virtue of that fact obtain or would obtain only remuneration lower than the minimum guaranteed in the sector under consideration'. The Court added, however, that the Treaty rules on freedom of movement for workers 'cover only the pursuit of effective and genuine activities, to the exclusion of activities on such a small scale as to be regarded as purely marginal and ancillary'.

In subsequent cases, the Court has provided clarification of its ruling in *Levin*. Thus, in *Kempf* v. *Staatssecretaris van Justitie*,[20] the Court held that, provided the person concerned was carrying on an effective and genuine activity, it made no difference that he supplemented the income he earned from it with financial benefits paid out of public

---

18. A striking recent example concerning the freedom to provide services is Judgment of 18 June 1991, case C 260/89 *ERT*, OJ No. C 201/5 of 31.7.1991. See also case 249/86 *Commission* v. *Germany* [1989] ECR 1263, para. 10; *Heylens, supra*, n.1, para. 14; *Rutili, supra*, n. 4, para. 32; and the Opinion delivered by A.G. van Gerven on 11 June 1991 in case C 159/90 *SPUC* v. *Grogan*.

19. Case 53/81 [1982] ECR 1035.

20. Case 139/85 [1986] ECR 1741.

funds. In *Lawrie-Blum* v. *Land Baden-Württemberg*,[21] the Court was asked whether a trainee teacher who conducted classes and received a salary constituted a worker for the purposes of Article 48. The Court explained that: 'The essential feature of an employment relationship . . . is that for a certain period of time a person performs services for and under the direction of another person in return for which he receives remuneration.' The Court took the view that these criteria were satisfied in the case of trainee teachers. By contrast, in *Bettray* v. *Staatssecretaris van Justitie*,[22] the Court held that Article 48 did not extend to a person employed under a scheme intended to improve the capacity for work of people who are unable to work under normal conditions. Although under the scheme in question the essential features of the employment relationship, as defined in *Lawrie-Blum*, were present, work which constituted a means of rehabilitation or reintegration, which was adapted to the physical and mental capacities of each person, and the purpose of which was to equip individuals to lead a normal life could not, in the Court's view, be regarded as 'effective and genuine economic activity' for the purposes of Article 48.

Although Article 48 only refers expressly to those who have already secured employment in another Member State, the Court held in *R.* v. *Immigration Appeal Tribunal, ex parte Antonissen*,[23] confirming indications given in its previous case-law,[24] that those in search of work also enjoyed rights of free movement under Article 48. Such persons do not, however, have the right to stay in the host State indefinitely, but only for long enough to enable them to familiarise themselves with the employment situation there and, where possible, to find a job. The Court held that a period of six months laid down by national law in such cases did not appear insufficient for these purposes. It added, however, that 'if after the expiry of that period the person concerned provides evidence that he is continuing to seek employment and that he has genuine chances of being engaged, he cannot be required to leave the territory of the host Member State.'

It will be apparent that all these criteria leave the national courts with considerable room for manoeuvre.

3.   THE RECOGNITION OF QUALIFICATIONS

One of the main obstacles to the free movement of persons in the Community is the disparity between the qualifications required for the exercise of certain professions in different Member States. Attempts to deal with this problem originally took the form of directives on the harmonization of the conditions for entry into specific professions. A major departure from this approach took place with the adoption in December 1988

---

21. Case 66/85 [1986] ECR 2121.

22. Case C 344/87 [1989] ECR 1621.

23. Judgment of 26 February 1991, case C 292/89, *The Queen* v. *Immigration Appeal Tribunal*, OJ No. C 74/9 of 20.3.1991.

24. See e.g., case 48/75 *Royer* [1976] ECR 497; *Levin, supra*, n. 19; case 316/85 *Centre Public d'Aide Sociale de Courcelles* v. *Lebon* [1987] ECR 2811.

of Directive 89/48/EEC on a general system for the recognition of higher-education diplomas awarded on completion of professional education and training of at least three years' duration.[25] This directive applies to 'any national of a Member State wishing to pursue a regulated profession in a host Member State in a self-employed capacity or as an employed person,' although it does not cover professions which are the subject of separate directives on the mutual recognition of diplomas (Art. 2).

It is not possible to deal with the detailed requirements of the directive in the space available here, but broadly speaking it lays down a general scheme designed to facilitate the pursuit of professional activities in the Member States by nationals of other Member States who hold qualifications awarded elsewhere in the Community. The general rule is laid down in Article 3, which provides:

> 'Where, in a host Member State, the taking up or pursuit of a regulated profession is subject to possession of a diploma, the competent authority may not, on the grounds of inadequate qualifications, refuse to authorize a national of a Member State to take up or pursue that profession on the same conditions as apply to its own nationals . . .'

if the applicant is qualified to exercise the profession concerned in another Member State. The national authorities are, however, permitted in certain circumstances to require nationals of other Member States to provide evidence of professional experience, to complete an adaptation period or to take an aptitude test (Art. 4).

Of particular interest in the present context is Article 8(2) of the directive, which requires the competent authority of the host State to deal promptly with applications to pursue regulated professions and to communicate the outcome in a reasoned decision within a specified time limit. It goes on: 'A remedy shall be available against this decision, or the absence thereof, before a court or tribunal in accordance with the provisions of national law.' The national courts may therefore be called upon to consider such matters as whether the host State was justified in requiring an adaptation period to be completed or an aptitude test to be taken. This may entail deciding whether the matters covered by the training received by the migrant in his State of origin 'differ substantially from those covered by the diploma required in the host Member State' or whether in the host State the profession in question 'covers matters which differ substantially' from those covered by the qualifications adduced by the applicant (Art. 4(1)(b)). In deciding such questions, the national courts will clearly enjoy a considerable degree of freedom, even if they ask the Court of Justice for assistance.

Where Directive 89/48/EEC is not applicable (for example because the profession in question does not involve the pursuit of a 'regulated professional activity' within the meaning of Art. 1(d)), the migrant may have to fall back on the rules laid down in the Treaty. The extent to which the Treaty requires the national authorities to examine whether qualifications awarded in other Member States should be treated as equivalent to those awarded in the host State was considered by the Court in *Vlassopoulou*,[26] a

---

25. OJ 1989 L19/16.
26. *Supra*, n. 1.

case on Article 52 of the Treaty the facts of which took place before the directive entered into force.[27]

In that case, the Court held that, when a national of a Member State seeks permission to exercise a profession in another Member State where the possession of particular qualifications is required, the authorities of the second State must examine the extent to which qualifications acquired by the migrant elsewhere in the Community should be treated as equivalent to those awarded under their national rules. If the foreign diploma does not entirely correspond with the national diploma, the national authorities are entitled to require proof that the migrant possesses the extra knowledge required, but they must make due allowance for knowledge already acquired in the host State and for the professional experience of the migrant. The Court added, reiterating its judgment in *Heylens*,[28] that the decision reached by the national authorities must be susceptible to review before the courts of the host State and that the migrant must be made aware of the reasons on which the decision is based.

The Court's decision in *Vlassopoulou* goes some way further than the earlier cases of *Thieffry* v. *Conseil de l'Ordre des Avocats à la Cour de Paris*[29] and *Patrick* v. *Ministre des Affaires Culturelles*,[30] where the equivalence of the qualifications concerned was not disputed. Even where Directive 89/48 does not apply, Member States may now find themselves under a positive obligation to consider the extent to which qualifications awarded in other Member States should be treated as equivalent to qualifications acquired under their national rules. The manner in which that obligation is discharged will ultimately be subject to the control of the national courts, which, even with the benefit of a preliminary ruling from the Court of Justice, may find themselves called upon to exercise a good deal of discretion.

4.   THE PUBLIC POLICY PROVISO

The rights conferred on workers by Article 48 are, by virtue of paragraph 3 of that Article, 'subject to limitations justified on grounds of public policy, public security or public health.' The rights enjoyed by the self-employed under Articles 52 and 59 are subject to similar limitations pursuant to Articles 56(1) and 66. Detailed rules for the application of these derogations are laid down in Council Directive 64/221/EEC.[31] In practice, the most frequently invoked head has been that relating to 'public policy', and a large body of case-law has developed on the meaning of this expression. As will be seen, however, much is entrusted to the discretion of the national courts.

It is clear that, as a derogation from a fundamental principle of the Treaty, the so-called public policy proviso is to be strictly construed. In particular, the Court's

---

27. For related decisions on Arts. 48 and 59 of the Treaty, see *Heylens, supra*, n. 1, and case 279/80 *Webb* [1981] ECR 3305 respectively. The latter case is considered further at n.52 below.

28. *Supra*, n. 1.

29. Case 71/76 [1977] ECR 765.

30. Case 11/77 [1977] ECR 1199.

31. *Supra*, n. 7.

decision in the *Rutili* case[32] suggests that Member States cannot justify recourse to the proviso on the basis of conduct which is permitted under the European Convention on Human Rights. Moreover, the Court has made it clear[33] that the derogations laid down in Articles 48(3) and 56(1) do not constitute a condition precedent to the exercise of the right of freedom of movement, but simply enable the Member States to limit that right in specific cases where this is properly justified. The Court's case-law also establishes that the Member States are not the sole judges of what their public policy requires and that steps taken by the Member States under the proviso are subject to control by the institutions of the Community, notably by the Court of Justice.[34] The Court has acknowledged, however, that 'the particular circumstances justifying recourse to the concept of public policy may vary from one country to another and from one period to another, and it is therefore necessary in this matter to allow the competent national authorities an area of discretion within the limits imposed by the Treaty.'[35] Both the Court and the Community legislature have taken steps to control the way in which that discretion is exercised. This has been done both by the elaboration of substantive criteria which must be satisfied if the public policy criterion is to be invoked and by the laying down of procedural safeguards[36] to protect the individual from abuse. Responsibility for the application of the concept of public policy in specific cases, however, rests ultimately with the national courts.

Under Article 3(1) of Directive 64/221/EEC, 'Measures taken on grounds of public policy or of public security shall be based exclusively on the personal conduct of the individual concerned.' The Court has held that such measures cannot therefore be justified on 'grounds extraneous to the individual case', such as their possible deterrent effect on others.[37] Mere association with a body or an organization which is considered by the national authorities to be socially harmful, however, may constitute personal conduct within the meaning of the directive if it 'reflects participation in the activities of the body or of the organization as well as identification with its aims and designs.'[38]

The fact that a migrant worker has broken the law of the host State is not in itself enough to justify recourse to the public policy proviso. A Member State wishing to rely on the proviso must establish 'the existence, in addition to the perturbation of the social order which any infringement of the law involves, of a genuine and sufficiently serious threat to the requirements of public policy affecting one of the fundamental interests of society.'[39] In order to satisfy this test, a Member State must be able to show that it adopts, 'with respect to the same conduct on the part of its own nationals repressive

---

32. *Supra*, n. 4.
33. See judgment of 5 February 1991, case C 363/89 *Roux* v. *Belgian State*, OJ No. C 56/6 of 5.3.1991.
34. See case 41/74 *van Duyn* v. *Home Office* [1974] ECR 1337, para. 18.
35. Ibid. See also joined cases 115 and 116/81 *Adoui and Cornuaille* v. *Belgium* [1982] ECR 1665, para. 8.
36. See in particular Arts. 6-9 of Directive 64/221/EEC.
37. See case 67/74 *Bonsignore* v. *Stadt Köln* [1975] ECR 297.
38. See *van Duyn*, *supra*, n. 34, at para. 17.
39. Case 30/77 *R.* v. *Bouchereau* [1977] ECR 1999, para. 35.

measures or other genuine and effective measures intended to combat such conduct.'[40] It is apparently no longer enough for a Member State to 'define its standpoint' on particular conduct and to take 'administrative measures' to counteract it.[41]

Cases in which the public policy proviso is invoked can pose a particular challenge to the national courts for a number of reasons. First, the Court of Justice's recognition that the requirements of public policy may vary means that the national courts are sometimes left to decide for themselves how those requirements are to be reconciled with the right to freedom of movement. Secondly, even where the principles applicable appear to be uniform, judicial attitudes to the effect they produce in particular cases may differ. Thirdly, the repugnant circumstances of many cases where the public policy proviso is in issue make it easy for national courts to lose sight of the fundamental importance of the right to freedom of movement.

A well known example of a case in which some of these difficulties may have led the national courts astray is *R. v. Secretary of State, ex parte Santillo*.[42] In that case, the applicant, an Italian national, had been convicted in England of a number of serious offences and sentenced to a term of imprisonment. At the same time, the trial judge had recommended that he be deported. About four and a half years later, in anticipation of the applicant's release from prison, the Secretary of State made a deportation order pursuant to the trial judge's recommendation. The applicant sought judicial review of the deportation order on the basis that, in view of the time which had elapsed since the recommendation was made, the order was incompatible with Article 9(1) of Directive 64/221/EEC, which prevents a decision ordering expulsion in cases such as this from being taken 'until an opinion has been obtained from a competent authority of the host country . . .'

The Divisional Court made a reference to the Court of Justice, which ruled that a recommendation for deportation made by a criminal court at the time of conviction could constitute 'an opinion . . . from a competent authority' within the meaning of the directive. It added, however, that such an opinion 'must be sufficiently proximate in time to the decision ordering expulsion to ensure that there are no new factors to be taken into consideration.' The Court explained that:

'A lapse of time amounting to several years between the recommendation for deportation and the decision by the administration is liable to deprive the recommendation of its function as an opinion within the meaning of Article 9. It is indeed essential that the social danger resulting from a foreigner's presence should be assessed at the very time when the decision ordering expulsion is made against him as the facts to be taken into account, particularly those concerning his conduct, are likely to change in the course of time.'[43]

40. See *Adoui and Cornuaille, supra,* n.35, at para. 8.
41. See *van Duyn, supra,* n. 34.
42. Case 131/79 [1980] ECR 1585.
43. See the operative part of the Court's ruling.

This ruling made it fairly clear that the Court of Justice regarded the period that had elapsed in the applicant's case as too long. Nevertheless, both the Divisional Court[44] and the Court of Appeal[45] refused to interfere with the order made by the Secretary of State, as they could find no evidence that the position had improved since the trial judge made his original recommendation. They seemed to regard the applicant as having the onus of establishing that his presence no longer constituted a social danger. Commentators have suggested that insufficient weight was given to the Community interest in securing freedom of movement. Such a view does not, of course, imply any condonation of the conduct in question.

5.   PUBLIC SERVICE AND OFFICIAL AUTHORITY

Article 48(4) of the Treaty provides: 'The provisions of this Article shall not apply to employment in the public service.' By virtue of Article 55(1), the provisions on the right of establishment 'shall not apply, as far as any given Member State is concerned, to activities which in that State are connected, even occasionally, with the exercise of official authority.' In accordance with Article 66, Article 55(1) also applies to the freedom to provide services.

Although Articles 48(4) and 56(1) are worded slightly differently, they are clearly related and, as derogations from the fundamental principle of freedom of movement, should be interpreted in the same restrictive manner.[46] As the Court explained in the *Lawrie-Blum* case,[47] 'Article 48(4) must be construed in such a way as to limit its scope to what is strictly necessary for safeguarding the interests which that provision allows the Member States to protect.' The Court went on to emphasize that the applicability of Article 48(4) did not depend on the legal classification of a post under national law, since this would allow the Member States to determine the scope of the exception. The Court stated that the expression 'employment in the public service':

'must be understood as meaning those posts which involve direct or indirect participation in the exercise of powers conferred by public law and in the discharge of functions whose purpose is to safeguard the general interests of the State or of other public authorities and which therefore require a special relationship of allegiance to the State on the part of persons occupying them and reciprocity of rights and duties which form the foundation of the bond of nationality. The posts excluded are confined to those which, having regard to the tasks and responsibilities involved, are apt to display the characteristics of the specific activities of the public service in the spheres described above.'

44. [1980] 3 CMLR 212.
45. [1981] 1 CMLR 569.
46. See the Opinion of Advocate-General Mayras in case 2/74 *Reyners* v. *Belgium* [1974] ECR 631, at p. 664.
47. *Supra*, n. 21.

The Court went on to describe these conditions as 'very strict', and it will not easily be convinced they are met. It has acknowledged, however, that their application 'gives rise to problems of appraisal and demarcation in specific cases.'[48] Nevertheless, it is well established that Article 48(4) cannot in principle be used to justify discrimination against workers from other Member States once they have been admitted to the public service.[49] Member States are not precluded, however, from reserving particular posts within the public service to their own nationals where this is justified having regard to the tasks which the holders of those posts may be called upon to perform.[50]

The Court has taken a similar approach to the scope of Article 55(1). In *Reyners* v. *Belgium*,[51] it held that Article 55 was confined to activities 'which in themselves involve a direct and specific connexion with the exercise of official authority.' In the context of a profession such as that of Belgian *avocat*, it did not therefore cover 'activities such as consultation and legal assistance or the representation and defence of parties in court, even if the performance of these activities is compulsory or there is a legal monopoly in respect of it.'

Again, the application of these criteria in particular cases leaves the national courts with considerable leeway.

6.   THE RULE OF REASON

In the *Webb* case,[52] the Court stated that 'the freedom to provide services is one of the fundamental principles of the Treaty and may be restricted only by provisions which are justified by the general good and which are imposed on all persons or undertakings operating in the said State (i.e., the State where the services are being provided) in so far as that interest is not safeguarded by the provisions to which the provider is subject in the Member State of his establishment.' Similar statements are to be found in the recent series of judgments on tourist guides.[53] They make it clear that certain types of restriction on the freedom to provide services will fall outside the Treaty if they can be justified in the public interest.

Since none of those cases was concerned with the public policy proviso contained in Article 56(1) and the exception concerned with the exercise of official authority was not in point, the legal justification for the class of restriction which the Court indicated would be compatible with the Treaty must lie elsewhere. It may well be that the case-law supports the existence of a rule of reason, analogous to the 'Cassis de Dijon'

---

48. See case 149/79 *Commission* v. *Belgium* [1980] ECR 3881, para. 12.
49. See e.g., case 33/88 *Allué and another* v. *Università degli Studi di Venezia* [1989] ECR 1591, para. 8.
50. See case 149/79 *Commission* v. *Belgium, supra*, n. 48, para. 21.
51. *Supra*, n. 46.
52. *Supra*, n. 27, para. 17.
53. Cases C 154/89, C 180/89 and C 198/89 *Commission* v. *France, Italy and Greece*, judgments of 26 February 1991.

doctrine[54] in the context of the free movement of goods, which may be invoked to take certain restrictions on the freedom to provide services outside the scope of the Treaty.[55] It seems that a similar doctrine may also be applicable in relation to the right of establishment.[56]

As in the case of goods, however, any such rule of reason which may be applicable in the services context cannot be invoked to justify national rules which discriminate on grounds of nationality. The Court made it clear in *Bond van Adverteerders* v. *Netherlands State*[57] that 'national rules which are not applicable to services without distinction as regards their origin and which are therefore discriminatory are compatible with Community law only if they can be brought within the scope of an express derogation.'

It would seem to follow that measures which do not discriminate on grounds of nationality, although not for that reason alone outside the scope of the Treaty prohibitions, are permissible if justified by the general interest. This umbrella term has been held to embrace a range of interests,[58] including rules of professional conduct,[59] the protection of the consumer,[60] the protection of intellectual property[61] and the safety of highway traffic.[62] Member States wishing to invoke the doctrine must show, however, that the national measures in question comply with the principle of proportionality, in other words that the same result could not have been achieved by less restrictive measures.[63] The application of that principle may leave some scope for the exercise of discretion by national courts.

---

54. See case 120/78 *Rewe-Zentrale AG* v. *Bundesmonopolverwaltung für Branntwein* [1979] ECR 649.

55. Strong support for this suggestion may now be found in the two Dutch *Mediawet* cases (Case C 288/89 *Stichting Collectieve Antennevoorziening Gouda* v. *Commissariaat voor de Media*, and case C 353/89 *Commission* v. *Netherlands*), and in Case C 76/90 *Säger* v. *Dennemeyer & Co Ltd*. All three judgments were delivered on 25 July 1991.

56. See case 107/83 *Ordre des Avocats au Barreau de Paris* v. *Klopp* [1984] ECR 2971; case 292/86 *Gullung* v. *Conseils de l'Ordre des Avocats du Barreau de Colmar et de Saverne* [1988] ECR 111; case 143/87 *Stanton* v. *Inasti* [1988] ECR 3877; joined cases 154 and 155/87 *RSVZ* v. *Wolf and Dorchain* [1988] ECR 3897.

57. Case 352/85 [1988] ECR 2085, para. 32.

58. See the catalogue given in the *Mediawet* cases (para. 14 of the judgment in case C 288/89 and para. 18 of the judgment in case C 353/89).

59. See e.g., case 33/74 *van Binsbergen* [1974] ECR 1299; case 39/75 *Coenen* v. *Sociaal-Economische Raad* [1975] ECR 1547.

60. See cases 220/83, 252/83, 205/84 and 206/84 *Commission* v. *France, Denmark, Germany and Ireland* ('*the Insurance* cases') [1986] ECR 3663, 3713, 3755 and 3817.

61. See case 62/79 *Coditel* v. *Ciné Vog Films* (No. 1) [1980] ECR 881.

62. See case 16/78 *Choquet* [1978] ECR 2293.

63. See e.g., *the Insurance* cases, *supra*, n. 60; case 427/85 *Commission* v. *Germany* [1988] ECR 1123.

7.   CONCLUSION

We are now in a position to list the main areas where the correct application of the Community rules on the free movement of persons may depend on an essentially discretionary assessment by the national courts.

In the context of Article 48, it is the national courts who ultimately decide whether particular individuals are carrying on effective and genuine economic activities, or whether any work in which they might be engaged can be ignored on the basis that it is purely marginal. Where a person seeking to rely on Article 48 has not yet found work, it is the national courts who have the final say over whether the individual in question has had a reasonable period in which to do so and whether, once that period has expired, 'he is continuing to seek employment and . . . has genuine chances of being engaged.'[64]

National judges are also increasingly likely to find themselves called upon to decide whether professional qualifications awarded in different Member States should be treated as equivalent.

Where the national authorities seek to rely on the public policy proviso, it is the national courts who will ultimately decide whether the presence of the individual concerned poses or would pose a sufficiently serious threat to the interests of the host State. Similarly, where Articles 48(4) or 55(1) are invoked, the national courts will in the last resort decide whether particular posts can be said to require a 'special relationship of allegiance' to the host State.[65]

As far as the rule of reason is concerned, it is perhaps true to say that, in principle, its application in particular cases offers less scope for the exercise of discretion by the national courts. Provided the national courts make proper use of the preliminary rulings procedure, the Court of Justice can control the content of the class of interests which are capable of taking national measures outside the scope of the Community rules. The question whether those interests are adequately protected by the rules applicable in the migrant's country of origin and the application of the principle of proportionality may, however, leave some room for the exercise of discretion by national judges.

We do not mean to suggest that the national courts cannot be trusted to apply the Community rules correctly or that the Court of Justice has been too liberal in conferring tasks on them. On the contrary, the scheme of the Treaty clearly envisages that a large part of the responsibility for seeing that Community law is properly applied will rest with the courts of the Member States. It is worth emphasising, however, the extent to which the correct application of the rulings of the Court of Justice in this area often involves more than merely deciding questions of fact. Sometimes it requires the exercise of discretion by the national courts and may even require them to make policy choices. Where this is the case, it is particularly important that the national courts give proper weight to the Community interest. This requires the utmost vigilance on their

64. See *ex parte Antonissen*, *supra*, n. 23.
65. See *Lawrie-Blum*, *supra*, n. 21.

part, as well as on the part of the Commission and the Court of Justice in the exercise of their supervisory functions.

THE FREE MOVEMENT OF PERSONS IN EUROPE – THE ROLE OF THE NATIONAL JUDICIARY

Richard Plender[*]

1.   INTRODUCTION

This report gives an account of the interpretation by the national judiciary of the provisions of Community law governing the free movement of persons. It aspires to complement the report of Mr Arnull and Mr Advocate-General Jacobs, which examines the jurisprudence of the Court of Justice of the European Communities on the role played by the courts of Member States, and the report of M. le Conseiller d'Etat Errera, which gives an account of the rules derived from the European Convention on Human Rights.

The case-law described in this report is drawn from judgments given in the twelve Member States of the European Communities. This report concentrates on national decisions which were final and, in particular, on cases not referred to the Court of Justice for preliminary ruling. It will soon become apparent to the reader that national courts have frequently addressed common problems; and more often than not, have done so without the benefit of the case-law developed in other Member States.

2.   THE TERM 'WORKER'

According to national jurisprudence, the term 'worker' denotes a natural person[1] genuinely engaged or seeking to engage in remunerative employment. The Marylebone magistrate took the view that the expression did not cover a Sardinian youth, where the only work in which he had been engaged was 'of the washing up in restaurants type'.[2] That decision is, perhaps, similar to that of the *Landgericht*, Wiesbaden, which held that an Italian national was not a 'worker' because he was an

---

[*] QC, London.

1. *Hof van Beroep*, Gent, 10 October 1986, *Naftikon Apomachikon Tamion* v. *P. Devos et al,* Jurisprudence du port d'Anvers, 1986, 148.

2. Marylebone magistrate, 25 March 1975, *R.* v. *Secchi* [1975] 1 CMLR 383.

H.G. Schermers et al., eds., Free Movement of Persons in Europe
© 1993, T.M.C. Asser Instituut, The Hague

'idle layabout'.[3] These are early decisions, preceding the European Court's ruling in the *Levin* case:[4] and in another early decision the term 'worker' was so construed as to exclude an Italian national in Germany who became unfit to work shortly after arriving there.[5] More recently the Immigration Appeal Tribunal in London held that a community national who entered another Member State, obtained employment there and thereafter held various posts with occasional periods of unemployment, and served imprisonment for a year preceding his deportation, was a 'worker';[6] and the *Bundesverwaltungsgericht*, following the *Levin* Case, took the view that a person exercising a professional occupation on a part-time basis could qualify as a 'worker', although the employment was subsidiary to his principal occupation as a farmer.[7]

On the position of unemployed Community nationals seeking employment in other Member States, national judicial decisions reflect the variations in State practice disclosed in the *Antonissen* case.[8] Thus, in the *Antonissen* case itself, the proceedings before the national court showed that a time limit of six months was imposed in the United Kingdom;[9] but in a case before the *Oberverwaltungsgericht*, Bremen, the period of three months was specified.[10] In several cases national courts have been urged, in all seriousness, to hold that persons engaged in prostitution and similar activities were 'workers' within the meaning of Article 48.[11] The uniformity of the courts' answer to this question is, perhaps, less surprising than the elaborate and scholarly attention given to it. Less obvious is the decision of the *Bundesverwaltungsgericht* of 5 November 1980 holding that a person engaging in study in a college of higher technical education cannot be characterised as a 'worker'. [12]

---

3. *Landgericht*, Wiesbaden, 14 November 1966, *City of Wiesbaden* v. *Barulli* [1968] CMLR 239; distinguishing *Verwaltungsgerichtshof*, Mannheim, DVBl. 1965, 504.

4. Case 53/81 *Levin* v. *Staatssecretaris van Justitie* [1982] ECR 1035.

5. *Landgericht*, Göttingen, 23 December 1963; *Re Expulsion of an Italian National* [1965] CMLR 285.

6. Immigration Appeal Tribunal, 17 November 1983, *Monteil* v. *Secretary of State* [1984] 1 CMLR 284.

7. *Bundesverwaltungsgericht*, 1 December 1987, *Raffeisenbank Gammesfeld* v. *Bundesrepublik*, BVerwE 78, 297.

8. Case C-292/89 *R.*v. *Immigration Appeal Tribunal, ex parte Antonissen*, judgment of 26 February 1991, OJ No. C-74/9 of 20.3.1991.

9. High Court, London, 14 June 1989, *R.*v. *Immigration Appeal Tribunal, ex parte Antonissen* [1989] 2 CMLR 957. The same period was mentioned by the High Court, London, on 25 March 1983 in *R.* v. *Secretary of State ex parte Ayub* [1983] Imm. AR 20.

10. *Oberverwaltungsgericht*, Bremen, 22 April 1988, DVBl. 1988, 279.

11. *Tribunal de première instance*, Liège, 29 November 1989, *Danielle Roux* v. *Belgium* [1990] Rev. de jurisprudence de Liège, Mons & Bruxelles 778; *Landgericht*, Frankfurt, 8 January 1982, *Guiseppa Cassaro* [1982] NJW 1955; *Bundesverwaltungsgericht*, 15 July 1980 *Maure Antoinette Falla* v. *Stadt Kiel Bundesverwaltungsgericht*, 15 July 1980, *Marie Lamperti* v. *Stadt Kiel* BVerwE 60, 284.

12. *Bundesverwaltungsgericht*, 5 November 1980, *Marcel Partigny* v. *Technische Hochschule Darmstadt* (1981) *Zeitschrift für das gesamte Familienrecht*, 406. Comparison may be made with case 66/85 *Lawrie-Blum* v. *Land Baden-Württemberg* [1986] ECR 2121.

3. NATIONALITY

A recurrent problem before national courts is the assessment of the rights enjoyed under Community law by nationals of third countries.[13] In principle, such nationals do not derive rights from that law since they are not 'workers'.[14] Thus, a national of a third country, married to an EEC national, does not acquire an independent right of residence even when issued with a residence permit as an accompanying member of the family.[15] Turkish nationals have been held to derive no rights of entry or residence under the EEC-Turkey Association Agreement.[16] Spanish, Portuguese and Greek nationals have been held to have no entitlement to benefit from the Community's rules relating to workers ending the expiry of the transitional periods specifically laid down for the purpose in the appropriate Acts of Accession.[17]

Confronted with the question whether nationals of third countries benefit from Community rules as members of the family of Community nationals, the courts of Member States have held that spouses derive such benefits, even when separated[18] but a 'common law' spouse does not derive such benefits.[19]

Decisions of national courts yield little support for the so-called principle of 're-verse discrimination' (whereby a national of a Member State is said to enjoy in his own State the rights conferred by Community law on a national of another Member

13. The definition of a 'national' is, according to the decisions of national courts, a matter for the law of the putative state of nationality, See *Cour de première instance*, Bruxelles, 28 May 1982. *D.L.* v. *O.M.* (1982) *Tijdschrift voor Vreemdelingenrecht* 121.

14. *Conseil d'Etat*, Belgium, 21 June 1979, *Sterea* v. *Belgium*, Rec. Cons. d'Etat (1979) 690; *Conseil d'Etat*, Belgium, 2 October 1986, *Forero* v. *Belgium, Administration Publique* 1986, 123; *Cour du travail de Liège*, 13 October 1987, *Office national de l'emploi* v. *Deak, Chronique de droit social*, 1988, 95 following Case 94/84 *Office national de l'emploi* v. *Deak* [1985] ECR 1873.

15. Court of Appeal, London, 16 June 1983, *R.* v. *Secretary of State, ex parte Sandhu* [1983] 3 CMLR 131, High Court, London, 17 November 1986, *R.* v. *Secretary of State, ex parte Botta* [1987] 2 CMLR 189; *Oberverwaltungsgericht*, Münster, 12 February 1990 [1990] NJW 889.

16. *Verwaltungsgerichtshof*, Baden-Württemberg, 10 May 1982 [1982] NJW 696; *Bundesverwaltungsgericht*, 9 February 1981 [1981] NJW 1919, Court of Appeal, London. *R.* v. *Secretary of State ex parte Narin* [1990] 2 CMLR 223; c.f., Case 12/86, *Demirel* v. *Stadt Schwabisch-Gmund* [1987] ECR 3719; Case C-192/89 *Sevince* v. *Staatssecretaris van Justitie* 20 September 1990.

17. *Cour d'Appel*, Montpellier, 26 May 1987, *Joseph Monllor* v. *Ministère Public, Cour de Cassation*, 7 June 1988, *Joseph Monllor* v. *Ministère Public* JCP 1988 I 17695; *Symvoulion Efeton Athinon*, 5 April 1985, Arbato Stellario; *Hessischer Verwaltungsgerichtshof*, 30 September 1988, *Informationsbrief Ausländerrecht* 1988, 323; *Sozialgericht*, Stuttgart, 29 July 1983; *Bundesverwaltungsgericht*, 24 June 1982, [1983] BVerwE 431.

18. High Court, London, 28 May 1982, *R.* v. *Secretary of State, ex parte Amarjit Singh Sandhu* [1982] CMLR 553; *Conseil d'Etat*, Belgium, 9 December 1988, *Ahmad Tanver* v. *Belgium*, [1989] Rev. de Jurisprudence de Liège, Mons et Bruxelles 466.

19. *Conseil d'Etat*, Belgium, 23 September 1983, *Assunta Petrilli and Abdellatif Fahmani* v. *Belgium* Rec. Cons. d'Etat, 1983, 1702. Remoter relatives, such as a nephew and brother or brother-in-law, are held to be excluded, unless dependent on the worker: *Conseil d'Etat*, Luxembourg, 19 November 1986, *Paradas and Paralta* v. *Ministère de la Justice*; *Conseil d'Etat*, Luxembourg, 19 November 1986, *Agostinho* v. *Ministère de la Justice*; *Cour du travail de Liège*, 17 November 1989, *Fazzolari* v. *Office nationale des pensions* (1990) *Journal des tribunaux du travail*, 154.

State in a similar situation). Where reliance has been placed on the principle of reverse discrimination in the context of Community rules governing the free movement of persons, this has been done in an effort to claim rights for members of the family of nationals of the Member State in which the principle was invoked[20] and for the purpose of resisting the surrender of a community national to a Member State other than this own, pursuant to extradition treaties and related arrangements.[21]

In some such cases the applications have been dismissed on the ground that there was no factor connecting the case with any of the situations envisaged by Community law. More often, reverse discrimination has been invoked in connection with establishment. In these cases national courts have often contented themselves with the observation that Article 52 of the EEC Treaty requires no more than respect for the standard of national treatment.[22]

4.   THE AMBIT OF COMMUNITY RIGHTS

The first right conferred by Community law on nationals of one Member State wishing to enter another such State for the purposes of employment is the right to enter the second State simply on production of a passport or national identity card. This right is, perhaps, of particular significance in the United Kingdom, where the grant of 'leave' to enter the kingdom is the cornerstone of all immigration control. The Immigration Appeal Tribunal in London has twice upheld the right of a Community national to enter without leave.[23] Courts in Belgium,[24] France[25] and Spain[26] have, however, upheld as in conformity with Community law the requirements imposed on aliens in those countries to register or hold permits.

20. Court of Appeal, London, 21 april 1988, *R.* v. *Secretary of State, ex parte Tombofa* [1988] 2 CMLR 609; Immigration Appeal Tribunal, London, 29 October 1981, *Gobind Singh Mansukhani* v. *Secretary of State* [1981] Imm. AR 184.

21. High Court, London, 7 March 1980, *Narinder Singh Virdee* [1980] 1 CMLR 709; High Court, London, 30 November 1979, *R.* v. *Governor, Brixton Prison ex parte Budlong* [1980] 2 CMLR 125.

22. *Conseil d'Etat*, Luxembourg, 8 November 1989, *Michèle Maret* v. *Ministère de l'éducation*; *Cour d'Appel*, Luxembourg, 27 March 1986, *Gaston Vergel* v. *Conseil de l'ordre du barreau de Diekirch*, 26 *Pas. Lux.* (1986) 333; *Cour de Cassation*, Paris, 10 May 1988, *Patrick Dupont*, 1988 (4) JCP 247; *Hof van Cassatie*, Belgium, 14 December 1976, *Openbaar Ministerie* v. *Herman Le Compte*, 1977 (1) Pas. Belge 430 *Symvoulio tis Epikrateias*, 24 March 1988, *Ioannis Spriopoulos* v. *Ygeias Ypourgon*, (1989) Armenopoulos 919; *Conseil d'Etat*, Belgium, 4 March 1982, *Canoot* v. *Belgian State*, Rec. Cons. d'Etat 1982, 474; *Cour d'Appel*, Caen, 2 February 1987, *Ministère Public* v. *Patrick Dupong*.

23. 19 January 1984, *Rubruck* v. *Secretary of State* [1984] 2 CMLR 499; 3 April 1984, *Lubberson* v. *Secretary of State* [1984] 3 CMLR 77. See also *Verwaltungsgerichtshof*, Baden-Württemberg, 30 April 1990 [1990] Inf. Aus. 294.

24. *Cour de Cassation*, Belgium, 30 September 1987, *Johannes van den Branden* v. *Josina Langenberg* 1988 (1) Pas. Belge 130.

25. *Tribunal administratif de Strasbourg*, 27 November 1980, *Joseph Weber* v. *Etat Français*; *Conseil d'Etat*, 9 March 1988, ditto, Rec. Cons. d'Etat, 9 March 1988.

26. *Tribunal Supremo*, Spain, 27 November 1989, *Joao* v. *XSA* [1990] La Ley 6.

German and French courts have held that discrimination between nationals of Member States is prohibited by Community law even in relation to the consequences of performance of national military service.[27] They have also applied the principle of non-discrimination in relation to the double taxation of frontier workers.[28]

The obligation to treat Community nationals equally in respect of 'social advantages' has been the source of much litigation at the national level. In a characteristically robust judgment, Lord Denning MR observed that nationals of other Member States have the same rights to local authority housing as 'true-born Englishmen'; nevertheless a family which left its home in Italy and claimed local authority housing in England was disqualified for it since the family had made itself intentionally homeless.[29] More recently, the Corte Costituzionale has held that the obligation of equal treatment assured for nationals of other Member States equal access to publicity-funded housing in Italy.[30] In the case of grants for university studies, English courts found (with some hesitation) that they should be available equally to nationals of all Member States.[31] Two German courts reached the conclusion, on the facts of particular cases, that the principle of non-discrimination did not require payment of grants to students at higher technical schools; and that no reference for preliminary ruling was required.[32]

A national court has held that the obligation imposed by national law to hold a driving licence issued by that State for the purpose of driving there (other than temporarily) was not incompatible with community law.[33] It has also been held that the detention of a person pending his extradition to another Member State, following the issuance of a warrant by the court of that State and its backing by the courts of the forum, was not incompatible with Community law.[34]

---

27. *Bundesarbeitsgericht*, 5 December 1969 *Salvatore Ugliola* [1970] NJW 1014; *Arbeitsgericht*, Köln, 14 February 1977, *Eric Louge* v. *Einkaufs-Kreditbank*; *Tribunal de Travail de Verviers*, 7 May 1980; *Crapanzano* v. *Copeland* (1980) *Journal des tribunaux du travail* 273.

28. *Bundesarbeitsgericht*, 15 October 1985. However, the Treaty was held inapplicable to Italian nationals resident in Switzerland, working for a German affiliate of a Swiss employer in Germany but near the Swiss border, and dismissed by their employer: *Arbeitsgericht Lörrach*, 2 March 1977, (1977) *Recht der Internationalen Wirtschaft* 646.

29. Court of Appeal, 12 December 1979, *De Falco* v. *Crawley Borough Council* [1980], *Lambert* v. *Ealing London Borough Council* [1982] 2 All ER 394.

30. *Corte Costituzionale*, 4 July 1989, Giur. Cost. 1989 - I, 1757.

31. High Court, Chancery Division, London, 16 July 1982, *MacMahon* v. *Department of Education and Science* [1982] 3 CMLR 91; High Court, Queen's Bench Division, 12 November 1984, *R.* v. *ILEA and Others ex parte Hinde* [1985] 1 CMLR 766.

32. *Hessischer Verwaltungshof*, 6 September 1979, *Marcel Partigny* v. *Technische Hochschule Darmstadt*; *Bundesverwaltungsgericht*, Berlin, 18 October 1979, 59 BVerwE 1. In the case of payments to victims of violence, the French *Commission pour Aide aux Victimes d'Actes Intentionnels de Violence* based its judgment of 6 January 1989 on a bilateral convention, thus avoiding the issue whether such payments are 'social advantages': *V.* v. *R.* (1989) *Journal des tribunaux* 463.

33. *Rechtbank van Eerste Aanleg*, Tongeren, 17 June 1982, *S.* (1982-3) *Rechtskundig Weekblad* 2691.

34. High Court, London, 4 May 1984, *Carthage Healy* [1984] 3 CMLR 575.

5. DIRECT EFFECT

The direct effectiveness of provisions of Community law has been acknowledged by national courts in several cases involving the free movement of workers.[35] In the case of *Daniel Cohn-Bendit*, the *Tribunal administratif de Paris*, 4th section, acknowledged the direct effectiveness of the Treaty provisions governing free movement of workers but held that the applicant had only acquired the status of worker by being offered employment after the decision ordering his expulsion; in this way the Tribunal found Article 48 to be unavailable to the applicant.[36] The effect of that controversial decision has now been much attenuated by the decision of the *Conseil* (2nd and 6th chambers together) date 8 July 1991 in the case of *Guiseppe Palazzi*. The Conseil there annulled a Decree of 1981 on the ground that it failed to confirm with Directive 64/221/EEC of 25 February 1964, since it did not provide for adequate procedural guarantees in advance of any refusal to review a residence permit.

In another recent decision, the Greek Council of State has struck down Greek legislation restricting access of nationals of other Member States to certain types of employment in the mining sector. The Council of State specifically stated that since 1 January 1991 Community law has formed an integral part of the law of Greece; and in accordance with Article 28 of the Constitution, it prevails over any provision to the contrary.[37] The *Cour d'Appel de Paris* held that Council Directive 80/987/ EEC of 20 October 1980[38] produced direct effects, so that guarantee institutions set up thereunder were obliged to guarantee payment of salaries of employees of French companies, irrespective of such employees' nationality (provided only that they were nationals of Member States).[39] The decision is remarkable since Italy and the United Kingdom, in another case, contended that the Directive did not produce direct effects.[40]

The direct effectiveness of Community provisions has also been acknowledged by national courts in the context of establishment. Thus, *the Cour d'Appel de Versailles* accepted that Council Directive 64/223/EEC of 25 February 1964 on Freedom of Establishment in Wholesale Trade[41] produced direct effects.[42] The *Cour d'Appel d'Aix en Provence* accepted the direct effect (and primacy) of Article

---

35. E.g., *Tribunal de première instance de Liège*, 6 May 1983, *Szocha* v. *Belgian State* [1985] 1 CMLR 12; *Conseil d'Etat*, Luxembourg, 19 December 1986, *Pierangelo Carli* v. *Ministre de la Justice*.

36. 11 July 1979, *Gazette du Palais* 1980 - II 194.

37. *Symvoulio tis Epikrateias*, 30 May 1986, *Ellinikoi Voxitai Distomou Anonymos Metalleftiki kai Viomichaniki Etairia* v. *Ypourgou Viomichaneias kai Energeias*, [1989] CDE 441.

38. OJ 1980 L 283/23.

39. *Cour d'Appel*, Paris, 18th Chamber, 1 February 1989, *Association Groupement Regional des Assedic de la Region Parisienne* v. *Yvan Tilmant*, *Gazette du Palais* 1989 - II 204.

40. Judgment of 19 November 1991, joined cases C-6/90 and C-9/90, *Francovich* v. *Italy*, *Bonifaci* v. *Italy*, OJ No. C-328/7 of 17.12.1991.

41. OJ Sp. Ed. 1963-4, 123.

42. 9 July 1986, *Direction de la Concurrence et des Prix des Hauts-de-Seine* v. *Conradi*.

52 of the EEC Treaty, when confronted with the claim of a national of a Member State to retain chambers as an avocat in more than one such State.[43]

In the context of freedom of establishment, however, the French *Conseil d'Etat* has applied the doctrine of direct effect in a controversial manner. Recalling that Article 189 of the Treaty makes Directives binding only as regards the ends to be achieved, it held that a Directive cannot be invoked by a national of a Member State save in support of a challenge to an individual administrative act. The *Conseil* deduced that a Community national could not invoke a Directive to secure the annulment of the implied administrative decision by which the *Ordre des vétérinaires* had refused to enrol him.[44]

Provision governing freedom to supply services have also been held, by a Luxembourg court, to produce direct effects.[45]

6.   DISCRIMINATION

The prohibition of discrimination on grounds of nationality is frequently invoked before national courts. In several cases involving access to employment, national courts and tribunals have applied that prohibition.[46] Thus, the *Pretura di Modena* acknowledged that this prohibition may be invoked by individuals, while rejecting the claim that discrimination is entailed in the policy of a university in offering only annual contracts of employment to language tutors.[47] The Belgian[48] and English[49] courts made a similar acknowledgment, while ruling that in principle it is not incompatible with the EEC Treaty for a Member State to require nationals of other Member States to obtain driving licences in the event of their permanent establishment in the State in question.

The prohibition of discrimination has arisen in several Member States in connection with taxation and social security, particularly where it is claimed that the application of a residence criterion is tantamount to discrimination on grounds of nationality. Thus, in Luxembourg it has been argued that Community law prohibits Member States from making the refund of excess tax deducted at source contingent

---

43. 23 October 1987, *Jean-Jacques Raynel* v. *Conseil de l'Ordre des avocats au barreau de Nice*.

44. 13 December 1985, *Gilbert Zakine*, (1989) CDE 441. For a criticism of the judgment see V. Constantinesco, (1988) *Revue trimestrielle de droit européen* 95.

45. *Cour d'Appel*, Luxembourg, 1 July 1970, *Association des Patrons - Epiciers de la Ville d'Esch-sur-Alzette* v. *Kohl*.

46. *Arbeitsgericht*, Dusseldorf, 8 June 1983 [1984] NJW 576; *Arbeidshof*, Antwerp, 13 February 1986, *Jos Blok* v. *Ministerie van Tewerkstelling en Arbeid*, (1986) *Journal des tribunaux* 401; *Pretura di Palermo*, 5 February 1982, *Carnesi* v. *ENEL* (1983) II *Rivista italiana di diritto del lavoro* 242.

47. 8 August 1990, *Anceschi* v. *Università degli Studi di Modena*, (1990) I Giustizia Civile 2995.

48. *Hof van Cassatie*, Belgium, 9 October 1979, *Procureur des Konings* v. *De Q.*, [1981] 3 CMLR 609.

49. High Court, London, 15 October 1982, *Farrall* v. *Department of Transport, The Times* LR 16 October 1982.

on the taxpayer's residence in the Grand Duchy throughout the fiscal year.[50] In France it has been contended that a worker temporarily stationed outside the Community by an employer having the nationality of another Member State does not forfeit his affiliation to the French social security scheme, since the employee of a French company would not do so.[51] It has also been contended in France (unsuccessfully) that a French law governing insolvency[52] conflicted with Articles 7 and 52 of the EEC Treaty in rendering the property of directors of insolvent companies liable to forfeiture since (it was said) directors of French nationality tended to have property in France and so were effected disproportionately and adversely.[53] In Germany it has been argued that the imposition of income tax on the basis of residence gives rise to unlawful discrimination, for frontier workers.[54] In Belgium, it was argued (unsuccessfully) that discrimination was involved in the rule providing for deduction of expenses of the conduct of a trade, excluding contributions paid to a foreign social security scheme.[55]

7. DEROGATIONS

It is axiomatic that derogations from the principle of freedom of movement for Community nationals must be construed strictly, by national courts as by the European Court.[56] Thus, national courts have often stated the proposition, based on the wording of Council Directive 64/221[57] that the expulsion of a community national cannot be justified on the sole ground that he or she has been convicted of an offence.[58] The Immigration Appeal Tribunal in London therefore found, in *Astrid Proll*'s case,[59] that even past involvement in the crimes of the Baader-Meinhoff gang did not amount to justification for the exclusion of a Community national from the United Kingdom; and the *Bayerischer Verwaltungsgerichtshof* held in *Nicola*

---

50. *Conseil d'Etat*, 21 June 1988, *Klaus Biehl* v. *Administration des contributions*.

51. *Commission de première instance du Contentieux de la securité sociale*, 4 January 1985, *Sarl Proudest* v. *CPAM*.

52. Law of 13 July 1967, Art. 99.

53. *Cour d'Appel*, Paris, 26 March 1982, *Claude de Daulces de Freycinet*, Gazette du Palais, 1982 - II, 13.

54. *Finanzgericht*, Köln, 23 May 1982, (1983) *Recht der Internationalen Wirtschaft* 384.

55. *Cour d'Appel*, Belgium, 12 January 1976, *B.E.* v. *Belgian State* (1977) Bulletin des Contributions 1495.

56. *Bundesverwaltungsgericht*, 29 May 1979 (suspended sentence); *Bundesverwaltungsgericht*, 20 June 1979 (failure to renew residence permit).

57. OJ Eng.Sp. Ed. 1963-4, p. 117, Art.3 (2).

58. *Conseil d'Etat*, Belgium, 7 October 1968, *Yvette Corveleyn* v. *Belgium*, (1969) CDE 343 (managing house of ill repute); *Conseil d'Etat*, Belgium, 2 December 1977, *Amerigo Vinciguerra* v. *Belgium*, (1977) *Recueil des arrêts du Conseil d'Etat*, 1381 (convictions abroad); *Raad van State*, Belgium 2 July 1987, *Hawwask* v. *Belgium*, (1988) *Tijdschrift voor bestuurwetenschappen en publiek recht* 561.

59. 12 April 1988 [1988] 2 CMLR 387.

Conte v. *Stadt Würzberg* [60] that the exclusion of a Community national could not be justified on the ground that she was infected with the AIDS virus. It has also been held that reliance on public funds cannot, by itself, warrant the deportation of a Community national.[61]

On the other hand, when confronted with cases of Community nationals with a demonstrated propensity to commit offences, national courts and tribunals have shown themselves very ready to uphold exclusions and deportations on the basis of public order.[62] The Court of Appeal has even stated that the European Court's words in the *Bouchereau case*[63] (requiring proof of a genuine and sufficiently serious threat to the requirements of public policy affecting one of the fundamental interests of society) were 'simply a somewhat fuller way of saying that the appellant's continued presence in the United Kingdom would be to its detriment.'[64]

The *Tribunal administratif de Papeete* in French Polynesia has held that in determining whether an exclusion was in conformity with the principles of Community law, it was necessary to apply the general principles of *excès de pouvoir*. Thus, the exclusion of a Member of the European Parliament could be justified only if strictly necessary from the protection of *ordre public*.[65]

In Belgian and Luxembourg, a recurrent problem has arisen of determining whether it was necessary in an individual case to consult the *Commission Consultative des Etrangers* before deporting an alien. In conformity with Council Directive 64/221/EEC,[66] Belgian and Luxembourg law requires consultation with the *Commission* 'save in cases of urgency'. The courts of those countries have generally been careful to require strict proof of urgency.[67] It is, of course, common for national

60. 19 May 1989.

61. Immigration Appeal Tribunal London, 18 August 1983, *Giangregario* v. *Secretary of State*, [1983] 3 CMLR 472.

62. *Conseil d'Etat*, Belgium, 10 September 1979, *Duijker* v. *Belgium*, (1975) *Rec. Cons. d'Etat* 723; Immigration Appeal Tribunal, London, 1 September 1981, *Denis Hayes* v. *Secretary of State*, [1981] Imm AR 123; *Conseil d'Etat*, Belgium, 11 September 1981, *Antonio Colucci* v. *Belgium* (1981) *Rec. Cons. d'Etat* 1686; *Areios Pagos*, 17 May 1985, *Arbato Stellario* v. *Symvoulio Efeton Athinon*, (1989) CDE 438; *Conseil d'Etat*, Belgium, 16 January 1987, *Amar Ayachi* v. *Belgium*, (1987) *Administration Publique* 23; *Hessischer Verwaltungsgerichtshof*, 2 February 1990, (1990) *Informationsbrief Ausländerrecht* 149.

63. Case 30/77 *R.* v. *Bouchereau* [1977] ECR 1990.

64. 21 December 1987, *R.* v. *Jacobo Escauriaza* [1983] 3 CMLR 281.

65. 23 December 1986, *Dorothée Piermont* v. *France*, (see also decision of *Conseil d'Etat*, France, 12 May 1989).

66. *Supra*, n. 57, Art. 9.

67. *Tribunal de première instance de Liège*, 5 March 1975, *Procureur du Roi* v. *Leon Peroval*, (1975) *Journal des tribunaux* 463; *Tribunal de première instance de Bruxelles*, 24 February 1976, *Ministère Public* v. *Jean-Pierre Paul*, (1976) *Pasicrisie belge* III, 26; *Conseil d'Etat*, Belgium, 18 June 1976, *Weiss* v. *Belgium*, (1976), *Rec. Cons. d'Etat* 615; *Raad van State*, Belgium, 11 May 1989, *R.W.* v. *Belgium* (1989) *Revue du droit des étrangers* 306; *Raad van State*, Belgium, 16 February 1989, *Christiane Denis* v. *Belgium* (1989) *Tijdschrift voor bestuurswetenschappen en publiek recht* 731; *Tribunal de Première Instance de Liège*, 19 January 1989, *C.* v. *Belgium*, (1989) *Revue du droit des étrangers* 27; *Conseil d'Etat*, Belgium, 26 February 1985, *M.C.* v. *Belgium* (1985) *Revue du droit des étrangers* 57; *Conseil d'Etat*, Luxembourg, 13 November 1980, *Claude Genin* v. *Ministre de la Justice*, 25 Pas. Lux. (1980) 97.

courts to require that sufficient reasons be given.[68] The Conseil d'Etat of Luxembourg, however, held that the exclusion of a German national was justified where the stated grounds were 'recent and serious criminal convictions abroad — has fraudulently given false information about his past judicial record — likely to constitute a threat to the requirements of public policy.'[69] In England, on the other hand, the court of Appeal quashed a criminal court's recommendation for deportation on the ground that the inferior court had given only a summary of its reasons, even though the alien had committed seven offences and (it was held at first instance) 'neither the Secretary of State nor the applicant could have had the slightest doubt about the material on which the justices acted.'[70]

In view of the wide divergences between the Member States' characterisations of the 'public service' it is, perhaps, surprising that national case-law on this subject shows a degree of uniformity. In Germany,[71] Italy[72] and Belgium[73] the 'public service' has been construed narrowly, for the purposes of applying the exception envisaged in Article 48(4) of the EEC Treaty.

8. ESTABLISHMENT

In the national case-law on freedom of establishment, it is possible to detect a tension between the principle of national treatment and the principle of freedom of movement. In this context, the former principle is most frequently invoked by national professional bodies seeking to exclude nationals of other Member States on the ground that they have not fulfilled the qualifications or will not practise under the title or designation or under the conditions applicable to nationals of the host State.

In the case of the legal profession, national rules prohibiting the maintenance of two places of business or chambers have proved problematical[74] but the existing uncertainties have been much reduced by the European Court's ruling in the *Klopp*

---

68. *Raad van State*, Belgium, 5 November 1975, *C.V.* v. *Belgium*, (1975) *Rec. Cons. d'Etat* 940; *Conseil d'Etat*, Luxembourg, 4 November 1988, *Rudolf Weber* v. *Ministre de la Justice*; *Conseil d'Etat*, Luxembourg, 5 July 1984, *Serge Gale* v. *Ministre de la Justice*; *Conseil d'Etat*, Luxembourg, *Maffie v. Ministre de la Justice*, 25 Pas. Lux. (1980) 95; *Conseil d'Etat* (Luxembourg) 23 April 1975, *Mohammed Subhani* v. *Ministre de la Justice*, 23 Pas. Lux. (1975)155.

69. 7 December 1978, *Staniczek* v. *Ministre de la Justice*, 24 Pas. Lux. (1978) 186.

70. Court of Appeal, 6 March 1984, *Dannenberg* v. *Secretary of State* [1984] 3 CMLR 456.

71. *Bundesarbeitsgericht*, 6 February 1980, (1980) *Juristenzeitung* 115 (see also *Bundesfinanzhof*, 18 May 1984, (1984) *Recht der Internationalen Wirtschaft* 831, (on naturalization expenses insured by a Community national assuming German nationality for purposes of entering public service).

72. Corte di Cassazione, 23 May 1987, *Taziano Tuzet*, Il Foro Italiano (1987 - II) 481.

73. *Cour d'Appel*, Brussels, 22 March 1988, *Van Dijk* v. *Belgium*, Pas. Belge (1988 - II) 157.

74. *Conseil de l'Ordre des avocats*, 10 June 1986, *Chambost*, Feuille de liaison de la Conférénce Saint-Yves (1987) No. 68, 46; *Cour d'Appel*, Metz, 22 December 1988, *Böhm & Korsec* v. *Ordre des avocats de Thionville*, *Gazette du Palais* (1989 - II) 17; *Cour de Cassation*, France, 18 May 1989, *Conseil de l'Ordre des avocats, Nice* v. *Raynel* [1990] 2 CMLR 190.

case and the *Gullung* case.[75] In few of the reported cases has the mutual recognition of law degrees presented difficulty; although it must be said that lawyers relying on such recognition have not done so when moving to Member States with radically different legal systems.[76]

For the medical, veterinary, pharmaceutical and paramedical professions, problems of a different order are presented to the national courts. These professions, unlike the legal professions, have as the object of their practice objective anatomies rather than territorial legal systems. This fact has facilitated the development of community legislation, particularly that governing the mutual recognition of qualifications, which is the basis for much of the national case-law.[77] Nevertheless, there remains the persistent problem that specialities in these areas of activity vary from Member State to Member State, so that even in the absence of any discrimination, qualifications and titles obtained in one such State may be unrecognized or even prohibited in another.[78] Thus, the French *Conseil d'Etat* has held that French professional body was under no obligation to recognize a qualification as a plastic surgeon obtained by a French national in Belgium: that qualification did not exist in French law.[79] It has also held that where a Community national wishes to establish himself in another Member State in order to carry on there a regulated medical profession, and neither qualifies under domestic law nor comes within any of the categories defined by domestic law as entitled to entry, residence and establishment as an EEC national, then not only may he be refused permission to carry on that profession: he may also be refused a permit to reside in that State.[80]

The application of the principle of national treatment has resulted in the rejection of claims by members of various non-medical professions to practise in Member

75. Case 107/83 *Ordre des Avocats au Barreau de Paris* v. *O. Klopp*, [1984] ECR 2971 and Case 292/86 *C. Gullung* v. *Conseils de l'ordre des avocats du barreau de Colmar*, [1988] ECR 111 respectively.

76. *Cour d'Appel*, Brussels, 27 January 1975, *Ihor Konyk*, Pas. Belge (1975 - II) 101; *Cour d'Appel*, Brussels, 3 December 1979, *Catherine D*. Pas. Belge (1980 - II) 31; *Cour d'Appel*, Douai, 13 July 1984, *Jean Connerotte* v. *Ordre des avocats de Lille*, Gazette du Palais (1984 - I) 736.

77. *Cour d'Appel d'Angers*, 30 March 1982, *Pierre Laumonier* v. *Ministère Public et al*, Gazette du Palais (1982 - I) 315; *Bayerischer Verwaltungsgerichtshof*, 9 April 1984, Bay. VerwBl (1984) 750; *Tribunal Supremo* (Spain) 27 October 1987, *Manuel Santolaya Mazo* v. *Administración Publica* [1988] La Ley No. 1096; *Corte di Cassazione*, 20 November 1988, *Giuseppe Viglietti*, Il Consiglio di Stato (1989 - II) 1419; *Conseil d'Etat*, Luxembourg, 31 March 1988, *Yvan Georges* v. *Ministère de la santé*; *Cour d'Appel d'Aix en Provence*, 23 January 1989, *Ministère Public et al* v. *Marc Bouchoucha*; *Conseil d'Etat*, Luxembourg, 14 June 1989, *Abdul Aziz Makhlouf* v. *Ministère de l'éducation et de la jeunesse*.

78. The European Court has, of course, ruled that legislation which 'applies without distinction to Belgian nationals and those of other Member States, and [whose] provisions and objectives do not permit the conclusion that it was adopted for discriminatory purposes or that it produces discriminatory effects' is not incompatible with Art. 52 EEC: Case 221/85 *Commission* v. *Belgium* [1987] ECR 719 at 737.

79. *Conseil d'Etat*, 11 July 1988, *Conseil departemental de l'Ordre des Medicins des Alpes Maritimes* v. Denis Bonc, Gazette du Palais (1989 - II) 18.

80. *Conseil d'Etat*, 9 March 1988, *Joseph Weber*, Gazette du Palais (1988 - II) 11. See also *Conseil d'Etat*, Belgium, 10 November 1989, *Marc Bataille* v. *Belgium*, Administration Publique (1989) 165.

States other than their own.[81] It should be said, however, that in early decisions the principle of national treatment provided the basis for the removal of certain restrictions on establishment[82] and the principle has not prevented national courts from adopting a liberal view towards problems arising in connection with the recognition of formal qualifications.[83] Recently, that principle has been invoked before national courts in a series of cases involving the fiscal treatment (or treatment in relation to social security contributions) of companies or individuals established in Member States other than their own. The tendency of the national courts has been to find that in the absence of discrimination, fiscal and similar rules imposing costs on persons exercising freedom of establishment are not incompatible with Community law.[84]

81. *Cour d'Appel*, Luxembourg, 2 December 1970, *Ministère Public* v. *Stefanetti*; *Conseil d'Etat*, Luxembourg, 8 April 1970, *Yves Calpo* v. *Ministre de l'économie et des classes moyennes*; *Symvoulio tis Epikrateias*, 8 January 1988. *Meyer Bridges Educational Trust Ltd* v. *Ypourgou Ethnikis Paideias*, (1988) *Armenopoulos* 263; *Corte di Cassazione*, 28 February 1989, *Guiseppe Vita*, *Il Foro Amministrativo* (1990) 1712; Tribunale Amministrativo Regionale del Piemonte, 12 July 1989, *Bruno Brayda* v. *Ministero dell industria commercio e agricoltura*, I *Tribunale Amministrativo Regionale* (1989 - I) 4318. See also Supreme Court (Ireland) 15 June 1983, *Robert Fearman & Co* v. *Irish Land Commission*, 6 J Ir. Soc. Eur. L (1982 - 3) 120, where it was held that a national of another Member State who formed a company in Ireland was entitled to no more favourable treatment than an Irish shareholder in an Irish company, when confronted with provisions for compulsory purchase of land of absent owners.

82. *Cour d'Appel*, Paris, 12 March 1974, *Von Kempis* v. *Geldorf* [1976] 2 CMLR 152; Controller of the Patent Office, London, 21 February 1975; High Court, London, 21 January 1977, *F.A. Bigger (Deceased)* [1977] 2 All ER 644; *Haug* v. *Registrar of Patent Agents* [1976] 1 CMLR 491.

83. *Conseil d'Etat*, Luxembourg, 21 November 1984, *Steichen* v. *Ministre de l'éducation nationale*, Feuille de liaison de la Conférence Saint-Yves (1985) 49; *Conseil d'Etat*, Luxembourg, 13 December 1985, *Scott Roger Cormack* v. *Ministre de la Justice*.

84. *Arbeidshof*, Brussels, 4 October 1982, *T.* v. *RISZV*, (1983-4) *Rechtskundig Weekblad* 872; *Hof van Cassatie*, Belgium, 18 June 1984, *John Philips* v. *Integrity Asbl.* [1986] 3 CMLR 673; *Hof van Beroep*, Brussels, 3 November 1987, (1988) *Journal de droit fiscal* (1988) 159; *Hof van Cassatie*, Belgium, 21 November 1988, *RSVZ* v. *Wolf*, Pasicrisie Belge (1989 - I) 315.

HUMAN RIGHTS AND THE FREE MOVEMENT OF PERSONS IN EUROPE
The role of the national judiciary in the Netherlands

P. van Dijk and M. Schreuder-Vlasblom[*]

1.   INTRODUCTION

Human rights and the free transborder movement of persons are closely interrelated. Possibilities to leave one's country of origin, in order to avoid persecution or other serious violations of human rights — civil and political, as well as economic, social and cultural rights — may be hampered by the restrictive asylum and immigration policies of other countries. Conversely, the removal of such obstacles to free movement improves the possibility of exercising various human rights including the right to leave and return to one's own country, to enter into, maintain or intensify family life and other relations, to exchange thoughts and information, to have access to education and work, and to exercise other human rights without the restriction of borders. Therefore, human rights law may be directly relevant to immigration law and policy and may influence the balancing of the public interest in a restrictive immigration and visa policy against the interests of the alien who wants to be admitted and claims that one or more of his or her human rights are at stake.

The national courts that consider appeals against either refusals of admission or intended expulsions can play an important role in securing a fair balance between these interests. For this the courts need legal rules that enable them to review the legitimacy of an administrative decision and its underlying policy. International law may provide supplementary standards for judicial review, especially in a situation like that of the Netherlands where the relationship between international and domestic law is determined by monistic rules.[1] The Dutch Constitution goes very far in attributing internal effect to provisions of international law. According to Article 93 of the Constitution, treaty provisions and decisions of international organizations

* Dr. P. van Dijk is a member of the Council of State of the Netherlands; Dr. M. Schreuder-Vlasblom is a member of the legal staff of the Judicial Division of the Council of State. The opinions expressed are those of the authors personally and do not necessarily reflect the views of the Council of State.

1. On this, see P. van Dijk, 'Domestic Status of Human Rights Treaties and the Attitude of the Judiciary; The Dutch Case', in M. Nowak et al., ed., *Progress in the Spirit of Human Rights; Festschrift für Felix Ermacora* (Kehl 1988) p. 631 at pp. 634-639.

that are of a generally binding character, (i.e., self-executing[2]), have binding effect within the legal order of the Netherlands after their publication. Article 94 stipulates that Dutch national law shall not be applied if and insofar as it is not compatible with a provision or decision referred to in Article 93. This means that international law may directly provide standards for review to the Dutch judiciary, which the latter has to apply with precedence over deviating standards ensuing not only from administrative directives, but also from general decrees, statutes, and even from the Constitution.

The rights and freedoms laid down in the European Convention on Human Rights (hereinafter: 'the European Convention' or 'the Convention')[3] must be secured to all persons, including non-nationals, within the jurisdiction of the States Parties to the Convention. Although this Convention does not offer an express legal foundation for challenging the legitimacy of a restrictive immigration and asylum policy, some of its provisions − especially Articles 3 and 8 − contain at least some clues to counterbalance in individual cases the general interest pursued by such a restrictive policy, by giving weight to certain rights of the alien concerned, whose protection requires admission into the State in question.

The role of the national judiciary in the Netherlands to ensure the rights and freedoms laid down in the European Convention with respect to aliens who apply for admission to, or who appeal against expulsion from the Netherlands, and the function of these rights and freedoms as legal standards at the disposal of the judiciary for that purpose, are the central issues of this report. The primary focus is on the Judicial Division of the Council of State (hereinafter: 'the Council of State'), which is the principal court in the Netherlands with jurisdiction in asylum and immigration cases.

2.   ACCESS TO COURT UNDER DUTCH ASYLUM AND
       IMMIGRATION LAW

Article 6 of the European Convention contains the basic guarantees of a fair trial. For the interpretation of this provision the European Court of Human Rights (hereinafter: 'the European Court'), in its *Delcourt* judgment, has formulated the following basic standard:

'In a democratic society within the meaning of the Convention, the right to a fair administration of justice holds such a prominent place, that a restrictive interpretation of Article 6 would not correspond to the aim and the purpose of that provision.'[4]

---

2. Thus the Supreme Court, judgment of 24 February 1960, NJ (1960) No. 483; judgment of 18 May 1962, NJ (1965) No. 604.
3. 213 UNTS 221; Trb. 1951 No. 154.
4. Judgment of 17 January 1970, ECHR A.11 (1970) p. 15.

This basic standard, combined with the position taken by the Court in its *Golder* judgment that Article 6 guarantees not only a fair trial in judicial procedures, but also *a right to* a judicial procedure and, consequently, a right of access to a court,[5] has substantially broadened the scope of application and the implications of Article 6. Nevertheless, the impact of this Strasbourg case-law on procedures in the Netherlands concerning asylum, admission and expulsion has been very limited to date. This is mainly because, according to the present Strasbourg case-law, claims of non-nationals for admission or against expulsion do not as such concern the 'determination of a civil right' within the meaning of Article 6.[6] Consequently, Article 6 applies only when the administrative decision denying such a claim also has a negative impact on a right of the applicant that is recognized as a 'civil right', for example the right to respect for his or her family life as is laid down in Article 8 of the Convention.[7] However, it should not be excluded that in the future Article 6 will be declared applicable to the determination of refugee status and to decisions on admission and expulsion, in view of the rights claimed under national law or under a treaty, such as the Geneva Convention relating to the Status of Refugees (hereafter: 'the Geneva Convention')[8] or the European Convention.

Article 13 of the European Convention grants a right to an effective — although not necessarily judicial — remedy against violations of the rights and freedoms laid down in the Convention. Since the Convention does not contain a right to asylum or, more generally, a right to be admitted into and to reside in a State Party to the Convention, Article 13 also applies only if the applicant has an arguable claim about violation of the prohibition of collective expulsion (the Fourth Protocol to the Convention) or if the refusal of admission or the intended expulsion may be claimed to constitute a violation of another right or freedom set forth in the Convention.

Outside this limited — and, as far as Article 6 is concerned, rather uncertain — applicability of Articles 6 and 13, and leaving aside the question to what extent these articles may be relied on by applicants as self-executing treaty provisions,[9] the availability of a judicial remedy or of any remedy at all against refusal of admission or against expulsion depends on whether national law provides such a remedy.

For the Netherlands the situation can be described as follows. In most cases, the alien concerned has the right to request a review of the decision by the Minister of Justice concerning residence permits from the same Minister of Justice. These cases are the following ones: (a) fictive or express refusal of a residence permit or settlement permit and refusal of admission as a refugee, and refusal to extend a residence permit; (b) granting or extension of a residence permit for a shorter period

5. Judgment of 21 February 1975, ECHR A.18 (1975) p. 13.

6. See e.g., Application No. 7902/77, *X*. v. *United Kingdom*, 9 D & R (1978) p. 224 at pp. 225-226.

7. See e.g., Applications Nos. 2991 and 2992/66, *Alam, Kahn and Singh* v. *United Kingdom*, X Yearbook (*Yearbook of the European Convention on Human Rights*) (1967) p. 478 at pp. 500-504.

8. Convention of 28 July 1951, 189 UNTS 137, Trb. 1951 No. 131 and Trb. 1954 No. 88; supplemented by a Protocol concerning the Status of Refugees of 31 January 1967, 606 UNTS 267, Trb. 1967 No.76.

9. This issue will be discussed *infra*, in section 4.

than was applied for, or under certain limitations or conditions; (c) unrequested changes in the limitations or conditions of the residence permit, or imposition of the obligation to report periodically to the police; (d) withdrawal of a residence permit, settlement permit or admission as a refugee; (e) declaration as *persona non grata*; (f) expulsion due to loss of the status that entitled the alien to a residence permit; and (g) expulsion after a stay of three months during which period the alien has reported to the police but has not been granted a residence permit.[10] If admission is refused at the border, such decision is not open to review by the Minister of Justice. However, the alien concerned may institute summary proceedings with the President of the District Court of The Hague, who may order the alien's admission for the purpose of filing a new request.

If a request for review by the Minister of Justice is declared admissable, it leads to a full reconsideration of the original decision. Appeals can be made either from a negative decision taken on review or, if after three months no decision has been taken, from the fictive rejection of the request. Such appeals are made to the Judicial Division of the Council of State, which is an independent tribunal with jurisdiction to review the decision for its conformity with the applicable domestic law, with general principles of good administration and with self-executing provisions of treaties and of decisions of international organizations, and for the absence of arbitrariness.

An exception is made for cases in which the negative decision by the Minister of Justice on review is in accordance with the advice of the Advisory Committee on Alien Affairs, and the alien concerned had not stayed in the Netherlands for a full year at the moment the decision was taken.[11] Although the Council of State has general supplementary jurisdiction to review administrative decisions, its review may be excluded by law. It has to be assumed that Article 34 of the Aliens Act is such an exclusion.[12] This would seem to leave a gap in the judicial review of decisions concerning aliens.[13] However, in those cases the alien concerned may institute summary proceedings with the President of the District Court of The Hague against his expulsion in a tort action against the State of the Netherlands. This action has developed in Dutch case-law into a fairly comprehensive judicial review of the challenged act or decision.[14] Therefore, in fact there is full access to the judiciary against the decision concerning expulsion.

In this context it should be mentioned that the creation of a general administrative jurisdiction in the Netherlands dates only from 1975. Before then gaps in the system

10. See Art. 29 Aliens Act (*Vreemdelingenwet*), Stb. 1965 No. 40.

11. Art. 34, para. 1(b) Aliens Act.

12. Since the granting of visas is not expressly regulated in the Aliens Act, the Council of State takes the position that it is not covered by the special regime of that Act and that the Council of State has jurisdiction to receive appeals against negative decisions.

13. Art. 102, para. 2 of the Aliens Decree (*Vreemdelingenbesluit*) provides that the exception does not apply to nationals of the other Member-States of the European Community with a special EC-status.

14. See e.g., Supreme Court, judgment of 27 June 1986, RvdW (1986) No. 139; judgment of 27 March 1987, AB (1987) No. 273.

of judicial review of governmental action were filled by the civil courts on the basis of an extensive interpretation of their general jurisdiction concerning property rights and other private rights and concerning contractual and non-contractual obligations,[15] which was assumed to also cover legal relations between private parties and public authorities, even if those relations were founded in public law. This general jurisdiction of the 'ordinary' courts has been preserved as a complementary jurisdiction in administrative disputes, also in cases of refusal of admission or threat of expulsion.

3.   LEGAL RULES TO BE APPLIED BY THE JUDICIARY IN
        THE NETHERLANDS

The legal protection of the right to free movement of persons depends not only on the right to judicial review of administrative action restricting free movement, but also on the availability of adequate legal rules on which such judicial review is based. These legal rules concern both the free movement of persons and the excercise of powers by national authorities.

    The goal of a greater freedom of movement within the European Community has been pursued through the adoption of elaborate Community legislation. Such legislation may either be directly applied by the national courts or has to be implemented by the national legislator within an indicated period. In both cases the national courts must give precedence to Community law whenever national law is not in conformity therewith. Thus Community law has become an important source of legal rules to be applied by the national courts in cases concerning movement of persons. This source also includes the case-law of the Court of Justice of the European Communities, which the national courts may elicit themselves by submitting issues to the Court for a preliminary ruling.

    These rules only apply, however, to a privileged group of nationals of the Member States and their relatives. Other sources of international law, such as the Refugee Convention, also apply to specific groups of aliens. Other international treaties, such as the European Convention, cover all aliens from the moment they find themselves under the jurisdiction of the State Party concerned. These international rules constitute only supplementary standards for review by national courts, albeit that in a constitutional system such as that of the Netherlands they have precedence. The national courts still have to rely mainly on their national law. We will, therefore, start with a short description of Dutch asylum law and immigration law.

    The legal history of the Aliens Act seems to indicate that the legislator started from the assumption that, to the extent that international commitments allowed, immigration into the Netherlands had to be confined to cases supported by the general interest or by a considerable individual interest of the alien concerned. In

15. Article 2 Judiciary Act (*Wet op de Rechterlijke Organisatie*).

order to give shape to a restrictive immigration policy, the legislator opted not for a system of detailed criteria and rules, but for a system of permits, which leaves a large margin to the authorities by attributing to them discretionary powers and by providing only vague standards. According to this system there are three main grounds for granting an alien a residence permit (for more than three months[16]): (a) international obligations;[17] (b) an essential interest of the Netherlands;[18] and (c) urgent humanitarian reasons.[19]

The Aliens Act is not very detailed in respect to the criteria for determining when to grant a residence permit. It expressly provides that the following aliens are entitled to indefinite residence in the Netherlands: (a) those who have a settlement permit; (b) those who have been admitted as refugees; and (c) those other categories of aliens designated by general decree.[20] For the rest the Act only stipulates that a residence permit or its renewal may be refused on grounds derived from the general interest[21] and that a residence permit may be withdrawn on certain grounds.[22] The establishment of more detailed criteria and rules for admission and expulsion is left to the competent authorities, without it even being stipulated that those criteria and rules have to be incorporated in formal legal regulations. In fact they are to be found in directives for the decision-making bodies, which are periodically collected and published in the Aliens Circular (*Vreemdelingencirculaire*).[23]

This regime, in which the legislature deliberately introduced the vague standard of 'general interest' in order to create a wide margin of discretion for the authorities, enabled the competent authorities to develop, in consultation with parliament, a restrictive immigration policy laid down mainly in directives and which left little scope for the judiciary to give its own interpretation and specification of these vague criteria and rules set by the legislature, independent of the interpretation and specification of the executive. In fact, the Council of State confines itself to examining whether the administrative directives are in conformity with the law and are not

16. Article 8 Aliens Act implies that any alien is entitled to a short stay, provided that he or she has the required travel and visa documents, has sufficient means of subsistence and does not constitute a threat to public order and national security.

17. One should think especially of refugees in the sense of the Refugee Convention, and of Benelux citizens and citizens of EC countries, but also, *inter alia*, of citizens of Suriname to which an agreement between the Netherlands and Suriname applies.

18. For instance aliens who are invited for a function or job for which there is no qualified person available in the Netherlands.

19. For instance for the purpose of family reunion, care in a foster home, medical treatment, education and the like.

20. Art. 10 Aliens Act.

21. Art. 11, para. 5 Aliens Act.

22. Art. 12 Aliens Act.

23. It is generally assumed, that the authorities themselves are bound by these directives and that their decisions may be reviewed for their conformity therewith. Thus, Council of State, decision of 21 June 1979, AB (1980) No. 9; decision of 10 February 1984, AB (1984) No. 423; decision of 29 April 1986, AB (1987) No. 250. Cf., Supreme Court, judgment of 27 March 1987, AB (1987) No. 273.

arbitrary or unreasonable.[24] Subsequently, decisions based on directives which can stand this test (which usually appears to be the case) are reviewed for their conformity with general principles of good administration. Those principles are partly of a procedural nature, in particular concerning due care in the examination of the request for admission or of the appeal against denials, withdrawals and expulsions,[25] and stating the reasons of the decision.[26] Partly they concern the contents of a challenged decision, in particular the principles of equality[27] and legal security.[28] Application of the latter principles leads, however, to a rather marginal review only, since these principles have mainly the effect of binding the authorities to criteria and rules laid down in their own directives, as far as these have been published and have been applied consistently. Consequently, in effect these principles tend to absorb the policy based upon these criteria and rules previously found to be not unreasonable. As a result, indirectly, the Council of State, too, uses those criteria and rules as standards for its judicial review.

Accordingly, it may be concluded that an adequate judicial review of administrative decisions concerning admission and expulsion of aliens requires more specific standards for review than the ones ensuing from the Aliens Act, in order to enable the judiciary to keep somewhat more distance *vis-à-vis* the policy laid down in administrative directives. As indicated above, international law may provide such supplementary standards for judicial review, especially in legal systems like that of the Netherlands where international law has internal effect within the national legal order.[29]

4.   HUMAN RIGHTS PROVISIONS TO BE APPLIED BY THE JUDICIARY IN THE NETHERLANDS

The most important international standards for reviewing decisions concerning the free transborder movement of persons are the ones contained in the law of the European Community, in the Refugee Convention and in bilateral and multilateral treaties concerning the treatment of aliens. In addition, however, the standards implied in human rights treaties have gained considerably in importance. In accordance with the subject of our presentation, we will concentrate on the latter category, with special emphasis on the European Convention on Human Rights.

---

24. See e.g., decision of 14 June 1979, RV (1979) No. 31, where it was held that the directives concerning family reunion did not take into consideration the different family relations in Cape Verde.

25. Council of State, decision of 18 May 1989, RV (1989) No. 5. Cf., Supreme Court, judgment of 13 March 1988, NJ (1988) No. 908.

26. Council of State, decision of 23 April 1985, AB (1986) No. 208.

27. Council of State, decision of 21 June 1979, AB (1980) No. 9; decision of 21 April 1987, R02.83.0925.

28. Council of State, decision of 27 January 1983, AB (1984) No. 363.

29. See *supra*, in the Introduction.

As far as the European Convention is concerned, an impact on judicial review of decisions concerning admission and expulsion is to be expected mainly from Articles 3, 6 and 8, which according to the case-law of both the Supreme Court and the Council of State are of a self-executing character.[30] Article 13 may also play a certain role, but its domestic status is much more ambiguous.[31] It should also be mentioned here that the case-law of the European Court of Human Rights has the same binding force within the Dutch legal order as the European Convention itself. The judgments of the European Court are not considered to be decisions of an international organization in the sense of Articles 93 and 94 of the Constitution; they are regarded to be incorporated into the provision or provisions of the Convention to which they relate. This means that the courts in the Netherlands may and must take these judgments into consideration when interpreting and applying a provision of the Convention; also those judgments which were pronounced in cases in which the Netherlands was not a party.[32]

In this context the question may be raised whether the national court is allowed to give a wider interpretation to self-executing provisions of the Convention than the interpretation laid down in the case-law of the European Court. Article 60 of the Convention[33] does not provide an answer to this question, because it is confined to the cases in which the national court (also) relies on rights and freedoms ensured under his national law or under another treaty, which leaves the question open as to what the situation is if the court only applies the Convention provision.

In a judgment of 10 November 1989,[34] the Supreme Court observed that its previous case-law had given a wider interpretation to the concept of 'family life' in Article 8 of the Convention than was subsequently done by the European Court in its *Berrehab* judgement of 21 June 1988.[35] The *Berrehab* case concerned the relationship between a father and his child after divorce in a situation where the father and the child did not live together. In its earlier case-law the Supreme Court had held

---

30. This position is implied in the standing case-law in which the applicability of these articles is examined. This case-law is listed annually in the *NJCM-Bulletin*. From the survey concerning 1988 the following examples may be mentioned. With respect to Art. 3: Supreme Court, judgment of 22 January 1988, NJ (1988) No. 891; Council of State, decision of 19 April 1988, RvdW (1988) No. 41. With respect to Article 6: Supreme Court, judgment of 19 February 1988, NJ (1988) No. 725; Council of State, decision of 10 May 1988, AB (1989)No. 86. With respect to Article 8: Supreme Court, judgment of 8 January 1988, NJ (1988) No. 857; Council of State, decision of 6 June 1988, RV (1988) No. 23.

31. It was declared to be not self-executing by the Council of State: decision of 29 July 1980, RV (1980) No. 46. A different position had been taken before by the Crown: Royal Decree of 22 October 1974, RV (1974) No. 27. If, and to what extent a new opening has been made by the Supreme Court in its judgment of 1 February 1991, RvdW (1991) No. 44, is still unclear.

32. See the judgment of the Supreme Court of 18 January 1980, NJ (1980) No. 483, where the Supreme Court applied the *Marckx* judgment of the European Court of 13 June 1979, ECHR A.31, delivered in a case against Belgium.

33. Art. 60 reads as follows: 'Nothing in this Convention shall be construed as limiting or derogating from any of the human rights and fundamental freedoms which may be ensured under the laws of any High Contracting Party or under any other agreement to which it is a Party.'

34. Judgment of 10 November 1989, NJ (1989) No. 628.

35. ECHR A.138 (1988) p. 14.

that the mere fact of the blood-tie between a parent and his or her child established a relationship that constituted 'family life' in the sense of Article 8 of the Convention.[36] The European Court, in its *Berrehab* judgment, held that even the family life that exists *ipso jure* between a child born out of marriage and his or her parents may be discontinued by 'subsequent events', which implies that 'family life' in the sense of Article 8 means *de facto* family life. Subsequently, the Supreme Court held that this interpretation by the European Court forced it to reconsider its own case-law, since this case-law was based directly on Article 8. This judgment indicates that the Supreme Court requires the Dutch courts to follow the interpretation of the European Court when they apply the European Convention.

This point of view is in conformity with the assumption according to which the case-law of the European Court is incorporated into the relevant provisions of the Convention and consequently shares the legal effect of these provisions within the domestic legal order. This assumption would seem to impede the national courts from ignoring a restrictive interpretation given by the European Court when using the provisions of the Convention as a standard for review. Indeed, the legal basis of such a review would otherwise become very weak, especially if it would lead to the decision — based on Article 94 of the Dutch Constitution — to set aside a provision of national law for its incompatibility with that provision of the Convention. On the other hand, one should not conclude too easily that the European Court has adhered to, or has rejected a certain interpretation of the Convention. In general, the Court declines to give general and abstract interpretations. It applies the Convention to the concrete case before it, with the result that its case-law is of a rather casuistic nature. And as its case-law shows, the Court is willing to develop and specify its opinion in later cases. In fact, one of the guiding factors for the Court is precisely the developments in the national legal systems of the States Parties to the Convention, including developments in national case-law.

The significance of the European Convention as a source of supplementary standards for judicial review is increased by the fact that several provisions of the Convention contain concepts that are also familiar to national law, but which have been given by the European Court (and the European Commission) an autonomous meaning, detached from any national legal system but to a certain degree based upon a comparison of the systems of the States Parties. This enables the courts in the Netherlands to review the challenged decision and the underlying policy in a somewhat more detached, independent way, and even permits deviation from a similar provision of the Constitution.

The role which the European Convention may play in this respect can be illustrated by describing recent developments in the case-law of the Council of State with respect to Article 8 of the Convention. This description will also show how important it is that the European Court in its judgments and the European Commission in its reports gradually give clear directions to the national courts about the way

36. Judgments of 22 February 1985, 12 December 1986 and 18 December 1987, NJ (1986) No. 3, NJ (1988) No. 188 and NJ (1988) No. 844 respectively.

in which the provisions and concepts should be interpreted and applied. Without such directions it may be difficult for a national court to dissociate itself from the familiar concepts and notions of national law and policy.

5. EXCURSUS: IMMIGRATION LAW AND 'FAMILY LIFE'

The administrative directives relating to the application of Article 11, paragraph 5 of the Aliens Act (grounds for (refusing) admission or renewal) provide for the granting of a residence permit, *inter alia*, on pressing humanitarian grounds, which are elaborated into more specific criteria, containing among others the criterion of family reunion. The required serious character of the humanitarian reasons, expressed in the word 'pressing' (*klemmend*), is reflected in the interpretation of the concept of 'family' which moreover in Dutch language stands for the narrow concept of '*gezin*' and not for the broader concept of '*familie*'. The applicant for admission must have belonged recently to an actual and uninterrupted (except as a result of the earlier departure of one or more members to the Netherlands) joint household with a person residing in the Netherlands, based on natural or legal family bounds.

Under this and certain more specific conditions the applicant will be granted a residence permit to enable him or her to rejoin the member or members of the family who already reside in the Netherlands. It should be noted that, contrary to renewal of permits enabling non-nationals to continue residence in the Netherlands in order not to interfere with their family life on Dutch territory, granting such a residence permit in a case of first admission amounts to affirmative action on the part of the author-ities, because respect for family life here consists in creating the conditions for the enjoyment of family life on Dutch territory through the granting of the permit. This explains the rather strict criteria for the existence of a family and for having belonged to that family, and the specific conditions for family reunion.

If on appeal from a negative decision concerning family reunion the applicant claims that the challenged decision constitutes a violation of his or her right to respect for his or her family life as guaranteed in Article 8 of the European Conven-tion, the Council of State will be called upon to review both the law and directives on which that decision is based and the decision itself for conformity with Article 8. For a long time the Council of State appeared to be inclined to connect the purpose and scope of this part of Article 8 to purpose and scope of the concept of family reunion according to the national directives and policy, a framework in which, as stated above, emphasis is on the presence of a family in the strict sense and on a set of exceptions. As a result of this orientation the Council of State tended to focus on the presence of family life under rather strict criteria, and — when family life was found to exist — on the issue of whether any of the grounds of limitation listed in paragraph 2 of Article 8 could justify the negative decision. And as far as the latter issue is concerned, the Council of State was inclined to hold in most cases that the exception to the right to family reunion which the authorities had found to be applicable, was covered by one of the grounds of the second paragraph. The condition that the limitation must be 'necessary in a democratic society' was not separately tested, as it was probably assumed to be met if the limitation was found to serve any of the listed grounds and to be provided by law. This approach inevitably resulted in a rather restrictive interpretation of the concept of 'family life', influenced by the strict meaning attached to the notion of 'family' within the national directives and policy concerning family reunion, while it came less to the fore that this concept in Article 8 had, according to the Strasbourg case-law,[37] an 'autonomous' meaning.[38]

This situation has changed. In its present case-law, the Council of State gives full recognition to the two main lines running through the Strasbourg case-law concerning Article 8, viz, (1) that 'the object of the Article is "essentially" that of protecting the individual against arbitrary interference by the public authorities'[39] and not that of providing a claim for affirmative action, and (2) that the concept of 'family life' in Article 8 is an autonomous concept.[40] It is, therefore, recognized by the Council of State that the purpose and scope of Article 8 may differ substantially from the purpose and scope of the regulations concerning family reunion under Dutch immigration law and policy, which are based upon a strict notion of 'family' and by definition imply a claim for affirmative action to make the reunion possible.

As far as the concept of 'family life' is concerned, the Council of State intends to follow the broad criteria laid down in the Strasbourg case-law: (a) a legal and genuine marriage establishes family life between the spouses,[41] which normally comprises cohabitation, but which is not an indispensible element;[42] (b) a child born of such a union is ipso iure part of that relationship and consequently has family life with each of the parents, although subsequent events may break that tie;[43] (c) in the case of an extra-marital relationship there may also be ties of family life between the partners, provided that they live together on a permanent basis and maintain a joint household;[44] (d) in the case of an illegitimate child the natural tie with a parent as a rule creates family life,[45] but here again subsequent events may

---

37. European Commission, report of 10 December 1977, *Marckx*, ECHR B.29 (1982) p. 44. Impliedly the European Court in its judgment of 13 June 1979 in the same case, ECHR A.31 (1979) p. 14.

38. See e.g., Council of State, decision of 10 April 1989, R02.86.1659; decision of 10 October 1989, R02.88.0736.

39. See e.g., judgment of 13 June 1979, *Marckx*, ECHR A.31 (1979) p. 15.

40. See n. 37.

41. Judgment of 21 June 1988, *Berrehab*, ECHR A. 138 (1988) p. 14. See Council of State, decision of 6 May 1989, No. R02.87.0968.

42. Judgment of 28 May 1985, *Abdulaziz, Cabales and Balkandali*, ECHR A.94 (1985) p. 32; judgment of 21 June 1988, *Berrehab*, ECHR A.138 (1988) p. 14

43. *Berrehab* judgment, *ibid*. See Council of State, decision of 6 December 1988, No. R02.88.1726; decision of 18 September 1990, No. R02.88.2615.

44. Applications 7289/75 and 7349/76, *X. and Y.* v. *Switzerland*, XX Yearbook (1977) p. 168 at p. 172. See Council of State, decision of 11 January 1990, No. R02.88.2800.

45. Judgment of 13 June 1979, *Marckx*, ECHR A.31 (1979) p. 14. See Council of State, decision of 5 July 1988, No. R02.88.0570.

indicate that no such special ties exist;[46] (e) relations between an adoptive parent and an adoptive child are also covered by Article 8;[47] relations between a foster parent and a foster child have not yet brought under family life, but are nevertheless covered by Article 8 as forming part of their private life;[48] (f) the recognition that 'family life' is an autonomous concept also implies that cultural patterns which prevail in western Europe are not decisive; thus a polygamous family is in principle also entitled to protection;[49] and (g) family life is not restricted to the marital or extra-marital relationship between partners, and to the relationship between children and their parents, but also includes the ties between other near relatives, for instance those between grandparents and grandchildren.[50]

As far as the purpose of Article 8 is concerned, the Council of State inferes from the Strasbourg case-law that this purpose is primarily to prevent the national authorities from interfering with the form, intensity and extent of the family life enjoyed by the persons concerned. This means, in the Council of State's opinion, that in the case of a request by an alien for admission or for a renewal of a residence permit, and in the case of an appeal against withdrawal of such a permit or against expulsion, the authorities must not interfere with the way in which and the legal basis on which the existing family life is or was maintained by the alien concerned with others at the moment the request or appeal was made or should have been made. By determining the scope of this prohibition of interference the Council of State follows the European Court in its statement in the *Abdulaziz* case:

'The duty imposed by Article 8 cannot be considered as extending to a general obligation on the part of a Contracting State to respect the choice by married couples of the country of their matrimonial residence and to accept the non-national spouses for settlement in that country.'[51]

In view of this purpose and scope of Article 8, and given the position of the Strasbourg organs that 'family life' in Article 8 is an autonomous concept, the Council of State on the one hand gives a broader interpretation to the concept of 'family life' as an autonomous concept than in the case of the national directives concerning family reunion, but on the other hand applies a rather strict test as to whether there has been an 'interference' with this family life.

---

46. This follows *a fortiori* from the *Berrehab* judgment, *supra*, n. 43. See Council of State, decision of 10 April 1989, No. R02.86.1659; decision of 30 October 1989, No. R02.88.0291.

47. Application 9993/82, *X.* v. *France*, 31 D & R (1983) p. 241. However, an adoption order against the wishes of the natural parent constitutes an interference with that parent's right to respect of his or her family life: Application 9966/82, *X.* v. *United Kingdom*, not published. See Council of State, decision of 29 June 1987, No. R02.83.3020; decision of 7 November 1989, No. R02.87.1705.

48. Application 8257/78, *X.* v. *Switzerland*, 13 D & R (1979) p. 448 at p. 453.

49. Impliedly: Application 2991/66, *Kahn* v. *United Kingdom*, X Yearbook (1967) p. 478. See Council of State, decision of 19 January 1990, No. R02.87.2500.

50. *Marckx* judgment, *supra*, n. 45, p. 21. See Council of State, decision of 14 February 1989, No. R02.87.0241.

51. Judgment of 28 May 1985, ECHR A.94 (1985) p. 34.

However, again following the Strasbourg case-law, the Council of State, after having found that the challenged decision does not constitute an interference with the family life of the applicant, will nevertheless examine whether there is a positive obligation on the part of the Dutch authorities, implied in the respect required by Article 8. As the European Court held in its *Marckx* judgment:

> 'in addition to this primarily negative undertaking, there may be positive obligations inherent in an effective "respect" for family life.'[52]

To determine whether the challenged decision refusing admission or leading to expulsion is in violation of any such 'positive obligation', the Council of State follows the Court's directive that:

> 'regard must be had to the fair balance that has to be struck between the general interest of the community and the interests of the individual, the search for which balance is inherent in the whole of the Convention.'[53]

It examines whether specific facts or circumstances have been put forward or have become known, in view of which the decision to refuse a residence permit to, or to expel the applicant displays a harshness of such a disproportion that the authorities by giving priority to the general interest of maintaining a restrictive immigration policy, have violated the applicant's right of respect for his or her family life.[54]

In examining that issue the Council of State takes also into account the Court's observation that:

> 'the Court cannot ignore that the present case is concerned not only with family life but also with immigration and that, as a matter of well-established international law and subject to its treaty obligations, a State has the right to control the entry of non-nationals into its territory.'[55]

This has as a result that the Council of State is inclined to give due weight to the public interest of a restrictive immigration policy for the Netherlands and that the private interests leading to a positive obligation to admit a non-national into its territory must indeed be of a pressing humanitarian character, for instance a situation where parents who live abroad, because of their age and/or physical or psychological condition are totally dependent on living with their children in the Netherlands.[56]

---

52. ECHR A.31 (1979) p. 15. See also the judgment of 28 May 1985, *Abdulaziz, Cabales and Balkandali*, ECHR A.94 (1985) p. 34 and the judgment of 17 October 1986, *Rees*, ECHR A.106 (1986) p. 15.

53. Judgment of 17 October 1986, *Rees*, ECHR A.106 (1986) p. 15. See also the judgment of 7 July 1989, *Gaskin*, ECHR A.160 (1989) p. 17.

54. See e.g., the decisions of 8 April 1991, Nos. R02.89.2080 and R02.89.1874, AB Kort (1991) No. 459.

55. Judgment of 28 May 1985, *Abdulaziz, Cabales and Balkandali*, ECHR A.94 (1985) p. 34.

56. Thus, impliedly, Council of State, decisions of 8 April 1991, Nos. R02.89.1888 and R02.89.1892.

However, the Council of State has not yet followed the European Court in transplanting the grounds of limitation of the second paragraph of Article 8 to the first paragraph as criteria for judging whether a positive obligation on the part of the authorities exist in relation to the applicant.[57] In our opinion, the issue of a positive obligation, which forms part of the first paragraph of Article 8 and relates mainly to the special facts and circumstances of the alien concerned, should not be mixed up with the issue of the justification of an interference, which forms part of the second paragraph and relates mainly to the general interests of the State. The system of Article 8 would seem to imply that, if a positive obligation on the part of the authorities to respect the family life of the applicant by granting him or her a residence permit is found to exist, and the conclusion is reached that this obligation has not been fulfilled, the State still may claim that this element of lack of respect of the applicant's family life in the sense of the first paragraph is justified under the second paragraph. It is difficult to see how the second paragraph could still function as an ultimate test, if a weighing of the same interests has already led the court to conclude that a positive obligation exists. Moreover, it is not clear what role the words 'necessary in a democratic society' play if the criteria of the second paragraph are incorporated in the notion of 'respect' of the first paragraph. As long as the Court's case-law on the issue is not well-established and unambiguous, the national courts may continue to develop their own case-law on the basis of what they consider to be the correct interpretation of Article 8.

The different approach which the Council of State has recently opted for has had as one of its main purposes precisely the restoration of the original function of the justification test under the second paragraph, which had lost almost all meaning in view of the broad application of the criterion 'economic well-being of the country', and to reserve that test as a strict test for those cases where an interference with family life or a positive obligation to respect family life is found to exist. This implies that, especially in cases of applications for admission, in fact the interference test of the first paragraph has to a certain extent taken over the screening function, which the justification test of the second paragraph performed until now. This would seem to be more in accordance with the purposes of the two paragraphs of Article 8 and their interrelationship.

6.   IMPEDIMENTS TO THE APPLICATION BY THE DUTCH
      JUDICIARY OF HUMAN RIGHTS STANDARDS FOR REVIEW

The extent to which the courts in the Netherlands are able to use provisions of human rights treaties as standards for reviewing decisions concerning admission and

---

57. The European Court, in its *Rees* judgment, ECHR A.106 (1986) p. 15, held as follows: 'In striking this balance the aims mentioned in the second paragraph of Article 8 may be of a certain relevance, although this provision refers in terms only to "interferences" with the right protected by the first paragraph — in other words is concerned with the negative obligations flowing therefrom'.

expulsion depends in the first place, as stated above, on the question of whether a certain provision is of a self-executing character as meant by Articles 93 and 94 of the Constitution. Besides this threshold, however, other problems may arise, related to the limited scope of the review by administrative courts. We will illustrate this in relation to some specific provisions of the European Convention.

6.1.   Article 3 of the European Convention: inhuman treatment

Under the Aliens Act the national authorities are expected, except in very special cases, to expel a non-national whose application for (an extension of) a residence permit has been refused. However, at present it is the 'official' policy in the Netherlands with respect to those asylum seekers from Afghanistan, Ethiopia, Iran, Iraq and Sudan,[58] who are not granted a residence permit, not to expel them, in view of the present situation in their countries of origin. This means that expulsion is dealt with separately and needs a separate decision. From the latter decision no appeal lies with the Council of State; the alien concerned can only address a civil court with a tort action.

This separation of decisions implies that a potential violation of Article 3 of the European Convention is an appropriate issue in a 'civil' action against an intended expulsion, but not necessarily so in an appeal to the Council of State against a refusal or withdrawal of a residence permit. Exactly because the expulsion decision is separate from that concerning refusal or withdrawal, according to the Council of State, the latter decision does not constitute in itself an inhuman or degrading treatment.[59] In fact, the alleged inhumanity of the challenged decision is connected with the inhuman treatment that is expected in the country of origin, an issue that arises only in case of an intended expulsion. Moreover, as far as the alleged inhumanity is claimed to be caused by the refusal or withdrawal of the permit, this argument is usually based on events that occurred after the challenged decision had been taken and pending the appeal proceedings before the Council of State, such as failed attempts to expel the applicant. According to existing case-law the Council of State cannot take such events into consideration in its review of the challenged decision, because that review only concerns the lawfulness of the challenged decision and should therefore be based on facts that had occurred at the time the decision was taken (*ex tunc* review).[60]

It may be a matter of dispute, however, whether and to what extent the decision to grant or to refuse a residence permit should nevertheless take into account the prospect, existing already at the time of the decision, that possible future expulsion could lead to a violation of Article 3 of the Convention. One could argue that the *ex*

---

58. These are the so-called 'Nawijn countries', named after the Head of the Directorate for Alien Affairs at the Justice Department. In fact, the same policy is followed in most of the cases with respect to Tamils from Sri Lanka, and more incidently with respect to asylum seekers from other countries.

59. State Council, decision of 14 March 1990, AB Kort (1990) No. 352.

60. Standing case-law; see e.g. Council of State, decision of 9 December 1977, AB (1978) No. 262. Recently, e.g., decision of 19 January 1990, No. R02.87.2500.

tunc principle does not necessarily impede the Council of State from addressing the question of whether Article 3 of the Convention, in conjunction with the principle of legal security, should have induced the authorities to grant or renew the residence permit or to decide not to withdraw it. So far, however, the Council of State has impliedly rejected or evaded the argument. In a recent decision it was held that, under the current policy of non-expulsion the applicant had no reason to fear an inhuman treatment in his country of origin (Iran) and that, consequently, there was not sufficient ground for the decision that the applicant should have been granted a residence permit for pressing humanitarian reasons.[61] If the alien concerned would nevertheless be threatened with expulsion, he could still institute summary proceedings with the President of the District Court of The Haque. Therefore, from the perspective of an effective judicial remedy, the Council of State's case-law cannot be said to leave a gap in this respect. On the other hand, from the perspective of legal certainty on the part of the applicant, it might be preferable for the Council of State to take into consideration the applicant's fear of the consequences of a possible future expulsion.

6.2 Article 3 of the Fourth Protocol to the European Convention: prohibition to expel nationals

Article 3 of the Fourth Protocol prohibits the State from expelling its own nationals or refusing them entry to the State's territory. This provision has been invoked before the Council of State especially in connection with the right to respect for family life in cases where one or more members of the family were Dutch citizens. The argument put forward claims that refusal of admission or expulsion of a non-national member of the family amounts to expulsion of also those family members who are Dutch citizens, who otherwise would be forced to break the family ties in violation of their right under Article 8 of the Convention.

The reply so far given by the Minister of Justice is to the effect that the decision refusing admission or withdrawing the residence permit of the non-national does not force the Dutch members of the family to leave the country; consequently their expulsion is not at issue. If they wish to follow the non-national family member to a foreign country in order to maintain the family ties, such decision would be their free choice, but it does not result in expulsion. Moreover, the latter are at all times free to return to the Netherlands. The Council of State, although in principle accepting the Minister's point of view as correct, in a recent case has indicated that Article 3 of the Fourth Protocol may nevertheless play an indirect role, at least when the Dutch member of the family is a child. In a case in which the German mother of a Dutch child was refused continued residence in the Netherlands, the Minister of Justice had rejected her reliance on Article 8 of the Convention with the argument that her child could in all reason be expected to follow her to Germany, so that her right to respect for her family life had not been interfered with. Next the appeal

61. Decision of 14 February 1991, R02.90.0934, AB Kort (1991) No. 347.

based upon Article 3 of the Fourth Protocol was rejected with the argument described above. The Council of State, however, held that Article 3 of the Fourth Prococol implies that it may be of particular interest to the Dutch child to be raised and educated in the Netherlands, the country where it may reside as a national. To give the mother in fact the choice of either depriving her child from this opportunity by taking him with her to Germany, or breaking the close ties with him by leaving him behind in the Netherlands, amounts to an interference in her right to respect for her family life. And also in the assessment of whether that interference is justified under the second paragraph of Article 8, the child's interest in being raised and educated in his country of nationality has to be taken into consideration.[62]

6.3 Article 6 of the European Convention: fair trial

As stated above, according to the current Strasbourg case-law, Article 6 of the Convention is not generally applicable to procedures concerning the admission or expulsion of aliens, unless a civil right — like the right to respect of family life — is involved. However, the question has still not been answered unequivocally whether Article 6 does apply with respect to the determination of refugee status, where in fact a person's whole status, including his civil rights, is at stake.

Dutch case-law is characterized by a certain caution on the issue. In its judgment of 8 April 1988, the Supreme Court held that the submission that Article 6 is applicable to procedures concerning admission or expulsion could not, in its unqualified form, be accepted as correct.[63] In some asylum cases the Council of State has been confronted with the question of whether Article 6 could have been violated as far as the requirement of a determination within a reasonable time was concerned. It subsequently passed the issue, not for reason of the inapplicability of Article 6, but for lack of legal consequences to be attached to any such violation. Thus, the Council of State held in a decision of 22 October 1990 that, assuming that Article 6 of the Convention applied to the determination of refugee status and assuming that the requirement of a determination within a reasonable time was violated, this could not result in the decision that, contrary to what had ultimately been determined about refugee status (the Council of State had rejected the appeal), the applicant should be recognized as a refugee. Consequently, the Council of State held that no reasonable interest of the applicant was served by annulment of the challenged decision on the ground of a violation of Article 6.[64] Indeed an annulment for exceeding the reasonable time would have as a consequence that the ultimate determination of the refugee status would be delayed even more, without this leading to a different outcome of the case.

62. Decision of 17 April 1991, No. R02.88.2462, AB Kort (1991) No. 582. Ultimately the State Council reached the conclusion that life in Germany differed so little from that in the Netherlands that the child's interests were outweighed by the interests of the State not to grant a residence permit to aliens who have not their own means of subsistence.

63. NJ (1988) No. 909.

64. No. R02.88.0178, AB Kort (1990) No. 1133.

In this context it should be mentioned that, in order to prevent as much as possible that a determination by a court within a reasonable time is blocked by a failure on the part of the authorities to make a decision, Dutch law allows appeal against fictive refusals after a certain period of time has lapsed.[65]

6.4   Article 13 of the European Convention: effective remedy

If, or to the extent that, Article 6 of the European Convention is considered not to be applicable to procedures concerning the admission or expulsion of aliens, Article 13 of the Convention might be of a certain relevance.

However, the effective remedy referred to in that provision is only guaranteed with respect to arguable claims about an alleged violation of a right or freedom laid down in the Convention. Since the right of an alien to be admitted to and reside in one of the States Parties to the Convention is not among those rights or freedoms, the applicant has in addition to argue that a refusal to admit him, or a decision to expel him, violates any of those rights or freedoms. Moreover, Dutch case-law concerning the direct applicability of Article 13 is unclear but still tends into the direction of a negation,[66] which would mean that reference to it by an applicant can have an indirect effect only. As a consequence, should national law deprive an alien of the effective remedy to which he is entitled under Article 13, by restricting access to, or the scope of jurisdiction of, the national authority mentioned in Article 13, such a provision could not be left aside by virtue of Article 94 of the Constitution, assuming, of course, that the case falls outside the range of Article 6.

However, as has been explained in section 3 above, under Dutch law there is as a rule access to a judicial body, even outside the limited range of Article 13, especially because of what is called 'the safety net function' of the civil courts. Nevertheless, from the perspective of the effectiveness of the remedy it would seem preferable for the alien concerned to have his claim determined by a court with general jurisdiction in asylum and immigration cases, because that court is likely to be more familiar with the relevant law, directives and policy. Uniformity of jurisprudence also argues in favour of general and exclusive jurisdiction on the part of the Council of State. From that perspective, it is to be welcomed that the Council of State is inclined to an extensive interpretation of the rules concerning its jurisdiction. Thus, the Council of State has assumed jurisdiction to consider appeals against refusals to grant a visa, although this category of decisions is not among those listed in Article 34 Aliens Act. Moreover, it has assumed jurisdiction to deal with all appeals from asylum seekers, even in those cases where Article 34, paragraph 1(b) Aliens Act excludes this review. The Council of State has done so in virtue of Article 94 of the Constitu-

---

65. See Art. 34, para. 2 Aliens Act: after three months. The absence of such a provision in fiscal law was held by the Supreme Court to be a lacuna which should be filled by the legislator. This holding was followed by the remarkable warning that in case of a continued absence of the required provision, the Supreme Court would recognize the possibility of appeal against a fictive negative decision by virtue of a reasonable interpretation of fiscal law in the light of Art. 6 of the Convention.

66. See *supra*, n. 31.

tion and giving precedence to Article 16 of the Geneva Convention, which guarantees for refugees access to court and national treatment on the territories of the States Parties to the Geneva Convention.[67] It equally declared the exception of Article 34 Aliens Act not applicable to American citizens because of Article V of the Treaty of Friendship, Commerce and Navigation between the Netherlands and the United States of America.[68]

In the second place, the Council of State is not prepared to refrain from determining refugee status for the mere reason that, even if the applicant should be found to be a refugee, he would not be entitled to admission on the basis of that status, for instance because he is in a position to return to a country of first asylum where he enjoyed an adequate protection against persecution.[69] This approach leads to a more restrictive recognition of the availability of a country of first asylum than was intended by the Dutch authorities. Furthermore, both the Council of State and the Supreme Court have adopted the position that — for lack of uniformity in the way the definition of refugee, laid down in Article 1(A) of the Geneva Convention, is interpreted and applied in the States Parties to the Geneva Convention — the responsability for that interpretation and application always rests with the State where an application for asylum is made, since this national interpretation and application, within the context of domestic law and policy, (co)determines the scope of the obligations imposed by the Geneva Convention on that State.[70] According to this case-law the State concerned is not allowed to refer to a decision on the refugee status of the applicant, made in another State, because that decision can determine and comply with the obligations of that other State only.

But even when the Council of State assumes jurisdiction to investigate the merits of an appeal and is not prepared to yield to another 'authority' in the sense of Article 13 of the European Convention, nor to a foreign judgment or decision, problems of effectiveness of the remedy thus available may still arise. In a report of 8 May 1990 the European Commission, dealing with Article 13 in an asylum case, stressed the necessity of a thorough review in the national procedure, in this case of the reasonableness of the fear of persecution posed by the applicants.[71] However, the thoroughness of even a judicial investigation may be impeded by the fact that the applicant — as a consequence of non-admission or expulsion — is not able to attend the hearing in person. In that situation obvious limitations are imposed on the possibilities of the applicant to produce evidence or at least to make his claim plausible, to fulfil formal conditions (terms, submission of certain documents) and to obtain adequate information and legal aid. It is then up to the court to compensate to the extent possible for these impediments by taking an active part in the fact-finding,

67. Decision of 20 December 1977, RV (1977) No. 97; decision of 2 May 1979, A-2.0896.

68. Treaty of 27 March 1956, 285 UNTS 231, Trb. 1956 No. 40. The decision of the Council of State is of 14 December 1978, RV (1978) No. 121.

69. Council of State, decision of 12 July 1978, RV (1978) No. 27.

70. Council of State, decision of 24 February 1986, RV (1986) No. 4; Supreme Court, judgment of 29 May 1987, NJ (1988) No. 56.

71. Vilvarajah and others v. United Kingdom (Application No. 13163/87).

by neutralizing as much as possible formal complications caused by the absence of the applicant and by seeing to it that the applicant receives adequate information about the formal and substantive aspects of the case. According to a recent decision of the Council of State, the same applies to the administrative procedure in first resort and in appeal. The Council of State annulled the refusal of admission because it had not been sufficiently investigated whether the applicants had meant to apply for asylum.[72]

7.   SOME CONCLUDING OBSERVATIONS

Dutch asylum law and immigration law are characterized by rather unspecified legal standards and by broad discretionary powers on the part of the administrative authorities, which are to be exercised for the purpose of maintaining the restrictive immigration policy presumably sought by the legislature.

Although under Dutch law aliens generally have access to a court in order to appeal against negative decisions concerning admission or continued residence, there is only a small margin for the court to review (the application of) immigration policy because of a deficiency of legal standards for such review. However, since Dutch constitutional law empowers and even obliges the court to apply self-executing provisions of treaties and of decisions of international organizations, and give them precedence over deviating provisions of domestic law, these provisions can also serve as complementary legal standards for judicial review. In asylum cases and immigration cases the most important sources of such standards are the law of the European Community, the Geneva Convention and the human rights treaties, especially the European Convention.

However, the extent to which these standards actually play an autonomous role in the national judicial review depends, *inter alia*, on the preparedness and ability of the national courts to give these provisions an interpretation and application that is sufficiently detached from national law and policy. That in turn depends, *inter alia*, on the stimulus and guidance the national courts receive. As far as the European Convention is concerned, it is the primary responsibility of the European Court and the European Commission to provide this stimulus and guidance. In addition to requiring a good knowledge of the different legal systems and legal practice in the individual States Parties to the Convention, which knowledge is guaranteed by the composition of Court and Commission, this task requires a creative, imaginative and sometimes bold reasoning, if necessary completed by abstract definitions and *obiter dicta*. Although under the European Convention there is no possibility for the national courts to refer questions of interpretation to the European Court for a preliminary ruling, the Court and the Commission should and can be aware of the issues which come up in national cases and should try to solve them in their case-law as fully as possible.

---

72. Decision of 15 June 1990, No. R02.87.0416.

In time, as the control at the borders within the European Community is lifted, it will be an inevitable task to establish Community rules and policy — at least harmonized national rules and policy — concerning asylum and immigration. Even now, a harmonization of criteria for the determination of refugee status would seem to be a prerequisite for the compatibility of the 'Schengen system' with the Refugee Convention, as the Council of State has pointed out in its advice to the government on ratification of the Schengen Convention.[73]

When drafting these Community rules and policy, or when harmonizing national rules and policy, due attention will have to be paid, not only to the Refugee Convention, but also to the European Convention, especially its Articles 3, 6, 8 and 13, in order to give full weight to legal protection and humanitarian considerations.

Even if it has not yet been recognized that the applicant in asylum and immigration cases can rely on Article 6 of the European Convention, and despite the still existing unclarity about the direct applicability of Article 13 of the Convention, the Dutch system of judicial review of administrative decisions concerning admission and expulsion of aliens is rather complete and contains adequate guarantees of legal protection. A decline in legal protection might occur if the administrative decisions are lifted from the national legal context and are made the object of intergovernmental cooperation without adequate provisions being made for appropriate substituting judicial review. Problems like the ones recently arisen with respect to the granting of Benelux visa may illustrate this danger.[74] This is one of the main objections to be made against both the Dublin Agreement of 15 June 1990 and the Schengen Convention of 19 June 1990: as extra-Community systems they do not share the legal status and legal guarantees of Community law, and in particular are not subject to the jurisdiction of the Court of Justice of the European Communities.

---

73. Advisory opinion of 8 April 1991, No. W02.91.0018. Hand. II (1990/91) 22 140 B.
74. See the judgment of the Benelux Court of Justice of 20 December 1988, RV (1988) No. 43.

FREE MOVEMENT OF PERSONS, HUMAN RIGHTS AND JUDICIAL POLICY: ASSESSMENT AND PROSPECTS
French law and practice

Roger Errera[*]

The law which applies to-day to foreigners in the EEC countries is the outcome of three basic trends. The first is the affirmation and consolidation of EC law. The second is the increasing protection afforded by other international instruments, be they bilateral, e.g., immigration treaties between two countries[1] or, more commonly, multilateral treaties, be they human rights treaties,[2] such as the European Human Rights Convention[3] the United Nations Covenant on Civil and Political Rights[4] or specialized instruments such as the 1951 Geneva Convention on Refugees[5] or the 1957 European Extradition Convention. Hence the increasing number of studies on international migration law.[6] The third and final trend is the evolution of domestic

---

[*] Conseiller d'Etat, Paris.
This paper sets out the author's personal views on the subject. Its contents are the author's sole responsibility and the opinions expressed are not necessarily held by the Conseil d'Etat.

1. See e.g., the 1968 Franco-Algerian Convention, as amended in 1984 and 1985.

2. Texts in Ian Brownlie, ed., *Basic Documents on Human Rights*, 2nd edn. (Oxford, 1981); F. Sudre, *Protection internationale et européene des droits de l'homme* (Paris, 1989).

3. J.E.S. Fawcett, *The application of the European Human Rights Convention*, 2nd edn. (Oxford, 1987); A.Z. Drzemczewski, *European Human Rights Convention in Domestic Law. A comparative study* (Oxford, 1985); G. Cohen-Jonathan, *La convention europeéene des droits de l'homme* (Paris, 1989); *Raisonner la raison d'Etat*, M. Delmas-Marty, ed. (Paris, 1989).

4. *The International Bill of Rights, The Convention on civil and political rights*, L. Henkin, ed. (New York, 1981).

5. Guy S. Goodwin-Gill, *The Refugee in International Law* (Oxford, 1983); 'Transnational legal problems of refugees', *Michigan Yearbook of International Legal Studies* (1982); F. Tiberghien, *La protection des réfugiés en France*, 2nd edn. (Paris, 1988); IRIRC, *International Bibliography of Refugee Literature* (Geneva, 1985); *Uncertain Haven: Refugee Protection on the Fortieth Anniversary of the 1951 United Nations Refugee Convention*, A Report of the Lawyers Committee for Human Rights (New York, 1991).

6. See *inter alia*, Guy S. Goodwin-Gill, *International law and the movement of persons between States* (Oxford, 1978); R. Plender, *International Migration law*, 2nd edn. (Dordrecht, 1988); *Basic Documents on international migration law*, R. Plender, ed. (Dordrecht, 1988); C. Leben, 'La circulation internationale des personnes et le droit international', *Annales de la faculté de droit et de science politique de l'université de Clermont-Ferrand*, 15 (1978) p. 627; Société française pour le droit international, *Les travailleurs étrangers et le droit international* (Paris, 1979); *La condition juridique de l'étranger, hier et aujourd'hui* (Nijmegen, 1988); *La liberté de circulation des personnes en droit international*, M. Flory and R. Higgins, eds. (Paris, 1989); *Immigrés et réfugiés dans les démocraties occidentales, Défis et*

H.G. Schermers et al., eds., Free Movement of Persons in Europe
© 1993, T.M.C. Asser Instituut, The Hague.

law, under the influence of the factors mentioned above and of social and political factors as well. The case-law is central here, including the policy of the courts (*la politique jurisprudentielle*), and their use of their law-making power at both the national and international level.

Any study on 'the role of the national judiciary in relation to human rights and the free movement of persons' must therefore be guided by the presence of such a context. One must also bear in mind the mutual relationship between the three main trends mentioned above as well as the present state of Europe regarding immigration and international migrations in general. One example of the former can be given: the place of fundamental rights in EC law and in particular in the case-law of the ECJ.[7] The evolution of the last thirty years is eloquent enough: in 1959 the ECJ declined jurisdiction to adjudicate on the violation by an EEC regulation of a right guaranteed by the Constitution of a member State.[8] It later went on to affirm that respect for fundamental rights was included in the general principles of law — the respect for which the Court had to enforce.[9] The third step consisted in openly taking its inspiration, from, *inter alia*, human rights treaties signed by Member States or with which they had collaborated (the European Human Rights Convention; the UN Covenants; ILO and UNESCO conventions).[10] The result was, in the case-law of

---

solutions, D. Turpin, ed. (Paris, 1989). On international labor and welfare law see G. Lyon-Cain and A. Lyon-Cain, *Droit social international et européen*, 7th edn. (Paris, 1991). For a recent comparative study of EEC law, see N. Guimezanes, *La circulation et l'activité économique des étrangers dans la Communauté européene. Droit communautaire, droits nationaux* (Paris, 1990).

7. See G. Cohen-Jonathan, 'La Cour des communautés européenes et les droits de l'homme', *Revue du Marché commun* (February 1978) p. 74; 'Les droits de l'homme dans les communautés européennes', in *Mélanges Eisenmann* (1975) p. 309; Manfred A. Dauses, 'La protection des droits fondamentaux dans l'ordre juridique communautaire', *Revue trimestrielle de droit européen* (1981) p. 401; Andrew Z. Drzemczevski, 'Fundamental Rights and the European communities. Recent developments', *Human Rights Review* (1977) p. 69; P. Pescatore, 'Les droits de l'homme et l'intégration européenne', 3 *Cahiers de droit européen* (1968) p. 620; 'The context and significance of fundamental rights in the law of the European Communities', *Human Rights Law Journal* (1981) p. 309; Hans G. Petersmann, 'The protection of fundamental rights in the European Communities', XXIII *European Yearbook* (1975) p. 179; Joseph H.H. Weiler, 'Protection of fundamental human rights within the legal order of the European Communities', in *International Enforcement of Human Rights*, R. Bernhardt and A.J. Jolowicz, eds. (Berlin, 1986). See also L. Collins, *European Community Law in the United Kingdom*, 4th edn. (London, 1990) p. 8 et seq.; J. Boulouis and R.M. Chevallier, *Grands arrêts de la Cour de justice des communautés européennes* I, 5th edn. (Paris, 1991) p. 91; O. Due, 'Le respect des droits de la défense dans le droit administratif communautaire', *Cahiers de droit européen* (1987) p. 383; Russell M. Dallen, Jr, 'An overview of the European Community protection of human rights, with some special reference to the United Kingdom', 27 CMLR (1990) p. 761; J. Schwarze, 'The Administrative Law of the Community and the Protection of Human Rights' 23 CMLR (1986) p. 401; T. Koopmans, 'European Public Law: Reality and Prospects', *Public Law* (1991) p. 53; Henry G. Schermers, 'The European Communities bound by fundamental human rights', 27 CMLR (1990) p. 249.

8. Case 1/58 *F. Stork & Co.* v. *ECSC [1959] ECR 17.*

9. Case 29/69 *E. Stauder* v. *City of Ulm* [1969] ECR 419, opinion Roemer p. 484; Case 11/70 *Internationale Handelsgesellschaft* v. *Einfuhr- und Vorratsstelle für Getreide und Futtermittel* [1970] ECR 1125, opinion Dutheillet de Lamothe p. 1140.

10. Case 4/73 *J. Nold* v. *Commission* [1974] ECR 491, opinion Trabucchi p. 510; case 36/75 *Rutili* v. *Minister for the Interior* [1975] ECR 1219, opinion Mayras p. 1237.

the ECJ, the affirmation and use of general principles of law (a technique familiar to other courts such as the French Conseil d'Etat), the scope of which is considerable:[11] the principle of proportionality;[12] that of legal certainty (*sécurité juridique*)[13] *audi alteram partem*, the right to an effective judicial review,[14] the non-retroactivity of penal provisions,[15] privacy and confidentiality,[16] in addition to such basic notions of EC law as equality of treatment and non-discrimination. This is indeed judicial law-making at its best.

This paper will focus on two important elements in the free movement of persons: on the one hand, family reunion and the right to family life; on the other, the influence of EC law on freedom of movement on the scope of judicial review. It will be centred on French law and practice and recent developments therein, in particular its relationship with the case-law of the ECJ and of the European Court of Human Rights.

1.   FREE MOVEMENT OF PERSONS, FAMILY REUNION AND THE RIGHT TO FAMILY LIFE

1.1   Free movement of persons under EC law

To whom does this right apply under EC law? The basic answer is to be found in a number of instruments:

— Regulation 1612/68 of the Council of 15 October 1968, amended by regulation 312/76 of 9 February 1976.
— Directive 68/360/EEC of the Council of 15 October 1968.
— Regulation 1251/70 of the Commission of 29 June 1970.
— Directive 72/194/EEC of the Council of 18 May 1972.
— Directive 74/148/EEC of the Council of 21 May 1973.

These texts mention, in addition to the worker, the spouse, descendants under 21 or dependent and the dependent ascendants of the spouses, irrespective of their nationality.[17]

---

11. On general principles of law in EC law, see J. Boulouis, *Droit institutionnel des communautés européennes*, 2nd edn. (Paris, 1900) p. 179 et seq.; Boulouis and Chevallier, op. cit. n. 7, at p. 78 et seq.; J. Schwarze, 'Tendencies towards a common administrative law in Europe', ELR (1991) p. 3.

12. Case 8/55 *Fédération Charbonnière de Belgique* v. *ECSC* [1956] ECR 245; case 154/78 *Ferriera Valsabbia and others* v. *Commission* [1980] ECR 907.

13. For a critical analysis of its use by the ECJ see Boulouis and Chevallier, op. cit. n. 7, at p. 82 et seq.

14. Case 222/84 *Johnston* v. *Chief Constable of the Royal Constabulary* [1986] ECR 1651, opinion Darmon p. 1654..

15. Case 63/83 *Regina* v. *Kent Kirk* [1984] ECR 2689, opinion Darmon p. 2720.

16. Case 136/79 *National Panasonic* v. *Commission* [1980] ECR 2033, opnion Warner p. 2061.

17. On the notion of dependent person see case 316/85 *Lebon* v. *C.P.A.S. Courcelles* [1987] ECR 2811. For the case of a wife living separated from her husband see case 267/83 *Diatta* v. *Land of Berlin* [1985] ECR 567.

In 1990 three directives extended this right to retired workers, students and other categories (Directives Nos. 90/364 EEC, 90/365 and 90/366, 28 June 1990).

1.2   The right to family reunion outside the EC framework

Family reunion is a fundamental right. Both the development of international migrations and the restrictions of all kinds invented by tyrannies — especially in Communist countries — have emphasized the social and legal importance of affirming and enforcing such a right. The latter is indeed only a part, a vital one no doubt, of the right to respect to family life under Article 8 of the ECHR. In spite of this the recognition in international law of such a right has been a belated one and remains partial, if not indeed tentative.

The Helsinki Final Act of 1975 contains a sentence that is relevant. The Participating States included the following aim:'to facilitate as far as possible the reuniting of migrant workers with their families.'[18] Two years later the European Convention on the legal status of migrant workers[19] was the first international multilateral legal instrument containing the clear affirmation of the right to family reunion. Such a right belongs to the spouse of a migrant worker lawfully employed and to the unmarried children thereof, minors under the relevant law of the receiving State and dependent on the migrant worker.[20] Reservations to this article are prohibited,[21] but temporary and geographically limited derogations are possible.[22] This Convention, however, has a limited scope. It applies only to migrants from the seven contracting States.[23]

Aliens living in France do have such a right. It has been affirmed and recognized in the following conditions: in a landmark 1978 decision[24] the Conseil d'Etat held that the right to a 'normal family life', as derived from the Preamble to the Constitution, was a general principle of law. It meant that a foreigner living lawfully in France is entitled to have his spouse and children come and live with him. The Government is empowered to regulate such a right on two grounds alone: public order and the welfare of the alien. The subsequent legislation and regulations apply

18. Final Act of the Conference on Security and Cooperation in Europe, 14 ILM (1975) 1293. Cooperation in the field of economics, of science and technology and of the environment. Cooperation in other areas: Economic and social aspects of migrant labour. On the Helsinki Act see O. Schachter, 'The twilight existence of non-binding international agreements', 71 AJIL (1977) p. 296.

19. ETS 93.

20. Art. 12.

21. Art. 36(1).

22. See Arts. 12-13.

23. France, the Netherlands, Norway, Portugal, Spain, Sweden, and Turkey. See J.B. Marie, 'International instruments relating to human rights as of 1 January 1991', 12 HRLJ, Nos. 1-2, p. 27. The Convention entered into force on 1 May 1983.

24. GISTI, 6 December 1978, p. 493; concl. Dondoux; RCDIP (1979) p. 139; D. (1979) p. 661, note Hamon; AJDA (1979) p. 38, note Dutheillet de Lamothe-Robineau; Droit ouvrier (1979) I, note Bonnechère.

this principle:[25] children must be under 18; the housing conditions must be adequate ones; the alien must establish that he has been residing there lawfully for one year and that he has adequate and sufficient income; a medical examination must take place abroad before the family is authorized to enter France.

The case-law of the Conseil d'Etat and of the lower administrative courts contains a number of refinements and additions on the meaning of the word 'spouse',[26] the notion of 'dependent children'[27] and on housing and income conditions.[28] A number of bilateral conventions contain specific conditions relating in particular to the minimum age of children.[29] The combination of agreements and of statutory law is, in turn, the source of an expanding case-law.[30]

1.3   The right to family life under Article 8 of the European Convention on Human Rights

The rights of aliens under the ECHR were not, for obvious reasons, paramount in the mind of the draftsmen. They have become more and more relevant in the course of time. Before studying the use of Article 8 by French courts some general reflections are in order.

25. See the *ordonnance* of 2 November 1945 (amended several times in the last 45 years) and the *décret* of 4 December 1984.

26. The relevant instruments do not elaborate on the meaning of the word 'spouse'. In an important 1980 decision the Conseil d'Etat held that polygamy was not a lawful ground for the refusal of a residence permit: July 11, 1980, *Ministre de l'Intérieur* v. *Mme Montcho*, p. 315; RA 1980, November-December, note Bienvenu-Trials; JCP (1981) II, 19629; concl. Rougevin-Baville; RCDIP (1981) p. 665. In French as well as in EC law 'spouse' means here married spouse: see case 59/85, *the Netherlands* v. *Reid* [1986] ECR 1291. For a comparative view see Plender, op. cit. n. 6, at pp. 382-384, 'The polygamous wife'. The Conseil d'Etat upheld the decision refusing family reunion to the wife of an alien in a case where the latter had abandoned his family and divorce proceedings existed: 6 June 1989, *Rezgui*.

27. A decision refusing the right to family reunion to a child who was not the legitimate child of the applicant and whose material and educative custody had been given to him by a Morrocan court has been quashed: 17 December 1987, *Mme Khattouf*, Limoges administrative Court, p. 501. The decision rightly established a link between parental authority and normal family life.

28. On housing conditions see 24 November 1989, *M. et Mme Masamba* (housing inadequate); on resources see 12 January 1990, *Moncef* (unemployed alien); 7 December 1990, *Keles*, p. 353 (low pension) and 28 September 1990, *Préfet de la Corrèze* v. *Ermiser*, p. 561.

29. Certain conventions stipulate a different maximum age for boys and girls: see e.g., the Franco-Portuguese convention of 11 January, 1977 on immigration, JO p. 2782: 18 for boys, 21 for girls. The same provision exists in the Franco-Spanish immigration convention of 25 January 1961, JO 23 March 1961, p. 2879. The Franco-Tunisian convention of 17 March 1988 (JO 11 February, 1989) refers to children who are minors 'in their country of origin', a clear reference to personal status. On the construction of the Franco-Algerian convention of 27 December 1968, as amended in 1985, see GISTI, 29 June 1990; D (1990) p. 560, note Sabourin.

30. This is true in particular of the Franco-Algerian convention of 1968. Its provisions on family reunion apply, for instance, when the husband, a Tunisian living in France, asks for his Algerian wife to join him: 19 September 1990, *Bouaoud*, p. 248.

a) The Convention rests on the principle of non-discrimination (Art. 14) and applies to 'everyone' within the jurisdiction of the contracting States (Art. 1). The Commission may receive applications from 'any person' (Art. 25).

While some clauses restrict the rights of aliens (see e.g., Art. 16 on political activity), most aim at their protection, such as Article 2(1) of the 4th Protocol (liberty of movement and freedom to choose one's residence lawfully within the territory of a State), Article 3(1) of the same Protocol (prohibition of collective deportation) and Article I of the 7th Protocol (procedural requirements in cases of expulsion).

b) There now exists a substantial case-law of the Court and of the Commission on Article 8 so far as it relates to the refusal of entry or expulsion of any alien, whenever the right to respect for family life is invoked. It may be summarised as follows:

— The Convention does not as such guarantee the right of an alien to reside in a certain country or the right not to be expelled or extradited from it.[31]

— Any measure taken against an alien must not infringe his rights under the ECHR.[32]

— Whenever the clause of Article 8(1) relating to the right to respect to one's family life is invoked, four questions have to be answered. Firstly, is there an effective family life? This is a matter of fact. The Court and the Commission take into account existing legal and *de facto* links.[33] Secondly, does the decision amount to an infringement of the right contained in Article 8(1)? The answer is in the affirmative when the decision will prevent family life from continuing elsewhere, e.g., in the country of origin of the alien, for social, economic or legal reasons, due to serious obstacles.[34] The relevant case-law takes into account the existence of effective links within the country of residence (birth, length of stay) and the absence of corresponding links in the country of which the alien is a citizen. Does the interference rest on one of the grounds listed in Article 8(2)?

And, finally, if so, was such an interference 'necessary' in a democratic society in order to attain such an aim? The case-law takes into account all the facts of the case, for example, in deportation cases the age of the alien, his criminal record and his general behaviour, and in other cases, all relevant matters.[35]

---

31. See Commission, 9203/80, 5 May 1981, DR 24, p. 237.

32. Commission, 17 December 1976, *Agee* v. *United Kingdom*

33. See Commission, 3110/67, *X.* v. *Federal Republic of Germany*, DR 27, p. 77; *European Yearbook*, XI, 494; 7289/76, *X. and Y.* v. *Switzerland*, DR 9, p. 57; 5302/71, *X.* v. *United Kingdom*, DR 44, p. 29; 2291/66 and 2292/66, *Alam and Singh* v. *United Kingdom, European Yearbook*, X, 478; 7229/75, *X.* v. *United Kingdom*, DR 12, p. 32.

34. See Commission 5269/71, DR 39, p. 104; 8245/78, DR 24, p. 98; 9492/81, DR 30, p. 232; 7647/76, DR 3, p. 137; 9088/80, DR 28, p. 160; 9478/81, DR 27, p. 243.

35. See the following decisions of the Court: 28 May 1985, *Abdulaziz, Cabales and Balkandali* v. *United Kingdom*; 21 June 1988, *Berrehab* v. *Netherlands*; 18 February 1991, *Moustaquim* v. *Belgium*; 20 March 1991, *Cruz Varas and others* v. *Sweden*; *Djeroud* v. *France*, 23 January 1991 (friendly settlement); *Beldjoudi* v. *France*, 26 March 1992.

1.4   The new case-law as an example of judicial policy

Until 1991, whenever an alien invoked Article 8(1) before French administrative courts against a deportation order the standard answer was that this was anyhow useless (*inopérant*); the latter word refers, in the French legal vocabulary, to a ground which cannot, in any event, be of any help to those who base their case on it.

Such case-law,[36] resting on barely reasoned decisions, was not consistent with the general case-law on the application of the ECHR.[37] It was in contradiction to Article 2 of the *ordonnance* of 2 November 1945 on foreigners, according to which this statute applies unless an international convention does so (*sous réserve des conventions internationales*).[38] The case-law was, moreover, totally inconsistent with the recent case-law inaugurated by the *Nicolo* decision of 1989[39] giving — at last — full effect to Article 55 of the Constitution under which treaties, once signed, ratified and published, take precedence over domestic statutes (a step that the Court de Cassation had already taken in 1975 in the *Vabre* case).

In three recent decisions the Conseil d'Etat held that Article 8 could be used whenever the legality of decisions taken against aliens (deportation on public order grounds; order to leave the country for those staying unlawfully) were challenged on such grounds.[40] This new judicial policy is of paramount importance for three reasons:

36. *Touami Abdesselem*, 25 July 1980, p. 820; *Chrouki*, 6 December 1985.

37. See e.g., on extradition, 16 February 1980, *Winter*, p. 87 (Art. 6(3) and (c)); 14 February 1987, *Urizar Margotto* (Arts. 3, 5 and 6); 20 May 1981, *Nicolaï and others*; on Arts. 10 and 14, 12 May 1989, *Ministre des départements et territoires d'outremer* v. *Piermont*, p. 444. See also a number of decisions relating to the scope of Art. 6: *Dollet*, 27 July 1979; AJDA (1980) 56; *Bidalou*, 5 May 1982, p. 662; *Gaudissart*, 25 November 1981; *Subrini*, 11 July 1984, p. 259; *Debout*, 27 October 1978, p. 395.

38. See Conseil constitutionnel, 9 January 1980, p. 29, and 3 September 1986, p. 135.

39. *Nicolo*, 20 October 1989 p. 190; JCP (1989) II, 21371, concl. Frydman; RFDA (1989) p. 813, concl. Frydman, note Genevois; RTDE (1989) p. 771, concl. Frydman, note Isaac; RFDA (1989) p. 993, note Favoreu and Dubouis; AJDA (1989) p. 788, note Simon; JDI (1990) p. 5; note Dehaussy; RCDIP (1990) p. 175, note Lagarde; D. (1990) p. 57, note Kovar and 135, note Salomon; RCDIP (1990) p. 94, note Boulouis; JCP (1990) I, 3429; H. Valvet, 'Le Conseil d'Etat et l'article 55 de la Constitution: une solitude révolue'; D. Ludet and R. Stolz, 'Die neue Rechtsprechung des franzözischen Conseil d'Etat zum Vorrang volkerrechtlicher Verträge', EuGRZ (1990) p. 93; C. Lerche, 'Ein Sieg für Europa? Anmerkung zum Urteil des Conseil d'Etat vom 20 Oktober 1989, Fall Nicolo, 50 ZaöRV (1990) p. 599. See also, on the supremacy of EEC regulations over statutes *Boisdet*, 24 September 1990; AJDA (1990) p. 863, note Honorat-Schwartz; ELR (1991) p. 144, note H. Cohen; *Public Law* (1990) p. 572, note R. Errera.

40. *Beldjoudi*, 18 January 1991, p. 18; *Belgacem*, 19 April 1991, p. 152, concl. Abraham; *Babas*, 19 April 1991, p. 162; AJDA (1991) p. 550, note Julien-Laferrière. *Belgacem* and *Beldjoudi* relate to deportation orders (expulsion); *Babas* to an order to leave for aliens staying unlawfully (*reconduite à la frontière*). The previous case-law on latter decisions was more restrictive even if it contained a welcome addition to the statute: see 29 June 1990; *Imambaccus*; *Préfet du Doubs* v. *Mme Olmos Quintero*, p. 192: RCDIP (1990) p. 682, note Turpin. For examples of recent decisions of the Conseil d'Etat implementing Article 8 of the EHRC and relating to deportation orders, see: 13 May 1991, *Badri*; 21 May 1991: *Bouarroudj*, 19 June 1991, *Bekchiche*; 8 July 1991, *Bouzizi*; 8 July 1991, *El Ghoul*; 8 July 1991, *Ministre de l'Intérieur* v. *Faker*. All these judgments uphold the legality of the deportation orders.

— The new case-law applies to all decisions relating to aliens whenever Article 8 and the right to family life is invoked: refusal of admission, refusal to issue or to renew a residence permit or visa.[40a]

— In reviewing such decisions in the light of Article 8 the Conseil d'Etat and the administrative courts will have to take into account the case-law of the European Human Rights Court and of the Commission.[41]

— The latter includes the use of the key concept of proportionality. The result of the new case-law will therefore be an extension of the scope of judicial review of the decisions mentioned above. Until now such a review was a rather restricted one (see below). On all these counts the direct influence of international law is as evident as it is welcome. It should be noted, however, that French domestic law already recognizes and protects, in many respects, the family interests of aliens: one example is the judicial affirmation of the right to family reunion (see above). Another example can be found in Article 25 of the *ordonnance* of 2 November 1945, already mentioned, which lists several categories of aliens who may not be expelled or ordered to leave the country because of their family or social situation.

2.   FREE MOVEMENT OF EC NATIONALS AND ITS INFLUENCE ON
         THE SCOPE OF JUDICIAL REVIEW: JUDICIAL POLICY
         RECONSIDERED

The scope of judicial review over administrative decisions in *excès de pouvoir* proceedings has depended traditionally in French administrative law on a series of factors such as the area covered, the wording of the applicable instrument, the nature of the decision challenged (in particular whether it relates to a right or a liberty) and, not in the least, the policy of the courts, what might be called the *politique jurisprudentielle*.[42] Although the administrative case-law on decisions relating to freedom of movement of EC nationals is not a very abundant one, it provides, on closer examination, a good example of the influence of EC law on the scope of judicial review. Three stages have been chosen as illustrations of the evolution.

40a. See three Conseil d'Etat's decisions of April 10, 1991: *Aykan*, *Minin*, and *Marzini*, commented by R. Errera in *Public Law* (1992) p. 343.

41. On Art. 8 of the ECHR see A.M. Connelly, 'Problems of interpretation of article 8 of the European Convention on Human Rights', 35 ICLQ (1986) p. 567. On the case-law relating to the right to family life see H. Storey, 'The right to family life and immigration case-law at Strasbourg', 39 ICLQ (1990) p. 328. G. Cvetic 'Immigration cases in Strasbourg. The right to family life under article 8 of the European Convention', 36 ICLQ (1987) p. 647. J. Madureira, *La jurisprudence des organes de la Convention européene des droits de l'homme et de la Charte sociale européene concernant l'entrée et la sortie des étrangers du territoire d'un Etat*, Conseil de l'Europe, Colloque 'Droits de l'homme sans frontières, (Strasbourg, 1989).

42. On the scope of judicial review in general see R. Chapus, *Droit administratif général*, I, 4th edn., (Paris, 1988) p. 663 et seq.; G. Vedel and P. Delvolvé, *Droit administratif*, II, 11th edn., (Paris, 1990) p. 336 et seq.

Stage 1:

Adjudicating on the legality of a decision taken against an EC national the court, having a choice between two instruments to attain the same result, chooses one of them, thus not avoiding a basic issue.

In 1973 the *préfet* of a *département* refused to issue eight EC nationals a residence permit and ordered them to leave the country. Two of them applied to the courts to annul the decision. The lower court rejected their claim. They appealed to the Conseil d'Etat, requesting it to quash the decisions on the ground that they violated both EC and national law. EC law consisted of Directive 64/221/EEC of 25 February 1964, Articles 6, 7 and 9. Article 6 mentions the grounds of public order, public security and public health which may be used to take a decision against an EC national. These grounds must be notified to him unless reasons relating to the security of the State prevent such notification. Under Article 7, unless the matter is an urgent one, the individual has 15 days to leave the country if he does not already have a residence permit. According to Article 9 an authority distinct from that which has jurisdiction to take the decision must have jurisdiction to hear the alien before the decision is taken.

Domestic law consisted of Article II of the *décret* of 5 January 1971 taken to implement the directive: the EC national to whom the issuance of a residence permit has been refused has the right, unless the matter is an urgent one, to be heard by a special committee set up by the *ordonnance* of 2 November 1945 on aliens to examine cases of deportation before the decision is taken.

Were the petitioners entitled to invoke against an *individual* decision the violation of a directive? The ECJ had answered the question in the affirmative on several occassions,[43] a policy approved by the *Commissaire du Gouvernement* in his conclusions. Following a custom consisting in not answering a question, albeit an important one, if the same result (in the circumstances the quashing of the decisions) might be attained by another route, the Conseil d'Etat annulled the decisions on the ground that they violated domestic law.[44] The reasoning of the judgment is far from

---

43. See case 7/90 *Franz Grad* v. *Finanzamt Traunstein* [1970] ECR 8825, opinion Roemer p. 842; case 33/70 *SpA SACE* v. *Ministry for Finance of the Italian Republic* [1970] ECR 1213, opinion Roemer, for directives in général. For Directive 64/221 of 25 February 1964, see case 48/75 *Royer* [1976] ECR 497; RCDIP (1977) p. 554; case 41/74 *Y.v.Duijn* v. *Home Office* [1974] ECR 1337; *CDE* (1975) p. 292; case 67/24 *C.A. Bonsignore* v. *Oberstadtdirektor Köln* [1975] ECR 297; *CDE* (1975) p. 299, concl. Mayras; case 36/75 *Rutili* v. *Minister for the Interior* [1975] ECR 1219; RCDIP (1976) p. 361; RTDE (1976) p. 135, note G. Lyon-Caen. See also D. Simon, 'Ordre public et libertés publiques dans les Communautés européennes', RMC (1976) p. 201; T. Hartley, 'Public policy and international free movement: a critical comment on the *Rutili* decision', ELR (1976) p. 473; On *Rutili*, *Bonsignore* and *Van Duyn* see L. Dubouis, 'Le juge administratif français et les mesures de police prises à l'encontre des étrangers (à propos de trois décisions récentes)', RCDIP (1976) p. 301; C. Tomuschat and G. Lyon-Caen, RTDE (1976) p. 135; CDE (1975) p. 302, note.

44. *Hill* and *Holzappel*, 8 October 1976, p. 402; D (1977) p. 316, concl. Guillaue; AJDA (1977) 130, note Nauwelaers-Fabius. See also M. Distel, 'Expulsion des étrangers, droit communautaire et respect des droits de la défense', D (1977) p. 316. For another application of the *décret* of 1970 see 9 March 1988, *Weber*, p. 112.

clair (to use a much disputed term) since both the directive and the *décret* are mentioned. Expediency has its own drawbacks.

Stage 2:

The basic issue of the direct effect of directives surfaced again two years later when, in the *Cohn-Bendit* case, the Conseil d'Etat refused to accept the right of an EC national to invoke, against an individual decision (a deportation order) an EC directive, thus putting itself in open dissent with the case-law of the ECJ.[45] The case-law inaugurated by *Cohn-Bendit* still seems valid to-day.[46] This is indeed a serious and much to be regretted disagreement on a basic issue of EC law and one which it is hoped will not last too long. That being said, the subsequent evolution of the case-law of both the ECJ and the Conseil d'Etat shows the relatively limited consequences of such a disagreement.[47]

— The ECJ's case-law has limited the possibility of directly invoking a directive in a three-fold way. Firstly, in time: the directive may be invoked only after the expiration of the delay given to the national authorities to enforce it.[48] Secondly, in relation to the contents of the directive: they must be unconditional and sufficiently precise, which is not always the case with all directives and with all parts of directives. They must, in particular, define rights that individuals may invoke against national authorities.[49] Thirdly, even when all the conditions are met, the directive may only be invoked against national public authorities, and not against another individual.[50]

45. *Ministre de l'Intérieur* v. *Cohn-Bendit*, 28 December 1978, p. 524; D (1979) p. 155, concl. Genevois, note Pacteau; and I.R. 89, note Delvolvé; RTDE (1979) p. 169, note Dubouis; AJDA (1979) p. 27, note Dutheillet de Lamothe-Robineau; JDI (1979) p. 589, note Goldman; JCP (1979) II, 19158, note Kovar; RCDIP (1979) p. 649. See also J. Boulouis, 'L' applicabilité des directives', RMC (1979) p. 104.

46. *Roland*, 30 April 1982; p. 547; 4 June 1982, *RJF* 1982, 394; *Zakine*, 13 December 1985, p. 515.

47. See R. Abraham, *Droit international, droit communautaire et droit français* (Paris, 1989) p. 144 et seq.; J. Boulouis, *Droit institutionnel des Communautés européennes*, 2nd edn., (Paris, 1990) p. 203 et seq.; J. Boulouis and R.M. Chevallier, *Les grands arrêts de la Cour de justice des Communautés européennes*, I, 5th edn., (Paris, 1991) p. 42 et seq.; J.C. Bonichot, 'Convergences et divergences entre le Conseil d'Etat et la Cour de justice des communautés européennes', RFDA (1989) p. 579 (see at p. 596 et seq.); On the ECJ case-law see Y. Galmot and J.C. Bonichot, 'La Cour de justice des communautés européennes et la transposition des directives en droit national', RFDA (1988); P. Pescatore, 'L'effet des directives communautaires: une tentative de démythification', D (1980) p. 171.

48. Case 148/78 *Pubblico Ministero* v. *Tullio Ratti* [1979] ECR 1629, opinion Reischl p. 1647; case 271/82 *V.R. Auer* v. *Ministère Public* [1983] ECR 2727; case 70/83 *G. Kloppenburg* v. *Finanzamt Leer* [1984] ECR 1075.

49. See case 21/78 *Delkvist* v. *Anklagemijndigheden* [1978] ECR 2327, opinion Mayras p. 2342; case 8/81 *Becker* v. *Finanzamt Münster* [1982] ECR 53, opinion Slynn p. 78; case 255/81 *R.A. Grendel* v. Finanzamt für Körperschaften [1981] ECR 2301; case 126/82 *Smit Transport* v. *Commission [1982] ECR* 73, opinion Reischl p. 95; *Auer, supra*, n. 48; case 301/82 *Clin Midy* v. *Belgium* [1984] ECR 251 opinion Mancini p. 261.

50. Case 152/84 *Marshall* v. *Southampton and South-West Hampshire Area Health Authority* [1986] ECR 723, opinion Slynn p. 725; case 372/85 *Ministère public* v. *O. Traen and others* [1987] ECR 1839, opinion Lenz p. 1851. For the case of public service companies (in the circumstances, British gas monopoly before the privatisation) see case 188/89 *Foster and others* v. *British Gas plc*, [1990] ECR I-3313. See generally S. Prechal, 'Remedies after *Marshall*', 27 CMLR (1990) p. 451; For two recent

— The case-law of the Conseil d'Etat, notwithstanding *Cohn-Bendit*, gives more and more weight to the implementation of directives.[51] The legality of national regulations in relation to them is reviewed.[52] The content of such regulations is closely examined, including any omissions. In addition, whenever a *décret* comes to be construed, it is construed in accordance with the directive.[53] Any regulation contrary to the objectives set by a directive is *ipso facto* unlawful.[54] Moreover, *Cohn-Bendit* allows the applicant to invoke the illegality of the national regulation on which the individual decision which is challenged rests.[55] Another technique consists in the applicant asking the administration to modify the national law so as to conform with a directive or EC regulation.[56] However, there are still other difficulties: when a litigant does not raise the issue of the incompatibility of a *décret* with the objectives of a directive, should the court itself raise the issue? That is what it must do when it has before it what is called a '*moyen d'ordre public*', i.e., a matter so important that even if no party raises it the Court must do so: e.g., the admissibility of the application, the jurisdiction of the author of the decision or, most importantly, the scope of the applicable law (*champ d'application de la loi*) The Conseil d'Etat answered the question in the negative in a recent decision,[57] which increases

comments of the ECJ's case-law see D. Curtin, 'The Province of Government: Delimiting the Direct Effect of Directives in the Common Law Context', ELR (1990) p. 195; P. Manin, 'L'invocabilité des directives: quelques interrogations', RTDE (1990) p. 669.

51. See D. de Bechillon, 'L'applicabilité des directives communautaires selon la jurisprudence du Conseil d'Etat', RDP (1991) p. 759.

52. 28 September 1984, *Confédération nationale des sociétés de protection de la nature*, p. 512; AJDA (1985) p. 695, concl. Jeanneney.

53. 9 March 1984, *Beaudroit*, p. 513.

54. 7 December 1984, *Fédération française des sociétés de protection de la nature*, p. 410; AJDA (1985) p. 83 note Schoettl-Hubac; 1 July 1988, *Fédération française des sociétés de protection de la nature*: p. 271; 7 October 1988, *Rassemblement des opposants à la chasse et autres*, p. 334; AJDA (1989) p. 34, concl. Guillaume; 8 February 1989, *Fédération nationale des internes et anciens internes des Lôpitaux des régions sanitaires*; 24 February 1989; *Rassemblement des opposants à la chasse*; 25 May 1990, *Ministre de l'envitonnement et Fédération Rhône-Alpes de protection de la nature. Fédération départementale des chasseurs de l'Isère et autres*, see also 3 December 1990, *Ville d'Amiens et autres*. On the effect of directives relating to the environment see L. Kramer, 'L'effet national des directives communautaires en matière d'environnement', *Revue juridique de l'environnement* (1990) p. 325.

55. See e.g., *Stasi*, Lyon Administrative Court, 25 October 1979, p. 534 declaring unlawful a section of Art. 14 of the *décret* of 5 January 1970, in that it did not contain the obligation to commmunicate to the EEC alien the reasons of his expulsion. The latter decison was quashed. See also Palazzi, 8 July 1991, commented by R. Errera in *Public Law* (1990) p. 614.

56. See 3 February 1989, *Compagnie Alitalia*, p. 44; concl. Chaid-Nourai, RFDA (1989) p. 391, notes *Dubouis and Beaud*; AJDA (1989) p. 387, note Fouquet; *Public Law* (1989) p. 650, note R. Errera; RTDE (1989) p. 509, note Vergès.

57. 11 January 1991, *Société Morgane* p. 9; AJDA (1991) III, note Honorat-Schwartz.

the difficulties besetting the issue and does not seem to be fully consistent with the case-law on the notion of *champ d'application de la loi*.[58]

Stage 3:

The direct influence of the ECJ's case-law on freedom of movement on the scope of judicial review.

As was said earlier the scope of judicial review in French law on decisions ordering the deportation of an alien or on refusing to issue or to renew a residence permit or a working permit or a visa is a rather restricted one. Such decisions may be quashed on one of the following grounds: lack of jurisdiction (*incompétence*); lack of jurisdictional fact:[59] error of law; unreasonableness (*erreur manifeste d'appréciation*)[60] abuse of power (*détournement de pouvoir*) or procedural irregularity. The source of such case-law lies in judicial self-restraint: administrative courts have, it is thought, been rather reluctant to review fully decisions relating to aliens, in view of the general wording of the statutes and the amount of discretion allowed to the administration.

The situation of EC nationals is, however, different: under a *décret* of 28 April 1981, which replaced that of 1970 mentioned above the administration may refuse to issue an EC national belonging to one of the eleven categories enumerated in Article I a residence permit only if he suffers from one of the illnesses listed in the annex to the *décret* or on grounds of *ordre public*. The same provision applies to deportation orders.

The scope of judicial review of decisions relating to EC nationals was bound to be directly affected by the law applying to them for the following reasons:

— the very wording of the *décret*: EC nationals have a *right* to enter and reside in an EC country whenever they belong to one of the categories mentioned *above*. In that respect the wording of the *décret* is very different from that of statutes and regulations applying to aliens in general, since it derives from EC texts, i.e., the Directives 64/221, 68/360 and 73/148/EEC.

— The case-law of the ECJ: we are here dealing with a right, as stated in the *Royer* decision.[61] As a result the residence permit has a merely declarative value,[62] hence the case-law of the ECJ on the right of EC nationals to an effective judicial review whenever one is dealing with rights arising from the Treaty of Rome and

---

58. On *moyens d'ordre public*, see R. Chapus, *Droit du contentieux administratif*, 2nd edn. (Paris, 1990) p. 468 et seq. On the notion of *champ d'application de la loi*, see ibid, p. 470 et seq. The existence of a treaty applicable in France and in contradiction to a statute *is a moyen d'ordre public*: see *Mlle Doyon*, 2 February 1990, p. 935.

59. See e.g., *Konaté*, 2 February 1981; D (1981) p. 353, note Pacteau. For a general comment on the scope of judicial review see J. Bell, 'The extension of judicial review over discretionary power in France', *Public Law* (1986) p. 99.

60. 3 February 1975, *Ministre de l'Intérieur* v. *Pardov*, p. 83; 8 December 1978, *Ministre de l'Intérieur* v. *Benouaret*, p. 502; D (1979) p. 339, concl. Hagelsteen.

61. Cf., *supra* n. 43.

62. 3 July 1980, 157/79; *Pieck*, p. 2171.

derived acts. This is indeed a general principle of EC law.[63] After the Heylens decision the duty to communicate reasons to the court and to the individual becomes a condition of the effectivity and of the efficiency of judicial review.[64] (Such a condition is satisfied in French administrative law).

It is also appropriate to mention the *Factortame* decision in this context.[65]

— The third reason comes from French administrative case-law itself. Whenever the administration restricts what is, under the law, a right or a basic freedom, or takes a decision derogating from a fundamental principle, the scope of judicial review is a full one. In 1990, two decisions of the Conseil d'Etat applied the new case-law. The first related to the refusal to issue an Italian an EC residence permit,[66] the second to a deportation order.[67]

3.   A WORD ON PERSPECTIVES

The remarkable achievements so far attained in the field of free movement of persons have been the result of EC norms robustly interpreted by the ECJ and duly implemented and applied by the national authorities and the judiciary. Much remains to be done, especially in relation to the professional aspects of freedom of movement within the EC. That being said one thing is clear: it is even more impossible today than yesterday not to take a hard look at the outer non-EEC world, in and out of Europe. In Europe the fall or disintegration of the Communist regimes and the difficult economic and social situation of these countries raise two major issues. The first is that of the date and of the conditions of the accession of Poland, Hungary and

---

63. Case 222/84 *Marguerite Johnston* v. *Chief Constable of the Royal Ulster Constabulary*, [1986] ECR 1651; case 222/86 *UNECTEF* v. *Heylens*, 3 CMLR (1986) p. 240, decided after a referral from the Lille *tribunal de grande instance*; B. Pommier, RMC (1988) p. 35, note. See L. Dubouis, 'A propos de deux principes généraux du droit communautaire (droit au contrôle juridictionnel effectif et motivation des décisions des autorités nationales qui porteraient atteinte à un droit conféré par la règle communautaire'), RFDA 1988, 691; L. Collins, *European Community Law in the U.K.*, 4th edn. (London, 1990) pp. 10 and 93 et seq.

64. See para. 18 of the *Johnston* decision quoting the European Human Rights Convention (Arts. 6 and 13).

65. Case C-213/89, *The Queen* v. *Secretary of State for Transport, ex parte Factortame Ltd and others* [1990] ECR I-2433; D (1990) p. 547, note Fourgoux; D. Simon and A. Barav, 'Le droit communautaire et la suspension provisoire des mesures nationales. Les enjeux de l'affaire Factortame', RMC (1990) p. 591; RFDA (1990) p. 912, note Bonichot; AJDA (1990) p. 832; note Le Mire; A.G. Toth, Comment, 27 CMLR (1990) p. 573; D. Oliver, 'Fishing on the incoming Tide', 54 MLR (1991) p. 442. On the conditions in which a national court may order a stay of execution of a national decision based on an EC regulation the legality of which is doubtful, see case 143/88 and 92/89 *Zuckerfabrik Süderdithmarschen AG* v. *Hauptzollamt Itzehoe* of 21 February 1991, OJ No. C 74/8 of 20.3.1991; AJDA (1991) p. 237, note Le Mire. See N.P. Gravells 'Effective protection of community law rights : Temporary disapplication of an Act of Parliament', *Public Law* (1991) p. 180; J.B. Auby, 'Le sursis à exécution de l'acte administratif pris en application d'un réglement communautaire', JCP (1991) p. 3530.

66. 24 October 1990, *Ragusi*, p. 289; AJDA (1991) p. 322, concl. Abraham, note Julien-Leferrière.

67. 19 November 1990, *Raso*, p. 901; AJDA (1991) p. 325; For a comment of both decisions see R. Errera, *Public Law* (1991) p. 136.

Czechoslovakia to the EC. The second is that of new international migrations from eastern Europe towards western Europe and beyond.

Outside of Europe the aggravation of the political and economical conditions in South East Asia, the Middle East and Africa and the suspension of immigration in EC and other west European countries raise the issue of the control of the entry and movement of non-EC nationals within EC territory.

Questions of jurisdiction, procedure and substance arise here together.[68] The choice of a treaty between several EC countries (instead of a directive) is a significant one. Although under Article 134 of the Schengen Convention of June 1990 the clauses of the Convention may be applied only if they are compatible with EC law, one salient fact remains: the ECJ has no jurisdiction to interpret the new Convention. Consequently, the task of the national courts, when they have to apply and construe it, will not be an easy one.

Questions relating to asylum and to the respect given by the Schengen Convention, to the Geneva Convention on Refugees raise complex issues, even constitutional ones in some countries.[69] Moreover, a brief comparison of the Schengen Convention and of that signed between the 12 EC countries in Dublin on 15 June 1990 relating to the determination of the State responsible for examining applications for asylum shows some discrepancies between the two instruments.

We are indeed entering new and perhaps harder times. Although there are many unknowns (those of the past are too easily forgotten) the accumulated legal wealth resulting from EC law, the European Convention on Human Rights and other instruments, duly implemented by the national judiciary, is our common heritage. Many components of this heritage predate our century:

'Au commencement du monde, alors que tout était commun, il était permis à chacun d'aller et de voyager dans tous les pays qu'il voulait. Or cela ne semble pas avoir été supprimé par la division des biens. Car les nations n'ont jamais eu l'intention d'empêcher, par cette division, les rapports des hommes entre eux; et, au temps de Noé, cela aurait certainement été inhumain.'[70]

68. See R. Plender, 'Competence, European Community and Nationals on non-member States', 39 ICLQ (1990) p. 599.

69. C. Norek, 'Le droit d'asile en France dans la perspective communautaire', RFDA (1989) p. 200; J.C. Paucelle, 'L'immigration et la libre circulation en Europe: enjeux et perspectives'. RFDA (1990) p. 516. On the implementation of the Geneva Convention in Europe see: M. Fullerton, 'Restricting the flow of asylum seekers in Belgium, Denmark, the Federal Republic of Germany and the Netherlands: new challenges to the Geneva Convention relating to the status of refugees and the European Convention on Human Rights', 29 Virginia Journal of International Law (1988) p. 33; M. Moussalli, 'Le problème des réfugiés en Europe. Action et recherche de solutions par les Etats, les institutions européennes et le Haut commissariat des Nations Unies pour les réfugiés', 4 International Journal of Refugee Law (1989) p. 528; A. Nayer, 'La Communauté européenne et les réfugiés', 22 Revue belge de droit international (1989) p. 133; D. Joly, 'Le droit d'asile dans la Communauté européenne', 1 International Journal of Refugee Law (1989) p. 365; G. Loescher, 'The European Community and Refugees', 65 International Affairs (1989) p. 617.

70. Francisco de Vitoria, Leçon sur les Indiens in Leçons sur les Indiens et sur le droit de la guerre, Introduction, traduction et notes par M. Barbier (Genève, 1966) p. 83, Vol. 3, Premier titre: 'Du droit de société et de communication'.

Institutional Problems and
Free Movement of Persons

INSTITUTIONAL PROBLEMS AND FREE MOVEMENT OF PERSONS
The legal and political framework for cooperation[*]

Jaap W. de Zwaan[**]

1.   INTRODUCTION

The abolition of obstacles to the freedom of movement of persons is one of the main objectives of the EEC Treaty.

For the purposes set out in Article 2 of the Treaty, Article 3(c) mentions the abolition of obstacles to the freedom of movement of, *inter alia*, persons as an explicit activity of the Community. Separate chapters of the Treaty offer, furthermore, a legal framework for the development of a Community policy concerning the free circulation more specifically of workers and self-employed persons.[1]

The entry into force of the Single European Act, in July 1987, confirmed the need to achieve the freedom of movement of persons, whilst making it a separate element of the internal market. This newly introduced legal concept, laid down in Article 8 A of the Treaty, is defined as follows:

'The internal market shall comprise an area without internal frontiers in which the free movement of goods, persons, services and capital is ensured in accordance with the provisions of the Treaty.'[2]

Notwithstanding the presence of this global framework for the development of a Community policy on the free movement of persons, activities in this area excepting those directly related to the right of residence of EC nationals in other Member States have to date been developed mainly in an intergovernmental context.

The main reason for this are the doubts and differences of opinion among Member States as to the nature and scope of Community competences in the field. More specifically, the exact meaning and implications of the concept of the internal market, as introduced by the Single European Act, leave room for divergent interpretations. The first question to arise is whether the internal market concept, which is drafted in a broad and dynamic but not very precise manner, in any way implies the abolition of controls

---

*   The text reflects the personal opinions of the author.
** Assistant Legal Adviser to the Ministry of Foreign Affairs in The Hague, The Netherlands.
1. Arts. 48, 52 and 59 EEC. See *infra*, in section 2.1.
2. Art. 13 of the Single European Act.

H.G. Schermers et al., eds., Free Movement of Persons in Europe

on persons at the internal frontiers. If so, a further question is to whom does this abolition of controls apply: to EC nationals alone or nationals of third countries as well. Another important point concerns the powers of the Community to provide for the necessary accompanying arrangements to be taken for example at external frontiers as a consequence of the abolition of internal controls and the completion of the internal market.

Whereas some claim that the Community is able to take all appropriate measures in this respect, others are of the opinion that the powers of the Community are restricted to establishing modalities required for the circulation of EC nationals within the Community. In this view arrangements concerning all other subjects are to be left to intergovernmental cooperation between Member States.[3]

In relation to these different understandings of the scope of Community powers, it has to be remembered that the removal of controls on persons at internal frontiers gives rise to a debate on other subjects, for example the organisation and nature of the controls to be carried out at external borders, the establishment of the conditions to be fulfilled by citizens of third countries for entry in the Community, the granting of a right of free circulation within the Community, and the development of common visa and asylum policies. The removal of controls at internal frontiers will also call for more intensive cooperation between the police and judicial authorities of the Member States.[4]

Doubts as to the competence of the Community to legislate in this field have also been fed by the attitude taken by the Commission itself. The Commission has, in fact, thus far refrained from presenting formal proposals to the Council on all relevant subjects. Apparently the Commission attaches more importance to achieving concrete results in this field by way of intergovernmental cooperation than trying to produce results in a purely Community framework.

Because the Commission has presented no concrete proposals to the Council, the Community has not yet been able to decide upon any major legislative measure in this field. Instead, a wide-ranging debate on the aspects of the free movement of persons has been conducted in different fora, all of them using the intergovernmental formula. In this connection in particular mention can be made, as frameworks for cooperation between the twelve Member States of the Community, of:
— the Ad Hoc Group on Immigration
— European Political Cooperation (Group on Legal Cooperation)

---

3. The supporters of the latter interpretation also refer to the Political Declaration by the Governments of the Member States on the free movement of persons, reflected in the Final Act to the Single European Act, according to which the Member States, in order to promote the free movement of persons, shall cooperate, without prejudice to the powers of the Community, in particular as regards the entry, movement and residence of nationals of third countries. Although this text makes an explicit reference to the powers of the Community, they consider the content of the declaration as a confirmation that national powers should prevail in this field.

4. Cf., the number of subjects included in the Schengen Convention of 19 June 1990. In fact, this Convention offers a complete and integral approach to the problems to be overcome, once the controls at internal frontiers have disappeared. See *infra*, in section 2.8.

— the Mutual Assistance Group
— TREVI
— CELAD

Reference should also be made to Schengen as a framework for cooperation between a smaller number of Member States.[5]

Furthermore, at least some specific subjects which are of relevance to the free movement of persons are under discussion in a still wider framework. Activities developed in the framework of the Council of Europe and the United Nations are of relevance here.

Because of the number of fora in which aspects of the circulation of persons are discussed it goes without saying that there is a need for the positions to be taken by the Member States in these talks to be coordinated. The European Council, meeting on Rhode, therefore decided in December 1988 to set up a Group of Coordinators, composed of representatives of the Member States.[6] Its primary task was to draw up a list of the fora discussing issues relating to the circulation of persons and a list of measures to be accorded priority between the Twelve.

What follows is a description of the most important fora and their principal activities. Consideration will also be given to the work of the Group of Coordinators. Because it is not possible, within the context of this paper, to depict all the activities of the different fora in full, attention will be focused on the more important.

An impression of the results and the effectiveness of cooperation in the field of the free movement of persons will be followed by an attempt to analyse the nature and extent of the Community's powers in this sphere. Finally some observations will be made on possible ways of taking advantage of the current Intergovernmental Conference on European Political Union[7] to amend the EEC Treaty by clarifying the Community's powers in this field and to establish a uniform framework for intergovernmental cooperation between Member States on specific aspects of this subject.

5. Cooperation in the framework of Benelux is also relevant in this context. A Convention concluded between the three countries concerned on shifting of controlls on persons from the internal borders to the external borders dates from 1960 and entered into force on 1 July 1960 (Convention between the Kingdom of Belgium, the Grand-Duchy of Luxembourg and the Kingdom of the Netherlands on the transfer of control of persons to the external frontiers of Benelux territory, Trb. 1960 Nos. 40 and 102).

6. The relevant conclusion was the following: 'The achievement of the Community's objectives, especially the area without internal frontiers, is linked to progress in intergovernmental cooperation to combat terrorism, international crime, drug trafficking and trafficking of all kinds. This cooperation will be stepped up in order to achieve rapid and concrete results which will enable the Community, for its part, to take the necessary measures to turn Europe into a tangible reality for its citizens. To this end each Member State will appoint a person responsible for the necessary coordination.'

7. The convening of the Conference, which started on 12 December 1990 in Rome, is based on Art. 236 EEC.

2. DIFFERENT FORA

2.1 European Economic Community

The legislation developed to date in the framework of the Community primarily concerns the right of establishment of EC nationals in other Member States. For workers the relevant instruments are Directive 68/360/EEC, Regulation 1612/68[8] and Regulation 1251/70,[9] for self-employed persons and those who provide services Directives 73/148/EEC[10] and 75/34/EEC.[11]

In June 1990 the Council adopted three directives concerning the right of residence of economically non-active EC nationals: Directive 90/364/EEC providing for a general arrangement, Directive 90/365/EEC concerning pensioned workers and the self-employed and Directive 90/366/EEC concerning the right of establishment of students.[12] The time limit for implementation of these directives expires on 30 June 1992. It should be noted that, under these directives, the granting of the right of residence to economically non-active persons is conditional: residence in the receiving Member State, in particular, has been made dependent on the possession of sufficient financial resources.[13]

Because the case-law of the Court of Justice regards tourists as receivers of services,[14] the conclusion can be drawn that nowadays in fact all EC nationals have the right to move freely in other Member States.[15]

In principle, however, the scope of the existing Community instruments is restricted to EC nationals. An exception to this principle is made in the legislation on the free movement of persons,[16] for members of the immediate family, and for displaced persons and refugees in Regulation 1408/71 on the application of social security schemes to employed persons and their families moving within the Community.[17]

---

8. See for both texts: OJ 1968 L 257/2 and following. In 1989 the Commission presented to the Council a proposal for an amendment to Regulation 1612/68, in order, *inter alia*, to increase the number of beneficiaries of the regulation: OJ 1989 C 100/6.

9. OJ 1970 L 142/24.

10. OJ 1973 L 172/14.

11. OJ 1975 L 14/10.

12. See for all three texts: OJ 1990 L 180/26, 28, 30. Art. 235 EEC served as the legal basis for all three directives. The European Parliament appealed to the Court of Justice against this choice of the Council, Case C-295/90 *European Parliament* v. *European Council*, Judgment of 7 July 1992. The Parliament is of the opinion that Art. 7 EEC, proposed by the Commission as the legal basis for all three texts, is the correct basis. In the proceedings the Commission intervened on the side of the Parliament. The United Kingdom and the Netherlands have intervened to support the Council's position.

13. See the first Articles of the directives concerned.

14. Case 186/87 *I.W. Cowan* v. *Trésor public* [1989] ECR 195; Cases 286/82 and 26/83 *G. Luisi and G. Carbone* v. *Ministero del Tesoro* [1984] ECR 377.

15. Judgment of 30 May 1991, Case C-68/89 *Commission of the European Communities* v. *Kingdom of the Netherlands*, not yet reported, consideration 10.

16. Art. 10 Regulation 1612/68 and Art. 1 Directive 73/148.

17. OJ 1971 L 149/2. See notably Art. 2.

At present, there is no Community measure on the removal or flexibility of controls on persons at frontiers between Member States. Except for the implications of the Benelux Convention of 1960 and pending the entry into force of the Schengen Convention of June 1990, such controls have therefore been retained within the Community. Although the Commission presented a proposal in 1985 for a regulation on the easing of controls on EC nationals at the internal EC frontiers,[18] this draft Regulation was never adopted by the Council.[19]

As far as the more recent results of Community activities are concerned, it is worth mentioning that the Council recently took final decisions on two Commission proposals which are also of relevance to our subject. One was a Commission proposal for a directive about controlling the acquisition and possession of firearms.[20] The other was a draft directive introducing a series of measures to combat money laundering.[21] Furthermore, the Council adopted on 18 June 1991 a common position on the Commission proposal for a regulation on the elimination of controls and formalities applicable to the cabin and checked baggage of passengers on intra-Community flights and the baggage of passengers on intra-Community sea crossings.[22]

In addition to these legislative developments, it can be stated that the Council working group on drugs provides a framework for Community anti-drug activities. An example of the concrete results of these activities is the Decision of the Council of 22 October 1990 authorizing the President of the Council to deposit the instrument of approval of the United Nations Convention (Vienna) against illicit traffic in narcotic drugs and psychotropic substances of December 1988 on behalf of the Community.[23]

2.2 Ad Hoc Group on Immigration

This group was set up on 20 October 1986, at a meeting of immigration ministers of the Member States and the Vice-President of the Commission in London. The meeting endorsed the objective of providing for free movement in the Community within the terms of the Single European Act. At the same time it was stressed that the goal of

18. Proposal for a Council Directive on the easing of controls and formalities applicable to nationals of Member States when crossing intra-Community borders, OJ 1985 C 47/5. Art. 235 EEC was proposed as the legal basis of the text. The proposal concerned a system whereby private vehicles would be permitted to cross borders at a reduced speed. In order to facilitate the control that was complied with the provisions concerning both the movement of persons and the movement of goods and in particular as regards the value or quantities of goods admitted free of charge, EC nationals could present a disc (bearing the letter E on a green background) affixed to the windscreen of their vehicle.

19. The Court of Justice has developed case-law on how to deal with EC nationals crossing internal borders: case 157/79 Regina v. Pieck [1980] ECR 2171; case 321/87 Commission of the European Communities v. Kingdom of Belgium [1989] ECR 997; Judgment of 30 May 1991, case C-68/89 Commission of the European Communities v. Kingdom of The Netherlands, not yet reported.

20. The re-examined Commission proposal for the draft directive is published in OJ 1990 C 265/6. A final decision on this proposal (second reading) was taken by the Council on 18 June 1991.

21. The re-examined Commission proposal for the draft directive is published in OJ 1990 C 319/9. The final decision was taken by the Council on 18 June 1991.

22. OJ 1990 C 212/8.

23. OJ 1990 L 326/56.

abolishing frontier formalities should remain compatible with the need to combat terrorism and drug trafficking.

The Ad Hoc Group is a group, composed of high level officials on immigration policy from the Member States. Where Community powers are involved, representatives of the Commission are invited to participate in the talks. The Council Secretariat provides the secretariat of the group. The Ad Hoc Group is assisted by subgroups on Asylum, Frontiers, Forged Papers, Visas and Data Processing.

According to the conclusions of the meeting of 20 October 1986 the group was instructed to examine:
— improved checks at the external Community frontiers;
— the contribution which internal checks can make;
— the role of coordination and possible harmonization of the visa policies of the Member States;
— the role and effectiveness of frontier controls at internal frontiers;
— the exchange of information about the operation of spot check systems;
— measures to achieve a common policy on eliminating the abuse of the right of asylum;
— ways in which the convenience of Community travellers can be improved.

To date, the group has drafted an Asylum Convention,[24] which was signed in Dublin on 15 June 1990 by eleven of the Member States and on 13 June 1991 by Denmark.[25] The Convention provides for a set of rules defining which Member State is responsible for dealing with asylum applications presented in one of the Member States. However, the text of the draft Convention leaves intact the principle of controls at internal frontiers. Furthermore the group has made considerable progress in formulating the External Frontiers Convention.[26] This refers to the conditions on which nationals of third countries may be granted admission to the territory of the Twelve. The convention also lays down a set of principles which are to be taken into account when a common visa policy is developed. However, the draft Convention does not depart from the principle of internal frontier controls.

Although they are undoubtedly important, therefore, neither the Asylum Convention and the External Frontiers Convention can be considered a decisive contribution towards the completion of the internal market as referred to in Article 8 A of the Treaty.

Another result of the work of the Ad Hoc Group was the drafting of a list of countries whose nationals are subject to visa requirements.

24. The official title is: Convention determining the State responsible for examining applications for asylum lodged in one of the Member States of the European Communities.

25. In the meantime a number of third countries have also expressed an interest in acceding to the Convention.

26. The official title is: Convention on the crossing of the external borders of the Member States of the European Communities.

2.3   European Political Cooperation

Several groups operate within the framework of European Political Cooperation (EPC) whose activities are of relevance to the free movement of persons. One deals with matters of legal cooperation (civil and penal matters). Another deals with questions concerning terrorism. The activities of the EPC Working Party on Drug Addiction should also be mentioned.

As regards criminal matters, special emphasis is currently being placed on the commitment to promote the ratification by States who have not already done so, of the Council of Europe Convention on Extradition of 13 December 1957, and to expedite the ratification of agreements concluded between the Twelve to improve judicial assistance in criminal matters.[27] Furthermore the desirability is being examined of ratifying agreements concluded in the Council of Europe to improve international judicial assistance in criminal matters.[28] Another project concerns the drafting of a Convention on the Enforcement of Foreign Decisions in Penal Matters, to be concluded between the Twelve. It is hoped that the text of this draft Convention will be open for signature at the meeting of Ministers of Justice scheduled for 13 November 1991. A final subject concerns the application of the Agreement on the use of fax in extradition procedures, some technical aspects of which still need to be clarified.

As far as civil matters are concerned the desirability of signing or ratifying several existing Conventions is under examination.[29]

27. Mention may be made of the following:
— the Agreement between the Member States on the application of the European Convention on the Suppression of Terrorism;
— the Agreement on the application between the Member States of the European Convention on the Transfer of Sentenced Persons;
— the Convention between the Member States on Double Jeopardy.
28. Apart from the European Convention on Extradition of 13 December 1957 (and its Additional Protocols) mention can be made of:
— the European Convention on the Suppression of Terrorism of 27 January 1957;
— the European Convention on Mutual Assistance in Criminal Matters of 20 April 1959 (and its Additional Protocols);
— the European Convention on the International Validity of Criminal Judgments of 28 May 1970;
— the European Convention on the Transfer of Proceedings in Criminal Matters of 15 May 1972;
— the European Convention on the Transfer of Sentenced Persons of 21 March 1983;
— the European Convention on the Compensation of Victims of Violent Crimes of 24 November 1983.
29. Mention can be made of:
— Convention between the Member States on simplification of the procedure for securing payment of alimony from abroad: signed by nine Member States in Rome on 6 November 1990;
— Draft Convention on the Transfer of Proceedings in Criminal Matters: signed by seven Member States on 6 November 1990;
— the Hague Convention on Civil Aspects of International Child Abduction of 1980;
— Luxembourg Convention on the Recognition and Enforcement of Decisions concerning Custody of Children and on Restoration of Custody of Children of 1980.

2.4   Mutual Assistance Group

The Mutual Assistance Group (MAG) is a forum composed of senior civil servants of the Member States. The MAG deals with the exchange of fiscal and customs information between Member States insofar as they are not Community matters. The group discusses legal and practical aspects of cooperation and the exchange of information, between customs services, on combating clandestine imports, including drugs.

The Mutal Assistance Group 1992 has drawn up a strategy for the application of customs regulations at the external borders after 1992. The group has also reached provisional agreement on a Protocol to be added to the Naples Convention of 1967 on Mutual Administrative Assistance between the Customs Authorities of the Member States. On the other hand agreement has not yet been reached on the creation of an information system for the exchange of customs information.

2.5   TREVI

The TREVI group was set up in December 1975 by the Ministers for Home Affairs (or Ministers with similar responsibilities) of the Member States meeting in Rome. The group is composed of the Ministers themselves and discusses matters of public order, more specifically terrorism and other forms of international crime. The group meets twice a year. The proceedings are prepared by a Committee of Senior Officials, which in its turn is assisted by sub-groups.

These days the attention of the Group is particularly focused on the consequences of the completion of the internal market by the end of 1992. Cooperation within TREVI is mainly of a practical nature. Priority is given to subjects which are of a general interest to the Twelve. On 13 June 1991 the Ministers agreed in principle to set up a European Drugs Intelligence Unit.

The possibility of establishing a separate secretariat for the TREVI Group is currently under discussion. The Commission of the European Communities has been fully associated with the activities of TREVI since the beginning of 1991.

2.6   Group of Coordinators

The Group of Coordinators on the free circulation of persons was set up in December 1988, as a result of discussions within the European Council. The relevant conclusion[30] refers to the need to achieve such common objectives as the internal market, while stressing the linkage with progress in intergovernmental cooperation in the field combating terrorism, international crime, drugs and illegal trade.

The Group of Coordinators, which is composed of representatives of the Member States, meets four or five times every six months. It has not set up any subgroups.

---

30. For the text: see *supra*, in section 1., n. 6.

The Group's primary task is to ensure coordination of all activities relating to the circulation of persons, be it in an intergovernmental framework or within the Community framework. To this end the group drew up the Palma Document, which was presented to the European Council in June 1989. The document reflects both the different fora which are active in this field and their respective activities. It also contains a list of priority measures to be taken by the Twelve. The Palma Document draws a distinction between:

— action at the external frontiers (competent fora: Ad Hoc Group, TREVI, MAG);
— action at the internal frontiers (Ad Hoc Group, TREVI, EC);
— action in connection with drug trafficking (EPC, TREVI, Council of Europe (Pompidou Group), UN, MAG);
— terrorism (TREVI, EPC);
— action in connection with admission to Community territory (Ad Hoc Group)
— action in connection with granting of asylum and refugee status (Ad Hoc Group, Council of Europe, UN);
— other activities (Ad Hoc Group);
— judicial cooperation in criminal and civil matters (EPC);
— goods carried by travellers (EC).

The Group of Coordinators has also made recommendations to the Ministers of Foreign Affairs on a procedure for providing information to the European Parliament; it has suggested removing the visa requirements for Hungary and Czechoslovakia, and has conducted a survey on immigration as requested by the European Council in Strasbourg.

However, it should be borne in mind that the Group is not an extra forum for debate. As things stand at present, the Group's sole responsibility is for coordination, and it is expected to give an impetus to and unblocking the whole complex of intergovernmental and Community work in the field of the free movement of persons. The Group regularly presents to the European Council a report of results in the area of the free movement of persons, including a timetable for their implementation.

2.7   CELAD

The 'Comité européen de la lutte antidrogue' (CELAD) was set up by the European Council, at its meeting in December 1989, on the initiative of the President of the French Republic. The group is composed of high-level officials of the Member States, while the Commission is invited to participate in its discussions where Community powers are involved.

The group is not a forum for negotiation. Its task is to coordinate of the activities of the Member States in relation to the campaign against the production of and trade in drugs. For example, in its report to the European Council of June 1990, CELAD suggested looking into how Member States might implement the provisions of the United Nations Convention of 1971 and the Vienna Convention of 1988, after their ratification. It has also developed a European plan to combat drugs.

The group meets four or five times every six months. It has set up an informal network of contacts with third countries, such as the United States, Canada, Sweden, Japan and Australia.

2.8   Schengen

'Schengen' is a forum for a limited number of Member States, which discusses all issues relating to the circulation of persons. The idea of removing controls on persons at the frontiers between the two countries was launched at the bilateral Franco-German summit in Saarbrücken on 13 June 1984. The three Benelux countries endorsed this political objective shortly afterwards.

Schengen is intended to act as the vanguard for the wider framework of the Twelve. Ideally all specific measures agreed in the Schengen-framework should serve as a model for the Community or be taken over by the Twelve.

The Schengen Agreement of 1985 was signed by the five countries concerned on 14 June 1985.[31] The Schengen Convention, to 'apply' the Schengen Agreement of June 1985, was subsequently signed on 19 June 1990.[32] The Schengen Convention provides for a series of measures, such as the abolition of checks at internal frontiers, the introduction of systematic controls at the external borders of the Schengen countries, the establishment principles to serve as the basis for a joint policy on visas, a list of criteria to determine which country should take responsability for applications for asylum submitted in one of the Schengen countries, modalities of cooperation between the police and the judicial authorities of the Schengen countries, and the establishment of an automatic information system (SIS). In addition, an Executive Committee has been set up, *inter alia*, to establish a set of implementation measures on a number of specific subjects referred to in the Agreement.

In November 1990 Italy signed the documents for accession to the Schengen Agreement of 1985 and the Schengen Convention of 1990. Spain and Portugal did so on 25 June 1991.

2.9   Council of Europe

A few years ago a working group was created within the Council of Europe with a mandate to study all the problems related to the free movement of persons. In May 1990 the Committee of Ministers charged the European Committee for Legal Cooperation, which includes a committee on free circulation, with this task.

The Pompidou Group, as it is called, also operates within the framework of the Council of Europe to discuss problems related to combatting drugs. Another group active within the Council of Europe is CAHAR, which deals with questions of asylum.

31. Published in the Trb. 1985 No. 102.
32. Published in the Trb. 1990 No. 145.

2.10   United Nations

The activities of the United Nations which are relevant for our subject are those concerning the fight against drugs. In this connection mention should be made of the Conventions of the United Nations dating from 1961, 1971 and 1988 respectively.

3.   RESULTS OF COOPERATION

To date the results achieved by cooperation within the different fora have been modest. Because of the Commission's reluctance to submit to the Council proposals for Community legislation for the purpose set out in Article 8 A of the Treaty, no major initiatives have been developed in the Community framework for the abolition of controls at internal frontiers or for the introduction of systematic controls at the external borders and other compensatory measures. Although this attitude on the part of the Commission may be explained by pragmatic considerations, the conclusion has to be drawn that the internal market still remains to be completed as far as the free movement of persons is concerned. The Commission was in fact the first to acknowledge this lack of progress, in the opinion it put forward before the opening of the Intergovernmental Conference on European Political Union.[33]

The results of the cooperation in an intergovernmental framework have also been somewhat limited. In fact the most important results are the signing of the Schengen Convention on 19 June 1990, and the accession of Italy, Spain and Portugal to the Schengen Agreement of 1985 and the Schengen Convention of 1990. However, it has to be kept in mind that cooperation within the framework of Schengen is a result achieved not by all twelve Member States, but only by a limited number of them. In fact some doubt is arising as to whether Schengen is really going to play the role originally forecast as trendsetter for the Community or the Twelve. For, instead of Schengen's achievements being taken over by the Community or the Twelve, at present individual EC Member States seem to prefer to apply for accession to the Schengen Agreement and the Schengen Convention. Thus, instead of serving as an example for the Community, Schengen might be showing a tendency to develop into an alternative to the Community.

Otherwise the draft Convention on Asylum concluded by the Twelve was signed only recently by all the Member States, and progress can be noted on the other draft convention namely that on controls at the external frontiers. However, both texts depart from the principle that controls at the internal frontiers should be maintained. To that extent there is room for doubt as to whether both conventions may be considered as concrete contributions to the achievement of the objective of Article 8 A of the Treaty.

Moreover, neither text provides for procedures for the settlement of disputes between the contracting parties, or for a mechanism for uniform interpretation by an independent tribunal. The same, however, is true for the Schengen Convention. In

33. See Commission document COM 90 (600) fin. of 23 October 1990.

particular, no provision is made for a role for the EC Court of Justice.[34] Without such mechanisms, the chances of the conventions being applied correctly leave to be desired.

It is difficult to judge to what extent the Group of Coordinators, set up in December 1988 by the European Council, has succeeded in streamlining the activities of the different fora and making them more efficient. In all probability, however, it may be concluded that the coordination provided to date is not sufficient. In fact, if it is planned to continue the existing situation, characterised as it is by numerous fora and so many diverse activities, there is an argument for changing the nature of the Coordinators' mandate to make them responsible for the course taken by negotiations in the different fora.

The European Council has also recognised that the present situation is unsatisfactory. Indeed, in the conclusions of its December 1990 meeting,[35] it expressed regret about the lack of progress in the field of the free movement of persons. The conclusion stressed the need for completion of the internal market by the end of 1992. The Commission was, moreover, invited to prepare a study on the enforcement of controls at the external frontiers of the Community. At the same time, the European Council called for consideration of how intergovernmental cooperation could be introduced within the scope of European Union. In this connection the European Council referred more specifically to home affairs, justice, immigration, visa policy, asylum law and the fight against drugs and organised crime.

4.   IS AN IMPETUS TO COMMUNITY ACTION NEEDED?

4.1   The Luxembourg non-paper

In April 1991, in the framework of the Intergovernmental Conference on European Political Union, the Luxembourg Presidency presented a non-paper containing a proposal for a Treaty on the Union.[36] Apart from amendments to the EC Treaties, the non-paper proposes separate chapters on intergovernmental cooperation in the field of on the one hand foreign and security policy and on the other home affairs and justice.

The home affairs and justice 'pillar' contains a series of procedural articles on cooperation in the field of the free movement of persons and cooperation between judicial authorities. The text presents a selection of subjects and decision-making procedures. In this connection the proposal is marked by the idea of linking certain subjects to a specific decision-making procedure, all, however, intergovernmental in character. Provision is also made for new items to be added to the list of subjects, on

---

34. However, as far as Schengen is concerned, it should be noted that the involvement of the EC Court of Justice would not have been an obvious step, since Schengen is a framework for cooperation between a limited number of Member States, and the EC Court was set up by all the Member States. Therefore, if it had been considered appropriate to accord the Court powers of interpretation, this would have required approval by all the EC Member States.

35. See for the text *Agence Europe*, special edition of 16 December 1990.

36. See for the text *Agence Europe*, Europe Documents No. 1709/1710 of 3 May 1991.

the basis of guidelines to be laid down by the European Council. Any additions to the list of subjects would, however, require, according to these proposals, ratification by national parliaments.

In fact the structure of the model is somewhat complex and obscure. In addition it is doubtful whether the proposed approach really presents the best answer to the problem. In fact it is remarkable that no attempt has been made to involve the Community more closely in this sector of cooperation.

Now, there would appear to be little doubt that progress towards more intensive Community involvement, at least from a legal point of view, is possible. A development in the framework of the Community seems all the more logical in the context of the Community's responsibility for completing the internal market by the end of 1992.

4.2   Community powers

It seems possible to interpret Article 8 A in such a way that this objective is supposed to imply, *inter alia*, the abolition of controls on persons at internal frontiers. Abolition is thus to be considered as a specific measure to remove internal obstacles not only to goods, services and capital, but also to the free movement of persons. Because the second paragraph of Article 100 A of the Treaty states that the procedures in the first paragraph of the article (application of the procedure for cooperation with the European Parliament[37] − qualified majority voting within the Council,[38] do not apply to the free movement of persons, the legislative measures concerned can be taken according to the procedures of Article 100 (consultation with the European Parliament - unanimity within Council).

An affirmative answer also seems possible to the follow-up question, on the existence of Community powers to take measures which are to be applied to third country nationals as well as EC nationals. In this connection it must be remembered for a start, that the notion of the free movement of persons is formulated, in Article 3 (c) of the Treaty, in a neutral way, that is to say without defining the nationality of the beneficiaries. Furthermore, the notion of 'worker' in Article 48 et seq. of the Treaty is also formulated in an abstract way, without explicit reference to the nationality of the persons concerned. In addition, the existing text of Article 59 of the Treaty provides, in its second paragraph, for the possibility of extending the provisions of 'this Chapter' to nationals of a third country who provide services and who are established within the Community.

Another point of reference on the involvement of the Community in matters concerning the circulation of third country nationals within the Community is Article

37. See Art. 149, para. 2, EEC.
38. See Art. 148, para. 2, EEC.

348 J.W. DE ZWAAN

238 relating to the conclusion, by the Community, of association agreements with third countries, a union of States or an international organisation.[39]

There is, therefore, room for an initial conclusion that, although secondary Community legislation[40] is thus far addressed primarily to nationals of the Member States, the text of the Treaty indicates in a number of places that specific actions of the Community in the field of the free movement of persons which also have relevance to third country nationals can in any event not be ruled out.[41]

However, should one be of the opinion that the existing Community powers are not sufficient for the achievement in full of the internal market objective as far as the movement of persons is concerned, it may be possible to invoke Article 235 EEC of the Treaty[42] as the legal basis for concrete legislative measures which are relevant to third country nationals as well as to EC nationals.

Once this conclusion has been drawn, the question arises of the extent to which the Community may be considered competent to take measures in this field, apart from, as indicated above, abolishing the controls at internal frontiers. In this regard it may be argued that the introduction of tighter controls at the external frontiers of the Community and the establishment of the modalities thereof may be decided by the Community, as a subject directly related to the abolition of internal frontier controls.

Furthermore, matters relating to the short-term stay of third country nationals in the Community could be dealt with by Community measures. Such matters include laying down the conditions for the entry of third country nationals to the Community; the right to free circulation within the Community as the direct consequence of entry and the adoption of a common visa policy, including drafting a list of third countries which are obliged to provide their nationals with visas.

It may even be possible to consider the establishment of a common asylum policy, albeit *a fortiori* related to the long-term stay of nationals of third countries, as a subject to be decided upon by the Community. Measures to be taken in this regard, could

39. In this connection reference could be made to recent Court decisions as, for example, Judgment of 20 September 1990, Case C-192/89, *S.Z. Sevince* v. *Staatssecretaris van Justitie*, [1990] ECR 3461 and Judgment of 31 January 1991, Case C-18/90, *Office National de l'Emploi* v. *Bahia Kziber*, [1991] ECR 199.
40. See *supra*, in section 2.1.
41. Reference may also be made to the judgment of the Court of 9 July 1987 in Cases 281, 283 to 285 and 287/85 *Federal Republic of Germany* v. *Commission*, [1987] ECR 3245. In this decision the Court, in interpreting Art. 118 of the Treaty, stressed that the employment situation and, more generally, the improvement of living and working conditions within the Community are liable to be affected by the policy pursued by the Member States with regard to workers from non-member countries (para. 16). The Court did not therefore accept the argument that migration policy in relation to non-Member States falls entirely outside the social field, in respect of which Art. 118 provides for cooperation between the Member States (para. 18). It made clear that the subject matter covered by the Commission Decision 85/381/EEC (OJ L 217/25) on 'notification and consultation' on the migration policies of the Member States in relation to non-member countries falls 'in the present stage of development of Community law' within the competence of the Member States (para. 30).
42. The text of the Article is as follows: 'If action by the Community should prove necessary to attain, in the course of the operation of the common market, one of the objectives of the Community and this Treaty has not provided the necessaruy powers, the Council shall, acting unanimously on a proposal from the Commission and after consulting the Assembly, take the appropriate measures.'

include laying down criteria for the designation of the Member State responsible for dealing with applications for asylum[43] and any harmonisation measures considered necessary.

All this should result in a Treaty regime governing the free movement of persons comparable to that of the existing Treaty regime on the circulation of goods, which indeed embraces not only rules for the circulation of goods within the Community but also ways of dealing with products originating from third countries, in the form of a common trade[44] and customs regime.[45]

On the other hand, the current Treaty text does not provide an appropriate legal framework for decision-making on such matters as cooperation between the police and the judical authorities of the Member States. Because in this context matters of criminal law — related for example to the fight against international crime — are at stake, activities of this kind cannot be brought within the purview of the existing Treaty objectives. Decisions on such activities, which complement the abolition of internal frontier controls, remain a matter for the individual Member States or for intergovernmental cooperation.

4.3   The Intergovernmental Conference on European Political Union

It remains to be seen whether and to what extent, the current Intergovernmental Conference will bring about new developments in the field of the free movement of persons. It is to be hoped that satisfactory results can be reached.

In this context a satisfactory solution could be to clarify the Community's powers in this field while at the same time creating a uniform framework for intergovernmental cooperation between Member States.

As far as clarifying the Community's powers is concerned, an idea could be to add an Article[46] to the Treaty stating that the Council is entitled to take appropriate measures as regards the entry, movement and residence of nationals of third countries.[47] It would be understood that the following subjects would fall under the scope of the new Article:
— the abolition of internal controls;
— the organisation of external frontier controls;
— the establishment of the conditions for entry to the Community by third country nationals;
— the right of free circulation of third country nationals within the Community;

---

43. See Title II, Chapter 7, Arts. 28-38 of the Schengen Convention of 19 June 1990.
44. See Art. 111 et seq. EEC.
45. See Art. 18 et seq. EEC.
46. The new article should be considered closely related to Arts. 8 A and 100 A.
47. The wording 'entry, movement and residence of nationals of third countries' corresponds to the text of the Political Declaration by the Governments of the Member States on the free movement of persons, which was included in the Final Act to the Single European Act and annexed to that Act.

— the establishment of a common visa policy;
— the establishment of a common asylum policy.[48]

For the decision-making on these matters the Commission should have the right of initiative. Because of the sensitive nature of the issues the decision-making within the Council itself should be unanimous. The European Parliament should at least be consulted. In view of the nature of the issues involved, it seems appropriate also to provide for consultation of the Economic and Social Committee.

As regards a uniform framework for intergovernmental cooperation, an idea could be to add several subjects to Article 220 of the EEC Treaty, being a framework for intergovernmental cooperation between Member States on areas which do not themselves fall under the scope of the Treaty but are nevertheless related to the objectives of the Community. The subjects to be incorporated in the Treaty could include the following:
— combating unauthorized immigration into and residence in the territory of the Member States by nationals of third countries;
— combating illegal trafficking, in particular illegal drug trafficking;
— customs cooperation in fields not falling within the powers of the European Communities;
— judicial cooperation in civil and criminal matters, with particular reference to the recognition and enforcement of judgments.[49]

The amendment to be made to Article 220 of the Treaty should be flexible in its wording. Thus, apart from taking the form of concluding international conventions, cooperation between Member States could be of a purely practical nature[50] or could take the form of coordination of the participation of the Member States in Conventions of the Council of Europe.[51]

A further advantage of cooperation within the framework of Article 220 is that, in all probability, the Court of Justice could be involved, through powers of uniform interpretation. Indeed, Member States have approved the granting to the Court of powers of uniform interpretation on several occasions in the past.[52]

It has been argued, however, that intervention by the Court, for example in asylum cases, is not to be welcomed, in particular because of the length of the proceedings. Such fears do not, however, seem to constitute a sufficient argument for not allowing

48. This summary of subjects implies that the items, mentioned in Art. A, para. 1 (a and b) of the Luxembourg non-paper on the so-called third pillar would be covered by the new Article.

49. The wording of the subjects is inspired by the wording of Art. A, para. 1 (c - g), of the Luxembourg non-paper concerning the third pillar.

50. An example is the achievement of cooperation between the judicial and police authorities of the Member States.

51. See *supra*, in section 2.3.

52. Examples are the Protocol of 3 June 1971 to the Convention of 27 September 1968 concerning the reciprocal recognition and enforcement of judgments of courts, and the Protocol of 3 June 1971 to the Convention of 29 February 1968 (not entered into force) concerning the reciprocal recognition of companies, both conventions being based on Art. 220 EEC. The two Protocols, dating from 19 December 1988 (OJ 1989 L 48), on the interpretation by the Court of Justice of the Convention on the law applicable to contractual obligations of 1980, although not based on Art. 220 EEC, can also serve as precedents.

the Court to play a role of ensuring a uniform interpretation. Even if it is thought that intervention by the Court might complicate the normal procedures because of the time factor, the establishment of special — and expedited — proceedings for this particular purpose cannot be ruled out. It would appear that appropriate arrangements should be worked out in consultation with the Court itself.

5.   CONCLUSION

The progress made to date towards the completion of the internal market, as far as the freedom of movement of persons is concerned, is modest. Except for the signing of the Schengen Convention by eight Member States and the signing of the Asylum Convention by all Twelve, there are no major developments to point at.

Furthermore, the activities which have been undertaken in a wide range of different fora suffer from a lack of transparency and consistency. Apparently the Group of Coordinators has difficulty in streamlining the activities of these fora in order to make their work more efficient.

Nevertheless the existence of a Treaty objective, the free movement of persons at the end of 1992 at the latest, must not be forgotten. If we still hope to achieve this objective in time, it seems advisable to consider seriously whether the Community itself could and should play a more important role in this field than it has done thus far.

In fact, it is not the absence of appropriate powers which rules out such action by the Community. On the contrary, it appears that the EEC Treaty already affords an adequate legal framework (reference may be made in particular to Articles 3(c), 8 A, 49, 59, 100, 100 A and 235), not only for the abolition of internal obstacles to freedom of movement, but also for a series of measures which may be considered necessary to supplement such abolition. Ultimately, too, advantage could be taken of the current Intergovernmental Conference on European Political Union to clarify Community powers and to provide for adequate modalities for intergovernmental cooperation in this sphere.

A further, significant advantage of more direct involvement of the Community might be that the Court of Justice would be able to play its traditional role of ensuring the correct application and interpretation of the Treaty.[53]

More direct Community involvement in the decision-making on legislation concerning the consequences of the free movement of persons within the Community is therefore to be welcomed. It is for the Governments of the Member States, meeting within the framework of the Intergovernmental Conference on European Political Union, to confirm this view and to provide for the relevant and appropriate arrangements to this end.

53. See Art. 164 EEC.

FREE MOVEMENT OF PERSONS AND THE DIVISION OF POWERS BETWEEN THE COMMUNITY AND ITS MEMBER STATES
Why do it the intergovernmental way?[*]

C.W.A. Timmermans[**]

1.   INTRODUCTION

1. 'Our objective is not merely to simplify existing procedures, but to do away with internal frontier controls in their entirety' (see the Commission in its White Paper on Completing The Internal Market of 1985).[1] Apparently the authors of the White Paper had little doubt as to the legal possibilities for the Community to realise these goals within the framework of the existing Treaties and powers to be derived therefrom, *even before* these were amended by the Single European Act (SEA). Let me add immediately that in view of the definition of the common market in the judgment in the *Schul* Case (15/81), the approach set out in the White Paper cannot be regarded as legally futuristic and exceeding Community powers.[2]

Yet, paradoxically the Community approach advocated by the White Paper, that is to enact the *indispensable* measures to compensate for the abolition of internal frontier controls by Community legislation, was not pursued even after the entry into force of the SEA and the consequent increase of Community competences. In view of the evident reticence of Member States to accept the Community approach in the sensitive area of immigration controls, asylum, visa, drugs control, crime prevention and the like, the Commission provisionally accepted the Member States' preference to follow the intergovernmental approach in order to avoid time-consuming and unprofitable debates on competences (para. 15 below). How delicate these issues remain in terms of competences, is clearly confirmed by the second 'non-paper' submitted by the Luxembourg Presidency to the intergovernmental Conference on political union. The so-called third pillar of the Union mentions a number of issues

---

[*] The views expressed are personal to the author.

[**] Adjunct Director-General, Legal Service, Commission of the European Communities.

1. Completing the internal market, White paper from the Commission to the European Council (Milan, 28-29 June 1985), Com (85) 310 fin; Bulletin EC, Suppl. 2/86.

2. Case 15/81 *Gaston Schul Douane Expediteur BV* v. *Inspector of Customs and Excise, Roosendaal*, [1982] ECR 1431 para. 33: 'The concept of a common market as defined by the Court in a consistent line of decisions involves the elimination of all obstacles to intra-Community trade in order to merge the national markets into a single market bringing about conditions as close as possible to those of a genuine internal market.'

H.G. Schermers et al., eds., Free Movement of Persons in Europe
© 1993, T.M.C. Asser Instituut, The Hague

relevant for our subject amongst the topics selected for cooperation in the judicial and internal affairs field, which cooperation was to be organised almost exclusively on an intergovernmental basis.

Addressing the subject allotted to me by the organisers of this Conference, thus risks remaining a theoretical exercise. Or, are the dice *not* definitely cast? One might be tempted to think so and not only because the work on the relevant conventions is not yet finished. In fact, the European Council seems to prepare the grounds for a more 'communautarian' approach, at least that is the impression given by the President's conclusions of the recent European Council meeting in Luxembourg (June 1991). In corroborating the 'underlying objectives' of the proposals submitted by Chancellor Kohl, the door for a more communautarian approach seems to have been set ajar, albeit in the context only of the Treaty on Political Union.

2.   Be that as it may, the issue of Community competences in this field, their scope and nature, raises important questions of principle on the interpretation of the SEA, but also of a more general institutional nature, justifying some comments.

2.   COMMUNITY POWERS

3.   Border controls are one of the classic instruments used by Member States in their policies regarding aliens, drugs, crime prevention/terrorism, etc. Abolishing all internal frontier controls between Member States to complete the internal market, more particularly as far as the free movement of persons is concerned, must therefore be balanced by accompanying measures replacing these controls. The problem has already been analysed in the White Paper of 1985, and was further refined as well as translated into a detailed working program by the Palma document.[3] The Schengen Convention reflects an integrated approach in this respect and could be regarded as a possible blueprint for Community-wide action in this field.[4] The gist of the necessary accompanying measures relates to policies regarding aliens (immigration controls, asylum, visa, extradition) and a regime ensuring respect of fundamental rights (privacy protection) in connexion with registration of personal data by centralised information systems. As far as the follow-up of the Palma program is concerned, these measures are covered by the Dublin Asylum Convention, the (as yet unsigned) Convention on crossing the external frontiers. Work on a special Convention regarding privacy protection is under way. The scope and contents of these (draft) Conventions, various other initiatives and bodies in which they are prepared, are amply discussed in other reports for this conference, which allows me to limit myself to these short references.

---

3.   See W. de Lobkowicz,'Quelle libre circulation des personnes en 1993?' *Revue du Marché Commun* (1990) p. 100; J.P.H. Donner, 'De ontwikkeling van het vrije verkeer van personen binnen de EG en de overeenkomst ter uitvoering van het akkoord van Schengen', SEW (1990) p. 766.

4.   See the article of P. Boeles and Donner, loc. cit. n. 3, SEW (1990) p. 686 et seq.; J.J.E. Schutte, 'Schengen, its meaning for the free movement of persons in Europe', CML Rev.(1991) 549.

4. The question to be addressed now is whether the Community can claim a competence on these issues. Before answering that question, we must first establish whether the abolition of all internal border controls between EC Member States is an obligation under Community law. In other words, how do we interpret Article 8A of the EEC Treaty? An important sub-question in this context is to what extent internal border controls on persons are still compatible with the EEC Treaty, now and at the date of expiry of the deadline laid down in Article 8A.

2.1   Does Article 8A impose an obligation to abolish all internal border controls?

5.   The wording of Article 8A EEC seems in itself sufficiently clear to allow for an affirmative answer to this question. Continuing internal border controls in an internal market defined as 'an area without internal frontiers' does not fit. One might add that the common understanding of the Europe 1992 programme is precisely the disappearence of the internal border controls. But that, I admit, is hardly a legal argument.

6.   For the interpretation of Article 8A in this respect the notion of border controls should first be defined. The definition of the Schengen Convention seems to me quite adequate: control at the frontier which, irrespective of any other motive, is carried out only because of the envisaged border crossing. So defined, normal police controls that may occur everywhere within the national territory under the conditions imposed by national law, fall outside the scope of border controls, even where they are carried out in a border region (para. 8 below). It could be argued that the very concept of the common market, as interpreted by the Court before the introduction by the SEA of Article 8A with its definition of the internal market, requires the abolition of internal border controls.[5] In any case the wording of Article 8A leaves little doubt on this point, particularly if account is taken of the origin of this Article and the Political Declaration adopted by the Conference on signature of the Single European Act in which Member States expressed their 'firm political will' to take the decisions necessary to implement the Commission's programme described in the White Paper of 1985.

7.   It is sometimes argued that Article 8A requires the abolition of border controls only with regard to nationals of Member States and leaves unaffected the power of Member States to continue border controls with regard to nationals of third countries. But, runs the usual counter-argument, how can they distinguish between EC nationals and others without maintaining overall border controls? Conceivably, there could be a special gate without control marked: 'EC nationals only', but in practice anybody could use it. Moreover why should the general objective of the free movement of persons under Articles 8A and 3 (c) of the EEC Treaty be so construed

---

5. See the ruling in the *Gaston Schul* case quoted in n. 2.

as to cover only nationals of Member States? The Council decision-making practice shows that the scope of this freedom is not necessarily limited to the measures provided for by title III of the Treaty relating to the free movement of workers and the right of establishment, which indeed confer direct benefits on Community nationals alone.[6] I just mention the Council directives on the right of residence for students and the general directive on right of residence which both refer in their preamble to the objective of Article 3 (c) EEC.[7]

Apart from that, the EEC Treaty itself as amended by the SEA demonstrates that the scope of the general objective of free movement of persons (Arts. 3c and 8A EEC) exceeds the realisation of the free movement in the limited sense of Title III under Articles 48 to 58 EEC. Article 100A, the general competence clause for Community legislation to realise the internal market, is expressed to be subject to the application of specific Treaty provisions (see Art. 100A (1)). That covers the various competence clauses in title III on free movement of persons (Arts. 49, 51, 54, etc.). Nevertheless Article 100A paragraph 2 excludes all provisions relating to the free movement of persons from its scope. That can only mean that the general objective of free movement of persons as part of the concept of the internal market under Article 8A exceeds the scope of free movement as set out in title III of the EEC Treaty. Member States have been clearly aware of this, as is shown by the two Declarations relating to this subject that were annexed to the Final Act of the Conference adopting the SEA.[8] More generally it appears rather artificial within the

---

6. Contrary to Art. 52 EEC, the wording of Art. 48, by referring generally to workers (of the Member States) does not explicitly limit the beneficiaries of this freedom to nationals of a Member State. That, however, is the generally accepted interpretation (see with further references U. Wölker in the forthcoming fourth edition of Von der Groeben Thiesing Ehlermann, *Kommentar zum EWG-Vertrag*, Vorbemerkung zu den Artikeln 48 bis 50, p. 30; for an interesting, more differentiated approach, see Donner, loc. cit. n. 3, at pp. 780-781. For related persons which according to Community legislation have derivative rights of free entry and residence, there is no nationality requirement (see Art. 10 Regulation 1612/68 (OJ 1968 L 257/2 and Art. 1 Directive 73/148/EEC, OJ 1973 L 172/14). Regulation 1408/71, OJ 1971 L 149/2 on social security for migrant workers applies also to refugees and stateless persons residing within a Member State. See more generally for the position of third country nationals under Community law, M. Hilf, 'Europaisches Gemeinschafsrecht und Drittstaatsangehörige', in *Staat und Völkerrechtsordnung, Festschrift für Karl Doehring*, (1989) p. 339; M. Maresceau, 'La libre circulation des personnes et les ressortissants d'Etats tiers', in *Relations extérieures de la CE et marché intérieur: aspects juridiques et fonctionnels*, Colloque 1986, P. Demaret, ed., Collège d'Europe No 45, p. 109 and P. Oliver, 'Non-Community Nationals and the Treaty of Rome', *Yearbook of European Law* (1985) p. 57.

7. Directive 90/366/EEC and Directive 90/364/EEC, OJ 1990 L 180.

8. There is first the general declaration of the Conference itself on Arts. 13 to 19 of the SEA: 'Nothing in these provisions shall affect the right of the Member States to take such measures as they consider necessary for the purpose of controlling immigration from third countries, and to combat terrorism, crime, the traffic in drugs and illicit trading in works of art and antiques.' In my view this declaration cannot be invoked to deny a Community competence which as such can be derived from the Treaty (para. 10 below). This is confirmed by the second declaration referred to, which is not a declaration adopted by the Conference itself but a political declaration of the Governments of the Member States in which they expressed their willingness 'in order to promote the free movement of persons' to cooperate on the subjects mentioned in the other declaration but 'without prejudice to the powers of the Community'. See more generally on the interpretative value of these declarations (with further references) J. Pipkorn in the

context of a Community social policy, and more particularly a labour market policy, to exclude third country workers already residing in a Member State as being irrelevant to the Community. Without necessarily accepting a principle of Community preference in this context,[9] it seems obvious that varying degrees of free movement of third country workers between Member States could reduce the practical impact of the freedom under Article 48 EEC for Community nationals and possibly also affect the conditions of competition between companies.

It should be added, to prevent confusion, that interpreting the objective of free movement of persons under Articles 3c and 8A EEC as including third country nationals (lawfully established within a Member State) would not automatically grant a right of free entry/residence or access to economic activities in other Member States. Indeed Articles 48 a.f. EEC do not apply to this class of persons. The rights just mentioned could therefore only be granted at the Community level by specific Community legislation to that effect (see also Art. 59 par. 2 EEC).[10]

Finally, an impartial support for a strict construction of Article 8A as imposing the abolition of *all* internal border controls can be derived from the preambles of both the Schengen Convention and the Asylum Convention and the External Frontiers Convention. Indeed, by explicitly linking the need for a common regime between Member States in the fields covered by the latter Conventions to the objective of an area without internal frontiers in which the free movement of persons is ensured, the draftsmen of these Conventions seem to accept that realising the objective of Article 8A EEC will also affect third country nationals.

2.2.   Compatibility of border controls with the EEC Treaty

8.   Before addressing the question as to whether the Community holds the necessary legislative powers to enact the measures which are indispensable to balance the disappearance of internal border controls, we should first consider to what extent these border controls are still permissible under the EEC Treaty and what the effect of Article 8A EEC might be in this respect.

Systematic or sporadic border controls on *persons* as earlier defined — controls at the frontier only carried out because of the envisaged border crossing — are still allowed under Community law. However, their scope must be fairly limited, as has been clarified by recent case-law of the Court of Justice. Relevant provisions are to be found in Article 3 of Directive 68/360/EEC and Article 3 of Directive 73/148/EEC which allow for identity controls of Community nationals at the internal borders.[11] These Directives only concern persons claiming free access to Member

---

forthcoming fourth edition of Von der Groeben Thiesing Ehlermann, *Kommentar zum EWG-Vertrag*, Artikel 8a, p. 204/205.

9. See in this respect Art. 16 of Regulation 1612/68, n. 6.

10. Third country nationals could, however, benefit indirectly from Arts. 59 et seq. as workers accompanying a service provider, see case 113/89 *Rush Portuguesa LDA Srl* v. *Office National d'Immigration* [1990] ECR I-417.

11. OJ 1968 L 257/13 and OJ 1973 L 172/14.

States as beneficiaries of one of the freedoms granted by Articles 48 (workers), 52 (establishment), or 59/60 (services) EEC. The Court has ruled in the recent *Hoffmann* case that Community nationals generally are to be considered as beneficiaries in those respects, more particularly because of the very wide scope of the freedom to supply and receive services. Border controls should therefore remain limited to *identity controls*, so that any further probing to establish whether the persons concerned are in fact in a position to invoke one of the Treaty freedoms granting free access is incompatible with Community law.[12]

I should add at once that the Court expressly reserved the possible application of the public order, etc., exception clause under Articles 48, 56 (and 66) EEC. However, earlier case-law had already clarified the limited possibilities which these provisions grant Member States to justify border controls. Systematic border controls can at any rate not be justified under these exception clauses; only in individual cases satisfying the strict criteria of necessity and proportionality as developed by the Court's case-law, could special control measures at the border be accepted.[13] Apart from these border controls properly so called, the Court has also limited the acceptability under the Treaty of non-discriminatory controls on persons as generally allowed under national law and thus not limited to borders or border regions. These controls (other than identity controls allowed under the above-mentioned Directives), *when* carried out at the border, will be incompatible with the principle of free movement if they are systematic and arbitrary and involve unnecessary constraints.[14] Accordingly even general, non-discriminatory controls are not entirely safe from the liberalising impact of the free movement principles of the Treaty.

9.   Since border controls still allowed under Community law are thus reduced, as far as EC nationals are concerned, to mere *identity controls*, the next question is whether the expiry of the time-limit for the completion of the internal market imposed by Article 8A will have any consequences for the lawfulness of these controls. Member States did not wish Article 8A to have any automatic effects in this respect as is stated in their express Declaration in the final Act of the Conference on the Single European Act. Given that this Declaration was adopted by the Conference itself, it cannot be disregarded when interpreting Article 8A. Thus the argument that border controls will be automatically rendered incompatible with the EEC Treaty from 1 January 1993 by virtue of Article 8A is open to question.

On the other hand it would be too simplistic to deny any effect to Article 8A in this respect. If the objective of removing all internal border controls is to be derived from Article 8A, this objective must be taken into account, according to the most

12. Judgment of 30 May 1991, case 68/89 *Commission of the European Communities* v. *Kingdom of the Netherlands*, not yet reported.

13. Judgment of 5 February 1991, case 321/87 *Commission of the European Communities* v. *Kingdom of Belgium* [1989] ECR 997, see also case 363/89, *Danielle Roux* v. *Belgian State*, not yet reported.

14. Case 321/87 *Commission of the European Communities* v. *Kingdom of Belgium* [1989] ECR 1011, para 15.

orthodox interpretation methods developed in the Court's case-law, when interpreting the other Articles of the Treaty. It would follow at the very least that, when interpreting the basic prohibitions on the free movement of goods, persons, services and capital (Arts. 30, 48, 52, 59/60 and 67) and the exception clauses relevant thereto, the objective of the removal of internal border controls from 1 January 1993 must be duly taken into account. That would mean, as far as the free movement of persons is concerned, that identity controls, as still allowed by Article 3 of both above-mentioned Directives, instead of being a token of liberalisation as was the situation before the SEA, now have to be regarded as restrictions to free movement to be abolished before the key date of 1 January 1993. A fairly radical solution would be to say that interpreting the basic Treaty provisions on free movement of persons in the light of Article 8A, warrants the conclusion that identity controls at the internal Community borders have to be regarded as restrictions of free movement prohibited by Articles 48, 52, 59 and 60 from 1 January 1993. That conclusion would not be very far removed from granting direct effect to Article 8A. It would surely be mere sophistry to attempt to refute that view on the basis that, far from accepting direct effect of Article 8A, this would be no more than a consequence of the direct effect of the basic Treaty prohibitions on free movement interpreted in the light of Article 8A.

Quite another, much less controversial, approach would be to apply the necessity and proportionality tests much more strictly having regard to Article 8A, when Member States seek to justify national measures restricting free movement by invoking imperative public interests. This test is only applicable where these national measures are indistinctly applicable to both the internal and the external, Community relevant situation. As for border controls the application of this test could be justified because they apply indiscriminately to aliens and nationals. Applying this test in concrete terms would require a judgment on the necessity of *first* achieving the indispensable accompanying measures at Community level before internal border controls can be abolished. What the outcome of this test should be, in other words which measures are really to be considered as indispensable in this respect, need not be answered here. Suffice it to say that border controls continuing after 1 January 1993 should be made subject to a strict test as to their compatibility with the basic prohibitions relating to free movement of persons. That effect of Article 8A seems to me a bare minimum.

If such controls are found to fall under these prohibitions, could the exception clauses of public policy, etc., of Articles 48(3) and 56 (and 66) provide for a possible outlet to continue the internal border controls? The argument would then have to be that the maintenance of these controls is indispensable to protect public policy and public safety in connexion with national policies on immigration, aliens, drugs control and the like. If the maintenance of border controls were to fail the test just mentioned under the basic Treaty prohibitions on free movement, it would seem highly unlikely that they could be saved by the backdoor of invoking the public policy exceptions. The reason for that is not only that justifying *systematic* controls seems almost excluded under these clauses in view of the case-law of the Court (above, para. 8); in addition, the stricter conditions to be applied when interpreting the basic Treaty provisions on free movement in the light of Article 8A EEC should equally have to be respected where the public policy exceptions are in issue.

2.3 Justification of Community powers

10. Assuming that border controls pass the tests just mentioned and survive 31 December 1992, could the Community then assert the necessary powers to legislate so as to establish the indispensable accompanying measures without which internal border controls can still be justified? In its White Paper of 1985 the Commission took the view that it could, without apparently seeing any difficulty in terms of Community competence. That view seems to me fully justified, especially since the coming into force of the Single European Act.

Indeed the situation seems to present a classic example for accepting Community competence. The removal of internal border controls, which is an essential element of the completion of the internal market, is impeded by divergencies between national laws and policies on a certain number of issues. Since the Treaty provides for a general competence clause for that very purpose, namely Article 100A, the conclusion seems to be self-evident. Although Article 100A paragraph 2 excludes the use of this legal basis precisely for matters relating to the free movement of persons, recourse may be had to the other general clause, Article 100. It could hardly be contested that the 'common market' referred to in the latter implies as the wider notion, the characteristics of the internal market as defined by Article 8A.

This interpretation could not be disputed on the basis that the mattters to be harmonised are traditionally considered to fall outside Community competence: immigration policy, national laws on aliens (asylum, visa), drugs control, crime prevention, arms control and so forth. That objection is only partially true on the one hand and not really relevant on the other. It is only partially true because the issues in question are already not entirely free from Community interference. A very old example is to be found in Directive 64/221/EEC harmonizing national laws and policies on handling the public policies exceptions under Articles 48(3), 56 (and 66) EEC. More recent examples are contained in the Directives on insider dealing and money-laundering.[15] More important, however, is to say that no sector of national law is *by its very nature* free from or protected against interference by Community law, unless the Treaties themselves explicitly say so or limit the possibilities for Community intervention (e.g., Arts. 223 and 224). Even criminal law, a subject of much recent discussion, is not safe from Community intrusion as the case-law of the Court clearly demonstrates.[16] In fact the situation *in law* is fairly clear: whenever

---

15. Directive 89/592/EEC, OJ 1989 L 334/30 and Directive 91/308/EEC, OJ 1991 L 166/77.

16. E.g., case 68/88 *Commission of the European Communities* v. *Hellenic Republic* [1989] ECR 2965.

the conditions for the exercise of existing Community powers are met, these powers may be exercised irrespective of the areas of national law involved.[17]

In conclusion, once it is established that a common regime at the external Community borders is *indispensable* to allow and compensate for the removal of internal border controls, the Community should be considered competent to lay down this common regime so as to realise one of the basic elements of the internal market.[18]

11. It is of course *understandable* that this reasoning, which appears flawless in law, is not readily accepted by all Member States in view of the political sensitivity of the subjects involved. Indeed, until recently it was fully legitimate to make a clear distinction between free movement of persons, related primarily to nationals of Member States, as a matter under Community competence on the one hand and policies regarding immigration, aliens, etc., a domain in principle left to Member States on the other hand. The progress of market integration, and in particular the coming into force of the SEA, have blurred this distinction and consequently changed the demarcation line between Community and national powers. Indeed, once the ambition to remove all internal border controls has been accepted as an explicit Community objective, it becomes impossible to continue to exclude in principle policies regarding third country nationals from the ambit of Community law.

Incidentally, this is a fairly general phenomenon, better known under the heading of 'the external dimension of the internal market'. Realising that a common market for goods extending to products originating in third countries would inevitably require a common external regime consisting of a common customs tarif and a common commercial policy, the draftsmen of the Treaty of Rome expressly provided for it. That a similar logic would have to be followed, as integration progressed, for the other fundamental Treaty freedoms, particularly regarding persons and services, has been much less widely acknowledged. Nevertheless, the evolution of Community harmonisation in a number of fields shows that the external dimension is more and more taken into account. Community legislation is rapidly evolving in this respect, somewhat surreptitiously one is sometimes inclined to think. Good examples are to be found in the financial services sector (banking, insurance, stock exchanges) and even company law.[19] As is well known, an early example is

---

17. As to the relevance of the declarations annexed to the Single European Act are concerned, see n. 8.

18. Cf., Donner, loc. cit. n. 3, at pp. 776-782; P. Gilsdorf, 'Die Kompetenz der Gemeinschaft zur Angleichung asylrechtlicher Bestimmungen in der EG', *Europarecht* (1990) p. 65; Hilf, op. cit. n. 6, at p. 359; Pipkorn, op. cit. n. 8, at pp. 203-204.

19. See e.g., the Second Banking Directive 89/646/EEC OJ 1989 L 386/1, the Insurance-services Directive 88/357/EEC OJ 1988 L 172/1 and the agreement between the EEC and Switzerland relating to direct insurance OJ 1991 L 205, see also Directives 79/279/EEC (general conditions for admission), OJ 1979 L 66/21, 80/390/EEC (prospectus), OJ 1980 L 1001, 82/121/EEC (continuous information), OJ 1982 L 48/26, 88/627/EEC (notification of shareholdings), OJ 1988 L 348/62, 89/592/EEC (insider dealing), OJ 1989 L 334/30. See finally in the company law field the Eleventh Directive 89/666/EEC

to be found in the transport sector.[20] It appears that with the external dimension of
the internal market in the sector of free movement of persons, an important new
chapter of Community activity is being, or will be, opened. Yet on reflexion this is
no more than a variation on an already well-known theme.

In summary, there can scarcely be any doubt that, the abolition of internal
border controls of *persons*, which is part of the completion of the internal market,
depends in part on the creation of a common regime on a number of issues related to
immigration and national rules and policies relating to aliens; and that to that extent
the Community is competent to enact such a regime by way of harmonisation
directives under Article 100 EEC.

2.4   Scope of Community powers

12. Accepting a Community power in this context does not necessarily mean that a
common, uniform Community policy must be enacted on these issues of immigration, aliens policy and so forth. As always in these cases, but it might be useful to
repeat that truism, Community regulatory powers are *functionally* limited to and
dependent upon the requirements of integration. In concrete terms, this means that
the scope of Community powers both as regards the limits and the intensity of
Community intervention remains restricted to the indispensable minimum regime
common to Member States which must be introduced to allow for the abolition of
the remaining internal border controls. The application of this rather vague criterion
is of course a matter of judgment for the Community itself, in the last resort subject
to the unanimous decision of Member States in the Council. The only point which I
can usefully add is that Community action for these purposes need not necessarily
take the form of a harmonization of the *substance* of national rules or policies;
laying down a framework for cooperation between national administrations or
transferring controls from the border to the interior might be attractive alternatives.[21]

2.5   Nature of Community powers

13. Where a Community power can be construed to enact the indispensable
accompanying measures to enable the abolition of the internal border controls, what
then is the nature of this power: exclusive, concurrent, or potential? This question
raises the fundamental problem of the delimitation of powers between the Community and its Member States. There is a vast amount of literature on the subject, opinions are divided, the case-law of the Court on the issue is abundant, and shows a

---

(disclosure by branches), OJ 1989 L 395/36.

20. Case 22/70 *Commission of the European Communities* v. *Council of the European Communities,
ERTA*, [1971] ECR 263.

21. See already the White Paper 1985 para. 29 and the transitional approach proposed by the
Commission to abolish frontier controls in relation to VAT.

variety in approaches.[22] This question must therefore be considered with care and caution. The suggestion that Community power to harmonise these matters on the basis of Article 100 EEC are not of an *exclusive* nature, in the sense that they do not exclude action by Member States as long as the Community power remains unused, does not appear to be particularly bold. Nevertheless — the point is not novel — where all Member States agree on the necessity of a common action on the level of the twelve and the Community enjoys the necessary power to act, the Community as such should act, not its Member States by negotiating agreements in an intergovernmental framework. To accept a free option for Member States between using the Community framework or an intergovernmental approach would be incompatible with basic principles of the Community legal system.[23] If, in such circumstances, the Community is competent, the Community should act, not only for constitutional reasons but also for very pragmatic ones linked to the superiority of the Community legal order compared with the results of a classic intergovernmental approach (below, para. 16). The view sometimes advanced that the general harmonization powers of the Community under Article 100 EEC are 'potential' powers (*compétences virtuelles*), which need not be used, if Member States prefer to opt for the intergovernmental way and enact the necessary rules by international treaties, cannot be accepted.[24] Applying the principle of subsidiarity in such a way would too easily undermine the Community and dilute its powers.

14. On the contrary, it would seem less objectionable if only a number of Member States were to agree on the necessity of a common regime and conclude a treaty to that effect (always assuming that Community powers as such are not exercised on the issue in question). As long as such 'regional' arrangements might be considered transitional, allowing for a final solution at the Community level and moreover fully respect Community law, they do not seem to pose any difficulty from a Community point of view.[25] The Schengen Convention which is expressly presented as an interim arrangement pending a final regime at the Community level (or by the twelve, see Arts. 136(2) and 142) and which is expressed to be subject to Community law as the superior rule of law (Art. 134), therefore seems fully in conformity with Community law.

22. See e.g., the detailed analysis by K. Lenaerts, *Le juge et la Constitution aux Etats-Unis d'Amérique et dans l'ordre juridique Européen* (1988).

23. See case 6/64 *Flaminio Costa* v. *ENEL* [1964] ECR 594: 'The transfer by the States from their domestic legal systems to the Community legal system of the rights and obligations arising under the Treaty carries with it a permanent limitation of their sovereign rights . . .' This concept has been consistently applied in the *Euratom* case 7/71 *Commission of the European Communities* v. *French Republic* [1971] ECR 1003. See also on this subject I.E. Schwartz in the forthcoming fourth edition of Von der Groeben Thiesing Ehlermann, *Kommentar zum EWG-Vertrag*, Artikel 220 p. 21 et seq., Artikel 235 p. 60 et seq.

24. See, however, Hilf, op. cit. n. 6, at pp. 358-359.

25. Cf., with the judgment in the *Kramer* case where the Court formulated similar conditions in a situation where an external Community competence had not yet become exclusive, cases 3, 4 and 6/76 [1976] ECR 1279.

15. The situation becomes more complicated where all Member States do agree on the necessity of a common regime for the twelve but *disagree* on the existence or the extent of Community powers to enact such a regime. That is precisely what has occurred in relation to the issues discussed in this paper. The Commission provisionally accepted the initiatives taken by Member States to achieve the necessary solutions by international treaties. This was not because in the Commission's view Member States have a free option between the Community and the intergovernmental approach, but because the Commission did not wish to lose time in doctrinal disputes on competences, which might delay the work to be done within the strict timetable imposed by the 1992 exercise. The Commission reserved the possibility of launching a Community initiative, were the intergovernmental attempts to fail or not produce sufficient results.[26]

16. Would not another solution have been for the Commission to insist on the Community approach and if the intergovernmental approach was nevertheless pursued, to start infringement procedures against Member States for breach of Community competence, or start an action under Article 175 EEC against the Council for failure to act (the latter action would have required the Commission first to submit the necessary proposals for Community action to the Council)? In the past the Commission has on various occasions brought fairly delicate and politically highly sensitive questions on the delimitation of powers between Community and Member States before the Court of Justice.[27] In the case in question the Commission has apparently preferred not to go for a judicial solution because of the delays this would inevitably have involved. Indeed, in all probability Member States would have suspended any further action awaiting the outcome of the Court's proceedings.

One might think by the way that on politically delicate issues like the ones in question it would be more attractive to ask the *opinion* of the Court under Article 228 paragraph 2 EEC instead of starting contentious procedures like an infringement procedure or a procedure for failure to act. The Court has already shown in the past its willingness to interpret quite generously the conditions of admissibility of such an application, notably in accepting questions on the division of external competences between Community and Member States.[28] Would it be too daring to suggest that the Court having already accepted to apply this procedure in a case where the Community as such did *not* envisage at all to conclude an agreement precisely because Member States argued to have remained competent,[29] could still go a step further by accepting to give an opinion on the division of competences between the Community and its Member States even in a situation where the treaty envisaged

26. See the Communication of the Commission of 7 December 1988 on the abolition of controls of persons at intra-Community borders (COM(88) 640 final) and the combined answer of Vice-President Bangemann to a number of written parliamentary questions, OJ 1991 C 141/6 and 7.
27. The obvious example is the *ERTA* case referred to in n. 20.
28. See Opinion 1/75 [1975] ECR 1355 and Opinion 1/78 [1979] ECR 2871.
29. See Opinion 1/75 referred to in the previous note.

would be concluded between Member States alone and would not involve the participation of third countries?

2.6 Advantages of a Community instrument

17. Generally speaking, using the Community framework instead of the classic instrument of an international treaty negotiated between the twelve EC Member States within an intergovernmental framework has some obvious advantages both in terms of efficiency and speed and, even more importantly, safeguards for a uniform application of the rules in question. Enacting the necessary rules by Community instrument instead of an international treaty will as a rule be more expeditious, since approval by national parliaments is not required.[30] The obvious objection to that is to refer to the deficient democratic legitimacy of the Community decision making process. Indeed, in the cases in hand (Art. 100 EEC), the European Parliament would have no more than an advisory role to play, the cooperation procedure not being applicable. This is a well-known debate, the terms of which might be changed by the way in the near future by the results of the intergovernmental conference on Political Union. I refrain from entering into the discussion, but only note that the perception by national parliaments themselves is not necessarily so negative as far as the Community system is concerned. Indeed, the Second Chamber of the Dutch Parliament in a debate on the Schengen Convention passed a resolution, asking the Government to opt for a Community approach to the issues covered by the Schengen Agreement and to raise the matter at Community level.[31] One of the reasons given was that realising the free movement of persons within the EC and enacting the necessary measures for that purpose should not increase the democratic deficit in Europe. The Dutch parliament obviously took the view that its powers to approve the treaties to be concluded were not sufficient to satisfy the necessary standards in this respect.

The attitude of the Dutch parliament might be explained by the fact that the Community decision-making procedure is normally of a much more open and transparent nature than the rather closed circuit of an intergovernmental negotiation. Since the European parliament is involved from the beginning in the decision-making process on a proposal submitted by the Commission, it is apparently considered to have more possibilities in practice to influence the final outcome than a national parliament which on the submittance of an international treaty can only say yes or no to the final result. In most cases saying no, is not a real option. A more machiavellian interpretation of the Dutch parliament's position might be that it hoped to improve, its own factual possibility of control and influence the Government's position on these issues because of the transparency of the Community's decision-making process, in the event that a Community approach was followed.

---

30. Cf., on the subject I.E. Schwartz, 'Verordnungen der Europäischen Gemeinschaften oder Übereinkommen unter den Mitgliedstaaten?', in *Festschrift für Caemmerer* (1978) p. 1067.

31. Motion by Van Traa, De Hoop and Scheffer of 13 June 1990, Second Chamber 19.326 No. 35.

Plainly, the argument that a Community instrument is more expeditious than a treaty, applies equally to future amendments of the regime in question. Moreover, an obvious disadvantage of a treaty approach is that each accession of a new Member State to the Community requires a new ratification procedure of the treaty in question by all Member States (see the example of the 1968 Brussels Convention on Enforcement of Judgments).

18. A second, more important, consequence of having a Community instrument is of course that the common regime so enacted benefits from the advantages deriving from the status of Community law: primacy over divergent national law, possibility of direct effect and the availability of the judicial mechanisms under the treaties to ensure a uniform interpretation of the rules in question, particularly the preliminary procedure of Article 177 EEC but also the infringement procedure of Articles 169 and 170 EEC. It might be added that the application of the Community rules in national legal practice automatically benefits also from the national system of legal review and legal protection which is not necessarily ensured with regard to the implementation of an international treaty, in so far it has not been incorporated into national law.[32]

19. Applying these general arguments to the issues considered in this paper, two further more specific advantages of a Community approach could be mentioned:
Let us suppose that a common regime on asylum enacted by a Community instrument was not limited to procedural matters but also applied to the substance of national asylum policies and practices. In that event, the underlying international regime to which all Member States are committed — the Refugees Convention of Geneva of 28 July 1951 as amended by the Protocol of New York of 31 January 1967 — would inevitably be drawn into the ambit of the Community legal order.[33] Whether it could be argued that in such a situation the Community itself becomes bound by this convention and will succeed to the Member States to the extent that the Community regime materially covers the subjects of the Convention — a kind of de facto succession as in the case of GATT[34] — requires further thought but does not seem to be entirely excluded. If so, the application of the Convention within Member States would benefit from the safeguards of a uniform interpretation under the preliminary procedure of Article 177 EEC. At any rate, it can be assumed in the light of earlier precedents of this kind that the Court of Justice will be prepared, when interpreting a Community instrument on asylum, to take into account the

---

32. See the example of the European Human Rights Convention in the United Kingdom.
33. To some extent that has been achieved already by Art. 1 (d) of Regulation 1408/71 on social security of migrant workers which uses the notion of 'refugee' and refers for its meaning to the Geneva Convention.
34. See joined cases 21-24/72 *International Fruit Company* v. *Productschap voor Groenten en Fruit*, [1972] ECR 1219.

Refugees Convention to which all Member States are a party.[35] Were that to happen, one of the main causes of divergence between actual Member States' policies on asylum might disappear: the varying interpretation of the notion of refugee under the Geneva Convention.[36]

In the same vein a similar evolution could occur with regard to human rights protection within this context. A Community regime on asylum would have to be structured *and* implemented in conformity with the human rights standards applying in the Community legal order under the control of the Court of Justice. This protection would also extend to the action by Member States implementing a Community regime.[37] Consequently, the harmonization effects of a Community regime would by itself spill over to the aspects of human rights protection within the scope of this regime. If so, problems in this respect created by a treaty approach in some Member States could possibly be solved at the same time.[38]

(b) A further advantage of a Community instrument instead of a Treaty approach would consist of better guarantees for transparency and legal security as far as implementing measures and procedures are concerned. The regime in question will not be realised by one set of rules complete in itself. The examples of the Schengen Convention, as well as the Dublin Asylum Convention and the Frontiers Convention indicate that in all probability the implementation of the common regime will require further rule-making by regulatory bodies. The Conventions in question attribute regulatory powers for that purpose to mixed committees. However, rule-making by such a procedure has some obvious disadvantages, not only in terms of transparency but also because the status of such rules is unclear; furthermore their uniform interpretation and application is not ensured. In some contracting parties, the Netherlands for instance, rules enacted by such mixed committees will probably be immediately applicable in national legal practice, in others, however, they will have the status of international agreements (in a simplified form), which are not automatically incorporated in the national legal order. No such problems would occur, were the regime to be enacted by Community instrument, the Community disposing of a well tried mechanism of rule-making by delegation with sufficient safeguards regarding the status of these rules, and their uniform interpretation by the European Court.

---

35. See case 89/76 *Commission of the European Communities* v. *Kingdom of the Netherlands* [1977] ECR 1355, case 289/86 *Happy Family* v. *Inspecteur der Omzetbelasting* [1988] ECR 3669 and *Witzemann*, Judgment of 6 December 1990, case C-343/89 [1990] ECR I-4477.

36. See Hilf, op. cit. n. 6, p. 347 with further references.

37. See for this phenomenon of 'incorporation' J. Weiler, 'The European Court at a Crossroad: Community Human Rights and Member State Action', in *Liber Amicorum Pierre Pescatore* (1987), p. 821; for recent examples see judgment of 18 October 1990, case C-297/88 *Massam Dzodzi* v. *Kingdom of Belgium*, [1990] ECR I-3763 and judgment of 25 July 1991, case C-353/89 *Commission of the European Communities* v. *Kingdom of the Netherlands*, OJ No. C 224/3.

38. See Hilf, op. cit. n. 6, at p. 361 et seq. and Gilsdorf, loc. cit. n. 18, at p. 67.

20. Accordingly, my personal conclusion is that in terms of legal techniques and mechanisms the quality of the Community legal order is highly superior to that of classic international public law, also for the subject-matter considered in this paper. That being so, the preference of some Member States for the intergovernmental approach is difficult to understand, but that might be a slightly naïve statement.

3. SUMMARY OF CONCLUSIONS

I. The obligation imposed upon the Community under Article 8A EEC to establish the internal market before 1 January 1993 implies the abolition of all internal border controls of persons between Member States. Continuing border controls only with regard to nationals from third countries is incompatible with this obligation.

II. Border controls in the strict sense with regard to EC nationals are only compatible with Treaty rules on free movement when they remain limited to *identity* controls. These controls do not automatically become illegal on the expiry of the deadline laid down by Article 8A EEC. However, since the basic Treaty rules on free movement have to be interpreted with due regard to Article 8A, continuing border controls (identity controls) after 31 December 1992 will have to be put to a strict test of necessity and proportionality. The main question to be considered will be whether the possible absence at that date of the indispensable accompanying measures to substitute internal border controls can justify continuing these controls.

III. The Community enjoys the necessary powers to enact the accompanying measures to the extent that it can be demonstrated that such measures are indispensable to allow for the abolition of the internal border controls. The legal basis for these measures should be Article 100 EEC.

IV. The scope of Community powers in this respect is functionally limited to the realisation of the objective of free movement, that is to enact the minimum regime required to compensate for and thus allow the abolition of internal border controls.

V. The Community powers are not exclusive. If, however, the necessity of a common regime at the level of the Twelve is acknowledged by all Member States and the competence of the Community to act is in principle accepted, action should be taken by the Community, not by the Member States negotiating international treaties. In Community law Member States are not free to opt between an intergovernmental or a Community approach. This does not exclude transitional regimes negotiated between a limited number of Member States, like the Schengen Agreement provided that Community law is duly respected.

VI. The Community approach presents some obvious advantages over an intergovernmental one in terms of speed (no ratification required on the national level), primacy over inconsistent national law, the existence of a judicial mechanism to ensure a uniform interpretation (Art. 177 EEC). To use a Community approach on the issues in question has moreover some specific advantages by facilitating a uniform interpretation in the Community of the international common law on asylum (Geneva Refugees Convention), and facilitating a Community solution to the problems related to the protection of human rights. Moreover using the Community framework would ensure better transparency and legal certainty with regard to implementing rules which the practical application of a common regime will require.

FREE MOVEMENT OF PERSONS – DEMOCRATIC CONTROL

Joost P. van Iersel[*]

1.   DEMOCRATIC CONTROL

The series of subjects which are in question in the realization of the free movement of persons in Europe form a multi-coloured pallet. However, they have in common that they were still recently considered to be in the exclusive dominion of the national State. It is not possible to predict to what extent sovereignty rights will gradually lose in power in this area. Ultimately, there exists a nexus between the area of justice and European integration in general. This coupling has resulted in the negotiations on 'Schengen'. Although the negotiations were concerned with a treaty, it was readily apparent that the interest of the parliaments became stronger due to the sensitivity of the subjects addressed. In any case, this occurred in the Netherlands which is one of the countries with a strong parliamentary regime. The influence of the Dutch parliament in the decision-making process of the Government is, when measured against international standards, remarkable.

I have been asked to illuminate certain aspects of democratic control. I will base my comments principally on experiences in my own country. However, I am of the opinion that these experiences also contain lessons for other Member States and for the European Community as such. In the long period of transition from the nation-state to a federal European Constitution with all its related conflicts, I am of the opinion that nationial parliaments must exercise their roles to the fullest extent. They remain an integral part of the democratic process and confer democratic legitimacy on what occurs in the management of the Community. This is particularly the case in those fields where sovereign national rights are still fully in place.

Briefly the involvement of the Dutch parliament in the negotiations on 'Schengen' can be described as follows. Initially the negotiations took place with silent approval from the parliament. Undoubtedly, this was also due to the fact that the discussions concerned intergovernmental negotiations about the realization of a treaty. However, later on the Schengen Convention dealt with a multitude of subjects worthy of publicity. In addition to the fact that the negotiations took longer and gradually became more public, this brought about active interference on the part of the parliament. In this process the uncertainty increased and parliament became

---

*   Member of the Second Chamber of the States General for the Christian Democratic Party (CDA), The Netherlands.

H.G. Schermers et al., eds., Free Movement of Persons in Europe
© 1993, T.M.C. Asser Instituut, The Hague.

increasingly annoyed with regard to the precise contents and reach of the Schengen Convention. In turn, this has led to the provision of more information from the side of the Government. In the result the position of parliament in the negotiations on treaties became more profiled. The general rule is that parliament subsequently accepts or rejects the result of negotiations. In the instant case the Second Chamber gradually asked for more information during the negotiations, which was provided in confidence. Thus, from a certain moment onward the Chamber actually became concretely involved in the negotiation process. Subsequently the Government informed parliament about the state of affairs and available options prior to negotiations starting. It was noted, however, that this method could slow the negotiations and even damage the ultimate result. Negotiation results were thus partly made dependent on the degree of parliamentary interference.

2.   NATIONAL SOVEREIGNTY

The free movement of persons is one of the four freedoms of the EC Treaty and of the Single European Act (Art. 8A) which until recently did not appeal greatly to political imagination. This freedom was only considered to be a free movement of workers who were not to be hindered by limiting provisions of the Member States. In a number of association treaties this freedom was interpreted in the same way. The Council of Ministers has dealt with great circumspection where broadening the concept of 'free movement' could affect national legal practice and traditions. This circumspection is also apparent in the suggestion of Luxembourg's chairmanship in the intergovernmental conference on the EPU where the chapter on Justice which deals with important parts of free movement is taken up in a separate column next to the chapters of the internal market on the one hand, and of foreign and security policy, on the other. However, it is unavoidable that a comprehensive arrangement for the entire topic of 'free movement' will come about. In the first place, the area which is designated by the Community gradually moves beyond strictly economically-based subjects. Secondly, it is questionable that one legal system continues to define different types of 'free movement', namely, one which is related to the functioning of the labour market and one for other matters. Therefore, it is understandable that a number of Member States are in favour of achieving a complete regulation of the free movement of persons. The complexity of the subject being dealt with, however, suggests on the contrary that only a partial arrangement between the participating Member States will result. The objective of a realization of a full common market, on the one hand, and the existing legal organization and legal opinions and traditions in the Member States, on the other, are still too disparate. In other words, the basis of national sovereignty is at stake and no State wants as yet to be limited in this respect.

3. ROLE OF THE NATIONAL PARLIAMENTS

There are further considerations which plead for a more active role for the national parliaments. In particular this is the case for States where parliaments play an active role in regard to European integration. This role varies in several States. For example, in France there is only a limited involvement. In the UK, Denmark, Germany, and the Netherlands there is a more intensive involvement with the integration process, as is reflected in the involvement with the Schengen process. In the Netherlands the involvement of parliament in EC matters became much more significant since the start of the 'Europe 1992' project in 1986. At the same time, the establishment of a standing committee for EC matters unquestionably has had a stimulating effect. Before that there was only a limited interest by European specialists in parliament and the discussion with the Government was limited to agricultural politics and general issues of economic, finance, and foreign policy.

The interest of the Dutch parliament increased as more subjects appeared on the agenda in Brussels which would significantly affect the life of the citizen. In the Netherlands a particular value is attached to the democratic functioning of the Community. The strengthening of the European institutions, and in particular the European parliament, is considered a necessity. However, this does not release the national parliaments from active involvement in the European dossier, each using its own traditions and methods of functioning. The national involvement is also a part of European democracy. Moreover, in the Netherlands Europolitics is rarely seen as a matter of foreign policy but much more as a subject of domestic policy, because the influence of 'Brussels' on national laws and regulations which directly affect the life of the citizen has increased so much. The result of this process is that the Dutch parliament gradually has been giving more attention to the EC and the standing committees in parliament regularly discuss subjects with ministers who are negotiating in the Council of Ministers in Brussels. This line of communication between government and parliament is strongly dependent on the type of information to which parliament is privy. Governments, conscious of their own interests are not very willing to provide sufficient information. Therefore, it took a long time before a satisfactory supply of information came into existence. As a result of the special intergovernmental negotiations on 'Schengen' it was even more difficult for the parliament to achieve the provision of information it required and the establishment of a satisfactory consultation procedure. As a result of pressure from parliament, a more positive practice has started to develop. This is also the case for a far broader range of EC issues.

4. POLITICAL REACH

In contrast to many other subjects, the Schengen dossier is certainly not a technical dossier. In the first place, it concerns a topic which directly affects the roots of national sovereignty. Secondly, the dossier deals with a number of aspects located in areas which have traditionally had nothing to do with the common market, while nevertheless being extremely sensitive to public opinion. These subjects include drug policy, asylum seekers, international terrorism, illicit drug trade, and criminal law. The subject is closely connected to fundamental aspects of the general interest. In the third place, the general interest is even more affected because the above-mentioned subjects are also part of national policy discussions apart from the European policy discussions. In the fourth place, the dossier concerns several relevant political questions which increase in importance due to the attraction of the Community in middle and eastern Europe and in North Africa. Against this background it is remarkable that the 'Schengen' negotiations took place without much interest from the outside. The Dutch parliament was initially also not interested, as I said before. The Second Chamber silently approved the Schengen Agreement of 14 June 1985. There appeared to be no problems. I am under the impression that the civil servants who were negotiating at that time also saw relatively few problems.

Only in 1988 did the political discussion commence. The interest of the parliament was primarily the result of publications in the press. From the moment that Schengen was on the agenda of the Chamber regular discussions took place between the Chamber and the Cabinet primarily based on the provision of information from the side of the Government. Thus far this has resulted in eight consultations between Government and parliament and two plenary debates. As a result of this exchange between the Chamber and the Cabinet a Dutch view has been established and worked out. This procedure reflects the state of affairs in the Netherlands with regard to subjects which are under consideration in the EC. As a result of the intergovernmental character of the negotiations, this was not the case during the first years of 'Schengen'. Each Member State has developed methods on the basis of own traditions to define national positions for discussions in the EC system. When a Member State has an active and reasonably independently functioning parliament, there will frequently be a detailed exchange of ideas about the most desirable position. In Member States where parliament plays a less profiled role, its vote with regard to national points for negotiation will not be heard as loudly. The situation is different from country to country sometimes to a large degree.

5.   PUBLIC OPINION

The experience in the Netherlands is that a critical position of the Chamber with regard to what should be decided in the EC operates beneficially on public opinion. Subjects become more lively when they are dealt with in a political forum. We have to admit that the effectiveness of the parliamentary procedure can be questioned. It is undeniable that intensive parliamentary procedures can have a slowing effect. At the same time, a positive correction of policies may result. Speaking for the Netherlands, the increased involvement of the parliament in EC topics has activated the interest of the media, has made the Government more aware of the complications which may arise, and has provided support for those elements in the central Government which are strongly in favour of a precise approximation between national and European law and practice. There is a mixture of objections and benefits, whereby the vision remains primarily that active involvement of the national parliament, next to that of the European parliament, is necessary to maintain the democratic character of the decision-making process and democratic control.

The above-mentioned theoretical concept about the interaction between Chamber and Cabinet is reflected in the Netherlands in the Schengen dossier. In the frequent and lengthy consultations of the parliament the accent lies clearly on the free movement of persons. The free movement of goods forms an important section of the Schengen Agreement, but it has not received any particular attention in parliamentary dealings. This is a weakness in parliamentary involvement because attention is understandably directed towards subjects which are media sensitive. This last effect can be strengthened because the outside lobbies also aim at those aspects. That is an inescapable given, but it can lead to a skewing of priorities in debate. Nevertheless, virtually all aspects of the free movement of persons in the framework of the Schengen negotiations are dealt with by the Second Chamber in the Netherlands.

6.   SENSITIVE SUBJECTS

Within the limited scope of this paper it is not possible to analyze the great variety of subjects involved. It is especially important to direct the attention of the reader towards certain structural elements. The interest of the Dutch parliament was primarily directed towards the question of asylum seekers. Presently, the EC is enjoying great popularity. Its attractiveness increases day by day. Despite national measures the tide of immigration of primarily illegal aliens does not seem to stop. Each participating Member State has an interest in the establishment of an asylum policy on a very strict basis or that the national policy on the subject remains prevalent. Gradually, this subject had received more attention in parliamentary dealings in the Netherlands. The Second Chamber has argued strongly for a European harmonisation of asylum policy. The common expulsion policy has also received much attention. Another subject which has aroused a lot of attention is the drug policy and its implications for the free movement of persons. In this case widely differing views of the Member States are involved. Particularly the French and the Germans have criticized Dutch policy. It formed a virtually insurmountable obstacle for the entire Schengen dossier. Lately more understanding has developed with regard to the Dutch drug policy because the effects of this policy are not at all negative and because the subject has been released from its ideological load. The facts are being regarded in a more business-like manner.

One of the positive side-effects of 'Schengen' is that interest has increased for medical, police, and juridical supervision for drug addicts, This issue was discussed at length in parliament and differences of opinion between the political parties emerged. These differences of opinion are naturally divided along the same lines as those in the similar discussion on the subject which has been addressed nationally for a long time. In a country such as the Netherlands where great interest has always been attached to the protection of individual privacy, it is no surprise that the issue of the Schengen Information System was regularly on the parliament's agenda.

Regarding this subject there is a clear relation with the domestic discussion about whether an obligation of identification should be instituted. In the Netherlands this has hitherto not been the case due to memories of World War II. Opinions have recently changed leading to a proposal of the Government which should provide for a limited but effective obligation of identification. Schengen and the practices elsewhere in Europe have aided this process. Another subject which enjoyed great attention was the issue of border controls. There is a close connection between judicial and police practices which, as is generally known, are based on lengthy traditions of legal practice and legal theory in each country.

7.   THREE REMARKS OF A GENERAL NATURE

This enumeration of subjects leads me to make three remarks of a general nature. First, as a result of the negotiations on 'Schengen' it has become clear that it will take a lot of time before the Community will be comprised of an *espace judiciaire*. Therefore, it is notable, but explicable, that Interior Affairs and Justice in the proposal of Luxembourg's chairmanship for a new treaty text has ended up in a separate or 'pillar' column corresponding to the arrangements for foreign and security policies. The predicted three-pillar structure does not, in my opinion, detract from the view that the common political aim of an integrated Europe, the *finalité politique*, is maintained in the composing of the new treaty text even though different decision-making procedures are envisaged for the different fields of policy. The unity of the EC Treaty may not be endangered. If this were to occur, the foundations of the integration process itself would be endangered.

My second remark is that 'Schengen', not surprisingly, does not envisage complete common arrangements but procedures which ensure free movement, thereby maintaining national concepts and practices intact. On top of that the national control mechanisms keep their existing meanings to an important extent. In this way the limits of integration in these specific non-economic areas remain visible.

My third remark is that as a result of the public discussion in the Netherlands which has been stimulated by the involvement of the parliament, national insights are again subjected to examination. This may also be the case in areas where European harmonization is not foreseeable for the time being. This means that those areas where strict national procedures and norms are in place will increasingly be influenced by the main trends in Europe. It is really enriching to see that there is a much greater exchange of information and that opinions are much more tested than was ever the case in the period of the exclusive nation State.

In other words, the fact that national regimes are being maintained in certain sectors does not at all impede a further convergence of views and practices. In other areas a parallel development can be seen. Public statements in the national parliaments can add to these developments in their own way. In this respect, I point to a resolution which the Dutch parliament approved in 1989 in which the Dutch Government was invited to test all new proposals or changes in the national legal system as to their foreseeable effects in relation to EC legislation. It seems logical to apply a similar rule with regard to existing or foreseeable legal proposals in other Member States. It is obvious that in areas where the national law is still strictly applicable a review possibility as described above faces stiff opposition in those cases where national sovereignty is felt to be at stake. Parliamentary interference in the Netherlands has shown this. In their Member States the situation is no different.

8.   NECESSITY OF SUFFICIENT INFORMATION

Of course, the public debate provides an excess of reasons for active lobbies. During 1988 a powerful lobby developed in the direction of social-democrats and left-leaning liberals which concentrated on the rights of asylum seekers and minorities in general. Hereunder I name the *Vereniging Vluchtelingenwerk Nederland* (Association for Refugee Work in the Netherlands), the *Nederlands Centrum Buitenlanders* (The Netherlands Centre for Foreigners), and the *Nederlands Juristen Comité voor de Mensenrechten* (The Netherlands Committee of Lawyers for Human Rights). These organisations disposed of the necessary inside information at that stage and they competently brought this information to the attention of the leaders of the various factions. These activities can benefit parliamentary discussions, but there is a danger of over-accentuation of certain aspects. It is obvious that, especially in the period that the Government provided little information to the Chamber, the interests supported by such organisations were given strong emphasis in the political discussion. There can be no other conclusion but that the Cabinet is well served by the balanced provision of information where it wants to establish a balanced political discussion.

In this case another fundamental point is in issue. At present, an intensive discussion is taking place regarding adaptations of the working procedures of the Second Chamber. Particularly the changes in the European context inspire new views leading to further adaptations. Integration and European legislation require a restructuring of methods and procedures. The road along which the relations between the parliament and the Government developed with regard to the Schengen dossier also raised the question whether there was a need for a general legal arrangement with regard to the provision of information before treaties are signed. The general opinion of the Chamber about this issue is positive due in part to the experiences of the Schengen dossier. Apart from 'Schengen' the position can be defended that a similar practice is warrantable in all those cases where the results of treaties directly influence the lives and circumstances of sectors of the population. Concretely, the introduction of such a procedure in the approval of a treaty would lead to an exchange of views between the Cabinet and the Chamber which is similar to the establishment of national law and rules, albeit that the margins for both would be much smaller in the international context, because it would be related to international negotiations. Presently the Government is ready to provide more information. The Chamber is aware of the narrow margins in the negotiation process within the EC and in respect of treaties although the narrowness of such margins may become sources of irritation. Parliament and the Government are increasingly confronted with diminishing national sovereignty.

9.   'SCHENGEN' AS A MODEL FOR THE EC?

It seems that the Schengen process has gradually had greater influence on the legal order of participating countries than was anticipated initially. 'Schengen' might thus become a forerunner of regulation within the EC context. Until recently the question was whether an EC arrangement would come into place at all and to what extent this would be a reflection of the Schengen Agreement itself. The circumstances have dramatically been altered. Recently Spain and Portugal have joined Schengen along with Italy, and Greece is soon to follow. Only the UK, which wants to guard its borders from fear of terrorist attacks, and Denmark are apprehensive thus far. All this is added to the fact that the negotiations on Schengen in the EC context are not running smoothly leads to the tentative conclusion that the Schengen Agreement will be of directive value for virtually the entire Community until the year 2000.

No argument needs to be made that the problems which have arisen between the five original participating countries only expand in intensity and depth as the number of participants increase. Moreover, dramatic change of circumstances results in an increase in problems. The Community gains in popularity daily. Foreigners and refugees come to Europe from a far to seek prosperity. The border of the Community will not be able to hold back immigration from North Africa, central and eastern Europe, and the Soviet Union. How can the borders of the southern European Countries be effectively protected against unwanted immigration, drug dealers, and international terrorists? Concerning the eastern part of our continent, the question does not become less timely now that the respective visa requirements are gone, the borders are open, and economic interdependence is becoming more intensive. The number of immigrants will increase as the differences between stability and instability, on the one hand, and rich and poor, on the other, become more polarized. Comparison with the United States becomes more apparent.

10.   CRITICAL OPINION OF THE PARLIAMENTS

Against this background, a more critical attitude may be expected from the national parliaments especially when the Member States run into more problems in the execution practices as a consequence of a too-liberalized free movement. It is not unthinkable that the opinion will prevail that orderless internal free movement within the Community is desirable, but only after an effective external border is guaranteed. Consequently a speedy signing of the Treaty regarding the external borders is of great importance. The Dutch Government has rightly coupled this treaty to the further elaboration of Article 8A of the Single European Act.

The influence of the Second Chamber in the Netherlands is not accurately measurable. Without doubt it is a partial mouthpiece for concerned groups in the country. Furthermore, the public debate has gained in intensity as a result of the political debates. Above all, discussion became more colourful because the Schengen dossier was deprived of all its technocratic character. In the meantime it is clear that the influence of the Chamber is greatest when not only the Government parties support certain opinions, but the largest possible majority does so. It is undeniable that the interest in the free movement of persons has decreased. Undoubtedly this is related to the dramatically changing circumstances of recent years, apart from the differences in legislation and execution practices in the various Member States.

Concerning the subjects on which the Dutch parliament exercises specific influence, I mention the material harmonisation of the asylum policy and the so-called compensating provisions. In the opinion of the Chamber not only should the admission policy be harmonized, but the deportation policy should also be harmonized. As a consequence of the pressure brought to bear by the Chamber, the Minister of Foreign Affairs pays full attention to this question while this prerequisite is also finding a positive response in other Member States. This subject is a priority of the Dutch presidency of the EC Council. A second demand made by the Dutch parliament concerns the so-called compensating measures. This means that the military police, which is no longer required for border traffic, is used elsewhere in the country in regard to alien control. Furthermore, in the view of the Second Chamber, the Government has to budget an extra Dfl. 100 million for this supervision. Lastly, the Chamber wants the Schengen Information System to be implemented in an original Dutch system.

The Dutch discussion has not ended. Especially in social-democrat circles which want to amend the Schengen Agreement with the aid of related factions in other Schengen countries, opposition is growing due to the way in which Schengen has foreseen the beginning of new floods of aliens. In contrast, the christian democrats are supporters of a clear division between well-founded and unfounded requests for asylum. The social democrats see eye to eye with two party-affiliated secretaries of State, namely, those for Justice and for Foreign Affairs, who are primarily responsible for the negotiations over Schengen. I do not share the opinions of the social-democrats. I am convinced that the results of negotiation must be accepted under the assumption that the aforementioned demand for compensating measures will be satisfied. One cannot renew discussions about issues when circumstances change. Above all, I am of the opinion that well-founded requests for asylum will be better dealt with in the framework of Schengen than is presently the case. In more general terms, the questioning of the results which have been achieved could endanger the entire process and could have damaging effects on other parts of the integration process.

The future looks as follows. In September 1991 the Second Chamber will receive written commentaries on the Schengen Agreement from lobbyist groups. The written exchange of opinions between the Chamber and the Cabinet is planned for the period from October to December. The plenary parliamentary debates in the Second and First Chambers of the States General will take place in the first half of 1992. Via this procedure, which does not diverge from the normal legislative procedure, the Dutch policy makers will integrate the international obligations into the national legal system. Throughout the consultations on the Agreement during the negotiation process, the Chamber gave form to its duty to exercise democratic control. In the legislative procedure her role as joint legislator will be given extra stature.

11.   CLOSING REMARK

One of the most remarkable developments of late is that Europe is well on its way to becoming a multi-racial society. For national communities this development has enormous consequences for which they are not prepared. Governments and parliaments are concerned to put this process on the best possible track. This means that in countries where there is an extensive degree of parliamentary control over government policy subjects such as free movement of persons in the EC will continue to receive much attention. This attention will be critical. Scepticism can easily gain the upperhand. At the same time it is perfectly clear that European integration and the free movement of persons are inextricably linked. For supporters of European unification it is essential to ensure that national legislation in the Member States will not diverge further and, on the other hand, that the arrangements which are being formed in the Member States are in accordance with the ultimate goal to liberalize the Community also for the movement of persons.

DEMOCRATIC CONTROL WITHOUT FRONTIERS?
The European parliament and free movement of persons

Mathilde M. van den Brink and Rob M.S. Vierhout[*]

1. INTRODUCTION

One of the objectives of the Treaty of Rome is the free movement of persons between the Member States of the European Community. To that end, it is imperative to abolish all types of frontier barriers between the Member States. The principle of the free movement of persons (goods, services and capital) was reiterated in the significant, though highly ambiguous, Article 8A of the 1987 Single European Act on the establishment of an internal market. The free movement of persons derives its importance from the fact that a real Community cannot exist without the concurrent free and unhampered movement and residence of the peoples living within its territory.

The Community is, however, primarily an economic community in terms of an internal or common market (cf., the objectives and Arts. 8A and 100 set out in the EEC Treaty). This means that the nationals of the Member States must be allowed free movement in relation to such economic considerations. As a consequence, the Community legislation that has been adopted or proposed thus far mainly refers to the freedom of movement for workers and the self-employed and, as of late, also for pensioners and students.

In recent years the debate over the free movement of persons has focused mainly on the political and legal dimensions. This can be explained by the increased attention given to the free movement of persons who cannot be principally regarded as economic subjects. The abolition of the internal borders of the Community means that non-EC citizens, such as immigrants, refugees, and even criminals, are, in principle, free to move around and to reside anywhere they want within the Community. More recently, both the debate and the legislation have focussed increasingly on the compensating safety measures at a national level and at the external borders that may be needed to offset the abolition of the internal frontiers.

This increased emphasis on internal safety has led to a shift in the decision-making procedures relating to the free movement of persons. The relevant decisions, which were made previously at a Community level, based on proposals from the European

* Mathilde van den Brink is a member of the European Parliament and part of the Socialist Group. She is a member of the Committee on Civil Liberties and Internal Affairs. Rob Vierhout is a staff member of the PvdA-Eurodelegation.

H.G. Schermers et al., eds., Free Movement of Persons in Europe
© 1993, T.M.C. Asser Instituut, The Hague.

Commission, are now made exclusively at the intergovernmental level with minimal social and parliamentary involvement.

We must then ask ourselves whether the course taken by the Member States does not infringe on democracy, particularly at a European level, and on the legal security of the European citizen.

The European Parliament (hereinafter the Parliament) is engaged in a continuous battle with both the Commission and the Council to counter the lack of democratic influence and control. The Parliament considers this to be a legitimate campaign on the grounds that where the Member States are involved in cross-border transactions, democracy also requires cross-border expression. In other words, the Community is or should be a a frontier-free democracy, so to speak, at least with respect to decisions affecting Community objectives.

The purpose of this report is to describe the role of the Parliament in achieving a freer movement of persons. First, we shall focus on the legal basis for regulation in this sphere, as well as on the political arena. Second, we will describe the legal margin of the Parliament and its relation to the Council and the Commission. We conclude the report with a brief consideration of the developments expected in this field, and some closing remarks.

2.   LEGAL BASIS

The free movement of persons within the Community is a task set down 35 years ago. As the Council of State stated justly in its notice regarding the Schengen Convention: 'the pursuit of the gradual abolition of identity controls at the internal frontiers of the Member States is included in the EEC Treaty.' [1]

The Treaty Articles that refer explicitly to the free movement of persons are 3(c), 8A, 48 to 58 and paragraphs 1 and 2 of Article 100A. The Articles 8A and 100A were added to the Treaty with the adoption of the 1987 Single European Act. These articles must be considered in conjunction with the 'Declaration on Article 8A of the EEC Treaty' and the 'Political Declaration by the Governments of the Member States on the Free Movement of Persons,' both of which are annexed to the Single European Act.

To date, regulation of the free movement of persons within the Community has been limited to freedom of movement for workers, the self-employed, and their families. Article 48 of the Treaty provides for freedom of movement for workers by requiring the abolition of any discrimination based on nationality between workers of the Member States as regards employment, remuneration and other conditions of work and employment. Workers also have the right to accept offers of employment made in another Member State and to reside there. Article 48 was the basis for Directive 68/360/

---

1. See notice No. WO2.91.0018 from the Council of State of 8 April 1991, p. 1.

EEC and Regulation 1612/68.[2] Article 52 of the Treaty provides for the freedom of establishment for the self-employed, and Directive 73/148/EEC provides for the right of residence for the families of the self-employed.

In 1990 the Council adopted laws on the right of residence (in a general sense) for 'EC nationals' (Directive 90/364/EEC), pensioners (Directive 90/365/EEC) and students (Directive 90/366/EEC).[3] As is the case for most Community legislation, the Member States are allowed to derogate from the provisions of these directives on grounds of public policy, public security or public health as is set out in the earlier Directive 64/221/EEC.[4]

When the White Paper was presented in 1985, it became clear that the Community wanted to place the free movement of persons within a wider context. Since a completed internal market would no longer have internal frontiers nor frontier controls, this required coordination of some national laws not explicitly referring to the right of residence.

The proposals the Commission was going to table on this subject were to take Art. 100A(2) or Article 235 as a legal basis.[5] However, since the Commission has never submitted any such proposals, the debate on the appropriate legal basis remains purely speculative.

The fact that the Commission did not submit the majority of the proposals planned can be attributed to the pronounced role played by the Member States (the Council of Ministers), and the European Commission's pragmatic attitude in this matter. Subsequently, the Council as an intergovernmental organization assumed control and designed a complex network, in collaboration with the Commission, for the development of the necessary regulation. The ensuing political arena is situated primarily at the intergovernmental level.

3.   THE POLITICAL ARENA

Ideally, the Community's political arena should feature only a handful of institutions: namely the Commission, the Council, the Parliament, the Court of Justice and, finally, the national parliaments. In reality, there are a great many unilateral consultative structures, working groups and ad hoc committees of an intergovernmental and often

2. In 1988, the European Commission introduced proposals to adjust Regulation 1612/68 (on freedom of movement for workers within the Community, OJ 1968 L 257/2) and EEC Directive 68/360 (on the abolition of restrictions on movement and residence within the Community for workers of Member States and their families, OJ 1968 L 257/13) within the framework of the internal market.

3. Arts. 48 to 51 cannot be considered as the legal basis for these three Directives since these Treaty provisions exclusively settle the freedom of movement for workers and not for persons in the wider sense. Art. 235 has been used as the legal basis, giving the Community the possibility of autonomously increasing the powers.

4. OJ 1964 L 56.

5. Although para. 1 of Art. 100A adopts the cooperation procedure for achieving the objectives set out in Art. 8A, Art. 100A(2) stipulates that the provisions of Para. 1 do not apply to the free movement of persons.

confidential character, which leads to ambiguous and complex influence and control procedures. Instead of a reduction in the number of consultative structures, we have witnessed an expansion, the result being a heightened probability of overlap and an increased lack of democracy and transparency. For the record we shall review these groups, though without being able to supply an exhaustive list.

The *Group of Coordinators* is the central unit. It was formed by high Member State officials, and was entrusted with establishing and implementing a schedule for the removal of the internal borders. The group was created in 1988 by the European Council of Rhodes.[6] The *Schengen Group* was originally constituted by the Benelux countries, Germany and France. The Schengen model can serve as an example for what is to be achieved eventually at an European level. Italy, Spain, Portugal and Greece recently joined the Schengen Convention. TREVI is the consultative structure working on political and legal cooperation in the field of terrorism, radicalism, extremism and international violence. It is the only consultative structure from which the Commission is systematically barred. The responsibility lies with the Home Secretaries and the Ministers of Justice. TREVI heads five sub-groups working on anti-terrorism, personal data files and the control of drug abuse. Other groups acting in the sphere of the control of drugs are *STAR (Ständige Arbeitsgruppe Rauschgift)* and *CELAD (Comité Européen pour la Lutte Anti-Drogue)* set up on the initiative of the French presidency in 1989.

The European Council in Strasbourg has commissioned TREVI to coordinate the Member States' actions in the spheres of drug prevention, social and health services, combatting drug trafficking, and international activities. This was followed by the creation of *GAFI (Groupe d'Action Financière)* in 1989, an alliance of the industrialized countries to combat drug trafficking. GAFI's actions are mainly directed against the laundering of drug money. The *Pompidou Group*, which comes under the European Council, also works on drug-related affairs.

Other created groups are the *Ad Hoc Group on Immigration* concerned with visa questions, asylum and immigration affairs, and the *Group of Legal Cooperation in the criminal sphere*. The latter works within the context of European political cooperation, and aims to conclude agreements on subjects such as legal aid, international validity of criminal judgments, transfer of criminal procedures and cross-border surveillance of persons.

The exact nature of the work carried out by these groups is unclear. The actions of these groups cannot be checked on by the national parliaments nor by the European Parliament. The European Commission officially acts as an observer to these groups but, in reality, is an active member. Much to the distaste of the Commission, it is barred from the TREVI activities at a ministerial level.

---

6. This time plan is included in the so-called secret Palma Document, which lists 46 necessary and 33 desirable measures, as well as the 'organs' responsible for the groundwork.

4.   THE QUESTION OF POWER

The Community has no power in the sphere of police and legal cooperation. The Treaty of Rome is quite explicit on this subject; it is simply not discussed. As a consequence, it is not an issue in the debate on Community competence. However, without jumping to conclusions, we can view closer cooperation in both spheres not only as inevitable, but, to a certain extent, as desirable and necessary. Collaboration or integration of this kind should preferably be conducted under the Community flag. However, reality has shown internal safety aspects to infringe as much on the sovereignty of countries as do external safety aspects. Hence cooperation is not likely to proceed beyond the intergovernmental level for the time being. Despite their previous statements, the Commission and the Member States are unwilling to settle matters at a Community level.

Quoting all the documents in which the need for cooperation is explicitly stated is beyond the scope of this report. We shall therefore address only four sources: the 1985 *White Paper* (see *infra*, par. 5),[7] two Declarations annexed to the Single European Act, and a report from the Commission on the progress made in this field.

The Declaration on Article 8A of the EEC Treaty states:

'The Conference wishes by means of the provisions in Article 8A to express its firm political will to take before 1 January 1993 the decisions necessary to complete the internal market defined in those provisions, and more particularly the decisions necessary to implement the Commission's programme described in the White Paper on the Internal Market.'

This Declaration has been adopted and seconds the implementation of the Commission's programme described in the White Paper. Proposals included in the programme must be submitted and fall under Community competence. The 'Political Declaration by the Governments of the Member States on the free movement of persons' states:

'In order to promote the free movement of persons, the Member States shall cooperate, *without prejudice to the powers of the Community* [emphasis added], in particular as regards the entry, the movement and residence of nationals of third countries. They shall also cooperate in the combating of terrorism, crime, the traffic in drugs and illicit trading in works of art and antiques.'[8]

Because of the italicized phrase, this Declaration does not infringe upon the Community's competence.

Finally, we can read in the 'Commission's report on the abolition of identity controls at the internal borders of the Community' that the powers of the Community for achieving the objectives mentioned under the Political Declaration — the free movement

---

7. COM (85) 310 fin.

8. See Treaty for the creation of the European Communities, EC Bureau for official publications, Luxembourg 1987, pp. 1067 and 1077.

of persons, capital, services and goods — are laid down in Article 8A of the EEC Treaty.[9]

Despite the apparent clear-cut role reserved for the Community, as reflected in the above-mentioned Declarations and reports, the Commission has chosen a different way of reaching its target of the free movement of persons.

5.   THE *REALPOLITIK* OF THE COMMISSION

Initially, the Commission was clear as to what its responsibilities were and how they were set out. On the subject of the establishment of the internal market the Commission's White Paper stated:

> 'It is the physical barriers at the customs posts, the immigration controls, the passports, the occasional search of personal baggage, which to the ordinary citizen are the obvious manifestion of the continued division of the Community — not the "broader and deeper Community" envisaged by the original Treaties but a Community still divided'

and

> 'the citizens shall regard the removal of the customs posts as the clearest proof for the unification of the Community into one single market.'[10]

These quotes point to the fact that free movement of persons is not only a matter of technical and material determinants, but also of political will.

If the Commission's objective of abolishing all internal frontier controls is to be reached, alternative means of protection need to be found, or, if they already exist, to be strengthened. Obvious examples are improving controls at the external frontiers of the Community; using spot checks at the internal frontiers and inland; and further enhancing cooperation between the national authorities concerned.[11]

Subsequently, the Commission indicated seven proposals that would have to be submitted over a two-year period in order to reach the set target: (1) simplified border controls (1987); (2) coordination of arms legislation (1987); (3) coordination of legislation on drugs (1987); (4) coordination of regulations on the right of asylum and refugee status (1988); (5) coordination of visa policies (1988); (6) coordination of the rules concerning extradition (1988); and (7) coordination of regulations on the status of nationals of third countries (1988).

Despite the clarity of its initial objectives, the documents and viewpoints successively published by the Commission continually expressed lower aims.

---

9. Report from the Commission on the abolition of the identity controls at the internal frontiers of the Community. COM (88) 640 fin. of 16 January 1989.

10. COM (85) 310 fin. p. 9, Section 24.

11. Ibid.

The 1989 'Commission Report on the Abolition of Identity Controls at the Internal Borders of the Community' states that, without prejudging its interpretation of the Treaty as modified by the Single European Act, the Commission proposes that Community legislation in this field be applied only to those cases where the legal security and uniformity provided by Community law constitutes the best instrument for achieving the desired goal.[12] In short, the Commission made an indirect plea for pragmatism, the promotion of intergovernmental cooperation and a renunciation of the right to introduce bills.[13]

Except for the proposal for a directive on the control of arms procurement and possession,[14] the Commission has either withdrawn all proposals or refrained from introducing any. The above-mentioned subjects were no longer considered in the successive annual legislative programmes of the Commission. As a result, the possibility of settling the free movement of persons within the framework of the Treaties has been lost. That means that democratic influence and control in this context will be out of the question, and citizens and institutions cannot introduce legal proceedings at the Court of Justice in Luxembourg.

6. THE EUROPEAN PARLIAMENT'S SCOPE OF ACTION

The processes taking place within the Community context generally supply a legitimate basis for the actions of the Parliament. The Parliament's actions in the strictly legal sense with respect to the free movement of persons are governed by the Treaty provisions described above.

The Parliament's regulatory role in the sphere of the free movement of persons is limited to consultation. The cooperation procedure under Article 149 EEC is normally used for Community legislation within the framework of the internal market. However, in the case of provisions concerning the free movement of persons and the interests of workers, Article 100 A(2) stipulates that the cooperation procedure does not apply. Accordingly, the Council shall take decisions in this context by unanimous vote. The cooperation procedure not only supplies the Parliament with the possibility of amending Commission proposals (two readings), but also enables the Parliament to oblige the Council to introduce unanimous decision-making if it rejects the common viewpoint of the Council. As far as the content is concerned the advisory or consulting procedure does not commit the Council or the Commission to anything, but it does impose a

12. COM (88) 640 fin.
13. We refer, for instance, to Commissioner Bangemann's statements in Parliament on 21 February 1991, indicating that the involvement of the Commission is particularly justified to prevent decisions being taken by these intergovernmental consultation forums contrary to Community law. Preliminary full report of meetings held 21 February 1991.
14. COM (87) 383 fin. amended by COM (89) 446 fin., again amended by COM (90) 453 fin.

waiting period for actions taken, pending the notification of the Parliament's opinion. [15] The approval procedure is the only instance where the Parliament can completely block decision-making in accordance with Article 203 (budget), Article 237 (entry of Member State candidate) and Article 238 (Association Agreement).

Since the Commission is the only institution with the right of initiative, the Parliament cannot take corrective measures in the event of negligence on the part of the Commission. The Parliament can, however, try to compel the Council and the Commission to action by instituting legal proceedings in the Court of Justice on the basis of Article 175 of the EEC Treaty. Article 175 stipulates that the Council and the Commission can be summoned before the Court of Justice by the Member States and the other institutions if, contrary to the Treaty, they fail to take a decision. The Parliament does not have other legal means at its disposal. There are, however, a number of parliamentary procedures which can increase both political and moral pressures.

The initiative report is the best known and most important procedure. It is a selective procedure used only with the approval of the majority in Parliament. The resolution pursuant to such a report obliges the Commission to nothing, but gives the Parliament the opportunity to express its views to the Commission, the Council and the public.

The Parliament can also use other instruments to clarify or publicize its views. Apart from the possibility of submitting oral or written questions, Parliament can enter into a monthly debate with both the Commission and the Council concluded by means of a resolution (Art. 58 of the Parliament's Rules of Procedure). Once a month, Parliament can adopt high-priority resolutions expressing its viewpoint on urgent and important matters. Finally, the Parliamentary Committees can at any time summon both Council and Commission representatives to their assembly to elaborate on certain views. The advantage of a Parliamentary Committee debate is that much more time is available than during a plenary session.

In short, the legislative role played by the Parliament is to a great extent dependent upon the legal basis chosen by the Commission for the Commission proposals. As explained above, the Treaty offers several possibilities for the introduction of bills in the sphere of the free movement of persons. The Political Declaration annexed to the Single European Act underlines the specific powers of the Community. Thus, the legal limits to the Parliament's actions have been clearly defined. However, effective action presupposes concrete steps taken by the Commission. But here lies the real 'sting in the tail'; the Commission has chosen the line of least resistance, and consequently the democratically elected institutions have become inoperative.

---

15. Even so, the Council has taken a decision several times without awaiting the Parliament's opinion. This is contrary to the Treaties, and has been recognized as such by the Court of Justice in a 29.10.1980 judgment, which held that consulting the Parliament is an essential procedural regulation (Cases 137/79 *Kohll* v. *Commission* [1980] ECR 2601 and 138/79 *S.A. Roquette Frères* v. *Council* [1980] ECR 3333). On 29.10.1990 the Parliament adopted a Resolution on the Council's obligation to await the Parliament's opinion. The so-called MEDINA Report on which this resolution was founded carries the number A3-0274/90.

7. PARLIAMENTARY ACTIVITIES

The Parliament has never resigned itself to accepting the state of affairs concerning the free movement of persons. It considers the course of action taken by the Council and the Commission as an infringement upon its democratic legitimacy and hence has regularly put up a stubborn resistance in an attempt to convince both the Commission and the Council to transfer the issue of the free movement of persons to the appropriate level, i.e., the Community level.

Since the 1989 elections, four resolutions on the free movement of persons have been adopted.[16] The gist of these resolutions is to grant the Community the responsibilities set out in the Treaties and to introduce proposals originally laid down in the White Paper. The Council of Ministers is requested to report regularly and openly to Parliament on the ongoing activities at intergovernmental level, and more importantly, regularly to consult Parliament on the matters under negotiation. Three of these resolutions are explicitly directed against the Schengen Convention and the Dublin Asylum Convention, both of which came about without any parliamentary involvement. The Parliament particularly objects to the Dublin Asylum Convention, which was signed by the twelve Member States (minus Denmark) on 12 March 1987, because it had already adopted a resolution on the right of asylum that pressed for the drawing up of minimum standards to guarantee those seeking asylum a particular degree of legal security and protection.[17] The Dublin Asylum Convention guarantees no such rights.

In addition to the four resolutions and countless questions, the Parliament is currently working on a report on the free movement of persons and the problems connected with national security within the Community.[18] The report's preliminary conclusions are: that the Commission should submit proposals dealing with the measures necessary to bring about the free movement of persons described in the Treaty by 1 December 1991; that the Commission should defer its cooperation to working groups for as long as Community responsibilities have not been clearly outlined; that the democratic element is an absolute necessity, and, therefore, the Parliament should be briefed continuously and allowed to take a stand; and, finally, that the Intergovernmental Conference on Political Union at Maastricht is to record even more

16. The resolutions adopted by the Parliament are: the resolution on the signing of the Supplementary Schengen Agreement (doc. B3-583/89) OJ 1989 C 323/98; the resolution on the free movement of persons in the internal market (joint resolution), OJ 1990 C 96/274; the resolution on the Schengen Convention, the Dublin Convention on the right of asylum, and the status of refugees of the Ad Hoc Group for Immigration (joint resolution), OJ 1990 C 175; the resolution on the harmonization of the policy on the entry into the territory of the Member States with a view to the free movement of persons (Art. 8A of the EEC Treaty) and the conclusion of an intergovernmental agreement between the twelve Member States (joint resolution).

17. See resolution on the right of asylum dated 12 March 1987, OJ 1987 C 99/167, pp. 167-171.

18. The Malangré report, PE 143.354/A/B. This Report has been adopted, (OJ 1991 C 267, pp. 197-201). Since the new Committee on Civil Liberties and Internal Affairs (see n. 19) the Parliament is very active in the field of free movement of persons. Reports in progress are: Cooney-report on right of asylum (A3-0337/92), Tsimas-report on free movement of persons (A3-0384/92), Van Outrive-report on Schengen (A3-0336/92) and the Van Outrive-report on Europol (PE 202-364).

explicitly all questions relating to the free movement of persons in a reformulated Treaty. The report also raises the interesting suggestion that the Legal Department of the Parliament should investigate whether the Commission is acting contrary to one of the Articles of the Treaty (e.g., Art. 3(c), 8A, 100A and 155), which would provide the basis for an action under Article 175 of the Treaty.

8.   INTERINSTITUTIONAL RELATIONS

By late 1988 the Commission had decided to disregard the policy lines on the free movement of persons set out in the White Paper and the Parliament became dependent on the willingness of the Commission and/or Council to keep the Parliament informed. Apart from the ocassional debates in Parliament, two information procedures were available.

First, the Parliament's committee on Legal Affairs and Citizens' Rights is usually informed on a half-yearly basis on the principal results of the activities initiated by the Ministers responsible for immigration affairs.[19] The quality of the (written) information ranges from extremely succinct to extremely lengthy. A second information channel is much more recent. On 7 May 1990 the Council of General Affairs (Ministers of Foreign Affairs) decided, under the Irish presidency, that the President of the Council responsible for immigration affairs and the President of the Parliamentary Committees concerned should begin meeting every six months. This meeting takes place after the half-yearly assembly of the competent ministers. Although several such meetings have taken place, they are of questionable merit because the information is supplied only after the meeting of the Council of Ministers and has usually already reached the Parliament through other channels. In addition, these meetings have been criticized because information is only supplied to a highly select number of members.

9.   THE FUTURE

The pragmatic, intergovernmental course the Commission has defended several times in Parliament is less effective than expected. Although the Schengen Convention hardly supports this conclusion, we must not forget that it has not yet been notified, and that the Council of State has expressed some tough criticisms on resolutions previously adopted by the Parliament. The Dublin Asylum Convention met with opposition from the Danish Government, and the Netherlands voiced reservations in the case of a continued refusal on the part of Denmark. The signing of the Agreement on the customs posts at the external borders was delayed due to a dispute between Great Britain and

---

19. In December 1991 the Parliament decided to create a new Committee which is called 'Civil liberties and Internal Affairs'. This now is the Committee responsible for all matters concerning free movement of persons, asylum, visa and police cooperation.

Spain on Gibraltar. In short, we find that matters have run less smoothly than expected; an opinion incidentally shared by the Commission.[20]

The Commission undoubtedly decided to turn back halfway rather than to completely lose its way when defining its views at the Maastricht Intergovernmental Conference on Political Union. The Commisson's notice on this matter stated that the principle that the freedom of movement, and the equality of treatment needed to exercise it, are rights enjoyed by Community nationals, flowing from the concept of a frontier-free area, and should be enshrined in the Treaty once and for all, as should the possibility of adopting the necessary measures by a qualified majority. With respect to non-EC nationals, the Commission proposed including Community competence in the Treaty that would require unanimous voting by the Council.[21]

The debate of the Intergovernmental Conference over Political Union is still in full swing and as yet insufficiently coherent to be able to say which part and in what shape will be incorporated in the new Treaty. We can, however, already conclude that there is a willingness to have police and legal cooperation play a part in the new Treaty in the same way as the European Political Cooperation is part of the Single European Act. Cooperation shall then take place at an intergovernmental level, but based on a treaty, which should be considered an advantage. Finally, police and legal cooperation should also be given a Community basis even if harmonization of legislation is desirable to a certain extent only, notably in the case of cross-border issues.

10.   CONCLUSION

We can consider the free movement of persons as a measure of European integration in that the success of European integration may be judged by the extent of freedom of movement. The fact that the executive power is well aware of this is shown by the repeated good intentions expressed in the manifold Declarations and documents. The gap between all those good intentions and concrete implementation is, however, still quite wide.

In conclusion, we should point out that parliamentary obstinacy and perseverance in insisting on Community regulation in the sphere of the free movement of persons is prompted by several concerns.

— First, the irritation that Parliament no longer has the opportunity to have a say, whereas the Commission does.

— Second, the conviction that matters of cross-border, European-wide significance should take shape and be controlled at the cross-border, European level.

— The notion that European union can only be developed further on the basis of democratic, i.e., supranational and not intergovernmental principles.

---

20. See Notice from the Commission dated 21 October 1990 concerning the draft for revision of the treaty for the creation of the European Economic Community in the matter of Political Union, COM (90) 600 fin. of 23 October 1990.
21. Ibid. p. 12

— Fourth, the belief that European regulation offers the European citizen better and more suitable scope for instituting legal proceedings.
— Fifth, the opinion that Community citizenship cannot be achieved by means of intergovernmental structures.
— Finally, Parliament wishes to make it clear that it has more to offer than just criticism on the free movement of persons. It wishes to, and can, take a constructive part in the process of deciding how we as a European society wish to give shape to the Europe of the future. This is only because it is the national and European Parliament that have been given a legitimate mandate by the citizens, as opposed to the officials, but also because their contributions have been shown to be of great benefit.

We quote from the note issued by the Dutch Government concerning the Dutch presidency entitled 'innovation in continuity': 'In a world where the need for international cooperation is becoming more imperative a supranational structure with strict rules applying to all the participants . . . gives comparatively more and better guarantees and opportunities for bringing the influence to bear than is possible in any strictly inter-governmental setting.[22] In the case of the free movement of persons there is a lack of political willingness to establish a supranational structure. The European Parliament's belief that it has right on its side in matters of competence takes nothing away from this reality. The only instrument left to the European Parliament is to increase political and moral pressure aimed at making it clear to both national parliaments and the public that fundamental parliamentary and civil rights are being infringed upon.'

22. Innovation in continuity, the Dutch presidency of the EC 1991, p. 18.

THREE QUESTIONS ABOUT FREE MOVEMENT OF PERSONS AND DEMOCRACY IN EUROPE

C.A. Groenendijk[*]

1. INTRODUCTION

The issue of free movement of persons and democracy in Europe raises at least three questions:
— Does the extension of the principle of free movement of persons itself affect democracy?
— What are the effects for democracy of the use of the intergovernmental model of rule-making concerning free movement?
— What is the role of the parliaments in the decision-making on this issue?

In this comment on the reports by Van Iersel and by Van den Brink and Vierhout I will try to find an answer to each of these three questions. My focus will be on the twelve Member States of the European Community. When discussing democracy I take three elements to be essential for that political system: (1) public debate and participation of a freely elected parliament in the making of rules that bind citizens, (2) the allocation of the powers of the State to separate public institutions, and (3) a system of parliamentary and judicial control of the executive. An important yardstick for measuring the quality of a democracy is its treatment of ethnic minorities living within the territory of the State.

2. DOES THE FREE MOVEMENT OF PERSONS AFFECT DEMOCRACY IN EUROPE?

The extension of the principle of free movement will provide many persons with greater rights to travel or migrate. Third country migrants with a residence permit issued by a Member State will be able to travel to other Member States without a visa. As of July 1992, the internal market will provide EC-citizens with the right to live in other Member States, even if they are not economically active. This will increase the possibilities for citizens of the Member States to vote with their feet and get away from undesirable economic, political or social situations. This option could

* Professor of Sociology of Law, Institute for Sociology of Law, Law Faculty, University of Nijmegen.

H.G. Schermers et al., eds., Free Movement of Persons in Europe
© 1993, T.M.C. Asser Instituut, The Hague

change the balance of power between citizens and local or national authorities to the advantage of citizens.

That prospect might partly explain the repeated requests by the authorities for more powers *vis-à-vis* individuals in the form of the 'compensatory measures' provided for in the 1990 Schengen Convention and in the Palma Document of the Group of Coordinators established by the European Council in 1988 at its Rhodos meeting. Both of these documents pertain to a range of issues concerning the relations between citizens and the State (police, criminal justice, immigration, residence rights, the right to possess firearms, etc.). I will leave aside the question of whether the powers sought under these documents, and which will be conferred if the recent treaties are ratified by the State Parties, are necessary for realizing legitimate aims, such as combating crime and preventing undesired immigration. But the enlargement of powers in the hands of government officials constitutes a potential danger for democracy. In discussions on the need for such compensatory measures, the effectiveness of the present level of control at the internal borders in Europe is often overestimated. Every tourist who has travelled recently within western Europe has been able to observe the drastic cutbacks in controls at the internal borders as opposed to the reinforcement of the controls at the outside borders of the Community (airports and maritime ports).

The abolition of internal border controls after 1992 will produce far less migration within the Community than is expected or feared. Since 1961 each extension of the free movement of persons within the Community has raised the same fears. Each time those fears of migration have proved to be without basis in reality. The absence of migration by citizens of the former German Democratic Republic to other EC-countries after the unification of Germany in October 1990, and the shortening of the transitional period for the free movement of workers set at the time of the entry of Portugal and Spain to the EC, are only the most recent examples of fears for migration that did not materialize.

In my opinion, the present policies entail yet another danger for democracy in Europe. A policy of granting freedom to work and live only to nationals of the Member States and not to non-EC nationals legally settled in the EC would reinforce the idea that there is a large group of second-class persons living in Europe that are excluded from full participation in public life. The separate entry ports, one for EC-passengers, another for non-EC-passengers, and the difference in speed of handling the queues at these ports convey a symbolic message to all passengers. That message will also have its effects within the Community. The officially supported distinction between EC-nationals and the eight million non-EC-nationals living in Europe will be a source of discrimination of the latter inhabitants of Europe. It will also be a cause of instability. Hence that policy will be a liability for democracy.

Some of those unavoidable side-effects of the policies established in the recent European treaties on migration could, however, be counteracted by a policy and a legislation granting equal treatment and security of residence to non-EC nationals legally settled within the Community.

3.   DEMOCRACY AND THE INTERGOVERNMENTAL MODEL
       OF RULE-MAKING

Both reports have raised the issue of the effect of the intergovernmental model for rule-making concerning free movement.

Van Iersel has pointed to the impact of the intergovernmental model on the power relationships between national parliaments and governments. The traditional procedures established for discussing draft Community legislation did not apply to the negotiation of the Schengen Convention, nor to the documents produced by the Ad Hoc Group Immigration or the Rhodos Group of Coordinators. Parliaments had to develop new special procedures once they became aware of the importance of the products of these new rule-making bodies. The lack of information among MP's made them dependent on the (selective) information supplied by pressure groups. It caused large discrepancies in the level of information within and between the national parliaments. In addition, the lack of information also made MP's dependent on the officials prepared to 'leak' draft texts. An informed public debate was further hampered by the fact that MP's and other outsiders only knew partial texts and often spoke on the basis of different versions of the draft conventions under discussion.

In their report Van den Brink and Vierhout have stressed another effect of the intergovernmental model of rule-making: it disturbs the delicate power relationships among the four main Community institutions. The Council acts in 'collaboration' with the Commission which is present at the negotiations as an observer only. The European Parliament and the Court of Justice are effectively excluded from control over the process of rule-making and the future application of the intergovernmental rules.

I would add yet another effect. The intergovernmental model also threatens to alter the *power relations between individual citizens and national authorities*. Existing legal remedies granted to citizens by national law might be excluded or prove to be less effective in the areas covered by the new treaties. In the first case submitted to the Benelux Court concerning immigration, the Dutch Ministry of Foreign Affairs argued that the intergovernmental nature of the Benelux rules on visas excluded national judicial remedies against decisions on visa applications.[1] The presence of an international court in the Benelux system proved to be a barrier against a policy to abolish national remedies through intergovernmental cooperation. Even if the competences of national courts are not restricted in law, it is probable that national judges will be reluctant to interfere with the decisions that are the

---

1. *Karim* v. *Minister van Buitenlandse Zaken*, Benelux Court 20 December 1988 *Jurisprudentie van het Benelux-Gerechtshof* 1988, p. 134; *Netherlands Yearbook of International Law* (1990) p. 404; European Law Digest (1989) p. 187; *Administratiefrechtelijke Beslissingen* (1990) No. 488 with note by H.J. Simon; *Rechtspraak Vreemdelingenrecht* (1988) No. 43 with note by C.A. Groenendijk; *Migranten-recht* (1989) p. 41 with note by W.A.C. Verouden; and (Belgian) *Tijdschrift voor Vreemdelingenrecht* No. 52, (1989) pp. 29-37.

outcome of bilateral diplomatic discussions and compromises,[2] or with decisions of the executive committees and working groups established by the Schengen Convention and the Dublin Asylum Convention. Thus, existing national remedies in this area in practice will become less effective, because no judicial protection at the European level is provided in the intergovernmental model. The gradual extension of judicial remedies in these areas that occurred in many European countries over the last decades, may be effectively curtailed or reversed.

4.   DISCREPANCIES IN INFORMATION

The discrepancies in information available to national parliaments resulting from the use of the intergovernmental model can be illustrated by two examples. Since 1987 the Dutch parliament regularly receives progress reports on the Schengen negotiations at the occasion of each half-yearly meeting of ministers of the Schengen group. Publications in the German press based on these Dutch progress reports prompted German MP's to request more information in 1989. The German Government provided the text of the latest draft of the Schengen Convention confidentially to a few German MP's in May 1989. However, Dutch MP's received such a draft only half a year later, a few weeks before the date originally set for signing the Convention.

In June 1989 the Rhodos Group of Coordinators agreed on a legislative programme generally known as the Palma Document. This document effectively supplemented and replaced large parts of the Commission's White Paper on the completion of the internal market.[3] The Palma Document was made public during a hearing of a House of Lords committee in July 1989 and was ordered to be printed.[4] Several months later the Dutch Government gave a copy of the same document to Dutch MP's. Some of them considered the document to be for confidential use only. However, by that time those MP's could have ordered the same information from HMSO in London.

The unclear status of the Palma Document — is it public or confidential information and what is its legal or political status? — did not stimulate public parliamentary debate on the document in the Netherlands. Instead, it made it harder for MP's and other outsiders to the negotiations to recognize the political importance of the Palma Document. This selective and partial provision of information opens up possibilities for manipulation of the national political debate by governments and pressure groups.

---

2. For instance the bilateral consultations on the issuing or the withdrawal of residence permits provided for in Art. 25 of the Schengen Convention.

3. COM(85)310 final.

4. House of Lords Select Committee on the European Communities, 1992: *Border Control of People*, Session 1988-89, 22nd report, London (HMSO) 1989 (HL Paper 90), Appendix 5, pp. 55-64.

5.   THE NEW COMMITTEES OF MINISTERS: BEYOND THE TRIAS
         POLITICA

Other effects of the intergovernmental model for democracy are highlighted by the
position and powers of the Committees of Ministers provided for in recent treaties.
Article 131 of the Schengen Convention provides for the establishment of an
Executive Committee. Both the Dublin Asylum Convention (Art. 18) and the draft
of the External Frontiers Convention (Art. 26) provide for a Committee of Government Representatives.

These committees are defined as having a variety of tasks. They will be
empowered to act as *legislators*: the committees will have the power to adopt
'rules', 'detailed provisions' or 'measures' and to make decisions on revising or
amending the respective conventions.[5] In addition, the committees will have clear
executive tasks: they will decide on the suspension of the application of the conventions by a State Party or on the extension of arrangements for the expulsion of third
country nationals to certain categories of aliens.[6]

Finally, the committees are entrusted with the supervision of the implementation
and the interpretation of the conventions. The exact wording of the relevant provisions varies among the conventions. The Schengen Executive Committee must
'ensure that the convention is implemented correctly.'[7] According to the Dublin
Asylum Convention the relevant committee should 'examine any question of a
general nature concerning the application or interpretation of this Convention.'[8] In
the draft of the External Frontiers Convention the committee is given the task 'to
take decisions necessary for the proper application of this Convention.'[9] This part of
their task could have both *executive* and *judicial* aspects. The issuance of binding
decisions as to the interpretation of rules or the resolution of conflicts about the
implementation of legislation are tasks that, in democratic states, are usually
assigned to the judiciary. Thus, these new ministerial committees and the working
groups comprising 'representatives of the Administrations of the Contracting
Parties', that are supposed to prepare the decision-making of the committees,[10]
could act as legislator, as executive and as judge as well.[11] Did the democratic
tradition of a certain separation of these three tasks make no sense after all?

---

5. Arts. 3, 12, 17 and 131 of the Schengen Convention; Art. 18(2) of the Dublin Asylum Convention
and Art. 26 of the Draft External Frontiers Convention.

6. Point 2 of the Joint Declaration of the six Schengen States at the occasion of the signature of the
Agreement with Poland concerning the re-admission of persons having entered or stayed irregularly,
concluded in Brussels on 29 March 1991, Trb. 1991, nr. 65.

7. Art. 131(2).

8. Art. 18(2).

9. Art. 26(3).

10. Art. 132(4) Schengen Convention, Art. 14(4) Dublin Asylum Convention and Art. 26(6) Draft
External Frontiers Convention.

11. See also H. Meijers, 'Schengen, an introduction', in H. Meijers et al., eds., *Schengen, Internationalisation of central chapters of the law on aliens, refugees, security and the police*, 2nd rev. edn.,
Stichting NJCM-Boekerij No. 21 (Leiden, 1992), pp. 5-7.

It is a bad omen that none of the three treaties contains any rule about publication of any decision of the committees. One small concession to democratic control has been made: the clause on a two months' postponement of the (final) decision-making by the committee upon request of a Member State. This *terme de grâce* could be used for consultation with the national parliaments. With respect to the Schengen Convention the two month period of postponement commences upon the submission of the draft decision to the committee.[12] Thus, governments and parliaments must be informed in time and respond very quickly.[13] In the draft of the External Frontiers Convention the two months deferral is possible only *after* a common position has been established on a proposal put to the committee.[14] However, after agreement has been reached in the committee, the possibilities for national parliaments to influence the final decision would be severely limited because the government's representative would have already committed himself to the common position.

The Dutch Council of State observed that considerable powers are granted to the Schengen Executive Committee, and that the Schengen Convention has 'serious shortcomings from the democratic point of view.'[15] After similar criticism had been voiced in the French Senate, the *Conseil Constitutionnel* in its July 1991 decision argued that the Schengen Convention does not grant direct effect to the decisions of the committee and that '*les mesures prises par les autorités françaises, à la suite des décisions dudit comité, seront elles-mêmes soumises au contrôle des juridictions françaises, dans le cadre de leurs compétences respectives.*'[16]

The accuracy of this position can be disputed from a strictly legal point of view. The legal effect of the future decisions of the Executive Committee will depend on the exact content of those decisions. More important, however, is that in practice national parliaments will be very limited in their ability to reject the implementing national legislation or administrative rules which implement an international decision, consented to by representatives of all States Parties including their own ministers. Moreover, a national judge asked to rule on the constitutionality of the national legislation implementing a decision of such a committee would think twice before interfering in a compromise reached at an international level. Neither would a

---

12. Art. 132(3).

13. In the Dutch bill concerning the ratification of the 1990 Schengen Agreement, after persistent pressure from the MP's a provision was added to the effect that the drafts of all decisions of the Schengen Executive Committee that will bind the Netherlands, will have to be presented to the Dutch parliament before the Executive Committee arrives at a decision on the draft. In exceptional cases the draft may be confidentially communicated to the MP's. In case parliament does not request a full debate within fifteen days after the communication this amounts to silent approval of the draft decision. The bill explicitly provides for the publication of all decisions of the Schengen Executive Committee in the Dutch official Treaties series (Art. 2 and Art. 3 of the bill, First Chamber Dutch parliament [Eerste Kamer] 1991-1992, 22140, No. 339). The bill was approved by the Second Chamber of the Dutch parliament in June 1992 by 146 to 13 votes.

14. Art. 26(5).

15. Sub 13 of the Opinion of 8 April 1991.

16. Decision of 25 July 1991, Journal Officiel of 27 July 1991, pp. 10001-10005.

national judge feel attracted by the possibility of divergent judicial opinions of courts in the different Member States, which could result in a situation that a committee decision is implemented in some States but not in other States on the ground that it is unconstitutional. National judges are more likely to accept the implementation measures because of their tendency to adopt a rather limited (marginal) appreciation of the constitutionality issue.

The treaty concluded in March 1991 between the Schengen countries and Poland is another example of the gradual exclusion of parliamentary control resulting from the intergovernmental model of rule-making in this area. The treaty with Poland in a way extends the Schengen system of responsibility for asylum requests, as laid down in the Schengen Convention, to the expulsion of all aliens considered undesirable in one of the Schengen States. This can be viewed as a *de facto* amendment of the Schengen Convention even before it comes into force through ratification. A Joint Declaration of the Schengen States stipulates that the new arrangement will provisionally (i.e., without prior consent of the national parliaments) be applied to Polish citizens only. But the Executive Committee can at any time decide to extend application of the new rules to all non-EC nationals in western Europe.[17] This extension also will be outside the control of any parliament. In addition, any other State of the world can — if it wishes to do so — become a party to this treaty with Poland, the Executive Committee consenting. All States can become involved in the Schengen system without any parliamentary approval being required. This is all the more surprising in the light of the argument that the close cooperation between the administrations of the Schengen States was justified because of the high and relatively uniform level of democratic and judicial protection of the rights of individuals in the Schengen States. Now, in principle, all States could become involved in the Schengen arrangements on immigration and aliens without any guarantee for the level of protection of human rights or the actual observance of international obligations (e.g., under the Geneva Convention on Refugees) in those States.

6. THE ROLE OF NATIONAL PARLIAMENTS

In his report Van Iersel points out that the Dutch parliament had some influence on the negotiation process. I would add that the repeated interest of Dutch parliament every six months since 1987 gave more attention and leverage for the interests not represented among the negotiators, e.g., the interests of third country immigrants living in Member States. It compensated for the rather one-sided expertise among negotiators (mainly police and criminal law experts and officials of immigration departments). I doubt whether this involvement of the Dutch parliament has really been a burden for the negotiations. But it did help to reinforce the rights of third country immigrants, to grant priority to the 1951 Convention on Refugees and to

17. See *supra*, n. 6.

improve the clauses on data protection in the Schengen Convention, the Dublin Asylum Convention and the Draft External Frontiers Convention.

But I disagree with Van Iersel when he depicts the role of Dutch parliament as an uninformed and innocent by-stander. His position that the Dutch parliament did not explicitly but tacitly agree with the 1985 Schengen Agreement, and that until 1988 it did not know what Schengen was all about, is only part of the truth.

In May 1985, two weeks before the Schengen Agreement was signed, a special meeting of two select committees of the Second Chamber of the Dutch parliament was held in the presence of several cabinet ministers. At this meeting most of the major items to be included in that agreement (drugs, police cooperation, visa policy, border control, control of aliens inside the country) were discussed. The meeting probably was held because some MP's got misgivings or doubts after reading the Benelux memorandum on this new form of European cooperation. A few days before the meeting the MP's 'confidentially' received the draft of the first Schengen Agreement. At the end of the meeting MP's of all three large political parties more or less wholeheartedly endorsed the project.[18] The Dutch Government received the green light to go ahead with Schengen.[19]

In May 1989, at the informal consultation between four members of the Bundestag and representatives of the German Government, the MP's discussed the drafts of the Schengen Convention they had just received. Since those MP's raised no major objections, this implied the informal consent of the main political parties with the Convention.

It is unclear whether the governments of the other Member States also received a similar informal parliamentary consent during or after 1985 to proceed with the signing of the Schengen Agreements.

The intergovernmental model appears to create a serious dilemma for MP's: they have the choice between refusing information that cannot be made public, or receiving the confidential information with the implication that not making objections will be interpreted as consent to its contents. In either case the main policy decisions would have to be made well before any informed public discussion of the issues would be possible. Such dilemmas do not reinforce democracy.

These dilemmas, however, are *not* part and parcel of the intergovernmental model. The United Nations and its specialised agencies have a long tradition of publishing drafts of the intergovernmental treaties prepared in these international organisations. The Council of Europe also publishes drafts of important conven-

18. Second Chamber Dutch Parliament [Tweede Kamer] 1984-1985, 18941, Nos. 1 and 2.

19. At this meeting in May 1985 the Dutch Government was asked and promised to inform parliament. The Dutch State Council in its opinion on the first Schengen Agreement stressed the necessity of giving the national parliament a role in policy-making and rule-making in the Schengen context, Second Chamber Dutch Parliament [Tweede Kamer] 1985-1986, 19326, B sub 3. This promise resulted in the progress report that later repeatedly provoked the public debate on the Schengen system in the Netherlands and elsewhere in Europe.

tions.[20] Such drafts allow for informed public discussion by affected individuals and organisations and by non-governmental experts.[21] The tendency of some European politicians, desiring to appear decisive, to set unrealistic short deadlines for reaching and drafting agreements, has been used as an excuse for not organizing a normal public and parliamentary debate. Public debate of new rules is an essential element of democracy. It makes democracy both an attractive and an efficient system of government. Rules that are established without the involvement of the persons and organizations that must comply with or apply them, run a great risk either to remain dead letters or to produce unexpected or undesirable side-effects.

For some MP's one of the attractions of the Schengen system, and the recent intergovernmental rule-making in Europe generally, appears to be that decision-making at the European level on those 'sensitive subjects' provides them with a welcome shield against national lobbies and pressure groups in areas that are political minefields. Cautious activities on issues such as immigration and asylum policy seldom bring in many voters. They mostly carry a great risk of losing votes. Rule-making under Schengen will enable MP's to tell their constituents: 'I do not agree with this rule or that decision, but it has been decided in Brussels.'[22]

7.   THE ROLE OF THE EUROPEAN PARLIAMENT

In their report Van den Brink and Vierhout highlight the role of the European parliament. In the fields of immigration of third country nationals and the cooperation of police and criminal justice authorities the European Parliament has very limited formal powers, but it uses these limited powers very intensively. The repeated questions, debates, motions and resolutions of the Parliament actually had several effects.

First, the activities of the Parliament emphasized the civil liberties issues raised by the Schengen Convention. The Schengen system could no longer be presented as merely a question of technical cooperation between police and immigration authorities. The translation of the Parliament's resolutions in the official Community languages extended public attention for Schengen to European countries other than the five countries originally involved in the Schengen Agreement.

20. For instance, the European Social Charter and the European Convention on the Legal Status of Migrant Workers were published in draft form.

21. See e.g., W.R. Böhning, 'The protection of Migrant Workers and International Labour Standards', 26 *International Migration* (1988) pp. 133-145, concerning the draft of the UN Convention on the Protection of the Rights of All Migrant Workers and Members of their Families.

22. In his report H.C. Taschner mentions the suspicion that European legislation is used as an 'alibi' for stricter national rules because 'Brussels requires it' (contribution to this Volume, pp. 432-433). At the formation of the German coalition Government in January 1991 the politicians agreed to let the decision on the hot issue of changing the clause on the right to asylum in the German constitution depend on the outcome of the decision-making about asylum policy by the Twelve Member States.

Second, the Parliament raised attention for the interests of unrepresented groups and interests, such as the third country immigrants, who were 'forgotten' in the early years of the negotiations.

Finally, the activities of the Parliament highlighted the democratic deficit of the intergovernmental model of legislation. It constantly questioned the legitimacy of this way of rule-making and thus made it less attractive for governments.

Compared with the results of interventions of national parliaments, the European Parliament's activities so far seldom gave rise to new information on the status of the secret negotiations. The national parliaments, probably due to their stronger constitutional position, were more often able (through parliamentary hearings, questions, or debates) to make new information available for public discussion. As of 1989, national and European officials started to leak information on the status of the negotiations and the drafts of texts. This tendency to leak information might be seen as a response to the repeated denunciation of the secrecy of the negotiations by the Parliament and others. Confidential or partial information, however, could not make up for the democratic deficit in the version of the intergovernmental model used by the Member States.

8. WHY IS COMMUNITY LEGISLATION MORE DEMOCRATIC?

Community rules on the law-making process provide for publication of drafts, the possibility of informed public debate on the issue, participation of the European Parliament and activities in the national parliaments prior to the adoption of the new rules. The present EC-treaty rules on law-making clearly are imperfect from the perspective of democratic participation. But the intergovernmental model certainly has a far larger 'democratic deficit'. This deficit has been increased by the refusal of the negotiating officials and politicians to publish a draft at any time during the negotiations. Was it really impossible to allow for six or at least three months between 1985 and 1990 for a public discussions of the draft of the Schengen Convention? Is the absence of such a 'time-out for democracy' an indication of the value of priorities of the negotiators? Is it a sign of their certainty or of a feeling of vulnerability about the project? Apart from that, the exclusion of judicial control at the European level, compared with Community law, further enhances the powers of the executive at the expense of the other organs and at the expense of the position of European citizens.

9. THE PRACTICAL ARGUMENT

In addition to all these principled arguments there also is a very practical argument for using Community legislation instead of intergovernmental decision-making in this area. It is doubtful whether the current detailed intergovernmental rules such as the rules on the responsibility for asylum requests, will ever work on a large scale in practice.

The intergovernmental model of both the Schengen Convention and Dublin Asylum Convention lacks the following features:

(1) it does not provide for a workable mechanism for solving disputes between national administrations, neither in individual cases nor in policy matters, unless all disputants agree with a certain solution;

(2) it has no instrument to oblige a State party to comply with its obligations other than diplomatic pressures, and;

(3) it has no suitable way to bring about a minimum of uniformity in the interpretation of the new rules by the legal and administrative authorities of the various parties.

The civil servants who 'represent the administrations' in the working groups have substantial discretion to agree on any interpretation of these Conventions. Their level of discretion raises serious questions about democratic control and the observance of the rule of law. 'In addition, in cases in which one of the government representatives does not agree with the majority view, then a solution or decision often cannot be reached'. Decades of practice of Article 32 of the European Convention on Human Rights demonstrates that a Committee of Ministers is not a body well-equipped to act as a substitute for a Court in deciding individual cases. Such a committee is unable to arrive at a unanimous decision if the State concerned believes that the decision would be contrary to its interests.[23]

In the 'sensitive' areas related to the free movement of persons (immigration policy, criminal and police policy) national traditions, particularities and emotions do play — and in my opinion should play — an important role. Moreover, in immigration matters national authorities often do not trust each other, because they are aware of a long tradition of cheating each other in their mutual efforts to get rid of undesirable aliens. In this field some mechanism for enforcement against unwilling national authorities should be provided, if one really wants the European cooperation to work in practice. In my view this is another compelling argument to pre-empt the fast-growing myriad of intergovernmental rules with Community legislation.

10.   A CONCLUSION: FOUR STEPS

Four steps could be taken in order to diminish the democratic deficit of the present system of rule-making on the free movement of persons in Europe.

First, the Court of Justice of the European Communities should be given jurisdiction to interpret and apply uniformly the new rules created under the Schengen and Dublin Conventions as a guarantee for the respect of the rule of law in the application of these rules (cf., Art. 164 EEC Treaty); by adding a provision similar to Article 177 EEC Treaty in a Protocol to the Schengen Agreement and to the Dublin

---

23. Even the rule that decisions are made by a majority of two-thirds of the members (in Art. 32 ECHR) did not solve those problems. Hence the Tenth Protocol to the ECHR, signed on 25 March 1992 introduces voting by simple majority in Art. 32(1) ECHR.

Asylum Convention[24], national courts whould be able to refer a case to the Court of Justice for a preliminary ruling.

Second, part of the Schengen *acquis* should be transferred to the Community legal sphere in two stages. Immigration related chapters should be 'translated' in Community law first in order to avoid the co-existence of two not identical sets of rules covering the same issues, one between the Schengen States and one between the twelve Member States. Police and criminal cooperation could, if the Council of Europe treaties in this area do not provide a suitable alternative, be transferred to Community law at a later stage.

Third, extension of the rights and powers of the European Parliament during the present revision of the EEC Treaty.

Fourth, and finally, a permanent advisory body under the European Commission should be established with the competence to develop an European migration policy.

If we do not take such steps, we should not be surprised to discover ourselves after 1992 on the road to a Europe of subjects instead of a Europe of citizens.

---

24. See the draft for such a Protocol in the Opinion of the Permanent Commission of Experts on international migration-, refugee-, and criminal law, (*Permanente commissie van deskundigen in internationaal vreemdelingen-, vluchtelingen- en strafrecht*), *De internationale aspecten van de Schengenverdragen*, Utrecht (September 1991) p. 19. In 1992 the Netherlands proposed to its Schengen partners two Protocols intended to extend the jurisdiction of the ECJ to the Schengen and Dublin Conventions and to the future External Frontiers Convention. One of the Protocols provides for competence of the ECJ to: (a) decide disputes between parties to the Schengen Convention and (b) on reference of national courts rule on questions of interpretation of certain chapters of the Schengen Convention. The Schengen States decided to study this issue.

Free Movement of
Various Categories of Persons

FREEDOM OF MOVEMENT AND EQUAL TREATMENT FOR STUDENTS IN EUROPE: AN EMERGING PRINCIPLE?

Walter van Gerven[*] and Peter van den Bossche[**]

1.   INTRODUCTION

1. For many years, education, not being part of economic life, was considered to be one of few areas which, notwithstanding the dynamics of European integration, unquestionably lay outside the ambit of Community powers and belonged to the hard core of the sovereignty of the Member States. Often the subject of delicate internal political compromises, the reflection of deeply rooted traditions and values, and a major source of expenditure, educational policy was a field in which Member States were understandably reluctant to allow Community 'meddling'.

2. It was of course recognized that some aspects of educational policy could be subject to Community law and action. The Treaty of Rome itself already provides proof of this (Arts. 57[1] and 128[2]) and the Court of Justice affirmed in 1974 in its important judgment in the *Casagrande* case[3] that the powers attributed to the Community for establishing a common market could not be limited by the fact that they encroached upon a substantive policy area, such as education, that had not been transferred 'as

---

[*]   Advocate-General at the Court of Justice of the European Communities.
[**]   Legal Secretary at the Court of Justice of the European Communities.
1. Art. 57 of the EEC Treaty provides: 'In order to make it easier for persons to take up and pursue activities as self-employed persons, the Council shall [. . .] issue directives for the mutual recognition of diplomas, certificates and other evidence of formal qualifications.' A real breakthrough in this respect was achieved only recently, as part of the internal market programme, with the adoption of Council Directive 89/48/EEC of 21 December 1988 on a general system for the recognition of higher-education diplomas awarded on completion of professional and training of at least three years' duration (OJ 1989 L 19/16.) On this Council directive, the earlier, sectoral directives on the mutual recognition of diplomas and qualifications as well as the relevant case-law of the Court of Justice, see: J. Laslett, 'The Mutual Recognition of Diplomas, Certificates and Other Evidence of Formal Qualifications in the European Community', *Legal Issues of European Integration* (1990/1) pp. 1-66.
2. Art. 128 of the EEC Treaty provides: 'The Council shall [. . .] lay down general principles for implementing a common vocational training policy capable of contributing to the harmonious development both of the national economies and of the common market.' On the basis of this provision, the Council adopted on 2 April 1963 Decision 63/266 laying down general principles for implementing a common vocational policy (OJ Eng. Sp. Ed. 1963-64, p. 25).
3. Case 9/74 *Casagrande* v. *Landeshauptstadt München* [1974] ECR 773.

H.G. Schermers et al., eds., Free Movement of Persons in Europe
© 1993, T.M.C. Asser Instituut, The Hague.

such' to the Community.[4] The Court thus ruled that the Community could indirectly and in an ancillary manner regulate matters that concerned education and held Community legislation concerning the access to education of children of migrant workers not to be *ultra vires*.[5] For many years to come, the Community would, however, steer clear of education; incursions and initiatives in this field of policy remained modest and mostly of an inter-governmental or non-binding nature.[6]

3.   Although the Single European Act did not itself explicitly increase the Community's powers in the field of education, the drive towards the realization of the internal market constituted in many respects a turning point with regard to the Community's involvement in education. In the latter part of the eighties there was within the Community a growing understanding and acceptance of the close links between, on the one hand, education and training and, on the other, the realization of the internal market, future wealth and prosperity, economic cohesion within Europe and international competitiveness. In its Communication to the Council of June 1989 on Guidelines for the Medium Term (1989-1992) on Education and Training, the Commission rightly observed that as a result of the Internal Market Programme, Europe was at last becoming a credible option and thus now constituted a new horizon for ordinary people, particularly young people at the start of their working life. To enable these young people to exploit this European horizon and survive in the internal market, education and training systems, however, will have to equip them with the appropriate skills.[7] Requests for such a 'Community dimension' in education and training, as a way of preparing young people for this new challenge, are formulated by employers and trade unions as well as by students and their parents. It is clear that one cannot operate on the internal market successfully without knowledge of other Community languages or knowledge of the culture and traditions of the other Member States. Furthermore, the advantages, both for the Community and for individuals, of students being able to study

---

4. See on this point, B. de Witte, 'The Scope of Community Powers in Education and Culture in the Light of Subsequent Practice', in Bieber and Ress, eds., *The Dynamics of EC-Law* (1987) pp. 261-281, at p. 262 et seq.

5. At issue was Art. 12 of Council Regulation (EEC) No. 1612/68 of 15 October 1968 on freedom of movement for workers within the Community, discussed in greater detail below.

6. See for example, the Commission's recommendations of 18 July 1966 on professional orientation (66/48/EEC), the Council's *'Orientations générales pour l'élaboration d'un programme d'activités au niveau communautaire en matière de formation professionnelle'* of 12 August 1971 (OJ 1971 C 81/5), the resolution of the Council of Ministers for Education meeting in the Council of 13 December 1976 concerning measures to be taken to improve the preparation of young people for work and facilitate their transition from education to working life (OJ 1976 C 308/1) and Council Resolution of 11 July 1983 concerning vocational training policies in the European Community in the 1980s (OJ 1983 C 193/2).

On the history of Community involvement in the educational arena, see K. Fogg and H. Jones, 'Educating the European Community - Ten Years On', 20 *European Journal of Education* (1985) p. 293.

7. COM(89)236 fin, p. 3. See also Commission of the EC, 'The Role of Education and Training in the Completion of the Internal Market', 3 *Social Europe* (1988) p. 36.

in other Member States are quite obvious, especially if, with increasing specialization, particular subjects are emphasized and developed in particular centres of education.[8]

4. While education remains in the first place a matter for the Member States[9] and while the Commission, well aware of the fact that in entering this field the Community is treading on the thin ice of Member States' sensibilities, emphasizes time and again its minimalist role under the principle of subsidiarity,[10] the need for a more active and broader involvement of the Community in the field of education is now generally recognized.[11] Today, the best known aspects of the emerging Community education policy are probably the Community's ERASMUS, COMETT, LINGUA and 'Youth for Europe' programmes and Council Directive 89/48/EEC of 21 December 1988 on a general system for mutual recognition of higher-education diplomas.[12] However, at least equally important to the new policy, and in many respects a *conditio sine qua non* for the success of programmes such as ERASMUS, is the establishment of the principle of freedom of movement and equal treatment for students. This paper has to do with the latter aspect of the emerging Community education policy and focusses on three questions, namely whether Community students have a right of entry to and residence in any Member State in which they wish to pursue their studies, whether these students have a right of access to educational institutions on the same conditions as nationals of the host Member State, and whether these students have the same rights to financial assistance from the host State as do nationals of that State. The practical importance of these questions is obvious and clearly is reflected in the case-law of the Court of Justice.[13] In the famous *Gravier* case, Françoise Gravier contended not without

8. See the Opinion of Advocate-General Slynn in case 293/83 *Gravier* v. *City of Liège* [1985] ECR 593 at 595.

9. In the *Gravier* case, for example, the Court of Justice held expressly that: '. . . educational organization and policy are not as such included in the spheres which the Treaty has entrusted to the Community institutions . . .' (para. 19 of the judgment).

10. See for example, the Commission's Communication of June 1989, referred to above in n. 7.

11. See also the draft treaty on Political Union, Part III, Policies of the Community, title XV, Education.

12. On the Council directive of 21 December 1988, see n. 1. On the Community's ERASMUS, COMETT, LINGUA and 'Youth for Europe' programmes, as well as other less well-known programmes, see for example, the Commission's Communication of June 1989, referred to above in n. 7, at pp. 9-19 and Annex A; G. Druesne, 'Le Programme ERASMUS', in Philip, ed., *L'enseignement supérieur et la dimension européenne*, (1989) pp. 63-72; K. Fahle, *Die Politik der Europäischen Gemeinschaften in den Bereichen Erziehung, Bildung und Wissenschaft* (1989) (with useful annexes); and K. Lenaerts, 'ERASMUS: Legal Basis and Implementation', and R. Bieber, 'Educational Aspects of Research and Technology Policies', in B. de Witte, ed., *European Community Law of Education* (1989) at respectively p. 113 et seq. and p. 83 et seq.

13. See for example, case 14/74 *Casagrande*, *supra*, n. 3, and case 293/83 *Gravier*, *supra*, n. 8; see also case 152/82 *Sandro Forcheri* v. *Belgian State* [1983] ECR 2323; case 293/85 *Commission* v. *Kingdom of Belgium* [1988] ECR 305; case 309/85 *Bruno Barra* v. *Belgian State and City of Liège* [1988] ECR 355; case 24/86 *Vincent Blaizot* v. *University of Liège* [1988] ECR 379; case 39/86 *Sylvie Lair* v. *Universität Hannover* [1988] ECR 3161; case 147/86, *Commission* v. *Hellenic Republic* [1988] ECR 1637; case 197/86 *Steven Malcolm Brown* v. *Secretary of State for Scotland* [1988] ECR 3205; case 263/86 *Belgian State* v. *René Humbel* [1988] ECR 5365; case 42/87 *Commission* v. *Kingdom of Belgium* [1988] ECR 5445; case 242/87 *Commission* v. *Council* (Erasmus) [1989] ECR 1425; joined cases 389 and 390/87 *C.B.C. Echternach and*

justification that if the concept of a European Community had any real meaning it must enable students to move to and study at education establishments in other Member States. As in so many other policy fields in which the Community legislature has not caught up with the reality of an increasingly integrated Europe, the Court's contribution to the establishment of the principle of freedom of movement and equal treatment for students has been particularly significant.[14]

5. Since Community law does not as yet recognize a general right of freedom of movement and equal treatment for students in the Community, there is no simple, straightforward answer to the questions on which this contribution will focus. Whether a student does or does not have a right of entry and residence, and does or does not have the same rights as national students regarding access to educational institutions and financial assistance, depends in fact on the status on which the Community student in question can rely. Four different 'situations' may be distinguished. First there are three situations of a specific nature, namely those in which the student can invoke the status of Community worker (points 6 to 11), the status of child of a Community worker (points 12 to 15) or the status of receiver of services (points 16 and 17) and then there is the situation in which the student can (only) invoke the general status of Community citizen (points 18 to 21).[15]

A. Moritz v. Netherlands Minister for Education and Science [1989] ECR 723; case C-308/89 Carmina di Leo v. Land Berlin, [1990] ECR I-4125.

14. See J. Lonbay, 'Education and Law: The Community context', in European Law Review (1990) pp. 363-387, who rightly observed: 'As is not uncommon on the Community scene, it is within the steel portals of the European Court that the battle of wills between the Member States, too timid to legislate directly, and the Community interests has been fought.' (p. 364.)

15. For recent contributions on the issues raised in this paper, see generally, O. Lenz, 'Zuständigkeiten und Initiativen der Europäischen Gemeinschaft im Bereich des Bildungswesens', 1 EG-Forum, Beilage zu IBW-Heft (1990); R. Waegenbaur, 'Die Einbeziehung der Hochschulen in den Europäischen Integrationsprozess', 25 Europarecht (1990) pp. 135-142; B. de Witte, 'Recht op Onderwijs zonder Grenzen?', Jura Falconis (1990) pp. 535-549; H. Lichtenberg, 'Freizügigkeit und Bildungswesen in der Europäischen Gemeinschaft an der Schwelle zum Gemeinsamen Binnenmarktes' in Festschrift für Ernst Steindorff (1990) pp. 1269-1286; E. Hennis, 'Access to Education in the European Communities', 3 Leiden Journal of International Law (1990) pp. 35-44; J. Fuchs, 'Bildung ohne Grenzen', 105 Deutsches Verwaltungsblatt (1990) pp. 245-246; J. Lonbay, 'Education and Law: The Community Context', European Law Review (1990) pp. 363-387; R. Kampf, 'Die richtige Rechtsgrundlage der Richtlinie über das Aufenthaltsrecht der Studenten', 25 Europarecht (1990) pp. 393-404; De Witte, 'Educational Equality for Community Workers and Their Families', in De Witte op. cit., n. 12, pp. 71-79; J. Flynn, 'Gravier: Suite du Feuilleton', in De Witte op. cit. n. 12, pp. 95-112; T.C. Hartley, 'La libre circulation des étudiants en droit communautaire', Cahiers de Droit européen (1989) p. 325; G. Isaac, 'L'enseignement supérieur et le champ d'application du Traité CEE', in Philip, ed., L'enseignement supérieur et la dimension européenne (1989) pp. 11-18; J. Flynn, 'Vocational Training in Community Law and Practice', Yearbook of European Law (1989) pp. 59-85; H. Gilliams, 'Van Gravier tot Erasmus: Over de Bijdrage van het Hof van Justitie tot de Uitbouw van een Europees Onderwijsbeleid', 15 Rechtskundig Weekblad (1989-1990) pp. 494-504; E. Traversa, 'L'interdiction de discrimination en raison de la nationalité en matière d'accès à l'enseignement', 25 RTDE (1989) p. 45; H. Conrad, 'Die Rechtsprechung des Gerichtshofs der Europäischen Gemeinschaften auf dem Gebiet des Bildungswesens', 22 Wiss.R 22. (1989) pp. 97-110.

2.   STUDENTS WITH THE STATUS OF COMMUNITY WORKER

6.   Freedom of movement for workers, laid down in Art. 48 (1) of the EEC Treaty as one of the fundamental freedoms of the Community, entails, by virtue of Article 48 (2), the abolition of any discrimination based on nationality between workers of the Member States as regards employment, remuneration and other conditions of work and employment. Article 48 (3) clarifies this sweeping provision by providing that this means that Community workers are to have the right of entry to[16] and of residence in the Member State in which they are[17] or were[18] employed.

7.   Secondary legislation and in particular Council Regulation (EEC) No. 1612/68 of 15 October 1968, one of the principal implementing regulations of Article 48 of the Treaty, have further clarified what freedom of movement for workers entails. In the context of this paper and in particular with regard to the right of access for Community workers to educational institutions, mention should of course be made of Article 7 (3) of the Regulation No. 1612/68 which provides that Community workers 'shall have access to training in vocational schools and retraining centres' 'under the same conditions as national workers'.[19] It will be noted, however, that Article 7 (3) only refers to 'vocational schools and retraining centres' and not to educational institutions in general, and while the Court of Justice has given to the concept of 'vocational training' in its judgments in the *Gravier* and *Blaizot* cases and its *ERASMUS* judgment an ever broader, more sweepy meaning, so as to include university courses,[20] the Court explicitly stated in its judgment of 21 June 1988 in the *Lair* case that 'vocational school' within the meaning of the Article 7 (3) of the above-mentioned regulation, 'refers exclusively to institutions which provide only instruction either alternating with or closely linked to an occupational activity, particularly during apprenticeship,'[21] which is not true of universities. Given its restricted scope, Article 7 (3) is therefore of limited use only. Unquestionably more useful is Article 7 (2) of the same regulation which provides that Community workers are to have the same social and tax advantages as national workers. The Court of Justice has always given a broad interpretation to the concept 'social advantages' and it can therefore be argued that access to educational institutions constitutes a 'social advantage' within the meaning of Article 7 (2). The Court has in a number of cases construed such advantages as being those by means of which the migrant worker is guaranteed the possibility of improving his living and working conditions and promoting his social advancement, regardless of whether they are available to national workers by reason of their objective status as workers or by the

16. See Art. 48 (3) (b).
17. See Art. 48 (3) (c).
18. See Art. 48 (3) (d) and Council Regulation (EEC) No. 1251/70 (OJ Eng. Sp. Ed. 1968 (II), p. 475).
19. Germany and Denmark suggested in their observations in the *Brown* case that an additional requirement, a connection with the worker's activity as a worker, is to be read into Art. 7 (3). The Court did not, however, adopt such a narrow interpretation.
20. See below, point 19.
21. Judgment in the *Lair* case, *supra*, n. 13, para. 26.

mere fact that they are residents in their national State and regardless of whether or not such advantages are directly linked to the contract of employment.[22] In the *Lair* case, the Court held that it followed from the broad definition it had given in previous judgments to the concept of 'social advantages' that 'a worker who is a national of another Member State and has exercised his right as such to freedom of movement is entitled in the same way as national workers to all advantages available to such workers for improving their professional qualifications and promoting their social advancement'.[23] Although the right of access to national educational establishments was not at issue in the *Lair* case, it is clear from the above that the Court would undoubtedly interpret Article 7 (2) as giving Community workers equal access to educational establishments as that enjoyed by national workers.[24]

8.   At issue in the *Lair* case was the question whether Community workers have the same rights as national workers to educational grants available in the host State. Miss Sylvie Lair, a French national who had worked in Germany as a bank clerk and in other capacities for a certain period of time and had on this ground claimed the status of Community worker,[25] contested the refusal by the University of Hanover to award her a maintenance and training grant for the pursuit of her university studies in Romance and Germanic languages and literature. In the light of what has been said above concerning the concept of 'social advantages', it will not come as a surprise that the Court ruled in its judgment that educational grants, such as the one refused to Lair, constituted a social advantage within the meaning of Article 7 (2) of Regulation (EEC) No. 1612/68[26] and that therefore Lair, to the extent that she was indeed a Community worker, was entitled to such grants on the same conditions as national workers. The Court reaffirmed this in its judgment of 27 September 1988 in the *Matteucci* case which concerned an Italian rhythmics teacher working in Brussels who had been refused a scholarship, available under the Belgian-German Cultural Agreement, to take a specialized course at the Hochschule der Künste, Berlin.[27]

While it has been argued that financial assistance for studies abroad does not contribute to the integration of the worker in the society of the host State, which is the objective of Article 7, it is clear after the *Matteucci* case that Community workers also have the same rights to financial assistance to study abroad as have the nationals of the host State.[28] In that judgment the Court furthermore ruled that a bilateral agreement which reserves the scholarships available under the agreement to nationals of the

22. Ibid., paras. 20 and 21.
23. Ibid., para. 22.
24. In the light of the judgment in the *Lair* case, in which the Court held that a student/Community worker was entitled, pursuant to Art. 7 (2), to a grant for maintenance and training with a view to the pursuit of university studies, it would be hard to maintain that a worker would be entitled to a grant for university studies but would not be entitled to access to a university on the same conditions as nationals.
25. As to the justification for this claim, see below, point 10.
26. Judgment in the *Lair* case, *supra*, n. 13, para. 24.
27. Case 235/87, *A. Matteuci* v. *Communauté française of Belgium and commissariat général aux relations internationales of the Communauté française of Belgium* [1988] ECR 5589, para. 11.
28. Ibid., para. 16.

Member States which are party to the agreement cannot prevent the application of the principle of equal treatment for national and Community workers established in the territory of one of the Member States.[29] It should be noted that so far as educational grants for studies at vocational schools are concerned, a Community worker could probably also rely on Article 7 (3) for the purpose of obtaining such grants on the same conditions as national workers. Advocate-General Slynn considered that the provisions of Article 7 (3) are not limited merely to the right to attend a course shorn of any right to a grant: if one of the conditions under which a national worker can attend such a course is that he obtains a grant, then a grant is one of the conditions available to the worker from another Member State.[30] This approach seems entirely consistent with the Court's case-law on Article 12, discussed below, which gives a right to children of Community workers to be admitted to the general educational, apprenticeship and vocational training courses of the host State under the same conditions as the nationals of that State. In the *Casagrande* case the Court held that this applied not only to rules relating to admission but also to 'general measures intended to facilitate educational attendance' which in that case covered means-tested educational grants in respect of children of national workers.[31] 'Under the same conditions' appears in both Articles 12 and 7 (3) and it can therefore be argued with force that these words should cover grants equally in both places.[32]

9. In view of the fact that students having the status of Community worker have a right of entry and residence (Art. 48 (3) of the Treaty) as well as the same rights of access to educational institutions (Art. 7 (2), and possibly 7 (3), of Regulation (EEC) No. 1612/68) and the same entitlement to educational grants as national workers (Art. 7 (2), and possibly 7 (3) of Regulation (EEC) No. 1612/68), it is evidently important to establish when a student can invoke the status of Community worker. As early as 1964 the Court held in its judgment in *Hoekstra*[33] that the concept of Community worker has a specific Community meaning; this concept does not vary from Member State to Member State and cannot be restricted by national rules. In its much cited judgment of 23 March 1982 in *Levin* the Court ruled that any person who pursues an economic activity which is effective and genuine, to the exclusion of activities on such a small scale as to be regarded as purely marginal and ancillary, is considered to be a Community worker within the meaning of Article 48 EEC and Regulation (EEC) No. 1612/68.[34] In a further attempt to clarify the concept of Community worker, the Court

---

29. Ibid., para. 23.

30. Advocate-General Slynn in his Opinions in the *Lair* case, supra, n. 13, at p. 3185, and the *Brown* case, supra, n. 13, at pp. 3230-3231.

31. See also case 68/74 *Alaimo* v. *Préfet du Rhône* [1975] ECR 109 which is to the same effect: Article 12 covers 'all the rights arising from admission to educational courses' given to a national's children.

32. Advocate-General Slynn in his Opinion in the *Lair* case, supra, n. 13, at pp. 3185-3186.

33. Case 75/63 *Unger (Hoekstra)* v. *Bedrijfsvereniging Detailhandel* [1964] ECR 177.

34. Case 53/81 *Levin* v. *Staatssecretaris van Justitie* [1982] ECR 1035, para. 17; see also case 344/87 *Bettray* v. *Staatssecretaris van Justitie* [1989] ECR 1621, para. 13. It should be noted that in the *Levin* case the Court held that the rules on freedom of movement for workers apply to persons who pursue or *who are desirous of pursuing* an economic activity. In its judgment of 18 June 1987 in case 316/85 *Lebon* v. *Centre*

W. VAN GERVEN AND P. VAN DEN BOSSCHE

held in its judgment in the *Lawrie-Blum* case of 3 July 1986 that the essential characteristic of the employment relationship is that for a certain period of time a person performs services for and under the direction of another person in return for which he receives remuneration.[35] Furthermore, the Court's case-law has made it clear that a Community worker within the meaning of Article 48 EEC may be a trainee[36] or work part-time or receive less than the minimum subsistence wage.[37]

10. In so far as a student pursues an activity which is effective and genuine (*Levin*) and satisfies the necessary characteristics of an employment relationship (*Lawrie-Blum*), he will thus be able to invoke the status of Community worker and have a right of entry and residence as well as the same rights of access to educational institutions and the same entitlement to educational grants as national workers. Few students, however, will work and study at the same time, in particular in the case of full-time studies; most will in fact have stopped working in order to pursue their studies or will be unemployed at the time when they commence their studies. The question therefore arises whether a student retains the status of Community worker when, in the host State, he gives up either his previous occupational activity or, if unemployed, his search for employment in order to pursue full-time studies. In the *Lair* case, the German and Danish Governments submitted that when Sylvie Lair became a student she ceased to be a Community worker and therefore no longer had the rights associated with the status of Community worker.[38] The Court pointed out, however, that it is clear from certain provisions of Community law[39] under which persons who have previously worked in

---

public d'aide sociale [1987] ECR 2811, para. 26, the Court made it clear, however, that the right to equal treatment with regard to social and tax advantages applies only to workers. Those who move in search of employment qualify for equal treatment only as regards access to employment in accordance with Article 48 of the Treaty and Arts. 2 and 5 of Regulation (EEC) No. 1612/68.

35. Case 66/85 *Lawrie-Blum* v. *Land Baden Württemberg* [1986] ECR 2121, para. 17; see also in the *Bettray* case, *supra*, n. 34, para. 12.

36. Judgment in the *Lawrie-Blum* case, *supra*, n. 35, para. 19 in which the Court held: 'The fact that teachers' preparatory service, like apprenticeships in other occupations, may be regarded as practical preparation directly related to the actual pursuit of the occupation in point is not a bar to the application of Article 48 (1) if the service is performed under the conditions of an activity as an employed person.' See also the *Brown* case, *supra*, n. 13, paras. 3 and 20 to 23.

37. *Levin, supra*, n. 34, para. 15; and case 139/85 *Kempf* v. *Staatssecretaris van Justitie* [1986] ECR 1741, para. 14.

38. Before starting her university studies in October 1984, Mrs Lair had worked in Germany as a bank clerk until 30 June 1981 and then went through alternate periods of unemployment and retraining, interspersed with brief periods of employment, the last of which came to an end in July 1983.

39. *Lair, supra*, n. 13, paras. 33. The Court refers (in paras. 34 and 35) to the following: Art. 48 (3) (d) of the Treaty which provides that persons who remain in the territory of a Member State after having been employed in that State are regarded as Community workers, and Commission Regulation (EEC) No. 1251/70 of 29 June 1970 on the right of workers to remain in the territory of a Member State after having been employed in that State, which implemented Art. 48 (3) (d); Council Directive 68/360/EEC of 15 October 1968 on the abolition of restrictions on movement and residence within the Community for workers of Member States and their families, which prohibits Member States in certain circumstances from withdrawing a residence permit from a worker solely on the ground that he is no longer in employment; Art. 7 (1) of Regulation (EEC) No. 1612/68 which provides that a Community worker who has become unemployed may

the host State but are no longer employed are nevertheless considered to be Community workers, that these 'workers' are guaranteed certain rights linked to the status of Community worker.[40] In the field of educational grants — the Court stated — such a link between the status of Community worker and a grant presupposes, however, some continuity between the previous occupational activity and the course of study; in other words, there must be a relationship between the previous occupational activity and the purpose of the studies, for a student to retain his status of Community worker and enable him to claim the same rights to educational grants as national workers. The Court immediately added that such continuity or relationship may not, however, be required where a migrant has involuntary become unemployed and is obliged by conditions on the job market to undertake occupational retraining in another field of activity.[41]

11. Another question which arose in the *Lair* case was whether a Member State is entitled to require that a national of another Member State applying for an educational grant must first have engaged in occupational activity for a minimum period within its territory. Under German law a person could only be given education grants if he had been engaged in full-time employment in the Federal Republic of Germany for at least *five* years and had therefore paid income tax and social security contributions.[42] Germany, the United Kingdom and Denmark, the three Member States which submitted written observations in the case, argued that a Member State was free to impose such a requirement. To regard a short-term period of employment, whether before going to university or during vacations, as qualifying for student maintenance grants, is, it was argued by those Member States, to give a wholly unjustified interpretation to the object and purpose of Regulation (EEC) No. 1612/68, which is to facilitate the taking-up of employment in and the integration of migrant workers into the host State. Advocate-General Slynn considered in his Opinion in the case that if a person is clearly a genuine Community worker, no 'time requirement' can be imposed but if this is not clear then a period of one year seemed to him to be a reasonable prerequisite in order to decide the question whether he is a worker for the purposes of Article 7. In its judgment in the *Lair*

---

not be treated differently from national workers in the same position as regards reinstatement or re-employment; Art. 7 (3) of the latter regulation which guarantees Community workers access, by virtue of the same right and under the same conditions as national workers, to training in vocational schools and retraining centres.

40. *Lair, supra*, n. 13, para. 36.

41. Interestingly, in case C-3/90 *Bernini* v. *Minister van Onderwijs en Wetenschappen*, pending before the Court, the question arises whether a Community worker in a case (such as the *Bernini* case) in which there must be considered to be (some) demonstrable link as regards content between the nature of the work previously undertaken and studies subsequently undertaken by the worker, retains the status of Community worker even if he did not become unemployed involuntarily and if he *goes to study*, not immediately after completing the work previously undertaken, but *some time later*.

42. The intention of the German legislature was clearly to make educational grants available only to foreigners who had contributed by their own work to the gross national product and thus to the social fund out of which the grants were financed. This is in fact an often-heard justification for limiting equal access and financial assistance to nationals.

case the Court, referring to its judgment of 6 June 1985 in the *Frascogna* case,[43] ruled, however, that Member States cannot unilaterally make the grant of the social advantages envisaged in Article 7 (2) of Regulation (EEC) No. 1612/68 conditional upon the completion of a given period of occupational activity.[44] As the Court noted, the arguments of the Member States in question were probably motivated by a desire to prevent certain abuses, for example where it may be established on the basis of objective evidence that a worker has entered a Member State for the sole purpose of enjoying, after a very short period of occupational activity, the benefit of the student assistance system in that State.[45] There was in the *Lair* case, however, definitely no question of abuse; Sylvie Lair had worked for at least two years and the fact that she initially came to Germany to work and not to study was undisputed.[46] This concern to avoid abuse appeared again in the *Brown* case and led the Court in its judgment to rule that a student, even if he is a Community worker, cannot rely on Article 7 (2) of Regulation (EEC) No. 1612/68 in cases in which the employment relationship is merely ancillary to the studies to be financed. Steven M. Brown was a student who had worked as a trainee in the United Kingdom for eight months before pursuing university studies in the same field at Cambridge University and of whom it had been established that he had entered into this employment relationship with a view to subsequently pursuing university studies. His employment was full-time, salaried employment described as 'pre-university industrial training' and it is important to note that he would not have been employed by his employer if he had not already been accepted for admission to university.[47]

We would like to add that when a person works only for a short period of time the question arises whether this work can still be considered to be effective and genuine (*Levin*) and/or satisfies the necessary characteristics of an employment relationship, one of which is work over a certain period of time (*Lawrie-Blum*). The Court is confronted with this question in the pending *Bernini* (C-3/90) and *Raulin* (C-357/89) cases. Both Bernini and Raulin claim the status of Community worker on the basis of the fact that they worked in the host State for respectively 10 weeks and 12 (five-hour) days.

3.   STUDENTS WHO CAN INVOKE THE STATUS OF CHILD
            OF A COMMUNITY WORKER

12. In addition to the rights granted to Community workers themselves, the Treaty and provisions adopted for its implementation also confer rights on the family, and in

---

43. Case 157/84 *Frascogna* v. *Caisse des dépôts et consignations* [1985] ECR 1739, para. 25.

44. *Lair, supra,* n. 13, para. 42.

45. *Lair, supra,* n. 13, para. 43.

46. The Court nevertheless acknowledged this concern for possible abuse and observed that such abuses are not covered by the Community provisions in question (Ibid., para. 43).

47. Also of interest is the fact that Cambridge University recommends but does not require electrical engineering students to obtain industrial experience before starting the course; however, it is obligatory to acquire eight weeks' experience before the end of the second year.

particular the children, of Community workers. It is obvious that workers will be deterred from moving to and taking up employment in other Member States and that freedom of movement for workers will not be realized if the members of his family will not be given the possibility of integrating into the host country and be treated on an equal footing with nationals. Of particular relevance in this context is once again Council Regulation (EEC) No. 1612/68. Article 10 (1) thereof confers on members of the family of a Community worker[48] the right to enter the territory of another Member State and to reside there[49] while Article 12, first paragraph provides:

'The children of a national of a Member State who is or has been employed in the territory of another Member State shall be admitted to that State's general educational, apprenticeship and vocational training courses under the same conditions as the nationals of that State, if such children are residing in its territory.'

13. With regard to the scope of the latter provision and in particular the persons to whom it applies, it must first of all be observed that Article 10 (1) defines as 'children', within the meaning of Regulation (EEC) No. 1612/68, descendants who are under the age of 21 years or are dependants. It is obvious that it may not always be easy to determine whether a person is a dependant and it is to be feared that, in the absence of a Community definition, this notion will be given a different meaning in each Member State. Some clarification would be welcome. Secondly, it should be noted that the enjoyment of the rights provided for in Article 12 is expressly made conditional upon the child's being resident in the territory of the host State. The application of this residence requirement is, however, not without its problems. Can a child keep his residence in the host State while (temporarily) living abroad to pursue his studies? What exactly does the notion of residence as stated in Article 12 entail? Does a child have to have his residence in the host State throughout the studies for which he claims financial assistance or is it sufficient that the child is residing in the host State when he applies for that assistance? These questions were first discussed in the context of the *Carmina di Leo* case (and of particular interest in this respect is the Opinion of Advocate-General Darmon, points 21-27) but in that case the Court did not need to tackle those questions in order to answer the question referred to it for a preliminary ruling. The Court may, however, not be able to avoid them in the *Bernini* case. In that case, Marina Bernini, an Italian national, whose father is and remains a Community worker in the Netherlands,

48. Under Art. 10 (1), members of the family of a worker are his spouse, his children and the dependent relatives in the ascending line of the worker or his spouse.

49. It should be noted that in accordance with Art. 4 of Council Directive 68/360/EEC of 15 October 1968 on the abolition of restrictions on movement and residence within the Community for workers of Member States and their families (OJ Eng. Sp. Ed. 1968 (II), p. 485), a special residence permit is to be issued as proof of the right of residence but as the Court noted in the *Echternach and Moritz* case, *supra*,n. 13, the issue of such a permit does not create the rights guaranteed by Community law, and the lack of a permit cannot affect the exercise of those rights (para. 25). In its judgment in the *Royer* case, the Court had already ruled that the right of nationals of a Member State to enter the territory of another Member State and reside there for the purposes intended by the Treaty is a right acquired independently of the issue of a residence permit by the competent authority of a Member State ([1976] ECR 497, paras. 31-32.).

moved, after having lived in that country for most of her young life, to Italy where she commenced studies in architecture at the University of Naples. Does she still meet the residence requirement of Article 12?

Finally, it should also be noted that Article 12 expressly refers to children of a national of a Member State who *is* or *has been* employed in the territory of another Member State. It is therefore clear that the status of 'child of a Community worker' (and consequently, if the child meets the residence requirement discussed above, the enjoyment of the rights provided for in Art. 12) does not necessarily depend on the parents still being employed in the host Member State. After the parents retirement the child will definitely retain the status of 'child of a Community worker'. The question arises, however, whether this is also the case after the parent leaves the Member State concerned to work or retire elsewhere. Confronted with this problem in the *Echternach and Moritz* case the Court held that Mr Moritz, in spite of the fact that his father no longer worked or resided in the Netherlands, nevertheless retained his status of 'child of a Community worker' for the purpose of *continuing* his studies there.[50]

14. With regard to the substantive scope of Article 12, it may first of all be observed that it clearly follows from its wording that it refers to any form of education, including university courses and primary and secondary school education. Secondly, it should be noted that as early as 1974, in the *Casagrande* case, and 1975, in the *Alaimo* case, both of them relating to the refusal to award educational grants, the Court interpreted Article 12 in its judgments as meaning that children of Community workers not only had a right to non-discriminatory access to education but also that 'general measures to facilitate educational attendance', such as educational grants, should be available to them on the same conditions as they were to children of nationals. In the *Alaimo* case the Court stated that the integration of a migrant worker's family into the society of the host country 'presupposes that, in the case of the child of a foreign worker who wishes to be admitted to an educational course, that child may take advantage of benefits provided by the laws of the host country relating to educational grants, under the same conditions as nationals who are in a similar position.'[51] As the Court recently observed in the *Echternach and Moritz* case, Article 12 would often indeed have no practical effect if it would be interpreted in any other way.[52] It is worth noting that in the latter case the Court also considered that, since it had interpreted Article 7 (2) as covering educational grants, Article 12 should be similarly interpreted.[53]

Finally, as regards the substantive scope of Article 12, mention should be made of the Court's ruling of 13 November 1990 in the *Carmina di Leo* case. Carmina di Leo, an Italian national, was the child of a Community worker in Germany, who, after finishing her secondary schooling in that country, started studying medicine at the University of Sienna and applied in Germany for an educational grant for these studies.

---

50. *Echternach and Moritz, supra*, n. 13, para. 23.
51. *Alaimo, supra*, n. 31, para. 5.
52. *Echternach and Moritz, supra*, n. 13, para. 34.
53. Ibid., para. 34.

Di Leo argued that since educational grants to study abroad are available to German students, they should, pursuant to Article 12, also be available to her, the child of a Community worker in Germany. The German and Dutch Governments argued in their observations to the Court that the equal-treatment requirement of Article 12 does not apply when studies outside the host State are concerned, first of all, because the child will leave the host State and thus no longer meet the residence requirement and, secondly, because studies abroad do not contribute to the child's integration into the host country, the objective of Article 12. In its judgment of 13 November 1990, the Court rejected those arguments and stated that it was clear from the wording itself of Article 12 that it was not limited to education within the host State. The Court held that:

> 'En effet, la condition de résidence, posée par l'article 12 du règlement no. 1612/68, précité, a pour but de réserver l'égalité de traitement quant aux avantages visés par cet article aux seuls enfants des travailleurs communautaires qui résident dans le pays d'accueil de leurs parents. En revanche elle n'implique pas que le droit à l'égalité de traitement dépende du lieu où l'enfant concerné suit l'enseignement.'[54]

However, whether this has any practical significance remains to be seen. Such will clearly not be the case if the residence requirement of Article 12 is construed narrowly, because in order to study in another country, it will almost certainly be necessary to live there. As indicated above, the forthcoming decision of the Court in the Bernini case will, it is to be hoped, clarify what exactly the residence requirement entails.

15. While Article 7 (2) of Regulation (EEC) No. 1612/68 clearly refers to Community workers and not to the children of Community workers, the question nevertheless arises whether in view of the Court's rulings in the Deak and Lebon cases, such children and possibly also other members of the worker's family can claim equal treatment as regards access to educational institutions and financial assistance on the basis of Article 7 (2).[55] In its judgment of 20 June 1985 in the Deak case the Court held that under Article 7 a Member State may not refuse to grant to the dependent children of a Community worker the benefits provided under its legislation for young people seeking work, on the ground that those children are nationals of another Member State.[56] In its judgment of 18 June 1987 in the Lebon case the Court affirmed its ruling in the Deak

---

54. Carmina di Leo, supra, n. 13, para. 12.
55. This question is raised in the Bernini case, supra, n. 41, pending before the Court.
56. Case 94/84 Office national de l'emploi v. J. Deak [1985] ECR 1873, para. 24. The Court had already held in its judgment in case 32/75 Cristini v. SNCF [1975] ECR 1085, and its judgment in case 63/76 Inzirillo v. Caisse d'allocations familiales Lyon [1976] ECR 2057 that the principle of equal treatment laid down in Art. 7 of Regulation (EEC) No. 1612/68 is also intended to prevent discrimination against descendants of a worker who are dependent on him. As the Court argued in its judgment in the Deak case (para. 23), a worker anxious to ensure for his children the enjoyment of the social benefits provided for by the legislation of the Member States for the support of young persons seeking employment would indeed be induced not to remain in the Member State where he had established himself and found employment if that State could refuse to pay the benefits in question to his children because of their foreign nationality. This result would run counter to the objective of the principle of freedom of movement of workers within the Community.

case but took the opportunity to make it clear (1) that only members of the worker's family within the meaning of Article 10 of the regulation[57] would benefit under Article 7, and (2) that they qualify only *indirectly* for the equal treatment accorded to the worker himself by Article 7; social advantages operate in favour of members of the worker's family only if such benefits may be regarded as social advantages, within the meaning of Article 7 (2), for the worker himself.[58] In the *Lebon* case the Community worker no longer supported financially the member of his family claiming the social advantage (the grant of the minimum means of subsistence). The Court therefore held that this advantage did not constitute for the Community worker a social advantage within the meaning of Article 7 (2) and concluded that the member of the family, who had also reached the age of 21 and was herself not a Community worker, had no right to equal treatment.[59] In light of this case-law the question thus arises whether a *dependent* child of a Community worker could claim equal treatment as regards access to educational establishments and to financial assistance on the basis of Article 7 (2).[60] This question should be answered in the affirmative. A dependent child is undoubtedly a member of the worker's family within the meaning of Article 10. Furthermore, access to educational institutions and access to financial assistance, whilst constituting in the first place advantages for the child, are also social advantages for the Community worker since they (may) represent substantial financial savings for the parent-Community worker who supports the child.[61] The fact that equal treatment of children of Community workers as regards access to educational institutions and financial assistance is specifically dealt with, and made subject to certain conditions (i.e., the residence requirement), in Article 12 does in our opinion not exclude that these children can claim equal treatment on the basis of Article 7 (2).[62]

4.   STUDENTS WHO CAN INVOKE THE STATUS OF RECIPIENT
            OF SERVICES

16. Under Article 59 of the EEC Treaty restrictions on freedom to provide services are, since the end of the transitional period, prohibited in respect of Community nationals who are established in a Member State other than that of the person for whom the services are intended. In its important judgment in the *Luisi and Carbone* case,[63] recently reaffirmed in its judgment in the *Cowan* case,[64] the Court held that, in order

---

57. See n. 47.

58. *Lebon, supra*, n. 34, para. 12.

59. Ibid., paras. 13 and 14.

60. The child would have an interest in so claiming if he does not meet the residence requirement under Art. 12.

61. See for the concept 'social advantages', point 7.

62. See on this point the Opinion of 11 July 1991 of Advocate-General Van Gerven in *Bernini, supra*, n. 41, point 22.

63. Joined cases 286/82 and 26/83 *G. Luisi and G. Carbone* v. *Ministero del Tesoro* [1984] ECR 377, para. 10.

64. Case 186/87 *I.W. Cowan* v. *Tresor public* [1989] ECR 195, para. 15.

to enable the services to be provided, the person for whom the services are intended may go to the State in which the person providing the services is established in order to receive the services there without being obstructed by restrictions. This was considered to be a necessary corollary of the right expressly conferred on the person providing a service by Article 60 of the Treaty. It may be noted that Council Directive 73/148/EEC[65] gave both the provider and the recipient of services a right of residence coterminous with the period during which the service is provided.

17. It follows that, if education is a service, students, the recipients of this service, would be entitled pursuant to Article 59 of the Treaty to go to another Member State to study there without any restriction being imposed on their right to do so; they would have a right of entry and residence and it would not be permissible by virtue of Article 7 of the Treaty, to impose restrictions on the right to follow a course of education — and thus to discriminate against them — by making access to educational institutions more difficult or more expensive or to discriminate against them by not making available to them educational grants available to nationals. The question which arises, however, is whether education constitutes a 'service' for the purposes of the Treaty. Article 60 provides that services are 'considered to be services within the meaning of this Treaty where they are normally provided for remuneration' and the Court added to this in its rulings in the *Walrave* and *Donà* cases[66] that certain activities are services within the meaning of the Treaty only in so far as they constitute economic activities (by reference to Art. 2). In the *Gravier* case, both Miss Gravier and the Commission relied principally on the argument that education is a service within the meaning of Article 59. In his Opinion in that case, Advocate-General Slynn argued that while some education is undoubtedly provided as part of an economic activity with the aim of covering costs and making a profit, this is not the case as regards 'state education' which is, on the contrary, provided as a matter of social policy. Rather than aiming at recovering the costs, the State bears all or a major part of the costs. Advocate-General Slynn considered that while education provided by a private organization with a view to profit is undoubtedly a service, education which is provided or substantially provided and paid for by the State is not provided for remuneration and therefore not a service for the purposes of the Treaty.[67] Furthermore, if an organization of a non-profit-making nature cannot take advantage of the freedom to provide services in other Member States conferred by the Treaty (see Art. 66 read in conjunction with the second paragraph of Art. 58), it seems to follow that would-be recipients of services provided by such an organization cannot rely on the Treaty either. In its judgment in the *Gravier* case the Court did not need to deal with this argument but in its judgment in the *Humbel* case, in which the argument re-emerged, it stated that the State, in establishing and maintaining a national educational system, is not seeking to engage in a gainful activity but is fulfilling its duties towards its own population in the social, cultural and

---

65. OJ 1973 L 172/14.
66. Case 36/74 *G. Sacchi* [1974] ECR 409 and case 13/76 *G. Donà* v. *M. Mantero* [1976] ECR 1333.
67. Advocate-General Slynn in his Opinion in *Gravier, supra*, n. 8, at p. 603.

educational fields, and that the system in question is, as a general rule, funded from the public purse and not by pupils or their parents.[68] The Court thus concluded that courses supplied in a technical school as part of the secondary education provided under the national educational system cannot be regarded as services for the purposes of Article 59.

It is correct to say that in the *Humbel* case the Court has virtually closed the door on the possibility of establishing the principle of freedom of movement and equal treatment for Community students by considering them of recipients of services. Only when the students take courses at private schools, i.e., institutions which provide education with a view to profit, are they recipients of services and have as such the right of entry and residence and are entitled to the same rights regarding access to such schools and to financial assistance (if any exists) as nationals of the host State.

5. STUDENTS WHO CAN ONLY INVOKE THE STATUS OF COMMUNITY CITIZEN

18. It is clear that most students cannot invoke the status of Community worker, child of a Community worker or recipient of services. Most students can invoke only the status of Community citizen. The question therefore arises whether a Community citizen has a right under the Treaty to enter another Member State for the purposes of education or to be admitted to study there on the same conditions, as regards fees and financial assistance, as those applying to that Member State's own nationals. It will be remembered that Article 7 of the Treaty prohibits discrimination of Community nationals on grounds of nationality. It does so, however, only within the scope of application of the Treaty. The question is therefore whether education, in general, comes within that scope.[69] Apart from the *Casagrande* case of 1974 to which we have already referred, the Court first considered this question in the *Forcheri* case, a case which concerned an enrolment fee to be paid by the spouse of a Commission official to study at the Institut Supérieur de Sciences Humaines Appliquées (mainly training social workers) because she was not of Belgian but Italian nationality.[70] The *Forcheri* case raised in particular the question whether access to educational courses, especially those concerning vocational training, fell within the scope of application of the Treaty. In its judgment of 13 July 1983, the Court considered, with reference to Article 128 of the Treaty and to Council Decision 63/266 of 2 April 1963 laying down general principles for implementing a common vocational policy,[71] that although it was true

68. *Humbel, supra*, n. 13, para. 18. The Court thus rejected the argument that it is irrelevant that a student may not pay the economic cost and that, as long as the person providing the services is paid, it does not matter who pays him.

69. As shown above, the education of Community workers and their children and private education definitely fall within the scope of application of the Treaty.

70. It should be mentioned that Mrs Forcheri could not invoke Art. 12 discussed above while she was not the child, but the spouse of a Community worker and the latter article only covers children.

71. See n. 2.

that educational and vocational training policy is not, as such, part of the area which the Treaty has allocated to the competence of the Community institutions, the 'opportunity' for such kinds of instruction falls within the scope of the Treaty. It therefore held that if a Member State organizes educational courses relating in particular to vocational training, to require of a national of another Member State 'lawfully established' in the first Member State (namely as the spouse of a Community worker) an enrolment fee which is not required of its own nationals in order to take part in such courses constitutes discrimination by reason of nationality, which is prohibited by Article 7 of the Treaty.[72]

In the *Gravier* case, the Court was again confronted with the question whether the requirement for non-exempted foreign students to pay an enrolment fee many times higher than the enrolment fee paid by Belgian students fell within the scope of application of the Treaty and constituted 'discrimination on grounds of nationality' within the meaning of Article 7. Unlike the situation in the *Forcheri* case, which concerned the spouse of a Community worker, that in the *Gravier* case concerned a student who was not yet 'lawfully established' in Belgium. Françoise Gravier, a French national who had never worked in Belgium and whose parents resided in France and, like her, had never worked in Belgium, went to the latter country in 1982 in order to study the art of strip cartoon at the Académie Royale des Beaux-Arts in Liège (a non-private school), on a four-year course of higher art education. In their observations submitted to the Court, the Danish and British Governments argued that Article 7 of the Treaty did not prevent a Member State from treating its own nationals more favourably in the area of education, particularly as regards access to education, scholarships, grants, etc. The Commission considered, on the contrary, that participation in vocational training is covered by the provisions of Articles 48, 52, 59 and 128 of the Treaty and therefore falls within the scope of application of the Treaty, and in particular of Article 7. In its judgment the Court first considered, as it had in the *Forcheri* case, that although educational organization and policy were not, as such, included in the spheres which the Treaty had entrusted to the Community institutions, access to and participation in courses of instruction and apprenticeship, in particular vocational training, were not unconnected with Community law. The Court referred in particular to Articles 7 and 12 of Council Regulation (EEC) No. 1612/68, discussed in detail above, Article 128 of the Treaty, Council Decision 63/266/EEC of 2 April 1963, and the Council's guidelines and resolutions concerning the problems of access to vocational training and its improvement throughout the Community, cited above.[73] The common vocational training policy referred to in Article 128 was thus gradually being established. This common policy, the Court observed, undoubtedly constituted an indispensable element of the activities of the Community, since the objectives of the Community included, *inter alia*, the free movement of persons, the mobility of labour and the improvement of the living standards of workers. Access to vocational training was, in particular, likely to promote free movement of persons throughout the Community, by enabling

72. *Forcheri, supra*, n. 13, paras. 17-18.
73. See n. 6.

them to obtain a qualification in the Member State where they intended to work and by enabling them to complete their training and develop their particular talents in the Member State whose vocational training programmes included the special subject desired.[74] The Court thus concluded that the conditions of access to vocational training fell within the scope of the Treaty and ruled that the imposition on students who were nationals of other Member States of a charge, a registration fee or the so-called 'minerval' as a condition of access to vocational training, where the same fee was not imposed on students who were nationals of the host Member State, constituted discrimination on grounds of nationality contrary to Article 7 of the Treaty.

19. The judgment in the *Gravier* case gave rise to two difficult questions with which the Court struggled in later cases, namely what forms of education fall within the concept of 'vocational training' and what should be understood by 'the conditions of access'.

With regard to the first question, it should be observed that in the *Gravier* case the Court ruled that vocational training is any form of education which prepares for a qualification for a particular profession, trade or employment or which provides the necessary training and skills for such a profession, trade or employment, whatever the age and the level of training of the pupils or students and even if the training programme includes an element of general education.[75] Although it defined 'vocational training' in broad terms, the judgment was not very helpful in establishing the furthermost limits of that concept, since courses in strip cartoon art are technical courses and therefore vocational training in the narrow sense of the word.

In the *Blaizot* case, however, the Court was asked whether university studies in veterinary medicine constituted vocational training. The Belgian Government submitted that for the purposes of Article 128 of the Treaty 'vocational training' did not refer to university education, which is essentially academic in nature, but to apprenticeship or technical training.[76] In its judgment of 2 February 1988, the Court *first* pointed out that neither the provisions of the Treaty, in particular Article 128 thereof, nor the objectives which those provisions, in particular those relating to freedom of movement for persons, sought to achieve, gave any indication that the notion of vocational training was to be restricted so as to exclude all university education. *Secondly*, it noted that it was accepted in all Member States that some university studies were intended to provide students with certain knowledge, training and skills as preparation for specific occupations. *Thirdly*, it observed that Article 10 of the European Social Charter, to which all but one Member State were contracting parties, treated university education as a type of vocational training. *Finally*, it considered that since certain studies were undertaken in universities in some Member States and not in others, the exclusion of university studies from the notion of vocational training would result in unequal

---

74. *Gravier, supra*, n. 8, para. 24.
75. Ibid., para. 30.
76. *Blaizot, supra*, n. 13, para. 13.

application of the Treaty in different Member States.[77] From all this the Court concluded that there was certainly no valid reason to exclude university studies as such from the notion of vocational training and, moreover, that, *in general*, university studies fulfilled the criteria of the *Gravier* definition of vocational training.[78] Only university courses which, because of their particular nature, were intended for persons wishing to improve their general knowledge rather than prepare themselves for an occupation did not fall within the scope of the concept of 'vocational training'.[79] The Court reaffirmed this broad interpretation of the notion of vocational training in its judgment in the *ERASMUS* case.[80]

There can be little doubt that almost all university education is now considered to constitute vocational training. But what about primary and secondary education? This question arose in the *Humbel* case, a case involving a year of basic general education in a technical secondary school which did not in itself meet the *Gravier* definition but which was an integral part of a programme of study that did meet that definition. In its judgment of 27 February 1988, the Court reiterated that, pursuant to the *Gravier* definition, neither the age and level of training of the pupils or students nor the fact that the course included an element of general education were relevant; all that was relevant was whether the education in question prepared for a qualification for, or provided the necessary training and skills for, a particular profession, trade or employment.[81] The Court added that the various years of a study programme, which formed a coherent single entity, should not be assessed individually but had to be considered within the framework of the programme as a whole. It thus held that a year of basic general education which was part of a programme forming an indivisible body of instruction which met the *Gravier* definition, nevertheless constituted vocational training.[82] *A contrario*, it follows, however, that all primary and most secondary school education, which is primarily if not exclusively basic general education, do not constitute vocational training.

20. The second question raised by the decision in the *Gravier* case is what should be understood by 'the conditions of access'. As was made clear by the Court in the *Gravier* case, an enrolment fee undoubtedly concerns the conditions of access. But do the rights of entry to and residence in the Member State in which one wishes to study, and the financial assistance to pursue the studies, also concern the conditions of access? If they

77. Ibid., paras. 17 and 18.

78. Ibid., paras. 19-20. The Court emphasized that university studies may be considered to prepare for a qualification for a particular profession and thus be vocational training not only where the final academic examination directly provides the required qualification for a particular profession but also in so far as the studies in question provide specific training and skills, that is to say where a student needs the knowledge so acquired for the pursuit of a profession, trade or employment, even if no legislative or administrative provisions make the acquisition of that knowledge a prerequisite for that purpose (para. 19).

79. In its judgment in the *Brown* case, *supra*, n. 13, the Court considered, referring to the *Blaizot* case, that in general university studies could be considered as vocational training (para. 15).

80. *ERASMUS* judgment, *Commission* v. *Council*, *supra*, n. 13, paras. 25 to 27.

81. *Humbel, supra*, n. 13, para. 10.

82. Ibid., paras. 12-13.

do, they fall within the scope of the Treaty for the purposes of Article 7 and to the extent to which they are available to the nationals of the host State, they may not, by virtue of the prohibition of discrimination on grounds of nationality laid down in that Article, be denied to nationals of other Member States. With regard to the rights of entry and residence, it should be observed that the Court will (for the first time) have an opportunity to clarify matters in the *Raulin* case,[83] now pending before it. In our opinion, however, the rights of entry and residence are clearly related to conditions of access to vocational training. Without them, there can obviously be no access to vocational training. Refusal to grant rights of entry and residence to nationals of other Member States who wish to follow a course of vocational training must therefore be regarded as discrimination prohibited by Article 7 of the Treaty. Article 7 thus guarantees to students the rights of entry and residence for the purpose of following a course of vocational training.

It should be noted, however, that as from 30 June 1992 there will be no longer any need to rely on this argument, since all Member States will, pursuant to Council Directive 90/366/EEC of 28 June 1990 on the right of residence for students, have 'recognized' the rights of entry and residence for Community students.[84] Article 1 of the directive provides that Member States are, in order to facilitate access to vocational training, to grant the right of residence to any student who is a national of a Member State and who does not enjoy this right under other provisions of Community law, provided that the student is enrolled in a recognized educational establishment for the principal purpose of following a vocational training course there and that they are covered by sickness insurance in respect of all risks in the host Member State.[85] It is important to note that the student will also have to assure the relevant national authority, by means of a declaration or by such alternative means as the student may choose that are at least equivalent, that he has sufficient resources to avoid becoming a burden on the social assistance system of the host Member State.

21. The question whether financial assistance concerns the conditions of access is even more difficult. It was tackled by the Court for the first time in the *Lair* case. In its judgment in that case, the Court held that, by virtue of its judgment in the *Gravier* case, only financial assistance intended to cover registration and other fees, in particular tuition fees, charged for access to education fell, as relating to conditions of access to vocational training, within the scope of the Treaty and that, consequently, the prohibition of discrimination on grounds of nationality laid down by Article 7 was applicable only to that extent[86] and, as Community law stood, was not applicable to

---

83. Case 357/89 *V.J.M. Raulin* v. *Minister van Onderwijs en Wetenschappen*, pending before the Court.

84. OJ 1990 L 180/30. Note that in case C-295/90, *Parliament* v. *Council*, pending before the Court, Parliament requests the annulment of this Directive because the latter is — according to Parliament — wrongly based on Art. 235 EEC Treaty instead of Art. 7(2) EEC Treaty.

85. It should also be noted that the spouse and the children of the student will have a right of residence (Art. 1) and be entitled, even if they are not nationals of a Member State, to take any employment or self-employed activity within the territory of the host State (Art. 2 (2)).

86. *Lair, supra*, n. 13, para. 14.

assistance given to students for maintenance and for training. That assistance, the Court went on to make clear, was, on the one hand, a matter of educational policy, which was not as such included in the spheres entrusted to the Community institutions (see *Gravier*), and, on the other hand, a matter of social policy, which fell within the competence of the Member States in so far as it was not covered by specific provisions of the Treaty.[87] The judgment in the *Lair* case was reaffirmed in the *Brown* case[88] and it is worth noting that while the Commission still argued in the *Lair* case that grants for maintenance and training concerned the conditions of access and therefore fell within the scope of the Treaty for the purposes of Article 7, in the *Brown* case it accepted that such was not the case.[89]

But is the distinction now made by the Court between, on the one hand, grants to cover registration and tuition fees and, on the other hand, grants for maintenance and training justified? Do not both equally concern access to vocational training? Referring to the *Casagrande* case, one could argue that conditions of access to vocational training not only include conditions on which students are initially admitted to a course but also cover what is needed to make it possible to attend the course. The student must have the means for his maintenance, books and equipment. Where national students receive maintenance grants, while students of another Member State have to provide for their own maintenance, there is, it is said, clearly discrimination. While acknowledging that the question is not an easy one, Advocate-General Slynn considered in the *Lair* case[90] and the *Brown* case[91] that the conditions of access did not cover such grants. In the *Brown* case the Advocate-General clarified this position by saying that although of course he realized that, if a student could not eat or have a bed he could not study, it did not seem to him that the means of subsistence had a sufficiently direct link with access to the course itself to fall within the principle of non-discrimination spelled out in the *Gravier* case.[92] However that may be, it seems obvious that the distinction between financial assistance to cover registration and tuition fees and financial assistance to cover costs of maintenance and training, in essence artificial and unsatisfactory, reflects the outcome of a seemingly unavoidable political compromise. In view of the different forms and levels of grants and of the differences which exist between the numbers of students moving into the various Member States, it is for many Member States probably unthinkable that nationals from other Member States should be entitled in full to educational grants available to their own nationals.[93]

87. Judgment of 9 July 1987 in joined cases 281, 283 to 285 and 287/85 *Germany and Others* v. *Commission* (migration policy) [1987] ECR 3203.

88. *Brown, supra*, n. 13, paras. 17-18.

89. As is shown in the Raulin case, supra, n. 83, problems may arise when a Member State's system of financial assistance to students does not distinguish between, on the one hand, assistance to cover registration and tuition fees and, on the other, assistance for maintenance and training.

90. See his Opinion in the *Lair* case, *supra*, n. 13, at p. 3188.

91. See his Opinion in the *Brown* case, *supra*, n. 13, at p. 3230.

92. Ibid.

93. Advocate-General Slynn in his Opinion in the *Gravier* case, *supra*, n. 8, at p. 597.

6.   CONCLUSION

22. Under the impetus of the internal market programme, the general public, especially young people and their parents, is increasingly concerned to ensure that Europe also offers an educational space for mobility and interchange.[94] However, Community law does not as yet recognize a general right of free movement and equal treatment for students in the Community. Nevertheless, and this is mainly due to the Court of Justice, a principle of freedom of movement and equal treatment for Community students is, albeit gradually and in a patchwork manner, emerging as one of the pillars of the Community's education policy. For the time being, only students who can invoke the status of Community worker or child of a Community worker and possibly, but this remains to be seen, other dependent members of a worker's family and students attending private schools are entitled to the same rights as national students. Community students who do not fall within these categories are, pursuant to the prohibition on grounds of nationality laid down in Article 7 of the Treaty, entitled to equal treatment as regards the conditions for access to vocational training. They have, however, only to a limited extent equal rights to educational grants.

As we have shown in this paper, Community law regarding freedom of movement and equal treatment for Community students is still in the making and the two cases pending before the Court may add new elements to it. However, in view of the complexity of the issues raised, the decisions of the Court cannot possibly serve as a substitute for detailed legislation. More legislative action in order to ensure that by the end of the decade Europe really offers an educational space for mobility and interchange would therefore be most welcome.

94. See the Commission's Communication of June 1989 on Guidelines for the Medium Term (1989-1992) on Education and Training, supra, n. 7, p. 1.

FREE MOVEMENT OF STUDENTS, RETIRED PERSONS AND OTHER EUROPEAN CITIZENS
A difficult legislative process

Hans Claudius Taschner[*]

1.   INTRODUCTION

The right of persons to move freely within the European Community is provided for by the Treaty establishing the European Economic Community. However, in accordance with the Treaty's goal of integrating the economies of the Member States, this right to free movement was originally restricted. Only persons that were 'economically active' were granted the right to move from their country of origin to any other Member State for the purpose of working there. These workers included blue-collar workers, white-collar workers, the self-employed and legal persons. And, almost as if to emphasize its connection with the right of establishment, the right to free movement originally ended when the activity itself ended. Any person that terminated his professional life had to return home; there was no further justification to stay.

And how about other persons? Does the right to move freely apply to pre-professionals such as students who are preparing for a profession in a Member State other than their country of origin? And does it apply to 'economically active' persons who have spent a lifetime working in one Member State (primarily their own) but now wish to spend their remaining years in another Member State of this Community? And finally, can citizens of the Member States exercise their desire to live in any part of the Community that they choose? Until recently the answer was simple and clear: there is no right to do so. States may admit foreigners to live on their territory and may make this admission depend upon the fulfilment of various conditions, but a right to come and to reside does not exist.

In December 1974, the Heads of States and Governments agreed at their Paris Summit that 'another working party will be instructed to study the conditions and the timing under which the citizens of the nine Member States could be given special rights as members of the Community'.[1] This agreement was intended to move the European Economic Community away from its original economic purpose, which

---

[*] EC Commission Brussels, Professor of Law, University of Saarbrücken.
  1. Point 11 of the Final Communique, Bull. EC, Suppl. 7/75 'Citizens Europe', p. 25.

H.G. Schermers et al., eds., Free Movement of Persons in Europe
© 1993, T.M.C. Asser Instituut, The Hague.

was a community of industry, commerce and agriculture, to create a 'Europe for everybody'.

The Commission was charged with developing ideas and elaborating proposals that, in the aggregate, would constitute an European citizenship.[2] The right to move to any place within the territories of all Member States constituting the 'European Community' — the restrictive characteristic of 'economic' was omitted — was considered to be one of the essential elements of an European citizenship. This right was to be supplemented later with other rights, such as the unrestricted passage through internal borders and the right to vote at local elections according to residence rather than nationality.

This new approach taken by the Community is important. It has been accepted that participation in the host country's economy should no longer be the basis of the freedom to move and to establish oneself. Instead, the new idea is that the basis of the right to move and to stay should be the fundamental right of every national of each Member State to live where he or she wishes to reside within the Community. In other words, the territory of a Member State should no longer be reserved to its own nationals.

It cannot be denied that the new approach is revolutionary with respect to traditional understanding. However, it lies exactly in line with the evolution of Europe from an economic system to a political entity. This new approach could have only been implemented through the Community's legislative process.

2.   THE STARTING POINT: THE 1979 PROPOSAL

On 31 July 1979, the Commission presented to the Council a 'draft directive on a right of residence for nationals of Member States in the territory of another Member State'.[3] In Article 1 of this draft directive, the Commission proposed that 'Member States shall . . . abolish restrictions on movement and residence in respect of nationals of another Member State who reside or wish to reside in their territory . . .' and who are not already beneficiaries of such a right due to directives and regulations already in force. This reference to legislation in force covered workers,[4] the self-employed,[5] and persons who wished to stay after having finished their professional life.[6] With respect to the latter category, the right to stay where a person has worked was considered only to be a prolongation of the original right to stay for work rather than a right based upon European citizenship. It was therefore restricted to that Member State in which the respective profession was exercised.

2. See the items discussed in the Bull. EC 7/75 *supra*, n. 1.

3. OJ 1979 C 207/14 (hereinafter referred to as 'draft directive').

4. See Directive 68/360/EEC OJ Eng. Sp. Ed. 1968(II), p. 485.

5. Directive 73/148/EEC, OJ 1973, L 172/14.

6. See Regulation (EEC) No. 1251/70, OJ Eng. Sp. Ed. 1968(II), p. 475; Directive 75/34/EEC, OJ 1975, L 14/10.

The method of excluding certain categories of persons from all other 'nationals of another Member State who reside or wish to reside in their territory' would have covered logically all citizens of all Member States. However, this single draft directive neglected the fact that the remaining persons, who would have been covered by the directive, belong to very different categories and sociological situations. As a consequence, the legal conditions for the right of residence had to be structured differently for different persons. This necessity was only revealed during the discussions of the Working Group of the Council, and led, as will be described later,[7] to new proposals from the Commission.

As a condition of the right to reside in another Member State, the Commission proposed in Article 4(2) of its draft directive that 'Member States may require those citizens to provide proof of sufficient resources to provide for their own needs and the dependent members of their family . . .' The Commission defended this principle against all attacks.

It should be noted however, citizen's right to reside anywhere within the territory of his own state is not subject to an obligation of having sufficient means to live there. Accordingly, if the right of residence for Member States' nationals should be created as a special right of an European citizen generally, it is arguable that the 'sufficient means' requirement should also not apply at the Community level. But this argument overlooks the fact that the social security systems of Member States still differ enormously, and any effort to harmonize these systems is met with formidable resistance, mainly by those Member States that have highly developed social security systems financed by their own taxpayers. This current inequality among the Member States does not allow renunciation of the sufficient means requirement, at least for the time being. Without such a condition, the fear of an uncontrolled flow of persons seeking residence for no other reason than to become beneficiaries of better social security than at home was, and is, completely justified. A realistic approach bars the way to abuse.

The Commission's draft directive did not provide a definition of the term 'sufficient means'. It provided only that 'Member States may not require such resources to be greater than the minimum subsistence level defined under their law.'[8] Any other definition would have allowed the Member States to lay down stricter financial conditions that would have rendered the right of residence illusory.

According to the Commission, other specific requirements, such as sickness insurance or proof of equivalent housing, would derive from the basic requirement that persons should have proof of sufficient resources. Consequently, it would be superfluous to make those requirements formal conditions to exercise the right of residence.

Who should be the beneficiary of this new citizen's right? Although the right clearly accrues to nationals of all Member States who have sufficient means to live on their own, it applicability to their families is a more complicated matter.

---

7. See *infra*, text accompanying nn. 12-17.
8. Draft directive, *supra*, n. 3, *Art. 4(2) second paragraph.*

The Commission suggested that the right of residence would be extended to all members of the beneficiary's family, even if they lack proof of sufficient resources as long as two conditions are met. First, the beneficiary must provide for their needs so that those persons also do not become a charge on the resources of the host country. Second, these family members must reside with the beneficiary within the territory of the host country, although not necessarily under the same roof (Art. 1(2)).

As far as the definition of 'family member' is concerned, the Commission proposed the 'large family': the second subparagraph 2 of Article 1(2) of the draft directive included in this notion the spouse, all — not only the common — relatives in the descending line under the age of 18, all other dependants in the descending line regardless of age, the spouses of those relatives, relatives in the ascending line, but only if they are dependant relatives and their spouses (even if they are not relatives of the beneficiary, such as stepfathers or stepmothers). In addition, Article 4(3) of the draft directive provided that the right of residence should not end at the decease of the beneficiary (Art. 4(3)).

For the Commission it went without saying that the nationality of all those persons would not play a role in the applicability of the right of residence; it was the family relationship alone that mattered. Thus, non-EC nationals who had the proper family connection would have had the right to residence under the draft directive.

The Commission went even further. Member States should favour the admission of any other member of the family, such as the beneficiary's or his spouse's brother or sister, uncle or aunt, as long as such relatives were dependants or living under the same roof in the country of origin (Art. 1(3)).

The legal basis of the draft directives should be Articles 56(2) and 235 of the EEC-Treaty. There was no doubt that Article 235 would be the correct legal basis. Article 3(c) provides for free movement of persons in general, and not specifically of Member State nationals. Articles 48 et seq., on the contrary, refer to this latter category of persons, and grant them the right of residence if they fulfil the respective conditions of being workers or self-employed persons. This leaves all persons not falling within these categories to be covered not by these articles, but rather by Article 3(c). Whenever a need 'to attain . . . one of the objectives of the Community should prove necessary and this Treaty has not provided the necessary powers,' Article 235 applies. This legal theory has been equally defended by the Council's Legal Service, leaving all those Member States who maintained that the Community had no competence in the matter without support.

3.   THE DISCUSSIONS IN THE COMMUNITY INSTITUTIONS

The European Parliament welcomed the Commission's proposal but insisted on having the draft directive enlarged in three principal respects:
(a) The requirement to prove sufficient means as a pre-condition to the exercise of the right of residence should not apply to students: 'students are like birds: they come, they fly away and should not be hindered to do so.'

(b) Member States should be obliged not only to respect a minimum subsistence level as defined under their law, but also to refer this level to that which is applicable with respect to their own nationals, preserving the principle of non-discrimination.
(c) The conditions to reside *with* the beneficiary on the territory of the host country should be relaxed: it should be sufficient to reside *also* in the host Member State.

The Commission amended its proposals accordingly.[9]

At the beginning, Council discussions of this draft directive went rather well. This hopeful start came to a halt at the turn of 1981-82, apparently due to the increased immigration of third country nationals into the European community, mainly as asylumseekers. The Member States' delegations could not be persuaded to distinguish between EC-nationals and third country nationals, even though the Commission's proposals only focused on the former. The preponderant opinion was that a foreigner is a foreigner.

Member State hostility was mainly directed against an increasing enrolment of students from other Member States. The statistics for 1985-86 reveal, however, that only a relatively small percentage of EC nationals were studying in another Member State, a much greater percentage of foreign students were non-EC nationals. For example, in the Federal Republic of Germany, only 5.5% of the students were from a Member State other than Germany against 94,5% non-EC nationals. Experience has shown that many students from developing countries whose vocational training (e.g. medical education) was believed to be a form of development aid did not return to their countries after their schooling, but rather stayed to exercise their profession in the host country where they hoped for a more profitable profession. Disregarding the statistical facts, the same was feared with respect to EC nationals. For this reason, the first suggestion made by the Commission, which accorded with the wishes of the European Parliament not to require proof of sufficient means to live was immediately rejected. The original proposal was then restored: students also must prove sufficient means and can only do so if they derive from a relative if the ascending line not living in the host country.

The biggest resistance was directed against the notion of 'family'. Step by step groups of relatives were taken out: no relatives in the ascending line of either the beneficiary or of his spouse: no relatives in the descending line beyond children. It was also demanded that all family members should be required to live with the beneficiary under the same roof in the host country. A further demand was made to restrict members of family to EC nationals, thereby leaving aside spouses (and children of a first marriage) having the nationality of a third country. It was argued that a rule which included those persons would open the doors to every sort of abuse (*marriages blancs*) and would permit uncontrolled immigration. A further demand was that children, even those having the nationality of a Member State, should only be beneficiaries if they are under 18 years of age. Other children still in educational systems and therefore dependent of their parents or handicapped and unable to live

9. See OJ 1980 C 188/7: *Art. 4(2) 1st sub-para.* as to students; *Art. 4(2) 2nd sub-para.* as to non-discrimination and *Art. 1(2) 1st sub-para.* as to beneficiaries.

on their own, should be excluded. Only very strong objections from the Commission's side stopped those demands of being inserted in the draft directive.

The Commission's view, which was met with this unexpected and mostly unjustified resistance, received enormous support from the Court of Justice of the European Communities in the *Gravier* case.[10] In this case, the Court granted all students the fundamental right to choose freely their place of education in order to prepare themselves for a profession. The Court did not expressly state a right of residence, because this was not its concern. In the Commission's view, however, it went without saying that a right of residence is the necessary precondition to the exercise of the right of free choice of education granted by the Court. If this were not the case, the right to choose a university would be virtually meaningless since the Member State concerned could prevent him from living there. The only way such education could be received without a right to residence would be through correspondence courses.

The Commission's view also received support from the Adonnino Report.[11] The Adonnino Committee confirmed the view 'that the right of a citizen of a Member State to reside in any other Member State of his free choice is an essential element of the right to freedom of movement.' But, referring to the discussions within the European Institutions since 1979, it considered evidence of sufficient resources to live on as an indispensable condition 'to avoid immigration motivated only by economic considerations because, in particular, the European social security systems have not been harmonised.' Otherwise, citizens would become 'an unreasonable burden on the public purse in the host country.'

Despite this support for the Commission's position, the Member States' representatives could not agree unanimously in the Council. The European Councils in The Hague in June 1986, in London in December 1986, and in Hannover in June 1988, expressed their firm wish to see the general right of residence realized. Each of them emphasized its importance in creating a Citizens' Europe - but in vain.

4.   THE FINAL REALISATION

In May 1989, Vice-President Bangemann, who was concerned with the inability of the Council to reach agreement, withdrew the proposal on behalf of the Commission. With all the new conditions to the directive, it had also become unacceptable to the Commission. The draft legislation had become more restrictive than the actual situation of EC nationals residing in other Member States, and the suspicion arose that Community legislation could be used as an excuse to redress

10. Case 293/83 *Gravier* v. *City of Liège* [1985] ECR 593. As to details see the report prepared by Van Gerven and Van der Bossche.
11. First Report to the European Council, Brussels 29/30 March 1985, published in Bull. EC Suppl. 7/85, No. 22 p. 14.

this situation and to introduce a stricter system thereby creating an alibi for these national rules: 'Brussels requires it'.

Immediately thereafter, the Commission proposed three new draft directives; these reflected the different sociological situations of the persons concerned: a directive on the right of residence for students,[12]another one on employees and self-employed persons who have ceased their occupational activity and wish now to live in another Member State (e.g., pensioners)[13] and a directive for all persons not yet covered by any of those directives or others already in force.[14]

Under these proposal, the conditions placed upon the exercise of the right of residence would be different for each category of persons. The beneficiary of the Student directive would be the student having the nationality of a Member State and his smaller family: spouse and children. First, a student normally does not wish to live with his parents in the country of education. Second, a person cannot qualify as a student unless he is formally enrolled in school; this should be self-evident. Finally, he and his family should be covered by a sickness insurance scheme.

The key problem with the Student directive again seemed to be the question of how to measure the requirement of sufficient means to subsist. The Commission dared to take a courageous step: no proof of those means would be necessary. Moreover, the student would even have the possibility to benefit from the social security system of the host country, provided that the beneficiary's country of origin would be obligated to reimburse the host country upon request, (art. 1(3)) so that the host country in the end would not bear the burden. This system would be combined with the right of the country of origin to concur with (or to object to) any renewal of the residence permit if the host country having paid social assistance has sought reimbursement, (Art. 2(1) 3rd subpara).

Under the proposed Pensioner directive the notion of family would be different: it is the same as defined in Article 10(1) of Regulation No. 1612/68 on freedom of movement for workers within the Community;[15] namely, spouse, relatives in the descending line under the age of 21 or supported and relatives in the ascending line if they are supported. This notion corresponds to the sociological status of pensioners. An even stronger argument is that it would have been incomprehensible for the public if workers and retired workers were allowed to be accompanied by a differently structured family since a pensioner's right of residence is based on the same legal grounds. Nationality should be irrelevant. However, the financial basis should be given: Article 1 of the proposal stated '. . . provided that they are recipients of an invalidity pension, or old age benefits or a pension in respect of an individual accident or desease.'[16] Sickness insurance should also be required of pensioners.

---

12. Proposal for a Council Directive on the right of residence for students, OJ 1989 C 191/2.

13. Proposal for a Council directive on the right of residence for employees and self-employed persons who have ceased their occupational activity, OJ 1989 C 191/3.

14. Proposal for a Council Directive on the right of residence, OJ 1989 C 191/5.

15. OJ 1968 L 257.

16. See *supra*, n. 13.

Finally, the proposed 'general' directive relates to 'nationals of Member States who do not enjoy this right [of residence] under other provisions of Community law.' This proposed directive uses the same notion of family as in the case of pensioners. In addition to proof of sickness insurance, the right is also condition on the requirement that the person has 'sufficient resources to avoid becoming a burden on the social security system of the host Member State during their period of residence.'(Art. 1)).[17]

The legal bases for these draft directives were proposed accordingly: for the Student directive, the legal basis should be Article 7, paragraph 2 of the EEC Treaty, because equal access to vocational or professional training — as granted by the Court of Justice in the *Gravier* case[18] — 'presupposes the possibility of being present on the territory of the Member State where the instruction is given and consequently the need for rules to ensure equal treatment,' as the Commission said in its explanatory memorandum to this draft.[19]

The legal basis for the Pensioner directive should be Articles 49 and 54 of the Treaty. 'The right of residence during the inactive part of a working life should also be granted to workers in paid employment and self-employed workers who have not exercised the right of freedom of movement during active periods of their working life, or who have exercised this right during an active period of their working life but in a Member State other than the one in which they wish to take up residence'.[20] In both cases the legal basis would allow a qualified majority voting on the Council pursuant to the cooperation procedure with the European Parliament under Article 149 of the Treaty.

Finally, the legal basis for the 'general' directive should be, according to the Commission, Article 100, 'because the abolition of obstacles to freedom of movement for persons is specifically listed in the action set out in Article 3(c).'[21] In this case, no majority vote and no cooperation procedure with the European Parliament would be required.

Apparently under pressure finally to reach agreement, the Council concentrated its efforts. It again insisted that all three categories of persons must meet the sufficient means requirement, and it therefore rejected the Commission's attempt to find a more favourable solution for students. The time is not ripe for a system in which the host country helps by granting social assistance and is reimbursed by the country of origin. However, after a dramatic Council meeting a compromise was found: students must also have the necessary means, but they may dispense with providing full proof of this situation. It is sufficient if they can make their assertions plausible and convince the competent authorities to believe them. The magic term to reach this compromise was the German word *Glaubhaftmachung*, which stems from

17. See *supra*, n. 14.
18. See *supra* n. 10.
19. COM (89) 275 final - SYN 199 - SYN 200 of 26 June 1989 No. 5, p. 6.
20. Idem at p. 7.
21. Idem.

the law of civil procedure and which became a foreign word even for the French and British delegations.

With respect to the two other groups of persons, namely pensioners and 'others', the Council determined that they are obliged to bring full proof of their pension or resources, the sufficiency of which is determined by whether they will 'avoid becoming a burden on the social security system of the host Member State.' The Council also determined that all beneficiaries of all three groups must be covered by a sickness insurance scheme.

As to the notion of family, the Council finally followed the distinction suggested by the Commission: the 'small family' in the case of the student, the 'large' for the two other groups. The Council also renounced the intention to restrict the right of residence to nationals of Member States and accepted the formula 'disregarding nationality'. Furthermore, it did not continue to insist on other conditions such as 'living under the same roof' of 'disposing of appropriate housing'. The delegations which sought to endure that these conditions are fulfilled at the point of entry decided to back down from their position. It would have been inconsistent with another fundamental right of European citizens to be created, namely, the uncontrolled passage through internal borders within the Community.

Conditioning the right of residence upon the requirement that the dependent member of the family lives with the beneficiary under the same roof would have been inhuman. Under such a rule, any matrimonial dispute involving an EC national and a non-EC national could result in the loss of the right of residence for the latter if the other spouse compelled him to leave the common roof and against the ruling of the Court of Human Rights. In the *Diatta* case,[22] the Court of Justice decided that separation of husband and wife having lived together does not end the right of residence. Only divorce does.

But another aspect of sociological evolution in nearly all Member States was left completely unrespected. The notion of 'family' as used in Community law is based on the traditional instrument to create such a community of life, the marriage. But how about 'modern' families, communities of life without marriage? If a man and a woman one not being an EC national, live together for decades and now wish — having more than sufficient means — to move to another Member State, does the 'spouse' being a non-EC national have a right of residence to be derived from that of the companion? The answer is no, unless the Court of Justice someday interprets term 'spouse' to include life companion. But it must be said that renouncing marriage to be the creating factor of a 'family' and allowing any less stronger link of human relationship as the basis for the genuine right of residence would open many doors to abuse.

The end of this legislative process was still dramatic, if one can speak of an end already. It should be described for the sake of completeness, even though it may be less relevant to the actual content of this new European citizen's right of residency.

22. Case 267/83 *Diatta* v. *Land Berlin* [1985] ECR 567.

On 21 December 1989, the Council agreed upon the three directives with the content as described above. The agreement was unanimous. But because the agreement was unanimous, the Council decided to replace — against the protest of the Commission — the three legal bases proposed by the Commission with Article 235[23] for all directives. The Council argued that its unanimity made the application of a majority rule provision superfluous. Its main intention was apparently to avoid a precedent for the application of Article 7.[24]

In so doing, the Council avoided the factual agreement to be the 'common position' pursuant to Article 149, which would have obliged the Council to re-consult the European Parliament. The Council also did not legally adopted the directives, but qualified its agreement as an *accord politique* with an 'orientation' as to the new legal bases. By letter from the Presidency it informed the European Parliament about the agreement and 'proceded to its new consultation'.

On 13 June 1990, the European Parliament insisted on the original legal bases and on its right to cooperate in adopting the two legal instruments, where cooperation was permitted.

The Council adopted on 28 June 1990 the three directives[25] without respecting the European Parliament's wish. The European Parliament contested the correctness of the procedure in the case of the Student directive and brought an action for annulment against the Council before the Court.[26] The Commission intervened in favour of the European Parliament. It is hoped that the Court limits the debate to the applicability of Article 7 and upholds the material agreement which was reached in such a cumbersome way.

23. The Council also went against the opinion of its own legal service, which follows the Commission's proposal as far as the student directive is concerned.

24. The second paragraph of Article 7 of the EEC Treaty provides for qualified majority voting for Community legislation proposed to the Council regarding the prohibition of discrimination on the grounds of nationality.

25. In an inverted order compared with the previous discussion: 'others': 90/364/EEC, OJ 1990 L 180/26; 'pensioners': 90/365/EEC, OJ 1990 L 180/28; 'students': 90/366/EEC, OJ 1990 L 180/30, all of 13 June 1990.

26. Case 295/90 *Parliament* v. *Council*.

THE FREE MOVEMENT OF PROFESSIONALS IN THE EUROPEAN COMMUNITY

F. Capelli[*]

1.   INTRODUCTION

In the following analysis of the Community regulation of professional activities, we will first draw a general picture of the rules and case-law regulating the matter. Second, we will examine the specific regulation of each professional activity, and, finally, we will examine briefly the innovations resulting from the enactment of Council Directive 89/48/EEC, which establishes a framework for the mutual recognition of diplomas.

2.   THE RULES ESTABLISHED BY THE TREATY

The issues being examined are regulated by the Treaty provisions on the right of establishment and the right to provide services. These are found in Title III, Chapters 2 and 3, Articles 52 to 58 on the right of establishment and Articles 59 to 66 on services.

Professionals are therefore subject to different rules according to whether they exercise their activity permanently in another Member State (right of establishment) or temporarily (right to provide services).

According to Article 52, the right of establishment 'shall include the right to take up and pursue activities as self-employed persons.' On the basis of Article 60, services are defined as services 'normally provided for remuneration, in so far as they are not governed by the provisions relating to freedom of movement for goods, capital and persons. 'Services' shall in particular include: (a) activities of an industrial character; (b) activities of a commercial character; (c) activities of craftsmen; (d) activities of the professions.'

As is the case with other rights established by the Treaty, the objective of the above-mentioned Treaty provisions is the achievement of real freedom for professionals to pursue their activities on both a permanent and temporary basis. This is sought through the abolition of all discrimination or restrictions based on nationality

---

[*] Advocate, Milan; Professor of Law, University of Parma.

H.G. Schermers et al., eds., Free Movement of Persons in Europe

within the European Community. Articles 52 and 60, in fact, establish the right of the provider of services, either in the case in which he operates permanently or temporarily in another Member State, to exercise his activity under the same conditions as imposed by the state on its own nationals.

The removal of obstacles implies the gradual abolition of existing restrictions on the freedom of establishment and the freedom to provide services as well as the prohibition against the introduction of new restrictions. Besides these two 'negative' duties imposed on the Member States, the Treaty envisions a 'positive' one on the Community institutions in relation to the issuance of directives for the mutual recognition of diplomas and for the coordination of national laws and regulations concerning the taking-up and pursuit of activities as self-employed persons.

The Treaty also includes two exceptions to the principle of the free movement of professionals. According to Article 55, those activities that are connected with the exercise of official authority are excluded from liberalization. Furthermore, according to Article 56(1) the liberalization rules do not prevent Member States from applying 'provisions laid down by law, regulation or administrative action providing for special treatment for foreign nationals on grounds of public policy, public security or public health.'

3. RULES ADOPTED BY COMMUNITY INSTITUTIONS

In 1962, through the issuance of two general programmes, the Council of Ministers implemented the rules contained in Articles 54 and 63 of the Treaty.[1] For each type of activity, the programmes (mentioned in Article 54, paragraph 1, and Article 63, paragraph 1) determined the general conditions and fixed the deadlines for the implementation of the freedom of self-establishment and the freedom to provide services. The programmes required the enactment of specific directives for the removal of obstacles to the access and exercise of activities by self-employed persons. The first stage of the liberalization process was to be implemented through the abolition of all discrimination based on nationality. The affirmation of the principle of equal treatment among citizens of Member States was, in fact, considered a necessary condition to enable the Community institutions to proceed to the second stage of the liberalization process, i.e., that of issuing directives regulating each particular profession.

The rules necessary to fully implement the two general programmes have not been adopted on time by the Community institutions. Once again, the Court of Justice has been instrumental in overcoming resistances on the part of the Member States.

---

1. General Programme on the abolition of restrictions to the freedom to provide services, OJ 2, 15 January 1962, p. 32. General programme on the abolition of restrictions to the freedom of establishment - OJ 2, 15 January 1962, p. 36. These programmes are mentioned explicitly in Articles 54(1) and 63(1) of the Treaty, respectively.

We will now examine the rights of professionals who move within the Community and the duties to which they are subject.

3.1   Admission, establishment and transfer

Admission to the territory of another Member State is granted subject to the presentation of an identity card or passport.[2].

The right of establishment in a Member State is granted in the case of the provider of services, for the period of time needed to provide services.[3] In contrast, those who exercise their profession permanently in another Member State may enjoy such right even after having terminated their work activity.[4] It is anticipated that the Member States will coordinate their special provisions concerning the transfer and establishment of foreigners on grounds of public policy, security or health.[5] While determining a series of duties and limits to the power of issuing national legislation, this coordination aims to ensure that such special provisions are not implemented in discriminatory or protectionist manner by the Member States.

3.2   Social security

The rules on social security, which were initially only for the benefit of workers, have been extended also to self-employed persons and their families through the issuance of specific regulations.[6]

3.3   Equal rights of men and women

The principle of equal treatment of men and women has been extended also to women who are self-employed or who participate in the self-employed activity of their husbands.[7]

3.4   Payment for services

In 1963, in order to implement Title V, letter b, of the general programme dealing with the removal of restrictions to provide services, the Council adopted a directive that requires Member States to abolish restrictions on the payment for services

---

2. Directive 73/148 of the Council dated 21 May 1973 (Art. 2 para. No. 1) OJ 1973 L 172/14.

3. Directive 73/148 (Art. 4, para. 2)

4. Directive 75/34 of the Council dated 17 December 1974, OJ 1975 L 14, 10. Directive 90/365 of the Council dated 28 June 1990, OJ 1990 L 180/28.

5. Directive 64/221 of the Council dated 25 February 1964, OJ 1964 L 56/850. Directive 75/35 of the Council dated 17 December 1974, OJ 1975 L 14/14.

6. Regulation 1390/81 of the Council dated 12 May 1981, OJ 1981 L 143/1. Regulation 3427/89 of the Council dated 30 October 1989, OJ 1989 L 331/1. Regulation 3795/81 of the Council dated 8 December 1981, OJ 1981 L 378/1.

7. Directive 86/613 of the Council dated 11 December 1986, OJ 1986 L 359/56.

provided and, consequently, to authorize the necessary foreign exchange transactions to make such payments.[8]

3.5   Responsibilities of the provider of services

In order to conclude our analysis, it is important to mention the proposal for a directive on the responsibilities of the provider of services, which was presented by the Commission to the Council in December 1990.[9] In contrast to the rules examined above, the purpose of the proposed directive is not simply to enable professionals from one country to exercise there activity under the same conditions as the citizens of the host country. Rather, it is to ensure that the citizens of each country receive the same protection from damages caused by the services being provided. This proposal is part of the Community action in defence of consumers and, once adopted, will have an affect on the exercise of some professions. It is based on the principle that the provider of services has the burden of proving the absence of negligence.

The term 'services', as defined in Article 1 of the proposed directives, includes only services that may cause damage to the health and well-being of fixed and moveable assets. Therefore, we may deduce that services of a consultative nature are not covered by this proposal. However, it may implicate health services or the design of real estate by engineers or architects.

4.   CASE LAW OF THE COURT OF JUSTICE

The absence of the directives which were to remove obstacles to the freedom of establishment and to provide services during the transitional period (contrary to what was required by the two general programmes of 1962) had enabled the Member States to continue to prevent the citizens of other Member States from practising their professions. This was achieved through the imposition of requirements based on nationality or residency.

The process of liberalization was initiated by the Court of Justice in 1974 through two fundamental decisions. The principles contained in Article 52 of the Treaty were affirmed by the Court in the *Reyners* case, implying the abolition of the requirement of nationality since the end of the transitional period in the case of professionals who plan to take advantage of their right of establishment.[10] Similarly, in the *Van Binsbergen* case, the Court affirmed the same principle with respect to the right to provide services by holding that the requirement of residence in the country in which a service is rendered is contrary to the provisions contained in Article 59.[11]

8. Directive 63/340 of the Council dated 31 May 1963, OJ 1963/86, p. 1609.

9. Proposal for a directive on the responsibility of the provider of services COM (90) 482 def. - SYN 308 dated 20 December 1990.

10. Case 2/74 *Jean Reyners* v. *Belgium* [1974] ECR 631.

11. Case 33/74 *Maria van Binsbergen* v. *Bestuur van de Bedrijfsvereniging* [1974] ECR 1299.

As is well-known, the affirmation by the Court of the direct applicability of Articles 52 and 59 of the Treaty has made the enactment of specific directives aimed at removing obstacles unnecessary. Furthermore, the decisions of the Court have required the abolition not only of all direct discrimination based on nationality and residency, but also a whole series of protectionistic regulations which, even if not openly discriminatory, limited the practice of professional activity. As an example of these indirect or hidden discriminatory practices, we may mention the requirement of establishment, of training or of undergoing State examinations to test the degree of knowledge of the language of the host country. The Court has also affirmed that the prohibition of discrimination does not 'concern only the rules relating to the exercise of a profession, but also the various general measures necessary to the exercise of these activities.'[12] Therefore, an Italian law that limited access to public housing and subsidized real estate mortgages only to Italian nationals has been ruled contrary to Articles 52 and 59 of the Treaty.[13]

Another limitation on the free exercise of professional activity is the requirement of a diploma from a national university. The drafters of the Treaty of Rome recognized that the different educational systems represented a major obstacle to free movement, and therefore they urged the enactment of directives for the mutual recognition of diplomas (Art. 57).[14]

The Court has laid down some important principles concerning this issue. In the *Thieffry* case, it affirmed that if the national of a Member State has his qualifications recognized as equivalent in the host Member State, and these qualifications entitle him to exercise his profession in the host country, it is considered sufficient to exercise his profession.[15]

However, we must point out that while it has been possible, through case law, to remove discriminatory practices based on nationality, it has not been possible to remove those barriers deriving from the different educational systems and from the requirements necessary to exercise a profession (such as training or the undergoing of state examinations). These obstacles may indeed be removed only through direct regulation aimed at the mutual recognition of diplomas and at the legal coordination of the systems of vocational training. In any case, the liberalization principles affirmed by the Court have been a guide to the legislative activity.

---

12. Case 63/86 *Commission of the European Communities* v. *Italy* [1988] ECR 29.

13. Ibid. With respect to Articles 52 and 59, the Court of Justice has also considered discriminatory a Greek law which subjected the purchase and rental of real estate to restrictions that were not imposed on its nationals, (Case 305/87 *Commission of the European Communities* v. *Greece* [1989] ECR 1461).

14. The General Programmes envision that for each category of services, the abolition of restrictions on the freedom to provide services must be accompanied, preceded or followed, if necessary, by the mutual recognition of diplomas, certificates or other degrees, and by the coordination of the provisions concerning these services, (Title V of the General Programme on the right of establishment and Title VI of the General Programme on the freedom to provide services).

15. Case 71/76 *Jean Thieffry* v. *Conseil de l'ordre des avocats à la Cour de Paris* [1977] ECR 765.

In order to conclude our examination of the Community's case-law on the free movement of professionals it is necessary to analyze the limitations set by the Court on the two exceptions listed in Articles 55 and 56 of the Treaty.

With respect to Article 55, we may now briefly indicate some elements that may be derived from the rulings of the Court :

(a) The exception must be interpreted in a restrictive manner,[16]

(b) The exercise of official authority must be direct and specific,[17]

(c) The exception may be applied only to certain activities and not to a whole professional category.[18] Concerning the practice of the law, the court has excluded consultative activities, legal assistance and the representation and defence of parties in judicial proceedings from the scope of activities that may be connected with the exercise of public authority.

(d) The content of these activities must be interpreted uniformly within the Community.[19]

With respect to Article 56 on the powers of the Member States to enact limitations on grounds of public policy, security or public health, the Court has placed limitations on the actions of the Member States. Besides setting up the guidelines that must be respected by Member States in the implementation of these provisions, such as expulsion from the territory or the denial of a permit of establishment,[20] the Court has affirmed some important principles on procedural matters.[21]

The analysis above shows the fundamental role of the Court in affirming the direct applicability of Articles 52 and 59, thus overcoming the national resistances and the subsequent absence of Community regulation during the 1970s.[22]

---

16. In the *Reyners* case, *supra*, n. 10, the Court of Justice stated that the relevance of the exceptions contained in Art. 55(1) may not exceed the objective which caused this exceptional clause to be inserted in the Treaty (pp. 42-44). The same opinion is contained in the case 147/86 *Commission of the European Communities* v. *Greece* [1988] ECR 1637.

17. *Reyners* case, *supra*, n. 10, pp. 45-47.

18. The Court of Justice has acknowledged that the exception contained in Art. 55 may be extended to a whole professional category only if the exercise of public authority may be an undistinguishable aspect of the whole professional activity. *Reyners* case, *supra*, n. 10, pp. 45-47.

19. *Reyners* case, *supra*, n. 10. Final remarks of the Adv. Gen. Mayras, p. 661.

20. We refer to the decisions on the following cases: case 30/77 *Regina* v. *Bouchereau* [1977] ECR 1999; case 131/79 *Regina* v. *Secretary of State for Home Affairs* [1980] ECR 1585; case 157/79 *Regina* v. *Pieck* [1980] ECR 2171; joined cases 115 and 116/81 *Adoui* v. *Belgium and city of Liège* and *Cournuaille* v. *Belgium* [1982] ECR 1665.

21. We refer to the main decisions on this matter: case 98/79 *Pecastaing* v. *Belgium* [1980] ECR 691; *Regina* v. *Secretary of State for Home Affairs*, *supra*, n. 20.

22. We refer to the main decisions of the Court of Justice on the professions:
- *Social security*
114/88 *Delbar* v. *Caisse Allocation Familiales de Roubaix-Tourcoing* [1989] ECR 4067
- *lawyers*
2/74 *Reyners* v. *Belgium* [1974] ECR 631; 71/76 *Thieffry* v. *Conseil de l'ordre des Avocats à la Cour de Paris* [1977] ECR 765; 107/83 *Ordre des Avocats au Barreau de Paris* v. *Onno Klopp* [1984] ECR 2971; 292/86 *Gullung* v. *Conseil de l'Ordre des Avocats du Barreau de Colmar et de Saverne* [1988] ECR 111; 427/85 *Commission of the European Communities* v. *Germany* [1988] ECR 1123;
- *medical and paramedical professions*

5. SECTORIAL DIRECTIVES

As we have already mentioned, Article 57 envisions the adoption of directives aimed at both the mutual recognition of diplomas and the coordination of national legislation with respect to access to and the exercise of professional activities. On the basis of Article 57, the Community has adopted specific regulations aimed at harmonizing the requirements of vocational training in order to make possible the recognition of diplomas meeting such requirements. The objective is not only to ensure an equivalent training level in order to achieve freedom of establishment and freedom to provide services through the recognition of diplomas, but also to enable professionals with significant experience in the country of origin to exercise their activity also given the absence of diplomas that meet the requirements of the host country.

A brief examination of the regulations relating to the various categories of professionals will enable us to assess the real impact of this legislative action on the liberalization process.

5.1 Medical and paramedical professions

Professionals in the health-care industry are the only ones who have benefitted from the issuance of specific regulations, both from the standpoint of the freedom of establishment and the freedom to provide services. The liberalization process of this industry has been facilitated by the fact that the level of vocational training is very similar (in terms of both the length of study and the level of instruction) in the

---

49/86 *Commission of the European Communities* v. *Italy* [1987] ECR 2995; 306/84 *Commission of the European Communities* v. *Belgium* [1987] ECR 675; 98, 162 and 258/85 *Bertini, Bisignani and others* v. *Regione Lazio e Unità sanitarie locali* [1986] ECR 1885; 246/80 *Broekmeulen* v. *Huisarts Registratie Commissie* [1981] ECR 2311; 96/85 *Commission of the European Communities* v. *France* [1986] ECR 1475;
(physician and dentist)
5/83 *Pretore di Lodi* v. *Rienks* [1983] ECR 4233;
(veterinary)
136/78 *Ministère Public* v. *Auer* [1979] ECR 437; 271/82 *Auer* v. *Ministère Public* [1983] ECR 2727; 29/84 *Commission of the European Communities* v. *Germany* [1985] ECR 1661;
(nurse)
221/85 *Commission of the European Communities* v. *Belgium* [1987] ECR 719
(clinical biology laboratory)
- *unregulated professions*
61/89 *Bouchoucha* v. *France* [1990] ECR I 3551; joined cases C-54/88, C-91/88 and C-14/89 Criminal Proceedings against Eleonora Nino and others [1990] ECR 3537;
- *technical professions*
36/87 *Commission of the European Communities* v. *Greece* [1988] ECR 4415;
(architect)
11/77 *Patrick* v. *Ministre des Affaires Culturelles* [1977] ECR 1199;
(architect)

different Member States. For each professional activity in the health industry, two directives have been issued: one relating to the mutual recognition of diplomas, the other on legislative coordination.

We will focus our examination on the directives on the medical profession. The activities involved are disciplined in basically the same way as the other professions in the health industry that have been liberalized.[23]

5.1.1   *Directive on coordination*

The directive on the coordination of national legislation details the minimum requirements (such as the length of study, the degree of knowledge that must be acquired for each subject taught, the access to specialization, and so on) which must be met in order for the Member States to grant diplomas.

5.1.2   *Directive on the mutual recognition of diplomas*

The directive on mutual recognition provides for the equivalence of diplomas granted in accordance with the minimum requirements set forth in the directive on legislative coordination.

If a diploma has been granted without meeting such minimum requirements, the recognition is subject to the release of a certificate, confirming that the medical profession has been exercised for a period of time specified in the directive.

The directives also envision rules aimed at favouring the exercise of the right of establishment and to provide services, such as the requirements on the access to the profession.

It is important to point out that the purpose of these directives is not completely to harmonize the different national educational systems. The preamble of directive 75/363 (the directive on coordination) states, in fact, that the coordination must be limited to the observance of minimum requirements, thus leaving the Member States free to organize their own teaching system.

5.2   Legal profession

The legal profession has not enjoyed the same degree of liberalization as the medical profession. Because the practice of the law requires specific knowledge of national legislation, it has not been possible to determine the minimum qualification require-

---

23. The following directives have been enacted on the health industry:
Directive 75/362 on the mutual recognition of diplomas; Directive 75/363 on the coordination of national provisions on the access and exercise of the activity, OJ 1975 L 167/1, 14.
Nursing - Directives 77/452 and 77/453, OJ 1977 L 176/1, 8.
Dentistry - Directives 78/686 and 78/687, OJ 1978 L 233/1, 10.
Veterinary - Directives 78/1026 and 78/1027, OJ 1978 L 362/1, 7.
Obstetrics - Directives 80/154 and 80/155, OJ 1980 L 33/1, 8.
Pharmacy - Directives 85/432 and 85/433, OJ 1985 L 253/34, 37.

ments that could serve as the basis for the mutual recognition of diplomas. As a consequence of the lack of legislative coordination, professionals are prevented in practice from exercising their activity permanently in another Member State.

The only directive which has been issued does liberalize the activities exercised by lawyers as providers of services.[24] Directive 77/249 disciplines the ethical standards that must be met in the exercise of the profession and allows lawyers to represent clients in judicial proceedings.

5.3   Technical professions

The adoption of coordination measures for the technical professions has been hampered by differences in the national educational systems. The only directive that has been issued dates back to 1985 and concerns the mutual recognition of diplomas for architects.[25]

In the absence of a specific directive on minimum requirements, the only one which must be met is that the diploma be granted only after completing a four-year university programme.

No agreement has been reached by the Council of Ministers regarding the engineering profession. However, it must be pointed out that, with respect to Italy, the directive which has been just examined enables engineers with a diploma in civil engineering to move to another Member State to practice that profession.

5.4   Final remarks

Our analysis has pointed out that the Community's legislative activity has had a limited role on the liberalization process of the different professional categories, except in the case of the health industry where a certain equivalence of the educational standards already existed. We must therefore conclude that what is missing is a precise commitment at the political level to determine minimum requirements, that would be valid in all Member States of the Community.

It is true that the coordination of national legislation has enabled the achievement of a minimum level of professional qualification in the case of some activities. However, further progress in the enactment of sectorial directives will require solutions to very complex problems.

First, it requires a long period of time to develop a single regulatory system for all types of professional activities, even in the absence of national resistance. Second, it is important to point out that the national provisions adopted for the

---

24. Directive 77/249, 22 March 1977, OJ 1977 L 78/17.
25. Directive 85/384, 10 June 1985, OJ 1985 L 223/15.

implementation of the Community directives have not always been in accordance with the directives.[26]

It is true that professional activities are not easily regulated by specific directives aimed at harmonizing occupational qualifications. Technological progress and the acquisition of new knowledge, especially in the legal field involve continual change in the educational systems in the form of the establishment of new faculties and new specialization programmes. The objective of harmonizing the different educational systems is not easy to achieve in a fast-changing environment.

6.   GENERAL FRAMEWORK FOR THE RECOGNITION OF DIPLOMAS — AN ANALYSIS OF DIRECTIVE 89/48

The enactment of directive 89/48 of 1988[27] represents an important step in the liberalization of professional activities, and a turning point in the Community's approach. An analysis of this directive will enable us to assess the actual degree of liberalization achieved in the case of professional activities and the problems that could arise in the implementation process.

The directive regulates the activity of all workers who — whether self-employed or not — intend to exercise their profession in another Member State either temporarily or permanently, except for those whose activity is already regulated by another specific directive (as in the case of the health-care industry). Directive 89/48 therefore differs from other directives in its horizontal approach to the issue. The directive defines the terms of 'regulated professional activity' and 'diploma'. A 'regulated professional activity' is defined as a profession whose exercise is subject to a higher education diploma which certifies that a three-year period of vocational training has been completed. The diploma must be granted by a competent authority of the Member State in which it has been pursued and must certify that its holder has obtained all the necessary qualifications to practice a regulated professional activity. It is therefore evident that an academic degree may not be regarded as a diploma, as this term is defined in the directive. As an example, in Italy, in order to exercise the profession of engineer, a diploma will require both the university degree and the certification that the state examination has been passed.

Since the recognition of diplomas is not subject to the preliminary harmonization of the systems of vocational training, other establishment of compensation mechan-

26. As an example, the Italian Law which implemented Directive 77/249 to facilitate the effective exercise by lawyers of the freedom to provide services (Law of 9 February 1982, Gazzetta Ufficiale 12 February 1982, n. 42) has been amply criticized; see comments by A. Annecchino in: *Professioni e servizi nella Cee* p. 301, (Padova, Cedam, 1985) and by M. Panebianco in *Diritto comunitario e degli scambi internazionali* (1981) p. 765.

27. Directive 89/48, 21 December 1988 on a general system on the recognition of higher education diplomas which certify the completion of at least three-years of a university programme, OJ 1989 L 19/16.

ism has been deemed necessary in order to compensate for the differences that exist among the educational and training levels in the different countries.

If such differences relate to the length of study, the recognition of a diploma in the host country may be subject to a period of professional experience. In contrast, if such differences relate to the content of the study or to the exercise of activities which were not required in the country of origin, the holder of the diploma may choose between a period of adaptation or an aptitude test. A restriction on this freedom of choice is provided for where the exercise of a profession requires precise knowledge of the national legislation. Although the directive addresses the legal profession, accounting and tax practices may also be included.

In any case, Member States retain ample flexibility in the evaluation of applications for the recognition of diplomas. However, the directive requires the competent authorities to communicate the outcome of the recognition process with a reasoned decision within four months from the filing of the petition. In the absence of such decision, or if the applicant wishes to object to the decision, a remedy may be sought before a court in accordance with national law.

In our opinion, despite the existence of procedural protection, serious efforts on the part of the Commission will be necessary to ensure that the directive is implemented correctly by the Member States. Particularly in those cases in which diploma recognition is subject to an aptitude test, the Member States could take advantage of this examination to discriminate against citizens of the other Member States.

As a final remark, in the case of those professions, particularly of a technical nature, in which the level of vocational training varies greatly among the Member States, an additional benefit of the liberalization process could be to induce countries with low qualification requirements to improve their educational system. Only through the implementation of this directive 89/48, will it be possible to decide, in the case of same professions, whether it is necessary to enact directives (such as those already examined for some professional activities) setting minimum qualification requirements.

7.   FURTHER DEVELOPMENTS

The case-law developed by the Court of Justice on the free exercise of professional services will also have an impact on the right of establishment of professionals. To an extent, this will result in developments which might not have been foreseen or intended, at least in the case of specific professions, such as the legal profession.

The example of the legal profession in Italy can be used to illustrate this point. Italian law provides that a lawyer may belong only to one bar association (there are as many bar associations as there are tribunals). Therefore, if a lawyer intends to exercise his profession in Milan he will belong to the Bar Association of Milan but will not be allowed to become a member of any other bar association in Italy. He may both defend and represent a client only in the court of appeal within the district where his bar association is located, i.e., the district of the Court of Appeal of Milan.

If a client's case is heard in the Court of Florence, since it is outside the Court of Appeal of Milan, he may defend his client but not represent him. In fact he has to appoint a lawyer belonging to the Bar Association of Florence who will represent the client at the tribunal proceedings. Otherwise, all judicial acts and proceedings are void and not taken into consideration by the Court of Florence.

The case-law developed by the Court of Justice enables a lawyer from Frankfurt, Paris or Brussels to defend and represent his client at the Court of Milan, as well as Florence, Rome or Turin, without necessarily belonging to any bar association in Italy.[28] The Court has clarified that the only obligation upon the lawyer is that of fixing his domicile with a lawyer belonging to the competent bar association. This case-law has provoked serious objections in Germany, and the German Law which was enacted after the ruling of the Court of Justice is still contrary to the principles affirmed by the Court.

If these principles are valid for lawyers, they must be also valid for other professions, for example that of *commercialista* (Italian tax accountant and business consultant, an expert in commercial law). A *commercialista* may represent and defend a client in Italian tax-related proceedings only if he belongs to the competent professional association. However, a professional from a Member State with qualifications equivalent to those of a *commercialista* may invoke the above-mentioned case-law of the Court of Justice, and be entitled to defend a client in Italian tax proceedings, simply by fixing his domicile with a colleague with whom he intends to cooperate.

The evolution in the case-law of the Court of Justice will have a wide range of consequences, since it will enable businessmen who operate in different countries to be assisted by the professionals of their home country.

With respect to the civil engineering profession, attention may focus on the liberalization process resulting from the introduction of the directives on public procurement for works and for services (the latter will soon be enacted).

As the technical, juridical, tax and accounting rules become more harmonized in the different countries, the easier it will become for professionals to continue assisting their clients in the different Member States. This process will be further enhanced by the integration resulting from the establishment of the single market in Europe.

At this point, one may wonder whether professionals will still be interested in taking advantage of their right of establishment since this would require them to be subject to examinations and/or training in order to exercise that profession. In fact, the case-law developed by the Court of Justice would enable professionals to practice their activity by simply fixing their domicile with colleagues with whom they intend to work.

---

28. Case 427/87 *European Commission* v. *Germany* [1988] ECR 1154. The ruling has been reaffirmed in the recent decision of case 294/89 *European Commission* v. *Republic of France*, OJ 1991 C 203/7.

In the case of both professionals and companies, there are several factors that may influence the choice to exercise the right of establishment in order to practice an economic activity. If the exercise of the right to provide services is economically convenient, it is obvious that the professional or the company will take advantage of such right whenever it presents greater returns.

For example, there are certain economic activities, such as in the fields of banking or insurance, where the exercise of the freedom to provide services is usually more convenient that the exercise of the right of establishment.

8.   CONCLUSION

Our analysis of Community legislation and case-law enables us to evaluate the level of liberalization that has been reached in the different professional activities. It is reasonable to assume that the correct and uniform implementation of directive 89/48 and the adoption of a general framework for the recognition of higher education diplomas[29] will facilitate the establishment of a free market of professional activities.

Moreover, the case-law developed by the Court of Justice concerning the free movement of services will, on the one hand, enable professionals to avoid unjustifiable restrictions against the right of establishment introduced by the Member States, and on the other, it will reduce the importance of the right of establishment for professionals, because they can reach the same objective through the freedom to provide services.

29. Proposal for a directive on a second general system on the recognition of diplomas, OJ 1989 C 263/1. Changes to the proposal, OJ 1990 C 217/4.

450

FREE MOVEMENT OF LEGAL PERSONS

Inne G.F. Cath[*]

1.   INTRODUCTION[**]

Natural persons are a creation of nature; legal persons of national law.[1] The EEC Treaty relates to economic activities that are physically carried out by natural persons, either as such or organized in the form of a legal person or persons. The decision whether to carry out economic activities as a natural or a legal person depends upon various factors, including not only the applicable fiscal regime and rules for the limitation of liability, but also organizational, commercial or even promotional purposes. This distinction between natural persons and legal persons relates to form, not to substance, and the economic operator should be free to select the form in which to conduct his economic activities. Intra-Community economic activities can be carried out either by cross-border movement of goods and/or services or by cross-border movement of the supplier or receiver of such goods and/or services. In the first case the emphasis is put upon the movement of the goods and/or services; in the second case the emphasis is on the movement of the supplier or receiver thereof. From the perspective of rights guaranteed and treatment received under the Treaty, the form selected should make no difference.

In the case-law of the Court of Justice the basic principle has emerged that — in the absence of Community harmonization — a particular economic activity should be carried out legitimately in *a* Member State in accordance with *its* rules and regulations. If this requirement is met, national obstacles to the cross-border exercise of such economic activity, whether relating to 'import' or 'export' thereof, should be justified from a Community perspective and proportionate to the non-economic public policy aim (if any) pursued by such obstacle. The burden of proof is incumbent upon the national authority invoking such national rule.[2]

---

* Member of the Bar of The Hague; the author is indebted for fiscal matters to Hans C. Bol.

** Editor's note: Unless indicated otherwise, all references to specific articles in this respect designate provisions of the EEC Treaty.

1. At Community level there is nowadays the 'European Economic Interest Grouping', created by Regulation 2137/85 of 25 July 1985 (OJ 1985, L 199/1). So far unsuccessful attempts have been made for a 'Societas Europea' (OJ 1970, C 124; EC-Bulletin 4/75).

2. Under Article 34 of the Treaty the Court applies a non-discrimination standard. See e.g., Case 15/79 *Groenveld* v. *Productschap voor Vee en Vlees* ECR [1979] 3409.

H.G. Schermers et al., eds., Free Movement of Persons in Europe

Another approach with the same objective in the absence of Community legislation on the matter, often applied with respect to the right of establishment, is the determination of equivalence, e.g., professional qualifications in a specific area or at a general level.[3] Account must be taken of qualifications obtained or controls exercised in the Member State of origin and unnecessary repetition of such controls or imposition of unnecessary or disproportionate additional requirements must be avoided: 'home country control'.[4]

The distinctions in the Treaty between free movement of persons, goods, services (and to a certain extent payments) and the rights of establishment of self-employed natural persons or legal persons should be seen as the result of the organization of the subject-matter in the Treaty rather than of any significant difference in substantive treatment. Except when specifically provided for otherwise under the Treaty (or its interpretation by the Court of Justice), there should be no national exceptions or 'reserved areas' that cannot be affected by the above principles on cross-border movement of economic activities, unless the subject-matter is completely harmonized at Community level and leaving no discretion to the Member States. In that case an 'objective legality test' could be applied comparing national legislation with the Community legislation concerned.[5]

The principles summarized above, could also apply to the free movement of legal persons. This report will focus upon intra-Community cross-border establishment of legal persons, not on cross-border provision of services by legal persons.[6]

2. RIGHT OF ESTABLISHMENT

The second paragraph of Article 52 of the Treaty provides self-employed natural persons with the right to take up and pursue activities and to set up and manage undertakings in particular companies or firms within the meaning of Article 58

---

3. See e.g., case 71/76, *Thieffry* v. *Conseil de l'ordre des avocats à la Cour de Paris* ECR [1977] 765; case 11/77 *Patrick* v. *Ministre des Affaires Culturelles* ECR [1977] 1199; case 136/78 *Ministère Public* v. *Auer* ECR [1979] 437; case 222/86 *UNECTEF* v. *Heylens* ECR [1987] 4097; the specific directives on harmonization of various medical professions; the 'General Services Directive': Directive 89/48/EEC of 21 December 1988 (OJ 1989/L 19/16).

4. See e.g., joined cases 110-111/79 *Ministère Public and A.S.B.L.* v. *Van Wesemael* ECR [1979] 35; case 279/80 *Webb* ECR [1981] 3305.

5. See e.g., case 51/76 *VNO* v. *Inspecteur der Invoerrechten en Accijnzen* ECR [1977] 113; case 38/77 *Enka* v. *Inspecteur der Invoerrechten en Accijnzen* ECR [1977] 2203; case 80/86 *Kolpinghuis* ECR [1987] 3969.

6. According to the case-law of the Court of Justice the rules on establishment apply (in substitution of the rules on provision of services) as of the moment a legal person acquires a permanent presence in another Member State, even if that presence does not take the form of a branch or an agency, but consists merely of an office managed by the undertaking's own staff or by a person who is independent but with authorization to act on a permanent basis for the undertaking as would be the case with an agency (case 205/84 *Commission* v. *Germany* ECR (1986) 3755 (Recital 21); see also case 220/83 *Commission* v. *France* ECR [1986] 3663; case 252/83 *Commission* v. *Denmark* ECR [1986] 3713: case 206/84 *Commission* v. *Ireland* ECR [1986] 3817: ('co-insurance cases').

under the conditions laid down for its own nationals by the law of the Member State where such establishment is effected. Article 58 provides that '[c]ompanies or firms formed in accordance with the law of a Member State and having their registered office, central administration or principal place of business within the Community shall — for the purpose of cross-border establishment — be treated in the same way as natural persons who are nationals of Member States.'

The right of *primary* establishment for self-employed natural persons is guaranteed by the first sentence of Article 52. This provision was given direct effect in the *Reyners* case.[7]Articles 52 and 58 do not distinguish between natural and legal persons in regard to the right of cross-border *primary* establishment.

Articles 52 and 58 guarantee nationals of a Member State (whether natural or legal persons) the right of *secondary* establishment in the territory of another Member State, i.e., 'the setting up of agencies, branches or subsidiaries.' The rights of primary and secondary intra-Community cross-border establishment may be limited by the operation of Articles 55 and 56. Article 55 relates to 'activities which in that State are connected, even occasionally, with the exercise of official authority.' Article 56 relates to '(. . .) the applicability of provisions laid down by law, regulation or administrative action providing for special treatment for foreign nationals on the grounds of public policy, public security or public health.'

These Treaty exceptions apply under the general proviso that these matters are not covered by exhaustive harmonization, leaving no room for additional national measures necessary and proportionate on a Community and non-economic basis.

The rights guaranteed under Article 52 for self-employed natural persons are confined to 'nationals of a Member State' (including nationals of Overseas Countries and Territories to which the provisions of Part IV of the Treaty apply). Excluded from its operation are self-employed nationals of non-EC countries.

Legal persons do not possess a passport. As a creation of national law, not of nature, the 'nationality' of legal persons is determined by 'the law of a Member State'. In addition, Article 58 requires that such legal persons have their registered office, central administration or principal place of business within the Community. Article 58 does not require that the 'registered office, central administration or principal place of business' be within the same Member State as the Member State of incorporation. Article 58 is 'neutral' in this respect.

The language of Article 58 further suggests that the requirements of 'registered office', 'central administration' or 'principal place of business' are alternative rather than cumulative. The text of Article 58, therefore, does not exclude — *prima facie* — the possibility that a legal entity formed in accordance with the law of Member State A, could have its 'registered office' in Member State B, its 'central administration' in Member State C and its 'principal place of business' in Member State D. In the event of primary establishment, it is even conceivable for a non-Community based legal person to set up a subsidiary corporation in accordance with the law of a Member State and then rely upon primary establishment throughout the Community

7. Case 2/74 *Reyners* v. *Belgium* ECR [1974] 631.

without effectively transferring its main (or indeed any) economic activities into the Community.

The General Programme on the abolition of restrictions on freedom of establishment, adopted on 18 December 1961[8] 'provides useful guidance for the implementation of the relevant provisions of the Treaty.'[9] The 1961 General Programme purports to set certain minimum requirements in order to abate the theoretical possibilities mentioned above. In the event that a legal person formed in accordance with the law of a Member State has only its 'registered office' within the Community, it can rely only upon the rights of *secondary* establishment, provided the activity of such legal person:

> '(. . .) présente un lien effectif et continu avec l'économie d'un État Membre (. . .), étant exclu que ce lien puisse dépendre de la nationalité, notamment des associés ou des membres des organes de gestion ou de surveillance ou des personnes détenant le capital social.'[10]

If this requirement is met, then Community law prohibits any formal or informal, direct or indirect, difference in treatment between 'national' legal entities and 'foreign' legal entities, that have established themselves cross-border on a secondary basis.

In addition, Title III of the 1961 General Programme provides a long and non-exhaustive list of examples of express or implied 'restrictions' on the freedom of secondary establishment, such as restrictions on access to economic activities in general, licensing or specific document requirements, imposition of specific conditions, prior practical training requirements, financial impediments, such as specific fiscal or other charges, guarantees or security, access to professional training, participation rights in legal entities, compensation in the social security system, different treatment in the event of expropriation, agreements to be concluded, public procurement, administrative concessions or licenses, purchase, sale or use of assets and intellectual property rights, loans, State aids, procedural rights and membership of professional associations. In view of the fact that even current national legislation may contain direct or indirect 'sins' against these clearly expressed examples, it is remarkable that the first case relating to the right of secondary establishment of legal persons only reached the Court of Justice at a very recent stage. This first case was decided by the Court of Justice in 1986. The following sections of this report analyze this first case and the subsequent decisions made by the Court in 1986 and 1988.

---

8. OJ, English Special Edition, Second Series, IX, p. 7.

9. Case 71/76, *Thieffry* v. *Conseil de l'ordre des avoates à la Cour de Paris*, (ECR) [1977] 765 (Recital 13).

10. See *supra*, n. 8, at p. 7; unfortunately the English text was not available.

3.   *COMMISSION* V. *FRANCE (AVOIR FISCAL)*[11]

This case concerned an action brought by the Commission under Article 169 of the Treaty against the French Government relating to the cumulative discriminatory effect of a number of provisions in the French *code générale des impôts* relating to tax credits (*avoir fiscal*) for French establishments of foreign-based legal entities. The French code made tax credits available only to French establishments of foreign-based legal entities organized in the form of a French legal entity (e.g., *société anonyme, s.a.*) and not to French establishments organized in the form of a branch or agency. The Commission's case was initially confined to French establishments of foreign-based *insurance* companies. However, during the proceedings the case was extended to French establishments of all foreign-based companies affected by these French tax provisions. This extension was accepted by the Court.

The Court held that the French tax provisions constituted a difference in treatment because (i) French establishments of foreign-based companies were treated differently from French companies, even though the French legislator in fact admitted that there was no objective difference between their positions, and because (ii) Article 52:

'. . . leaves traders free to choose the appropriate legal form in which to pursue their activities in another Member State and that freedom of choice must not be limited by discriminatory tax provisions.'[12]

The arguments put forward in defence by the French Government and rejected by the Court are noteworthy in this context. First, the French Government argued that the difference in treatment was objectively justified because it was based upon the (international) tax law distinction between residents and non-residents, which is to be found in all legal systems and is internationally accepted: tax law notions of residence should equally be used as the connecting factor in application of Articles 52 and 58. In addition, the French Government submitted that branches and agencies of foreign-based companies enjoy various other advantages over French companies, thereby balancing out any disadvantages with respect to the issue of tax credits. Moreover, a 'pragmatic' argument was made to the effect that these disadvantages are, in any event, insignificant and may be easily avoided by setting up a subsidiary in France.

Although the Court conceded that a distinction based on the location of the registered office of a company or the place of residence of a natural person might, under certain conditions, be justified in an area such as tax law,[13] it nevertheless rejected this proposition on the grounds that tax-based notions of residence (i) cannot serve as a proper and objective justification for differences in treatment

11. Case 270/83, *Commission* v. *France* (ECR) [1986] 273.
12. Ibid., Recital 22.
13. Ibid., Recital 19.

between 'national' and 'foreign' legal entities and (ii) Article 58 uses as the connecting factor with the legal system of a particular State not the notion of residence, but that of 'registered office' which also may include a branch or agency.[14] The 'pragmatic' submissions of the French Government were equally rejected.

In its second line of argument, the French Government sought to justify the difference in treatment by reference to the absence of harmonization of national tax systems, double taxation agreements concluded between the Member States and expressly recognized in Article 220 and the necessity of preventing tax evasion. In response, the Court held that neither the absence of harmonization nor the risk of tax evasion permitted 'any derogation from the fundamental principle of freedom of establishment on such grounds.'[15]

The Court rejected the argument on double taxation agreements because (i) such agreements do not deal with the case at issue, and (ii) the rights conferred by Article 52:

'(. . .) are unconditional and a Member State cannot make respect for them subject to the contents of an agreement concluded with another Member State. In particular, that article does not permit those rights to be made subject to conditions of reciprocity imposed for the purpose of obtaining corresponding advantages in other Member States.'[16]

In many of its basic assumptions and notions, (international) tax law differs from the principles underlying Articles 52 and 58. This means that these Treaty rules may provide a legal basis for significant inroads into national tax law systems (and, hence, the principle of reciprocity upon which double taxation agreements rest) as an instrument to pursue certain (desired) national policy and budgetary objectives.

However, this expectation is somewhat tempered by the judgments of the Court in two joined cases relating to fiscal restrictions of the freedom to provide cross-border services by insurance companies.[17]

According to Belgian tax law premiums for, *inter alia*, life insurance and pension schemes are tax deductible, provided such premiums are 'payable in Belgium'.[18]

The same treatment was denied by the Belgian tax authorities to premiums payable to German insurance companies for the same type of policies by a German national, resident in Belgium. Obviously, such difference in tax treatment would render the conclusion of such policies with insurance companies based in other Member States, very unattractive and, hence, prove to be a formidable barrier to the

14. Ibid., Recitals 18 and 20.
15. Ibid., Recital 25.
16. Ibid., Recital 26.
17. Joined cases C-204/90 *Bachmann* v. *Belgium* and C-300/90 *Commission* v. *Belgium*, 28 January 1992, not yet published.
18. Similar restrictions exist in other tax laws such as Art. 45(5) Netherlands' Income Tax Act ('Wet Inkomstenbelasting') where tax deductible premiums must be payable to insurance companies or natural persons (under certain conditions), established in the Netherlands, with certain exceptions for immigrating foreigners, provided the insurance relationship existed at least three years prior to (tax) residence in the Netherlands).

cross-border provision of such services (and cross-border movement of (employed) persons without any clear justification other then national (budgetary) interests: this was the conclusion of the Commission and the Advocate-General.

The Court accepted that this difference in treatment constituted a restriction on free movement of (employed) persons and provision of services, but yielded to the justification proposed by the Belgian government (and other governments) by the introduction of a new 'rule of reason' exception on these freedoms, denominated *cohérence fiscale*: in the absence of harmonisation in the field of tax law mainte-nance of the (budgetary) linkage between tax deductibility for premiums and tax imposition on payments made by insurance companies under these policies is neces-sary and not disproportionate as other means of ensuring such *cohérence fiscale* (e.g., guarantees or even deposits by the foreign-based insurance companies for such tax payments) were considered insufficient.[19]

This finding is for various reasons, which cannot be dealt with exhaustively in this context, both in reasoning and result less than convincing. For example, in other fields restrictions on freedoms, guaranteed under the Treaty, of a less far-reaching nature have been deemed unjustified, or at least disproportionate. (See, e.g., the cases referred to in footnotes 4 and 5, where national authorities were required in their licensing policy to take account of licenses provided and controls executed in this respect in the Member State of origin ('home country control')). Furthermore, many international double taxation agreements fully accept, or are even designed on this basis. In the event of cross-border movement that premiums will have been deducted for which no (more or less) 'corresponding' revenues are generated for the state by taxation of payments under such policies. Consequently a situation may have arisen for certain Member States, such as the Netherlands, which have con-cluded many international double taxation treaties that cross-border movement in or out of the Community receives more favourable tax treatment than movement within the Community. This consequence was taken into account by the Court, but it was left to the Council to find appropriate solution.

The second case in this field presented the issue (although not formally responded to) of whether this same principle applies with respect to the right of pri-mary establishment and particularly, within the field of social security.

4.   CASE 79/85, *SEGERS* V. *BEDRIJFSVERENIGING*[20]

This case involved Segers, a Dutch national, who established himself in the Nether-lands and exercised his professional activities as a natural person mainly in the Netherlands. Segers wished for a variety of business reasons to incorporate himself. In the Netherlands the foundation of a private limited liability company (*Besloten Vennootschap*, or B.V.), which is the usual legal vehicle for smaller businesses,

19. Ibid., Recitals 23-25, *supra*, n. 17.
20. Case 79/85, *Segers* v. *Bedrijfsvereniging* (ECR) [1986] 2375.

requires not only a notarial deed containing the articles of association and accompanying documents, but also consent by the Ministry of Justice to create the legal person. This consent relates both to the legal correctness of the documents required and presented to the Ministry and the 'morality' of the persons wishing to form the legal person. In practice, this Ministerial consent is subject to considerable administrative delays (up to four months), even when the documentation presented and the antecedents of the founder(s) are beyond reproach.

Segers could not await this period of time and transferred his business into a 'private company limited by shares' (Ltd.) in accordance with English company law where comparable consent requirements and accompanying delays do not exist. In addition, the legal form of a 'limited' company is better known in international business than a Dutch 'B.V.'. Segers became, in equal parts with his wife, shareholder of Slenderose Ltd. The registered office was in London, and Segers was the sole managing director. The English company was not only registered in England, but also *in its own right* at the Commercial Registry of the Chamber of Commerce competent for the place where Segers was resident in the Netherlands.

As the sole managing director of Slenderose Ltd. Segers applied for registration with the *Bedrijfsvereniging voor Bank- en Verzekeringswezen, Groothandel en Vrije Beroepen* (Banking, Insurance, Wholesale Trade and Professions Association), which is the authority in charge of the due operation of the mandatory employees' social security system in force in the Netherlands. According to the case-law in force at that time (later repealed) of the Supreme Administrative Court of Social Security Matters in the Netherlands (*Centrale Raad van Beroep*) the notion of an employee relationship was extended to managing directors, even if they owned 50% or more of shares in the company.[21] The application was refused by the *Bedrijfsvereniging* on the ground that this case-law applied only to directors of companies incorporated and with a registered office in the Netherlands and not to directors of companies incorporated and having a registered office abroad.

The *Centrale Raad van Beroep* asked the Court of Justice, *inter alia*, whether such distinction between the director/shareholder of a private limited liability company established in the Netherlands and that of a private limited liability company incorporated under the law of another Member State would be compatible with the freedom of establishment within the Community, even if the foreign company did not carry out any actual business in the Member State of incorporation.

As a matter of principle and by reference to the 1961 General Programme, which prohibits all provisions and administrative practices that 'deny or restrict the rights to participate in social security schemes, in particular sickness . . . insurance schemes,'[22] the Court held that the discriminatory treatment of employees in connection with social security protection 'indirectly restricts the freedom of companies

---

21. Centrale Raad van Beroep (CRB) 10 December 1968 (RSV 1969, 40-41); repealed: CBR 4 October 1985 (RSV 1986, 21).

22. *Supra*, n. 8, at p. 8.

of another Member State to establish themselves (. . .) in the Member State concerned.'[23]

The principle is clear. However, the Court added the phrase 'through an agency, branch or subsidiary', which points in the direction that this ruling is only valid for the right of *secondary* establishment, not of *primary* establishment, as was the case presented by Segers.

In response to the significance of the fact that the English company clearly did not conduct business in the United Kingdom, the Court quoted the two requirements of Article 58, to which it added: 'Provided that those requirements are satisfied, the fact that the company conducts its business through an agency, branch or subsidiary, solely in another Member State is immaterial.'[24]

This wording seems to suggest — at any rate in so far as secondary establishment is concerned — that 'registered office', 'central administration' or 'principal place of business' are not cumulative, but alternative requirements.

From a practical point of view in the *Segers* case, it mattered little whether the principle set forth above was intended to apply to primary establishment: having received the answer of the Court of Justice, the *Centrale Raad van Beroep* granted Segers his sickness benefit.

From the point of view of doctrine, the question of the scope of the principle does not seem without importance. Secondary establishment does not affect the territoriality of the existence and functioning of a legal person dependent upon the 'charter' granted by the national law of a Member State. The second sentence of Article 52 essentially guarantees the freedom 'to choose the appropriate legal form in which to pursue (. . .) activities in another Member State.'[25]

However, this freedom of choice is limited to those legal forms that exist and function according to the national law of the Member State of *establishment*. As such, it does not imply that the legal form of the Member State of origin could be chosen (for whatever reason).

Primary establishment would imply the possibility of actual 'export' from the Member State of origin and 'import' to the Member State of establishment of foreign legal persons retaining in an unaltered form their original legal 'charter'. In the absence of exhaustive harmonization of company law on the basis of Article 54(3)(g), free movement of legal persons in the true sense and comparable to the free movement of goods, services or natural persons would imply, in principle, recognition of foreign legal persons, existing and functioning in accordance with the law of the Member State of origin, unless a national rule of a non-economic nature, justified and proportionate from a Community perspective, could oppose such recognition. If direct effect were to be granted to Article 58, harmonization could be confined to those elements of national company law which are justified and proportionate.

23. *Supra*, n. 20, Recital 15.
24. *Supra*, n. 20, Recital 16.
25. See *supra*, n. 12.

A major obstacle appears to be the applicability of private international law: the age-old discussion between the doctrine of incorporation and that of *siège réel*.[26] Under the doctrine of incorporation a foreign corporation created in accordance with a foreign legal system and having its statutory seat (e.g., registered office) in a foreign State is recognized as such by the host State in which the company operates. Within the Community this system prevails in various forms in the Netherlands, the United Kingdom, Ireland and Denmark. It also applies in the United States, where company law varies from state to state. Under the doctrine of incorporation a legal person should be able to move its seat to another country without losing its original corporate 'charter'.

Under the system of *siège réel*, recognition of a foreign company is denied, or made dependent upon the 're-creation' of the foreign company in accordance with the requirements of the legal system of the host State, or at least application of certain of its mandatory requirements, if the real centre of the company's activities or decision-making has moved to that State. This may even imply a certain legal schizophrenia, because the company — in order to have a valid existence — must comply with the legal requirements both of the State of incorporation and of the host State, whereas under the doctrine of incorporation only one legal system is applicable. In practice, the 'old' company is liquidated and a 'new' company is created. The system of *siège réel* prevails in all the other Member States.

The rationale of the doctrine of incorporation is legal certainty: a company's statutory seat is an objective fact, whereas determination of its centre of decision-making or of its main economic activities implies a difficult subjective assessment, which may vary from country to country and lead to more than one seat (dual residence). In addition, transfer of the company's seat does not imply liquidation and/or winding up of its assets. The doctrine of *siège réel* is generally defended on the grounds that abuse of foreign and more lenient company law should be prevented or that certain mandatory requirements of domestic substantive law are of such primary importance for public policy considerations that these must apply (*règles d'application immédiate*).

Between recognition under the doctrine of incorporation and only limited or no recognition under the doctrine of *siège réel* private international law has developed a third option: 'the doctrine of social priorities'.[27] Under this doctrine a foreign legal person may be recognized as such, subject to the possibility of application of certain domestic substantive rules of a public policy nature. An example of this type of domestic legislation is the successive United Kingdom's Companies Acts, under which the existence of a foreign company depends on the law under which it was incorporated, but which impose certain requirements, such as registration and the

---

26. See e.g., C.W.A. Timmermans, pre-advies Nederlandse Vereniging van Internationaal Recht (Deventer, 1980); E.A. Brood, De vestigingsplaats van vennootschappen (Deventer, 1984); I.G.F. Cath, 'Freedom of Establishment of Companies: a New Step Towards Completion of the Internal Market', *Yearbook of European Law* (1986) pp. 247, 249-252 (and literature quoted).

27. P. Vlas, *Rechtspersonen in het Internationaal Privaatrecht* (Deventer, 1982) pp. 62-79.

preparation and delivery of accounts, when the foreign company establishes a place of business in the United Kingdom.

A similar approach would be conceivable in those Member States where certain rules of employees' participation are considered to be of primary public policy importance. An example is Dutch law, which applies the doctrine of incorporation, where the advisory rights of the Works Council of a Dutch-based company or the SER-Merger Guidelines must be observed in the event of a merger or take-over, even if seller and purchaser of the company concerned are located abroad, acquisition negotiations take place abroad and the acquisition agreement is signed and executed abroad, and is subject to foreign law. Neither seller nor purchaser themselves are subject to these requirements, but nevertheless these must be taken into account: otherwise these could be easily circumvented by the foundation of foreign-based companies.

Registration as well as the preparation and delivery of accounts has now largely been harmonized on the basis of Article 54(3)(g) in the First Directive (registration) and the Fourth and Seventh Directive (single company and group accounting) of the Communities. Employees' participation is still a matter of debate, e.g., the proposed Fifth Directive on the structure of the public limited liability company and the now aborted 'Vredeling proposal' for a directive on cross-border employees' consultation rights.[28] It would seem that continuing harmonization in the field of company law should resolve the most pertinent barriers to full acceptance of the doctrine of incorporation.

Another obstacle could be international tax law but for a different reason: a national state's interest to raise as much fiscal revenue as feasible as opposed to the need to avoid double taxation for companies operating internationally. The residence of a legal person is an essential factor in determining its (national) tax liability and, hence, 'residence' is usually defined as broad as possible in national tax law. In principle, the worldwide profits of a legal person are taxed in its country of residence, even if the legal person concerned is incorporated under the laws of a different State. The consequences of dual residence can be mitigated either by unilateral measures of the State which could claim residence or by double taxation treaties, whereby the right to levy taxes is, wholly or in part, renounced. In order to determine residence various criteria can be used, such as:[29]

— the State where the legal person is incorporated;
— the State where the legal person has its statutory seat;
— the State where the founders or shareholders of the legal person are resident;
— the State on whose territory the income is realised or its principal facilities are located;

28. First Directive 68/151/EEC of 9 March 1968 (OJ 1968, L 65); Fourth Directive 78/660/EEC of July 1978 (OJ 1978, L 222); Seventh Directive 83/349/EEC of 13 June 1983; proposed Fifth Directive (OJ 1983, C 240) and 'Vredeling Directive' (OJ 1983, C 217); see also Council Resolution 21 July 1986 (OJ 1986, C 203).

29. E.A. Brood, op cit. n. 26, at pp. 90-96.

— the State where the formal or real management of the legal person is situated, varying between options such as 'top management' to 'day-to-day' management. The last criterion is usually the most important.

A practical example: according to Article I: 10(2) of the Netherlands Civil Code, a Dutch legal person must be incorporated in accordance with Dutch law and have its statutory seat in the Netherlands, even if its main economic activities or centre of decision-making is located abroad. It cannot transfer its statutory seat abroad, unless legislation both in the Netherlands and abroad specifically provides for this possibility.[30] So far Dutch legislation only provides for the possibility of transferring a Dutch legal person's statutory seat to the Netherlands Antilles in the event of war, threat of war, revolution or comparable exceptional circumstances.[31] The transfer of the statutory seat is effected by a shareholders' resolution amending the articles of association of the company, for which amendment — contrary to the normal procedure — no prior consent from the Ministry of Justice is required, provided the requirements of legislation are met and consent is given by the Ministry of Justice in the Netherlands Antilles. Otherwise the Dutch legal person ceases to exist upon transfer of its statutory seat.[32]

Under Dutch corporate income tax law, a company that ceases to exist according to Dutch law must provide an accounting to the Dutch tax authorities of its assets at real economic value, add its fiscal reserves to profits made and repay government (fiscal) benefits received.[33] However, because the Netherlands applies the criterion of transfer of statutory seat deriving from the doctrine of incorporation rather than the doctrine of *siège réel*, a Dutch company may transfer its main economic activities, its centre of decision-making (or any other connecting factor relevant for application of the doctrine of *siège réel*) abroad. Technically, a Dutch company that did so would remain liable in the Netherlands for taxes on worldwide profits as a company established in the Netherlands,[34] but such tax liability would then usually be governed by double taxation treaties to which the Netherlands is a party, with the result that the Dutch incorporated company would no longer be taxed in the Netherlands under the operation of any such treaty.

As a matter of principle Dutch company law and tax law effectively prohibit 'exit' of a Dutch company in so far as the transfer of the statutory seat is concerned. However, exit of its *siège réel* — in contrast to the English tax system prior to 1988, which gave rise to the *Daily Mail* case[35] — is generally covered by a double

30. Article II: 66 and II: 177 BW ('Netherlands Civil Code'), Asser-Van der Grinten, *Handboek voor de Naamloze en de Besloten Vennootschap* (Zwolle, 1989) No. 80, pp. 117-118.

31. Rijkswet vrijwillige zetelverplaatsing ('Act on Voluntary Transfer of Seat'), 9 March 1967 (Stc. 1967 No. 161) as amended and replacing a similar statute of 26 April 1940 (Stc. 1940 No. 200) just prior to the German invasion of the Netherlands on 10 May 1940.

32. See *supra*, n. 27; see Asser-Van der Grinten, op. cit. n. 30, at pp. 118-119; see also *infra*, n. 54.

33. Art. 8 Wet Vennootschapsbelasting ('Corporate Income Tax Act'); see also *Nederlandse belasting jurisprudentie op vier internationale gebieden* (Amsterdam, 1986) pp. 21-22.

34. Art. 2 (4) Wet Vennootschapsbelasting ('Corporate Income Tax Law') and Art. 1 (3) Wet Dividendbelasting ('Dividend Withholding Tax Act').

35. For an overview, see J. Lever, 26 CMLRev. (1989) p. 327.

taxation treaty with the result that in its practical implications there are no restrictions on 'fiscal exit'. It may be a different matter if the *siège réel* of a Dutch
incorporated company is transferred to a country which applies the *siège réel*
doctrine and requires that such Dutch company be terminated and 're-created' in
accordance with the company law of the host State.

According to a 1866 judgment of the Supreme Court of the Netherlands, foreign
legal persons, validly existing in the state of their statutory seat, must be recognized
in the Netherlands (for all practical purposes) on an equal footing with Dutch
companies. This recognition of foreign companies is not subject to international
treaties, but based upon an independent rule of Dutch law expressed in statute since
1956.[36] This recognition of foreign legal persons is subject to the limitation that the
statutory seat of the foreign legal entity remains abroad, unless the statute specifically provides otherwise. If a foreign company transfers its statutory seat to the
Netherlands it loses its corporate existence under Dutch law.[37] Recognition of a
foreign company established in the Netherlands on the basis of its *siège réel* may
give rise to Dutch tax liability mitigated, if possible, by the operation of any double
taxation treaty on the same basis as described above.

The discussion on incorporation versus *siège réel* in the field of company law is
reflected in Article 220 which provides, *inter alia*, that the Member States shall, so
far as is necessary, enter into negotiations with a view to securing for the benefit of
their nationals the mutual recognition of companies or firms within the meaning of
Article 58 and the retention of legal personality in the event of transfer of their seat
from one country to another.

Article 220 also provides for the possibility of treaties between the Member
States with a view to securing for the benefit of their nationals the abolition of
double taxation within the Community. Apparently, for reasons undisclosed, it was
felt upon conclusion of the Treaty that, especially with respect to free movement of
legal persons within the Community, both for civil and tax law purposes further
treaties should be concluded, 'so far as is necessary'. The question then arises
whether and to what extent there effectively exists such a necessity under the
operation of Article 52 et seq.

In the *avoir fiscal* case the Court of Justice held in respect of treaties on the
abolition of double taxation within the Community:

> 'It must first be noted that the fact that the laws of the Member States on corporation tax
> have not been harmonized cannot justify the difference of treatment in this case. Although
> it is true that in the absence of such harmonization, a company's tax position depends on
> the national law applied to it, Article 52 of the EEC Treaty prohibits the Member States
> from laying down in their laws conditions for the pursuit of activities by persons exercis-
> ing their right of establishment which differ from those laid down for its own nationals.'

---

36. HR March 23, 1866 W 2781; see also Asser-Van der Grinten, op. cit. n. 30, at pp. 123-127; see
also *infra*, n. 53.

37. See Asser-Van der Grinten, op. cit. n. 30, at pp. 123-127.

'Furthermore, the risk of tax avoidance cannot be relied upon in this context. Article 52 of the EEC Treaty does not permit any derogation from the fundamental principle of freedom of establishment on such a ground (. . .).'[38]

Article 220 need not necessarily constitute an obstacle to application of the Treaty rules, either for tax law purposes or for private international law purposes in as far as 'import' of foreign legal persons on a secondary establishment basis is concerned. The question then arises if and to what extent the same would apply should the matter relate to cross-border establishment on a primary basis, especially regarding 'exit' from the original Member State of incorporation.

5.   *THE QUEEN* V. *H.M. TREASURY AND COMMISSION OF INLAND REVENUE (EX PARTE* DAILY MAIL)*[39]

The question was put squarely before the Court of Justice in the *Daily Mail* case. Daily Mail and General Trust PLC, a limited company incorporated under English law whose registered office was in the United Kingdom, contemplated a full-fledged transfer of central management and control from the United Kingdom to the Netherlands, without losing its legal personality, or ceasing to be a company incorporated in the United Kingdom, in order to establish residence in the Netherlands. Daily Mail made no secret of the fact that the proposed transfer of central management and control was purely tax-driven in order to avoid substantial English capital gains tax liabilities for the sale of a significant part of its non-permanent assets with a view to use the proceeds to buy its own stock.

The United Kingdom's Income and Corporation Taxes Act 1970 prohibits companies resident for tax purposes in the United Kingdom from ceasing to be resident without the consent of the Treasury. When protracted negotiations with the Treasury did not produce the desired results, Daily Mail applied to an English Court for a declaratory judgment to the effect that Articles 52 and 58 of the EEC Treaty precluded the Treasury from requiring prior consent for transfer of central management and control to another Member State or, alternatively, implied for Daily Mail the right to obtain such consent unconditionally. The matter was referred to the Court in Luxembourg.[40]

The Court of Justice recognized Daily Mail's claim under Article 58 to the same right of primary establishment in another Member State as that conferred by Article 52 on natural persons. According to Daily Mail the transfer of central management and control did in fact amount to establishment in another Member State because the centre of decision-making would be located there, constituting a genuine and effective economic activity in another Member State. The Court also recognized that

38. *Supra*, n. 11, Recitals 24-25.
39. Case 81/87, *The Queen* v. *Treasury and Commissions of Inland Revenue, Ex parte Daily Mail and General Trust PLC* ECR [1988] 5483.
40. See for details, Lever, op. cit. n. 35, at pp. 327-328.

the joint existence in both Member States of the doctrine of incorporation did not constitute as such an obstacle to the right of primary establishment under Article 58. It observed as a matter of principle that Article 52 and consequently Article 58 not only purport to ensure equal treatment in the host Member State, but also:

'(. . .) prohibit the Member State of origin from hindering the establishment in another Member State of one of its nationals or of a company incorporated under its legislation which comes within the definition contained in Article 58.'[41]

Having so found, the Court emphasized that the national laws of the Member States differ widely in regard to both the factor providing a connection to the national territory required for the incorporation of a company and the question whether a company incorporated under the legislation of a Member State may subsequently modify that connecting factor: incorporation versus *siège réel*. The Court then continued with language which appears to clarify, if not confirm, its findings in the *Segers* case:

'The Treaty has taken account of that variety in national legislation. In defining, in Article 58, the companies which enjoy the right of establishment, the Treaty places *on the same footing*, as connecting factors, the registered office, central administration or principal place of business of a company.'[42]

The Court further conceded that neither Article 220 nor harmonization under Article 54(3)(g) have resolved these differences in national legislation, which in other, closely related fields of Community law have in the past not precluded the Court from granting direct effect to certain Treaty provisions, provided the conditions of clarity, precision and non-reserve are met. However, the Court concluded that these differences in national legislation 'are not resolved by the rules concerning the right of establishment but must be dealt with by future legislation or conventions.'[43]

Therefore, free circulation of legal persons in as far as the right of primary establishment is concerned is effectively considered not to exist, at least in as far as 'export' of legal persons on a primary establishment basis is concerned.[44]

The question may be asked why differences in national company law should constitute an unsurmountable obstacle to the operation of Article 58, which in itself is sufficiently precise, clear and without reservation in order to qualify for direct effect. A possible explanation is that other Treaty provisions that have been granted direct effect deal mainly with real persons and physical things, whereas legal persons are 'creatures of the law' and, in the present state of Community law, 'creatures of national law', which 'exist only by virtue of the varying national

41. *Supra* n. 39, Recital 16.
42. *Supra*, n. 39, Recital 21 (emphasis added).
43. *Supra*, n. 39, Recital 23.
44. See e.g., C.W.A. Timmermans, note on the *Daily Mail* case in 'Sociaal-Economische Wetgeving' 1 (1991) pp. 66, 70-71.

legislation which determines their incorporation and functioning.'[45] However, an element of intangibility has not precluded services, e.g., television signals, from becoming subject to application of the Community rules.[46]

Another hypothesis could be the alternative of secondary establishment, e.g., 'in this case by opening an investment management office in the Netherlands' or 'by taking part in the incorporation of a company in another Member State' where Article 221 ensures the same treatment as that available to nationals as regards participation in the capital of a new company. The existence of alternative options does not as such justify non-operation of the Treaty rules. In the *avoir fiscal* case this type of argument was not accepted by the Court.[47]

A further hypothesis could be possible negative consequences for national tax systems as recognized by the Court in the *avoir fiscal* case in an unspecified manner. However, it was also emphasized that the risk of tax avoidance did not on that ground permit any derogation from the fundamental principle of freedom of establishment.[48]

Advocate-General Darmon proposed in his opinion a different, more economic, approach. While accepting as a matter of principle the possibility that transfer to another Member State of the central management of a company may constitute a form of exercise of the right of establishment, the Advocate-General emphasized the need for appropriate criteria for the national courts to assess elements of facts that show whether such a transfer reflects a genuine integration of that company into the economic life of the host Member State.

This approach purports to resolve the same problems with which experts in private international law and international tax law have been wrestling for a long time: how to find appropriate assessment criteria both for the purpose of mutual recognition and retention of legal personality in the event of transfer of seat and for the avoidance of double taxation within the Community while at the same time retaining the basic principles of Article 52 et seq. In this respect it has been observed that under Dutch fiscal case-law, in order to resolve this type of problem, 16 different tests have been developed over the last century in order to establish residence, which under Dutch tax law should be determined 'according to the circumstannces'.[49] Following the approach proposed by the Advocate-General, and giving national courts some guidance in this matter, would have required the Court to resolve not only the incorporation versus *siège réel* discussion, but also various complex issues of international taxation.

It has been argued that the approach endorsed by the Advocate-General — mandatory authorization to transfer if genuine economic activity exists subject to the limitation that the company meets its tax liability in the Member State of origin —

---

45. *Supra*, n. 30, Recital 19.
46. See e.g., case 52/79 *Procureur du Roi* v. *Debauve* (1980) ECR 833; case 352/85 *Bond van Adverteerders and others* v. *The Netherlands* (1988) ECR 2085.
47. *Supra*, n. 39, Recital 17.
48. See *supra*, n. 11, Recital 23.
49. Art. 4 Algemene Wet Rijksbelastingen ('General Tax Act'); see *supra*, n. 33, pp. 21-40, at p. 28.

would have amounted to a derogation, on fiscal grounds, of the principles of freedom of establishment in view of the Court's finding of inadmissibility of fiscal derogations in the *avoir fiscal* case.[50] The logic of the argument is appealing. However, it seems debatable whether for that reason preference should be given to the Court's finding. Doing so could result in an even greater derogation from the Treaty principles on freedom of establishment of legal persons or, in the alternative, could qualify this issue as a matter immune from Community treatment to be left to the unilateral or treaty-making discretion of the Member States. On the other hand, developing assessment criteria, as suggested by the Advocate-General, would have amounted to the enormous task of comparing twelve different national civil law and tax law systems within the community, double taxation agreements between Member States, comparing these to international standards and models, such as the model OECD double taxation treaty, and finding common denominators.[51]

For all practical purposes it seems that in the area of free movement of legal persons a distinction can be made between secondary establishment 'protected' by the Treaty, and the 'unprotected' area of primary establishment, to be left to 'future legislation or conventions'. This raises the question if and when these differences in national legislation will be resolved to a sufficient degree in order to grant full operation to the rules concerning the right of establishment. Would it suffice to adopt (in whatever form) the draft 1968 Brussels Convention on the Mutual Recognition of Companies or Firms (with attached Protocol) on the basis of Article 220 or a regulation on the basis of Article 54(3)(g)? Or would even further-reaching harmonization on the basis of this Treaty provision (or any other 'harmonizing provision' of the Treaty) be required?

The draft 1968 Brussels Convention[52] as it stands now is basically an 'agreement not to agree'. Articles 1 and 2 of this Convention provide for acceptance in principle of the doctrine of incorporation. However, Articles 3 and 4 of the Convention leave the possibility for the contracting parties to issue a declaration to the effect that they will apply the doctrine of *siège réel*. So far the Convention has been signed by the 'old Six', and the Member States which apply the doctrine of the *siège réel* have indeed issued the declarations provided for under Article 3 of the Convention. The Netherlands have not issued any declaration and also may not be able to do so in view of existing Dutch legislation, at least not without altering the same.[53]

---

50. *Lever*, op. cit. n. 35, at p. 329.

51. E.A. Brood, op. cit. n. 26, at pp. 90-96.

52. Convention on the Mutual Recognition of Companies, of 29 February 1968; see, *inter alia*, Supplement 13/73 EC-Bulletin.

53. This is closely linked to a peculiarity of Dutch law, where, in order to implement the Hague Convention on Recognition of 1 June 1956, a statute was enacted which provides an independent rule of Dutch private international law which states that 'the Netherlands is not a country whose law takes into consideration the *siège réel*, as provided for in Art. 2 of this Convention (. . .)' (Act of 7 October 1959, Stb. 1959 No. 347).

Commentators have argued that under the operation of Articles 52 and 58 of the EEC Treaty there is no need for a Convention on the basis of Article 220 because due application of these Treaty provisions, also with respect to the right of legal entities to primary establishment, should effectively resolve the issue in favour of the doctrine of incorporation.[54] However, in the *Daily Mail* case the Court held differently, although it could be argued that these findings are limited to 'exit' on a primary basis of legal persons.[55]

A traditional argument against unlimited adoption of the doctrine of incorporation is the possibility of abuse of company law to the effect that economic entities will choose the legal vehicles of those Member States which are the most lenient in their company laws, thereby avoiding application of stricter rules in their home country: this is the so-called 'Delaware effect'. Unlimited recognition of such foreign legal entities on a primary establishment basis in other Member States could lead to the general erosion of national company law standards.

In fact, the *Segers* case provides an example of the application and consequences of this argument by a Member State that admittedly applies the doctrine of incor- - poration. In that case the argument of the *Bedrijfsvereniging* not to treat the English 'Limited' on an equal footing with a Dutch 'B.V.' was based upon the alleged need to reduce the general possibility of abusive 'company shopping' within the Community and thereby avoid preventive control by the Dutch Ministry of Justice. This argument was made in spite of the fact that the *Bedrijfsvereniging* admitted in the specific case of Segers that no such abusive intent had been established.[56]

From the perspective of Dutch company law practice this argument, even on an abstract level, carries little weight. Control by the Ministry of Justice is confined to an examination of the correctness of documentation regarding the company and the antecedents of the persons that present themselves as founders and future owners and/or directors of the company to be founded. As opposed to continuous review of documentation, which must be presented to the Ministry for its consent on even the slightest proposed modification of the articles of association, review of antecedents of persons involved in such company is confined to a written undertaking by the company to the Ministry not to change ownership or management structure within one year from the date of consent (leaving, if desired, sufficient room for manoeuvre). In addition, there is always the possibility of purchasing an existing company.

Apart from these practical considerations relating to the specific situation in the Netherlands, the Treaty rules provide for the possibility, if necessary, to combat possible abuse or even fraud without affecting the principles laid down in Articles 52 and 58. According to Article 56 these principles 'shall not prejudice the applicability of provisions laid down by law, regulation or administrative action providing for special treatment for foreign nationals on grounds of public policy, public

---

54. See *supra*, n. 26.
55. See *infra*, n. 44.
56. See *supra*, n. 20, Recital 9-10.

security or public health.' Combat of abuse of company law (or fraud) could be qualified under the exception of public policy, provided the conditions for application of this exception are met.

The Segers judgment does not provide many details on the specific requirements for application of Article 56 in this framework. A proportionality test was applied:

> 'Although the need to combat fraud may therefore justify a difference of treatment in certain circumstances, the refusal to accord a sickness benefit to a director of a company formed in accordance with the law of another Member State cannot constitute an appropriate measure in that respect.'[57]

The public policy exception also exists in the framework of the free movement of workers (Art. 48), where the Court has laid down certain principles:[58]

(i) measures should have an appropriate legal basis in national law;

(ii) 'public policy' is a Community concept, subject to review by the Court and as a derogation to fundamental Community principles should be narrowly construed;

(iii)measures are not justified on the grounds of general prevention;

(iv) individual measures can only be taken if the person concerned represents 'a genuine and serious threat to the requirements of public policy affecting one of the fundamental interests of society'.[59]

(v) the reasons for such measures in an individual case should be specified and communicated to the person affected, providing for the opportunity of full judicial review.[60]

The application of Article 56 may be based on the rationale that (i) the right of cross-border establishment exists and (ii) may subsequently be limited by the operation of Article 56. In literature[61] the view has been defended that a difference in treatment justified in order to combat possible abuse or fraud may also lead to non-application of the basic principles of cross-border establishment on the basis of the 'anti-circumvention' recitals of the Court in, for example, the *Van Binsbergen* case[62] relating to cross-border provision of services or the *Leclerc* case[63] relating to free movement of goods.

This seems to suggest that in situations where the Treaty applies (i.e., not in purely national situations), in addition to the well-known exceptions found in the Treaty itself or developed on a 'rule of reason' basis, a further type of exception would exist. Second, it seems debatable whether there is any real need for such

---

57. *Supra*, n. 20, Recital 17.

58. Case 36/75, *Rutili* v. *Minister for the Interior* ECR [1975] 1219; case 41/74 *Van Duyn* v. *Home Office* ECR [1974] 1337; case 67/74 *Bonsignore* v. *Stadt Köln* ECR [1975] 306; case 30/77 *Regina* v. *Bouchereau* ECR [1977] 1999; case 48/75 *Royer* ECR [1976] 497.

59. *Bouchereau supra*, n. 58, at p. 2014.

60. See also case 222/86 *UNECTEF* v. *Heylens*, ECR [1987] 4097.

61. See C.W.A. Timmermans, *Tot Vermaak Van Slagter* (Deventer, 1988) pp. 321, 324-326.

62. Case 33/74 *Van Binsbergen* v. *Bedrijfsvereniging Metaalnijverheid* ECR [1974] 1299 (Recital 13).

63. Case 224/83 *Leclerc* v. *Au Blé vert* ECR [1985] 1 (Recital 27).

'other exceptions'. If for the purposes of anti-circumvention full operation of the Community rules in an individual case should be limited, then exceptions formulated in the Treaty or recognized as such by the Court should provide a sufficient legal basis to do so without recourse to non-application as such of the Treaty rules.

Furthermore, non-operation of the Community rules in order to combat abuse or circumvention of Community law otherwise applicable is not entirely the same as combat of circumvention, abuse or even fraud of national company law by the operation of Community law. In such cases Community law should prevail, limited by Community exceptions, whereas in the first situation Community law cannot be applied. In addition, although it is conceded that from a practical point of view the results may not differ widely, it seems that the tests developed in the free movement of workers cases above are possibly easier to apply than the following:[64]

'(. . .) a Member State cannot be denied the right to take measures to prevent the exercise by a person providing services whose activity is entirely or principally directed towards its territory of the freedom guaranteed by Article 59 for the purpose of avoiding the professional rules of conduct which would be applicable to him if he were established within that State.'

'(. . .) where it is established that the books in question were exported for the sole purpose of re-importation in order to circumvent legislation of the type of issue.'

This test — as with most 'anti-circumvention tests — requires a determination of subjective intent, which is difficult to apply in practice. In addition, it is interesting to note certain translation differences: the English text uses the notion 'where it is established', leaving a rather large discretion to a national court, whereas the Dutch text (in a rough translation) relates to the case where 'it would appear from objective circumstances,' which seems to leave less room.

This also raises the question if and to what extent the Court could have ruled differently if the case had related to secondary establishment. In this respect the Court held that the Treaty provisions not only aim at ensuring that foreign nationals and companies are treated in the host Member State in the same way as nationals of that State but that they:

'also prohibit the Member States of origin from hindering the establishment in another Member State of one of its nationals or of a company incorporated under its legislation which comes within the definitions contained in Article 58.'[65]

This finding points in the direction that impediments to 'exit' may indeed be prohibited in the case of secondary establishment. This argument is strengthened by the Court's endorsement of the Commission's view (expressed in its submissions) that otherwise the rights guaranteed by Article 52 et seq. would be rendered mean-

64. See *supra*, nn. 62 and 63.
65. *Supra*, n. 39, Recital 16.

ingless if the Member State of origin could *prohibit* undertakings from leaving in order to establish themselves in another Member State. The wording 'prohibited' leaves some room for doubt as to whether the same would apply in cases in which departure is only rendered more difficult. However, it seems defensible by reference to the Court's case-law in the *avoir fiscal* case, among others, that the notion of impediment to departure should be interpreted in the widest possible manner. In the *Daily Mail* case, these findings were of little assistance to Daily Mail because the requirement of consent only applied in the event of primary transfer of seat.

As set out above, the Netherlands is technically even stricter on 'exit' of Dutch-companies than the United Kingdom prior to the 1988 amendment of fiscal legislation: the transfer of the statutory seat abroad automatically terminates the existence of a Dutch company and gives rise to full tax accountability to the Dutch fiscal authorities. However, as long as the statutory seat is retained in the Netherlands and transfer of *siège réel* is covered by a double taxation treaty, the fiscal result may be that there is no impediment on 'exit'. Therefore, a case similar to the *Daily Mail* case is less likely to arise in the Netherlands.

With respect to natural persons the Court has emphasized that no impediments to departure can be imposed. In this respect the Court has expressly referred to Directive No. 73/148/EEC,[66] which guarantees nationals of Member States such rights.

Articles 1 and 2 of the Directive provide nationals of a Member State (including spouses, children younger than 21 years and certain dependent relatives) with the right to leave their Member State of origin for the purpose of establishment or provision of services in another Member State. The only restriction imposed is possession of a valid identity card or passport which *must* be provided by the Member State of origin. The Directive does not allow for conditions to be imposed in providing a passport.

This may have considerable implications for national tax laws including income tax laws. Any derogation from 'exit prohibitions' not expressly allowed under this directive, such as non-compliance with payment obligations of taxes or social security premiums due, or even a 'well-found suspicion' to that effect[67] or provision to 'take on board' national tax obligations upon emigration to another Member State[68] seem in principle at odds with the finding of the Court in the *avoir fiscal* case that the risk of tax avoidance cannot be relied upon as a valid derogation from the fundamental principle of freedom of establishment, a principle which was repeated for natural persons in relation to 'exit prohibitions' in the *Daily Mail* case.

---

66. Directive 73/148/EEC of the Council of 21 May 1973 on the abolition of restrictions on movement and residence within the Community for nationals of Member States with regard to establishment and the provision of services (OJ 1973, L 172/14).

67. Compare, e.g., Art. 6 (a) Netherlands' Interim Passport Act (Interimwet paspoorten); Stb. 1988, 35.

68. Compare Arts. 27(3) and 44(a) Netherlands Tax Collection Act (Invorderingswet), as revised in 1991, concerning tax treatment of life insurance and pension policies upon departure from the Netherlands.

However, as this case, and especially the *Bachmann* and *Commission* v. *Belgium* cases purport to show, a certain degree of caution would seem to be required. The emergence of 'cohérence fiscale' almost twenty years after *Dassonville*,[69] where the Court recognised for the first time certain other 'rule of reason' exceptions, the Court appears to show a certain reluctance to encroach too much upon the highly 'sensitive' area of national governments' central social-economic (income) policy and revenue generating instrument: direct taxation.

In this respect the recent discussions on the 'Treaty of Maastricht' may not have been of great assistance in decreasing this reluctance, especially as certain of its provisions suggest an increase rather then a decrease in 'national sovereignty' in fiscal matters.[70] As for the fate of 'Maastricht' itself only the future can tell.

69. Case 8/74 *Procureur des Konings* v. *Dassonville* [1974] ECR 837.
70. Compare, e.g., its (new) Art. 73d.

FREE MOVEMENT OF WORKERS AND FREEDOM TO PROVIDE SERVICES
Considerations on the employees of the provider of services with specific references to France

Alain Desmazières de Séchelles[*]

1. INTRODUCTION

Free movement of workers and freedom to provide services are well-known concepts to the readers. From the point of view of EEC law relating to the movement of natural persons within the territory of the European Community, there are few legal problems. The inevitable litigation that occurs in this field can be considered negligible when compared to the general phenomenon of free movement of persons within the Community.

Free movement of workers within the Community takes place pursuant to Articles 48 to 51 of the Treaty of Rome. In addition to their uncontested supremacy over national law, these Treaty provisions have been directly effective since 1 January 1970, as recognised by the Court of Justice.[1] Prior to this date, Articles 48 to 51 were already implemented by Council Regulation 1612/68 of 15 October 1968.[2] In addition, Council Directive 64/221/EEC of 25 February 1964[3] and Council Directive 68/360/EEC of 15 October 1968,[4] the latter referring specifically to Regulation 1612/68, serve as the legal basis for national legislation that organises and facilitates free movement of workers within the Community.

Freedom to provide services within the Community takes place pursuant to Articles 59 to 66 of the Treaty of Rome. These Treaty provisions also have priority over national law and have been directly effective since 1 July 1970.[5]

---

[*] Advocate, Member of the Paris Bar.

1. See cases 167/73 *Commission* v. *French Republic* [1974] ECR 359, 371-372; case 41/74 *Y. van Duyn* v. *Home Officer* [1974] ECR 1337.

2. OJ 1968 L 257/2, p. 475, Eng. Sp. Ed., 1968(II).

3. OJ 1964 L 850/64, p. 117, Eng. Sp. Ed., 1963-1964.

4. OJ 1968 L 257/13, p. 485, Eng. Sp. Ed., 1968(II).

5. See e.g., case 33/74 *Binsbergen* v. *Bedrijfsvereniging Metaalnijverheid* [1974] ECR 1299; case 36/74 *Walrave and Koch* v. *Union Cycliste Internationale* [1974] ECR 1405; case 39/75 *Coenen* v. *Sociaal Economische Raad* [1975] ECR 1547; joined cases 110 and 111/78 *Ministère Public and A.S.B.L.* v. *Van Wesemael* [1979] ECR 35; case 279/80 *Webb* [1981] ECR 3305; joined cases 62 and 63/81 *Seco* v. *E.V.I.* [1985] ECR 223; case 76/81 *Transporoute* v. *Minister of Public Works* [1982] ECR 417, case 220/83

H.G. Schermers et al., eds., Free Movement of Persons in Europe
© 1993, T.M.C. Asser Instituut, The Hague

This matter has been more difficult to organise and implement than the free movement of workers. The Court of Justice had to construe these Articles broadly in order to establish that they forbid:
— all discrimination against the provider of services based on nationality or residence in a Member State other than the one where the services are provided;[6] and
— any other prohibition or hinderance of activities related to the services provided;[7] and
— any dissimulated or covert form of discrimination which, although based on apparently neutral criteria, leads to a discriminatory result.[8]

Before Articles 59 to 66 were recognised as having a direct effect with such a broad scope, many directives had to be adopted in order to eliminate national restrictions to freedom of services. These directives were adopted in accordance with the 1961 General Programme established by the Council for the abolition of restrictions on the freedom to provide services.[9] Most of these directives are technical and will not be examined here except for Council Directive 64/224/EEC of 25 February 1964[10] concerning the accomplishment of freedom of establishment and of freedom to provide services in the activities of commercial intermediates, industry and craftsmanship, which is discussed here as an example of legal uncertainty and wrong legal basis.

But a few directives enacted in accordance with the 1961 Programme are of a general nature. For example, Council Directive 64/221/EEC of 25 February 1964[11] is also applicable in the field of services. Together with Council Directive 73/148/EEC of 21 May 1973,[12] it serves as the legal basis for national legislation that organises free movement of natural persons providing services within the Community.

In France it is the same text: *Décret* 81-405 of 28 April 1981[13], which addresses both the free movement of workers and freedom to provide services. In accordance with this *Décret*, an EC national who seeks or obtains employment in France may go there, without the need of a visa, 'under mere cover' of his passport or national identity card. The worker may apply for work in France and, upon proof of employment, may apply and obtain an EEC national residence card for a duration of five years renewable for subsequent periods of ten years. The worker's family may also go to France to apply for and obtain EEC national residence cards for the same duration. Applications for

---

Commission v. *France* [1986] ECR 3702, case 252/83 *Commission* v. *France* [1986] ECR 3742; case 205/84 *Commission* v. *Germany* [1986] ECR 3793; case 206/86 *Commission* v. *Ireland* [1986] ECR 3843.

   6. See case 33/74 *Binsbergen* v. *Bedrijfsvereniging Metaalnijverheid* [1974] ECR 1299.

   7. See case 33/74 *Binsbergen* v. *Bedrijfsvereniging Metaalnijverheid* [1974] ECR 1299; case 39/75 *Coenen* v. *Sociaal Economische Raad* [1975] ECR 1547; case 279/80 *Webb* [1981] ECR 3305.

   8. See joined cases 62 and 63/81 *Seco* v. *E.V.I.* [1982] ECR 223.

   9. OJ 2/32 of 15 January 1962 (hereinafter cited as '1961 Programme').

   10. OJ 869/64 of 25 February 1964, English Special Edition, 1963-1964, 126.

   11. *Supra*, n. 3.

   12. OJ 1973 L 172/14.

   13. JORF 29 April 1981 p. 1208, replacing *Décret* 77-1044 of 1 September 1977, JORF 18 September 1977 p. 4633 and *Décret* 79-1051 of 23 November 1979, JORF 7 December 1979 p. 3083.

residence cards must be made within *three months* of arrival on French territory by the persons concerned.[14]

In accordance with the same *décret*, an EEC national who seeks to provide services in France may also go there, without a visa, 'under mere cover' of his passport or national identity card. If the services to be provided do not last more than three months, the person providing services may stay in France without any permit 'under mere cover' of his passport or national identify card. If performance of the services lasts longer than three months, the person providing the services may apply for and obtain a residence permit valid for the duration of the performance of services but limited to one year.[15] Applications for these temporary residence permits must be made within *three months* of the arrival on French territory by the EC national who comes to provide services.

Examination of these basic situations shows that the legal situation in France for nationals of other Member States who go there as salaried workers or as self-employed natural persons providing services may be considered as satisfactory in the light of Community law. There is, of course, some litigation on these matters but, as stated above, it can be considered as negligible from a statistical point of view when compared to the general phenomenon of free movement of physical persons. One can presume that the same satisfactory situation prevails in the other Member States.

Of course, one could question the three-months time limits which are imposed upon:
— the worker and his family to apply for the EC national residence card from the day they arrive on French territory;
— the person providing services to apply for a temporary residence permit for the duration of the service when it exceeds such three-months period.

These three-months time limits are a bit short when one takes into account the recent *Antonissen* judgment by the Court of Justice of 26 February 1991[16] which states that a six-month delay (and even more concerning free movement of workers) would be more appropriate. The flexibility which is suggested by the Court of Justice in the case of a worker who is earnestly looking for employment for more than three, or even six, months after arrival in another Member State should also apply to a person providing services.

One could also question the maximum period of one year for a temporary residence permit granted to a person providing services. Indeed, a one-year period for such permits is not included in either the relevant Directive 73/148/EEC or the previous directive which it replaced, Directive 64/220/EEC of 25 February 1964.[17]

It is interesting to note that a one-year period for temporary residence permits is referred to in Article 6(3) of Directive 68/360/EEC, which relates to the free movement of workers. However, this provision does not apply to the person providing services, but rather to his employees.[18] The French *Décret* has assimilated the provider of

---

14. Ibid. Art. 6.
15. Ibid. Art. 10.
16. Case C-292/89, *The Queen* v. *Immigration Appeal Tribunal, (ex parte) G.D. Antonissen*, OJ 1991, C 74/9 (not yet reported).
17. OJ 1964, No. 845/64 of 4.4.1964.
18. See *supra*, n. 4, Article 6(3).

services with his personnel. This wrongful assimilation is amusing when one considers, as we shall see, that *Décret* 81-405 does not make any explicit specific reference to the employees of the provider of services.

These two criticisms of French *Décret* 81-405 of 28 April 1981, although relevant, only reveal small inconsistencies with Community law. Such inconsistencies have little effect on the freedom to provide services, especially with respect to self-employed natural persons providing services.[19]

Indeed a three-month period is not excessively short especially when one considers that national authorities, who have the burden of proof, do not know exactly when such period begins since the compulsory stamping at the border of passports or other documents is now prohibited.

Moreover, one can hardly expect services provided by natural persons to last more than a few months. This corresponds to the concept of services, in the traditional sense, i.e., services provided by self-employed natural persons for a short period of time and with no or very few personnel.

A much more important criticism which could be made against *Décret* 81-405 is that it does not contain any specific, clear or express provisions about the employees of the person providing services. It would be a mistake to blame the French authorities for this defect, since it is due to the defects, the contradictions, and the lack of clarity on this point in both the relevant Community directives, which the *Décret* aims to implement, and community regulations with which the *Décret* must conform.

These drafting defects within the Community legislation and the French *Décret* (and probably other national implementation measures) were probably due to the influence of the traditional concept of the provider of services (i.e., a self-employed highly skilled and/or qualified individual). The employees of the providers of service have a complicated, ambiguous and contradictory status. Although the relevant Community legislation does not ignore employees of the provider of services, their status under Community law was not made clear prior to the *Rush Portuguesa* decision, discussed in part 3 of this report.

2.   BEFORE CLARIFICATION BY THE COURT OF JUSTICE, FREE MOVEMENT OF THE EMPLOYEES OF THE PROVIDER OF SERVICES: FREE MOVEMENT OF WORKERS OF FREEDOM TO PROVIDE SERVICES?

According to the traditional concept of the provider of services (i.e., a self-employed highly skilled or qualified individual) the only personnel who would accompany him

---

19. Reference is made to Mr Errera's contribution to this volume: 'Free movement of persons, human rights and judicial policy: assessment and prospects' as far as the Palazzi judgment of the French Conseil d'Etat is concerned, which reveals another incompatibility of *Décret* 81-405 with Council Directives 64/221/EEC and 68/360/EEC (CE 8 July 1991, Palazzi, Dalloz 1991, IRP 228).

or her would be particularly skilled and/or trustworthy employees in small numbers. A good example is a physician's or architect's assistant.

This traditional concept is reflected in the 1961 Programme[20] which recites the need to ensure free movement not only of providers of services considered as natural persons (*'ces ressortissants'* — 'these nationals') but also of any specialised personnel or personnel occupying a trustworthy position and accompanying the person providing services or acting on his behalf.[21]

It was probably believed in 1961 that should the person providing services have some highly specialized and trustworthy personnel and should such employees travel with him or on his behalf, then such personnel should be allowed to move freely *on the basis of the Treaty provisions relating to freedom to provide services* (Art. 59 et seq.)

On the other hand, Community secondary legislation did not totally ignore the personnel of the persons providing services. Instead, it seems to have based, strangely enough without distinction, the free movement of all such personnel on the Treaty provisions relating to the free movement of workers (Art. 48 et seq.).

Council Directive 64/224/EEC of 25 February 1964[22] concerning the accomplishment of freedom of establishment and freedom to provide services in the activities of commercial intermediates, industry and craftsmanship, which apparently has not been repealed, states in its fifth recital:

'Whereas the position of paid employees accompanying a person providing services or acting on his behalf will be governed by the provisions laid down in pursuance of Articles 48 and 49 of the Treaty;'[23]

Moreover, the superseded Regulation 38/64 of 25 March 1964[24] *relating to free movement of workers* within the Community provided:

'Any salaried worker (employee) national of a Member State having his residence on the territory of a Member State and whose employer provides a service on the territory of another Member State, either by virtue of the legislation of the latter Member State or in conformity with a Council Directive enacted pursuant to Article 63 of the Treaty, has the right to exercise in the conditions foreseen in this regulation his activity for the account (or on behalf) of his employer, whether he accompanies him or not.'[25]

20. *Supra*, n. 9.
21. *'Le personnel spécialisé ou le personnel occupant un poste de confiance accompagnant le prestataire ou exécutant la prestation pour son compte.'* (translation by author).
22. *Supra*, n. 10.
23. Ibid., fifth recital.
24. OJ 1964, No. 965/64 of 17.4.1964.
25. Ibid., Art. 1(2) (author's translation from French text).

This provision corresponds to the third recital of this former Regulation which provided:

> 'Whereas it is necessary to abolish the restrictions on employment within the Community of the workers of a Member State accompanying a person providing services or acting on his behalf in the territory of another Member State to the extent that these restrictions constitute a hindrance to the providing of services in a field of activity which has been liberated ...'[26]

At the time it was very clear that Community secondary legislation considered that *all* the employees of the provider of services moved pursuant to the rules governing the free movement of workers. According to that concept, freedom to provide services required the elimination of obstacles to the free movement of the employees of the provider of services; but the legal basis for that elimination was the free movement of workers and *not* freedom to provide services.

This concept, contained within superceded Regulation 38/64 and reflected also in Directive 64/224/EEC, was somewhat different from the concept contained within the 1961 Programme, which made a distinction between the specialised and/or trusted employees and other employees. When Regulation 38/64 was replaced by Regulation 1612/68 the distinction was dropped. In fact, Regulation 1612/68 is silent on the issue of employees of the providers of services. Directive 73/148/EEC of 21 May 1973[27] is also silent with regard to the employees of the provider of services.

Council Directive 68/360/EEC of 15 October 1968[28] relating to the abolition of restrictions on movement and residence of workers makes an elliptical reference to the personnel of the provider of services:

> 'Where a worker is employed for a period exceeding three months but not exceeding a year in the service of an employer in the host State or in the employment of a person providing services, the host Member State shall issue him a temporary residence permit, the validity of which may be limited to the expected period of the employment.'[29]

According to this provision, the employee of a person providing services receives the same treatment as the temporary foreign employee (for example, a seasonal worker) of a local employer. The presence of the employee of the person providing services in the State of performance is also, according to that provision, considered as *employment* in that Member State, which is not surprising since Directive 68/360/EEC concerns free movement of workers.

These inaccuracies, ambiguities and, as we shall see, errors relating to the status of the employees of the provider of services and to the legal basis for their freedom of movement were regrettable and surprising in the light of the Treaty of Rome itself, which, by virtue of the reference made in Article 66 to Article 58, expressly foresees

---

26. Ibid., third recital (author's translation from French text).
27. OJ 1973 L 172/14.
28. *Supra*, n. 4.
29. Ibid., Art. 6(3).

that freedom to provide services is not only enjoyed by natural persons but also by companies and firms. By definition a company can only provide services through its personnel.

The French *Décret* 81-405, which implements both Directive 68/360 and Directive 73/148/EEC is also silent on this particular point. In practice, and because the wording of the *Décret* contains no explicit specific provision that may lead to distinctions on this point, the employees of the provider of services are granted temporary residence permits for the duration of the work to be performed (Articles 1e, 11 and 12 of the *Décret*).[30] In the absence of explicit specific provisions about them they are considered as coming to France to exercise a salaried activity on a temporary basis ('*venant en France excercer une activité salariée à titre temporaire*').

To sum up:

— When specialised employees or employees occupying a position of trust moved from one Member State to another with, or on behalf of, a person providing services, one could *theoretically* consider, in the light of the 1961 Programme, that they moved pursuant to Articles 59 to 66 of the Treaty of Rome (freedom to provide services).

— When other categories of personnel (non-specialised and/or not occupying trust positions) moved with the provider of services it was believed that this freedom of movement took place pursuant to Articles 48 to 51 of the Treaty of Rome (free movement of workers).

— In practice, taking more or less consciously into account the unsatisfactory wording of Community secondary legislation, the French national authorities made no distinction between the two categories of salaried workers, and granted provisional residence permits for the duration of the work to be done (subject to a maximum of one year) apparently pursuant only to free movement of workers.

In theory, both the distinction (i.e., basing free movement of the unqualified personnel on the principle of free movement of workers) and the lack of distinction at national authority level (i.e., basing free movement of *all* the employees of the provider of services on the mere principle of free movement of workers) has proved to be incorrect.

In practice, this conceptual confusion has had no damaging consequences for the Community and did not jeopardize the freedom to provide services, since the relevant Treaty provisions relating to both free movement of workers and freedom to provide services were held to be directly effective at the same time, namely, as of 1 January 1970.

The only problem which could have arisen from the use of this erroneous legal basis was that, since the employees of the provider of services moved pursuant to free movement of workers, and since they were deemed to be employed in the Member State where the services were performed, labour relations (including level of salary) in such Member State of performance could have been governed by the labour laws of such

30. Omiclasseur 'Eléments du droit de l'immigration' Office des Migrations Internationales (Paris, 1991) A. 18 p. 116 II 2.

Member State and not by the labour laws of the State of origin (the State of the seat of the provider of services and of the residence of his employees).

On the one hand, the imposition upon the provider of services of the labour laws of the place of performance could have jeopardized the freedom to provide services (subject perhaps to compulsory minimums on the basis of public order). On the other hand, one could have feared distortion of competition and disturbances in the labour market due to performances of services at social costs and conditions other than those prevailing on the market of the Member State of performance.

But the erroneous legal basis for free movement of the employees of the providers of services did not cause practical problems until the middle of the 1970s because prior to that time:
— the original Member States of the EEC had little unemployment. Some were short of labour; and
— the Member States afforded to their workers reasonably equivalent standards of living and of social protection.

For these reasons, the providing of services in another Member State at an extensive level with many employees was probably not worthwhile. Undertakings tended to keep to their own Member States. In other words, the presence in the various Member States of nationals of other Member States as employees of providers of services was presumably only a marginal phenomenon. The conditions of activity in France of these employees were probably considered to be satisfactory and not a phenomenon that deserved examination from the point of view of labour law.

As economic conditions changed, and with the most recent accessions to the European Communities, the question of the legal basis of the free movement of employees of the provider of services was re-examined. Solutions that had been unquestioned (although questionable) were challenged. The long-forgotten distinction between the specialised and/or trusted personnel of the provider of services and his other employees was rediscovered. This matter was brought to the scrutiny of the Court of Justice of the European Communities.

3.   THE *RUSH PORTUGUESA* JUDGMENT: THE BEGINNING OF A CLARIFICATION OF THE STATUS OF THE EMPLOYEES OF THE PROVIDER OF SERVICES

The distinction between specialised and/or trusted personnel and the other employees of the provider of services was revived or rediscovered as a result of the accession of Greece, Portugal and Spain to the European Communities.

Article 45(1) of the Acts of Accession of Greece[31] provided for a six-year transition period for the free movement of workers between Greece and the other nine Member States. During this transitional period Greek workers, as is the case with non-EC nationals, required a residence permit and a working permit. This transitional period

31. OJ 1979 L 291/17.

for Greece ended on 1 January 1988 without any problems as far as the present subject is concerned.[32]

Similarly, Articles 55 and 56 (for Spain)[33] and 215 to 218 (for Portugal)[34] of the Acts of Accession of Spain and Portugal provided for a six-year transition period for free movement of workers. This transition period, which was originally due to expire on 1 January 1993, was shortened by Council Regulation 2194/91 of 25 June 1991[35] and expired on 31 December 1991 (except for Luxembourg, which reserved a 31 December 1992 deadline).

Because the Acts of Accession of Spain and Portugal did not contain any transitional period relating to freedom to provide services, several questions were brought into focus regarding the status of employees of the provider of services.[36] During the transition period relating to the free movement of workers, a provider of services could move freely from Spain or Portugal to another Member State when necessary for the performance of his services. But could he move with his personnel (or send his personnel on his behalf?). And if so, all his personnel? In other words, were there any limits upon the types of personnel that could move freely with the person providing services?

On the one hand, if free movement of the employees of the provider of services was based on free movement of workers, then the Spanish or Portuguese provider of services might have had to leave his workers behind. This could have jeopardized freedom to provide services, especially for companies which enjoyed this freedom pursuant to Articles 66 and 58 of the EEC Treaty. On the other hand, if free movement of the employees of the provider of services was based on freedom to provide services, then the Spanish or Portuguese provider of services could travel with his employees. If this was accepted, however, the question was whether he could come with *all* his employees or only those whose movement was believed to be based on freedom to provide services; for example his specialised and/or trusted personnel.

Confronted with this problem, the French Government responded by adopting *Décret* 86-1267 of 8 December 1986[37], which stated bluntly that 'in order to exercise a salaried professional activity in France', Greek, Spanish and Portuguese nationals needed working permits, like non-EEC nationals.

In the absence of any specific provisions on the employees of the providers of service (also a category unknown in Décret 81-405 discussed above) this meant that the Greek, Spanish and Portuguese employees of Greek, Spanish and Portuguese providers

32. One should note that in its Judgment of 23 March 1983, case 77/82 *Peskeloglou* v. *Bundesanstalt für Arbeit* [1983] ECR 1085 the Court of Justice confirmed that transitional periods concerning accessions are to be interpreted and applied in a restrictive way and that nationals of Member States in a transitional period should not be treated quite the same as non-EC nationals. If a Member State diminishes the rights of nationals, such changes do not apply to EC nationals to the transition period. They continue to enjoy as vested rights the status which was applicable to non-EC nationals on the day of accession.

33. OJ 1985 L 302/35.

34. OJ 1985 L 302/88.

35. OJ 1991 L 206/1.

36. There were a few minor provisions relating to certain services destined for Portugal.

37. JORF 12 December 1986 p. 14917.

of service were treated like non-EEC nationals and needed *working permits* as well as *residence permits*.

This lead to some litigation before the Tribunal Administratif of Versailles, which resulted in an Article 177 reference to the Court of Justice.

It was clear that the freedom to provide services would be jeopardized unless at least some of the personnel of the providers of services were granted access to the territory of the Member State of performance. Therefore, the distinction between specialised and/or trusted personnel and other personnel had to be examined by the Court of Justice.

This distinction was supported before the Court of Justice by the French Government and (perhaps with less vigour) by the Commission of the European Communities. Advocate-General van Gerven[38] suggested in his opinion another distinction, more favourable to freedom to provide services, based on the indispensable character of the personnel (especially as far as skills and possibility of local recruitment are concerned) for the orderly providing of services.

In its Rush Portuguesa judgment of 27 March 1990,[39] the Court of Justice renewed and gave new light to the discussion by doing away altogether with a distinction dating from 1961, which had been neither expressly repealed nor clearly endorsed by Community secondary legislation. Furthermore, the 1964 conceptions of Community secondary legislation were also disavowed by the Court of Justice.

We now know that the provider of services may move from one Member State to another with *all* his employees. This right is necessary in order to avoid discrimination contrary to Article 60 EEC. For example, if a French provider of services may move within France with *all* his employees, then it would be discriminatory to maintain that a Portuguese provider of services could not also move from Portugal to France with *all* his personnel.

All the employees of the provider of services move pursuant to Articles 59 and 60. The legal basis for their freedom to move is therefore the freedom to provide services and *not* the free movement of workers.

Nevertheless, the Rush Portuguesa judgment leaves open many questions. The Court was careful to specify that the decision was only valid between Portugal and the other Member States for the providing of services in the field of construction and public works. The Court stated that its decision may not apply to all services. More specifically, the decision does not apply to services providing manpower to other undertakings. Although undoubtedly a service, the providing of manpower is governed by the transitional period concerning free movement of workers. The authorities of the Member States remain free to proceed to the exact qualifications or requalifications of the services rendered, provided that they do not use arbitrary powers which would hinder freedom to provide services.

The Court's careful, step-by-step and casuistic approach, which leads to distinctions based upon the object of the service in question, is probably governed by its concern to

---

38. See C-113/89 Rush Portuguesa [1990] ECR I-1425.
39. Ibid., at 1439.

safeguard some of the fundamental principles of Community law: irreversibility, unconditionality, restrictive application of transition periods, maximum *effet utile* of freedom to provide services, and protection of *acquis communautaire* as of 1 January 1970 and *a fortiori* as of 1 January 1986. And, at the same time, this approach is probably based upon the Court's recognition of the need to preserve a degree of stability in the labour markets, as was sought by the Member States in the use of a transitional period for the free movement of workers.

This teleological approach in the way the transitional period is construed and applied can also be found in the recitals of Council Regulation 2194/91, which shortened the transitional period.

The question that remains is whether this approach leaves uncertainties regarding the legal basis for the free movement of *all* the employees of the provider of services? I do not believe so. As a rule, *all* the employees of the provider of services *move pursuant to the freedom to provide services*. If there are any exceptions, it is only when and because the service in question concerns the labour market so much that it is submitted to the transitional provisions governing free movement of workers. While free movement of workers plays a role, the legal basis for free movement of *all* the personnel of the provider of services is based primarily upon the freedom to provide services.

Finally, the Court added in ground 18 of its Rush Portuguesa judgment, that Community law did not prevent the Member States from extending the benefits of their social legislation and collective agreements to the activities on their respective territories of the employees of the providers of services, even those who are domiciled outside the Member State.

The French Government immediately seized on this aspect of the judgment to issue a *Circulaire* of 2 May 1991 on rules applying to undertakings moving temporarily to provide services in France in the field of construction.[40] In this matter the *Circulaire* states that the provider of services must conform to French social law, including minimum wages, for work performed in France.

Although this is not exactly a problem of Community law, one can doubt the legality and binding force and effect of the extension, by way of a mere *Circulaire*, of French domestic law to foreign labour contracts between the foreign provider of services and his personnel domiciled in the Member State of origin, which is also the Member State of employment and the Member State where the provider of services has his seat and principal establishment. One must remember that the Court of Justice did not state that national labour laws of the State of performance of the services were automatically applicable to such labour relationships. It only stated that EEC law did not prevent such an extension.

One could argue that the *Circulaire* is no more than a reminder of the rule of equality of treatment and salaries of French and Spanish workers, on the one hand, and French and Portuguese workers, on the other, as was foreseen by respectively the

---

40. See Feuillets Rapides Francis Lefebvre (1991) F 31-91 p. 28.

Franco-Spanish Convention of 29 December 1933[41] and the Franco-Portuguese Convention of 11th January 1977.[42] However, the weakness in this argument is that these Conventions only concern the situation of Spanish and Portuguese employees employed in France by French employers and not by Spanish and Portuguese providers of services.

The French *Circulaire* also states that since the provider of services has no access to the French labour market, he cannot solicit or recruit French complementary personnel needed for the performance of his services. This is a very surprising statement. The Court of Justice never stated that the provider of services has no access to the labour market of the Member State of performance. It merely stated, in ground 15 of its judgment, that the *employees* of the provider of services who move with their employer for the sake of performing services, do not have access to the labour market of the Member State of performance. This explains why they are not subject to the transition period relating to free movement of workers. The use of the *Circulaire* to prevent EC undertakings providing services in France from recruiting complementary staff there, on the spot, would probably constitute an obstacle to the freedom to provide services contrary to Articles 59 and 60.

4.   CONCLUSION

Of course, the shortening of the transitional period relating to free movement of workers between Spain and Portugal and the rest of the Community has simplified the matter considerably. When both freedoms are exercised simultaneously, distinctions between their respective legal bases lose some relevance.

The Rush Portuguesa judgment will nevertheless serve as a useful precedent for future extensions of the Community and also for future commercial and association agreements, not to mention the GATT negotiations on free trade in services. The basic rule is now clear: free movement of *all* the employees of the provider of services is based on the freedom to provide services.

The residual problem of the legal basis for the free movement of the employees of the provider of services, as a criterion of applicability of the local social laws of the State of performance of the services to the work performed there by such employees, may be completely obsolete if the Member States proceed unilaterally to the extension of such laws according to the suggestion (or *nihil obstat*) of the Court of Justice. These extensions must nevertheless be accompanied by harmonisation of the social policy of the Member States. If the national laws differ too much, their application may hinder freedom to provide services contrary to Articles 59 and 60.

The *Rush Portuguesa* case revealed that the employees of the providers of services do not find the place they deserve in the Community secondary legislation or the various implementing national regulations. Both Community and national measures in

41. JORF 17 January 1934 p. 442.
42. JORF 17 May 1977 p. 2787.

this field are unsatisfactory in this respect, especially because of the legal uncertainty that results from the lack of clear, specific and express provisions (not to speak of erroneous legal basis). These measures do not correspond to the quality standards required of 'law' by either the Court of Justice or the European Court of Human Rights. Therefore, the legislative institutions of the Community should 'scrap' or update certain regulations and directives, that have become unnecessary, obsolete or perhaps even invalid as a result of the Court of Justice's repeated recognitions of the direct effect of Articles 48 to 51 and 59 to 66 of the EEC Treaty as of 1 January 1970, as well as of its clarification of their respective scopes of application.

FREE MOVEMENT OF NON-EC NATIONALS
A review of the case-law of the Court of Justice

Willy Alexander[*]

1.   INTRODUCTION

This report will examine the case-law of the Court of Justice regarding the legal status of non-EC nationals under Community law. I believe that this issue has been the subject of the following thirteen judgments (I have added the nationality of the persons concerned):

1. Case 40/76 *Karmaschek* [1976] ECR 1669 (Yugoslavia)
2. Case 65/77 *Razanatzimba* [1977] ECR 2235 (Madagascar)
3. Joined Cases 62 and 63/81 *Seco* [1982] ECR 223 (not mentioned)
4. Joined Cases 35 and 36/82 *Morson* and *Jhanjan* [1982] ECR 3723 (Suriname)
5. Case 283/83 *Meade* [1984] ECR 2631 (USA)
6. Case 267/83 *Diatta* [1985] ECR 567 (Senegal)
7. Case 94/84 *Deak* [1985] ECR 1873 (Hungary)
8. Case 131/85 *Gül* [1986] ECR 1573 (Cypriot national of Turkish origin)
9. Case 12/86 *Demirel* [1987] ECR 1573 (Turkey)
10. Case C-113/89 *Rush Portuguesa* [1990] ECR I-1417. Actually, this case dealt with EC nationals (Portuguese employees). I have included it in my list because they did not at the time yet enjoy the full rights of EC nationals.
11. Case C-192/89 *Sevince* [1990] ECR I-3461 (Turkey)
12. Case C-18/90 *Kziber* [1991] ECR I-199 (Morocco)

Although various Community regulations and directives grant rights to stateless persons and refugees, there is no reported case-law dealing with this matter. Therefore, it will not be discussed in this report.

An analysis of the judgments cited above must take account of the fact that non-EC nationals may have rights or benefits either directly under an EC instrument or indirectly as a result of their relationship with an EC national. Because of the fundamental nature of this distinction this report is divided into two parts. The first

---

*   Member of the Bar of The Hague, Barents & Krans, The Hague, Brussels.

H.G. Schermers et al., eds., *Free Movement of Persons in Europe* part deals with the rights and benefits that non-EC nationals derive from their relationship with an EC national; the second part addresses direct rights under an EC instrument.

2.   DERIVED RIGHTS AND BENEFITS

A large number of regulations and directives grants certain rights to members of the families of EC nationals, irrespective of the family members' nationality. In addition, it appears from two of the cases listed above that non-EC nationals may derive certain benefits from the fact that they are employed by an EC firm exercising its freedom to provide services.

2.1   Relatives of EC nationals

Freedom of movement of EC nationals requires that obstacles to their mobility be eliminated, in particular as regards their right to be joined by family members and the conditions for the integration of that family into the host country.[1] Consequently, the numerous Community regulations[2] and directives[3] which seek to facilitate the free movement of employees, self-employed persons, (retired) pensioners, students and nationals who wish to reside in a Member State other than their own, also grant rights to the relatives of these persons.

---

1. Preamble to Regulation No. 1612/68.
2. Council Regulations 1612/68 on freedom of movement for workers within the Community, OJ 1968 L 257/2; Commission Regulation 1251/70 on the right of workers to remain in the territory of a Member State after having been employed in that State, OJ 1970 L 142/24; Council Regulation 1408/71 on the application of social security schemes to employed persons, to self-employed persons and to members of their families moving within the Community, last consolidated text in OJ 1983 L 230/8.
3. Council Directive 64/221/EEC on the co-ordination of special measures concerning the movement and residence of foreign nationals which are justified on the grounds of public policy, public security and public health, OJ 1964/850; Council Directive 68/360/EEC on the abolition of restrictions on movement and residence within the Community for workers of Member States and their families, OJ 1968 L 257/13; Council Directive 72/194/EEC extending to workers exercising the right to remain in the territory of a Member State after having been employed in that State the scope of Directive 64/221/EEC, OJ 1972 L 121/32; Council Directive 73/148/EEC on the abolition of restrictions on movement and residence within the Community for nationals of Member States with regard to establishment and the provision of services, OJ 1973 L 172/14; Council Directive 75/34/EEC concerning the right of nationals of a Member State to remain in the territory of another Member State after having pursued therein an activity in a self-employed capacity, OJ 1975 L 14/10; Council Directive 75/35/EEC extending the scope of Directive 64/221/EEC to include nationals of a Member State who exercise the right to remain in the territory of another Member State after having pursued an activity in a self-employed capacity, OJ 1975 L 14/14; Council Directive 77/486/EEC on the education of children of migrant workers, OJ 1977 L 199/32; Council Directive 90/364/EEC on the right of residence, OJ 1990 L 180/26; Council Directive 90/365/EEC on the right of residence for employees and self-employed persons who have ceased their occupational activity, OJ 1990 L 180/28; Council Directive 90/366/EEC on the right of residence for students, OJ 1990 L 180/30.

The circle of beneficiaries of these derived rights is not always exactly the same. In most cases, it comprises the spouse of the holder of the original right and their descendants who are dependants. It also often includes the dependent relatives in the ascending line of the holder of the original right and his spouse. The term 'spouse', contained in these regulations and directives, refers to a marital relationship only; however, if a Member State grants certain advantages to unmarried companions of its nationals, it cannot refuse to grant them to those of workers who are nationals of other Member States without being guilty of discrimination on grounds of nationality, contrary to Articles 7 and 48 of the Treaty.[4]

Where there is no holder of an original right, there cannot be a beneficiary of a derived right. This has been the core of the rulings in joined cases 35 and 36/82 *Morson* and *Jhanjan*, in case 283/83 *Meade* and in joined cases C-297/88 and C-197/89 *Dzodzi*.

Mrs Morson and Mrs Jhanjan had applied for permission to reside in the Netherlands in order to install themselves with their daughter and son respectively. Since these were Dutch nationals who were employed in their own country and who had never exercised their right to freedom of movement within the Community, the cases had, as the Court stated, no factor linking them with any of the situations governed by Community law. Accordingly, the Treaty provisions on freedom of movement and the rules adopted to implement them did not apply.[5]

Mr Meade, an US national, Mrs Meade, an UK national who was unemployed, and their two children, UK nationals, had been resident in France where Mr Meade was self-employed. The Court ruled that in these circumstances neither Regulation 1408/71 nor Article 48 of the Treaty prevented family allowances from being withdrawn pursuant to French legislation on the ground that one of the children was pursuing a course of study in the United Kingdom.[6]

On the same ground as in the *Morson* and *Jhanjan* case, the Court held that Mrs Dzodzi, widow of a Belgian national, could not rely on Regulation 1612/68, Directive 68/360/EEC, Regulation 1251/70 and Directive 64/221/EEC[7] for her application to remain in Belgium.[8] However, under Article 40 of the Belgian Law on access to the territory of the State for aliens and the residence, establishment and expulsion of aliens, the foreign spouse of a Belgian national, whatever his or her nationality, is treated as a Community national. The Court of Justice held that if the national court considers that as a result of reference to Community law, a provision of Community law is applicable to a purely domestic situation, such as the one in the *Dzodzi* case, the Court of Justice has jurisdiction to give a preliminary ruling on the

---

4. Case 59/85 *Reed* v. *The Netherlands*, [1986] ECR 1283 at 1300 and 1303.
5. Joined cases 35 and 36/82 *Morson* v. *The Netherlands* and *Jhanjan* v. *The Netherlands* [1982] ECR 3723, at 3734-3738.
6. Case 238/83 *Caisse d'Allocations Familiales* v. *Meade* [1984] ECR 2631, at 2637-2639.
7. See *supra*, nn. 2 and 3.
8. Paras. 20-28 of the judgment.

interpretation of that provision of Community law.[9] Acting on this basis, the Court of Justice defined, in its *Dzodzi* judgment, the right of residence and the right to remain in the territory which Directive 68/360/EEC and Regulations 1612/68 and 1251/70 confer upon the spouse of a worker who is a national of a Member State, employed or previously employed in the territory of another Member State; and the scope of the legal protection required by Articles 8 and 9 of Directive 64/221/ EEC.[10]

The derived rights include the right to install themselves with the holder of the original right,[11] a conditional right to remain permanently in the host State,[12] admission to normal education on the same conditions as the nationals of that State,[13] the right to take up work,[14] and benefits under the social security system of that State.[15]

Moreover, Article 7(2) of Regulation 1612/68 provides that a worker, who is a national of a Member State shall enjoy in the territory of another Member State the same social and tax advantages as national workers. The Court of Justice has held that this principle of equal treatment is also intended to prevent discrimination against the worker's widow and against his dependent relatives in the descending and in the ascending line.[16] As a result, this provision bestows a wide range of benefits upon the worker's relatives, including reduced railway fares for large families,[17] interest-free loans on the birth of a child,[18] a guaranteed income for old persons[19] and unemployment benefits for school leavers.[20] In case 94/98 *Deak* the Court has stated that this principle applied without regard to the nationality of those family members.[21]

In case 267/83 *Diatta* the Court ruled that a member of a migrant worker's family is not required to live permanently with him in order to qualify for a right of residence under Article 10 of Regulation 1612/68. Mrs Diatta was married to a French national working in Berlin. After some time she had separated from him with the intention of divorcing. The Court held that Article 10 must not be interpreted restrictively. Its interpretation of that provision corresponds to the spirit of Article 11

9. Paras. 29-43 of the judgment.

10. Paras. 44-69 of the judgment.

11. Art. 10(1) Reg. 1612/68; Art. 1 Dir. 73/148; Art. 1 Dir. 75/34; Art. 1 of Directives 90/364, 365 and 366.

12. Art. 3 Reg. 1251/70.

13. Art. 12 Reg. 1612/68; Art. 2 Dir. 77/486.

14. Art. 11 Reg. 1612/68.

15. Art. 3 Reg. 1408/71.

16. Case 32/75 *Cristini* v. *SNCF* [1975] ECR 1085, at 1095; case 63/76 *Inzirillo* v. *Caisse d'Allocations Familiales*, [1976] ECR 2057, at 2068; case 261/83 *Castelli* v. *ONPTS*, [1984] ECR 3199, at 3213; case 256/86 *Frascogna* v. *Caisse des dépôts et consignations* [1987] ECR 3431, at 3443.

17. Case 32/75 *Cristini* [1975] ECR 1085.

18. Case 65/81 *Reina* v. *Landeskredit Baden-Württemberg* [1982] ECR 33.

19. Case 261/83 *Castelli* [1984] ECR 3199.

20. Case 94/84 *Deak* v. *ONEM* [1985] ECR 1873.

21. [1985] ECR, at 1887.

of the same Regulation, which gives the member of the family the right to take up any activity as an employed person throughout the territory of the Member State. Moreover, the marital relationship cannot be regarded as dissolved so long as it has not been terminated by the competent authority.[22]

Article 11 of Regulation 1612/68 was also the subject-matter of case 131/85 *Gül*. Under this Regulation, the spouse and the children of an EC-national who is pursuing an activity as an employed or self-employed person in a Member State other than his own, are entitled to take up any activity as an employed person throughout the territory of that same State, even if they are not nationals of any Member State. The Court in *Gül* held that, in order to pursue an occupation such as the medical profession, the spouse of a migrant worker who is a non-EC national must meet the same requirements as those imposed by the host Member State on its own nationals. The migrant worker may rely on the principle of non-discriminatory treatment which is provided for in Article 3(1), first indent, of Regulation 1612/68. With regard to the worker's access to employment within the medical profession and to the practice of that profession, it is immaterial whether his qualifications are recognized under the legislation of the host Member State alone or pursuant to Directive 75/363/EEC.[23]

In respect of social security, the Court has stressed, in case 40/76 *Kermaschek*, that Regulation 1408/71 refers to two clearly distinct categories: the workers on the one hand, and the members of their families and their descendants on the other. The persons belonging to the second category can only claim derived rights of social security acquired through their status as a member of the family or a descendant of the holder of the original right. As a result, the spouse of a worker cannot claim, under Article 67 et seq., unemployment benefits on account of her own unemployment; she is only entitled to the benefits provided by the national legislation for the members of the family of unemployed workers. The Court added expressly that the nationality of the members of the family does not matter for this purpose.[24]

This principle has been confirmed in case 94/84 *Deak*. A national of a non-member country who is the member of a family of a national of a Member State cannot rely on Regulation 1408/71 in order to claim unemployment benefits granted, under the legislation of the host State, to young persons seeking employment.[25] However, as has been mentioned above, such benefits constitute a social advantage to which he is entitled under Article 7(2) of Regulation 1612/68.

2.2 Employees of a firm providing services in another Member State

Under Articles 59 and 60 of the Treaty, a firm established in a Member State is allowed to provide services in another Member State under the same conditions as

22. [1985] ECR, at 589-591.
23. [1986] ECR, at 1588-1594.
24. [1976] ECR, at 1676-1678.
25. [1985] ECR, at 1884-1885.

are imposed by that State on its own nationals. The Court has made it clear that this freedom carries with it the right for such a firm to use its own staff, regardless of their nationality, for that purpose.

Joined cases 62 and 63/81 *Seco* involved Luxembourg legislation governing contributions to old-age and invalidity insurance. By virtue of the Social Insurance Code workers employed in Luxembourg are in principle compulsorily insured. Half of the contributions must be paid by the employer and half by the worker. However, the Government may exempt from insurance foreigners who are temporarily resident in the Grand Duchy. In that case the employer is nevertheless liable for his share of contributions, although they do not entitle the worker concerned to any social benefit. It appeared from the papers before the Court that the reason for this was, on the one hand, that it would be unfair to collect contributions from workers residing in Luxembourg only temporarily, whilst, on the other hand, the temptation for employers to use foreign labour in order to alleviate the burden of paying their share of social security contributions must be avoided. Nevertheless, in practice the employer's share is no longer required to be paid in respect of workers who are temporarily in Luxembourg, if they are nationals of a Member State.

Seco and Dequenne were French undertakings carrying out work in the Grand Duchy, employing for that purpose workers who were not nationals of a Member State and who remained compulsorily affiliated to the French social security scheme during the entire duration of the work carried out in Luxembourg. The Court held that the extension of the obligation to pay the employer's share of social security contribution to employers established in another Member State who are already liable under the legislation of that State for similar contributions in respect of the same workers and the same periods of employment, constituted a discrimination prohibited under Articles 59 and 60(3) of the Treaty. As a consequence of this legislation employers established in another Member State in fact have to bear a heavier burden than those established within the national territory. The Court added that a Member State's power to control the employment of non-EC nationals may not be used to impose a discriminatory burden on an undertaking from another Member State enjoying the freedom to provide services.[26]

The problem in case C-113/89 *Rush Portuguesa* resulted from the fact that, while the freedom of providing services was already fully applicable between Portugal and the older members of the Community, Article 216 of the Act of Accession of Spain and Portugal provided for a derogation from freedom of movement for workers until 1 January 1993. When a Portuguese undertaking arranged for Portuguese workers to go to France for the purpose of carrying out work which it had sub-contracted there, the French immigration office claimed payment from it of the special contribution payable by an employer employing foreign workers in breach of the provisions of the labour code.

The Court declared that Articles 59 and 60 EEC preclude a Member State from prohibiting a provider of services established in another Member State from

26. [1982] ECR, at 232-236.

travelling freely within its territory with the whole of its staff, or from making the movement of the staff in question subject to restrictions such as a requirement to carry out on-the-spot recruitment or to obtain work permits. To impose such conditions on the provider of services of another Member State would be to discriminate against him in relation to his competitors established in the host country who are able to avail themselves of their own staff and would, moreover, affect his capacity to provide the services. However, the derogation of Article 216 of the Act of Accession applies whenever the access by Portuguese workers to the employment market of other Member States and the system governing the entry and residence of Portuguese workers requiring such access, were in issue. It would also preclude workers coming from Portugal from being made available through the intermediary of an undertaking providing services.[27]

It appears from these two judgments that the freedom to provide services in another Member State implies the right to employ non-EC nationals for that purpose, and that the host State may not make this freedom subject to restrictive conditions. It is too early to define the precise scope of this principle. It seems, however, that it can only be relied upon by the provider of services established in another Member State, even if it may result in benefits for non-EC nationals by facilitating their temporary employment elsewhere in the Community.

3.   DIRECT RIGHTS

Several agreements concluded under Articles 228 and 238 of the Treaty between the Community and third countries make provision for the way in which the Member States shall treat nationals of those countries. These provisions may, moreover, be implemented by acts adopted by a Joint Council instituted by the agreement.

The Court has always held that such agreements and acts are, as far as the Community is concerned, acts of one of the Community institutions within the meaning of Article 177(1)(b) of the Treaty, and that the provisions of these agreements and acts form, from their entry into force, an integral part of the Community legal system. On this ground it has accepted jurisdiction to give preliminary rulings concerning the interpretation of such provisions.[28]

The Court has further held that such rules of Community law, resulting from agreements with non-member countries, can be directly applicable and, consequently, relied upon by nationals of these countries. A provision in such an agreement or in an act adopted for its implementation must be regarded as being directly applicable when, regard being had to its wording and the purpose and nature of the agreement itself, the provision contains a clear and precise obligation which is not

---

27. Paras. 12-16 of the judgment.
28. See as regards the rights of non-EC nationals: for agreements: case 12/86 *Demirel* [1987] ECR, at 3750; for implementing acts: case C-192/89 *Sevince* at 3501, para. 10 of the judgment.

subject, in its implementation or effects, to the adoption of any subsequent measure.[29]

These principles have been applied in respect of the 1963 Association Agreement concluded with Turkey and its implementation, the 1975 Lomé Convention and the 1976 Cooperation Agreement with Morocco. Each of these three agreements will be discussed below.

3.1   The Association Agreement concluded with Turkey[30]

This Association Agreement with Turkey and its implementation by the Council of Association were at issue in case 12/86 *Demirel* and in case C-192/89 *Sevince*. Mrs Demirel, a Turkish national, had entered the Federal Republic of Germany to rejoin her husband, who had the same nationality and who had been living and working in Germany since entering that country in 1979. She was ordered to leave the country because her husband did not fulfil the German conditions for family reunification in the case of non-EC nationals. These conditions had been tightened between 1982 and 1984 by increasing from three to eight years the period during which the foreign national was required to have resided continuously and lawfully on German territory.

According to Article 12 of the Association Agreement with Turkey, the contracting parties agreed to be guided by Articles 48, 49 and 50 of the EEC Treaty for the purpose of progressively securing freedom of movement for workers between them. Article 36 of the Additional Protocol gives the Council of Association exclusive powers to lay down detailed rules for the progressive attainment of freedom of movement for workers. Decision No. 1/80 of this Council prohibits, with regard to Turkish workers who are already duly integrated in the labour force of a Member State, any further restrictions on the conditions governing access to employment. In the sphere of family reunification no decision of that kind had been adopted. Article 7 of the Association Agreement provides that the contracting parties are to refrain from any measures liable to jeopardize the attainment of the objectives of the Agreement.

The question was whether the provisions quoted above conferred rights on individuals such as the spouse and the minor children of a Turkish worker established within the Community. The Court's reply was negative. Article 12 of the Association Agreement and Article 36 of the Additional Protocol were held not to be sufficiently precise and unconditional for that purpose. And, the Court also held, it was not possible to infer from Article 7 of the Agreement a prohibition on the introduction of further restrictions on family reunification.[31]

---

29. For agreements: case 12/86 *Demirel* [1987] ECR, at 3752; for implementing acts: case C-192/89 *Sevince* [1990] ECR I at 3502, para. 15.

30. OJ 1963 C 113/2. The Additional Protocol of 1970 has been published in OJ 1973 C 113/18.

31. [1987] ECR, at 3752-3754.

On the other hand, in case C-192/89 *Sevince* the Court ruled that certain provisions of Decisions Nos. 2/76 and 1/80 of the Association Council have direct effect in the Member States. That ruling applies to Article 2(1)(b) of Decision No. 2/76 and Article 6(1), third indent, of Decision No. 1/80, under which, after five and four years respectively of legal employment in an EC Member State, a Turkish worker is to enjoy free access to any paid employment of his choice in that State. It also applies to Article 7 of Decision No. 2/76 and Article 13 of Decision No. 1/80, which both contain a stand-still clause to prevent new restrictions on the access to employment on behalf of workers having legal right of residence and employment within the territory of the contracting States. Neither the fact that these two Decisions make provision for the adoption of implementing measures, nor the non-publication of these Decisions, nor certain narrow safeguard clauses were considered to affect this rule of direct effect.[32]

The two Decisions are confined to regulating the right of access to employment of the Turkish worker, without referring to his right of residence. However, the Court declared that these two aspects of his personal situation are so closely interrelated that, by acknowledging the right of a Turkish worker to free access to any employment of his choice, after a certain period of legal employment in that Member State, these provisions necessarily imply the existence, at least as from that moment, of a right of residence for that person.[33]

It was, however, of no avail to Mr Sevince because he was not deemed to have a 'legal employment' within the meaning of Article 2(1)(b) of Decision No. 2/76 and Article 6(1), third indent, of Decision No. 1/80. That term does not cover the situation of a Turkish worker authorized to engage in employment during the period of suspension of operation of a decision refusing him a right of residence, against which he has lodged an appeal which has been dismissed.[34]

3.2 The Lomé Convention

Case 65/77 *Razanatsimba* concerned the interpretation of Article 62 of the Lomé Convention of 1975.[35] This Article provides that, as regards the arrangements that may be applied in matters of establishment and provision of services, the Afro-Carribean-Pacific States (ACP), on the one hand, and the Member States, on the other, shall treat nationals and companies or firms of Member States and nationals and companies of the ACP States respectively on a non-discriminatory basis.

Razanatsimba had the professional qualifications enabling him to seek admission to the French bar. The question was whether the legal condition that he must be French, in so far as international agreements do not provide otherwise, formed an

32. Paras. 16-26 of the judgment.
33. Paras. 28-29 of the judgment.
34. Paras. 30-33 of the judgment.
35. OJ 1976 L 25/2.

impediment to his admission. Razanatsimba argued that that would be contrary to the principle of non-discrimination laid down in Article 62 of the Lomé Convention.

According to the Court, the interpretation of that provision raised two questions:
(i) Does it oblige either the ACP States or the EC Member States to give to the nationals of a State belonging to the other group treatment identical to that reserved to their own nationals? The reply to that question was negative. The wording of the Article referred to the two groups of States bound by the Lomé Convention and provided that any State belonging to one of the groups shall treat nationals of any State belonging to the other group on a non-discriminatory basis.
(ii) Is a national of one ACP State (in this case: Madagascar) entitled under it to invoke the particular advantages accorded in matters of establishment by a Member State (France) to another ACP State (the Malagasy Republic)? The Court declared that it is not contrary to the rule as to non-discrimination laid down in Article 62 for a Member State to reserve more favourable treatment to the nationals of one ACP State, provided that such treatment results from the provisions of an international agreement comprising reciprocal rights and advantages.[36]

3.3   Cooperation agreements

The EEC has concluded cooperation agreements, *inter alia*, with Algeria,[37] Morocco,[38] Tunisia[39] and Yugoslavia.[40] These agreements each contain a provision which states that workers of that country's nationality and any members of their families living with them shall enjoy, in the field of social security, treatment free from any discrimination based on nationality in relation to nationals of Member States in which they are employed. This clause, as contained in Article 41(1) of the Cooperation Agreement with Morocco, was the subject-matter of a ruling in case C-18/90 *Kziber*.

Mrs Kziber, a Moroccan national, lived with her father, who has the same nationality and who retired in Belgium after having been employed in that country. She had appealed against a refusal of the Belgian authority to grant her the special unemployment benefits provided by Belgian legislation for school leavers which the Court of Justice had already, in case 94/98 *Deak*, defined as a social advantage within the meaning of Article 7(2) of Regulation 1612/68.[41]

The Court held, in the first place, that the prohibition on discrimination contained in Article 41(1) was capable of direct application.[42] It further declared that the concept of 'social security' contained in that Article has a meaning analogous to that found in Regulation 1408/71, and that Article 4 of this Regulation includes unem-

---

36. [1977] ECR at 2238-2239.
37. OJ 1978 L 263/2.
38. OJ 1978 L 264/2.
39. OJ 1978 L 265/2.
40. OJ 1983 L 41/2.
41. See *supra*, n. 19.
42. Paras. 17-23 of the judgment.

ployment benefits, including the type at issue, as a branch of social security.[43] It then stated that the concept of 'worker' encompasses not only workers in active employment but also those who have withdrawn from the employment market because of age or of a work accident.[44] All of these determinations led to the ruling that the principle of freedom from any discrimination based on nationality in the field of social security, contained in Article 41(1) of the Cooperation Agreement with Morocco, means that Member States are precluded from refusing to grant an unemployment benefit, which its legislation makes available to young persons seeking work, to a member of the family of a worker of Moroccan nationality residing with him, on the ground that the person seeking work is a Moroccan national.[45]

In his Opinion delivered in the *Kziber* case the Advocate-General Van Gerven submitted that in cases 40/76 *Kermaschek* and 94/84 *Deak* the Court held that Regulation 1408/71 entitles members of the family of a worker who is a national of a Member State only to the benefits which the national legislation provides for the members of the family of unemployed workers. In particular, he argued that it does not entitle those relatives to unemployment benefits granted to young persons seeking employment, such as the benefits at issue in the main proceedings.[46] He then submitted that the rule of equal treatment of workers of Moroccan nationality does not allow the members of their families to claim more rights than those accruing to relatives of nationals of other Member States.[47] The Court did not make clear why it rejected the reasoning of its Advocate-General. One might perhaps defend the Court's result with the argument that a literal interpretation of Article 41(1) of the Cooperation Agreement with Morocco appears to require a treatment of Moroccan workers and of members of their families equal to that of the nationals of the Member State in which they are employed, and not merely equal to the treatment which that Member State must give to nationals of another Member State and their relatives.

4.   CONCLUSIONS

Under Community law the rights of non-EC nationals to entry, residence, work, social security benefits, education and other social and tax advantages are based either on their relationship with EC nationals or firms or on their status as a national of a country with which the Community has concluded an international agreement. The attitude of the Court of Justice varies widely depending on which of these grounds is invoked. The reason is that the former ground is related to the freedom of

43. Para. 25 of the judgment.
44. Para. 27 of the judgment.
45. Paras. 28-29 of the judgment and ruling.
46. For a discussion of these cases, see *supra*, text accompanying nn. 24-25.
47. Para. 18 of the opinion.

movement within the common market, while the latter ground concerns the Community's external relations.

Whenever the freedom of movement within the common market is at stake, the Court is quick to condemn everything which might stand in its way. In the case of free movement of persons, the achievement of the objectives of family reunification and integration in the host Member State had far-reaching consequences. The fact that this also benefits relatives who are nationals of third countries is not so much the Court's achievement; the numerous regulations and directives stipulate that the various rights are extended to the spouse and the relatives irrespective of their nationality. In contrast, in the case of freedom to provide services, the Court can be credited with deciding that the nationality of the employees of the provider of services should not constitute an obstacle.

Different rules apply in the field of international agreements.

The recent *Kziber* case stands alone. This case resulted in the grant, to a relative of a worker from a third country, of certain rights falling within the scope of Regulation 1408/71, while previous case-law had denied such rights to relatives of workers from another Member State. In addition, it is the only one of the cases examined above in which a national of a third country was successful in invoking a provision of an international agreement.

In principle, the Court of Justice is prepared to regard a provision in an international agreement as being directly applicable. In practice, however, the Court is reluctant to render a judgment which would deprive the Community of any room for further negotiations with the other contracting partner. It can avoid such a decision either by denying direct effect, as it did in the *Demirel* case, or by adopting a restrictive interpretation of the scope of the provision, as in the *Razanatsimba* case.

This approach of the Court appears to be in line with its general attitude in cases involving the effects of international agreements in the legal order of the Community. I note, however, that the consequences of this approach can be harsh in cases involving the free movement of persons. Take the *Demirel* case as an example. The Court could have declared that the obligation to refrain from any measures liable to jeopardize the attainment of the objectives of the Association Agreement with Turkey is 'a clear and precise obligation which is not subject, in its implementation or effects, to the adoption of any subsequent measure.' Furthermore, it could have held that the increase from three to eight years of the period during which a foreign worker is required to have resided continuously and lawfully on German territory before being entitled to family reunification constitutes an infringement of that obligation. Ultimately, this is a matter of appreciation. The Court appears to have been deeply impressed by the problems that the presence of 1,500,000 Turkish immigrants caused to the Federal Republic of Germany. Personally, I would be inclined to be more impressed by the inhumanity of a rule which compels a lawful immigrant to wait eight years before being allowed to enjoy family life again.

FREE MOVEMENT AND INTEGRATION OF NON-EC NATIONALS AND THE LOGIC OF THE INTERNAL MARKET

T. Hoogenboom[*]

1. INTRODUCTION

Discrimination against aliens, particularly against those who are not nationals of one of the Member States, is a source of concern of the European Community. This concern has been expressed repeatedly by the Council, the Commission and the European Parliament. This topical and highly sensitive issue is one of extreme political and legal complexity. This complexity is a consequence of two conflicting positions: first, the conviction that it is no longer possible to delay integrative measures at a Community level, and, second, the traditional view that the Member States have retained certain sovereign rights in the field of the treatment of aliens. The Member States' view of their sovereignty, which is discussed in sections 5 and 6 of this report, is apparently difficult to reconcile with the requirements of the internal market. The conflict is evidenced by the on-going debate regarding the powers of the Community and the possible transfer of the powers of the Member States to the Community.

In both material and formal terms, the position of non-EC nationals residing within the Community gives rise to tension, not only for the people themselves, but also for EC nationals. Among the material factors causing this tension are governmental efforts at immigration control, the poor education and high unemployment of immigrants in the Community, and the existence of racist and xenophobic attitudes. European Governments have suggested several traditional solutions, such as a radical restriction of immigration by exercising more vigilant control at the outer borders, harmonization of visa and admission policies and the promotion of integration. Formal factors which impede effective action at a Community level are the supposed lack of competence of the Commission and the Council, the traditional view that the Member States hold of their sovereignty in the field of immigration law, and the vast differences between the economies of certain of the Member States.

If this tension is not alleviated, Community principles will be corrupted, and there will be a huge waste of social and human resources. It may be possible to find

---

[*] Practising lawyer and lecturer at the University of Amsterdam.

H.G. Schermers et al., eds., Free Movement of Persons in Europe
© 1993, T.M.C. Asser Instituut, The Hague

solutions for the formal problems either by granting powers to the European institutions, or by making use of intergovernmental conventions to harmonize provisions relating, *inter alia*, to the law relating to aliens. Recent examples of these conventions are the Schengen Conventions[1] and the Dublin Asylum Convention.[2] The Member States have shown a preference for the intergovernmental approach, although it has not, in the Commission's view, produced significant results.[3] The intergovernmental path also has the disadvantage of failing to involve the European Parliament and the Court of Justice. Thus, for example, the measures that are being prepared by the Ad Hoc Immigration Group[4] lack the necessary openness and have little or no democratic legitimacy. Because intergovernmental treaties are excluded from the scope of the EEC Treaty, their legitimacy is generally not subject to review by the Court of Justice. It is therefore doubtful whether uniform implementation of the regulations and legal protection against their application can be assured.

An alternative formal solution that is also being considered is the granting of nationality to non-EC nationals while allowing them to retain their original nationality.[5]

2.   THE ISSUE

Non-EC nationals who are permanently[6] and legally residing within the Community are usually in a position that is both formally and materially weak and unequal. Their status is reflected in the debate on whether the right to free movement of persons can, or indeed should, be granted to them. This matter is, rightly, often linked to that of integration. After all, integration is primarily a means of removing gross inequalities between various population groups. A prohibition against the free movement of certain persons is a structural factor confirming inequality. The issue

---

1. Agreement between the Kingdom of the Netherlands, the Kingdom of Belgium, the Federal Republic of Germany, the French Republic and the Grand Duchy of Luxembourg on the Gradual Abolition of Checks at the Common Borders, done at Schengen 14 June 1985, Trb. [Dutch Treaties Series] 1985 No. 102 and the Convention applying the Schengen Agreement of 14 June 1985 between the Governments of the States of the Benelux Economic Union, the Federal Republic of Germany and the French Republic on the gradual abolition of checks at their common borders, 30 ILM (1991) 68.

2. Convention determining the State responsible for examining application for asylum lodged in one of the Member States of the European Communities, done at Dublin 15 June 1990, 30 ILM (1991) 425.

3. Commission of the European Communities, Commission Opinion of 21 October 1990 on the proposal for amendment of the Treaty establishing the European Economic Community with a view to political Union, COM(90) fin. p. 12.

4. An informal working party which is, among other things, drafting the Convention on the crossing of the external borders of the Member States of the European Community.

5. See *infra*, text accompanying notes 38-39.

6. A definition of the concept of permanent residence does not necessarily require the adoption of a yardstick measured in terms of a minimum number of years, as is done by the Council of Europe. See Council of Europe, Parliamentary Assembly, Report on the right of permanent residence for migrant workers and members of their families, Doc. 5904. For example, it is also possible to adopt the periods imposed under various national rules regarding permanent residence of aliëns.

to be discussed in this report is whether depriving permanently and legally-resident non-EC nationals of free movement within the Community accords with the fundamental principles of the Community on the one hand, and with the idea of justice, which can be distilled from the Community's principles and policies on the other.

With a view to the changes the internal market will bring, it is reasonable to ask whether withholding the right to free movement is compatible with the logic of the internal market. The question is particularly relevant in the light of the internal market programme, which has renewed interest in the concept of European citizenship. At present, European citizenship is a common, factual relationship among nationals of the Member States. If this concept is transformed from the realm of European rhetoric into a legal status,[7] it would emphasize the fact that there are two sorts of persons living within the territory of the EEC: EC citizens, on the one hand, and persons who can be regarded as second-class residents, on the other.[8] In other words, the grim picture the Commission painted as far back as 1976 could become reality.[9]

3.   THE LOGIC OF THE INTERNAL MARKET AND THE POSITION OF NON-EC NATIONALS

The persons referred to in this report as 'non-EC nationals' are asylum seekers, stateless persons, gypsies, and both legal and illegal migrant workers. The legal position of these groups differ, particularly with respect to admission policies. However, after they are admitted, their relationship to the Community and to the Member States is comparable. For practical reasons this report is restricted to a discussion of legally resident migrant workers and their families. They form the largest group. But the remarks can be regarded *mutatis mutandis* as being equally relevant to the other groups. From a legal point of view, the position of illegal immigrants is so different from that of legal immigrants that it would not be fruitful to compare their position to that of EC nationals.

In this report the Community principles which will be adopted as a yardstick for assessing the position of legally resident aliens are the ones which pervade the Community's whole legal system, namely, free movement of persons, equal treatment and social justice. This section will discuss the right to *free movement of persons* and the related right to equality of treatment.

The right to free movement of persons encompasses the right to reside in another Member State in order to work there, even when the person in question is not a

7. In accordance with proposals by the Commission, see Commission of the European Communities, 'First Contributions of the Commission to the Intergovernmental Conferences on Political Union' SEC(91) 500, as partly reproduced in *Migration News Sheet* No. 98/1991-05 (May 1991) p. 8.

8. Advisory Council for Ethnic Minorities, Memorandum A social Europe for one and all, The Hague 1989, pp. 17 and 21.

9. Commission of the European Communities, Action programme in favour of migrant workers and their families, Bull. EC, suppl. 3/76.

national of that State. In accordance with prevailing Community legislation, Member States are obliged to admit to their territory those persons to whom the right of free movement applies. All that is required is that a valid identity document or valid passport be shown.[10] The States are thus entitled to request that these documents are shown at their borders and to refuse entry to persons who are unable to meet this requirement. The right to free movement may be regarded as fundamental in the context of the Community.[11]

In addition to the right to free movement of persons in order to work, it is possible to distinguish a *right of residence*, as has been laid down in several recent Council directives relating to students and persons who are no longer employed.[12] This right of residence has for some time applied to citizens of the Benelux within the Benelux area.

Finally, there is the *right to travel freely* or the *right of circulation*, which applies to non-EC nationals in certain areas, including the Benelux area, and which will apply within the Schengen area after the 1990 Schengen Convention has been ratified.[13] The right to travel freely may be distinguished from the other forms of mobility in that it only permits persons to stay within the territory of a State that is party to the agreement for a very limited period of time, namely three months. In contrast, the right to free movement and the right of establishment also give nationals of the Member States or of the Benelux the right to take up residence elsewhere within the Community or the Benelux respectively, under certain conditions.

The significance of the rights to free movement of persons and to equal treatment (Arts. 3(c) and 48-66 of the EEC Treaty) is clear. These rights are intended to enable the residents of the Community to look for work in another Member State, if necessary. The exercise of these rights is seen as a means of realizing the common market. Pursuant to Community law, the right to equality of treatment — or in other words, the prohibition on discrimination on grounds of nationality — and the right to free movement can be invoked by EC citizens in many fields, ranging from working conditions to social security. According to the EEC Treaty, EC citizens enjoy the right to free movement of persons. Under Articles 7 and 48(2) of the Treaty, they may not be subjected to discrimination on grounds of nationality.

---

10. Art. 3(1) of EEC Directive 68/360; Art. 3(1) of EEC Directive 73/148.

11. See e.g., Court of Justice in case 152/73, *Sotgin* v. *Deutsche Bundespost* [1974] ECR 153; see further R.O. Plender, 'The right to free movement in the European Communities', in J.W. Bridge et al. (eds.), *Fundamental Rights* (London, 1973) pp. 306-317; R.O. Plender,'La libre circulation des personnes en droit européen', in M. Flory and R. Higgins (eds.), *Liberté de circulation des personnes en droit international* (Paris, 1988) pp. 55-75; see also the preamble to EEC Regulation 1612/68.

12. The Community directives relating to the right of residence include: Council Directive of 28 June 1990 on the right of residence, OJ L 180/26; Council Directive on the right of residence for employees and self-employed persons who have ceased their occupational activity, OJ L 180/28; and Council Directive of the Council of 28 June 1990 on the right of residence for students, OJ L 180/30.

13. The right to travel freely or the right of circulation is reflected in Article 8 of the Convention on the transfer of control of persons to the external borders of the Benelux area and Art. 21 of the 1990 Schengen Convention.

Article 2 of the EEC Treaty sets out its general aims and objectives. By establishing a common market and approximating the economic policies of Member States, the Community seeks to promote, *inter alia*, the raising of the standard of living of the peoples of Europe. One of the means of achieving this is the abolition of obstacles to freedom of movement for persons. In this context, Article 8A of the EEC Treaty is especially significant. The relevant part of the Article states: 'The Community shall adopt measures with the aim of progressively establishing the internal market over a period expiring on 31 December 1992 . . .' The internal market is defined in paragraph two of the Article as 'an area without internal frontiers in which the free movement of goods, persons, services and capital is ensured in accordance with the provisions of this Treaty.'

Non-EC nationals represent a considerable market potential. The current working population of non-EC nationals comprises approximately four million people. If the families of these workers are also counted, there will problaly be more than ten million of these people distributed throughout the twelve Member States in 1993.[14] They are active in both the labour and consumer markets. Restricting their presence in twelve markets, which are sheltered from one another in this respect, is contrary to the objective of the common employment and consumer market set out in Article 2 of the EEC Treaty. Furthermore, any such restriction can easily lead to unfair competition, and is at cross purposes with the goals of the internal market. Or, in the words of Böhning and Werquin:

'In any labour market, statutorily imposed restrictions on economically active persons introduce rigidities and inefficiencies; that is to say, the market-clearing mechanism cannot work as well as it would in the absence of such restrictions. Inefficiencies incur lower output and lower employment. As the establishment of the Single Market is, in essence, an attempt to render the Member States' economies more efficient and competitive, the maintenance of twelve national policies that have the effect of confining a considerable part of the EC's labour force — some 2.5 to 3 million persons — to twelve segregated territories, conflicts with the very goals of the Single European Market.'[15]

In other words, the authors believe that the logic of the internal market is contrary to the exclusion of non-EC nationals from the free movement of persons. I would put it more forcefully: this restriction frustrates one of the primary objectives of Community law — raising the standard of living. This objective, which according to the preamble of the Treaty is to be achieved by the elimination of the barriers dividing

---

14. In 1989, which was even before the operations regularizing the status of illegal immigrants in Italy and Spain, the Commission estimated their number at 8,179,000, or 2.55 % of the total population. See Commission of the European Communities, The social integration of third country migrants residing on a permanent and lawful basis in the Member States, SEC(89) 924 fin., table 1.

15. W.R. Böhning and J. Werquin, 'Some Economic, Social and Human Right Considerations concerning the Future Status of Third-Country Nationals in the Single European Market' ILO-Working Paper (Geneva, 1990) p. 9.

Europe, a means on which the Single European Act places its primary emphasis,[16] simply cannot be served by such a restriction. It therefore corrupts Community principles.

4.   THE LOGIC OF THE INTERNAL MARKET AND THE NECESSITY
        OF INTEGRATION OF NON-EC NATIONALS

The various developments within national labour markets will entail certain restrictions. This will, in turn, create a greater need for freedom of movement. There is nothing to indicate that this need will be limited to EC nationals. In the view of the Economic and Social Committee, the Community should pursue a dual aim without delay. First, the Community should harmonize the legal and administrative regulations and relevant Member State measures. Second, the Community should ensure that the conditions for implementing the free movement of non-EC nationals are laid down on the same footing as for EC nationals.[17]

However, the internal market is not only an economic concept. The reference to European citizenship already suggests that a market-oriented approach can be supplemented by a line of reasoning focusing on the material differences between nationals of non-member countries and those of the Member States. To put it briefly, the difference is that, in general, non-EC nationals who belong to certain ethnic groups have proportionately less access to social institutions such as work, housing and education than nationals of the Member States. According to a Commission report, non-EC nationals belong to 'the most disadvantaged economic categories of the host country's society from which many are unable to break free owing to the living, education and working conditions inherent in that situation.'[18]

Attempts to improve these conditions were relatively late in getting under way. The receiving societies were initially only interested in the work and not in the workers. Policies of the Member States and the Community that were aimed at integration came too late, if at all. The northern Member States realized belatedly that the workers they had imported from Turkey and North Africa in the sixties and early seventies did not come simply to work and then allow themselves be sent back home afterwards. They arrived as 'guest workers' but became immigrants. The Member States also realized belatedly that their societies' capacity to absorb these people was limited if the government did too little to encourage integration. The result has been vulnerable groups of immigrants, uncertain about their future, dreaming of returning to their country of origin but knowing that they and their children no longer have a

16. See P.J.G. Kapteyn and P. VerLoren van Themaat, *Introduction to the Law of the European Communities*, 2nd edn. L.W. Gormley, ed., Deventer (1989) p. 75.

17. Economic and Social Committee, Own-initiative opinion on the Status of migrant workers from third countries (91/159/05) OJ 1991 C159/12.

18. Commission of the European Communities, The social integration of third-country migrants residing on a permanent and lawful basis in the Member States, SEC(89) 924 fin., p. 22.

future there. And, in many cases, these groups of immigrants are living in poverty with the bleak prospect of lack of work.

The official view of the Member States is that integration can only succeed if immigration is limited. The logic of the internal market implies that the internal frontiers will be abolished and border checks removed to the outer frontiers. The officially propagated Community policies on integration are based on the need to restrict immigration by harmonization of visa regulations and stricter border controls.[19] Immigrant groups will find this policy paradoxical and threatening, and this in turn may prove counterproductive in terms of integration. The situation is aggravated because immigration will certainly continue, despite the official stop on immigration. As has been recognized in a draft communication from the Commission to the Council, two possible reasons to expect continued immigration are the Member States' humanitarian obligations to allow families to reunite and to admit persons seeking asylum.[20] Apart from the flow of immigrants from the traditional emigration countries, it is expected there will be an influx, albeit temporary and limited, from the eastern European countries. Because immigration is going to continue, the question is not so much how best to integrate the existing migrant populations, but rather what a social and legal system that is directed towards integration should be like. Integration should not be understood simply as a unilateral attempt to teach newcomers the norms and values of western European society. Instead, integration policies should also endeavour to reinforce the values of hospitality and equality of treatment which underlie west European society.

Where does the logic of the internal market stand in relation to this type of attempt to achieve integration? If the internal market were regarded merely as a form of economic cooperation in the narrow sense of the word, it would be difficult to justify a common attempt to achieve integration. But the rules that govern the internal market are expressly concerned with more far-reaching interests than purely economic ones. This is evidenced not only in the preamble of the EEC Treaty, but also in that of the Single European Act. This refers to the decision of the Twelve to promote democracy, based on the fundamental rights that are acknowledged in the Member States, in the European Convention on the Protection of Human Rights and Fundamental Freedoms, and in the European Social Charter, especially those of freedom, equality and social justice.

Community law, to the extent it is laid down in the Single European Act, claims to be based on social justice, and, moreover, social justice as a fundamental right.[21] In the legal culture of western Europe, social justice is a name that is given to efforts to create equal rights and distribute scarce goods equitably. In the above characterization, what counts is that non-EC nationals are given proportionate access to social

---

19. See Commission of the European Communities, Policies on immigration and the social integration of migrants in the European Community; Experts' Report drawn up on behalf of the Commission of the European Communities, SEC(90) 1813 fin., p. 17.

20. *Migration News Sheet* No. 99/1991-06 (June, 1991) p. 1.

21. The terminology of the preamble is not clear. Views on social justice constitute the starting-point from which the creation of rights should follow social justice cannot in itself be seen as a right.

institutions. The Economic and Social Committee has warned that, unless the two paths of (1) the harmonization of regulations promoting integration and (2) the laying down of conditions for the free movement of persons, are followed, the proper working of the internal market will be jeopardized, and further discrimination against non-EC nationals will be certain to occur.[22] This development would infringe upon one of the dominant legal norms in both the Community and the Member States: the prohibition of discrimination.

5.   THE LOGIC OF THE INTERNAL MARKET AND THE POWERS OF THE COMMUNITY

The intractability of issues related to the phenomenon of free movement of non-EC nationals is particularly evident in the battle for the powers of the Community. This battle is being waged at various levels. It is primarily about the interpretation of provisions in the EEC Treaty governing the free movement of persons. It has been argued that the Community also has the power to regulate the free movement of non-EC nationals, in a manner similar to the regulations applying to EC nationals. There are convincing arguments in favour of this, because the Treaty does not restrict free movement and equality of treatment to EC nationals. Article 3(c) expressly refers to the free movement of *persons*, without limiting it to EC nationals, and Articles 7, which contains the prohibition on discrimination, and 48(1), which provides for the free movement of workers, do not expressly reserve these norms for citizens who are nationals of one of the Member States. In contrast, treaty provisions on the right of establishment and freedom to provide services are expressly limited to the nationals of Member States.[23]

This has led several authors to state that the draftsmen of the Treaty wanted to leave open the possibility that non-EC nationals might indeed fall under these favourable provisions. One also frequently comes across a different opinion.[24] But the Treaty in no way compels one to take the view that the free movement of workers from third countries cannot be included within the scope of Articles 3(c), 7,

22. Economic and Social Committee, *supra* n. 17.

23. See Arts. 52 and 59 of the EEC Treaty. Article 48(2) requires the abolition of discrimination based on nationality only for 'workers of the Member States.'

24. See in support of the view that the regulation of the legal position of citizens from third countries does not fall outside the scope of the Treaty, for example, Kapteyn, VerLoren van Themaat and Gormley, op. cit. n. 16 pp. 415-416 and R.O. Plender, *International Migration Law*, Dordrecht (1988) pp. 197-198; see also for a recent summary H. Verschueren, 'Het arrest Rush Portuguesa. Een nieuwe wending aan het vrij verkeer van werknemers in het Europese gemeenschapsrecht' [The Rush Portuguesa decision. A new turn in the free movement of workers in European community law], *Migrantenrecht* (1990) pp. 188 and 191, n. 11. For the opposite view see Verschueren, pp. 188 and 191, n. 10 and B. Sundberg-Weitman, *Discrimination on grounds of nationality*; Free Movement of Workers and Freedom of Establishment under the EEC Treaty, Amsterdam (1977) pp. 100-101; see also P. Oliver, 'Non-Community Nationals and the Treaty of Rome', 5 YEL (1985) pp. 59-60.

8a and 42-51, or that the organs of the Community are not competent to regulate the free movement of non-EC nationals.

The free movement of these residents is indeed also the subject of secondary legislation. Article 10 of EEC Regulation 1612/68, concerning the free movement of workers within the Community, provides that the spouse of a worker who is a national of a Member State and is employed in the territory of another Member State, as well as his children under the age of 21 and all other dependent children or ascendent relatives of the worker and his spouse, *in all cases irrespective of their nationality*, may take up residence with the worker in question. According to Article 11 of this regulation, the spouse and children under 21 or dependent on a worker may accept employment on the territory of the Member State where the worker is working. This right is conditional on the worker's exercise of the right of free movement. If the worker does not exercise the right, the spouse, children or other relatives may not exercise it either.[25] Article 4 of Regulation 1408/71 on the application of social security schemes to employed persons and their families moving within the Community contains a similar favourable provision. These regulations are intended to avoid the nationality of the spouse and relatives from forming an obstacle to free movement of workers.

On the other hand, Regulation 1408/71 shows that the Community institutions derive their regulatory power in respect of workers from third countries from the Treaty, in particular Article 48. In Articles 1 and 2, stateless persons and admitted refugees and their relatives are expressly referred to as beneficiaries.

Curiously, however, in the *Meade* case the Court of Justice, albeit in an incidental and relatively obscure passage, within a preliminary ruling that has no further bearing on stateless persons or refugees, seems to have taken the view that Article 48 of the Treaty only ensures the free movement of workers for workers of the Member States, possibly with the intention of thus demonstrating that the provision relates solely to workers who are nationals of one of the Member States. But the Court of Justice did not state it so explicitly. It quoted Article 48 of the EEC Treaty in the following words: 'By virtue of Article 2(1), Regulation 1408/71 is to 'apply to workers . . . who are nationals of one of the Member States . . . as also to the members of their families'. Similarly, Article 48 guarantees free movement of persons only to workers of the Member States. As is clear from the documents before the Court, the national court raised its question in the context of the case of a child whose father is a national of a non-member country and whose mother is not employed. Under those conditions, Regulation 1408/71 does not apply to this case.'[26] Nevertheless, we cannot be certain of the view taken by the Court of Justice, because it did not define the term 'workers' in Article 48 as meaning 'workers who are nationals of one of the Member States'.

---

25. Joined cases 35 and 36/82, *Morson and Jhanjan* v. *Netherlands* [1982] ECR 3723; joined cases C 297/89 and C 197/89, *Massam Dzodzi* v. *Belgium* [1990] ECR 3783.

26. Court of Justice in case 238/83, *Meade* [1984] ECR 2631 consideration 7. For a discussion of *Meade* and the limits it may impose on free movement of workers, see C. Greenwood, 'Nationality and the Limits of the Free Movement of Persons in Community Law', 8 YEL (1988) pp. 205-207.

Those who advocate a restrictive view of Articles 3(c), 8a, 7 and 48-51 base themselves primarily on case-law dealing with Community secondary legislation, in which the significance of these provisions for the free movement and equality of treatment of citizens from third countries was not the main issue.

The Court of Justice has also clarified its position on non-EC nationals who have been recruited by a person to provide services in one of the Member States, other than that of the person for whom the services are intended (see Arts. 59 and 60 of the Treaty). The authorities of the Member State where the services are being provided may not take any restrictive measures in respect of the employees as long as the service continues. This supports a limited right of free movement; namely to the Member State where the services are to be provided and for as long as the service lasts.[27]

The above discussion demonstrates that the EEC Treaty does not limit the free movement of persons to persons or workers who are nationals of one of the Member States. Secondary legislation does impose limits, although it nevertheless expressly grants certain rights to nationals of third countries. This is also the view taken by the Member States and the Council.[28] In its 1985 White Paper on Completing the Internal Market, the Commission implicitly adopted the stance that the Community has powers in this respect. After all, according to the White Paper, the Commission aims to promote a directive on the harmonization of the regulations concerning the status of non-EC nationals.[29]

However, the Commission has refrained from proposing this legislation because of the practical difficulty of achieving a majority of Council votes, much less unanimity.[30]

The Community certainly has the power to promote close cooperation between the Member States in the social field. The Commission is explicitly charged with this task under Article 118 of the EEC Treaty. It has used these powers twice in respect of non-EC nationals. The first time was in 1985 when the Commission adopted a decision setting out a procedure for prior communication and consultation on migration policies in relation to non-member countries.[31]

This 1985 Commission decision can be seen as the first regulatory deed that directly attempted to intervene in the policies of the Member States in respect of non-EC nationals. Its aim was, *inter alia*, to harmonize national legislation in the field of immigration law.

West Germany, France, the Netherlands, Denmark and the United Kingdom, which are the richer Member States with more or less highly developed social

27. Court of Justice, decision of 27 March 1990, case C-113/89 *Rush Portuguesa* [1990] ECR 1439; see also Verschueren, op. cit. n. 24, p. 188.

28. For the Council's view see Council Resolution of 27 June 1980 on guidelines for a Community labour market policy, OJ 1980 C 168/1.

29. COM (85) 310, fin., para. 48.

30. Unanimity in such cases is prescribed in Art. 100A(2) of the EEC Treaty.

31. Commission Decision of 8 July 1985, setting up a prior communication and consultation procedure on migration policies, No. 85/381/EEC, OJ 1985 L 217/25.

security systems, felt that this 1985 Commission decision impinged on their sovereignty in the field of immigrants and immigration rules. They appealed to the Court of Justice.[32] The basic contention of these Member States was that migration policies concerning non-member countries either did not fall within the social field within the meaning of Article 118 or only partly within such field. The most far-reaching contention was put forward by the French Republic: the whole of immigration law, being law that relates to national public policy and public security, was outside the competence of the Community. In addition, the applicant Member States argued that the 1985 Commission decision was not limited to arranging a consultation procedure. By laying down the aim of the consultations (i.e., the harmonization of the national regulations) the Commission allegedly sought to determine the outcome of these consultations; it was argued that this exceeded the Commission's procedural powers.

The Court of Justice had to decide two separate issues. First, whether the cooperation between the Member States in the social field aimed at in Article 118 included migration policies in respect of non-member countries. Second, whether the task that is entrusted to the Commission in Article 118, of arranging consultation, implies that this institution is empowered to adopt binding decisions.

The Court rejected the contention that migration policies in respect of non-member countries falls completely outside the scope of Article 118. In answer to the first issue, the Court held that social integration policies fall within the scope of Article 118 because they are directly connected with problems in the fields of employment and working conditions. However, the cultural integration of immigrant communities from non-member countries is in some respects related to and the consequences of migration policies, the need for cultural and social integration applies to immigrant communities as a whole, without distinction between migrant workers and other aliens, and, therefore its relationship to employment and working conditions is tenuous. The Court held that migration policies can only pertain to the social field within the meaning of Article 118 to the extent that they relate to the situation of workers from non-member countries in connection with these workers' impact on the community labour market and working conditions.

In answer to the second issue, the Court held that when the Commission is only competent to set up a consultation procedure, it cannot prescribe the intended aim of those consultations, and cannot prevent the Member States from applying draft treaties, agreements or provisions that the Commission believes are not in accordance with the policies and actions of the Community.[33]

---

32. Court of Justice in cases 281, 283-285 and 287/85, *Germany and others* v. *Commission* [1987] ECR 3254; the application of the Netherlands was declared inadmissible as being out of time.

33. Apart from this, the Court noted that the competence of the Commission should remain restricted to the organization of a procedure for communication and consultation: '(. . .) and that in the present stage of development of Community law the subject-matter of the notification and consultation falls within the competence of the Member States.', see [1987] ECR 3254. Thus it cannot be ruled out that Community law will develop in such a way that the Commission will acquire competence in these fields. This may be possible within the context of the Internal Market after 1992.

In summary the 1985 decision was therefore declared void to the extent that the Commission was not empowered either (1) to extend the communication and consultation procedure to areas connected with the cultural integration of workers/nationals of non-member countries and their families, or (2) to set the objective of such communication and consultation procedures as establishing conformity between draft national measures and Community policies and actions.

The second time the Commission used its powers under Article 118 was in 1988, when a decision appeared which was almost identical to that of 1985, but which met the Court's objections.[34]

The Commission has various means of assisting non-EC nationals in connection with social or development action programmes entrusted to the Commission, especially when these programmes contribute to education and training. Similarly, there are also ways to admit non-EC nationals who have been born and bred in a Member State, and are legally resident there, to the Community's exchange and cooperation programmes (for students, young workers and schoolchildren). In view of the Court of Justice's ruling in *Germany and others* v. *Commission,* discussed above, the Commission is also empowered to promote close cooperation between the Member States in respect of employment for non-EC nationals. This is why it can promote the creation of a right of access to labour, even if that right were not available in the Member State where the non-EC national in question has been admitted. According to a draft communication to the Council, the Commission does indeed have this in mind. Opportunities for cross-border labour, which in fact amount to the free movement of persons, could be sought for certain categories of non-EC nationals who are permanent residents in one of the Member States, such as treaty refugees or non-EC nationals who are employed as guest workers.[35]

6.   THE LOGIC OF THE INTERNAL MARKET AND THE UPHOLDING OF THE SOVEREIGNTY OF THE MEMBER STATES

Legislative action by the Community is often complicated by the attitude the Member States have adopted towards their sovereignty. The proceedings before the Court of Justice discussed above clearly demonstrate this obstacle. A further, express reservation of sovereignty was made in the Single European Act. In a general declaration accompanying Articles 13 (which incorporated Art. 8A into the EEC Treaty) to 19 of the Single European Act, the contracting parties laid down the following:

'Nothing in these provisions shall affect the right of the Member States to take such measures as they consider necessary for the purpose of controlling immigration from third

---

34. Commission decision of 8 June 1988, setting up a prior communication and consultation procedure on migration policies in relation to non-member countries, No. 88/384/EEC, OJ L 183/35.

35. See *supra*, n. 20.

countries, and to combat terrorism, crime, the traffic in drugs and illicit trading in works of art and antiques.'

Based on the conventional concept of legal competence under international law, the clause on measures in respect of immigration is not surprising. It becomes surprising when read in combination with the Political Declaration by the governments of the Member States on the Free Movement of Persons, which was also made in the Single European Act. This Declaration reads as follows:

'In order to promote the free movement of persons, the Member States shall cooperate, without prejudice to the powers of the Community, in particular as regards the entry, movement and residence of nationals of third countries. They shall also cooperate in the combating of terrorism, crime, the traffic in drugs and illicit trading in works of art and antiques.'

Taking both of these declarations together, it can be deduced that the Member States wish to retain their power to control immigration into their territories, but that they nevertheless acknowledge the powers of the Community in the fields of entry, movement and residence of non-EC nationals. Although it is true that these declarations do not have the force of treaty provisions,[36] they can be utilized in the interpretation of treaty provisions, and are certainly politically significant.[37] These declarations demonstrate that, unlike its power in the field of the free movement of EC nationals, the Community's power in this respect is not regarded as exclusive. From the point of view of a clear demarcation of competence between the Community and the Member States, this is open to considerable objections. These objections may to some extent be removed if the forthcoming Treaty amendments, resulting from the recent intergovernmental conferences on political union, were to lay down the powers of the Community in no uncertain terms. The effectiveness of the Community's institutions would be greatly enhanced if the present requirement of unanimity were no longer to apply to the Council's decisions on matters relating to the free movement of persons.

Paradoxically, the traditional view of sovereignty as regards the Community may also contribute to nationals actually being granted free movement. Although it is by no means ruled out that nationality may give rise to rights under community law,[38] it is up to the Member States to determine who their nationals are. Giving a person the nationality of a Member State may also be giving him the benefits of the EEC

---

36. See A.G. Toth, 'The legal status of the declarations annexed to the Single european act', 23 CML Rev. (1986) pp. 803-812 and G.M. Borchardt and K.C. Wellens, 'Soft law in het gemeenschapsrecht' [Soft law in community law], *Sociaal-Economische Wetgeving* (1987) pp. 688-695.

37. An illustration of the political significance is the debate in the Dutch Second Chamber on the signing of the 1990 Schengen Convention. The State Secretary justified the intergovernmental path, which was not well received in the House, by referring to the political declaration; see the Proceedings of the Second Chamber, Hand. II 1989-1990, p. 77/4253.

38. See Court of Justice case 36/75 *Rutili* v. *Ministre de l'Intérieur* [1975] ECR 1753.

Treaty. This is the path the Netherlands seems to wish to take.[39] Those people who do not object to dual nationality may thus be given the opportunity to acquire Dutch nationality by means of a flexible naturalization procedure. In any case this attitude is a reflection of a systematic policy of integration that has been followed for years.

7.   THE LOGIC OF THE INTERNAL MARKET AND THE CONTROL OF
       NON-EC NATIONALS CROSSING THE INTERNAL BORDERS

The final matter to be considered in this report is the position on non-EC nationals who wish to cross the internal borders of the Community. Under Article 8A of the EEC Treaty, the internal market is an area without internal frontiers. This is an area in which the internal border controls have been moved to the external borders of the Community. The Benelux and Schengen areas are other examples of this type of system. The topics which have been regulated in the Schengen Agreement and Schengen Convention will also have to be worked out in the context of the internal market. In fact, the Schengen area is viewed as a precursor — or to use the jargon of the builders of Europe: a testing ground, a laboratory[40] — of the internal market. This means that the movement of aliens, as regulated in the 1990 Schengen Convention, will serve as a model for the regulation contained in any treaty between the Twelve. According to Article 21 of the Schengen Convention, aliens who are legally resident in one of the Schengen countries may avail themselves of a right to move freely within the territory of the other Schengen countries for a period of up to three months. It is reasonable to conclude that the Schengen Convention is not intended to allow aliens to stay for consecutive and successive three month periods in each of the Schengen countries.[41] Article 22 of the 1990 Schengen Convention provides for another, very important, restriction. Nationals of third countries who enter another Schengen country must report to the appropriate authorities on, or within three days of, entry into that country.[42] This means that border controls, even the borders

---

39. See the Netherlands Government's memorandum 'Rechtspositie en sociale integratie' [legal position and social integration], announced and summarized in Stc. (1991) No. 94.

40. See e.g., the statement by the Commission, reproduced in AE 30 November 1989, No. 5142 (n.s.) and that of the Dutch Government in Hand. II 1988-1989, 19 326, No. 10, p. 6. The Commission even calls the '*pilot function*' of the 1990 Schengen Convention its '*raison d'être*', see AE 16 December 1989, No. 5142 (n.s.); see also the answer of the Commission to written question No. 413/89, OJ 1990 C 90/11.

41. This conlusion implies a restriction that can be contrasted with the present situation. At the moment it is still the case, according to the Netherlands government, that aliens who visit the Benelux, France and Germany in succession within a period of six months may stay in each of the three areas without a residence permit (although they may require three visas), as long as they do not stay in each of the areas longer than three months, and may in principle take up permanent residence within the territory of the three. Hand. II 1988-1989, 19 326, No. 13, pp. 19-20.

42. It is true that some form of duty to report does exist in the Benelux countries, but its maintenance has been eroded with the passage of time. Aliens who propose to stay longer than eight days in one of the Benelux countries, otherwise than in hotels, are obliged to report to the appropriate authorities in that country. See Article 1 of the Decision of the working group for the movement of persons on the reporting of aliens, m/p (60) 4, of 20 June 1960.

themselves, will remain in existence. It is hard to maintain that this is in accordance with the logic of the internal market. Although it will actually be possible to cross the internal frontiers without being subject to checks, the abolition of border controls may also lead to the development of more refined and effective domestic control.

Free movement of persons may therefore mean more control being exercised in respect of certain groups of residents. It is not only non-EC national who may face these increased controls; there is a real danger that the domestic freedom of EC nationals will also be subject to more restrictions than is currently the case. Freedom thus generates lack of freedom. This, too, may lead to a corruption of the Community principles of freedom of movement.

8.   CONCLUSION

When one compares the material differences between nationals of the Member States and non-EC nationals who have legally settled in the Member States, it is evident that there are formal inequalities in the application and use of the rights and principles codified in Community law. In particular, non-EC nationals are denied the right of free movement of persons. The EEC Treaty as such does not impose any express requirement to promote equality, in this matter. Moreover, the development of the internal market has not yet resulted in a solution to this problem. Continued inequality between EC nationals and non-EC nationals in this matter constitutes a perversion of Community principles and, on a number of points, is contrary to the logic of both the internal market suggested by Article 8A of the EEC Treaty, and of the principles which underlie the free movement of persons within the Community. This potential breach could be removed by explicitly granting non-EC nationals who are permanently resident in the Community the right to free movement as set forth in Article 3(c) and Articles 48-66 of the Treaty, on the same footing as EC nationals and based on the same secondary legislation as applies to EC nationals.

GENERAL REMARKS ON THE FREE MOVEMENT OF VARIOUS CATEGORIES OF PERSONS

M.R. Mok[*]

The enormous differences between the standards of living in the several parts of our planet are likely to constitute the most delicate and the most dangerous problem of the present-day world. If development programmes work at all, which is controversial, they only work slowly and sometimes their effect merely matches the consequences of population growth.

It is not surprising that many people from the less favoured parts of the world, Africa in the first place, but also Asia, Latin America and last but not least eastern Europe, seek to begin a new life in prosperous countries, especially OECD countries.

From an idealistic point of view it would be attractive if the wealthy peoples of Europe and North America were willing to share their profusion with their less favoured brethren from elsewhere and to sacrifice a considerable part of their spending abilities. But we do not live in an idealistic world and even less in an ideal one. Many western Europeans are ready to pay from time to time some 'Ecus' in order to fight hunger in Africa, but if their governments were to admit thousands of Africans, the same Europeans would, at the next general election, vote for the local 'Le Pen'.

European lawyers may discuss in clean legal language the equal rights in the Common Market of aliens from non-EC countries and turn up their noses at xenophobia and racism, but they would do better to ask their neighbour, their nephew or their cleaning-woman how much of their prosperity the latter would be ready to give up in order to admit more hungry Africans.

Equal rights for third-country citizens constitute mainly a political problem, much more than a legal one. Turning nonetheless to the legal aspects of the problem, I shall pass by problems relating to special agreements, concluded with third countries, referring you instead to Professor Weiler's excellent report.

All persons are equal before the law and are entitled without any discrimination to the equal protection of the law, as Article 26 of the International Covenant on Civil and Political Rights states. And, as we all know, Article 7 EEC Treaty pro-

---

[*]   Advocate-General, the Netherlands, Supreme Court, The Hague.

H.G. Schermers et al., eds., Free Movement of Persons in Europe
© 1993, T.M.C. Asser Instituut, The Hague

hibits any discrimination on grounds of nationality, without being expressly limited to EC nationals.

Unfortunately (although fortunately for lawyers) those rules do not define the notion of discrimination. To give an example: there can be little doubt that nationality, irrespective of whether it concerns the nationality of a Member State or of a third country, provides no valid reason for instance for paying different wages for the same labour. But on the other hand it is a principal characteristic of the concept of nationality of a certain State that such nationality entitles a holder of that nationality to admission to the territory of that State. It makes no sense to contend that foreigners are discriminated against when they are deprived of the same right of admission.

The EEC Treaty contains the principle of the free movement of persons — the theme of this Colloquium — but at the same time it makes clear in its Article 48, that for the main category of persons in this context, workers, discrimination based on nationality between workers *of the Member States* shall be abolished. The same applies to free establishment (Art. 52) and services (Art. 59).

The Court of Justice had confirmed that the free movement of persons does not apply as a general rule to nationals of third countries, not even when they are members of the family of a migrant worker who himself is a national of a Member State (e. g., in 1982 in the *Morson* Judgment:) I refer to the reports of Dr Plender and Mr Alexander).

Free movement within the Community of migrant workers from third countries necessitates a common policy of recruitment and admission of such workers. Again I give an example: Member State A has a lack of mechanics of a special kind. It recruits them in a third country, say Utopia. Member State B has no lack of those mechanics, but has better conditions of employment. Should the Utopians, recruited by the authorities (or by enterprises with the consent of the authorities) of A, be permitted to move freely from A to B? I would say: not if the decision to recruit and to admit them has been taken by the authorities of A alone; not even when this has been done after a consultation or information procedure within the Community. What I have pointed out for migrant workers will mainly apply as well to the other categories of non-EC nationals.

It does not seem to be excluded that a legal basis for a common policy with regard to the recruitment and admission of migrant workers from third countries may be found, even though Article 118 does not provide for it, as the Court of Justice has already decided.

When the barriers, i.e, the checkpoints at the internal frontiers, disappear, control of the movement of third country nationals will in practice become more difficult. That, however, cannot in itself justify the free movement of aliens from third countries.

The united Europe cannot admit just any member of the world population, but it should not solve this problem by the simple solution of excluding everybody. I am aware that I have spoken of admission more than of stay. For those, or for certain of those persons, who are legally staying in EC countries at the moment that a common admission policy comes into force, transitory rules will be required.

My conclusion is that the completion of the Common Market should neither result in the opening of undesired and unchecked loopholes in the territory of the Member States, loopholes touting the presumed paradise to those who are outside, nor in the erection of a sort of new iron curtain around the Community's territory.

It seems unlikely that all the necessary preparation will be finished before the end of 1992.

COMMENTS ON THE FREE MOVEMENT OF VARIOUS CATEGORIES OF PERSONS

David O'Keeffe[*]

1. My main criticism of Professor Taschner's paper is that he ignores the fundamental point of the legality of the three directives on the right of residence. It should be noted that it is nowhere stated in the three directives that the right of equal treatment applies to the beneficiaries of the directives. However, that this is so is probable, as they are based on Article 235, but this would have to be read into them, by judicial interpretation.

The question arises whether the directives are compatible with Article 7 of the EEC Treaty. Their key feature is that a beneficiary may not become a charge on the public funds of the host State, and is thus excluded from access to the social security system. As the *Kempf* case[1] demonstrates, such exclusion is not permitted in the case of beneficiaries of the right of free movement who are workers, who derive their rights directly from Article 48 of the EEC Treaty. The conclusion to be drawn is that at least on first sight, the three directives are incompatible with Article 7.

During the colloquium, Advocate-General Van Gerven appeared to implicitly recognise this when he argued that the restrictions contained in the directive on the right of residence for students could be justified on the ground of objective justification, linked presumably to Article 128.[2] While acknowledging the persuasive authority of this opinion, I tend to take a different view. In any event, the same objective justification does not present itself, nor did the Advocate-General offer it, in respect of the other two directives on the right of residence. In my opinion, the better approach is to consider that the three Directives have created a group of second-class Community citizens, who enjoy less rights than those who can claim rights directly under the Treaty (for example, workers under Art. 48). This second-class character emerges not only in relation to the fact that the beneficiary of the directives may not become dependent on the social security system of the host State,

---

[*] Allen & Overy Professor of European Law, University of Durham
1. Case 139/85 [1986] ECR 1741.
2. The legal basis for the directive on the right of residence for students is being challenged by the European Parliament: see case C-295/90 *European Parliament* v. *Council*, OJ 1990, C 285/13.

H.G. Schermers et al., eds., Free Movement of Persons in Europe

but also because the definition provided in the directives of the family is more restricted than under the conventional Community rules regarding migrants.[3]

I suggest that this legislative development is not one which can be welcomed whole-heartedly. Although it is good that a general right of residence now exists, the conditions to which it is subject make one doubt whether any *real* difference has been made in practice, as those who qualify under the directives would very likely have also qualified for residence permits under national law. Moreover, the directives constitute a dangerous precedent. Article B of Part Two of the draft Treaty on the Union of the Luxembourg Presidency prepared for the IGC's states that every union citizen shall have the right to move and reside freely within the territory of the Member States under the conditions laid down in the Treaty and by the measures adopted to give it effect. The danger is that the secondary legislation which will be prepared to give effect to this right will in fact be modelled, in the case of the economically non-active, on the three new directives, which are unsatisfactory for the reasons mentioned above, in that they create a class of second-rate Community citizen.

2. At page 435 of his Volume, Professor Taschner refers to the notion of the 'family'. He maintains that the Council ignored the sociological evolution of the notion of family in nearly all Member States. It is not quite correct to say that this was ignored. The Council had a very far-reaching proposal indeed on the table, in the form of an amendment by the European Parliament, inspired by the judgment of the Court of Justice in *Reed*.[4] In that case, the Court of Justice had to deal with the Dutch rule that the unmarried alien companion of a Dutch national within a stable relationship as defined by Dutch law is treated as a spouse for the purposes of immigration requirements and for authorisation to work in the Netherlands. The Court held that a British citizen who was a migrant worker in the Netherlands was entitled to the same treatment in respect of his unmarried partner. The Court's ruling *cannot* be held to introduce an EEC-wide right; it only sought to give equal treatment to Dutch nationals and to EEC nationals within the Netherlands on the basis that the right was created by Dutch law. Nevertheless, the European Parliament sought to introduce such a rule into the draft directive on the right of residence.[5] The Parliament therefore went far beyond the application of the *Reed* case as intended by the Court, but of course its amendment was, perfectly legitimately,

3. Art. 10 of Regulation 1612/68 and Art. 1 of Directive 73/148/EEC grant rights to descendants who are under the age of 21 years or are dependants whereas Directives 90/364/EEC on the general right of residence and 90/365/EEC on the right of residence for those who have ceased their occupational activity exclude a right of residence for descendants who are not dependants. Likewise, whereas Art. 10 (2) of Regulation 1612/68, and Art. 1 (2) of Directive 73/148/EEC, provide that Member States shall facilitate the admission of any other member of the family if dependent on the worker or living under his roof in the country whence he comes, these other family members are not mentioned in the Directives 90/364/EEC and 90/365/EEC. Directive 90/366/EEC on the right of residence for students gives the right of residence only to the student's spouse and their dependant children.

4. Case 59/85 *Reed* [1986] ECR 1283.

5. OJ 1990, C 15/70 et seq.

inspired by a political aim rather than the strict meaning to be drawn from the *Reed* case.

For its part, the Council could draw comfort from the Court's judgment in *Reed*, where the Court was asked by the *Hoge Raad* whether for the purposes of Article 10 (1) (a) of Regulation 1612/68, a person who has a stable relationship with a worker within the meaning of that provision is to be treated as his 'spouse'. The Court replied in the negative. During the colloquium, Professor Mok criticised the posing of this question by the referring Court — indeed, as Advocate-General he had specifically asked it not to do so. I tend to share his view: the Court of Justice has rarely been asked to deal with such issues, and is unaccustomed to interpreting a legal term on the basis of social developments which must take account of all the Community, and not merely the situation in one Member State, particularly where it concerns a social institution as fundamental as the family. On the other hand, the Court when confronted with a straightforward non-discrimination issue is proverbially liberal, and indeed inventive, as it proved to be in the *Reed* case. One suspects that the Court felt that interpretation of Article 10 in the way suggested, touching the definition of family which is fundamental in the laws of all Member States, was a matter for the Council, and the Council in its rejection of the Parliament's amendment to the draft residence directive showed that it was not willing to take that step.[6]

3. In their Report, Advocate-General van Gerven and Mr van den Bossche rightly state that it is an unsatisfactory political compromise reached by the Court whereby Community law makes a distinction between requiring a Member State to give a non-national student financial assistance to cover registration and tuition fees, on the one hand, and imposing no such requirement in the case of financial assistance to cover the costs of maintenance and training, on the other. This is the result of the *Lair*[7] and *Brown*[8] jurisprudence. They also perceptively note that for many Member States it is unthinkable that nationals from other Member States should be entitled in full to educational grants available to their own nationals.

It is interesting to note that the Court seems to have appreciated the 'link-point' by making the distinction between the two forms of financial assistance mentioned above, in the case of foreign students coming to a Member State, whereas the Court has been far more adventurous as regards education grants for the children of migrant workers, even where the link with the host State of residence of the parents

---

6. During the Colloquium, Professor Jessurun d'Oliveira raised the question of Danish homosexual marriages, and their consequences for the law concerning the free movement of persons. I take the view that the situation here is on all fours with that in the *Reed* judgment, and that the rationale of non-discrimination expressed in that case applies in the case of an EC national and his or her partner who wish to contract a homosexual marriage in Denmark. The interesting questions raised of recognition of the marriage should, at least in theory, be no more difficult than the question of the recognition of e.g., foreign legal polygamous marriages, with which national courts are reasonably familiar.

7. Case 39/86 *Lair* v. *Universität Hannover* [1988] ECR 3161.

8. Case 197/86 *Brown* v. *Secretary of State for Scotland* [1988] ECR 3205.

518   D. O'KEEFFE

is very tenuous indeed. Thus, in the *Di Leo* case,[9] the Court held that the daughter
of a migrant must be able to avail of an educational grant from the host State of her
migrant worker parents, whereas she was to study in the Member State of origin, of
which she was moreover a national. The link between the migrant's child and the
host State is attenuated by the very fact of the grant of the social advantage in
question.

Likewise, in the *Matteucci* case[10] the Court held that the daughter of Italian
migrants living in Belgium must be able to avail of the benefits of scholarships
available under the bilateral Cultural Agreement between Belgium and Germany.
The point as regards the link between a migrant or migrant's child and the host State
was made by France and the defendant national authority in their observations in this
case that Article 7, paragraph 2 of Regulation 1612/68 imposes obligations on the
host State only in respect of training provided in its own territory and that it is not
binding on the host Member State where the training in question is provided in the
territory of another Member State. The Court held instead that where a Member
State gives its national workers the opportunity of pursuing training provided by
another Member State, that opportunity must be extended to Community workers
established in its territory. The Court's judgment is particularly noteworthy in that in
its result-oriented judgment, it seemed to have accepted that the cultural agreement
at issue fell outside the scope of the Treaty, but noted that insofar as refusal to give
access to the scholarships in question might jeopardise the right of Community
workers to equal treatment, the application of Community law cannot be precluded
on the ground that it would affect the implementation of a bilateral cultural agreement.

The conclusion to be drawn from this is that the Court appears to be far braver
in the case of extending the right to equal treatment to migrants' children, even
where the link with the host Member State is very tenuous indeed, as in these cases,
and to be correspondingly less brave where a student comes to a Member State
without being the child of a migrant. Objectively, in terms of promoting European
integration, there is no justification for the distinction. On the other hand, the
concept of linkage with a Member State is politically sensitive, and has received
cautious handling from the Court of Justice.[11]

4.   In his Report, Mr Hoogenboom makes the point that 'freedom . . . generates
lack of freedom', by way of pointing to the phenomenon of internal checks springing
up to replace external ones. This is not a new perception,[12] but it is certainly a valid

9. Judgment of 13 November 1990, Case C-308/89 *Di Leo* v. *Land Berlin*, ECR [1990] I-4185.

10. Case 235/87 *Matteucci* v. *Kingdom of Belgium* [1988] ECR 5589.

11. Case 24/74 *Biason* [1974] ECR 999. See also Judgment of 12 July 1990, Case 236/88 *Commission*
v. *France*, ECR [1990] I-3163.

12. Rüter, (1985) *Delikt en Delinkwent*, editorial, quoted in L.D.H. Hamer, 'Free Movement of
Persons: An Exploration from a Dutch Perspective', (1989) *Legal Issues of European Integration* no. 1, p.
49 characterised the removal of person checks as a magician's disappearance-tricks; the checks will
inevitably return somewhere in the interior.

observation which appears particularly telling under the Schengen Agreement. The example he uses is the reporting requirement imposed on third country nationals by Article 22 of the Schengen Convention.

An interesting parallel can be made with the *Messner* case,[13] which also dealt with a reporting requirement, this time applicable to EC citizens. The case is largely a simple repetition of the *Watson and Belmann* judgment[14] but it is striking that, in view of the imperatives of the internal market, the Court of Justice's reasoning remained unchanged in the 13 years separating the two cases. The Court, unlike Advocate-General Mischo, did not specifically refer to the concept of the internal market as laid down in Article 8A. Rather, it reiterated its *Watson and Belmann* ruling to the effect that 'Community law has not excluded the power of Member States to adopt measures enabling the national authorities to have an exact knowledge of population movements affecting their territory.'

The conclusion to be drawn from this judgment is that the Court was undoubtedly as aware as its Advocate-General of the implications of its judgment for the achievement of the internal market. The Court thus would seem to have made a deliberate choice in holding that certain internal controls, such as a reporting requirement, may be legitimate. On the other hand, in its recent *Commission* v. *Belgium* judgment,[15] the Court gave some indication of what it considers acceptable when carrying out external controls: to be permissible, frontier controls of the type at issue in that case must be carried out sporadically and unsystematically.[16]

The problem here is that what seems reasonable in the Community context is dictated by the differing national backgrounds of the judges and national legal cultures. Thus, it is not surprising that the reporting requirement was upheld in *Messner*: such requirements exist in all Member States except Ireland or France. The point to be made is that in some legal cultures, internal requirements/controls such as compulsory identity documents or residence reporting requirements is quite usual even in the case of nationals of that State, and thus appears suitable as a means of control for EC migrants. Whereas in other Member States, the application of such rules to nationals of the host State would be unacceptable because they are seen to be particularly invasive,[17] and their application to EC migrants would thus constitute discriminatory treatment which would have to be objectively justified.

5.   My final point concerns the position of non-nationals. I agree with Mr Hoogenboom's analysis at p. 505 of this Volume that the Court in *Meade*[18] did not decide the point whether Article 48(2) of the EEC Treaty in referring to 'workers of the

---

13. Case 265/88 *Messner* [1989] ECR 4209.
14. Case 118/75 *Watson and Belmann* [1976] ECR 1185.
15. Case 321/87 *Commission* v. *Belgium* [1989] ECR 997.
16. The Court also noted that the circumstances in which a control is carried out can colour the legitimacy of the control.
17. See Hamer, op. cit. n. 12, at p. 58.
18. Case 238/83 *Meade* [1984] ECR 2631.

Member States' implied that such workers must be citizens of the Member States.[19] However, as Advocate-General Mancini points out in his Opinion in that case, if such were not the case, there would be a strange dissonance between Article 48 on the one hand, and the parallel provisions of Article 69 of the ECSC Treaty and Article 96 of the EAEC Treaty on the other hand, which specifically refer to workers who are nationals of the Member States. I conclude that Article 48 must be interpreted as referring only to workers who are nationals of the Member States.

On the other hand, I support Mr Hoogenboom's thesis that non-EC nationals who are permanently resident in the EC should be granted freedom of movement, and thus, one presumes, would be covered by the prohibition on the ground of nationality, contained in Articles 48-66 of the EEC Treaty and secondary legislation, to which Mr Hoogenboom refers though without making specific reference to the equal treatment principle. My reasoning however, would be somewhat different. If, in *Cowan*,[20] the Court extended the equal treatment principle enshrined in Article 7 of the Treaty to recipients of services following the judgment in *Luisi and Carbone*,[21] it seems perverse, in the context of the dynamics of creating rules for the single market, to deny that protection merely on the ground that the recipient of the service does not have Community nationality. To be sure a jurisprudential jump would be necessary, as it seems reasonably clear that in *Luisi and Carbone* the Court envisaged[22] that the recipients of services would be Community nationals, though the *Cowan* judgment is much more ambiguous in this regard.[23] Nevertheless, it is submitted, such an interpretation would reflect the aims of Article 3(c) of the Treaty. Taking this argument to its logical conclusion, and affording the protection of the equal principle clause to *all* recipients of services who find themselves in the Community, irrespective of nationality or residence, is unlikely in the current stage of the development of European integration. Nevertheless, in the context of creating the single market, it is surely unacceptable that this fundamental principle of Community law does not apply to third country nationals, given the dimensions of their presence in the Community and given the vocation of Community law as a legal system for an evolving European union. It would seem likely that change in this area, if it will come at all, will have to be judicially-inspired; as Mr Hoogenboom points out,[24] change by means of legislation is not practicable.

---

19. In contrast, Arts. 52 and 59 of the Treaty, however, provide that the self-employed and providers of services must be nationals of a Member State.

20. Case 186/87 *Cowan* [1989] ECR 195.

21. Joined cases 286/82 and 26/83 *Luisi and Carbone* [1984] ECR 377.

22. See for example, points 10 and 12 of the judgment.

23. The *Cowan* judgment does not refer to Community nationals; it refers to 'persons in a situation governed by Community law': see point 10 of the judgment.

24. At pp. 506-507 of this Volume.

REPORT OF THE CONFERENCE ON
FREE MOVEMENT OF PERSONS IN EUROPE
12 AND 13 SEPTEMBER 1992

REPORT OF THE CONFERENCE

INTRODUCTION

This report provides an account of only the central issues discussed during the Conference. It is hoped that this may serve the purpose of offering extra information regarding the individual reports.

The first day of the colloquium was chaired during both the morning and afternoon sessions by Henry G. Schermers. During the second day the chairmen were Cees Flinterman (morning) and Piet Jan Slot (afternoon). Henry G. Schermers, again presided over the closing session.

1.   BENELUX EXPERIENCES OF THE ABOLITION OF BORDER
        CONTROL

In the Benelux there was a loosening in practice of the controls operated at the external borders in spite of the fact that there existed an aspiration to maintain them, both externally as well as internally, at the same high level. An example of this loosening was given by the migration of people from Surinam after that country gained its independence and who were permitted to join their relatives in the Netherlands by way of Paris and Belgium, although in practice they needed a Dutch visa to enter the country (*Kruijtbosch*).

Although the Benelux Convention on the free movement of persons has been in force for 30 years, only one case concerning a topic as important as visa policy 'reached' the Benelux Court. The conclusion was drawn that in the area of free movement of persons the need for such a jurisdiction is less necessary as this area concerns obligations between States and not between States and private individuals. The latter is the case in the European Communities where the European Court of Justice guarantees a uniform interpretation of Community law in applying Article 177 EEC. Consequently, the preliminary procedure of Article 177 EEC is more frequently applied than the equivalent procedure before the Benelux Court (*Donner, Schermers*).

The Schengen agreements could benefit largely from the Benelux experiences. That is why there is relatively more stress on the strengthening of the controls at the external frontiers in Schengen than there was in the Benelux (*Donner*). The necessity to insert into the Schengen Convention the issue of harmonisation of legislation on weapons and ammunition came about as a result of the enormous rise

H.G. Schermers et al., eds., *Free Movement of Persons in Europe*
© 1993, T.M.C. Asser Instituut, The Hague.

in armed robberies in the Netherlands due to the ease with which criminals can get hold of weapons in Belgium (*H.H.A.M. Peek*).

There are two approaches to the realization of free movement of persons in Europe; the intergovernmental solution and the Community approach. The latter is based on cooperation within the Twelve, as expressed in the Palma document, which is also of a practical nature. Whereas the Benelux Convention signed at Brussels on 11 April 1960 had only 18 Articles, the Schengen Convention of 1990 contains 142 Articles. The approach in the Palma document is still wider and can probably not be contained in one single document. There is thus a risk that the pragmatic list of essential measures is getting too long; the Benelux arrangements managed to operate a successful free-travel area on the basis of a document that was merely 18 articles long (*Fortescue*).

If one compares the institutional framework of Benelux with Schengen one can see that the Committee of Ministers of the Benelux has delegated its powers of decision-making in this field to the working party on free movement of persons. The division of powers is clear. The competence of the Executive Committee in the Schengen Agreement, on the other hand, is more vague (*Kruijtbosch*).

2.   IS THE EUROPEAN ECONOMIC COMMUNITY EMPOWERED?

The best prospect of progress lies in avoiding questions about Community powers.[1] The Commission has had some difficulties with this choice for pragmatism, especially in the first half of 1989. On the one hand, there was the opinion of Delors pleading for competence to be given to the Commission, and, on the other, there was the opinion of Bangemann who seemed to be content with the Palma approach, i.e., coordination of intergovernmental activities within the European Council. There was much pressure from the European Parliament to abandon the Palma approach in favour of that of the Commission. From a political point of view the Commission of the EC has from the beginning viewed the Schengen process in positive terms. The observer status of the Commission in Schengen is useful in order to avoid conflicts with regard to compatibility with existing Community law and with Community aspirations. This objective will be achieved by articles 134 and 142 of the Schengen Convention. The first article makes it clear that the Schengen provisions can be implemented only in harmony with Community law and the second article that Schengen can in no way prevent the twelve Member States of the Community from advancing further in an intergovernmental framework (*Fortescue*).

Thus while the Schengen process took place outside the Community framework, it has already received the approval of the Commission of the EC and the European Parliament. The Commission has described this initiative as a 'dynamic element in

---

1. Report Donner, see pp. 19-22, 25-26, *supra*.

the completion of the internal market' and has qualified the political commitment by the Member States concerned as an 'especially positive element'.[2]

3.   THE SCHENGEN INFORMATION SYSTEM (SIS)

The Schengen Convention provides for the creation of a joint information system which will furnish the law enforcement authorities of all signatory countries with access to information on persons and objects circulated as wanted for the purpose of police controls and checks at external borders. An information system such as this, that leads to direct action by law enforcement officers at the request of a foreign authority, is new, not only in Europe, but in the whole world. As a consequence, the system is introducing new aspects in international police cooperation. The SIS is one of the essential compensatory measures for the abolition of checks on persons at internal borders. At the same time the Convention of Schengen places a burden on the external border control authorities to perform their duties also in the interests of other Member States.

The value placed on border controls varies widely in political and police debates. Unfortunately, little is known about the percentage of major crimes solved as a result of border controls. However, whatever ones views of such value one aspect is important and worth considering. As long as the infrastructure for border control exists, large-scale random control, even on tourist peak days, remains possible and in times of need the system can be tightened. If this infrastructure disappears such controls will no longer be possible.

Three questions can be asked in respect to the SIS:

i)   Is it a necessary compensatory measure?

ii)   Does it meet the requirements of border control authorities and of police authorities?

iii) Will it work while ensuring a balance between serving public interests and pro-tecting private rights?

Two aspects may be mentioned. Police information is by its nature restricted as it deals with suspects or criminals. Therefore, there are two general restrictions on information dissemination. Firstly, that the police itself is not readily prepared to share or to circulate it widely. This, they believe, does not serve their own effectiveness. Secondly, that the protection of citizens demands the objective regulation of the way in which information is spread and the extent thereof. Therefore in the Netherlands, police information systems are organized on local,

---

2. Commission report concerning the removal of controls on persons at the internal frontiers of the Community, COM (88) 640 fin. of 16 January 1989, p. 9 (Annex). See also the Commission Communication to the Council and Parliament, SEC (92) 877 final, Brussels, of 8 May 1992. The aim of this communication is to determine the interpretation which the Commission intends to place on Article 8A. See finally the second report of the Committee on Civil Liberties and Internal Affairs on the entry into force of the Schengen Agreements of 5 November 1992. Rapporteur: L. van Outrive (European Parliament, A3-0336/92).

regional and national levels. Information that the local police may find interesting need not always be spread nationwide and may thus be restricted. This idea is in general also the basis of the Schengen Information System as laid down in Article 94 of the Schengen Convention, stating that the Contracting Party, when providing a report, shall determine whether the importance of the case warrants the inclusion of the report in the system. That might also create a problem with the growing number of Schengen partners. What may be of sufficient interest to be notified to five bordering countries, as was the case in the first discussions on Schengen, may not necessarily be worth spreading among so many Schengen partners covering so many thousands of square kilometres.

The second aspect concerns the degree to which the SIS functions as an information system. One should bear in mind that the SIS is a search and not a research system. It answers the question: is X in it, yes or no, and if so, what action is to be taken? It provides no information, for example, about the numbers of certain types of persons in a certain category of age or nationality. In the negotiations on Schengen it appeared that countries were not willing to establish a search system through which they would pass sensitive information data that would be accessible to all partner police authorities. However, the need for sensitive information data has recently been developing within the Twelve; the European Council in Luxembourg ordered as a starting point that a report on the foundation of a European Police Intelligence Bureau be prepared. The SIS discussions paved the way for these developments. The Schengen cooperation as such, however, will have to deal with a restricted information system and the bilateral exchange of information without such an infrastructure (*H.H.A.M. Peek*).

The Schengen Information System seems to become the policeman's dream and the citizen's nightmare (*Hondius*). Therefore the public in- and outside of Europe will be informed of the existence of this system, its safeguards and the legal protection concerned by articles in the press until ratification by the national parliaments (*Schattenberg*).

4.	RELATIONSHIP BETWEEN SCHENGEN, OTHER
	INTERNATIONAL RULES AND NATIONAL LEGAL
	SYSTEMS

If there existed no obligation on individual countries under the Geneva Convention to deal with asylum requests no asylum seeker would ever become a refugee with corresponding rights as 'non-refoulement' and easy assimilation and naturalisation under that convention. This is essential for the effectiveness of the Geneva Convention. In the spirit of this convention certain subjective or objective links between the asylum seeker and a certain country make it compulsory for that country to decide individually on the request to be classified as a refugee. Because these links are not mutually exclusive there exists multiple competence on differing signatories to the convention to deal with requests. The Schengen Convention, on the other hand, imposes an order of priority on these links, as if these were mutually exclusive, thereby making only one state responsible for dealing with the request for asylum. The number of countries dealing with a request is thus reduced by, say, eleven and it is open to question what the other signatories would have said in any procedure relating to such request. The Dutch Council of State rightly takes the position that a country which has the individual obligation under the Geneva Convention to deal with a request to be classified as a refugee cannot fully and definitely delegate this obligation to other countries on the basis of a regional agreement. That country has a responsibility towards the other countries that have signed the Geneva Convention and towards the UNHCR (*Jessurun d'Oliveira*).

The Geneva Convention itself does not deal with the way applications should be processed by the contracting states, it merely mentions national law in that respect. There is a variety of national systems; in the U.K. or the U.S. immigration authorities do it autonomously with the possibility of appeal to tribunals etc.. In France the 'Office de protection des refugiés et apatrides' was created in 1952, two years before France ratified the Geneva Convention, in order to fill the gap between the dissolution of the IRO and the creation of the High Commissioner for Refugees. In Belgium, until the recent reform, it was the office of the High Commissioner for Refugees itself which had to determine the status of refugee. The legal status of refugee law is not the same in all countries. Sometimes it has a constitutional status, sometimes it is based only on a convention. The right of asylum as laid down in a constitution may also differ from the Geneva Convention, as is the case in France. However, a statute with the provision excluding the processing of any applications from asylum seekers would constitute a breach of the Convention. In other cases states retain their freedom on how to process such applications. It is an open question whether states are free to provide (as has been done in the Schengen Convention) that in certain cases people staying on the territory of one country must have their application processed by another country. One of the dimensions of this question is the possible constitutional status of refugee. It is not possible to give a direct and complete answer to this question that is valid for all countries (*Errera*).

It should be said that the Geneva Convention only prohibits 'refoulement', i.e. returning someone to the state where he claims to have been persecuted. There is no obligation under the Geneva Convention on the national governments to ascertain whether persons are true refugees in so far as that would leave all asylum seekers within the national borders and admit them to the labour market and the social security system. It is only in relation to returning them that the Geneva Convention clearly contains an obligation to find out whether someone is a refugee. That is also the reason why in the Schengen Convention the basic rule is that an application has to be processed by one of the signatories, a principle that can also be found in the Dublin Convention. An expulsion by the Netherlands of an asylum seeker to Germany, a Schengen Member State, with the guarantee that Germany will treat the case according to its obligations, can hardly constitute 'refoulement' under the Geneva Convention (*Donner*).

The reason for the omission in the Geneva Convention of the right to make an application had to do with the moment of drafting. There was then a great shortage of labour and no migration from Eastern Europe in view. Refusals were expected therefore to be exceptional rather than the norm. The reasons for the omission of matters of procedure in the Schengen arrangements are less obvious but were probably due to the fact that governments were reluctant to be seen to cede national control to any intergovernmental agency at a time of substantial unemployment in Western Europe and a sensitivity over questions of immigration and race relations (*Plender*).

There is at this moment a growing number of refugees and asylum seekers in Europe while only a small number of the latter will ultimately be recognised as refugees. There is also uncertainty relating to all these applications, the status of these applicants and the cooperation on refugee status between EC states. Legal principles should therefore be (re-)affirmed at the constitutional level. Chapter 7 of the Schengen Convention (Arts. 29, 30 and 32) deals with the responsibility for the processing of applications for asylum, while Articles 32 and 29 paragraph 4 emphasize the role of national law. As one thus has to 'fall back' on national law in applying the Schengen Convention one must bear in mind that in many Member States, e.g., France, Germany and Italy, the right to asylum is laid down in the Constitution. Questions may arise about the compatibility of the Schengen Convention and these constitutions. A decision of the French Conseil Constitutionnel of July 1991 is relevant to this issue. In France refugee law and the right to asylum are contained in two different legal instruments: (1) the preamble to the French Constitution which states: 'Any person persecuted because of his action in favour of liberty has the right of asylum on the territories of the republic'; and (2) Article 1A of the Geneva Convention on Refugees

There are two important differences between these two instruments, in scope as well in the extent of the conferred rights. In scope the Constitution is narrower (only persecution) but the extent of the right is broader (the right to enter the country/the right to asylum).

According to the standard procedure in France the bill of ratification of the Schengen Convention was sent to the Conseil Constitutionnel in May-June 1991. In the referral the issue was raised as to the compatibility of the Schengen Convention and the right to asylum as stated in the Constitution (not as stated in the Geneva Convention, as this would concern the relationship between treaties). The Conseil Constitutionnel answered, somewhat ambiguously, quoting the Constitution and Articles 29, paragraphs 4, 30 and 32 of the Schengen Convention, that these stipulations (Art. 29 para. 4) will have to be applied in favour of persons asking for the right of asylum stated in the Constitution. The Conseil could also have considered that as the right of asylum, taken together for the sake of the argument with the right to be recognised as a refugee, is a constitutional right, no treaty can deprive someone of the right to request national authorities to proceed with an application. It did not consider that point probably for two reasons. The legal reason is that the constitutional right of asylum is not the same as that stated in Article 1A of the Geneva Convention. The probable factual consideration is that such a decision would have 'opened the floodgates' at an awkward moment.

This decision means that, irrespective of the Geneva Convention, when someone qualifies as an asylum seeker and fulfills the (narrower) conditions set out in the Constitution, then, in principle, the government is strongly urged to use the faculty granted to them by art. 29 paragraph 4 of the Schengen Convention. This decision may be important for possible future cases before constitutional courts in other Member States in which the compatibility of the Schengen Convention with national constitutions may be considered and questioned (*Errera*).

With regard to the position of the Geneva Convention on the Status of Refugees in the United Kingdom it should perhaps be clarified that although it can be said that its provisions cannot be invoked in national courts in the U.K., its crucial provisions are incorporated in the British immigration rules. They can be relied upon by asylum seekers and they are regularly invoked before adjudicators, with a right of appeal to a tribunal. Courts in application for judicial review interpret and apply these terms and not long ago, the House of Lords in a particular case also looked at the *travaux préparatoires* in different language versions and at certain case law, interpreting and applying the terms of the provisions just as an international tribunal would do (*Plender*).

5.   RECENT AND FUTURE DEVELOPMENTS

The EC Ministers of Immigration decided in Athens to work together within the framework of cooperation between diplomatic and consular posts in the countries of origin in reporting on the situation in those countries. This first step is not yet operational but is again receiving attention under the [present] Dutch EC presidency. A second step will be made during this presidency to elaborate on a proposal for a European clearing house for existing information on the topic of countries of origin. This system will have no legal character and the reports will not be binding upon Ministers of Justice or on the judiciary. A further step of a more legal character would be necessary and one could think of being assisted by Amnesty International or of cooperation within the framework of the UNHCR (*De Jong*).

It would have been unthinkable a year and a half ago that any group of Western European governments would be prepared to receive a document dealing with questions on the protection of national minorities or even minority languages. Until then only topics such as the rights of migrant workers and the protection of their culture and cultural rights were received. Matters concerning national minorities have now been brought to the attention of all governments cooperating in the Council of Europe, which at the present time also includes Hungary and Czechoslovakia.

   Hungary delivered the text of a draft convention relating to the protection of national minorities. It had been elaborated by a special body consisting of eminent constitutional lawyers from different countries: the so-called Venice Commission for Democracy through Law. The text of a draft convention on the protection of national and regional languages was, on the other hand, an initiative of the Conference of local and regional authorities in Europe. Most people have no illusions about the fate of these two texts as many governments, particularly in Western Europe, immediately stated that the texts were unacceptable for a number of reasons.

These two existing texts will, however, serve in the coming years as important reference documents. The text on minority and regional languages will have the greatest chance of success, because its drafters have accepted the possibility that it could be utilized as a recommendation. The drafters of the text on national minorities have stated that it only makes sense if the text becomes a treaty. The two texts are now on the agenda of the Committee of Ministers of the Council of Europe and that is in itself a remarkable fact (*Hondius*).

6.   IS HARMONISATION OF ASYLUM LEGISLATION AND POLICY
        NECESSARY?

It is doubtful whether there exists a political will to execute the decision of the Council of Ministers in Luxembourg (1991) to harmonise asylum policies. Possibly this decision attempts to institute a quota system by another name. With regard to the need for harmonisation of social security matters it should be noted that there has been no noticeable flow of migration from countries with a less 'beneficial' system of social security to other countries. The arguments concerning the need for harmonisation therefore do not hold, no more than the argument of the present large number of asylum applications in the different countries (*M. van Traa*).

Three questions should here be distinguished. One concerns the present lack of harmonisation of asylum policies, one concerns the political will for such harmonisation and one states that there is no need to harmonise social security as there has been no substantial migration of EC nationals. In answering the first two questions mention should be made of the fact that the Dutch Ministry of Justice has produced documents on, e.g., the philosophy of asylum harmonisation, on the country of first asylum, on manifest ill-foundedness, on the above-mentioned clearing house and a general working program. Therefore, one may conclude that there does exist a political will to harmonise asylum policies. The concern of the [present] Dutch EC presidency is that there should be harmonisation at a reasonably high level of rights for the asylum seekers. Harmonisation of social security is then needed because during the asylum procedure asylum seekers have some rights and many countries may individually try to lower their standards to prevent the influx of asylum seekers (*De Jong*).

Harmonisation of the procedures relating to asylum requests is very important and there is a need for an instrument to harmonise these procedures to a far greater degree than is presently the case. The existing recommendations of the Parliamentary Assembly of the Council of Europe or the Executive Committee of the United Nations High Commissioner for Refugees are not sufficient. A right to have a hearing before return of an asylum seeker to a country in which he has established at least an arguable case that he would face persecution, would be a good starting point. That is also the case for the establishment of a consultative committee to receive requests for guidance by a procedure analogous to a reference for a preliminary ruling. Harmonisation of procedures would resolve some of the present substantive difficulties. Procedure often determines substance. Multiple application and asylum shopping, lawful or not, are not to be encouraged and are commonly the results of disparities in national procedures (*Plender*).

Getting a grip on migratory streams into Europe will be realized by harmonising asylum law and procedures. As this is a highly political area for which only Article 1 of the Geneva Convention gives certain interpretative guidelines, it is uncertain whether the required harmonisation will be done by treaty or by Community directive. The question now under consideration is whether a regulation like the one contained in the Schengen Convention and Agreement is a sufficient basis to start the process of abolishing border controls. But, on the other hand, it would probably take another ten years first to harmonise procedural and material asylum laws (*Donner*).

7. WHAT ARE THE ADVANTAGES OF SCHENGEN?

This question has been answered by the politics of Europe. A choice has been made for an internal market, which implies the absence of frontier controls. The Dutch parliament, when approving the Schengen Agreement of 1985, declared the abolishment of internal border controls to be an objective. It is apparently considered to be an advantage for European citizens. If we look at the U.S.A. we see that in the '70s certain states still retained border controls while a complete freedom of movement of persons was established only by the decision of the Supreme Court in 1941 in *Edwards* v. *California* and finally, that the whole system of penal cooperation between states and the federation is based on penalising the cross-border movements of criminals, as e.g. in the Fugitive, Witness and Felon Act.

There is no clear distinction between the interests of the government and the interests of the private citizen, because these interests are connected. The police do not exist just for the pleasure of civil servants and to keep some people busy. In the same way, aliens legislation is a protection in the interest of citizens against an unrestricted access to public goods like education, social security and even the labour market. Therefore, it should be stressed that as border controls and legislation on aliens exist in the interests of the collective group, when eliminating the obstacles resulting therefrom compensatory measures will also primarily be in the interests of this group. If one looks at the present flow of migration and the numbers of migrants it must be seriously doubted whether the European states will be able to continue to absorb such numbers of asylum seekers for any length of time. It is therefore fully understandable that procedures should be chosen that take into account the fact that only 20% of the migrants are potential refugees. The benefit for the individual lies in the freedom of movement itself while promotion of the legitimate interests of the collective group is primarily aimed at by treaties such as Schengen (*Donner*).

8. HARMONISATION OF THE CONCEPT OF PUBLIC ORDER?

The suggestion was made, as the Standing Committee of Experts had done in its opinion on the Schengen treaties, to take steps towards harmonising the concept of public order in the direction of the meaning already acribed to it in Community law in connection with the free movement of EC citizens. In that field of law it is a reasonable but not too strict concept, with the burden of proof on the state that a person is an actual threat to the public order. Where that is not the case a state should not refuse entry to such an alien (*Boeles*).

A common concept of public order is developing in the present process of integration. This concept will in its turn become a national concept as it is introduced into the legislation of the Member States (*De Jong*).

9. DOES THERE EXIST A RIGHT TO MOVE FREELY WITHIN THE COMMUNITY?

'Human rights and the free movement of persons: the role of the European Commission and Court of Human Rights' was the first report in line to be discussed. In his oral presentation Schermers drew the attention of the audience to three topics, which currently play an important role in the proceedings of the European Commission of Human Rights: (i) the Fourth Protocol to the European Convention on Human Rights; (ii) Rule 36 of the Rules of Procedure of the ECHR; and (iii) the problem of the so-called 'second generation' immigrants. With respect to the last two topics the reader is referred to the Schermers Report.

Regarding the Fourth Protocol to the European Convention on Human Rights (hereinafter: the Convention) a vivid discussion was activated on whether there actually exists a right to move freely within the Community. Briefly, the Fourth Protocol guarantees to all persons lawfully within the territory of a State that is a party to the Convention the right to move freely within that State. The European Community has not acceded to the Convention. As a legal consequence, the right to move freely within the Community does not exist. Notwithstanding this consequence, this right could nevertheless be assumed to exist. The Court of Justice of the European Communities (hereinafter: Court of Justice) has stated that the content of the Convention is part of the general principles of law which have to be applied by the Community. Therefore, as a general principle of Community law there exists a fundamental right to move freely within the Community. This right, if it can be construed, is further not to be reserved exclusively to Community citizens. Article 2 of the Fourth Protocol to the Convention is applicable to everyone lawfully within the terrytory of a Member State. Article 14 of the Convention prohibits discrimination between nationals and non-nationals (*Schermers*).

Because of the willingness of the Court of Justice to apply the Convention as a general principle of Community law it was submitted that it would make no difference whether the EC is a party to the Convention or not (*Weiler*). In opposition to this view it was pointed out that the Fourth Protocol, unlike the Convention, has not been ratified by all Member States of the European Community. Therefore, before becoming a party to the Fourth Protocol the Community will have to make a separate decision to accede. Further, and more importantly, the non-overall application of the Convention makes it highly uncertain whether the general principles of law to be applied by the Court of Justice also cover the Fourth Protocol (*Van Dijk*). However, the Court of Justice, instead of referring to treaties to which the Member States are parties, always refers to 'international treaties for the protection of human rights on which the Member States have collaborated or of which they are signatories.'[3] In casu, this has been the case as all Member States cooperated closely in the drafting of the Fourth Protocol. In this cooperation an argument might be found that the general principles of law also cover the Fourth Protocol (*Schermers*).

With the question 'Are we all nomads . . . ?' the right of persons not to move was brought to the discussion, a right that is conceptually distinct from the right to move freely within the Community. The Community has recognized this right, which can be derived from Regulation 1251/70 of the Commission of 29 June 1970[4] on the right of workers to remain in the territory of a Member State after having been employed in that State (*H. Storey*). It was added that the right not to move has been laid down in Article 8 of the Convention which contains the right of private life and the right of protection of one's home. The possibility for governments to evict persons from their homes would infringe Article 8 in practically all cases. However, exemptions are possible under Article 8(2) of the Convention (*Schermers*).

10.   ROLE OF THE NATIONAL JUDICIARY

In his commentary concerning the reports of Arnull and Jacobs and Van Dijk and Schreuder-Vlasblom, Gormley underlined the necessity of 'piercing the intergovernmental veil' with regard to the establishment of the free movement of persons within the Community:

'Both of these papers stress the need for national courts to give precedence to European provisions in a manner detached from national law and policy. Only if the initiative comes from institutions representing the wider European interest rather than from intergovernmental cooperation founded in national self-interest, rather than in the detachment of the pursuit of wider goals, can a foundation be laid which directs national courts as to the correct approach.'

---

3. See, e.g., the *Second Nold* Case, Case 4/73, 14 May 1974, co. 13, [1974] ECR 507.
4. OJ 1970 L142/24.

10.1   Rule of Reason

Gormley concluded that the paper by Arnull and Jacobs concentrated:

> 'understandably on the interpretation of the concepts of a worker, the headings of Article
> 48 EEC,[5] the mutual recognition of qualifications and the application *mutatis mutandis* in
> relation to persons of the rule of reason which the Court developed in relation to the free
> movement of goods'.[6]

With respect to the rule of reason the degree to which the Court of Justice allows the courts of the Member States a margin of discretion in their application of the rules on the free movement of persons was highlighted. In the summer of 1991 the Court of Justice dealt with three cases in which it had the opportunity to clarify this issue.[7] The effect of these three judgments was that the prohibition contained in Article 59 EEC was extended to all restrictions on the freedom to provide services even if such restrictions have a non-discriminatory character. However, the Court of Justice still recognizes that national non-discriminatory restrictions on the freedom to provide services can be justified by mandatory requirements of public policy (*Jacobs/Arnull*).

In some of these cases the Court of Justice delivered a catalogue of the permitted requirements and, furthermore, acknowledged that objectives of cultural policy are also capable of falling within that catalogue. With respect to objectives of cultural policy stress was laid upon the considerable convergence between the case-law of the Court of Justice on the free movement of services and the case-law on the free movement of goods. In the 'Cinéthèque' case[8] the Court of Justice seemed to have accepted that the pursuance of cultural policy can also justify non-discriminatory obstacles to the free movement of goods. The case-law of the Court seems to establish that the effect of the mandatory requirements is the same as that of Article 36 EEC. In other words, the mandatory requirements constitute derogations from Article 30 EEC rather than a true rule of reason. That means that in the case of non-discriminatory obstacles to the import of goods, Article 36 EEC is not a complete statement of the circumstances in which national obstacles may be justified. And because of the convergence between the case-law on Article 30 EEC and the case-law on Article 59 EEC, it seems that the same reasoning could be defended in the field of services. Thus, the effect of the mandatory requirements in the field of

---

5. In this respect Gormley referred to the Commission's action in relation to the application of Article 48(4) EEC: Freedom of movement of workers and access to employment in the public service of the Member States, OJ 1988 C72/2.

6. See Gormley, Prohibiting Restrictions on Trade within the EEC, (Amsterdam, 1985) Chapter 3.

7. Two of them are the so called Dutch Mediawet cases: Case C-288/89 *Stichting Collectieve Antennevoorziening Gouda and Others* v. *Commissariaat voor de Media* and Case C-353/89 *Commission* v. *the Netherlands*. The other judgment was in Case C-76/90 *M. Säger* v. *Dennemeyer & Co Ltd*. All three judgments were delivered on 25 July 1991 and have not yet been reported.

8. Case 60 and 61/84 *Cinéthèque SA and Others* v. *Féderation Nationale des Cinémas Français* [1985] ECR 2857.

services is not to define the scope of the prohibition contained in Article 59 EEC, but merely to broaden the circumstances in which non-discriminatory restrictions on the freedom to provide services can be justified. As a consequence, however, this approach raises the question of how to reconcile it with the Court's case-law to the effect that derogations from fundamental principles of the Treaty have to be construed in a strict sense (*Jacobs/Arnull*).

10.2 Practice

In his oral presentation of Plender's report Arnull accentuated the point that national courts frequently have to address common problems without the benefit of the case-law of the Court of Justice. The guidelines laid down by the Court of Justice have been followed fairly faithfully by the national courts but even a correct judicial follow-up at the national level does not in practice always lead to uniform results. According to commentator Gormley, Arnull and Jacobs also:

> '. . . expressly do not suggest that national courts cannot be trusted to apply Community rules correctly but there are well-known instances of national courts clearly acting in a manner incompatible with the requirements of Community law.'[9]

In this respect mention was made of the refusal by the French *Conseil d'État* in its judgment in the *Cohn-Bendit* case[10] to recognize that Directives can have a direct effect. This notorious judgment has now been corrected by the Conseil d'État in its 'Palazzi' judgment of 8 July 1991. The *Conseil d'État* decided that a national regulation (*in casu* the Décret of 28 April 1981 concerning the rights of EC nationals in France), adopted to give effect to Directive 64/221/EEC of 25 February 1964 but which failed to do so correctly, was unlawful and that an individual decision based on that measure was also unlawful. This decision seems very much to be a recognition of the fact that Directive 64/221/EEC confers certain rights on the applicant which the *Conseil d'État* considers itself bound to protect. If this assumption is correct the decision represents a welcome 'reveillement' by Europe's most distinguished administrative tribunal (*Arnull*). This decision will lead to a governmental reform of the Décret of 1981 and can be considered a 'by-product' of the Nicolo decision.[11] Both judgments are an example of the consistency and the accelerating increase in the new case-law of the *Conseil d'État* in the last two years (*Errera*).

---

9. Gormley mentioned the judgment of the English Divisional Court, Queen's Bench Division and the Court of Appeal in *R.* v. *Secretary of State for the Home Department, ex parte Santillo* [1980] 3 CMLR 212 & [1981] 1 CMLR 569. Arnull and Jacobs discuss Santillo in their paper, see Gormley (1986) 23 CMLRev. 287 at 302.

10. *Ministre de l'Intérieur* v. *Cohn-Bendit*, 28 December 1978, (1979) RTDE 1570. See Report Errera, p. 328, *supra*, n. 45.

11. *Nicolo*, 20 October 1989, RTDE (1989) 771. See Report Errera, p. 325, *supra*, n. 39.

With respect to the above-mentioned 'anomalies' or undesired attitudes of national courts, Gormley further remarked that,

'Hitherto the Commission's response has been political rather than legal[12] but the time may well come when in response to a sufficiently flagrant national judicial decision the Member State will be called to account under the procedure of Article 169 EEC. The reluctance to use this procedure in relation to judgments of national courts has traditionally been founded on an understandable desire not to prejudice the spirit of cooperation between the Community and national judiciaries in the context of Article 177 EEC. In only one instance has the Commission gone so far as to issue a reasoned opinion to a Member State on account of a ruling of a national court but the differentiating factor was that the ruling affected the ability of the Commission to exercise its inspection powers in the competition field under Regulation 17/62.[13] A more co-operative attitude may perhaps be achieved by the somewhat more agreeable vehicle of ensuring that members of national judiciaries are trained in Community law.'

Further, Plender stated in his report that it is difficult for national courts to assess the rights under Community law possessed by nationals of third countries. As non-EC nationals are not 'workers' in the sense of EEC law,[14] they do not derive rights from Community law. Thus:

'Spanish, Portuguese and Greek nationals have been held to have no entitlement to benefit from the Community's rules relating to workers ending the expiry of the transitional periods specifically laid down for the purpose in the appropriate Acts of Accession.'[15]

In opposing this view mention was made of the judgment of the Court of Justice in Case 113/89 *Rush Portuguesa Lda* v. *Office National d'Immigration*.[16] In that case the Court had to answer a question posed by the *Tribunal Administratif* Versailles whether the right of a Portuguese firm to provide services in one of the Member States could be made subject to conditions, in particular to the 'import' of Portuguese labour.[17] This case offered a good example of a question which had first been brought up before the Court and which had finally had a political 'follow-up'. This 'follow-up' was Regulation No. 2194/91 of 25 June 1991 on the transitional period for freedom of movement of workers between Spain and

---

12. See Kapteyn & VerLoren van Themaat, *Introduction to the Law of the European Communities*, (2nd. ed. Deventer/London, 1989), 279 and examples and literature cited there.
13. The matter concerned an order of a German court preventing the Bundeskartellamt from assisting the Commission in an inspection of premises owned by Hoechst AG.
14. See Report Plender, pp. 228-289, *supra*, for relevant national and European case-law.
15. Report Plender p. 288 *supra*.
16. [1990] ECR 1417.
17. The facts in this case were that the building company Rush Portuguesa Lda was sub-contracted by a French firm to carry out constructionworks in connection with the development of the TGV Atlantique railway. By bringing its own Portuguese workers Rush Portuguesa infringed the French Code du Travail, an infringement for which the Office National d'Immigration started proceedings and sought payment of a specific endowment.

Portugal, on the one hand, and the other Member States, on the other.[18] The regulation gave Portuguese and Spanish workers the same rights as citizens of the other Member States with respect to freedom of movement (*I. Jalles*).

10.3   Decline of legal protection

Van Dijk and Vlasblom noted that a:

' . . . decline in legal protection might occur if the administrative decisions are lifted from the national legal context and are made the object of intergovernmental cooperation without adequate provisions being made for substituting judicial review.'[19]

According to Gormley this is one of several fundamental objections to Schengen in particular and he explained that:

'Not only is the Community interest left out of account with the Commission's right of initiative being side-stepped through intergovernmental action but there is no democratic input whatsoever at the European level — even the scarcely adequate participation of the European Parliament in the adoption of Community legislation at least provides a platform for the views of members of European-wide political groups. Whilst the aim of Schengen is clearly laudable the modalities of achieving the aim are perhaps less so. Any trends towards intergovernmental cooperation (specifically to take the initiative away from the Commission as the British government now openly emphasises) must not be at the expense of judicial protection at the Community and national levels.'

10.4   Fiscal preliminary rulings?

As double-taxation matters influence economic activities the suggestion was made to include in bilateral double-taxation treaties concluded between Member States of the Community a clause of the same nature as Article 177 EEC Treaty. This has also been done, e.g., in the Protocol to the Judgments Convention of 27 September 1968. If such a clause were to become part of double taxation treaties between Member States, not only could the collision of equal terms between tax law and community law be minimized but also the legal security for legal persons in the Community and maybe the freedom of movement could be furthered (*M.C.E.M. Draaisma/P.E.L. Janssen*).

---

18. OJ 1991 L206/1.
19. Van Dijk and Vlasblom, report p. 318 *supra*.

11.   IS THE EUROPEAN COURT OF JUSTICE COMPETENT TO
         INTERPRET THE SCHENGEN AGREEMENTS?

Under the heading 'Institutional problems and free movement of persons', De
Zwaan dedicated his report and presentation to the legal and political framework for
the cooperation concerning the abolition of obstacles to the freedom of movement of
persons. In the light of the rather marginal progress in cooperation made in order to
achieve the Treaty objective of free movement of persons by the end of 1992 he
pleaded for a more important role for the European Community. One of the
significant advantages could be that:

   ' . . . the Court of Justice would be able to play its traditional role of ensuring the correct
   application and interpretation of the Treaty.'[20]

The Court of Justice should be given the competence to interpret the Schengen
Agreement. The endowment of such a new competence in the 'Schengen area'
would in practice, however, lead to considerable problems because currently only a
limited number of Member States cooperate under the 'umbrella' of the Schengen
Agreement. By way of the adoption of two protocols a rather technical solution was
advanced to cope with these problems. One protocol would give the Court of Justice
the jurisdictional competence to interpret the Schengen Agreement and should be
signed and adhered to by all twelve Member States. The other protocol would then
be concluded only by the 'Schengen Member States'. In this protocol they would
agree to submit themselves to the jurisdiction of the Court of Justice with respect to
all future disputes concerning the interpretation and application of the Schengen
Agreement. Other solutions, such as the creation of a separate Schengen Court and
the endowment of jurisdictional competence on the Benelux Court (in an enlarged
composition) could be envisaged (*De Zwaan*).

   The proposition to provide the Court of Justice with the power to interpret the
Schengen Agreement met with some strong opposition. This would not be a sound
and wise legal policy as the Schengen Agreement has neither been signed nor
ratified by all Member States. Another option could be a more indirect approach
along the lines of Article 177 EEC, i.e., the possibility for a national court to request
the Court of Justice to render a preliminary ruling on a question in which a
'Schengen' issue is present (*Errera*).

   On the other hand, it was put forward that in practice the functioning of the
Schengen Agreement would not be hindered by an inadequate level of legal
protection. The formulation of Article 2, paragraph 1 of the Schengen Convention is
sufficiently clear to be applied by every national court.[21] Furthermore, other
instruments exist which could provide for a sufficient level of legal protection, such

   20. De Zwaan, p. 351 *supra*.
   21. Art. 2: 'Internal borders may be crossed at any point without any checks on persons being carried
out'.

as the existing procedures for the areas that directly concern private law (or the laws and treaties on privacy) and the possibility of mutual recognition of judicial decisions by each of the national courts. With respect to the Schengen area it would be necessary to become accustomed to the idea that uniformity in the Community is not a constitutional principle as it is for the concept of the common market. Therefore, the Schengen area is not yet ready to be developed by judicial decisions. In this respect there is the possibility for the Member States to use the public policy clauses of the Treaty, which are commonly defined. However, in practice the Member States choose not to use these clauses because the number of possibilities to invoke them in accordance with Community law is too limited for their purposes (*Donner*). However, the public policy clauses of the Treaty still leave Member States a considerable discretion to impose restrictions on the free movement of persons. For example, the Court of Justice found that systematic border controls in general are under no circumstance compatible with an exception such as that provided by Article 56 EEC, but that in individual cases, complying with the strict criteria of necessity and proportionality, the possibility to impose special control measures could be accepted (*Timmermans*).[22]

12.   WHY DO IT THE INTERGOVERNMENTAL WAY?

In his report with the stimulating title Timmermans concluded among other things:

'The obligation imposed upon the Community under Article 8a EEC to establish the internal market before 1 January 1993 implies the abolition of all internal border controls of persons between Member States.(. . .)'
'The Community approach presents some obvious advantages over an intergovernmental one in terms of speed (no ratification required on the national level), primacy over inconsistent national law, the existence of a judicial mechanism to ensure a uniform interpretation (Art. 177 EEC).(. . .)'[23]

This provoked some critical remarks. With respect to the reluctance of the Member States to connect formally the common actions on the external frontiers of the Community and an agreement aimed at reducing the level of internal frontier checks two arguments on behalf of the Member States were advanced. Firstly, that Member States are not likely to leap in the dark by removing the internal checks before they are convinced of the effectiveness of common efforts to strengthen the external frontiers. Secondly, the fact that the public policy clauses of the Treaty protect national restrictions on the free movement of persons. The discretionary margin that these clauses offer to the Member States can also be found in the Express Declaration in the Final Act of the Conference on the Single European Act (*Brown*). And the advantages, summed up by Timmermans, of doing it the Community way,

22. See also Report Timmermans, p. 357 *supra*.
23. Report Timmermans, pp. 367-368 *supra*.

can as easily be seen contrariwise as reasons for doing it the intergovernmental way (*Donner*).

The intergovernmental approach which led to the Schengen Agreement could, given the assumption of an existing Community competence, actually be interfering with it. Therefore, Community competence should be exercised along the lines which have been set down by Article 176 EEC, where all Member States agree on the necessity of effective supervision by the Court over common action. Such an exercise would leave the Community a margin to operate in a situation where only some Member States are prepared to undertake action. Any acceptance that the intergovernmental approach is unconstitutional or incompatible with Community law would completely frustrate any further progression. Such a 'thesis of exclusivity' of Community powers is only defensible in a situation where all Member States acknowledge the competence of the Community to act. As long as this is not the case transitional regimes established by intergovernmental cooperation should be acceptable (*Timmermans*).[24]

13.   FREE MOVEMENT OF NON-EC NATIONALS

In his oral presentation Alexander reviewed the case-law of the Court of Justice and analyzed the position of non-EC nationals, in particular the scope of exception to the rule that non-EC nationals are denied the Community right of free movement. Such a positivist approach contrasts with a more idealistic approach in which this rule is examined by means of a test called 'the logic of the internal market' (*Hoogenboom*). With regard to invoking fundamental human rights by non-EC nationals there is the possibility that in individual cases this might improve the situation of a migrant from a third country. For example, by invoking the right to respect for family life, the chances for success in establishing a right to reside may increase. But remedies of this kind cannot achieve a treatment which is equal to that given to EC nationals. The decisive difference in treatment lies in the right to work. The main goal advanced by establishing the free movement of persons in Community law is that of making it possible to seek and find employment in another Member State. That right belongs to nationals of Member States, but not to those of third countries. If we want to eliminate the present discrimination against non EC nationals it will therefore be necessary to expand the notion of human rights under Community law (*Alexander*).

---

24. Report Timmermans, p. 367 *supra*.

14.   THE CONCEPT OF SPOUSE

With respect to the terms 'family' and 'spouse' Taschner in his paper — analyzing the three 'Residence Directives'[25] — stated the following:

> 'But another aspect of sociological evolution in nearly all Member States was left completely unrespected. The notion of "family" as used in Community law is based on the traditional instrument to create such a community of life, the marriage. But how about "modern" families; communities of life without marriage? If a man and a woman, one not being an EC national, live together for decades and now wish — having more than sufficient means — to move to another Member State, does the spouse being a non-EC national have a right of residence to be derived from that of the companion? The answer is no, unless the Court of Justice someday interprets the term "spouse" to include companion. But it must be said that renouncing marriage to be the creating factor of a "family" and allowing any less stronger link of human relationship as the basis for the genuine right of residence would open many doors to abuse.'[26]

A restriction of the concept of spouse only to officially married people can cause several problems. In Denmark there exists the legal possibility to conclude a lesbian or homosexual 'marriage'. According to the applicable Danish law only one of the parties has to hold Danish nationality. The question which arises as a consequence is whether this civil marriage, concluded in accordance with the law in Denmark, being a Member of the European Community, allows the couple involved to move freely to other Member States. The different national views on this point may infringe Article 7 EEC and lead to discrimination between homosexuals and heterosexuals. Further, problems of reverse-discrimination can arise. For example, the national policy of a Member State to allow homosexual couples to enter the national territory only if they are officially married, would lead to a discrimination against nationals of other Member States where the possibility for homosexuals to conclude a civil marriage does not exist (*Jessurun d'Oliveira*).

But the Council — in trying to reach an agreement on the final version of the 'Residence' directives simply did not take these 'modern' problems into consideration (*Taschner*). The answer to the question as to the scope of the concept of spouse is therefore not to be found in an interpretation of the Council's original intentions. Such an interpretation would automatically have as a consequence that the concept of spouse is only reserved to a heterosexual spouse (*Weiler*). The term 'spouse' in the directives should be regarded as a Community term which is open to interpretation by the Court of Justice (*Taschner*). The Court of Justice would be competent to decide on the scope of the concept of spouse and to state whether this

---

25. Council Directive 90/364/EEC of 28 June 1990 on the right of residence, OJ 1990 L180/26; Council Directive 90/365/EEC of 28 June 1990 on the right of residence for employees and self-employed persons who have ceased their occupational activity, OJ 1990 L180/28 and Council Directive 90/366/EEC of 28 June 1990 on the right of residence for students, OJ 1990 L180/30.

26. Report Taschner, p. 435 *supra*.

concept is limited to heterosexual couples only. Thus, as a consequence, the Court could find that homosexual couples are also covered by the term 'spouse', even if this is contrary to the original intention of the Council (*Weiler/Taschner*). Such a competence of the Court of Justice could be constructed by underlining the fact that the Council is bound by the general prohibition on discrimination as found in Article 7 EEC and further in the general Treaty provisions on free movement (*Weiler*).

On the other hand, why let the Court of Justice take the lead in matters concerning the future development of family law in which the concept of spouse is dominant? It is obvious that the Court finds itself under a duty to promote certain values. But it is a different matter to perform this duty in an area which is politically highly sensitive — in some Member States more than in others — and also, in one which is outside the scope of Community law as far as the consequences of such performance are concerned. Reference can be made in this respect to Case 59/85 *State of the Netherlands* v. *Anne Florence Reed*.[27] In that case the Court of Justice was presented with two questions by the Dutch Supreme Court (*Hoge Raad*): (i) is a Member State, which treats unmarried couples from other Member States in a manner different to that in which it treats its own unmarried couples, acting in a discriminatory manner contrary to Articles 7 and 48 EEC[28] and (ii) would it be contrary to EEC law if a more extensive interpretation were to be given to the concept of spouse than is presently customary?[29] The Court of Justice found that it was only competent to decide on the first question. With respect to the second question the Court held that no reason could be adduced to show that the common notion of spouse as contained in the secondary Community legislation should be extended by its own interpretation (*Koopmans*).

With respect to the example of the Danish homosexual couple it can be said - on the assumption that the relevant Danish law is contrary to another Member State's 'ordre public' — that the latter State may refuse the homosexual couple the right to enter its national territory. The Danish law being legal at least in Community terms, there should be no reason for reverse or 'backward' rights, or for an enforcement of the Danish rights outside the Danish territory (*Taschner/O'Keeffe*). As a consequence, problems may arise for couples who are legally married under the law of one Member State but are not recognized as such under the law of another (*O'Keeffe*). In this respect it is not the point that the Member States should recognize the Danish homosexual spouse for the purpose of the free movement of persons but

27. [1986] ECR 1283.
28. [1986] ECR 1299, para. 7: '(1) In the light of the provisions of Article 10 of Regulation No 1612/68, does discrimination prohibited by Articles 7 and 48 of the EEC Treaty arise where, as part of its policy on aliens, a Member State treats a person who has a stable relationship with a worker who is a national of that Member State as the spouse of such a worker, but does not grant the same treatment to a person who has a stable relationship with a worker who is a national of another Member State but is employed and resides in the first-named Member State?'.
29. [1986] ECR 1299, para. 7: '(3) Must Article 10 (1) (a) of Regulation No 1612/68 be interpreted as meaning that in certain circumstances a person who has a stable relationship with a worker within the meaning of that provision is to be treated as his "spouse"?'.

that the Court of Justice should scrutinize the national 'ordres publics'. The result of such an examination might be that the Court finds that the national notion of 'ordre public' of a particular Member State is contrary to its own conception of fundamental human rights (*Weiler*).

15. APPLICATION OF DIFFERENT STANDARDS FOR THE RIGHT OF ENTRY AND FOR THE RIGHT OF RESIDENCE OF NON-EC NATIONALS

The current practice in the Community to use equal criteria for the right of entry and for the right to reside and to remain met with criticism. On this point Community law fully corresponds with the relevant national laws. This application of equal criteria is difficult to understand from a legal point of view and impossible from a human point of view. A different regime for the right of entry and for the right to reside could lead to a better policy in handling the problem of the non-EC national. It would then be much easier to apply certain standards of equal protection and treatment without discrimination on the basis of nationality (*Koopmans*).

It could even be said that once a person is established in a country (for a long period) it would be contrary to the fundamental notion of human rights that this person could be expelled from that country. One should bear in mind in this respect Case 249/86, *Commission* v. *Germany*[30], where the Court of Justice had to deal with a similar problem and where it opted for a similar sort of reasoning. That case concerned the requirement of Article 10(3) of Regulation 1612/68 that worker immigrants should, in the event that they want their family to join them, have available housing that is considered normal for national workers. The German authorities interpreted this provision in the sense that a migrant must have housing for his family members throughout the total period of the residence in Germany. The Court of Justice considered this obligation as an 'one-off obligation' and declared:

' . . . that by adopting and retaining provisions in its national legislation which make renewal of the residence permit of members of the family of Community migrant workers conditional on their living in appropriate housing, not only at the time when they install themselves with the migrant worker concerned but for the entire duration of their residence, the Federal Republic of Germany has failed to fulfil its obligations under Article 10(3) of Regulation No 1612/68 of the Council of 15 October 1968.'[31]

But a plea for the application of different standards with respect to the right of entry and to the right to reside is opposed to the system of the three 'Residence' directives. For example, with respect to the right of entry the 'Pensioners' and 'Students' directive require that every person who wants to enter a Member State should have

---

30. [1989] ECR 1263.
31. [1989] ECR 1294.

sufficient means to support himself, and consequently is not dependent on public funds. If, in respect of residence his personal circumstances change in such a way that he becomes dependent on public funds, both directives offer the Member State the possibility to expel him (*Weiler/O'Keeffe*). Mention was made of the fact that in the second draft of the Student directive the Commission tried to persuade the Member States to renounce this requirement for those students who do not have adequate private means. Where the foreign student becomes a burden on the social security funds of the host country, the host country should support him but would be entitled to reimbursement by the home country of the student. The representatives of the Member States, however, thought this was an unacceptable approach (*Taschner*).

DOCUMENTATION

THE SCHENGEN AGREEMENT OF 14 JUNE 1985
(Unofficial Translation)

AGREEMENT BETWEEN THE GOVERNMENTS OF THE STATES OF THE BENELUX ECONOMIC UNION, THE FEDERAL REPUBLIC OF GERMANY AND THE FRENCH REPUBLIC ON THE GRADUAL ABOLITION OF CONTROLS AT THE COMMON FRONTIERS.

The Governments of the Kingdom of Belgium, the Federal Republic of Germany, the French Republic, the Grand Duchy of Luxembourg and the Kingdom of the Netherlands, Hereinafter referred to as the Parties,

Aware that the increasingly closer union of the peoples of the Member States of the European Communities should be manifested through freedom to cross internal frontiers for all nationals of the Member States and in the free movement of goods and services,

Anxious to affirm the solidarity between their peoples by removing the obstacles to free movement at the common frontiers between the States of the Benelux Economic Union, the Federal Republic of Germany and the French Republic,

Considering the progress already achieved within the European Communities with a view to ensuring the free movement of persons, goods and services,

Prompted by the will to succeed in abolishing controls at the common frontiers in the movement of nationals of the Member States of the European Communities and to facilitate the movement of goods and services,

Considering that application of this Agreement may require legislative measures which will have to be submitted to the national parliaments in accordance with the constitutions of the signatory States,

Having regard to the Declaration of the Fontainebleau European Council of 25 and 26 June 1984 on the abolition at the internal frontiers of police and customs formalities in the movement of persons and goods,

Having regard to the Agreement concluded at Saarbrücken on 13 July 1984 between the Federal Republic of Germany and the French Republic,

Having regard to the conclusions adopted on 31 may 1984 following the meeting at Neustadt-Aisch of the Ministers for Transport of the Benelux States and the Federal Republic of Germany,

Having regard to the memorandum of the Governments of the Benelux Economic Union on 12 December 1984 forwarded to the Governments of the Federal Republic of Germany and the French Republic,

H.G. Schermers et al., eds., Free Movement of Persons in Europe
© 1993, T.M.C. Asser Instituut, The Hague.

Have agreed as follows:

TITLE I
Measures applicable in the Short Term

Article 1

As soon as this Agreement enters into force and until all controls are abolished completely, the formalities at the common frontiers between the States of the Benelux Economic Union, the Federal Republic of Germany and the French Republic shall be completed, for the nationals of the Member States of the European Communities, in accordance with the conditions laid down below.

Article 2

In regard to the movement of persons, from 15 June 1985 the police and customs authorities shall as a general rule carry out a simple visual check on private vehicles crossing the common frontier at a reduced speed, without requiring such vehicles to stop.

However, they may carry out more thorough controls by means of spot checks. These shall be carried out where possible, in special bays in such a way that the movement of other vehicles crossing the frontier is not hampered.

Article 3

To facilitate the visual check, the nationals of the Member States of the European communities presenting themselves at the common frontier in a motor car may affix to the windscreen of the vehicle a green disc measuring at least 8 centimetres in diameter. This disc shall indicate that they have complied with the rules of the frontier police, are carrying only goods permitted under the duty-free arrangements and have complied with exchange regulations.

Article 4

The Parties shall endeavour to reduce to a minimum the time spent at common frontiers on account of the checks on the carriage of persons by road for hire or reward.

The Parties shall seek solutions enabling them to forego, by 1 January 1986, the systematic control at the common frontiers of the passenger waybill and licences for the carriage of persons by road for hire or reward.

Article 5

By 1 january 1986 common control points shall be set up in the adjacent national control offices in so far as that is not already the case and in so far as actual circumstances permit. Consideration shall subsequently be given to the possible introduction of common control points at other frontier posts in the light of local conditions.

Article 6

Without prejudice to the application of more favourable arrangements between the Parties, the latter shall take the measures required to facilitate the movement of nationals of the Member States of the European Communities resident in the municipalities locates in the proximity of the common frontiers with a view to allowing them to cross such frontiers outside the approved crossing points and outside the opening times of the control points.

The persons concerned may benefit from these advantages provided that they transport only goods permitted under the duty-free arrangements and comply with exchange regulations.

Article 7

The Parties shall endeavour to approximate as soon as possible their visa policies in order to avoid any adverse consequences that may result from the easing of controls at the common frontier in the field of immigration and security. They shall take, if possible by 1 January 1986, the steps necessary with a view, in applying their procedures for the issue of visas and admission to their territory, to taking into account the need to assure the protection of the entire territory of the five States against illegal immigrants and activities which could jeopardize security.

Article 8

With a view to easing the controls at the common frontiers and in the light of the significant differences in the laws of the States of the Benelux Economic Union, the federal Republic of Germany and the French Republic, the Parties shall undertake to

THE SCHENGEN AGREEMENT OF 14 JUNE 1985

combat vigorously on their territories illicit drug trafficking and to coordinate effectively their action in this area.

Article 9
The Parties shall reinforce the cooperation between their customs and police authorities, notably in fighting crime, particularly illicit traffic in drugs and arms, the unauthorized entry and residence of persons and customs and tax fraud and smuggling. To that end and in accordance with their national laws, the Parties shall endeavour to improve the exchange of information and to reinforce it where information likely to be of interest to the other Parties in combating crime is concerned.

The Parties shall reinforce in the context of their national laws mutual assistance in respect of irregular capital movements.

Article 10
With a view to assuring the cooperation provided for in Article 6, 7, 8 and 9, meetings between the competent authorities of the parties shall be held at regular intervals.

Article 11
In regard to the cross-frontier carriage of goods by road, the Parties shall forego, from 1 July 1985, the systematic completion at the common frontier of the following controls:
- control of driving and rest periods Council Regulation (EEC) No 543/69 of 25 March 1969 on the harmonization of certain social legislation relating to road transport and AETR);
- control of the weight and size of commercial vehicles; this provision shall not exclude the introduction of automatic weighing systems with a view to spot checks on weight;
- controls on the technical state of the vehicles.

Measures shall be taken to prevent the duplication of controls within the territories of the Parties.

Article 12
From 1 July 1985 control of documents giving details of transport operations not carried out underer licence or quota pursuant

to Community or bilateral rules shall be replaced at the common frontiers by spot checks. The vehicles carrying out the transport under these systems shall be distinguished when crossing the frontier by means of a visible symbol.

The competent authorities of the Parties shall determine the features of this symbol by common agreement.

Article 13
The Parties shall endeavour to harmonize by 1 january 1986 the systems for the licensing of commercial road transport in force among them for cross-frontier traffic with the aim of simplifying, easing and possibly replacing licenses for journeys by licenses for a period of time, with a visual check on the crossing of the common frontiers.

The procedures for converting the licenses for journeys into licenses for periods shall be agreed on a bilateral basis, account being taken of the road transport requirements in the different countries concerned.

Article 14
The Parties shall seek solutions to reduce the waiting times of rail transport at the common frontiers caused by completion of frontier formalities.

Article 15
The Parties shall recommend to their respective rail transport companies:
- to adapt technical procedures in order to reduce to a minimum the waiting time at the common frontiers;
- to do everything possible to apply to certain types of carriage of goods by rail to be defined by the rail companies, a special routing system such that the common frontiers can be crossed rapidly without any appreciable stops (goods trains with reduced waiting times at frontiers).

Article 16
The Parties shall harmonize the opening times and dates of customs posts for waterway traffic at the common frontiers.

TITLE II
Measures Applicable in the Long Term

Article 17
In regard to the movement of persons the Parties shall endeavour to abolish the controls at the common frontiers and transfer them to their external frontiers. To that end, they shall endeavour to harmonize in advance, where necessary, the laws and administrative provisions concerning the prohibitions and restrictions which form the basis for the controls and to take complementary measures to safeguard security and combat illegal immigration by nationals of States that are not members of the European Communities.

Article 18
The Parties shall open discussions, notably on the following matters, account being taken of the results of the short-term measures:
(a) drawing up arrangements for police cooperation on the prevention of delinquency and on search;
(b) examining any difficulties in applying agreements on international judicial assistance and extradition in order to determine the most appropriate solutions for improving cooperation between the Parties in those fields;
(c) seeking means to permit the joint combating of crime, inter alia, by studying possible introduction of a right of pursuit for police officers, taking into account existing means of communication and judicial assistance.

Article 19
The Parties shall seek to harmonize laws and regulations, in particular on:
— drugs,
— arms and explosives,
— registration of travellers in hotels.

Article 20
The Parties shall endeavour to harmonize their visa policies and conditions for entry to their territories. In so far as necessary, they shall also prepare for harmonization of their rules governing certain aspects of the law on aliens in regard to nationals of States that are not members of the European Communities.

Article 21
The Parties shall undertake common initiatives within the European Communities:
(a) to arrive at an increase in the duty-free allowances granted to travellers;
(b) to remove in the context of the community allowances, restrictions which might remain on entry to the Member States in respect of goods whose possession is not prohibited for their nationals.

The Parties shall take steps within the European Communities to attain harmonized charging in the country of departure of VAT on tourism transport services within the European Communities.

Article 22
The Parties shall endeavour both among themselves and within the European Communities:
— to increase the duty-free allowance for fuel to bring it into line with the normal contents of bus and coach tanks (600 litres);
— to harmonize the taxation of diesel fuel and increase the duty-free allowances for the normal contents of lorry tanks.

Article 23
The Parties shall also endeavour in the area of road transport to reduce, at the adjacent national control offices, waiting times and numbers of stopping points.

Article 24
In regard to the movement of goods, the Parties shall seek means to transfer to the external frontiers or to within their own territories the controls now carried out at the common frontiers.

To that end, they shall take, where necessary, common steps among themselves and within the European Communities to harmonize the provisions which form the basis for the controls of goods at the common frontiers. They shall ensure that these measures are without prejudice to the necessary protection of the health of persons, animals and plants.

Article 25
The Parties shall develop their cooperation with a view to facilitating the customs clearance of goods crossing a common frontier,

thanks to a systematic, automatic exchange of the necessary data collected by means of the single document.

Article 26

The Parties shall examine how taxes (VAT and excise duties) can be harmonized in the framework of the European Communities. To that end they shall support the initiatives undertaken by the European Communities.

Article 27

The Parties shall examine whether, on a reciprocal basis, the limits on the duty-free allowances granted at the common frontiers to frontierzone residents, as authorized under Community Law, can be abolished.

Article 28

Any conclusion on a bilateral or multilateral basis of arrangements similar to this Agreement with States that are not Parties thereto shall be preceded by consultation between the Parties.

Article 29

This Agreement shall apply also to the Land of Berlin, unless a declaration to the contrary is made by the Government of the Federal Republic of Germany to the Governments of the States of the Benelux Economic Union and the Government of the French Republic within three months of entry into force of this Agreement.

Article 30

The measures provided for in this Agreement which are not applicable as soon as it enters into force shall be applied by 1 January 1986 as regards the measures provided for in Title I and if possible by 1 january 1990 as regards the measures provided for in Title II, unless other deadlines are fixed in this Agreement.

Article 31

This Agreement shall apply subject to the provisions of Articles 5 and 6, and 8 to 16 of the Agreement concluded at Saarbrücken on 13 July 1984 between the Federal Republic of Germany and the French Republic.

Article 32

This Agreement shall be signed without being subject to ratification or approval or subject to ratification or approval followed by ratification or approval.

This Agreement shall be applied on a provisional basis from the day following its signature. This Agreement shall enter into force thirty days after deposit of the last instrument of ratification or approval.

Article 33

The Government of the Grand Duchy of Luxembourg shall be depository of this Agreement.

In witness whereof, the representatives of the Governments duly empowered to that effect have signed this Agreement.

Done at Schengen, Grand Duchy of Luxembourg, on 14 June 1985, the German, French and Dutch texts of this Agreement being equally authentic.

552

THE SCHENGEN CONVENTION OF 19 JUNE 1990
(Unofficial Translation)

APPLYING THE SCHENGEN AGREEMENT OF 14 JUNE 1985 BETWEEN THE GOVERNMENTS OF THE STATES OF THE BENELUX ECONOMIC UNION, THE FEDERAL REPUBLIC OF GERMANY AND THE FRENCH REPUBLIC, ON THE GRADUAL ABOLITION OF CHECKS AT THEIR COMMON BORDERS

The Kingdom of Belgium, the Federal Republic of Germany, the French Republic, the Grand Duchy of Luxembourg and the Kingdom of the Netherlands, hereinafter called the Contracting Parties,

Taking as their basis the Schengen Agreement of 14 June 1985 on the gradual abolition of checks at their common borders,

Having decided to implement the intention expressed in that agreement of bringing about the abolition of checks at their common borders on the movement of persons and facilitating the transport and movement of goods,

Whereas the Treaty establishing the European Communities, supplemented by the Single European Act, provides that the internal market shall comprise an area without internal frontiers,

Whereas the aim pursued by the Contracting Parties coincides with that objective, without prejudice to the measures to be taken to implement the provisions of the Treaty,

Whereas the implementation of that intention requires a series of appropriate measures and close co-operation between the Contracting Parties,

Have agreed as follows:

TITLE I
Definitions

Article 1

Internal border	shall mean the common land borders of the Contracting Parties, their airports for internal flights and their sea ports for regular trans-shipment connections exclusively from or to other ports within the territories of the Contracting Parties not calling at any ports outside those territories;
External borders	shall mean the Contracting Parties' land and sea borders and their airports and sea ports, provided they are not internal borders;

H.G. Schermers et al., eds., Free Movement of Persons in Europe
© 1993, T.M.C. Asser Instituut, The Hague.

Internal flight	shall mean any flight exclusively to or from territories of the Contracting Parties not landing within the territory of a Third State;
Third State	shall mean any State other than the Contracting Parties;
Alien	shall mean any person other than a national of a Member State of the European Communities;
Alien reported as a person not to be permitted entry	shall mean any alien listed reported as a person not to be permitted entry in the Schengen Information System in accordance with Article 96;
Border crossing point	shall mean any crossing point authorized by the competent authorities for the crossing of external borders;
Border control	shall mean a check made at a border in response solely to an intention to cross that border, regardless of any other consideration.
Carrier	shall mean any natural or legal person whose occupation it is to provide passenger transport by air, sea or land;
Residence permit	shall mean an authorization of any type issued by a Contracting Party giving the right of residence within its territory. This definition shall not include temporary admission to residence within the territory of a Contracting Party for the purpose of the processing of an application for asylum or an application for a residence permit;
Application for asylum	shall mean any application submitted in writing, orally or otherwise by an alien at an external border or within the territory of a Contracting Party with a view to obtaining recognition as a refugee in accordance with the Geneva Convention of 28 July 1951 relating to the Status of Refugees, as amended by the New York Protocol of 31 January 1967 and as such obtaining the right of residence;
Applicant for asylum	shall mean any alien who has submitted an application for asylum within the meaning of this Convention, on which no final decision has been taken;
Processing of an application for asylum	shall mean all the procedures for examining and taking a decision on an application for asylum, including measures taken in implementation of a final decision thereon, with the exception of the determination of the contracting Party responsible for the processing of an application for asylum under this Convention.

TITLE II
Abolition of checks at internal borders and movement of persons

CHAPTER 1
Crossing internal frontiers

Article 2

1. Internal borders may be crossed at any point without any checks on persons being carried out.

2. Where public policy or national security so require, however, a Contracting Party may, after consulting the other contracting Parties, decide that for a limited period national border checks appropriate to the situation will be carried out at internal borders. If public policy or national security require immediate action, the Contracting Party concerned shall take the necessary measures and shall inform the other Contracting Parties thereof at the earliest opportunity.

3. The abolition of checks on persons at internal borders shall not affect either Article 22 below or the exercise of police powers by the competent authorities under each Contracting Party's legislation throughout its territory, or the obligations to hold, carry and produce permits and documents provided for in its legislation.

4. Checks on goods shall be carried out in accordance with the relevant provisions of this Convention.

CHAPTER 2
Crossing external borders

Article 3

1. External borders may in principle be crossed only at border crossing points during the fixed opening hours. More detailed provisions, and exceptions and arrangements for minor border traffic, as well as the rules applicable to special categories of maritime traffic such as yachting and coastal fishing, shall be adopted by the Executive Committee.

2. The Contracting Parties undertake to introduce penalties for the unauthorized crossing of external borders at places other than crossing points or at times other than the fixed opening hours.

Article 4

1. The Contracting Parties guarantee that as from 1993 passengers on flights from Third States who board internal flights will first be subject, upon arrival, to personal and hand baggage checks in the airport of arrival of their external flight. Passengers on internal flights who board flights bound for Third States will first be subject, on departure, to personal and hand baggage checks in the airport of departure of their external flight.

2. The Contracting Parties shall take the measures required for checks to be carried out in accordance with paragraph 1.

3. Neither paragraph 1 nor paragraph 2 shall affect checks on registered luggage; such checks shall be carried out either in the airport of final destination or in the airport of initial departure.

4. Until the date laid down in paragraph 1, airports shall, by way of derogation from the definition of internal borders, be considered as external borders for internal flights.

Article 5

1. for visits not exceeding three months entry into the territories of the Contracting Parties may be granted to an alien who fulfils the following conditions:
   a) in possession of a valid document or documents permitting them to cross the border, as determined by the Executive Committee;
   b) in possession of a valid visa if required;
   c) if applicable, submits documents substantiating the purpose and the conditions of the planned visit and has sufficient means of support, both for the period of the planned visit and to return to their country of

origin or to travel in transit in a Third State, into which their admission is guaranteed, or is in a position to acquire such means legally;

d) has not been reported as a person not to be permitted entry;

e) is not considered to be a threat to public policy, national security or the international relations of any of the Contracting Parties.

2. Entry to the territories of the Contracting Parties must be refused to any alien who does not fulfil all the above conditions unless a Contracting Party considers it necessary to derogate from that principle on humanitarian grounds or in the national interest or because of international obligations. In such cases permission to enter will be restricted to the territory of the Contracting Party concerned, which must inform the other contracting Parties accordingly.

These rules shall not preclude the application of special provisions concerning the right of asylum or of the provisions of Article 18.

3. An alien who holds a residence permit or a return visa issued by one of the contracting Parties or, if required, both documents, shall be permitted to enter in transit, unless their name is on the national list of persons reported as not to be refused entry which is held by the Contracting Party at the external borders of which they arrive.

Article 6

1. Cross-border movement at external borders shall be subject to checks by the competent authorities. Checks shall be made in accordance with uniform principles, within the scope of national powers and national legislation, account being taken of the interests of all Contracting Parties throughout the Contracting Parties' territories.

2. The uniform principles referred to in paragraph 1 shall be as follows:

a) checks on persons shall include not only the verification of travel documents and of the other conditions governing entry, residence, work and exit but also checks to detect and prevent threats to the national security and public policy of the Contracting Parties. Such checks shall also cover vehicles and objects in the possession of persons crossing the border. They shall be carried out by each Contracting Party in accordance with its legislation, in particular as regards searches.

b) All persons must be subject to at least one check making it possible to establish their identities on the basis of their presentation of travel documents.

c) On entry aliens must be subject to a thorough check as defined in (a).

d) On exit checks shall be carried out as required in the interest of all Contracting Parties under the law on aliens in order to detect and prevent threats to the national security and public policy of the Contracting Parties. Such checks shall be made in all cases in respect of aliens.

e) If such checks cannot be made because of particular circumstances priorities must be established. In this connection, entry checks shall in principle take priority over exit checks.

3. The competent authorities shall use mobile units to exercise surveillance on external borders between crossing points; the same shall apply to border crossing points outside normal opening hours. This surveillance shall be carried out in such a way as not to encourage people to circumvent the checks at crossing points. The surveillance procedures shall, where appropriate, be fixed by the Executive Committee.

4. The Contracting Parties undertake to deploy enough appropriate officers to conduct checks and maintain surveillance along external borders.

5. An equivalent level of control shall be exercised at external frontiers.

Article 7

The Contracting Parties shall assist each other and shall maintain constant, close co-operation with a view to the effective exercise of checks and surveillance. They shall in particular exchange all relevant, important information, with the exception of data relating to named individuals, unless otherwise provided in this Convention, shall as far as possible harmonize the instructions given to the authorities responsible for checks and shall promote the uniform training and retraining of officers manning checkpoints. Such co-operation may take the form of the exchange of liaison officers.

Article 8

The Executive committee shall take the necessary decisions relating to the practical procedures for implementing border checks and surveillance.

CHAPTER 3
Visas

Section 1
Visas for short visits

Article 9

1. The Contracting Parties undertake to adopt a common policy on the movement of persons and in particular on the arrangements for visas. They shall give each other assistance to that end. The Contracting Parties undertake to pursue by common agreement the harmonization of their policies on visas.

2. The visa arrangements relating to Third States, the nationals of which are subject to visa arrangements common to all the Contracting Parties at the time when this Convention is signed or later, may be amended only by common agreement of all the Contracting Parties. A Contracting Party may exceptionally derogate from the common visa arrangeements with respect to a Third State for over-riding reasons of national policy that require an urgent decision. It must first consult the other contracting Parties and, in its decision, must take account of their interests and of the consequences of that decision.

Article 10

1. A uniform visa valid for the entire territory of the Contracting Parties shall be introduced. This visa, the period of validity of which shall be determined by Article 11, may be issued for visits not exceeding three months.

2. Until this visa is introduced the Contracting Parties shall recognize their respective national visas, insofar as these are issued on the basis of common conditions and criteria determined within the framework of the relevant provisions of this Chapter.

3. By way of derogation from paragraphs 1 and 2 above each Contracting Party shall reserve the right to restrict the territorial validity of the visa in accordance with common arrangements determined in the context of the relevant provisions of this Chapter.

Article 11

1. The visa provided for in Article 10 may be:
   a) a travel visa valid for one or more entries, provided that neither the length of a continuous visit nor the total length of successive visits may exceed three months in any half year as from the date of first entry;
   b) a transit visa allowing its holder to pass through the territories of the Contracting Parties once, twice or exceptionally several times en route to the territory of a Third State, provided that no transit shall last longer than five days.

2. Paragraph 1 shall not preclude a Contracting Party from issuing a new visa, the validity of which is limited to its own territory, within the half year in question if necessary.

Article 12

1. The uniform visa provided for in Article 10 (1) shall be issued by the diplomatic and consular authorities of the Contracting Parties and, where appropriate, by the authorities of the Contracting Parties designated under Article 17.

2. The Contracting Party competent to issue such a visa shall in principle be that of the principal destination. If this cannot be determined the visa shall in principle be issued by the diplomatic or consular post of the Contracting Party of first entry.

3. The Executive Committee shall specify the implementing arrangements and, in particular, the criteria for determining the principal destination.

Article 13

1. No visa shall be apposed on a travel document that has expired.

2. The period of validity of a travel document must be greater than that of the visa. taking account of the period of use of the visa. It must enable an alien to return to his country of origin or to enter a third country.

Article 14

1. No visa may be apposed to a travel document if that travel document is valid for none of the Contracting Parties. If a travel document is valid only for one Contracting Party or for a number of Contracting Parties the visa to be apposed shall be limited to the Contracting Party or Parties in question.

2. If a travel document is not recognized as valid by one or more of the Contracting Parties a visa may be issued in the form of an authorization in place of a visa.

Article 15

In principle the visas referred to in Article 10 may be issued only if an alien fulfils the conditions of entry laid down in Article 5(1)(a), (c), (d) and (e).

Article 16

If a Contracting Party considers it necessary to derogate, on one of the grounds listed in Article 5 (2), from the principle enunciated in Article 15 by issuing a visa to an alien who does not fulfil all the conditions of entry referred to in article 5 (1), the validity of this visa shall be restricted to the territory of that Contracting Party, which must inform the other Contracting Parties accordingly.

Article 17

1. The Executive Committee shall adopt common rules for the examination of applications for a visa, shall ensure their correct implementation and shall adapt them to new situation and circumstances.

2. The Executive Committee shall also specify the cases in which the issue of a visa shall be subject to consultation with the central authority of the Contracting Party to which application is made and, where appropriate, the central authorities of other Contracting Parties.

3. The Executive Committee shall also take the necessary decisions regarding the following points:
   a) the travel documents to which a visa may be apposed;
   b) the bodies responsible for the issue of visas;
   c) the conditions governing the issue of visas at borders;
   d) the form, content, and period of validity of visas and the charges to be imposed for their issue;
   e) the conditions for the extension and refusal of the visas referred to in (c) and (d) above, in accordance with

the interests of all the Contracting Parties;

f) the procedures for the limitation of the territorial validity of visas;

g) the principles governing the preparation of a common list of aliens reported as not to be permitted entry, without prejudice to Article 96.

Section 2
Visas for long visits

Article 18

Visas for visits of more than three months shall be national visas issued by one of the Contracting Parties in accordance with its own legislation. Such a visa shall enable its holder to transit through the territories of the other Contracting Parties in order to proceed to the territory of the Contracting Party which issued the visa, unless he fails to fulfil the conditions of entry referred to in Article 5(1)(a), (d) and (e) or he is on the national reporting list of the Contracting Party through the territory of which he seeks to transit.

CHAPTER 4
Conditions governing the movements of aliens

Article 19

1. Aliens holding a uniform visa who have legally entered the territory of a Contracting Party may move freely within the territories of all the Contracting Parties throughout the period of validity of their visas, provided they fulfil the conditions of entry referred to in Article 5(1)(a), (c), (d) and (e).

2. Pending the introduction of a uniform visa, aliens holding a visa issued by one of the Contracting Parties who have legally entered the territory of one Contracting Party may move freely within the territories of all the Contracting Parties during the period of validity of their visa up to a maximum of three months from the date of first entry, provided they fulfil the conditions of entry referred to in Article 5(1)(a), (c), (d) and (e).

3. Paragraphs 1 and 2 shall not apply to visas of which the validity is subject to territorial limitation in accordance with Chapter 3 of this Title.

4. This Article shall apply without prejudice to Article 22.

Article 20

1. Aliens not subject to a visa requirement may move freely within the territories of the Contracting Parties for a maximum period of three months during the six months following the date of first entry, provided they fulfil the conditions of entry referred to in Article 5(1)(a), (c), (d) and (e).

2. Paragraph 1 shall not affect the rights of each Contracting Party to extend beyond three months the visit of an alien within its territory in exceptional circumstances or in implementation of a bilateral agreement concluded before the entry into force of this Convention.

3. This Article shall apply without prejudice to Article 22.

Article 21

1. An alien holding a residence permit issued by one of the Contracting Parties may, under cover of that permit and of a travel document, both documents still being valid, move freely for up to three months within the territories of the other Contracting Parties provided he fulfils the conditions of entry referred to in Article 5(1)(a), (c) and (e) and is not on the national reporting list of the Contracting Party concerned.

2. Paragraph 1 shall also apply to an alien holding a provisional residence permit issued by one of the Contracting Parties and a travel document issued by that Contracting Party.

3. The Contracting Parties shall communicate to the Executive Committee a list of the documents which they issue that are valid as residence permits or provisional residence permits and travel documents within he meaning of this Article.

4. This Article shall apply without prejudice to Article 22.

Article 22

1. An alien who has legally entered the territory of one of the Contracting Parties shall be obliged to declare himself, in accordance with the conditions imposed by each Contracting Party, to the competent authorities of the Contracting Party the territory of which he enters. Such declaration may be made, at each Contracting Party's choice, either on entry or, within three working days of entry, within the territory of the Contracting Party which he enters.

2. An alien resident within the territory of one of the Contracting Parties who enters the territory of another Contracting Party shall be subject to the obligation to declare himself referred to in paragraph 1.

3. Each Contracting Party shall enact exceptions to paragraphs 1 and 2 and shall communicate them to the Executive Committee.

Article 23

1. An alien who does not fulfil or who no longer fulfils the short visit conditions applicable within the territory of a Contracting Party must in principle leave the territories of the Contracting Parties without delay.

2. An alien who holds a valid residence permit or temporary residence permit issued by another Contracting Party must enter the territory of that contracting Party without delay.

3. Where such an alien has not left voluntarily or where it may be assumed that he will not so leave or if his immediate departure is required for reasons of national security of public policy, he must be expelled from the territory of the contracting Party within which he has been arrested as laid down in the national expulsion, the Contracting Party concerned may allow the person concerned to remain within its territory.

4. Expulsion may be effected from the territory of that State to the alien's country of origin or to any other State to which he may be permitted entry, in particular under the relevant provisions of the re-entry agreements concluded by the Contracting Parties.

5. Paragraph 4 shall not preclude the application of national provisions on the right of asylum, of the Geneva Convention of 28 July 1951 relating to the Status of Refugees as amended by the New York Protocol of 31 January 1967, or of paragraph 2 of this Article or Article 33(1) of this Convention.

Article 24

Subject to the Executive Committee's definition of the appropriate practical criteria and arrangements, the Contracting Parties shall compensate each other for any financial imbalances resulting from the compulsory expulsion provided for in Article 23 where such expulsion cannot be effected at the alien's expense.

CHAPTER 5
Residence permits and reporting as a person not to be permitted entry

Article 25

1. Where a Contracting Party considers issuing a residence permit to an alien who has been reported as a person not to be permitted entry it shall first consult the reporting Contracting Party and shall take account of its interests; the residence permit shall be issued only on serious grounds, in particular of a humanitarian nature or pursuant to international obligations.

    If a residence permit is issued the reporting Contracting Party shall withdraw the report but may put the alien concerned on its national reporting list of persons not to be permitted entry.

2. Where it emerges that an alien holding a valid residence permit issued by one of the Contracting Parties has been reported as a person not to be permitted entry the reporting Contracting Party shall consult the Party which issued the residence permit in order to determine whether there are sufficient grounds for the withdrawal of the residence permit.

    If the residence permit is not withdrawn the reporting Contracting Party shall withdraw the report but may put the alien in question on its national reporting list.

CHAPTER 6
Measures relating to organized travel

Article 26

1. Subject to the obligations arising out of their accession to the Geneva Convention of 28 July 1951 relating to the Status of Refugees, as amended by the New York Protocol of 31 January 1967, the Contracting Parties undertake to incorporate the following rules in their national legislation:

a) If an alien is refused entry into the territory of one of the Contracting Parties the carrier which brought him to the external border by air, sea or land shall be obliged to assume responsibility for him again without delay. At the request of the border surveillance authorities the carrier must return the alien to the Third State from which he was transported, to the Third State which issued the travel document on which he travelled or to any other Third State to which he is guaranteed entry.

b) The carrier shall be obliged to take all necessary measures to ensure that an alien carried by air or sea is in possession of the travel documents required for entry into the territory of the Contracting Parties.

2. The Contracting Parties undertake, subject to the obligations arising out of their accession to the Geneva Convention of 28 July 1951 relating to the Status of Refugees, as amended by the New York Protocol of 31 january 1967, and in accordance with their constitutional law, to impose penalties on carriers who transport aliens who do not possess the necessary travel documents by air or sea from a Third State to their territories.

3. Paragraph 1(b) and paragraph 2 shall also apply to carriers of groups by coach over international road links, with the exception of border traffic.

Article 27

1. The Contracting Parties undertake to impose appropriate penalties on any person who, for purposes of gain, assists or tries to assist an alien to enter or reside within the territory of one of the Contracting Parties contrary to the laws of that Contracting Party on the entry and residence of aliens.

2. If a Contracting Party is informed of the facts referred to in paragraph 1 which constitute an infringement of the legislation of another Contracting Party, it shall inform the latter accordingly.

3. Any Contracting Party which requests another Contracting Party to prosecute on the grounds of the infringement of its own legislation, offences such as those referred to in paragraph 1, must specify, by means of an official denunciation or a certificate from the competent authorities, the provisions of law which have been infringed.

CHAPTER 7
Responsibility for the processing of applications for asylum

Article 28
The Contracting Parties hereby reaffirm their obligations under the Geneva Convention of 28 July 1951 relating to the Status of Refugees as amended by the New York Protocol of 31 January 1967, without any geographical restriction on the scope of those instruments, as also their commitment to co-operate with the United Nations High Commissioner for Refugees in the implementation of those instruments.

Article 29
1. The Contracting Parties undertake to process any application for asylum lodged by an alien within the territory of any one of them.

2. This obligation shall not bind a Contracting Party to authorize every applicant for asylum to enter or to remain within its territory.

   Every Contracting Party shall retain the right to refuse entry or to expel any applicant for asylum to a Third State on the basis of its national provisions and in accordance with its international commitments.

3. Regardless of the Contracting Party to which an alien addresses an application for asylum, only one Contracting Party shall be responsible for processing that application. It shall be determined by the criteria laid down in Article 30.

4. Notwithstanding paragraph 3 every Contracting Party shall retain the right, for special reasons concerning national law in particular, to process an application for asylum even if under this Convention the responsibility for doing so is that of another Contracting Party.

Article 30
1. The Contracting Party responsible for the processing of an application for asylum shall be determined as follows:
   a) If a Contracting Party has issued to the applicant for asylum a visa of any type, or a residence permit, it shall be responsible for processing the application. If the visa was issued on the authorization of another Contracting Party, the Contracting Party who gave the authorization shall be responsible.
   b) If two or more Contracting Parties have issued to the applicant for asylum a visa of any type or a residence permit, the Contracting Party responsible shall be the one which issued the visa or the residence permit that will expire last.
   c) As long as the applicant for asylum has not left the territory of the contracting Parties the responsibility defined in accordance with (a) and (b) shall subsist even if the period of validity of the visa of any type of the residence permit has expired. If the applicant for asylum has left the territory of the Contracting States after the issue of the visa or the residence permit, these documents shall be the basis for the responsibility as defined in (a) and (b) unless they

have expired in the interval under national provisions.

d) If the Contracting Parties exempt the applicant for asylum from the requirement for a visa, the Contracting Party across the external borders of which the applicant for asylum has entered the territory of the Contracting Parties shall be responsible.

Until the harmonization of visa policies is completed, and if the applicant for asylum is exempted from the requirement for a visa by certain Contracting Parties only, the Contracting Party across the external border of which the applicant for asylum has entered the territory of the Contracting Parties by means of an exemption from the requirement of a visa shall be responsible, subject to (a), (b) and (c).

If the application for asylum is submitted to a Contracting Party which has issued a transit visa to the applicant — whether the applicant has passed passport checks or not — and if the transit visa was issued after the country of transit has ascertained from the consular or diplomatic authorities of the Contracting Party of destination that the applicant for asylum fulfilled the conditions for entry into the Contracting Party of destination, the Contracting Party of destination shall be responsible for processing the application.

e) If the applicant for asylum has entered the territory of the Contracting Parties without being in possession of one or more documents permitting the crossing of the border, determined by the Executive Committee, the Contracting Party across the external borders of which the applicant for asylum has entered the territory of the Contracting Parties shall be responsible.

f) If an alien whose application for asylum is already being processed by one of the Contracting Parties submits a new application the Contracting Party responsible shall be the one processing the first application.

g) If an alien on whose previous application for asylum a Contracting Party has already taken a final decision submits a new application, the Contracting Party responsible shall be the one that processed the previous request unless the applicant has left the territory of the Contracting Parties.

2. If a Contracting Party has undertaken the processing of an application for asylum in accordance with Article 29(4) the Contracting Party responsible under paragraph 1 of the present Article shall be relieved of its obligations.

3. If the Contracting Party responsible cannot be determined by means of the criteria laid down in paragraphs 1 and 2 the Contracting Party to which the application for asylum was submitted shall be responsible.

Article 31

1. The Contracting Parties shall endeavour to determine as quickly as possible which of them is responsible for the processing of an application for asylum.

2. If an application for asylum is addressed to a Contracting Party which is not responsible under Article 30 by an alien resident within its territory that Contracting Party may request the Contracting Party responsible to take responsibility for the applicant for asylum in order to process his application for asylum.

3. The Contracting Party responsible shall be bound to take responsibility for the applicant for asylum referred to in paragraph 2 if the request is made within six months of the submission of the application for asylum. If the request is not

made within that time the Contracting Party to which the application for asylum was submitted shall be responsible for processing the application.

Article 32

The Contracting Party responsible for the processing of an application for asylum shall process it in accordance with its national law.

Article 33

1. If an applicant for asylum is illegally within the territory of another Contracting Party while the asylum procedure is in progress the Contracting Party responsible shall be bound to take him back.

2. Paragraph 1 shall not apply where the other Contracting Party has issued an applicant for asylum with a residence permit valid for one year or more. In this case responsibility for the processing of the application shall be transferred to the other Contracting Party.

Article 34

1. The Contracting Party responsible shall be bound to take back an alien whose application for asylum has been finally rejected and who has entered the territory of another Contracting Party without being authorized to reside there.

2. Paragraph 1 shall not, however, apply where the Contracting Party responsible expelled the alien from the territories of the Contracting Parties.

Article 35

1. The Contracting Party which granted an alien the status of refugee and gave him the right of residence shall be bound, provided that those concerned are in agreement, to be responsible for processing any application for asylum made by a member of his family.

2. A family member for the purposes of paragraph 1 shall be the spouse or the unmarried child less than 18 years old of the refugee or, if the refugee is an unmarried child less than 18 years old, his father or mother.

Article 36

Any Contracting Party responsible for the processing of an application for asylum may, on humanitarian grounds based on family or cultural reasons, ask another Contracting Party to assume that responsibility in so far as the person concerned so wishes. The Contracting Party to whom such a request is made shall consider whether it can grant it.

Article 37

1. The competent authorities of the Contracting Parties shall at the earliest opportunity send each other details of:
   a) an new rules or measures adopted as regards the law of asylum or of the treatment of applicants for asylum no later than their entry into force;
   b) statistical data concerning the monthly arrivals of applicants for asylum, indicating the principal countries or origin, and decisions on applications for asylum in so far as they are available;
   c) the emergence of, or significant increases in, certain groups of applicants for asylum and any information available on this subject;
   d) any fundamental decisions as regards the law of asylum.

2. The Contracting Parties shall also guarantee close co-operation in the collection of information on the situation in the countries of origin of applicants for asylum with a view to reaching a common assessment.

3. Any instruction given by a Contracting Party concerning the confidential processing of the information that it com-

municates must be complied with by the other Contracting Parties.

Article 38

1. Every Contracting Party shall send every other Contracting Party that requests it the information it holds on an applicant for asylum that is necessary for purposes of
   - determining the Contracting Party responsible for processing the application for asylum;
   - processing the application for asylum;
   - implementing the obligations arising under this chapter.

2. Such information may concern only
   a) the identity (name and forename, any previous names, appellations or aliases, date and place of birth, present nationality and any previous nationalities of the applicant for asylum and, where appropriate, the members of his family);
   b) the identity and travel documents (references, periods of validity, dates of issue, issuing authorities, place of issues, etc.);
   c) any other particulars necessary for establishing the applicant's identity;
   d) places of residence and the itineraries of journeys;
   e) residence permits or visas issued by a Contracting Party;
   f) the place where the application for asylum was submitted;
   g) where appropriate, the date of submission of any previous application for asylum, the date of submission of the present application, the point reached in the procedure and the import of the decision taken.

3. In addition, a Contracting Party may ask another Contracting Party to inform it of the grounds invoked by an applicant for asylum in support of his application and, where appropriate, the grounds for the decision taken on it. The Contracting Party requested shall consider whether it can comply with the request made to it. In any case the communication of such information shall be subject to the consent of the applicant for asylum.

4. Exchanges of information shall be effected at the request of a Contracting Party and may be effected only between the authorities the designation of which has been communicated by each Contracting Party to the Executive Committee.

5. The information exchanged may be uses only for the purposes set out in para-graph 1. Such information may be communicated only to the authorities and jurisdictions responsible for
   - determining the Contracting Party responsible for the processing of an application for asylum;
   - processing an application for asylum;
   - implementing obligations arising under this Chapter.

6. A Contracting Party that communicates information shall ensure it is correct and up to date.
   If it emerges that this Contracting Party supplied information that was not correct or should not have been communicated the recipient Contracting Parties shall be informed without delay. They shall be bound to correct that information or to delete it.

7. An applicant for asylum shall be entitled to be informed, at his request, of the information exchanged regarding him as long as it is available.
   If he ascertains that this information is incorrect or should not have been communicated he shall be entitled to require its correction or deletion. Cor-

rections shall be effected as laid down in paragraph 6.

8. In each Contracting Party concerned the communication and receipt of information exchanged shall be recorded.

9. Information communicated shall be preserved no longer than the time necessary for the purposes for which it was exchanged. The need for its preservation must be assessed in due course by the Contracting Party concerned.

10. Information communicated shall in any case have at least the same protection as that laid down in the law of the recipient Contracting Party for information of a similar nature.

11. If information is not processed automatically but in another manner each Contracting Party must take appropriate measures to ensure that this Article is complied with by means of effective checks. If a Contracting Party has a service of the type referred to in paragraph 12 it may instruct that service to carry out those checks.

12. If one or more Contracting Parties want to computerize the processing of all or part of the information referred to in paragraph 2 and 3, computerization shall be authorized only if the Contracting Parties concerned have adopted legislation relating to such processing that implements the principles of the Council of Europe Convention of 28 January 1981 for the Protection of Individuals with regard to Automatic Processing of Personal Data and if they have entrusted an appropriate national body with the independent control of the processing and use of data communicated under this Convention.

TITLE III
Police and security

CHAPTER 1
Police co-operation

Article 39

1. The Contracting Parties undertake to ensure that their police authorities shall, in compliance with national legislation and within the limits of their responsibilities, assist each other for the purposes of preventing and detecting criminal offenses, in so far as national law does not stipulate that the request is to be made to the legal authorities and provided the request or the implementation thereof does not involve the application of coercive measures by the requested Contracting Party. Where the requested police authorities do not have jurisdiction to implement a request, they shall forward it to the competent authorities.

2. The written information provided by the requested Contracting Party under paragraph 1 may not be used by the requesting Contracting Party as evidence of the criminal offence other than with the agreement of the relevant legal authorities of the requested Contracting Party.

3. Requests for assistance referred to in paragraph 1 and the replies to such requests may be exchanged between the central bodies responsible in each Contracting Party for international police co-operation. Where the request cannot be made in good time by the above procedure, it may be addressed by the police authorities of the requesting Contracting Party directly to the competent authorities of the requested Party, which may reply directly. In such cases, the requesting police authority shall as soon as possible inform the central body responsible in the requested Contracting

Party for international police co-operation of its direct application.

4. In border regions, co-operation may be covered by arrangements between the responsible Ministers of the Contracting Parties.

5. The provisions of this Article shall not preclude more detailed present or future bilateral agreements between Contracting Parties with a common border. The Contracting Parties shall inform each other of such agreements.

Article 40

1. Police officers of one of the Contracting Parties who, within the framework of a criminal investigation, are keeping under observation in their country, a person who is presumed to have taken part in a criminal offence to which extradition may apply, shall be authorized to continue their observation in the territory of another Contracting Party where the latter has authorized cross-border observation in response to a request for assistance which has previously been submitted. Conditions may be attached to the authorization.

    On request, the observation will be entrusted to officers of the Contracting Party in whose territory it is carried out.

    The request, for assistance referred to in the first subparagraph must be sent to an authority designated by each of the Contracting Parties and having jurisdiction to grant or to forward the requested authorization.

2. Where, for particularly urgent reasons, prior authorization of the other Contracting Party cannot be requested, the officers conducting the observation shall be authorized to continue beyond the border the observation of a person presumed to have committed offences listed in paragraph 7, provided that the following conditions are met:

    a) the authorities of the Contracting Party designated under paragraph 5, in whose territory the observation is to be continued, must be notified immediately, during the observation, that the border has been crossed;

    b) a request for, assistance submitted in accordance with paragraph 1 and outlining the grounds for crossing the border without prior authorization shall be submitted without delay.

    Observation shall cease as soon as the Contracting Party in whose territory it is taking place so requests, following the notification referred to in (a) or the request referred to in (b) or where authorization has not been obtained five hours after the border was crossed.

3. The observation referred to in paragraphs 1 and 2 shall be carried out only under the following general conditions:

    a) The officers conducting the observation must comply with the provisions of this Article and with the law of the Contracting Party in whose territory they are operating, they must obey the instructions of the local responsible authorities.

    b) Except in the situations provided for in paragraph 2, the officers shall, during the observation, carry a document certifying that authorization has been granted.

    c) The officers conducting the observation must be able at all times to provide proof that they are acting in an official capacity.

    d) The officers conducting the observation may carry their service weapons during the observation save where specifically otherwise decided by the requested party: their use shall be prohibited save in cases of legitimate self-defence.

e) Entry into private homes and places not accessible to the public shall be prohibited.

f) The officers conducting the observation may neither challenge nor arrest the person under observation.

g) All operations shall be the subject of a report to the authorities of the Contracting Party in whose territory they took place; the officers conducting the observation may be required to appear in person.

h) The authorities of the Contracting Party from which the observing officers have come shall, when requested by the authorities of the Contracting Party in whose territory the observation took place, assist the enquiry subsequent to the operation in which they took part, including legal proceedings.

4. The officers referred to in paragraphs 1 and 2 shall be:

   — as regards the Kingdom of Belgium: members of the 'police judiciaire près les Parquets', the 'gendarmerie' and the 'police communale' as well as customs officers, under the conditions laid down in appropriate bilateral agreements referred to in paragraph 6, with respect to their powers regarding illicit traffic in narcotic drugs and psychotropic substances, traffic in arms and explosives, and the illicit carriage of toxic and dangerous waste;

   — as regards the Federal Republic of Germany, officers of the 'Polizeien des Bundes und der Länder' as well as, with respect only to illegal traffic in narcotic figs and psychotropic substances and arms traffic, officers of the 'Zollfahndungsdienst' (customs investigation service) in their capacity as auxiliary officers of the public ministry;

   — as regards the French Republic: officers and criminal police officers of the national police and national 'gendarmerie' as well as customs officers, under the conditions laid down in appropriate bilateral agreements referred to in paragraph 6, with respect to their powers regarding illicit traffic in narcotic drugs and psychotropic substances, traffic arms and explosives, and the illicit carriage of toxic and dangerous waste;

   — as regards the Grand Duchy of Luxembourg: officers of the 'gendarmerie' and the police as well as customs officers, under the conditions laid down in appropriate bilateral agreements referred to in paragraph 6, with respect to their powers regarding illicit traffic in narcotic drugs and psychotropic substances, traffic in arms and explosives, and the illicit carriage of toxic and dangerous waste;

   — as regards the Kingdom of the Netherlands: officers of the 'Rijkspolitie' and the 'Gemeentepolitie' as well as, under the conditions laid down in appropriate bilateral agreements referred to in paragraph 6, with respect to their powers regarding illicit traffic in narcotic drugs and psychotropic substances, traffic in arms and explosives and the illicit carriage of toxic and dangerous waste, officers of the fiscal information and research service responsible for entry and excise duties.

5. The authority referred to in paragraphs 1 and 2 shall be:

   — as regards the Kingdom of Belgium: the 'Commissariat général de la Police judiciaire';

   — as regards the federal Republic of Germany: the 'Bundeskriminalamt';

- as regards the French Republic: the 'Direction centrale de la Police judiciaire';
- as regards the Grand Duchy of Luxembourg: the 'Procureur général d'Etat';
- as regards the Kingdom of the Netherlands: the 'Landelijk Officier van Justitie' responsible for cross-border observation.

6. The Contracting Parties may, at bilateral level, extend the scope of this article and adopt additional measures in implementation thereof.

7. the observation referred to in paragraph 2 may take place only for one of the following criminal offences:
   - assassination,
   - murder,
   - rape,
   - arson,
   - counterfeiting,
   - armed robbery and receiving of stolen goods,
   - extortion,
   - kidnapping and hostage taking,
   - traffic in human beings,
   - illicit traffic in narcotic drugs and psychotropic substances,
   - breach of the laws on arms and explosives,
   - use of explosives,
   - illicit carriage of toxic and dangerous waste.

Article 41

1. Officers of one of the Contracting Parties following, in their country, an individual apprehended in the act of committing one of the offenses referred to in paragraph 4 or participating in one of those offenses, shall be authorized to continue pursuit in the territory of another Contracting Party without prior authorization where given the particular urgency of the situation it was not possible to notify the competent authorities of the other Contracting Party by one of the means provided for in Article 44 prior to entry into that territory or where these authorities have been unable to reach the scene in time to take over the pursuit.

   The same shall apply where the person pursued has escaped from provisional custody or while serving a custodial sentence.

   The pursuing officers shall, not later than when they cross the border, contact the competent authorities of the Contracting Party in whose territory the pursuit is to take place. The pursuit will cease as soon as the Contracting Party on the territory of which the pursuit is taking place so requests. At the request of the pursuing officers, the competent local authorities shall challenge the pursued person so as to establish his identity or to arrest him.

2. The pursuit shall be carried out in accordance with one of the following procedures, defined by the declaration provided for in paragraph:
   a) The pursuing officers shall not have the right to apprehend.
   b) If no request to cease the pursuit is made and if the competent local authorities are unable to intercede quickly enough, the pursuing officers may apprehend the person pursued until the officers of the Contracting Party in the territory of which the pursuit is taking place, who must be informed without delay, are able to establish his identity or arrest him.

3. Pursuit shall be carried out in accordance with paragraphs 1 and 2 in one of the following ways as defined by the declaration provided for in paragraph 9:
   a) in an area or during a period as from the crossing of the border, to be established in the declaration;
   b) without limit in space or time.

4. In a declaration referred to on paragraph 9, the Contracting Parties shall define the offenses referred to on paragraph 1 in accordance with one of the following procedures:
   a) The following offences:
      - assassination,
      - murder,
      - rape,
      - arson,
      - counterfeiting,
      - armed robbery and receiving of stolen goods,
      - extortion,
      - kidnapping and hostage taking,
      - traffic in human beings,
      - illicit traffic in narcotic drugs and psychotropic substances,
      - breach of the laws on arms and explosives,
      - use of explosives,
      - illicit carriage of toxic and dangerous waste,
      - taking to flight after an accident which has resulted in death or serious injury.
   b) Extraditable offences.

5. Pursuit shall be subject to the following general conditions:
   a) The pursuing officers must comply with the provisions of this Article and with the law of the Contracting Party in whose territory they are operating: they must obey the instructions of the competent local authorities.
   b) Pursuit shall be solely over land borders.
   c) Entry into private homes and places not accessible to the public shall be prohibited.
   d) The pursuing officers shall be easily identifiable, either by their uniform or by means of an armband or by accessories fitted to their vehicle; the use of civilian clothes combined with the use of unmarked vehicles without the beforementioned identification is prohibited; the pursuing officers must at all times be able to prove that they are acting in an official capacity.
   e) The pursuing officers may carry their service weapons; their use shall be prohibited save in cases of legitimate self-defence.
   f) Once the pursued person has been apprehended as provided for in paragraph 2 (b), for the purpose of bringing him before the competent local authorities he may be subjected only to a security search; handcuffs may be used during his transfer; objects carries by the pursued person may be seized.
   g) After each operation mentioned in paragraphs 1, 2 and 3, the pursuing officers shall present themselves before the local competent authorities of the Contracting Party in whose territory they were operating and shall give an account of their mission; at the request of those authorities, they must remain at their disposal until the circumstances of their action have been adequately elucidated, this condition shall apply even where the pursuit has not resulted in the arrest of the pursued person.
   h) The authorities of the Contracting Party from which the pursuing officers have come shall, when requested by the authorities of the Contracting Party in whose territory the pursuit took place assist the enquiry subsequent to the operation in which they took part, including legal proceedings.

6. A person who, following the action provided for in paragraph 2, has been arrested by the competent local authorities may, whatever his nationality, be

held for questioning. The relevant rules of national law shall apply by analogy.

If the person is not a national of the Contracting Party in the territory of which he was arrested, he shall be released no later than six hours after his arrest, not including the hours between midnight and 9.00 in the morning, unless the competent local authorities have previously received a request for his provisional arrest for the purposes of extradition in any form whatever.

7. The officers referred to in the previous paragraphs shall be:
   - as regards the Kingdom of Belgium: members of the 'police judiciaire près les Parquets', the 'gendarmerie' and the 'police communale' as well as customs officers, under the conditions laid down in appropriate bilateral agreements referred to in paragraph 10, with respect to their powers regarding illicit traffic in narcotic drugs and psychotropic substances, traffic in arms and explosives, and the illicit carriage of toxic and dangerous waste;
   - as regards the Federal Republic of Germany: officers of the 'Polizeien des Bundes und der Länder' as wel as, with respect only to illegal traffic in narcotic drugs and psychotropic substances and arms traffic, officers of the 'Zollfahndungsdienst' custom investigation service) in their capacity as auxiliary officers of the public ministry;
   - as regards the French Republic: officers and criminal police officers of the national police and national 'gendarmerie' as well as customs officers, under the conditions laid down in the appropriate bilateral agreements referred to in paragraph 10, with respect to their powers regarding illicit traffic in narcotic drugs and psychotropic substances, traffic in arms and explosives, and

the illicit carriage of toxic and dangerous waste;
   - as regards the Grand Duchy of Luxembourg: officers of the 'gendarmerie' and the police as well as customs officers, under the conditions laid down in the appropriate bilateral agreements referred to in paragraph 10, with respect to their powers regarding illicit traffic in narcotic drugs and psychotropic substances, traffic in arms and explosives, and the illicit carriage of toxic and dangerous waste;
   - as regards the Kingdom of the Netherlands: officers of the 'Rijkspolitie' and the 'Gemeentepolitie' as well as, under the conditions laid down in the appropriate bilateral agreements referred to in paragraph 10, with respect to their powers regarding the illicit traffic in narcotic drugs and psychotropic substances, traffic in arms and explosives and the illicit carriage of toxic and dangerous waste, officers of the fiscal information and research service responsible for entry and excise duties.

8. This Article shall be without prejudice, where the Contracting Parties are concerned, to Article 27 of the Benelux Treaty of 27 June 1962 on Extradition and Mutual Assistance in Criminal Matters as amended by the Protocol of 11 May 1974.

9. On signing this Convention, each Contracting Party shall make a declaration in which it shall define, on the basis of paragraphs 2, 3 and 4 above, the procedures of implementing pursuit in its territory for each of the Contracting Parties with which it has a common border.

A Contracting Party may at any moment replace its declaration by another declaration, provided the latter does not restrict the scope of the former.

Each declaration shall be made after consultations with each of the Contracting Parties concerned and with a view to obtaining equivalent arrangements on both sides of internal borders.

10. The Contracting Parties may, on a bilateral basis, extend the scope of paragraph 1 and adopt additional provisions in implementation of this Article.

Article 42

During the operations referred to in Articles 40 and 41, officers operating on a territory of another Contracting Party shall be regarded as officers of that Party with respect to offences committed against them or by them.

Article 43

1. Where, in accordance with Articles 40 and 41 of this Convention, officers of a Contracting Party are operating in the territory of another Contracting Party, the first Contracting Party shall be responsible for any damage caused by them during the course of their mission, in accordance with the law of the Contracting Party in whose territory they are operating.

2. The Contracting Party in whose territory the damage referred to in paragraph 1 is caused shall repair such damage under the conditions applicable to damage caused by its own officers.

3. The Contracting Party whose officers have caused damage to whomsoever in the territory of another Contracting Party shall reimburse in full to the latter any sums it has paid out to the victims or other entitled persons.

4. Without prejudice to the exercise of its rights vis-à-vis third parties and without prejudice to paragraph 3, each Contrac-

ting Party shall refrain, in the case provided for in paragraph 1, from requesting reimbursement of the amount of the damages it has sustained from another Contracting Party.

Article 44

1. In accordance with the relevant international agreements and account being taken of local circumstances and the technical possibilities, the Contracting Parties shall set up, in particular in border areas, telephone, radio, and telex lines and other direct links to facilitate police and customs co-operation, in particular for the transmission of information in good time for the purposes of cross-border observation and pursuit.

2. In addition to these short-term measures, they will in particular examine the following possibilities:
   a) the exchange of equipment or the assignment of liaison officials provided with appropriate radio equipment;
   b) the widening of the frequency bands used on border areas;
   c) the establishment of a common link for police and customs services operating in these same areas;
   d) co-ordination of their programmes for the procurement of communications equipment, with a view to achieving the introduction of standardized compatible communications systems.

Article 45

1. The Contracting Parties undertake to take the measures required to guarantee that:
   a) the managers of establishments providing lodging or their employees insure that aliens accommodated therein, including nationals of the other Contracting Parties as well as those of other Member States of the European Communities, with the

exception of accompanying spouses or minors or members of travel groups, personally complete and sign declaration forms and confirm their identity by the production of a valid identity document;

b) the declaration forms thus completed will be kept for the competent authorities or forwarded to whom where such authorities deem this necessary for the prevention of threats, for criminal proceedings or to ascertain what has happened to persons who have disappeared or who have been the victim of an accident, save where national law provides otherwise.

2. Paragraph 1 shall apply by analogy to persons staying in any accommodation provided by professional lessors, in particular tents, caravans and boats.

Article 46

1. In particular cases, each Contracting Party may, in compliance with its national legislation and without being asked, send the contracting Party concerned any information which may be of interest to it in helping prevent future crime and to prevent offences against or threats to public order and security.

2. Information shall be exchanged, without prejudice to the arrangements for co-operation in border areas referred to in Article 39 (4), through a central body to be designated. In particularly urgent cases, the exchange of information within the meaning of this Article may take place directly between the police authorities concerned, save where national provisions provide otherwise. The central body shall be informed of this as soon as possible.

Article 47

1. The Contracting Parties may conclude bilateral agreements providing for the secondment, for a specified or unspecified period, of liaison officers from one Contracting Party to the police authorities of the other Contracting Party.

2. The secondment of liaison officers for a specified or unspecified period is intended to promote and to accelerate cooperation between the Contracting Parties, particularly by providing assistance.

a) in the form of the exchange of information for the purposes of fighting crime by means both of prevention and of punishment;

b) in complying with requests for mutual police assistance and legal assistance in criminal matters;

c) for the purposes of missions carried out by the authorities responsible for the surveillance of external borders.

3. Liaison officers shall have the task of giving advice and assistance. They shall not be competent to take independent police action. They shall supply information and perform their duties in accordance with the instructions given to them by the Contracting Party of origin and by the Contracting Party to which they are seconded. They shall make report regularly to the head of the police service to which they are seconded.

4. The Contracting Parties may agree within a bilateral of multilateral framework that liaison officers from a Contracting Party seconded to third States shall also represent the interests of one or more other Contracting Parties. Under such agreements, liaison officers seconded to third States shall supply information to other Contracting Parties when requested to do so or on their own initiative and shall, within the limits of their powers, perform duties on behalf of such Parties. The Contracting Parties shall inform one another of their inten-

tions as regards the secondment of liaison officers to third States.

CHAPTER 2
Mutual assistance in criminal matters

Article 48

1. The provisions of this Chapter are intended to supplement the European Convention of 20 April 1959 on Mutual Assistance in Criminal Matters as well as in relations between the contracting Parties which are members of the Benelux economic Union, Chapter II of the Benelux Treaty on Extradition and MutualAssistance in Criminal Matters of 27 June 1982, as amended by the Protocol of 11 May 1974, and to facilitate, the implementation of these agreements.

2. Paragraph 1 shall not affect the application of the broader provisions of the bilateral agreements in force between the Contracting Parties.

Article 49
Mutual assistance shall also be afforded:

a) in proceedings brought by the administrative authorities in respect of offences which are punishable in one of the two Contracting Parties or in Contracting Parties by virtue of being infringements of the rules of law, where the decision may give rise to proceedings before a criminal court;

b) in proceedings for compensation in respect of unjustified prosecution or conviction;

c) in proceedings in non-contentious matters;

d) in civil proceedings joined to criminal proceedings, as lang as the criminal court has not yet given a final ruling in the criminal proceedings;

e) to communicate legal statements relating to the execution of a sentence or measure, the imposition of a fine or the payment of costs of proceedings;

f) in respect of measures relating to the suspension of delivery of a sentence or measure, conditional release or the postponement or suspension of execution of a sentence or measure.

Article 50

1. The Contracting Parties undertake to afford each other, in accordance with the Convention and the Treaty referred to in Article 48, mutual assistance as regards infringements of their rules of law with respect to excise duty, value added tax and customs duties. Customs provisions are the rules laid down in Article 2 of the Convention of 7 September 1967 between Belgium, the Federal Republic of Germany, France, Italy, Luxembourg and the Netherlands on mutual assistance between customs administrations, as well as Article 2 of Council Regulation (EEC) No 1468/81 of 19 may 1981.

2. Requests based on evasion of excise duties may not be rejected on the grounds that the country requested does not levy excise duties on the goods referred to in the request.

3. The requesting Contracting Party shall not forward or use information or evidence obtained from the requested Contracting Party for enquiries, proceedings or procedures other than those referred to in its request, without the prior assent of the requested Contracting Party.

4. The mutual assistance provided for in this Article may be refused where the alleged amount of duty underpaid or evaded is no more than ECU 25,000 or where the presumed value of the goods exported or imported without authorization is no more than ECU 100,000, unless, given the circumstances or the identity of the accused, the case is

deemed to be extremely serious by the requesting Contracting Party.

5. The provisions of this Article shall also apply when the mutual assistance requested concerns infringements punishable only by a fine as infringements of the rule of law on proceedings brought by the administrative authorities, where the request for assistance emanates from a judicial authority.

Article 51

The Contracting Parties may not make the admissibility of letters rogatory for search or seizure dependent on conditions other than the following:

a) the offence giving rise to the letters rogatory is punishable under the law of both Contracting Parties by a custodial sentence or a security measure restricting liberty of a maximum of at least six months or is punishable under the law of one of the two Contracting Parties by an equivalent penalty and under the law of the other Contracting Party as an infringement of the regulations which is prosecuted by the administrative authorities where the decision may give rise to proceedings before a criminal court;

b) execution of the letters rogatory is consistent with the law of the requested Contracting Party.

Article 52

1. Each Contracting Party may address procedural documents directly by post to persons who are in the territory of another Contracting Party. The Contracting Parties shall send the Executive Committee a list of the documents which may be forwarded in this way.

2. Where there is reason to believe that the addressee does not understand the language in which the document is drafted, the document — or at least the important passages in it — must be translated into (one of) the language (s) of the

Contracting Party in the territory of which the addressee is staying. If the authority forwarding the document knows that the addressee speaks only another language, the document — or at least the important passages thereof — must be translated in that other language.

3. An expert or witness who has failed to answer a summons to appear, sent to him by post, shall not, even if the summons contains a notice of penalty, be subjected to any punishment or measure of restraint, unless subsequently he voluntarily enters the territory of the requesting Party and is there again duly summoned. The authority sending a summons to appear by post shall ensure that it does not involve penalties. This provision shall be without prejudice to Article 34 of theBenelux Treaty on Extradition and Mutual Assistance in Criminal Matters of 27 June 1962 as amended by the Protocol of 11 May 1974.

4. If the offence on which the request for assistance is based is punishable under the law of both contracting Parties as an infringement of the regulations which is being prosecuted by the administrative authorities where the decision may give rise to proceedings before a criminal court, the procedure outlined in paragraph 1 must in principle be used for the forwarding of procedural documents.

5. Notwithstanding paragraph 1, procedural documents may be forwarded through the legal authorities of the requested Contracting Party where the addressee's address is unknown or where the requesting Contracting Party requires a formal service.

Article 53

1. Requests for assistance may be made directly between legal authorities and returned through the same channels.

2. Paragraph 1 shall not prejudice the possibility of requests being sent and returned between Ministries of Justice or through the intermediary of national central offices of the International Criminal Police Organization.

3. Requests for the temporary transfer or transit of persons provisionally under arrest or detained or who are the subject of a measure depriving them of their liberty, and the periodic or occasional exchange of data from the judicial records must be effected through the Ministries of Justice.

4. Within the meaning of the European Convention of 20 April 1959 on Mutual Assistance in Criminal Matters, Ministry of Justice means, where the Federal Republic of Germany is concerned, the Federal Minister of Justice and the Justice Ministers or Senators of the Federal States.

5. Information laid with a view to proceedings in respect of infringements of the legislation on driving and rest time, in accordance with Article 21 of the European convention of 20 April 1959 on Mutual Assistance in Criminal Matters or with Article 42 of the Benelux Treaty on Extradition and Mutual Assistance in Criminal Matters of 27 June 1962, as amended by the Protocol of 11 May 1974, may be sent by the legal authorities of the requesting Contracting Party directly to the legal authorities of the requested Contracting Party.

CHAPTER 3

Application of the Non bis in idem principle

Article 54

A person who has been finally judged by a Contracting Party may not be prosecuted by another Contracting Party for the same offences provided that, where he is sentenced, the sentence has been served or is currently being served or can no longer be carried out under the sentencing laws of the Contracting Party.

Article 55

1. A Contracting Party may, when ratifying, accepting or approving this Convention, declare that it is not bound by Article 54 in one or more of the following cases:

   a) where the acts to which the foreign judgment relates tool place in whole or in part in its own territory; in the latter case, this exception shall not however apply if the acts took place in part in the territory of the Contracting Party where the judgment was given;

   b) where the acts to which the foreign judgment relates constitute an offence against State security or other equally essential interests of that Contracting Party;

   c) where the acts to which the foreign judgment relates were committed by an official of that Contracting Party in violation of the obligations of his office.

2. A Contracting Party which has made a declaration regarding the exception referred to on paragraph 1 (b) shall specify the categories of offences to which this exception may apply.

3. A Contracting Party may at any moment withdraw a declaration relating to one or more of the exceptions referred to in paragraph 1.

4. The exceptions which were the subject of a declaration under paragraph 1 shall not apply where the Contracting Party concerned has, in respect of the same acts, requested the other Contracting Party to prosecute or has granted the extradition of the person concerned.

Article 56

If further proceedings are brought by a Contracting Party against a person who has been finally judged for the same offences by another Contracting Party, any period of deprivation of liberty served on the territory of the latter Contracting Party on account of the offences in question must be deducted from any sentence handed down. Account will also be taken, to the extent that national legislation permits, of sentences other than periods of imprisonment already undergone.

Article 57

1. Where a Contracting Party accuses an individual of an offence and the competent authorities of that Contracting Party have reason to believe that the accusation relates to the same offences as those for which the individual has already been finally fudged by another Contracting Party, these authorities shall, if they deem it necessary, request the relevant information from the competent authorities of the Contracting Party in whose territory judgment has already been delivered.

2. The information requested shall be provided as soon as possible and shall be taken into consideration as regards further action to be taken in the proceedings in progress.

3. At the time of ratification, acceptance or approval of this Convention, each Contracting Party will nominate the authorities which will be authorized to request and receive the information provided for in this Article.

Article 58

The above provisions shall not preclude the application of wider national provisions on the 'non bis in idem' effect attached to legal decisions taken abroad.

CHAPTER 4
Extradition

Article 59

1. The provisions of this Chapter are intended to supplement the European Convention of 13 September 1957 on Extradition as well as, in relations between the Contracting Parties which are members of the Benelux Economic Union, Chapter I of the Benelux Treaty on Extradition and Mutual Assistance in Criminal Matters of 27 June 1962, as amended by the Protocol of 11 May 1974 and to facilitate the implementation of these agreements.

2. Paragraph 1 shall not affect the application of the broader provisions of the bilateral agreements in force between Contracting Parties.

Article 60

In relations between two Contracting Parties, one of which is not a party to the European Convention on Extradition of 13 September 1957, the provisions of the said convention shall apply, subject to the reservations and declarations made at the time of ratifying this Convention or, for Contracting Parties which are not parties to the Convention, at the time of ratifying, approving or accepting the present Convention.

Article 61

The French Republic undertakes to extradite, at the request of one of the Contracting Parties, persons against whom proceedings are being taken for offences punishable under French law by deprivation of liberty or under a detention order for a maximum period of at least two years and under the law of the requesting Contracting Party by deprivation of liberty or under a detention order for a maximum period of at least a year.

Article 62

1. As regards interruption of prescription only the provisions of the requesting Contracting Party shall apply.

2. An amnesty granted by the requested Contracting Party shall not prevent extradition unless the offence falls within the jurisdiction of that Contracting Party.

3. The absence of a charge or an official notice authorizing proceedings, necessary only under the legislation of the requested Contracting Party, shall not affect the obligation to extradite.

Article 63

The Contracting Parties undertake, in accordance with the Convention and the Treaty referred to in article 59, to extradite between themselves persons being prosecuted by the legal authorities of the requesting Contracting Party for one of the offences referred to on Article 50 (1), or being sought by them for the purposes of execution of a sentence or detention order imposed in respect of such an offence.

Article 64

A report included in the Schengen Information System in accordance with Article 95 shall have the same force as a request for provisions arrest under Article 16 of the European Convention on Extradition of 13 September 1957 or Article 15 of the Benelux Treaty on Extradition and Mutual Assistance in Criminal Matters of 27 June 1962, as amended by the Protocol of 11 May 1974.

Article 65

1. Without prejudice to the option to use the diplomatic channel,requests for extradition and transit shall be sent by the relevant Ministry of the requesting Contracting Party to the relevant Ministry of the requested Contracting Party.

2. The relevant Ministries shall be:
   - as regards the Kingdom of Belgium: the Ministry of Justice;
   - as regards the Federal Republic of Germany: the Federal Ministry of Justice and the Justice Ministers or Senators of the Federal States;
   - as regards the French Republic: The Ministry of Foreign Affairs;
   - as regards the Grand Duchy of Luxembourg: the Ministry of Justice;
   - as regards the Kingdom of the Netherlands: the Ministry of Justice.

Article 66

1. If the extradition of a wanted person is not obviously prohibited under the laws of the requested Contracting Party, that Contracting Party may authorize extradition without formal extradition proceedings, provided that the wanted person agrees thereto in a statement made before a member of the judiciary after being examined by the latter and informed of his right to formal extradition proceedings. The wanted person may have access to a lawyer during such examination.

2. In cases of extradition under paragraph 1, a wanted person who explicitly states that he will not invoke the rule of speciality may not revoke that statement.

CHAPTER 5
Transfer of the execution of criminal judgments

Article 67

The following provisions shall apply between the Contracting Parties who are parties to the Council of Europe Convention of 21 March 1983 on the Transfer of Sentenced Persons, for the purposes of supplementing that Convention.

Article 68

1. The Contracting Party in whose territory a sentence of deprivation of liberty or a detention order has been imposed in a judgment which has obtained the force of res judicata in respect of a national of another Contracting Party who, by escaping to his own country, had avoided the execution of that sentence or detention order, may request the latter Contracting Party, if the escaped person is in its territory, to take over the execution of the sentence or of the detention order.

2. The requested Contracting Party may, at the request of the requesting Contracting Party, prior to the arrival of the documents supporting the request that the execution of the sentence or of the detention order or part of the sentence be taken over, and prior to the decision on that request, take the convicted person into police custody or take other measures to ensure that he remains in the territory of the requested Contracting Party.

Article 69

The transfer of execution under Article 68 shall not require the consent of the person on whom the sentence or the detention order has been imposed. The other provisions of the Council of Europe Convention of 21 March 1983 on the Transfer of Sentenced Persons shall apply by analogy.

CHAPTER 6
Narcotic drugs

Article 70

1. The Contracting Parties shall set up a permanent working party to examine common problems relating to the combating of offences involving narcotic drugs and to draw up proposals, where necessary, to improve the practical and technical aspects of co-operation between the Contracting Parties. The working party shall submit its proposals to the Executive Committee

2. The working party referred to in paragraph 1, the members of which are nominated by the relevant national authorities, shall include representatives of the police and of the customs authorities.

Article 71

1. The Contracting Parties undertake as regards the direct or indirect sale of narcotic drugs and psychotropic substances of whatever type, including cannabis, and the possession of such products and substances for sale or export, to take, in compliance with the existing United Nations Conventions,[*] all measures necessary for the prevention and punishment of the illicit traffic in narcotic drugs and psychotropic substances.

2. The Contracting Parties undertake to prevent and to punish by administrative and penal measures the illegal export of narcotic drugs and psychotropic substances, including cannabis, as well as the sale, supply and handling of such products and substances, without prejudice to the relevant provisions of Articles 74, 75 and 76.

3. To combat the illegal importation of narcotic drugs and psychotropic substances, including cannabis, the Contracting Parties shall strengthen the checks on the movement of persons and goods and of means of transport at their external borders. such measures shall be drawn up by the working party provided for in Article 70. This working party

---

[*] Single Conventions on Narcotic Drugs of 1961 as amended by the 1972 Protocol amending the 1961 Single Convention on Narcotic Drugs, the 1971 Convention on Psychotropic Substances, the United Nations Convention of 20 December 1988 on Illicit Traffic in Narcotic Drugs and Psychotropic Substances.

shall consider inter alia the reassignment of some of the police and customs staff released from internalborder duty, as well as recourse to modem drug-detection methods and sniffer dogs.

4. To ensure compliance with this Article, the contracting Parties shall specifically maintain surveillance on places known to be used for drug trafficking.

5. The Contracting Parties shall do all in their power to prevent and combat the negative effects of the illicit demand for narcotic drugs and psychotropic substances of whatever kind, including cannabis. The measures adopted to this end shall be the responsibility of each Contracting Party.

Article 72

The Contracting Parties shall, in accordance with their constitution and their national legal system, ensure that legislation is enacted to permit the seizure and confiscation of assets deriving from illicit traffic in narcotic drugs and psychotropic substances.

Article 73

1. The Contracting Parties undertake, in accordance with their constitution and their national legal system, to take measures to allow monitored deliveries to take place in the illicit traffic in narcotic drugs and psychotropic substances.

2. In each individual case, a decision to allow monitored deliveries will be taken on the basis of prior authorization by each of the Contracting Parties concerned.

3. Each Contracting Party shall retain responsibility for and control over the operation on its own territory and shall be empowered to intervene.

Article 74

With respect to legal trade in narcotic drugs and psychotropic substances, the Contracting Parties agree to transfer inside the country, wherever possible, checks conducted at the border and arising from obligations under the United Nations Conventions listed in Article 71.

Article 75

1. As regards the movement of travellers to the territory of the Contracting Parties or within such territory, individuals may carry narcotic drugs and psychotropic substances in connection with medical treatment, provided they produce at any check a certificate issued or authenticated by a competent authority of the State of residence.

2. The Executive Committee shall adopt the form and content of the certificate referred to in paragraph 1 and issued by one of the Contracting Parties, with particular reference to the data regarding the nature and quantity of the products and substances and the duration of the journey.

3. The Contracting Parties shall notify each other of the authorities responsible for the issue and authentication of the certificate referred to on paragraph 2.

Article 76

1. The Contracting Parties shall, if necessary, and in accordance with their medical, ethical and practical usage, adopt the appropriate measures for the monitoring of narcotic drugs and psychotropic substances subjected in the territory of one or more Contracting Party to more rigorous checks than in their own territory so that the effectiveness of such checks is not prejudiced.

2. Paragraph 1 shall also apply to substances frequently used for the man-

ufacture of narcotic drugs and psychotropic substances.

3. The Contracting Parties shall notify each other of the measures taken in order to monitor the legal trade in the substances referred to in paragraphs 1 and 2.

4. Problems experienced in this connection shall be regularly raised in the Executive Committee.

CHAPTER 7
Firearms and ammunition

Article 77

1. The Contracting Parties undertake to bring into line with the provisions of this Chapter their national laws, regulations and administrative provisions relating to the purchase, possession, sale and surrender of firearms and ammunition.

2. This Chapter covers the purchase, possession, sale and surrender of firearms and ammunition by natural and legal persons; it does not cover their supply to the central and territorial authorities, the armed force or the police, nor the purchase or possession by them of firearms and ammunition nor the manufacture of firearms and ammunition by public undertakings.

Article 78

1. For the purposes of this Chapter, firearms shall be classified as follows:
   a) prohibited arms,
   b) arms subject to authorization,
   c) arms subject to declaration.

2. The locking mechanism, the magazine and the barrel of firearms shall be subject mutatis mutandis to the provisions which apply to the weapon of which they form or are intended to form a part.

3. For the purposes of this Convention, 'short firearms' means firearms with a barrel which is not more than 30 cm long or with a total length of not more than 60 cm; 'long firearms' means all other firearms.

Article 79

1. The list of prohibited firearms and ammunition shall include the following items:
   a) firearms normally used as war firearms;
   b) automatic firearms, even if they are not war firearms;
   c) firearms disguised as other items;
   d) armour-piercing, explosive or incendiary ball ammunition and projectiles for such ammunition;
   e) ammunition for pistols and revolvers with dum-dum or hollow-pointed projectiles and such projectiles.

2. The competent authorities may, in special cases, grant authorizations for the firearms and ammunition referred to on paragraph 1, if public order and security do not preclude it.

Article 80

1. The list of firearms, the purchase and possession of which is subject to authorization, shall include at least the following firearms if they are not prohibited:
   a) semi-automatic or repeater short firearms;
   b) single-shot short firearms with centrefire;
   c) single-shot short firearms with rimfire, with a total length under 28 cm;
   d) semi-automatic long firearms of which the magazine and chamber can contain more than three cartridges;
   e) repeater semi-automatic long firearms with a smoothbore barrel, the barrel of which is not longer than 60 cm;

f) semi-automatic civilian firearms which resemble automatic war firearms.

2. The list of firearms subject to authorization shall not include:
   a) arms used as warning devices, teargas guns or alarms, provided that it can be technically proved that such arms cannot be concerted, using ordinary tools, to fire ball ammunition and provided the firing of an irritant substance does not cause irreversible injury to persons;
   b) semi-automatic long firearms of which the magazine and chamber cannot contain more than three cartridges without being reloaded, provided that the loader is immovable or that it can be proved these firearms cannot be converted, using ordinary tools, into firearms of which the magazine and chamber can contain more than three cartridges.

Article 81
The list of firearms subject to declaration shall include, if such arms are neither prohibited nor subject to authorization:
a) repeater long firearms;
b) single-shot long firearms with a rifled barrel or barrels;
c) single-shot short firearms with rimfire with a total length exceeding 28 cm;
d) the arms listed in Article 80 (2)(b).

Article 82
The list of arms referred to in Articles 79, 80 and 81 shall not include:

a) firearms, the model or year of manufacture of which, save in exceptional cases, predates 1 January 1870, provided that they cannot fire ammunition intended for prohibited or authorized arms;
b) reproduction of arms under (a), provided what they cannot be used with metal-case cartridges;

c) firearms adapted, in accordance with technical procedures guaranteed by the stamp of an official body or recognized by such a body, so that they cannot fire ammunition.

Article 83
A permit to purchase and possess a firearm listed in Article 80 may be issued only:
a) if the person concerned is over 18 years of age, with the exception of dispensations for hunting and sport purposes;
b) if the person concerned is not unfit to purchase or possess a firearm as a result of mental illness or any other mental or physical disability;
c) if the person concerned has not been convicted of an offence or if there are no other indications that he might be a danger to public order and security;
d) if the reasons given by the person concerned for purchasing or possessing firearms can be considered legitimate.

Article 84
1. Declarations in respect of the firearms mentioned in Article 81 shall be entered in a register kept by the persons referred to in Article 85.

2. If a firearms is disposed of by a person not referred to in Article 85, a declaration of disposal must be made in accordance with the detailed rules to be laid down by each Contracting Party.

3. The declarations referred to in this Article must contain the necessary details to identify the persons and the arms concerned.

Article 85
1. The Contracting Parties undertake to subject to an obligation of authorization persons who manufacture firearms subject to authorization and persons selling such firearms, and to subject to an obligation of declaration persons who manufacture firearms subject to

declaration and persons selling such firearms. Authorization in respect offirearms subject to authorization shall also cover firearms subject to declaration. The Contracting Parties shall make effective checks on persons who manufacture arms and persons who sell arms.

2. The Contracting Parties undertake to adopt measures to ensure that, as a minimum requirement, all firearms are marked durably with a serial number permitting their identification and carry the manufacturer's mark.

3. The Contracting Parties shall oblige manufacturers and dealers to keep a register of all firearms subject to authorization or to declaration; the register must make it possible rapidly to determine the nature of firearms, their origin and the purchaser.

4. As regards firearms subject to authorization subject to Articles 79 and 80, the Contracting Parties undertake to adopt measures to ensure that the serial number and the manufacturer's mark on the firearm are reproduced on the permit supplied to its holder.

Article 86

1. The Contracting Parties undertake to adopt measures prohibiting legitimate holders of firearm subject to authorization or declaration from transferring these arms to persons not holding a permit for their purchase or a declaration certificate.

2. The Contracting Parties may authorize the temporary transfer of such firearms in accordance with procedures which they lay down.

Article 87

1. The Contracting Parties shall incorporate in their national legislation provi-

sions permitting permits to be withdrawn from persons who no longer satisfy the conditions for the issue of permits laid down in Article 83.

2. The Contracting Parties undertake to take appropriate measures, including seizure of firearms and withdrawal of permits and to punish in an appropriate way infringements of the laws and administrative provisions applicable to firearms. Such penalties may provide for the confiscation of firearms.

Article 88

1. Persons who have a permit to purchase a firearm shall not require an authorization to purchase ammunition for such firearms

2. The purchase of ammunition by persons who do not have a permit to purchase arms shall be subject to the system governing the arm for which the ammunition is intended. Such authorization may cover a single category or all categories of ammunition.

Article 89

The lists of firearms which are prohibited, subject to authorization or subject to declaration may be amended or supplemented by the Executive Committee to take account of technical developments, economic trends and State security.

Article 90

The Contracting Parties shall have the right to adopt more stringent laws and provisions on the purchase and possession of firearms ammunition.

Article 91

1. The Contracting Parties agreed, on the basis of the European Convention of 28 June 1978 on the Control of the Acquisition and Possession of Firearms by

change of information on the acquisition of firearms by persons — whether private individuals or retailing gunsmiths — normally resident or established in the territory of another Contracting Party. A retailing gunsmith is deemed to be any person whose professional activity consists, in whole or in part, in trade in or the retailing of firearms.

2. The exchange of information shall concern:
   a) between two Contracting Parties having ratified the Convention referred to in paragraph 1, the firearms listed in Annex 1 (A)(1)(a) to (h) of that Convention;
   b) between two Contracting Parties at least one of which has not ratified the Convention referred to in paragraph 1, firearms which are subject to authorization or declaration in each of the Contracting Parties.

3. Information regarding the acquisition of firearms shall be communicated without delay and shall include the following data:
   a) the date of the acquisition and the identity of the purchaser, viz.:
      — in the case of a physical person: name, forenames, date and place of birth, address and passport or identity card number, and date of issue and indication of the issuing authority, whether gunsmith or not;
      — in the case of a legal person: the name or business name and registered place of business as well as the name, forenames, date and place of birth, address and passport or identity card number of the person authorized to represent the legal person;
   b) the model, manufacturer's number, calibre and other characteristics of the firearm in question as well as its serial number.

4. Each Contracting Party shall designate the national authority responsible for sending and receiving the information referred to in paragraph 2 and 3 and shallnotify the other Contracting Parties without delay of any change in the identity of that authority.

5. The authority designated by each Contracting Party may forward the information notified to it to the competent local police authorities and to the authorities responsible for checks at the borders, for the purposes of preventing or prosecuting punishable offences and breaches of the rules.

TITLE IV
The Schengen Information System

CHAPTER 1
Setting up of the Schengen Information System

Article 92

1. The Contracting Parties shall set up and maintain a joint information system, hereinafter referred to as the Schengen Information System, consisting of a national section in each of the Contracting Parties and a technical support function. The Schengen Information System shall enable the authorities designated by the Contracting Parties, by means of an automated search procedure, to have access to reports on persons and objects for the purposes of border checks and controls and other police and customs checks carried out within the country in accordance with national law and, in the case of the single category of report referred to on Article 96, for the purposes of issuing visas, the issue of residence permits and the administration of aliens in the context of the application of the provisions of this Convention relating to the movement of persons.

2. Each Contracting Party shall set up and maintain, for its own account and at its own risk, its national section of the Schengen Information System, the data file of which shall be made materially identical to the data files of the national sections of each of the other Contracting Parties using the technical support function. To ensure the rapid and effective transmission of data as referred to on paragraph 3, each Contracting Party shall observe, when creating its national section, the protocols and procedures which the Contracting Parties have jointly established for the technical support function. Each national section's data file shall be available for the purposes of automated search in the territory of each of the Contracting Parties. It shall not be possible to search the data files of other Contracting Parties' national sections.

3. The Contracting Parties shall set up and maintain jointly and with joint liability for risks, the technical support function of the Schengen Information System, the responsibility for which shall be assumed by the French Republic; the technical support function shall be located in Strasbourg. The technical support function shall comprise a data file which ensures that the data files of the national sections are kept identical by the on-line transmission of information. The data file of the technical support function shall contain reports on persons and objects where these concern all the Contracting Parties. The data file of the technical support function shall contain no data other than those referred to in this paragraph and in Article 113 (2).

CHAPTER 2
Operation and utilization of the Schengen Information System

Article 93
The purpose of the Schengen Information System shall be in accordance with this convention to maintain public order and security, including State security, and to apply the provisions of this Convention relating to the movement of persons, in the territories of the Contracting Parties, using information transmitted by the system.

Article 94
1. The Schengen Information System shall contain only the categories of data which are supplied by each of the Contracting Parties and are required for the purposes laid down in Articles 95 to 100. The Contracting Party providing a report shall determine whether the importance of the case warrants the inclusion of the report in the Schengen Information System.

2. The categories of data shall be as follows:
   a) persons reported
   b) objects referred to in Article 100 and vehicles referred to in Article 99.

3. The items included in respect of persons, shall be no more than the following:
   a) name and forename, any aliases possibly registered separately;
   b) any particular objective and permanent physical features;
   c) first letter of second forename;
   d) date and place of birth;
   e) sex;
   f) nationality;
   g) whether the persons concerned are armed;
   h) whether the persons concerned are violent;
   i) reason for the report;
   j) action to be taken.

Other references, in particular the data listed in Article 6, first sentence of the Council of Europe Convention of 28 January 1981 for the Protection of Individuals with regard to Automatic Processing of Personal data, shall not be authorized.

4. Insofar as a Contracting Party considers that a report in accordance with Articles 95, 97 or 99 is incompatible with its national law, its international obligations or essential national interests, it may subsequently add to the report in the data file of the national section of the Schengen Information system a note to the effect that the action referred to will not be taken in its territory in connection with the report. Consultations must be held in this connection with the other Contracting Parties. If the reporting Contracting Party does not withdraw the report it will continue to apply in full for the other Contracting Parties.

Article 95

1. Data relating to persons wanted for arrest for extradition purposes shall be included at the request of the judicial authority of the requesting Contracting Party.

2. Prior to making a report, the reporting Contracting Party shall check whether the arrest is authorized by the national law of the requested Contracting Parties. If the reporting Contracting Party has doubts, it must consult the other Contracting Parties concerned.

   The reporting Contracting Party shall send the requested Contracting Parties together with the report, by the swiftest means, the following essential information relating to the case:
   a) the authority which issued the request for arrest;
   b) whether there is an arrest warrant or a document having the dame force, or an enforceable judgment;

c) the nature and legal classification of the offence;
d) a description of the circumstances in which the offence was committed, including the time, place and degree of participation in the offence by the person reported;
e) as far as possible, the consequences of the offence.

3. A requested Contracting Party may add to the report in the file of the national section of the Schengen Information system a note prohibiting arrest in connection with the report, until such time as the note is deleted. The note shall be deleted no later than 24 hours after the report is included, unless the Contracting Party refuses to make the requested arrest on legal grounds or for special reasons of expediency. Where, in particularly exceptional cases, this is justified by the complexity of the facts underlying the report, the above time limit may be extended to one week. without prejudice to a qualifying note or a decision to refuse arrest, the other Contracting Parties may make the arrest requested in the report.

4. If, for particularly urgent reasons, a Contracting Party requests an immediate search, the Party requested shall examine whether it is able to withdraw its note, The Contracting Party requested shall take the necessary steps to ensure that the action to be taken can be carried out without delay if the report is validated.

5. If the arrest cannot be made because an investigation has not been completed or owing to a refusal by the requested Contracting Party, the latter must regard the report as being a report for the purposes of communicating the place of residence of the person concerned.

6. The requested Contracting Parties shall carry out the action to be taken as requested in the report in compliance with extradition Conventions in force and with national law. They shall not be required to carry out the action requested where one of their nationals is involved, without prejudice to the possibility of making the arrest in accordance with national law.

Article 96

1. Data relating to aliens who are reported for the purposes of being refused entry shall be included on the basis of a national report resulting from decisions taken, in compliance with the rules of procedure laid down by national legislation, by the administrative authorities or courts responsible.

2. Decisions may be based on a threat to public order or national security and safety which the presence of an alien in national territory may pose.

   Such may in particular be the case with:
   a) an alien who has been convicted of an offence carrying a custodial sentence of at least one year;
   b) an alien who, there are serious grounds for believing, has committed serious offences, including those referred to on Article 71, or against whom there is genuine evidence of an intention to commit such offenses in the territory of a Contracting Party.

3. Decisions may also be based on the fact that the alien has been the subject of a deportation, removal or expulsion measure which has not been rescinded or suspended, including or accompanied by a prohibition on entry or, where appropriate, residence, based on non-compliance with national regulations on the entry or residence of aliens.

Article 97

Data relating to persons who have disappeared or to persons who, in the interests of their own protection or in order to prevent threats, need to be placed provisionally in a place of safety at the request of the competent authority or the competent judicial authority of the reporting Party, shall be included in order that the police authorities can communicate their whereabouts to the reporting Party or can remove the person to a place of safety for the purposes of preventing him from continuing his journey, if so authorized by national legislation. This shall apply in particular to minors and to persons who must be interned by decision of a competent authority. Communication of the information shall be subject to the consent of the person who has disappeared, if of full age.

Article 98

1. Data relating to witnesses, to persons summoned to appear before the judicial authorities in connection with criminal proceedings in order to account for acts for which they are being prosecuted, or to persons who are to be notified of a criminal judgment or of a summons to appear in order to serve custodial sentence, shall be included, at the request of the competent judicial authorities, for the purposes of communicating their place of residence or domicile.

2. Information requested shall be communicated to the requesting Party in accordance with national legislation and with the Conventions in force concerning mutual judicial assistance in criminal matters.

Article 99

1. Data relating to persons or vehicles shall be included, in compliance with the national law of the reporting Contracting Party, for the purposes of discreet surveillance or specific checks, in accordance with paragraph 5.

2. Such a report may be made for the purposes of prosecuting criminal offenses and for the prevention of threats to public safety:

a) where there are real indication to suggest that the person concerned intends to commit or is committing numerous and extremely serious offences, or

b) where an overall evaluation of the person concerned, in particular on the basis of offences committed hitherto, gives reason to suppose that he will also commit extremely serious offenses in future.

3. In addition, a report may be made in accordance with national law, at the request of the authorities responsible for State security, where concrete evidence gives reason to suppose that the information referred to on paragraph 4 is necessary for the prevention of a serious threat by the person concerned or other serious threats to internal or external State security. The reporting Contracting Party shall be required to consult the other Contracting Parties beforehand.

4. For the purposes of discreet surveillance, the following information may in whole or in part be collected and transmitted to the reporting authority when border checks or other police and customs checks are carried out within the country:

a) the fact that the person reported or the vehicle reported has been found;

b) the place, time or reason for the check;

c) the route and destination of the journey;

d) persons accompanying the person concerned or occupants of the vehicle;

e) the vehicle used;

f) objects carried;

g) the circumstances under which the person or the vehicle was found.

When such information is collected, steps must be taken to ensure that the discreet nature of the surveillance is not jeopardized.

5. In the context of the specific checks referred to in paragraph 1, persons, vehicles and objects carried may be searched in accordance with national law, in order to achieve the purpose referred to in paragraphs 2 and 3. If the specific check is not authorized in accordance with the law of a Contracting Party, it shall automatically be converted, for that Contracting Party, into discreet surveillance.

6. A requested Contracting Party may add to the report in the file of the national section of the Schengen Information System a note prohibiting, until the note is deleted, performance of the action to be taken pursuant to the report for the purposes of discreet surveillance or specific checks. The note must be deleted no later than 24 hours after the report has been included unless the Contracting Party refuses to take the action requested on legal grounds or for special reasons of expediency. Without prejudice to a qualifying note or a refusal decision, the other Contracting Parties may carry out the action requested in the report.

Article 100

1. Data relating to objects sought for the purposes of seizure or of evidence in criminal proceedings shall be included in the Schengen Information System.

2. If a search brings to light the existence of a report on an item which has been found, the authority noticing the report shall contact the reporting authority in order to agree on the requisite measures. For this purpose, personal data may also be transmitted in accordance with this Convention. The measures to be taken

by the Contracting Party which found the object must comply with its national law.

3. The categories of object listed below shall be included:
   a) motor vehicles with a capacity in excess of 50 cc which have been stolen, misappropriated or lost;
   b) trailers and caravans with an unladen weight in excess of 750 kg which have been stolen, misappropriated or lost;
   c) firearms which have been stolen, misappropriated or lost;
   d) blank documents which have been stolen, misappropriated or lost;
   e) identification documents issued (passports, identity cards, driving licences) which have been stolen, misappropriated or lost;
   f) bank notes (registered notes).

Article 101

1. Access to data included in the Schengen Information System and the right to search such data directly shall be reserved exclusively for the authorities responsible for
   a) border checks;
   b) other police and customs checks carried out within the country, and the co-ordination of such checks.

2. In addition, access to data included in accordance with Article 96 and the right to search such data directly may be exercised by the authorities responsible for issuing visas,, the central authorities responsible for examining vasa applications and the authorities responsible for issuing residence permits and the administration of aliens within the framework of the application of the provisions on the movement of persons under this Convention. Access to data shall be governed by the national law of each Contracting Party.

3. Users may only search data which are necessary for the performance of their tasks.

4. Each of the Contracting Parties shall communicate to the Executive Committee a list of the competent authorities which are authorized to search the data included in the Schengen Information directly. That list shall indicate for each authority the data which it may search, and for what purposes.

CHAPTER 3
Protection of personal data and security of data under the Schengen Information System

Article 102

1. The Contracting Parties may use the data provided for in Articles 95 to 100 only for the purposes laid down for each type of report referred to in those Articles.

2. Data may be duplicated only for technical purposes, provided that such duplication is necessary for direct searching by the authorities referred to on Article 101. Reports by other Contracting Parties may not be copied from the national section of the Schengen Information System in other national data files.

3. In connection with the types of report provided for in Articles 95 to 100 of this Convention, any derogation from paragraph 1 in order to change from one type of report to another must be justified by the need to prevent an imminent serious threat to public order and safety, for serious reasons of State security or for the purposes of preventing a serious offence. The prior authorization of the reporting Contracting Party must be obtained for this purpose.

4. Data may not be used for administrative purposes. By way of derogation, data included in accordance with Article 96 may be used, in accordance with the national law of each of the Contracting Parties, only for the purposes of Article 101 (2).

5. Any use of data which does not comply with paragraphs 1 to 4 shall be considered as a misuse in relation to the national law of each Contracting Party.

Article 103

Each Contracting Party shall ensure that, on average, every tenth transmission of personal data is recorded in the national section of the Schengen Information System by the data file managing authority for the purposes of checking the admissibility of searching. The recording may be used only for this purpose and shall be deleted after six months.

Article 104

1. The law applying to reports shall be the national law of the reporting Contracting Party, unless more rigorous conditions are laid down in this Convention.

2. In so far as this Convention does not lay down specific provisions, the law of each Contracting Party shall apply to data included in the national section of the Schengen Information System.

3. In so far as this Convention does not lay down specific provisions concerning performance of the action requested in the report, the national law of the Contracting Party requested which carries out the action shall apply. In so far as this Convention lays down specific provisions concerning performance of the action requested in the report, responsibility for the action to be taken shall be governed by the national law of the requested Contracting Party. If the action requested cannot be performed,

the requested Contracting Party shall inform the reporting Contracting Party without delay.

Article 105

The reporting Contracting Party shall be responsible for the accuracy, up-to-dateness and lawfulness of the inclusion of data in the Schengen Information System.

Article 106

1. Only the reporting Contracting Party shall be authorized to amend, supplement, correct or delete data which it had introduced.

2. If one of the Contracting Parties which has not made the report has evidence to suggest that an item of data is legally or factually inaccurate, it shall advise the reporting Contracting Party thereof as soon as possible; the latter must check the communication and, if necessary, correct or delete the item in question without delay.

3. If the Contracting Parties are unable to reach agreement, the Contracting Party which did not generate the report shall submit the case to the joint supervisory authority referred to in Article 115 (1) for its opinion.

Article 107

Where a person has already been the subject of a report in the Schengen Information System, a Contracting Party which introduces a further report shall come to an agreement on the inclusion of the reports with the Contracting Party which introduced the first report. The Contracting Parties may also adopt general provisions to this end.

Article 108

1. Each of the Contracting Parties shall designate an authority which shall have central responsibility for the national section of the Schengen Information System.

2. Each of the Contracting Parties shall make its reports via that authority.

3. The said authority shall be responsible for the correct operation of the national section of the Schengen Information system and shall take the measures neces-sary to ensure compliance with the provisions of this Convention.

4. The Contracting Parties shall inform one another, via the Depositary, of the authority referred to in paragraph 1.

Article 109

1. The right of any person to have access to data relating to him which are included in the Schengen Information System shall be exercised in accordance with the law of the Contracting Party before which it invokes that right. If the national law so provides, the national supervisory authority provided for in Article 114 (1) shall decide whether information shall be communicated and by what procedures. A Contracting Party which has not made the report may communicate information concerning such data only if it has previously given the reporting contracting Party an opportunity to state its position.

2. Communication of information to the person concerned shall be refused if it may undermine the performance of the legal task specified in the report, or in order to protect the rights and freedoms of others. It shall be refused in any event during the period of reporting for the purposes of discreet surveillance.

Article 110

Any person may have factually inaccurate data relating to him corrected or have legally inaccurate data relating to him deleted.

Article 111

1. Any person may, in the territory of each Contracting Party, bring before the courts or the authority competent under national law an action to correct, delete or provide information or obtain compensation in connection with a report concerning him.

2. The Contracting Parties shall undertake amongst themselves to execute final decisions taken by the courts or authorities referred to on paragraph 1, without prejudice to the provisions of Article 116.

Article 112

1. Personal data included in the Schengen Information System for the purposes of locating persons shall be kept only for the time required to achieve the purposes for which they were supplied. No later than three years after their inclusion, the need for their retention must be reviewed by the reporting Contracting Party. This period shall be one year in the case of reports referred to in Article 99.

2. Each of the Contracting Parties shall, where appropriate, set shorter review periods in accordance with its national law.

3. The technical support function of the Schengen Information System shall automatically inform the Contracting Parties of a scheduled deletion of data from the system, giving one month's notice.

4. The reporting Contracting Party may, within the review period, decide to retain the report if its retention is necessary for the purposes for which the report was made. Any extension of the report must be communicated to the technical support function. The provisions of paragraph 1 shall apply to report extension.

Article 113

1. Data other than those referred to in Article 112 shall be retained for a maximum of ten years, data relating to identity documents issued and to registered bank notes for a maximum of five years and those relating to motor vehicles, trailers and caravans for a maximum of three years.

2. Data deleted shall continue to be retained for one year in the technical support function. During that period they may be consulted only for the purposes of subsequently checking their accuracy and the lawfulness of their inclusion. Afterwards they must be destroyed.

Article 114

1. Each Contracting Party shall designate a supervisory authority responsible, in compliance with national law, for carrying out independent supervision of the data file of the national section of the Schengen Information System and for checking that the processing and utilization of data included in the Schengen Information System are not in violation of the rights of the person concerned. For this purpose the supervisory authority shall have access to the data file of the national section of the Schengen Information System.

2. Any person shall have the right to ask the supervisory authorities to check the data concerning him which are included in the Schengen Information System, and the use which is made of such data. That right shall be governed by the national law of the Contracting Party to which the request is made. If the data have been included by another Contracting Party, the check shall be carried out in close co-ordination with that Contracting Party's supervisory authority.

Article 115

1. A joint supervisory authority shall be set up, with responsibility for supervising the technical support function of the Schengen Information System. This authority shall consist of two representatives of each national supervisory authority. Each Contracting Party shall have one vote. supervision shall be carries out in accordance with the provisions of this Convention, of the Council of Europe convention of 28 January 1981 for the Protection of Individuals with regard to the Automatic Processing of Personal Data, taking into account recommendation R (87) 15 of 17 September 1987 of the Committee of Ministers of the Council of Europe regulating the use of personal data in the police sector, and in accordance with the national law of the Contracting Party responsible for the technical support function.

2. As regards the technical support function of the Schengen Information system, the joint supervisory authority shall have the task of checking that the provisions of this Convention are properly implemented. For this purpose it shall have access to the technical support function.

3. The joint supervisory authority shall also be competent to examine any difficulties of application or interpretation which may arise during the operation of the Schengen Information System, to study problems which may arise with the exercise of independent supervision by the national supervisory authorities of the Contracting Parties or in the exercise of the right of access to the system, and to draw up harmonized proposals for the purpose of finding joint solutions to problems.

4. Reports drawn up by the joint supervisory authority shall be forwarded to the

authorities to which the national supervisory authorities submit their reports.

Article 116

1. Each Contracting Party shall be responsible, in accordance with its national law, for any injury caused to a person through the use of the national data file of the Schengen Information System. This shall also be the case where the injury wascaused by the reporting Contracting Party, where the latter included legally or factually inaccurate data.

2. If the Contracting Party against which an action is brought is not the reporting Contracting Party, the latter shall be required to reimburse, on request, sums paid out as compensation, unless the data were used by the requested Contracting Party in contravention of this Convention.

Article 117

1. With regard to the automatic processing of personal data which are transmitted pursuant to this Title, each Contracting Party shall, not later than when this Convention enters into force, make the national arrangements necessary to achieve a level of protection of personal data at least equal to that resulting from the principles of the Council of Europe Convention of 28 January 1981 for the Protection of Individuals with regard to the Automatic Processing of Personal Data, and in compliance with Recommendation R (87) 15 of 17 September 1987 of the Committee of Ministers of the Council of Europe regulating the use of personal data in the police sector.

2. The transmission of personal data provided for in this Title may take place only where the arrangements for the protection of personal data provided for in paragraph 1 have entered into force in the territory of the Contracting Parties concerned by the transmission.

Article 118

1. Each of the Contracting Parties shall undertake, in respect of the national section of the Schengen Information System, to take the measures necessary to:
   a) prevent any unauthorized person from having access to installations used for the processing of personal data (checks at the entrance to installations);
   b) prevent data media from being read, copied, modified or removed by unauthorized persons (control of data media);
   c) prevent the unauthorized entry of data into the file and any unauthorized consultation, modification or deletion of personal data included in the file (control of data entry);
   d) prevent automated data processing systems from being used by unauthorized persons by means of data transmission equipment (control of utilization);
   e) guarantee that, with respect to the use of an automated data processing system, authorized persons have access only to data for which they are responsible (control of access);
   f) guarantee that it is possible to check and establish to which authorities personal data may be transmitted by data transmission equipment (control of transmission);
   g) guarantee that it is possible to check and establish a posteriori what personal data has been introduced into automated data processing systems, when and by whom (control of data introduction);
   h) prevent the unauthorized reading, copying, modification or deletion of personal data during the transmission of data and the transport of data media (control of transport);

2. Each Contracting Party must take special measures to ensure the security

of data when it is being transmitted to services located outside the territories of the Contracting Parties. Such measures must be communicated to the joint supervisory authority.

3. Each Contracting Party may designate for the processing of data in its national section of the Schengen Information System only specially qualified persons subject to security checks.

4. The Contracting Party responsible for the technical support function of the Schengen Information System shall take the measures laid down in paragraphs 1 to 3 in respect of the latter.

CHAPTER 4
Apportionment of the costs of
the Schengen Information System

Article 119

1. The costs of setting up and using the technical support function referred to in Article 92 (3), including the cost of cabling for connecting the national sections of the Schengen Information System to the technical support function, shall be defrayed jointly by the Contracting Parties. Each Contracting Party's share shall be determined on the basis of the rate for each Contracting Party applied to the uniform basis of assessment of value-added tax within the meaning of Article 2 (1)(c) of the Decision of the Council of the European Communities of 24 June 1988 on the system on the Communities' own resources.

2. The costs of setting up and using the national section of the Schengen Information System shall be borne by each Contracting Party individually.

TITLE V
Transport and movement of goods

Article 120

1. The Contracting Parties shall jointly ensure that their laws, regulations or administrative provisions do not unjustifiable impede the movement of goods at internal borders.

2. The Contracting Parties shall facilitate the movement of goods at internal borders by carrying out formalities relating to prohibitions and restrictions at the time goods are cleared through customs for release for consumption. Such customs clearance may, at the option of the party concerned, be conduced either within the country or at the internal border. The Contracting Parties shall endeavour to encourage customs clearance within the country.

3. Insofar as it is not possible in certain spheres to achieve the simplifications referred to on paragraph 2 in whole or in part, the Contracting Parties shall endeavour to bring about the conditions therefor amongst themselves or within the framework of the European Communities.

   This paragraph shall apply in particular to the monitoring of compliance with rules concerning transport permits, to technical inspection of means of transport, to veterinary checks and animal health checks, veterinary checks on health and hygiene, to plant health checks and to the monitoring of transport of dangerous goods and waste.

4. The Contracting Parties shall endeavour to harmonize formalities concerning the movement of goods at external borders and to monitor compliance therewith in accordance with uniform principles. The Contracting Parties shall, to that end, work closely together within the Executive Committee, within the frame-

work of the European Communities and within other international fora.

Article 121

1. The Contracting Parties shall, while complying with Community law, waive the checks and cease to require submission of the plant health certificates, prescribed by Community law for certain plants and plant products.

   The Executive Committee shall adopt the list of plants and plant products to which the simplification specifies in the first sentence above shall apply. It may amend this list and shall set the date of entry into force for such amendments. The Contracting Parties shall inform each other of the measures adopted.

2. Should there be a danger of harmful organisms being introduced or propagated, a Contracting Party may request the temporary reinstatement of the surveillance measures prescribed by Community law, and may implement them. It shall immediately inform the other Contracting Parties thereof in writing, giving the reasons for its decision.

3. Plant health certificates may continue to be used as the certificate required by virtue of the law on the protection of species.

4. The competent authority shall, upon request, issue a plant health certificate when a consignment is intended in whole or in part for re-exportation, in so far as plant health requirements are met in respect of the plants or plant products concerned.

Article 122

1. The Contracting Parties shall step up their co-operation in order to endure the safe transport of dangerous goods, and undertake to harmonize the national provisions adopted pursuant to international Conventions in force. They undertake, moreover, particularly with a view to maintaining the existing level of safety, to:
   a) harmonize their requirements in respect of the vocational qualifications of drivers;
   b) harmonize the procedures for and the frequency of checks conducted in the course of transport and within undertakings;
   c) harmonize the descriptions of offences and the legal provisions concerning the relevant sanctions;
   d) ensure a permanent exchange of information, and of experience acquired, with regard to the measures implemented and the checks carried out.

2. The Contracting Parties shall step up their co-operation in order to conduct checks on transfers of dangerous and of non-dangerous waste across internal borders.

   To that end, they shall endeavour to adopt a common position as regards the amendment of Community Directives on the monitoring and management of transfers of dangerous waste and in respect of the introduction of Community acts concerning non-dangerous waste, with the aim of setting up an appropriate infrastructure for the disposal thereof and of introducing standards on such disposal harmonized at a high level.

   In the absence of Community rules on non-dangerous waste, checks on transfers of such waste shall be conducted on the basis of a special procedure whereby transfers to the point of destination lay be checked at the time of processing.

   The provisions of the second sentence of paragraph 1 above shall also apply to this paragraph.

Article 123

1. The Contracting Parties undertake to consult each other for the purposes of abolishing amongst themselves the current obligation to provide a permit for the export of strategic industrial products and technologies, and to replace such a permit if necessary, by a flexible procedure in instances where the countries of first and final destination are Contracting Parties.

   Subject to such consultations, and in order to guarantee the effectiveness of such checks as may prove necessary, the Contracting Parties shall, by co-operating closely within a co-ordination system, endeavour to conduct such exchanges of information as are appropriate in the light of national legislation.

2. With regard to products other than the strategic industrial products and technologies referred to in paragraph 1, the Contracting Parties shall endeavour, on the one hand, to have export formalities conducted within the country and, on the other, to harmonize their monitoring procedures.

3. Within the framework of the objectives set out in paragraphs 1 and 2 above, the Contracting Parties shall undertake consultations with the other partners concerned.

Article 124

The number and frequency of checks on goods during movements of travellers at internal borders shall be reduced to the lowest level possible. Further reductions in and the final abolition of such checks will depend on the gradual increase of travellers' exemptions and on future developments in the rules applicable to travellers crossing borders.

Article 125

1. The Contracting Parties shall conclude arrangements on the secondment of liaison officers from their customs administrations.

2. The secondment of liaison officers shall be for the general purposes of promoting and accelerating co-operation between the Contracting Parties, in particular within the framework of existing Conventions and Community acts on mutual assistance.

3. The duties of liaison officers shall be of a consultative nature, and to provide assistance. They shall not be empowered to take customs administration measures on their own initiative. They shall provide information and shall perform their duties in accordance with the instructions given to them by the Contracting Party of origin.

TITLE VI
Protection of personal data

Article 126

1. With regard to the automatic processing of personal data transmitted pursuant to this Convention, each Contracting Party shall, no later than the time of entry into force of this Convention, adopt the national provisions required to achieve a level of protection of personal data at least equal to that resulting from the principles of the Council of Europe Convention of 28 January 1981 for the protection of individuals with regard to automatic processing of personal data.

2. Personal data for which this Convention provides may not be transmitted until after the provisions for the protection of personal data as specified in paragraph 1 have entered into force within the territory of the Contracting Parties involved in such transmission.

3. The following provisions shall, moreover, apply in respect of the automatic

processing of personal data transmitted pursuant to this Convention:

a) the data may be used by the recipient Contracting Party solely for the purposes for which this Convention stipulates that such data may be transmitted; such data may be used for other purposes only with the prior authorization of the Contracting Party which transmitted the data and in compliance with the legislation of the recipient Contracting Party; such authorization may be granted insofar as the national legislation of the Contracting Party transmitting the data permits;

b) the data may be used only by the judicial authorities and by the departments and authorities carrying out a task or performing a function in connection with the aims mentioned in paragraph (a);

c) the Contracting Party transmitting the data shall be obliged to ensure the accuracy thereof; should it note, either on its own initiative or further to a request by the person concerned, that the data are inaccurate or should not have been transmitted or provided, the recipient Contracting Party or Parties must be informed thereof forthwith, the latter shall be obliged to correct or destroy the data, or state that such data are inaccurate or should not have been transmitted;

d) a Contracting Party may not plead that another Contracting Party had transmitted inaccurate data in order to avoid its liability under its national legislation vis-a-vis an injured party; if damages are awarded against the recipient Contracting Party because of its use of inaccurate data transmitted, the Contracting Party which transmitted the data shall refund in full to the recipient Contracting Party the sums paid in damages;

e) the transmission and receipt of personal data must be recorded both in the data file from which they originated and in the data file in which they are incorporated;

f) the joint supervisory authority mentioned in Article 115 may, at the request of one of the Contracting Parties, issue an opinion on the difficulties of implementing and interpreting this Article.

4. This Article shall not apply to the transmission of data provided for under title II, Chapter 7 and in Title IV. Paragraph 3 shall not apply to the transmission of data provided for under Title III, Chapters 2, 3, 4 and 5.

Article 127

1. Where personal data are transmitted to another Contracting Party pursuant to the provisions of this Convention, the provisions of this Convention, the provisions of Article 126 shall apply to the transmission of data from a non-automated data file and to their incorporation in another non-automated data file.

2. Where, in cases other than those governed by Article 126 (1), or by paragraph 1 of the present Article, personal data are transmitted to another Contracting Party pursuant to this Convention, Article 126 (3) shall, with the exclusion of subparagraph (e), apply. The following provisions shall also apply:

a) a written record shall be kept of the transmission and receipt of personal data; this obligation shall not apply where there is no need, in order to use them, to record such data, particularly if they are not used or are used only very briefly;

b) the recipient Contracting Party shall guarantee, for the use of transmitted data a level of protection at least equal to that stipulated under its national legislation for the use of data of a similar nature;

c) access to data and the conditions under which it shall be granted, shall be governed by the national legislation of the Contracting Party to which the person concerned applies.

3. This Article shall not apply to the transmission of data provided for under Title II, Chapter 7, and Title III, Chapters 2, 3, 4 and 5 as also in Title IV.

Article 128

1. The transmission of personal data for which this Convention makes provision may not take place until the Contracting Parties involved in that transmission have instructed a national supervisory authority to monitor independently, in respect of the processing of personal data in data files, compliance with the provisions of Article 126 and Article 127 and the provisions adopted in implementation thereof.

2. Insofar as the Contracting Party has, in accordance with its national legislation, instructed a supervisory authority to monitor independently, in one or more areas, compliance with the provisions on the protection of personal data not incorporated in a data file, that Contracting Party shall instruct the same authority to supervise compliance with the provisions of this Title in the areas involved.

3. This Article shall not apply to the transmission of data provided for under Title II, Chapter 7 and in Title III, Chapters 2, 3, 4, and 5.

Article 129

With regard to the transmission of personal data pursuant to Title III, Chapter 1, the Contracting Parties undertake, without prejudice to the provisions of Articles 126 and 127, to implement a level of protection for personal data which complies with the principles of Recommendation R (87) 15 of 17 September 1987 of the Committee of Ministers of the Council of Europe regulating the use of personal data in the police sector. Moreover, with regard to transmission pursuant to Article 46, the following provisions shall apply:

a) the data may be used by the recipient Contracting Party solely for the purposes indicated by the Contracting Party which provided such data and in compliance with the conditions imposed by that Contracting Party;

b) the data may be forwarded only to police departments and authorities; such data may be communicated to other departments only with the prior authorization of the Contracting Party which provided them;

c) the recipient Contracting Party shall, upon request, inform the Contracting Party which transmitted the data of the use made of them and of the results thus obtained.

Article 130

If personal data are transmitted through a liaison officer as referred to on Article 47 or Article 125, the provisions of this Title shall apply only where that liaison officer transmits such data to the Contracting Party which seconded him to the territory of the other Contracting Party.

TITLE VII
Executive Committee

Article 131

1. An Executive Committee shall be set up for the implementation of this Convention.

2. Without prejudice to the special powers granted to it by this Convention, the general purpose of the Executive Committee is to ensure that this Convention is implemented correctly.

Article 132

1. Each of the Contracting Parties shall have one seat on the Executive Committee. The Contracting Parties shall be represented on the Committee by a Minister responsible for the implementation of this Convention; he may be assisted by the requisite experts who may participate in the deliberations.

2. The Executive Committee shall take its decisions unanimously. It shall draw up its own rules of procedures; in this connection it may provide for a written procedure for the taking of decisions.

3. At the request of the representative of a Contracting Party, the final decision of a draft on which the Executive Committee has taken its decision may be postponed until no more than two months after the submission of that draft.

4. The Executive Committee may set up Working Parties comprising representatives of the Administrations of the Contracting Parties in order to conduct preparations for decisions or for other work.

Article 133

The Executive Committee shall meet in the territory of every Contracting Party in turn. It shall meet as often as necessary in order to discharge its duties effectively.

TITLE VIII
Final Provisions

Article 134

The provisions of this Convention shall apply only in so far as they are compatible with Community law.

Article 135

The provisions of this Convention shall apply subject to the provisions of the Geneva Convention of 28 July 1951 relating to the Status of refugees, as amended by the New York Protocol of 31 January 1967.

Article 136

1. A Contracting Party which envisages conducting negotiations on border checks with a Third State shall inform the other Contracting Parties thereof in good time.

2. No Contracting Party shall conclude with one or more Third States agreements simplifying or abolishing border checks without the prior agreement of the other Contracting Parties, subject to the right of the Member States of the European Communities to conclude such agreements jointly.

3. The provisions of paragraph 2 shall not apply to agreements on local border traffic since these agreements comply with the exemptions and arrangements laid down under Article 3 (1).

Article 137

This Convention shall not be the subject of any reservations, save for those referred to in Article 60.

Article 138

As regards the French Republic, the provisions of this Convention shall apply only to the European territory of the French Republic.

As regards the Kingdom of the Netherlands, the provisions of this Convention shall apply only to the territory of the Kingdom of the Netherlands situated in Europe.

Article 139

1. The present Convention shall be subject to ratification, acceptance or approval. The instruments of ratification, acceptance or approval shall be deposited with the Government of the Grand Duchy of Luxembourg, which shall notify all the Contracting Parties thereof.

2. This Convention shall enter into force on the first day of the second month following the deposit of the final instrument of ratification, acceptance or approval. The provisions concerning the setting up, activities and jurisdiction of the Executive Committee shall apply as from the entry into force of this Convention. The other provisions shall apply as from the first day of the third month following the entry into force if this Convention.

3. The Government of the Grand Duchy of Luxembourg shall notify all the Contracting Parties of the day of entry into force.

Article 140

1. Any Member State of the European Communities may become a Party to this Convention. Such accession shall be the subject of an agreement between that State and the Contracting Parties.

2. Such an agreement shall be subject to ratification, acceptance or approval by the acceding State and by each of the Contracting Parties. It shall enter into force on the first day of the second month following the deposit of the final instrument of ratification, acceptance or approval.

Article 141

1. Any Contracting Party may submit to the depository a proposal to amend this Convention. The depository shall forward that proposal to the other Contracting Parties. At the request of one Contracting Party, the Contracting Parties shall re-examine the provisions of the Convention if, in their opinion, there has been a fundamental change in the condition obtaining when the Convention entered into force.

2. The Contracting Parties shall adopt amendments to this Convention by mutual consent.

3. Amendments shall enter into force on the first day of the second month following the date of deposit of the final instrument of ratification, acceptance or approval.

Article 142

1. When Conventions are concluded between the Member States of the European Communities with a view to the completion of an area without internal frontiers, the Contracting Parties shall agree on the conditions under which the provisions of the present Convention are to be replaced or amended in the light of the corresponding provisions of such Conventions.

The Contracting Parties shall, to that end, take account of the fact that the provisions of this Convention may provide for more extensive co-operation than that resulting from the provisions of the said Conventions.

Provisions which are in breach of those agreed between the Member States of the European Communities shall in any case be adapted in any circumstances.

2. Amendments to this Convention deemed necessary by the Contracting Parties shall be subject to ratification, acceptance or approval. The provision contained in Article 141 (3) shall apply, it being understood that the amendments will not enter into force before the said Conventions between the Member States of the European Communities come into force.

In witness whereof, the undersigned, duly authorized to that end, have hereunto set their hands.

Done at Schengen, this nineteenth day of June in the year one thousand one hundred and ninety, in a single original, in the Dutch, French and German languages, all three texts being equally authentic, which shall be deposited in the archives of the Government of the Grand Duchy of Luxembourg, which shall transmit a certified copy to each of the Contracting Parties.

For the Government of the Kingdom of Belgium,

For the Government of the Federal Republic of Germany,

For the Government of the French Republic,

For the Government of the Grand Duchy of Luxembourg,

For the Government of the Kingdom of the Netherlands.

FINAL ACT

At the time of signing, the Convention implementing the Schengen Agreement of 14 June 1985 between the Governments of the States of the Benelux Economic Union, the Federal Republic of Germany and the French Republic regarding the gradual abolition of checks at their common borders, the Contracting Parties adopted the following statements:

1. *Joint statement concerning Article 139*

The signatory States shall, prior to the entry into force of the Convention, inform each other of all circumstances of significance for the matters covered by the Convention and for its entry into force.

The Convention shall not enter into force until the prior conditions for its implementation are fulfilled in the signatory States and check at external borders are effective.

2. *Joint statement concerning Article 4*

The Contracting Parties undertake to make every effort to comply with this deadline simultaneously and to preclude any shortcomings in security. Before 31 December 1992, the Executive Committee shall examine what progress has been made. The Kingdom of the Netherlands stresses that difficulties in meeting the deadline in a particular airport cannot be excluded but that this will not give rise to any shortcomings in security. The other Contracting Parties will take account of this situation although this may not be allowed to lead to difficulties for the internal market.

In the event of difficulties the Executive Committee shall examine the optimal conditions for the simultaneous implementation of these measures at airports.

3. *Joint statement regarding Article 71 (2)*

In so far as a Contracting Party derogates from the principle referred to on Article 71 (2) in connection with its national policy on the prevention and treatment of addiction to narcotic drugs and psychotropic substances, all contracting parties shall adopt the requisite administrative measures and penal sanctions to prevent and penalize the illicit import action and export action of such products and substances, particularly towards the territory of the other Contracting Parties.

4. *Joint statement concerning Article 121*

The Contracting Parties shall, while complying with Community law, waive the checks and cease to require submission of the plant health certificates, prescribed by Community law for the plants and plant products

a)   listed under 1 below, or

b)   listed under 2 to 6 below and originating in one of the Contracting Parties:

    1) Cut flowers and parts of plants suitable for ornamental purposes of:
    Castanea
    Chrysanthemum

   Dendranthema
   Dianthus
   Gladiolus
   Gypsophila
   Prunus
   Quercus
   Rosa
   Salix
   Syringa
   Vitis

2) Fresh fruit of:
   Citrus
   Cydonia
   Malus
   Prunus
   Pyrus

3) Wood of:
   Castanea
   Quercus

4) Growing medium constituted wholly or in part of earth or solid organic matter such as parts of plants, turf and bark with humus, but not constituted entirely of turf.

5) Seeds

6) Live plants listed below and appearing under the CN Code listed below in the Customs Nomenclature published in the Official Journal of the European Communities of 7 September 1987.

CN Code	Description
0601 20 30	Bulbs, tubers, tuberous roots and rhizomes, in growth or in flower: orchids,hyacinths, narcissi and tulips
0601 20 90	Bulbs tubers, tuberous roots and rhizomes, in growth or in flower: other
0602 30 10	Rhododendron simsii (Azalea indica)
0602 99 51	Outdoor plants: perennial plants
0602 99 59	Outdoor plants: other
0602 99 91	Indoor plants: flowering plants with buds or flowers, excluding cacti
0602 99 99	Indoor plants: other

5) *Joint statement on national asylum policies*

The Contracting Parties shall make an inventory of national asylum policies with a view to the harmonization thereof.

6) *Joint statement concerning Article 132*

The Contracting Parties shall inform their national Parliaments of the implementation of this Convention.

Done at Schengen this nineteenth day of June in the year one thousand nine hundred and ninety, in a single original, in the Dutch, French and German languages, all three texts being equally authentic, which shall be deposited in the archives of the Government of the Grand Duchy of Luxembourg, which shall transmit a certified copy to each of the Contracting Parties.

For the Government of the Kingdom of Belgium,

For the Government of the Federal Republic of Germany,

For the Government of the French Republic,

for the Government of the Grand Duchy of Luxembourg,

For the Government of the Kingdom of the Netherlands.

MINUTES

Further to the Final Act of the Convention implementing the Schengen Agreement of 14 June 1985 between the Governments of the States of the Benelux Economic Union, the Federal Republic of Germany and the French Republic regarding the gradual abolition of checks at their common borders, the Contracting Parties adopted the following joint statement and took note of the following unilateral declarations made in respect of the said Convention:

I) Statement on the scope of the Convention

    The Contracting Parties note that, after the unification of the two German States, the scope of the Convention shall under international law also extend to the current territory of the German Democratic Republic.

II) Declarations by the Federal Republic of Germany concerning the interpretation of the Convention

    1) The Convention has been concluded in the light of the prospective unification of the two German States.

        The German Democratic Republic is not a foreign country in relation to the Federal Republic of Germany.

        Article 136 shall not apply in relations between the Federal Republic of Germany and the German Democratic Republic.

2) This Convention shall not jeopardize the arrangements agreed in the Germano-Austrian exchange of letters of 20 August 1984 simplifying checks at their common borders for nationals of both States. Such arrangements will however have to be implemented in the light of the over-riding security and immigration requirements of the Schengen Contracting Parties so that such facilities will in practice be restricted to Australian nationals.

III) Declaration by the Kingdom of Belgium concerning Article 67

The procedure which will be implemented internally for taking over the execution of a foreign judgment will not be that specified in the Belgian law on the transfer of sentenced persons between States, but rather a special procedure which will be determined when this Convention is ratified.

Done at Schengen, this nineteenth day of June in the year one thousand nine hundred and ninety, in a single original, in the Dutch, French and German languages, all three texts being equally authentic, which shall be deposited in the archives of the Government of the Grand Duchy of Luxembourg, which shall transmit a certified copy to each of the Contracting Parties.

For the Government of the Kingdom of Belgium,

For the Government of the Federal Republic of Germany,

For the Government of the French Republic,

For the Government of the Grand Duchy of Luxembourg,

For the Government of the Kingdom of the Netherlands.

JOINT STATEMENT
by the Ministers and State Secretaries
meeting in Schengen on 19 June 1990

The Governments of the Contracting Parties to the Schengen Agreement will commence or continue discussions in the following spheres in particular:

— improving and simplifying practice in respect of extradition;
— improving co-operation on proceedings in respect of road traffic offences;
— arrangements for the mutual recognition of loss of entitlement to drive motor vehicles;
— possibilities of reciprocal collection of fines;
— introduction of rules on reciprocal transfers of criminal proceedings including the possibility of transferring the accused person to his country of origin;
— introduction of rules on the repatriation of minors who have been unlawfully removed from the authority of the person responsible for exercising parental authority;
— further simplification of checks on commercial movements of goods.

Done at Schengen, this nineteenth day of June in the year one thousand nine hundred and ninety, in a single original, in the Dutch, French and German language, all three texts being equally authentic, which shall be deposited in the archives of the Government of the Grand Duchy of Luxembourg, which shall transmit a certified copy to each of the Contracting Parties,

For the Government of the Kingdom of Belgium,

For the Government of the Federal Republic of Germany,

For the Government of the French Republic,

For the Government of the Grand Duchy of Luxembourg,

For the Government of the Kingdom of the Netherlands.

TREATY ON EUROPEAN UNION

Relevant texts of the Treaty on European Union, its Annexes and the Final Act as signed in Maastricht 7 February 1992.

(...)

TITLE I
Common Provisions

Article A

By this Treaty, the High Contracting Parties establish among themselves a European Union, hereinafter called 'The Union'.

This Treaty marks a new stage in the process of creating an ever closer union among the peoples of Europe in which decisions are taken as closely as possible to the citizen.

The Union shall be founded on the European Communities, supplemented by the policies and forms of cooperation established by this Treaty. Its task shall be to organize, in a manner demonstrating consistency and solidarity, relations between the Member States and between their peoples.

Article B

The Union shall set itself the following objectives:

— to promote economic and social progress which is balanced and sustainable, in particular through the creation of an area without internal frontiers, through the strengthening of economic and social cohesion and through the establishment of economic and monetary union, ultimately including a single currency in accordance with the provisions of this Treaty;

— to assert its identity on the international scene, in particular through the implementation of a common foreign and security policy including the eventual framing of a common defence policy, which might in time lead to a common defence;

— to strengthen the protection of the rights and interests of the nationals of its Member States through the introduction of a citizenship of the Union;

— to develop close cooperation on justice and home affairs;

— to maintain in full the 'acquis communautaire' and build on it with a view to considering, through the procedure referred to in Article N(2), to what extent the policies and forms of cooperation introduced by this Treaty may need to be revised with the aim of ensuring the effectiveness of the mechanisms and the institutions of the Community. The objectives of the Union shall be achieved as provided in this Treaty and in accordance with the conditions and the timetable set out therein while respecting the principle of subsidiarity ad defined in Article 3b of the Treaty establishing the European Community.

Article C

The Union shall be served by a single institutional framework which shall ensure the consistency and the continuity of the activities carried out in order to attain its objectives while respecting and building upon the 'acquis communautaire'.

The Union shall in particular ensure the consistency of its external activities as a whole in the context of its external relations, security, economic and development policies. The Council and the Commission shall be responsible for ensuring such consistency. They shall ensure the implementation of these policies, each in accordance with its respective powers.

Article D

The European Council shall provide the Union with the necessary impetus for its development and shall define the general political guidelines thereof.

The European Council shall bring together the Heads of State or of Government of the Member States and the President of the Commission.

They shall be assisted by the Ministers for Foreign Affairs of the Member States and by

H.G. Schermers et al., eds., Free Movement of Persons in Europe
© 1993, T.M.C. Asser Instituut, The Hague.

a Member of the Commission. The European Council shall meet at least twice a year, under the chairmanship of the Head of State or of Government of the Member State which holds the Presidency of the Council.

The European Council shall submit to the European Parliament a report after each of its meetings and a yearly written report on the progress achieved by the Union.

Article E

The European Parliament, the Council, the Commission and the Court of Justice shall exercise their powers under the conditions and for the purposes provided for, on the one hand, by the provisions of the Treaties establishing the European Communities and of the subsequent Treaties and Acts modifying and supplementing them and, on the other hand, by the other provisions of this Treaty.

Article F

1. The Union shall respect the national identities of its Member States, whose systems of government are founded on the principles of democracy.

2. The Union shall respect fundamental rights, as guaranteed by the European Convention for the Protection of Human Rights and Fundamental Freedoms signed in Rome on 4 November 1950 and as they result from the constitutional traditions common to the Member States, as general principles of Community law.

3. The Union shall provide itself with the means necessary to attain its objectives and carry through its policies.

TITLE II
Provisions amending the Treaty establishing the European Economic Community with a view to establishing the European Community.

Article G

The Treaty establishing the European Economic Community shall be amended in accordance with the provisions of this Article, in order to establish a European Community.

A. *Throughout the Treaty:*
1) The term 'European Economic Community' shall be replaced by the term 'European Community'.
B. *In Part One 'Principles':*
2) Article 2 shall be replaced by the following:
'Article 2
The Community shall have as its task, by establishing a common market and an economic and monetary union and by implementing the common policies or activities referred to in Articles 3 and 3a, to promote throughout the Community a harmonious and balanced development of economic activities, sustainable and non-inflationary growth respecting the environment, a high degree of convergence of economic performance, a high level of employment and of social protection, the raising of the standard of living and quality of life, and economic and social cohesion and solidarity among Member States.'

3. *Article 3 shall be replaced by the following:*
'Article 3
For the purposes set out in article 2, the activities of the Community shall include, as provided in this Treaty and in accordance with the timetable set out therein:
a) the elimination, as between Member States, of customs duties and quantitative restrictions on the import and export of goods, and of all other measures having equivalent effect;
b) a common commercial policy;
c) an internal market characterized by the abolition, as between Member States, of obstacles to the free movement of goods, persons, services and capital;
d) measures concerning the entry and movement of persons in the internal market as provided for in Article 100c;
e) a common policy in the sphere of agriculture and fisheries;
f) a common policy in the sphere of transport;
g) a system ensuring that competition in the internal market is not distorted;
h) the approximation of the laws of Member States to the extent required for the functioning of the common market;

i)   a policy in the social sphere comprising a European Social Fund;

j)   the strengthening of economic and social cohesion;

k)   a policy in the sphere of the environment;

l)   the strengthening of the competitivenes of Community industry;

m)   the promotion of research and technological development;

n)   encouragement for the establishment and development of trans-European networks ;

o)   a contribution to the attainment of a high level of health protection;

p)   a contribution to education and training of quality and to the flowering of the cultures of the Member States;

q)   a policy in the sphere of development cooperation;

r)   the association of the overseas countries and territories in order to increase trade and promote jointly economic and social development;

s)   a contribution to the strengthening of consumer protection;

t)   measures in the spheres of energy, civil protection and tourism.'

(...)

C.   *The following Part shall be inserted:*

'PART TWO
Citizenship of the Union

Article 8

1.   Citizenship of the Union is hereby established. Every person holding the nationality of a Member State shall be a citizen of the Union.

2.   Citizens of the Union shall enjoy the rights conferred by this Treaty and shall be subject to the duties imposed thereby.

Article 8a

1.   Every citizen of the Union shall have the right to move and reside freely within the territory of the Member States, subject to the limitations and conditions laid down in this Treaty and by the measures adopted to give it effect.

2.   The Council may adopt provisions with a view to facilitating the exercise of the rights referred to in paragraph 1; save as otherwise provided in this Treaty, the Council shall act unanimously on a proposal from the Commission and after obtaining the assent of the European Parliament.

Article 8b

1.   Every citizen of the Union residing in a Member State of which he is not a national shall have the right to vote and to stand as a candidate at municipal elections in the Member State in which he resides, under the same conditions as nationals of that State. This right shall be exercised subject to detailed arrangements to be adopted before 31 December 1994 by the Council, acting unanimously on a proposal from the Commission and after consulting the European Parliament; these arrangements may provide for derogations where warranted by problems specific to a Member State.

2.   Without prejudice to Article 138 (3) and to the provisions adopted for its implementation, every citizen of the Union residing in a Member State of which he is not a national shall have the right to vote and to stand as a candidate in elections to the European Parliament in the Member State in which he resides, under the same conditions as nationals of that State. This right shall be exercised subject to detailed arrangements to be adopted before 31 December 1993 by the Council, acting unanimously on a proposal from the Commission and after consulting the European Parliament; these arrangements may provide for derogations where warranted by problems specific to a Member State.

Article 8c

Every citizen of the Union shall, in the territory of a third country in which the Member State of which he is a national is not represented, be entitled to protection by the diplomatic or consular authorities of any Member

State, on the same conditions as the nationals of that State.
Before 31 December 1993, Member States shall establish the necessary rules among themselves and start the international negotiations required to secure this protection.

Article 8d
Every citizen of the Union shall have the right to petition the European Parliament in accordance with Article 138d.
Every citizen of the Union may apply to the Ombudsman established in accordance with Article 138e.

Article 8e
The Commission shall report to the European Parliament, to the Council and to the Economic and Social Committee before 31 December 1993 and then every three years on the application of the provisions of this Part. This report shall take account of the development of the Union. On this basis, and without prejudice to the other provisions of this Treaty, the Council, acting unanimously on a proposal from the Commission and after consulting the European Parliament, may adopt provisions to strengthen or to add to the rights laid down in this Part, which it shall recommend to the Member States for adoption in accordance with their respective constitutional requirements.'

D. *Parts Two and Three shall be grouped under the following Title:*

'PART THREE
Community Policies'

and in this Part:

10) *The first sentence of Article 49 shall be replaced by the following*:
'As soon as this Treaty enters into force, the Council shall, acting in accordance with the procedure referred to in Article 189b and after consulting the Economic and Social Committee, issue directives or make regulations setting out the measures required to bring about, by progressive stages, freedom of movement for workers, as defined in Article 48, in particular:'

11) *Article 54 (2) shall be replaced by the following:*
'2. In order to implement this general programme or, in the absence of such programme, in order to achieve a stage in attaining freedom of establishment as regards a particular activity, the Council, acting in accordance with the procedure referred to in Article 189b and after consulting the Economic and Social Committee, shall act by means of directives.'

12) *Article 56 (2) shall be replaced by the following:*
'2. Before the end of the transitional period, the Council shall, acting unanimously on a proposal from the Commission and after consulting the European Parliament, issue directives for the coordination of the abovementioned provisions laid down by law, regulation or administrative action. After the end of the second stage, however, the Council shall, acting in accordance with the procedure referred to on Article 189b, issue directives for the coordination of such provisions as, in each Member state, are a matter for regulation or administrative action.'

13) *Article 57 shall be replaced by the following:*
'Article 57
1. In order to make it easier for persons to take up and pursue activities as self-employed persons, the Council shall, acting in accordance with the procedure referred to in Article 189b, issue directives for the mutual recognition of diplomas, certificates and other evidence of formal qualifications.

2. For the same purpose, the Council shall, before the end of the transitional period, issue directives for the coordination of the provisions laid down by law, regulation or administrative action in Member States concerning the taking up and pursuit of activities as self-employed persons, The Council, acting unanimously on a proposal from the Commission and after consulting the European Parliament, shall decide on directives the implementation of which involves in at least one Member State amendment of the existing principles

laid down by law governing the professions with respect to training and conditions of access for natural persons. In other cases the Council shall act in accordance with the procedure referred to in Article 189b.

3. In the case of the medical and allied and pharmaceutical professions, the progressive abolition of restrictions shall be dependent upon coordination of the conditions for their exercise in the various Member States.'

(...)

23) *The following Article shall be inserted:*

Article 100c

1. The Council, acting unanimously on a proposal from the Commission and after consulting the European Parliament, shall determine the third countries whose nationals must be in possession of a visa when crossing the external borders of the Member States.

2. However, in the event of an emergency situation in a third country posing a threat of a sudden inflow of nationals from that country into the Community, the Council, acting by a qualified majority on a recommendation from the Commission, may introduce, for a period not exceeding six months, a visa requirement for nationals from the country in question. The visa requirements established under this paragraph may be extended in accordance with the procedure referred to in paragraph 1.

3. From 1 January 1996, the Council shall adopt the decisions referred to in paragraph 1 by a qualified majority. The Council shall, before that date, acting by a qualified majority on a proposal from the Commission and after consulting the European Parliament, adopt measures relating to a uniform format for visas.

4. In the areas referred to in this Article, the Commission shall examine any request made by a Member State that it submit a proposal to the Council.

5. This Article shall be without prejudice to the exercise of the responsibilities incumbent upon the Member States with regard to the maintenance of law and order and the safeguarding of internal security.

6. This Article shall apply to other areas if so decided pursuant to Article K. 9 of the provisions of the Treaty on European Union which relate to cooperation if the fields of justice and home affairs, subject to the voting conditions determined at the same time.

7. The provisions of the conventions in force between the Member States governing areas covered by this Article shall remain in force until their content has been replaced by directives or measures adopted pursuant to this Article.

(...)

TITLE VI
Provisions on Cooperation in the Fields of Justice and Home Affairs

Article K

Cooperation in the fields of justice and home affairs shall be governed by the following provisions.

Article K. 1

For the purposes of achieving the objectives of the Union, in particular the free movement of persons, and without prejudice to the powers of the European Community, Member States shall regard the following areas as matters of common interest:
1. asylum policy;
2. rules governing the crossing by persons of the external borders of the Member States and the exercise of controls thereon;
3. immigration policy and policy regarding nationals of third countries:
   a) conditions of entry and movement by nationals of third countries on the territory of Member States;

b) conditions of residence by nationals of third countries on the territory of Member States, including family reunion and access to employment;

c) combatting unauthorized immigration, residence and work by nationals of third countries on the territory of Member States;

4. combatting drug addiction in so far as this is not covered by 7 to 9;

5. combatting fraud on an international scale in so far as this is not covered by 7 to 9;

6. judicial cooperation in civil matters;

7. judicial cooperation in criminal matters;

8. customs cooperation;

9. police cooperation for the purposes of preventing and combatting terrorism, unlawful drug trafficking and other serious forms of international crime, including if necessary certain aspects of customs cooperation, in connection with the organization of a Union-wide system for exchanging information within a European Police Office (Europol).

Article K. 2

1. The matters referred to in Article K. 1 shall be dealt with in compliance with the European Convention for the Protection of Human rights and Fundamental Freedoms of 4 November 1950 and the Convention relating to the Status of Refugees of 28 July 1951 and having regard to the protection afforded by Member States to persons persecuted on political grounds.

2. This Title shall not affect the exercise of the responsibilities incumbent upon Member States with regard to the maintenance of law and order and the safeguarding of internal security.

Article K. 3

1. In the areas referred to in Article K. 1, Member States shall inform and consult one another within the Council with a view to co-ordinating their action. To that end, they shall establish collaboration between the relevant departments of their administrations.

2. The Council may:

— on the initiative of any Member State or of the Commission, in the areas referred to in Article K. 1 (1) to (6);

— on the initiative of any Member State, in the areas referred to in Article K1 (7) to (9):

a) adopt joint positions and promote, using the appropriate form and procedures, any cooperation contributing to the pursuit of the objectives of the Union;

b) adopt joint action in so far as the objectives of the Union can be attained better by joint action than by the Member States acting individually on account of the scale or effects of the action envisaged; it may decide that measures implementing joint action are to be adopted by a qualified majority;

c) without prejudice to Article 220 of the Treaty establishing the European Community, draw up conventions which it shall recommend to the Member States for adoption in accordance with their respective constitutional requirements.

Unless otherwise provided by such conventions, measures implementing them shall be adopted within the Council by a majority of two-thirds of the High Contracting Parties.

Such conventions may stipulate that the Court of Justice shall have jurisdiction to interpret their provisions and to rule on any disputes regarding their application, in accordance with such arrangements as they may lay down.

Article K. 4

1. A Coordinating Committee shall be set up consisting of senior officials. In addition to its coordinating role, it shall be the task of the Committee to:

— give opinions for the attention of the Council, either at the Council's request or on its own initiative;

— contribute, without prejudice to Article 151 of the Treaty establishing the European Community, to the preparation of the Council's discussions in the areas referred to in Article K.1 and, in accordance with the conditions laid down in Article 100d of the Treaty establishing the European Community, in the areas referred to in Article 100c of that Treaty.

2. The Commission shall be fully associated with the work in the areas referred to in this Title.

3. The Council shall act unanimously, except on matters of procedure and in cases where Article K.3 expressly provides for other voting rules.

   Where the Council is required to act by a qualified majority, the votes of its members shall be weighted as laid down in Article 148 (2) of the Treaty establishing the European Community, and for their adoption, acts of the Council shall require at least fifty-four votes in favour, cast by at least eight members.

Article K. 5

Within international organizations and at international conferences in which they take part, Member States shall defend the common positions adopted under the provisions of this Title.

Article K. 6

The Presidency and the Commission shall regularly inform the European Parliament of discussions in the areas covered by this Title. The Presidency shall consult the European Parliament on the principal aspects of activities in the areas referred to in this Title and shall ensure that the views of the European Parliament are duly taken into consideration. The European Parliament may ask questions of the Council or make recommendations to it. Each year, it shall hold a debate on the progress made in implementation of the areas referred to in this Title.

Article K. 7

The provisions of this Title shall not prevent the establishment or development of closer cooperation between two or more Member States in so far as such cooperation does not conflict with, or impede, that provided for in this Title.

Article K. 8

1. The provisions referred to in Articles 137, 138 to 142, 146, 147, 150 to 153, 157 to 163 and 217 of the Treaty establishing the European Community shall

apply to the provisions relating to the areas referred to in this Title.

2. Administrative expenditure which the provisions relating to the areas referred to in this Title entail for the institutions shall be charged to the budget of the European Communities.

   The Council may also:

   — either decide unanimously that operating expenditure to which the implementation of those provisions gives rise is to be charged to the budget of the European Communities; in that event, the budgetary procedure laid down in the Treaty establishing the European Community shall be applicable;

   — or determine that such expenditure shall be charged to the Member States, where appropriate in accordance with a scale to be decided.

Article K. 9

The Council, acting unanimously on the initiative of the Commission or a Member State, may decide to apply Article 100c of the Treaty establishing the European Community to action in areas referred to in Article K. 1 (1) to (6), and at the same time determine the relevant voting conditions relating to it. It shall recommend the Member States to adopt that decision in accordance with their respective constitutional requirements.

TITLE VII
Final Provisions

(...)

Article Q

This Treaty is concluded for an unlimited period.

Article R

1. This Treaty shall be ratified by the High Contracting Parties in accordance with their respective constitutional requirements. The instruments of ratification shall be deposited with the government of the Italian Republic.

2. This Treaty shall enter into force on 1 january 1993, provided that all the instruments of ratification have been deposited, or, failing that, on the first day of the month following the deposit of the instrument of ratification by the last signatory State to take this step.

(...)

FINAL ACT OF THE CONFERENCE

I. the Treaty on European Union
(...)
II. Protocols
(...)
III. Declarations
(...)

2. *Declaration on Nationality of a Member State*
The Conference declares that, wherever in the Treaty establishing the European Community reference is made to nationals of the Member States, the question whether an individual possesses the nationality of a Member State shall be settled solely by reference to the national law of the Member State concerned. Member States may declare, for information, who are to be considered their nationals for Community purposes by way of a declaration lodged with the Presidency and may amend any such declaration when necessary.

(...)

31. *Declaration on asylum*
1. The Conference agrees that, in the context of the proceedings provided for in Articles K. 1 and K. 3 of the provisions on cooperation in the fields of justice and home affairs, the Council will consider as a matter of priority questions concerning Member States' asylum policies, with the aim of adopting, by the beginning of 1993, common action to harmonize aspects of them, in the light

light of the work programme and timetable contained in the report on asylum drawn up at the request of the European Council meeting in Luxembourg on 28 and 29 June 1991.

2. In this connection, the Council will also consider, by the end of 1993, on the basis of a report, the possibility of applying Article K. 9 to such matters.

32. *Declaration on Police Cooperation*
The Conference confirms the agreement of the Member States on the objectives underlying the German delegation's proposals at the European Council meeting in Luxembourg on 28 and 29 June 1991.

For the present, the Member States agree to examine as a matter of priority the drafts submitted to them, on the basis of the work programme and timetable agreed upon in the report drawn up at the request of the Luxembourg European Council, and they are willing to envisage the adoption of practical measures in areas such as those suggested by the German delegation, relating to the following functions in the exchange of information and experience:
— support for national criminal investigation and security authorities, in particular in the coordination of investigations and search operations;
— creation of data bases;
— central analysis and assessment of information in order to take stock of the situation and identify investigative approaches;
— collection and analysis of national prevention programmes for forwarding to Member States and for drawing up Europe-wide prevention strategies;
— measures relating to further training, research, forensic matters and criminal records departments.
Member States agree to consider on the basis of a report, during 1994 at the latest, whether the scope of such cooperation should be extended.

(...)

AGREEMENT ON THE EUROPEAN ECONOMIC AREA

The European Economic Community,
The European Coal and Steel Community,
The Kingdom of Belgium,
The Kingdom of Denmark,
The Federal Republic of Germany,
The Hellenic Republic,
The Kingdom of Spain,
The French Republic,
Ireland,
The Italian Republic,
The Grand Duchy of Luxembourg,
The Kingdom of the Netherlands,
The Portuguese Republic,
The United Kingdom of Great Britain and Northern Ireland

and

The Republic of Austria,
The Republic of Finland,
The Republic of Iceland,
The Principality of Liechtenstein,
The Kingdom of Norway,
The Kingdom of Sweden,
The Swiss Confederation

hereinafter referred to as the Contracting Parties;

(...)

PART I
OBJECTIVES AND PRINCIPLES

Article 1

1. The aim of this Agreement of association is to promote a continuous and balanced strengthening of trade and economic relations between the Contracting Parties with equal conditions of competition, and the respect of the same rules, with a view to creating a homogeneous European Economic Area, hereinafter referred to as the EEA.

2. In order to attain the objectives set out in paragraph 1, the association shall entail in accordance with the provisions of this Agreement:
   a) the free movement of goods;
   b) the free movement of persons;
   c) the free movement of services;
   d) the free movement of capital;

   e) the setting up of a system ensuring that competition is not distorted and that the rules thereon are equally respected; as well as
   f) closer cooperation in other fields, such as research and development, the environment, education and social policy.

Article 2

For the purposes of this Agreement:
a) the term 'Agreement' means the main Agreement, its Protocols and Annexes as well as the acts referred to therein;
b) the term 'EFTA States' means the Contracting Parties which are, members of the European Free Trade Association;
c) the term 'Contracting Parties' means, concerning the Community and the EC Member States, the Community and the EC Member States, or the Community, or the EC Member States. The meaning to be attributed to this expression in each case is to be deduced from the relevant provisions of this Agreement and from the respective competencies of the Community and the EC Member States as they follow from the Treaty establishing the European Economic Community and the Treaty establishing the European Coal and Steel Community.

Article 3

The Contracting Parties shall take all appropriate measures, whether general or particular, to ensure fulfilment of the obligations arising out of this Agreement.

They shall abstain from any measure which could jeopardize the attainment of the objectives of this Agreement.

Moreover, they shall facilitate cooperation within the framework of this Agreement.

Article 4

Within the scope of application of this Agreement, and without prejudice to any special provisions contained therein, any

H.G. Schermers et al., eds., Free Movement of Persons in Europe
© 1993, T.M.C. Asser Instituut. The Hague.

discrimination on grounds of nationality shall be prohibited.

(...)

PART II
FREE MOVEMENT OF GOODS

(...)

PART III
FREE MOVEMENT OF PERSONS, SERVICES AND CAPITAL

CHAPTER 1
Workers and self-employed persons

Article 28
1. Freedom of movement for workers shall be secured among EC Member States and EFTA States.

2. Such freedom of movement shall entail the abolition of any discrimination based on nationality between workers of EC Member States and EFTA States as regards employment, remuneration and other conditions of work and employment.

3. It shall entail the right, subject to limitations justified on grounds of public policy, public security or public health:
   a) to accept offers of employment actually made;
   b) to move freely within the territory of EC Member States and EFTA States for this purpose;
   c) to stay in the territory of an EC Member State or an EFTA State for the purpose of employment in accordance with the provisions governing the employment of nationals of that State laid down by law, regulation or administrative action;
   d) to remain in the territory of an EC Member State or an EFTA State after having been employed there.

4. The provisions of this Article shall not apply to employment in the public service.

5. Annex V contains specific provisions on the free movement of workers.

Article 29
In order to provide freedom of movement for workers and self-employed persons, the Contracting Parties shall, in the field of social security, secure, as provided for in Annex VI, for workers and self-employed persons and their dependants, in particular:
   a) aggregation, for the purpose of acquiring and retaining the right to benefit and of calculating the amount of benefit, of all periods taken into account under the laws of the several countries;
   b) payment of benefits to persons resident in the territories of Contracting Parties.

Article 30
In order to make it easier for persons to take up and pursue activities as workers and self-employed persons, the Contracting Parties shall take the necessary measures, as contained in Annex VII, concerning the mutual recognition of diplomas, certificates and other evidence of formal qualification, and the coordination of the provisions laid down by law, regulation or administrative action in the Contracting Parties concerning the taking up and pursuit of activities by workers and self-employed persons.

CHAPTER 2
Right of establishment

Article 31
1. Within the framework of the provisions of this Agreement, there shall be no restrictions on the freedom of establishment of nationals of an EC Member State or an EFTA State in the territory of any other of these States. This shall also apply to the setting up of agencies, branches or subsidiaries by nationals of any EC Member State or EFTA State

established in the territory of any of these States.

Freedom of establishment shall include the right to take up and pursue activities as self-employed persons and to set up and manage undertakings, in particular companies or firms within the meaning of Article 34, second paragraph, under the conditions laid down for its own nationals by the law of the country where such establishment is effected, subject to the provisions of the Chapter relating to capital.

2.   Annexes VIII to XI contain specific provisions on the right of establishment.

Article 32
The provisions of this Chapter shall not apply, so far as any given Contracting Party is concerned, to activities which in that Contracting Party are connected, even occasionally, with the exercise of official authority.

Article 33
The provisions of this Chapter and measures taken in pursuance thereof shall not prejudice the applicability of provisions laid down by law, regulation or administrative action providing for special treatment for foreign nationals on grounds of public policy, public security or public health.

Article 34
Companies or firms formed in accordance with the law of an EC Member State or an EFTA State and having their registered office, central administration or principal place of business within the territory of the Contracting Parties shall, for the purposes of this Chapter, be treated in the same way as natural persons who are nationals of EC Member States or EFTA States.

'Companies or firms' means companies or firms constituted under civil or commerciallaw, including cooperative societies, and other legal persons governed by public or private law, save for those which are non-profit-making.

Article 35
The provisions of Article 30 shall apply to the matters covered by this Chapter.

(. . .)

PART IV
COMPETITION AND OTHER COMMON RULES

(. . .)

PART V
HORIZONTAL PROVISIONS RELEVANT TO THE FOUR FREEDOMS

(. . .)

PART VI
COOPERATION OUTSIDE THE FOUR FREEDOMS

(. . .)

PART VII
INSTITUTIONAL PROVISIONS

(. . .)

PART VIII
FINANCIAL MECHANISM

(. . .)

PART IX
GENERAL AND FINAL PROVISIONS

(. . .)

INDICES

TABLE OF INTERNATIONAL LEGISLATION
(The footnotes were not indexed)

MULTILATERAL LEGISLATION

7 December 1944
  Chicago Convention on international civil
      aviation, 138, 180-181
10 December 1948
  Universal Declaration of Human Rights
      general references, 155, 181, 239
      art. 13, 154
4 November 1950
  European Convention on human rights
      (ECHR)
      general references, 71, 140, 161, 163,
          198, 227, 235-247, 252-253, 261,
          275, 279, 299-300, 302, 304-306,
          310, 312, 316-320, 324-325, 332,
          503 532-533
      art. 1, 324
      art. 3, 191, 239-243, 299, 305, 312-
          313, 318
      art. 5, 238, 155
      art. 6, 272, 299-300, 305, 314-315,
          318
      art. 7, 181
      art. 8, 133, 191, 239, 243-245, 261,
          263, 299-300, 305-311, 313-314,
          318, 322-326, 533
      art. 9, 263
      art. 10, 155, 263
      art. 11, 263
      art. 13, 55, 57, 272, 300, 305, 315-
          316, 318
      art. 14, 244, 324, 532
      art. 16, 324
      art. 25, 241, 324
      art. 32, 401
      art. 60, 247, 305
  Fourth Protocol (1963)
      general references, 130, 154, 236-238,
          300, 532
      art. 2, 130, 155, 236-239, 324, 532
      art. 3, 313-314, 324
      art. 4, 182
  Seventh Protocol (1984)
      general references, 246
      art. 1, 246-247, 324

18 April 1951
  Treaty establishing the European Coal and
      Steel Community
      art. 69, 520
28 July 1951
  Geneva Convention on the status of refu-
      gees
      general references, 15, 23, 152, 163-
          164, 166-167, 169, 171-175, 177-
          181, 188-189, 197, 199-205, 209,
          302, 304, 332, 365-366, 368, 397,
          526-529
      art. 1, 142-143, 153, 176, 200, 316,
          528, 531
      arts. 2-34, 200
      art. 3, 178, 181
      art. 8, 202
      art. 9, 202
      arts. 12-24, 143
      art. 16, 316
      art. 17, 201
      art. 24, 202
      art. 25, 201-202
      art. 26, 130
      art. 27, 180
      art. 28, 181, 203
      art. 29, 14, 202
      art. 31, 137-138, 143, 181
      art. 32, 14, 143, 202
      art. 33, 137, 143-144, 176, 181
      art. 35, 173
  Protocol (1967), 14, 140, 189, 200-201
25 March 1957
  Treaty establishing the European Economic
      Community
      art. 2, 335, 419, 501
      art. 3(c), 194, 335, 347, 351, 355-356,
          388, 430, 434, 500, 504, 506,
          511, 520
      art. 5, 91, 256
      art. 6, 327
      art. 7, 229, 262, 273, 293, 419-420,
          421-422, 424-426, 434, 436, 487,
          500, 504, 506, 512, 515, 518,
          520, 541-542

25 March 1957, cont.,
  Treaty establishing the EEC, cont.,
    art. 8A, 21, 43, 102, 169, 193-195,
      216, 335, 340, 345, 347, 351,
      354-359, 367, 370, 376, 379-380,
      383, 384, 388, 501, 505-506, 508,
      510-511, 519, 539
    art. 30, 358, 534
    art. 36, 106, 110, 534
    arts. 42-51, 505
    art. 48, 21, 116, 217, 259, 262, 264-
      265, 270, 272-273, 275-276, 278-
      279, 281-282, 284, 287, 291, 295,
      347, 356-359, 380, 409, 411-412,
      421, 468, 476, 487, 492, 500,
      505, 513, 515, 519-520, 534, 542
    arts. 48-50, 203, 266
    arts. 48-51, 472, 478, 484, 506
    arts. 48-58, 355
    arts. 48-66, 273, 500, 511, 520
    arts. 48 et seq., 258, 347, 430, 476
    art. 49, 259, 351, 355, 434, 476, 492
    art. 50, 259, 492
    art. 51, 355
    art. 52, 21, 116, 217, 274, 278, 289,
      293, 357-358, 381, 421, 437-438,
      440, 441-442, 451-452, 454-455,
      458, 462-464, 467, 513
    arts. 52-58, 437
    arts. 52 et seq., 462, 465, 469
    art. 54, 355, 434, 438, 458, 460, 464,
      466
    art. 55, 281-282, 284, 438, 442, 452
    art. 56, 264, 278-279, 281-282, 357-
      359, 430, 438, 442, 452, 467-468,
      539
    art. 57, 405, 441, 443
    art. 58, 419, 451-452, 454-455, 458,
      462-464, 467, 469, 477, 480
    art. 59, 21, 217, 273, 278, 347, 351,
      356, 358, 418-421, 440-442, 469,
      481, 483, 489-490, 506, 513,
      534-535
    arts. 59-60, 357-358
    arts. 59-66, 437, 472-473, 478, 484
    art. 59 et seq., 476
    art. 60, 358, 419, 437-438, 481, 483,
      489-490, 506
    art. 63, 438, 476
    art. 66, 264, 278, 281, 357-359, 419,
      477, 480
    art. 67, 358
    art. 85, 91

25 March 1957, cont.,
  Treaty establishing the EEC, cont.,
    art. 86, 91
    art. 100, 347, 351, 359, 361-362, 364,
      367, 379, 434
    art. 100A, 347, 351, 355, 359, 380-
      381, 385, 388
    art. 118, 506-508, 513
    art. 128, 405, 420-422, 515
    art. 149, 385, 434, 436
    art. 155, 388
    art. 164, 401
    art. 169, 365, 454, 536
    art. 170, 365
    art. 175, 363, 386, 388
    art. 176, 540
    art. 177, 255-256, 260, 274, 365, 368,
      401, 481, 491, 523, 536-539
    art. 189, 292
    art. 203, 386
    art. 220, 350, 455, 462-464, 466-467
    art. 221, 465
    art. 223, 359
    art. 228, 256, 363, 491
    art. 233, 32, 38
    art. 235, 21, 348, 351, 381, 430, 436,
      515
    art. 237, 386
    art. 238, 204, 257-258, 348, 386, 491
25 March 1957
  Treaty establishing the European Atomic
      Energy Community
    art. 96, 520
13 December 1957
  European Convention on extradition
    general references, 66, 155, 319, 341
    art. 3, 145-146
13 December 1957
  European Agreement on regulations govern-
      ing the movement of persons,
      158-159
3 February 1958
  Treaty establishing the Benelux Economic
      Union, 32
20 April 1959
  European Convention on mutual assistance
      in criminal matters, 77
20 April 1959
  European Agreement on the abolition of
      visas for refugees, 140, 159, 203

11 April 1960
Benelux Convention on the free movement
of persons
general refences, 13, 31-39, 191-192,
339, 523-524
art. 1, 33
art. 2, 33, 191
art. 3, 33
art. 4, 33, 37, 39
art. 5, 36
art. 7, 33
art. 12, 33, 35-36
art. 13, 33
art. 15, 33
16 December 1961
European Agreement on travel by young
persons on collective passport
between the Member States of the
Council of Europe, 159
18 October 1961
European Social Charter
general references, 133, 503
art. 10, 422
art. 19, 133
6 May 1963
European Convention on the reduction of
multiple nationality, 156
19 December 1966
International Covenant on Civil and Political Rights
general references, 319
art. 12, 154, 236
art. 17, 133
art. 23, 133
art. 26, 512
1 August 1975
Helsinki Final Act, 322
24 November 1977
European Convention on the legal status of
migrant workers, 162, 322
16 October 1980
European Agreement on transfer of responsibility for refugees, 140, 163,
203, 205
28 January 1981
Convention of Strasbourg for the protection
of individuals with regard to
automatic processing of personal
data, 49-50, 53-54, 113, 160
14 June 1985
Schengen Agreement
general references, 9, 34-35, 37-38,
43-44, 51, 84, 86, 109, 171, 192,
242, 344-345, 372-373, 376, 398,

14 June 1985, cont.,
Schengen Agreement, cont.,
401, 510, 524, 531, 538, 540
art. 17, 43, 192
art. 20, 192
art. 28-38, 170
17/28 February 1986
Single European Act (SEA)
general references, 20, 37, 43, 76, 91,
102, 107, 116, 169, 194, 228,
335, 339, 352-355, 357-360, 370,
376, 379-380, 383, 385-386, 389,
406, 502-503, 508-509
art. 13, 102, 508
Declaration on Article 8A of the EEC
Treaty, 380, 383
Declaration on Articles 13-19 of the Single
European Act, 91, 107
25 May 1987
EC Convention on double jeopardy, 17
15 June 1990
Dublin Convention determining the state
responsible for examining applications for asylum lodged in one
of the Member States of the European Communities (Dublin Asylum Convention)
general references,14, 19, 24, 164,
170-172, 177, 179, 195, 230, 239,
318, 332, 340, 345, 351, 353,
366, 387-388, 394, 398, 401-402,
498, 527
art. 9, 175
art. 15, 19
art. 18, 26, 395
19 June 1990
Schengen Convention
general references, 6, 9-18, 22, 24, 27,
29, 37-39, 44-45, 48-54, 57, 65-
66, 68-69, 76, 84, 86, 93, 109-
110, 170-176, 178-181, 192-193,
216, 222-225, 228, 318, 332, 339,
344-346, 351, 353-354, 356, 362,
364, 366, 369-370, 380, 382,
387-388, 392-401, 498, 500, 510,
523-529, 531
art. 2, 10, 538
art. 5, 11, 13, 16, 56
art. 6, 11
art. 9, 12, 37-38
art. 10, 12
art. 12, 13
art. 18, 11
art. 19, 13

19 June 1990, cont.,
Schengen Convention, cont.,
art. 20, 13
art. 21, 13-14, 510
art. 22, 13, 510, 519
art. 23, 13
art. 24, 13-14
art. 25, 11, 14, 56
art. 26, 13, 179-180
art. 27, 13
art. 28, 15, 173
arts. 28-38, 170
art. 29, 15, 173-175, 528-529
art. 30, 14, 173, 528
art. 31, 174
art. 32, 174, 176, 177, 528
art. 33, 15
art. 34, 15
art. 35, 14
art. 37, 15
art. 38, 18-19, 54
art. 39, 16
art. 39-91, 38
art. 40, 67
art. 41, 17, 67-69
art. 46, 53
art. 47, 67
art. 49, 17
art. 50, 17
art. 53, 17

19 June 1990, cont.,
Schengen Convention, cont.,
art. 61, 17
art. 64, 16
art. 65, 17
art. 68, 17
art. 72, 17
art. 73, 17
art. 74, 18
art. 75, 18
art. 91, 18
art. 94, 526
art. 95, 16
art. 96, 12, 54
art. 99, 52
art. 101, 12
art. 109, 52
art. 110, 55
art. 111, 55
art. 116, 19, 55-56
arts. 120-125,38
art. 126, 18, 54
art. 127, 18
art. 128, 18, 54
art. 129, 18
art. 131, 395
art. 134, 19, 332, 362, 524
art. 135, 15, 173, 176-177
art. 136, 19, 362
art. 142, 19, 362, 524

EUROPEAN COMMUNITY LEGISLATION

Directives

64/220/EEC, 474
64/221/EEC, 131, 218, 228-229, 232, 262, 273, 278-280, 291, 293-294, 327, 330, 359, 381, 472-473, 487-488, 535
64/223/EEC, 291
64/224/EEC, 473, 476-477
68/151/EEC, 460
68/360/EEC, 131, 194, 218, 273, 321, 330, 338, 356-358, 380, 472, 474, 477-478, 487-488
69/169/EEC, 121
72/194/EEC, 131, 321
73/148/EEC, 218, 321, 330, 338, 356-358, 381, 419, 470, 473-474, 477-478
74/651/EEC, 121
75/34/EEC, 338
75/363/EEC, 344, 489
77/249/EEC, 445

78/660/EEC, 460
80/987/EEC, 291
83/181/EEC, 122
83/183/EEC, 122
83/349/EEC, 460
85/348/EEC, 121
87/198/EEC, 121
89/48/EEC, 276-278, 407, 437, 446-447, 449
89/592/EEC, 359
90/364/EEC, 194-195, 216, 219, 322, 338, 355, 381, 436, 515-517, 541, 543-544
90/365/EEC, 194-195, 216, 219, 322, 338, 381, 436, 515-517, 541, 543-544
90/366/EEC, 195-196, 216, 219, 322, 338, 355, 381, 424, 436, 515-517, 541, 543-544
91/308/EEC, 359

Regulations

17/62,	536
38/64,	476-477
1612/68,	21, 131, 194, 227, 231, 267-271, 273-274, 321, 338, 381, 409-411, 414-415, 417, 421, 433, 472, 477, 487-489, 494-495, 505, 517-518, 543

1251/70,	131, 268, 274, 321, 338, 487, 533
1408/71,	338, 487, 489, 494, 505
312/76,	321
1468/81,	112
2194/91,	480, 482, 536-537

Decisions

63/266/EEC,	420-421

TABLE OF CASES OF THE COURT OF JUSTICE
OF THE EUROPEAN COMMUNITIES

8/55	Fédération Charbonnière de Belgique v. High Authority of the European Coal and Steel Community [1954 to 1956] ECR 245	321
1/58	Friedrich Stork & Co. v. High Authority of the European Coal and Steel Community [1959] ECR 17	320
75/63	Mrs M.K.H. Hoekstra (née Unger) v. Bestuur der Bedrijfsvereniging voor Detailhandel en Ambachten (Administration of the Industrial Board for Retail Trades and Businesses) [1964] ECR 177	203, 411
6/64	Flaminio Costa v. ENEL [1964] ECR 585	362
29/69	Erich Stauder v. City of Ulm, Sozialamt [1969] ECR 419	260, 320
9/70	Franz Grad v. Finanzamt Traunstein [1970] ECR 825	327
11/70	Internationale Handelsgesellschaft mbH v. Einfuhr- und Vorratsstelle für Getreide und Futtermittel [1970] ECR 1125	320
22/70	Commission v. Council [1971] ECR 263 (ERTA)	361, 363
33/70	SpA SACE v. Ministry for Finance of the Italian Republic [1970] ECR 1213	327
7/71	Commission v. French Republic [1971] ECR 1003	362
21-24/72	International Fruit Company NV, Kooy Rotterdam NV, Velleman en Tas NV and Jan Van den Brink's In- en Exporthandel NV v. Produktschap voor Groenten en Fruit [1972] ECR 1219	365
4/73	J. Nold, Kohlen- und Baustoffgroßhandlung v. Commission [1974] ECR 491	237, 260, 274, 320
8/73	Hauptzollamt Bremerhaven v. Massey-Ferguson GmbH [1973] ECR 897	253
152/73	Giovanni Maria Sotgiu v. Deutsche Bundespost [1974] ECR 153	500
155/73	Guiseppe Sacchi [1974] ECR 409	419
167/73	Commission v. French Republic [1974] ECR 359	472
2/74	Jean Reyners v. Belgian State [1974] ECR 631	281, 282, 440, 442, 452
8/74	Procureur du Roi v. Benoît and Gustave Dassonville [1974] ECR 837	471
9/74	Donato Casagrande v. Landeshauptstadt München [1974] ECR 773	271, 405, 411, 416, 420, 425
24/74	Caisse Régionale d'Assurance maladie de Paris v. Giuseppina Biason [1974] ECR 999	518
33/74	Johannes Henricus Maria van Binsbergen v. Bestuur van de Bedrijfsvereniging voor de Metaalnijverheid [1974] ECR 1299	283, 440, 468, 472, 473
36/74	B.N.O. Walrave and L.J.N. Koch v. Association Union Cycliste Internationale, Koninklijke Nederlandsche Wielren Unie and Federation Española Ciclismo [1974] ECR 1405	273, 419, 472
41/74	Yvonne van Duyn v. Home Office [1974] ECR 1337	279, 327, 280, 468, 472

67/74	Carmelo Angelo Bonsignore v. Oberstadtdirektor der Stadt Köln [1975] ECR 297	279, 327, 468
68/74	Mr Angelo Alaimo v. Préfet du Rhône [1975] ECR 109	411, 416
1/75	Opinion of the Court [1975] ECR 1355	363
7/75	Mr. and Mrs. Fracas v. Belgian State [1975] ECR 679	227
32/75	Anita Cristini v. Société nationale des chemins de fer français [1975] ECR 1085	417, 488
36/75	Roland Rutili v. Minister for the Interior [1975] ECR 1219	262, 263, 264, 265, 273, 275, 279, 320, 327, 468, 509
39/75	Robert Gerardus Coenen and Others v. Sociaal- Economische Raad [1975] ECR 1547	283, 472, 473
48/75	Jean Noël Royer [1976] ECR 497	276, 327, 330, 415, 468
118/75	Lynne Watson and Allessandro Belmann [1976] ECR 1185	218, 263, 272 273, 519
2/76	Maria Mascetti v. Commission [1976] ECR 1975	265
3,4 and 6/76	Cornelis Kramer and others [1976] ECR 1279	362
13/76	Gaetano Donà v. Mario Mantero [1976] ECR 1333	273, 419
40/76	Slavica Kermaschek v. Bundesanstalt für Arbeit [1976] ECR 1669	485, 489, 495
51/76	Verbond van Nederlandse Ondernemingen v. Inspecteur der Invoerrechten en Accijnzen [1977] ECR 113	451
63/76	Vito Inzirillo v. Caisse d'Allocations Familiales de l'Arrondisement de Lyon [1976] ECR 2057	417, 488
71/76	Jean Thieffry v. Conseil de l'ordre des avocats à la Cour de Paris [1977] ECR 765	278, 441, 442, 451, 453
89/76	Commission v. Kingdom of the Netherlands [1977] ECR 1355	366
90/76	S.r.l. Ufficio Henry van Ameyde v. S.r.l. Ufficio Centrale Italiano di Assistenza Assicurativa Automobilisti in Circolazione Internazionale (UCI) [1977] ECR 1091	274
11/77	Richard Hugh Patrick v. Ministre des Affaires Culturelles [1977] ECR 1199	278, 443, 451
30/77	Regina v. Pierre Bouchereau [1977] ECR 1999	279, 294, 442, 468
38/77	Enka BV v. Inspecteur der Invoerrechten en Accijnzen, Arnhem [1977] ECR 2203	451
65/77	Jean Razanatsimba [1977] ECR 2229	485, 493, 496
1/78	Opinion of the Court (Rubber) [1979] 2871	257, 363
16/78	Criminal Proceedings v. Michel Choquet [1978] ECR 2293	283
21/78	Knud Olof Delkvist v. Anklagemyndigheden [1978] ECR 2327	328
110 and 111/78	Ministère Public and Chambre Syndicale des Agents Artistiques et Impressarii de Belgique, A.S.B.L. v. Willy van Wesemael and Others [1979] ECR 35	472
120/78	Rewe-Zentral AG v. Bundesmonopolverwaltung für Branntwein [1979] ECR 649	283
136/78	Ministère Public v. Vincent Auer [1979] ECR 437	443, 451
148/78	Pubblico Ministero v. Tullio Ratti [1979] ECR 1629	328
154/78	SpA Ferriera Valsabbia and Others v. Commission [1980] ECR 907	321

15/79	P.B. Groenveld B.V. v. Produktschap voor Vee en Vlees [1979] ECR 3409	450
44/79	Liselotte Hauer v. Land Rheinland-Pfalz [1979] ECR 3727	260, 269, 274
62/79	SA Compagnie Générale pour la Diffusion de la Télévision, Coditel, and Others v. SA Ciné Vog Films and others [1980] ECR 881	283
98/79	Josette Pecastaing v. Belgian State [1980] ECR 691	442
131/79	Regina v. Secretary of State for Home Affairs, ex parte Mario Santillo [1980] ECR 1585	280, 442
136/79	National Panasonic (UK) v. Commission [1980] ECR 2033	260, 321
137/79	Jean Kohll v. Commission [1980] ECR 2601	386
138/79	SA Roquette Frères v. Council [1980] ECR 3333	386
149/79	Commission v. Belgium [1980] ECR 3881	282
157/79	Regina v. Stanislaus Pieck [1980] ECR 2171	229, 330, 338, 442
804/79	Commission v. United Kingdom of Great Britain and Northern Ireland [1981] ECR 1045	256, 266
246/80	C. Broekmeulen v. Huisarts Registratie Commissie [1981] ECR 2311	443
279/80	Criminal proceedings agains Alfred John Webb [1981] ECR 3305	278, 282, 451, 472, 473
8/81	Ursula Becker v. Finzanzamt Münster-Innenstadt [1982] ECR 53	328
15/81	Gaston Schul Douane Expediteur BV v. Inspecteur der Invoer- rechten en Accijnzen, Roosendaal [1982] ECR 1409	352, 354
53/81	D.M. Levin v. Staatssecretaris van Justitie [1982] ECR 1035	275, 276, 287, 411, 412, 414
62 and 63/81	SECO SA and Desquenne & Giral SA v. Établissement d'Assurance contre la Vieillesse et l'Invalidité [1982] ECR 223	254, 472, 473, 485, 490
65/81	Francesco Reina and Letizia Reina v. Landeskreditbank Baden-Württemberg [1982] ECR 33	488
76/81	SA Transporoute et Travaux v. Minister of Public Works [1982] ECR 417	472
104/81	Hauptzollamt Mainz v. C.A. Kupferberg & Cie. KG a.A. [1982] ECR 3641	258, 262, 265
115 and 116/81	Rezguia Adoui v. Belgian State and City of Liège; Dominique Cornuaille v. Belgian State [1982] ECR 1665	279, 280, 442
255/81	R.A. Grendel GmbH v. Finanzamt für Körperschafte in Hamburg [1982] ECR 2301	328
35 and 36/82	Elestina Esselina Christina Morson v. State of the Netherlands and Head of the Plaatselijke Politie within the meaning of the Vreemdelingenwet; Sewradjie Jhanjan v. State of the Netherlands [1982] ECR 3723	485, 487, 505
77/82	Anastasia Peskeloglou v. Bundesanstalt für Arbeit [1983] ECR 1085	480
126/82	D.J. Smit Transport BV v. Commissie Grensoverschrijdend Beroepsgoederenvervoer [1983] ECR 73	328

152/82	Sandro Forcheri and his wife, Marisa Forcheri, née Marino v. Belgian State and asbl Institut Supérieur de Sciences Humaines Appliquées - École Ouvrière Supérieure [1983] ECR 2323	407, 420, 421
271/82	Vincent Rodolphe Auer v. Ministère Public [1983] ECR 2727	328, 443
286/82 and 26/83	Graziana Luisi and Giuseppe Carbone v. Ministero del Tesoro [1984] ECR 377	338, 418, 519
301/82	SA Clin-Midy and Others v. Belgian State [1984] ECR 251	328
5/83	Criminal proceedings against H.G. Rienks [1983] ECR 4233	443
63/83	Regina v. Kent Kirk [1984] ECR 2689	321
70/83	Gerda Kloppenburg v. Finanzamt Leer [1984] ECR 1075	328
107/83	Ordre des avocats au barreau de Paris v. Onno Klopp [1984] ECR 2971	283, 296, 442
220/83	Commission v. French Republic [1986] ECR 3663	283, 451, 472
229/83	Association des Centres distributeurs Édouard Leclerc, SA Thouars distribution et autres v. Sàrl 'Au blé vert', Georges Lehec, SA Pelgrim, Union syndicale des libraires de France, Ernest Marchand and Jeanne Demée, née Palluault [1985] ECR 17	468
238/83	Caisse d'Allocations Familiales de la Région Parisienne v. Mr and Mrs Richard Meade [1984] ECR 2631	485, 487, 505, 519
252/83	Commission v. Kingdom of Denmark [1986] ECR 3713	283, 451, 473
261/83	Carmella Castelli v. Office National des Pensions pour Travailleurs Salariés (ONPTS) [1984] ECR 3199	488
267/83	Aissatou Diatta v. Land Berlin [1985] ECR 567	254, 267-271, 327, 435, 485, 487, 489
270/83	Commission v. French Republic [1986] ECR 273	454-456, 462, 465, 466, 470
293/83	Françoise Gravier v. City of Liège [1985] ECR 593	273, 407, 409, 419, 421, 422, 423, 424, 425, 432, 434
29/84	Commission v. Federal Republic of Germany [1985] ECR 1661	229, 443
60/84 and 61/84	Cinéthèque SA and Others v. Fédération Nationale des Cinémas Français [1985] ECR 2605	261, 264
94/84	Office national de L'emploi v. Joszef Deak [1985] ECR 1873	288, 417, 485, 488, 489, 494, 495
152/84	M.H. Marshall v. Southampton and South West Hampshire Area Health Authority (Teaching) [1986] ECR 723	274, 328
157/84	Marie Frascogna v. Caisse des dépôts et consignations, Bordeaux [1985] ECR 1739	414
205/84	Commission v. Federal Republic of Germany [1986] ECR 3755	283, 451, 473
206/84	Commission v. Ireland [1986] ECR 3817	283, 451, 473
222/84	Marguerite Johnston v. Chief Constable of the Royal Ulster Constabulary [1986] ECR 1651	263, 321, 331
306/84	Commission v. Kingdom of Belgium [1987] ECR 675	443

59/85	State of the Netherlands v. Ann Florence Reed [1986] ECR 1283	321, 487, 516, 517
66/85	Deborah Lawrie-Blum v. Land Baden-Württemberg [1986] ECR 2121	276, 281, 284, 412, 414
79/85	D.H.M. Segers v. Bestuur van de Bedrijfsvereniging voor Bank- en Verzekeringswezen Groothandel en Vrije Beroepen [1986] ECR 2375	456-463, 467, 468
96/85 98, 162 and	Commission v. French Republic [1986] ECR 1475	443
258/85	Michele Bertini and Giuseppe Bisignani and Others v. Regione Lazio and Unità sanitarie locali [1986] ECR 1885	443
131/85	Emir Gül v. Regierungspräsident Düsseldorf [1986] ECR 1573	485, 489
139/85	R.H. Kempf v. Staatsecretaris van Justitie [1986] ECR 1741	275, 412, 515
221/85	Commission v. Kingdom of Belgium [1987] ECR 719	296, 443
281, 283, 284, 285 and		
287/85	Federal Republic of Germany and Others v. Commission [1987] ECR 3203	348, 507
293/85	Commission v. Kingdom of Belgium [1988] ECR 305	407
309/85	Bruno Barra v. Belgian State and City of Liège [1988] ECR 355	407
316/85	Centre public d'aide sociale de Courcelles v. Marie Christine Lebon [1987] ECR 2811	231, 276, 321, 411, 417, 418
352/85	Bond van Adverteerders and Others v. the Netherlands State [1988] ECR 2085	283, 465
372, 373 and		
374/85	Ministère public v. Oscar Traen and Others [1987] ECR 2141	328
427/85	Commission v. Federal Republic of Germany [1988] ECR 1123	283, 442
12/86	Meryem Demirel v. Stadt Schwäbisch Gmünd [1987] ECR 3719	254, 255-267, 269, 271, 485, 491, 492, 496
24/86	Vincent Blaizot v. University of Liège and Others [1988] ECR 379	273, 407, 409, 422
39/86	Sylvie Lair v. Universität Hannover [1988] ECR 3161	407, 409, 410, 411, 412, 413, 414, 424, 425, 517
45/86	Commission v. Council [1987] ECR 1493 ('General Tariff Preferences')	253
49/86	Commission v. Italian Republic [1987] ECR 2995	443
63/86	Commission v. Italian Republic [1988] ECR 29	441
80/86	Criminal proceedings against Kolpinghuis Nijmegen BV [1987] ECR 3969	451
147/86	Commission v. Hellenic Republic [1988] ECR 1637	407, 442
197/86	Steven Malcolm Brown v. Secretary of State for Scotland [1988] ECR 3205	407, 409, 411, 412, 414, 423, 425, 517

222/86	Union nationale des entraîneurs et Cadres techniques profession els du football (Unectef) v. Georges Heylens and Others [1987] ECR 4097	272, 275, 278, 331, 451, 468
249/86	Commission v. Federal Republic of Germany [1989] ECR 1263	264
256/86	Maria Frascogna v. Caisse des dépôts et consignations [1987] ECR 3431	488
263/86	Belgian State v. René Humbel and Marie Thérèse Humbel, née Edel [1988] ECR 5365	407, 419, 420, 423
289/86	Vereniging Happy Family Rustenburgerstraat v. Inspecteur der Omzetbelasting, Amsterdam [1988] ECR 3669	366
292/86	Claude Gullung v. Conseil de l'Ordre des avocats du barreau de Colmar et de Saverne [1988] ECR 111	283, 296, 442
36/87	Commission v. Hellenic Republic [1988] ECR 4415	443
42/87	Commission v. Kingdom of Belgium [1988] ECR 5445	407
81/87	The Queen v. H.M. Treasury and Commissioners of Inland Revenue, ex parte Daily Mail and General Trust PLC [1988] ECR 5483	461, 463-471
143/87	Christopher Stanton and SA belge d'assurances l'Étoile 1905 v. Inasti (Institut national d'assurances sociales pour travailleurs indépendants) [1988] ECR 3877	283
154 and 155/87	Rijksinstituut voor de Sociale Verzekering der Zelfstandigen (RSVZ) v. Heinrich Wolf and NV Microtherm Europe and Others [1988] ECR 3897	283
186/87	Ian William Cowan v. Trésor Public [1989] ECR 195	273, 338, 418, 519
235/87	Annunziata Matteuci v. Communauté française of Belgium and commissariat général aux relations internationales of the Communauté française of Belgium [1988] ECR 5589	410, 518
242/87	Commission v. Council [1989] ECR 1425 (Erasmus)	407, 423
302/87	European Parliament v. Council [1988] ECR 5615 (Comitology)	253
305/87	Commission v. Hellenic Republic [1989] ECR 1461	273, 441
321/87	Commission v. Kingdom of Belgium [1989] ECR 997	339, 357, 519
344/87	I. Bettray v. Staatssecretaris van Justitie [1989] ECR 1621	276, 411
389 and 390/87	G.B.C. Echternach and A. Moritz v. Netherlands Minister for Education and Science [1989] ECR 723	407, 415, 416
427/85	Commission v. Federal Republic of Germany [1988] ECR 1154	448
5/88	Hubert Wachauf v. Federal Republic of Germany [1989] ECR 2609	264
33/88	Pilar Allué and Carmel Mary Coonan v. Universitàdegli Studi di Venezia [1989] ECR 1591	282
C-54/88, C-91/88 and C-14/89	Criminal Proceedings against Eleonora Nino and others [1990] ECR 3537	443
68/88	Commission v. Hellenic Republic [1989] ECR 2965	21, 359
C-70/88	European Parliament v. Council [1990] ECR I-2041 (Chernobyl)	253
114/88	Patrick Delbar v. Caisse d'allocation familiales de Roubaix-Tourcoing [1989] ECR 4067	442

C-143/88 and
C-92/89   Zuckerfabrik Süderdithmarschen AG v. Hauptzollamt Itzehoe
                    and Zuckerfabrik Soest v. Hauptzollamt Paderborn
                    [1991] ECR I-415   331
C-236/88   Commission v. French Republic [1990] I-3163   518
C-265/88   Criminal proceedings against Lothar Messner ECR [1989] 4209   218, 519
C-297/88 and
C-197/89   Massam Dzodzi v. Belgian State [1990] ECR I-3763   218, 366, 505
C-61/89   Criminal proceedings against Marc Gaston Bouchoucha
                    [1990] ECR I-3551   443
C-68/89   Commission v. Kingdom of the Netherlands, Judgment of
                    30 May 1991, not yet reported   218, 231, 338,
                                                                             339, 357
113/89   Rush Portuguesa LDA Srl v. Office National d'Immigration
                    [1990] ECR I-417   356, 475, 479-
                                                                             483, 485, 490,
                                                                             491, 504
C-154/89   Commission v. French Republic [1991] ECR I-659   282
C-180/89   Commission v. Italian Republic [1991] ECR I-709   282
C-188/89   A. Foster and Others v. British Gas plc [1990] ECR I-3313   328
C-192/89   S.Z. Sevince v. Staatssecretaris van Justitie
                    [1990] ECR I-3461   256, 258, 265,
                                                                             266, 288, 348,
                                                                             485, 491, 492,
                                                                             493
C-198/89   Commission v. Hellenic Republic [1991] ECR I-727   282
C-213/89   The Queen v. Secretary of State for Transport, ex parte
                    Factortame Ltd and Others [1990] ECR I-2433   331
C-260/89   Elliniki Radiophonia Tiléorassi AE v. Dimotiki, Eteria
                    Pliroforisis, Sotirios Kouvelas, Judgment of 18 June 1991,
                    not yet reported   252, 264, 275
C-288/89   Stichting Collectieve Antennevoorziening Gouda and Others,
                    Nederlandse Vereniging voor Erkende Reclame Adviesbureaux
                    v. Commissariaat voor de Media, Judgment of 25 July 1991,
                    not yet reported   283
C-292/89   The Queen v. The Immigration Appeal Tribunal, ex parte
                    Gustaff Desiderius Antonissen [1991] ECR I-745   218, 231, 276,
                                                                             284, 287, 474
294/89   Commission v. French Republic, Judgment of 10 July 1991,
                    not yet reported   448
C-308/89   Carmina di Leo v. Land Berlin, Judgment of 13 November 1990,
                    not yet reported   408, 416, 417,
                                                                             518
C-340/89   Irene Vlassopoulou v. Ministerium für Justiz, Bundes- und
                    Europaangelegenheiten Baden-Württemberg, judgment of
                    7 May 1991, not yet reported   272, 277, 278
C-343/89   Max Witzemann v. Hauptzollamt München-Mitte
                    [1990] ECR I-4477   366
C-353/89   Commission v. Kingdom of the Netherlands, Judgment of
                    25 July 1991, not yet reported   283, 366
C-357/89   V.J.M. Raulin v. Minister for Education and Science, Judg-
                    ment of 26 February 1992, not yet reported   414, 424, 425
C-363/89   Danielle Roux v. Belgian State, Judgment of 5 February 1991,
                    not yet reported   279, 357

C-3/90	M.J.E. Bernini v. Minister for Education and Science, Judgment of 26 February 1992, not yet reported	413, 414, 415, 417
C-6/90 and		
C-9/90	Andrea Francovich v. Italian Republic, Bonifaci v. Italian Republic, Judgment of 19 November 1991, not yet reported	291
C-10/90	Maria Masgio v. Bundesknappschaft, Judgment of 7 March 1991, not yet reported	273
C-18/90	Office national de l'emploi (Onem) v. Bahia Kziber [1991] ECR 1-199	204, 228, 348, 485, 494, 495, 496
C-76/90	Manfred Säger v. Dennemeyer & Co Ltd, Judgment of 25 July 1991, not yet reported	283
C-159/90	The Society for the protection of Unborn Children Ireland Limited v. Stephen Grogan and others, Judgment of 4 October 1990, not yet reported	252, 264, 275
C-204/90	Hans-Martin Bachmann v. Belgian State, Judgment of 28 January 1992, not yet reported	455, 471
C-295/90	European Parliament v. Council, Judgment of 7 July 1992, not yet reported	338, 424, 515
C-300/90	Commission v. Kingdom of Belgium, Judgment of 28 January 1992, not yet reported	455

GENERAL INDEX

(The footnotes were not indexed)

Accession of UK and Ireland to the EC (1972), 203

Accession of Greece to the EC (1979), 288, 479-480, 536

Accession of Spain and Portugal to the EC (1985), 216-220, 288, 479-480, 490-491, 536

Adjudication on immigration matters in the UK and Ireland, 211-213, 229-230

Aliens, 10-11, 13-14, 34, 53-57, 64, 125-153, 177-188, 193, 196, 201-202, 205-208, 210, 227-232, 236, 238-239, 241-242, 246-247, 248-251, 253, 263, 265, 289, 294-295, 298-304, 309, 311, 313, 322-327, 330, 358, 377, 395, 397-398, 401, 497-498, 507, 510, 512-513, 516

Aliens, admission of —, 11, 13, 20, 33, 55-56, 174, 183-188, 190, 239 192-193, 197, 200, 243, 299, 301, 309, 314-315, 318, 324, 487, 532

Aliens, illegal —, 23, 43, 51, 137-138, 141, 149, 160-161, 164, 181, 184, 187, 192-193, 207, 217, 225, 236, 373, 499

Aliens, law on —, 11, 22, 166, 183-185, 192, 198, 199, 207, 210, 213-214, 217, 219-220, 222, 224, 229, 231, 301-304, 307, 312, 315-317, 359, 487, 498, 531

Aliens, policy on —, 12, 33, 190, 239, 353, 358, 360-361

Association agreements (of the EC), 204, 255-259, 264-266, 288, 348, 370, 386, 483, 492-493, 496

Asylum, 13-15, 19, 29, 38, 44, 53-54, 135, 138, 142, 144-146, 153, 163, 166-168, 171-173, 175-182, 185, 188-190, 192, 195-196, 227, 239-240, 247, 299-300, 302, 312, 314-317, 332, 344-346, 350, 352-353, 359, 372-373, 375, 387, 397, 399-400, 499, 503, 527-529

Asylum, refugees and stateless persons (CAHAR), Ad Hoc Committee of experts on the legal aspects of territorial —, 14, 163, 170, 197, 344

Asylum, concept of the country of first —, 163, 196, 316, 530

Asylum, application for —, 13-15, 19, 54, 152, 163, 170-171, 173-177, 188-190, 196-197, 212, 225, 230, 316, 332, 340, 344, 349, 377, 526-528, 530

Asylum, right of —, 117, 143-146, 163, 174, 194, 225, 230, 239-241, 300, 340, 384, 387, 527-528

Asylum policy, 15, 24-26, 28, 197, 298-299, 336, 365-366, 373, 377

Asylum policy/law, harmonisation of —, 15, 24-25, 189-191, 193, 195-197, 318, 349, 350, 365-366, 373, 377, 530-531

'Asylum shopping', 173, 177, 185, 189, 531

Benelux, 5, 13, 31-39, 62, 86, 93-94, 109, 171, 191-192, 227, 318, 339, 344, 382, 393, 398, 500, 510, 523-524

Benelux Court of Justice, 31, 34-35, 38, 393, 523, 538

Border controls, 5-26, 27-30, 43-45, 50-51, 93-94, 99-114, 223-225, 510-511, 525, 531, 539

Border controls, abolition of —, 5-26, 27-30, 31-39, 43-45, 51, 104, 106, 108-109, 112, 184-185, 187-188, 191-194, 216, 222, 235, 318, 335-336, 339-340, 344-345, 347-349, 352-356, 358, 361, 367, 380, 383-385, 392, 503, 511, 513, 523, 531

Borders/Frontiers, external —, 6-8, 10-14, 22-25, 27, 31, 33, 34, 43-45, 50-51, 63-64, 68, 112-114, 171-172, 184-186, 188, 191-193, 216, 250, 336, 340, 342-346, 348, 353, 360, 376, 379, 384, 388, 392, 395-396, 398, 510, 525

Bundeskriminalamt, 82-83, 89

'Cassis de Dijon' doctrine, 282-283

Carriers' liability, 137-138, 179-180

Citizens, rights of non —, 227

Citizenship, British —, 205-206

Citizenship, Commonwealth —, 205-207, 213

Citizenship, EC/Community —, 20, 250-251, 390, 408, 420, 516

Citizenship, European —, 216-217, 221-222, 249, 428-429, 499, 502

Citizenship, Irish —, 205-206

Circulation, right/freedom of —, 13-14, 33-34, 184-185, 187-188, 192-193, 195, 216, 224, 266, 335-337, 342-344, 348-349, 464, 500

Colonial ties, 36, 158, 169, 205, 230

Comité Européen pour la Lutte Anti-Drogue (CELAD), 112, 337, 343-344

Common area of travel (U.K. and Ireland), 200, 213-214, 227

'Communitization', 75-76, 81-88, 230-231

Community framework, 364-367

Companies, *see* Legal persons

Competence, European Community —, 6, 19-22, 28, 93-96, 169-170, 181, 194-195, 258, 335-336, 347-349, 352-355, 359-364, 367, 383, 389-390, 421, 430, 497, 504-505, 507, 508-509

Cooperation agreements (of the EC), 204, 228, 492, 494-495

Coordinators, Group of —; set up by the December 1988 Rhodos European Council, 22, 29-30, 112, 195, 337, 342-343, 346, 351, 382, 392-394

Council of Europe, 49-50, 65-66, 78, 94, 113, 135, 154-165, 170, 191, 197-198, 203, 205, 337, 341, 343-344, 350, 398, 402, 529-530

Council of Ministers [European Communities], 371, 381, 387-388

Council of State, opinion of Dutch — on the Schengen Convention, 9, 52-53, 175-177, 180, 318, 380, 388, 396, 527

Crime, international —, 61, 70-73, 77, 81-83, 84-85, 88, 92-93, 95, 342, 349

Criminal justice, cooperation on —, 7-8, 10, 16-18, 21, 26, 45-49, 25-26, 63-69, 70-74, 75-92, 93-96

Criminal law, 93-96

Criminal law, harmonisation of —, 7, 10, 17-18, 25, 44, 64-65, 71, 73-74, 82

Customs cooperation, 66, 99-114, 350

Custom's Mutual Assistance Group 1992 (MAG '92), 99, 112-113, 337, 342-343

Data protection, 18-19, 46-50, 52-57, 71, 73, 113, 187, 397-398, 526

Declaration by the Governments of the Member States [EC] on the Free Movement of Persons, Political —, 380, 383, 386, 509

Democratic control, 73, 85, 182, 369, 373, 378-379, 396, 401

Democratic deficit, 182, 364, 400-401

Direct applicability, 204, 315, 318, 441-442

Direct effect, 20, 221, 253-254, 259-261, 264-266, 273-275, 291-292, 328, 358, 365, 396, 452, 458, 464, 473, 484, 491-493, 496, 535

Diplomas, recognition of —, 116, 277-278, 407, 437-438, 441, 443-447, 449

Discrimination, 161-162, 177-178, 181, 204, 229-231, 244, 250, 254, 262, 262, 265, 273-274, 282, 288-289, 290, 292-293, 297, 321, 324, 380, 392, 409, 420-422, 424-425, 431, 437

Discrimination, cont.,
438, 441, 473, 481, 487-488, 490, 494-495, 497, 500, 504, 512-513, 517, 532, 540-543

Discrimination, reverse —, 178-179, 288-289, 541

Drugs, 10, 17-18, 45, 50, 72, 78, 87-89, 94, 100-103, 106-114, 160-161, 339-340, 342, 343, 350, 382, 383, 508-509

Duty-free, 104, 121

Education, 112, 142, 158, 277, 287, 298, 405-426, 431-433, 441, 444-447, 449, 488, 495, 502, 508, 517-518, 531

Employees, 116, 128, 194, 291, 293, 433, 457, 460, 472, 474-486, 489, 496, 506

Establishment, freedom/right of —, 24, 116, 218, 220, 281, 283, 291-292, 295, 297, 338, 355, 357, 381, 427, 437-440, 443-444, 447-449, 451-458, 462-466, 468-470, 473, 476, 500, 504, 513

European Committee for Legal Cooperation, 156, 344

European Commission [European Communities], 9, 21, 27, 29, 72, 75, 82, 87, 91-92, 101, 103, 113, 199, 237, 254, 260, 266, 268-270, 285, 306, 316, 317, 324, 336, 339-340, 342-343, 345-346, 350, 352, 363-364, 379-389, 393, 402, 406-407, 428-436, 447, 497-499, 506-508, 524, 536-537, 544

European Commission of Human Rights, 191, 198, 238-245, 326

European Council, 23, 75, 80, 88, 195, 347, 353, 524

European Court of Human Rights, 71, 191, 198, 238-245, 299, 305, 321, 326, 435, 484

European Drugs Intelligence Unit (EDIU), 72-73, 101-102, 342

European Parliament, 51, 92, 270, 294, 343, 347, 350, 364, 371, 373, 380, 382, 385, 390, 393, 399-400, 402, 430-431, 434, 436, 497-498, 516, 524, 537

European Political Cooperation, 22, 80, 336, 341, 389

European Political Union (EPU), 20, 76, 88, 91, 93, 194, 337, 345, 349, 351

Europol, 72-73, 75, 82-84, 85, 88-92, 102, 526

Excise, 100, 103-105, 117, 122

Expulsion, 13, 14-15, 55, 132, 136-138, 176-178, 182, 190, 196, 202, 217, 220, 236-247, 268, 271-270, 280, 291, 293, 299-305, 309-318, 324, 326, 373, 395, 397, 442, 487, 527, 543-544

Extradition, 7, 16-17, 38, 45, 47, 53, 64, 66, 70, 117, 127, 136, 143-148, 150, 155, 237-241, 244-245, 289-290, 319, 341, 353, 384

Family life, right to –, 55, 57, 133-134, 239, 243-246, 255, 270, 288-289, 298, 300, 305-311, 313-314, 321-324, 326, 414-418, 431-432, 495-496
Firearms, 10, 17-18, 22, 94, 45, 47, 72, 103, 106, 339, 392, 523-524
Fiscal aspects, 29, 64, 99-100, 103-106, 111-112, 114, 115-122, 202, 290, 292-293, 297, 342, 450, 453-456, 460-463, 465-466, 470-471, 537
'four freedoms', 20, 28, 30, 43, 102, 115-116, 335, 347, 358, 370, 379, 384, 501
Fraud, 71, 73, 104-105, 467-469
Frontiers/Borders, external –, see Borders/Frontiers
Frontiers, draft Convention on the External –, 23, 68, 340, 345, 353, 356, 366, 395-396, 398

GATT (General Agreement on Tariffs and Trade), 260, 365, 483
Germany, consequences of the unification (1990) of –, 44, 156, 392
Goods, controls on –, 10, 37-38, 43, 50, 99-100, 102, 106-108, 111-112
Goods, free movement of –, 32, 103, 106, 115, 263, 283, 347, 358, 360, 373, 384, 450-451, 458, 468, 501, 534
Group on Legal Cooperation, 336, 382
Gypsies, 36, 156, 161-162, 178, 499

Identity cards/documents, 36, 46-47, 158, 160-161, 180, 186, 188, 225, 289, 439, 470, 473-474, 500, 519
Immigration, 6-8, 10-11, 20-26, 28, 36, 43, 55, 62, 68, 107, 110-113, 117, 142, 149, 161-163, 166-169, 178, 185, 188, 190, 192, 195, 199-200, 205-214, 218-219, 222-223, 225, 228-232, 239, 241, 244, 246, 249-251, 254, 289, 298-299, 302-303, 308, 310, 317-318, 319-320, 332, 339-340, 343, 346, 350, 352-353, 358-361, 373, 376, 382, 388, 392-393, 397-402, 431-432, 496, 497-499, 502-503, 506-509, 516, 528
Immigration, Ad Hoc Group on –, 22, 112, 195, 336, 339-340, 343, 382, 393, 498
Inhuman(e) treatment, 55, 239-241, 243, 312-313
Integration, economic –, 6, 23, 31, 32, 427
Integration, political –, 32, 115

Integration, social –, 6, 23-24, 26, 191, 185, 191, 410, 413, 415-416, 498, 502-504, 507-508
Intergovernmental, 71, 77, 80, 89-90, 94-95, 155-157, 168, 170, 181-182, 194-195, 197-198, 335-337, 342-343, 345-346, 349-353, 362-364, 367, 369-372, 380-381, 383, 385, 387-391, 393-395, 397-401, 498, 509, 524, 528
Intergovernmental conference (on European Political Union) (1991), 345, 516
Intergovernmental cooperation, 195, 232, 318, 336-337, 342, 346, 349-351, 385, 389, 393, 524, 533, 537, 539-540
Internal market, 5, 20-21, 24-25, 38, 43, 61, 63, 93, 99, 100, 102-106, 110, 112, 114, 115-117, 121-122, 168-170, 193, 232, 335-336, 340, 342, 345-348, 351-355, 357, 359-361, 367, 370, 379, 381, 383, 384-385, 391, 394, 406, 426, 448, 497, 499, 501-504, 508, 510-511, 519-520, 525, 531, 539-540
Interpol, 47, 66, 70, 75-80, 82-90, 92

Judicial assistance, 7, 10, 16-18, 21-22, 25, 341
Judicial cooperation, 8, 16-17, 63, 69, 94

Languages, draft European Charter for Regional or Minority –, 157, 529-530
Leave a country, right to –, 235-236
Legal persons, 116, 427, 449-471, 478, 480, 493, 537
Local and Regional Authorities, Standing Conference of –, 157, 530
Lomé Convention, 492-494
Luxembourg non-paper, draft Treaty on the European Political Union (1991), 222, 232, 346-347, 352, 370, 374, 516

Maastricht, Treaty/Summit of –, 72, 249, 387, 389, 471
Migrant workers, 120, 162, 165, 256, 259, 262, 265-266, 268-269, 271, 279, 322, 406, 409, 413, 416, 488-489, 499, 507, 513, 516-518, 529, 543
Migration policy, 402, 506-507
Migration, European Committee on –, (CDMG), 197
Minorities, 133, 157, 190, 375, 391, 529-530
Minorities, draft European Convention for the protection of –, 157, 529-530
Missing persons, 72, 161

National courts, 221, 228, 253, 255, 267, 270, 272-285, 286-297, 298, 302, 305-307, 311, 317, 322, 393, 402, 465, 469, 487, 505, 529, 533, 535-536, 538-539

Nationality, aspects of —, 74, 116, 120, 126, 135, 140, 145, 155-158, 161-162, 167, 169, 162, 177, 199, 201-202, 204-206, 208, 217, 223, 225, 229-230, 250-251, 262, 265, 273, 281, 283, 288, 291-293, 314, 321, 347, 380, 409, 420-422, 424, 426, 428, 430-431, 433, 435, 437-438, 440-441, 452-453, 473, 486-491, 492, 494-496, 498, 500, 505, 509, 510, 513, 520

Nationals, 203-204

Non-EC nationals, *see* Third country nationals

Nordic countries/cooperation, 5, 13, 22, 61-69, 81, 85, 227-228

Ordre public, *see* Public order

'Palma' document, 28-30, 91, 195, 343, 353, 392, 394, 524

Penises, tiger —, 109

Pensioners, 322, 379, 381, 416, 433-435, 486, 494, 543

Police cooperation, 7-8, 10, 16-18, 22, 25-26, 61-62, 64-69, 72, 75-92, 94, 112, 344, 349, 389, 398-399, 402, 525-526

Privacy, 10, 16, 22, 43-51, 52-53, 57, 113, 321, 353, 373, 539

Private life, 55, 57, 245, 309, 533

Proportionality, 56, 283-284, 321, 326, 357-358, 367, 468, 539

Public order, 7-8, 12, 33, 53-55, 80, 130, 137, 158, 161, 186-188, 202, 236, 245-246, 294, 322-323, 329-330, 342, 357, 387, 479, 532, 542-543

Public policy, 105-106, 202, 217, 224, 228, 232, 262-263, 265, 278-282, 284, 294-295, 358-359, 381, 438-439, 442, 450, 452, 459, 460, 467-468, 507, 534, 539

Pursuit, trans/cross-border —, 37, 44, 113

Pursuit, hot —, 10, 17, 38, 68, 72-73, 86, 93, 109

Refoulement, 15, 137, 143, 145, 176-178, 181, 196, 526

Refugees, 10, 15, 18-19, 23, 34, 130, 135, 138, 139-146, 149, 151-153, 158-159, 162-164, 166-170, 173-178, 180-181, 194, 196-197, 200-203, 205, 209, 212, 225, 230, 238, 240, 300-304, 316, 318, 338, 366, 375-376, 379, 397, 485, 505, 508, 526-528, 531

Refugee status, 14, 117, 138-146, 148, 174, 152-153, 163, 176-177, 188-190, 196-197, 199-200, 203, 205, 225-226, 228, 230, 300, 314, 316, 318, 343, 384, 527-529

'Refugees in orbit', 173, 178, 189, 195

Remain, right to —, 116, 146, 207, 229, 237, 242, 271, 488, 533, 543

Retired persons, *see* Pensioners

Residence, right of —, 130-131, 188, 222, 254, 267-270, 288, 335, 338, 355, 381, 419, 424, 428-435, 488, 493, 499-500, 515-516, 541, 543-544

Residence permit, 11, 13-14, 56, 64, 129-134, 136-137, 149-151, 167, 173, 188, 219, 229, 231, 238-239, 288, 291, 300-301, 303, 307, 309-313, 326-327, 330, 391, 433, 474, 477, 479, 543

Rule of law, 78, 95, 362, 401, 462

Rule of reason, 282-284, 456, 468, 471, 534-535

Saarbrücken, Agreement of — (1984), 9, 36-37, 43, 86, 344

Schengen Information System (SIS), 12, 16, 18, 43-51, 52-53, 55-57, 68, 71, 87, 93, 109, 223, 232, 344, 373, 377, 525-526

Security, national —, *see* Public order

Self-employed persons, 116, 277-278, 335, 338, 379-381, 427-428, 430, 433-434, 437-439, 446, 451-452, 474-475, 486-487, 489

Services, freedom to provide —, 281-283, 338, 347, 418-419, 437-440, 443-444, 449, 472-483, 486, 489-491, 496, 504, 506, 534-536

Single (European) Market, *see* Internal market *and* White Paper

Social assistance, 23, 225, 231, 424, 433-434

Social security, 162, 190, 202, 204, 222, 228, 236, 292-293, 297, 338, 413, 429, 432-435, 439, 453, 456-457, 470, 488-490, 494-495, 500, 505, 515, 527, 530-531, 544

Sovereignty of the Member States, 5, 8, 70, 161, 197, 369-371, 375-376, 405, 497, 507-509

Spouse, rights of —, 132, 134, 151, 256, 267-271, 288, 321-323, 420-421, 430-431, 433, 435, 487-489, 492, 496, 505, 516-517, 541-543

Stateless persons, 125-126, 135, 156, 161-162, 485, 499, 505

Students, 122, 290, 322, 338, 355, 379, 381, 405-414, 417-436, 486, 500, 508, 515-518, 543-544

Subsidiarity, principle of —, 95, 362, 407

Supremacy of Community law, 204, 221, 263, 472

Supremacy of international law, 157

Taxes, *see* Fiscal aspects

Terrorism, 36, 79-80, 94-95, 106-107, 148, 160, 340-343, 353, 372, 382-383, 509

Third country nationals (*see also* Aliens), 7, 13, 20-26, 54, 169, 195, 223, 238, 252, 254, 332, 379, 389, 392, 397, 430-431, 435, 479, 485-486, 489-492, 495, 497-506, 508-511, 512-513, 519-520, 540

Transit, 110, 137, 152, 187-188, 192-193, 195, 225

TREVI, 22, 61-62, 65-69, 72, 75-80, 84-85, 89-92, 101, 112-113, 337, 342-343, 382

United Nations, 78, 239, 337, 345, 398

United Nations High Commissioner for Refugees (UNHCR), 141, 173, 176, 179-181, 189, 197, 225, 527, 529-530

VAT, 29, 100, 103-105, 117-118

Visa, 13-14, 24, 36, 127-129, 150, 171, 173, 185-187, 193, 203, 211, 223-225, 315, 318, 326, 330, 352-353, 359, 376, 382, 391, 473, 503, 523

Visa, common —, 12-13, 33

Visa application, 50, 393

Visa policy, 7, 10-12, 22, 24, 35, 37-38, 44, 64, 117, 193, 223, 298, 336, 340, 346, 348, 350, 384, 398, 497, 523

Visa requirements, 11-12, 29, 36, 44, 186, 224, 340, 343

Vocational training, 422-426

Weapons, *see* Firearms

White Paper on the Single Market, 91, 99, 115-118, 120, 169, 194, 352-354, 359, 381, 383-384, 387-388, 394, 506

Workers (*see also* Employees), 21, 116, 120-121, 133, 162, 164-165, 170, 203-204, 218-220, 227, 232, 250, 255-262, 265-272, 275-276, 278-279, 282, 286-293, 321-322, 335, 338, 347, 335, 356-357, 370, 379-380, 385, 392, 406, 408-421, 426-428, 430, 433-434, 439, 446, 468-469, 472-483, 487-496, 499, 501-508, 513, 515-520, 529, 533-534, 536-537, 543

LIST OF PARTICIPANTS

H.S.J. Albers, University of Leiden, Leiden

W. Alexander, Barents & Krans, Advocaten, The Hague

Th. Antoniou, University of Athens, Athens

A. Arnull, Court of Justice, Luxembourg

H.A.H. Audretsch, Europa Instituut, Utrecht

P.J. Baauw, University of Utrecht, Utrecht

M.H. Bastiaans, T.M.C. Asser Instituut, The Hague

L.A.N.M. Barnhoorn, T.M.C. Asser Instituut, The Hague

P.T. Benschop, Advies Commissie Vreemdelingen, The Hague

E.M.L. Blanco, T.M.C. Asser Instituut, The Hague

P. Boeles, Everaert c.s., Lawyers, Amsterdam

J.J. Bolten, University of Utrecht, Utrecht

M. Bonn, Ministry of Justice, The Hague

J.M. Bonnes, Catholic University of Brabant, Tilburg

J.H.M. van Bonzel, Ministry of Foreign Affairs, The Hague

E.C.A.M. Boot, Utrecht

J. Borgesius, Judge Court of Appeal, Aerdenhout

M. van den Brink, Member European Parliament, Utrecht

E.R. Brouwer, University of Amsterdam, Amsterdam

O.W. Brouwer, Stibbe, Blaisse & De Jong, Lawyers, Brussels

M.R. Brown, H.M. Customs and Excise, London

W. Bulterman, Attorney at Law, Laren

F. Capelli, University of Parma, Parma

A. Carnelutti, Institute of Political Studies, Paris

I.G.F. Cath, Buruma & Maris, Lawyers, The Hague

F. van Craeyenest, Council of the European Communities, Brussels

P. Cullen, University of Edinburgh, Edinburgh

D. Curtin, Europa Instituut, Leiden

R. Czartoryski, Ambassy of Poland, The Hague

X. Denoël, University of Liège, Liège

A. Desmazières de Séchelles, Lawyer French Bar, Paris

H.W. Diender, University of Groningen, Groningen

P. van Dijk, Council of State, The Hague

A. Mc.Donnell, Europa Instituut, Leiden

J.P.H. Donner, Scientific Council for Government Policy, The Hague

M.C.E.M. Draaisma, Open University of Heerlen, Heerlen

A.M.A. Driessen, Ministry of Economic Affairs, The Hague

J. Th. Drop, Advies Commissie Vreemdelingen, The Hague

L.M. Ebbekink, Buruma & Maris, Lawyers, The Hague

T. Eijsbouts, University of Amsterdam, Amsterdam

R. Errera, Conseil d'Etat, Paris

S.M. Evers, Pels Rijcken & Droogleever Fortuyn, The Hague

J.J. Feenstra, Nauta Dutilh, Lawyers, Rotterdam

M.A. Fierstra, Court of Justice, Luxembourg

C. Fijnaut, Erasmus University, Rotterdam

A.R. Filius, Pels Rijcken & Droogleever Fortuyn, The Hague

C. Flinterman, University of Limburg, Maastricht

H. Fode, Ministry of Justice, Copenhagen

A. Fortescue, Commission of the EC, Brussels

C. Garbarino, University of Siena, Siena

J.P. Gardner, British Institute of International and Comparative Law, London

W.J.M. van Genugten, Catholic University of Brabant, Tilburg

W. van Gerven, Court of Justice, Luxembourg

R. Glaser, European Commission, The Hague

L.W. Gormley, University of Groningen, Groningen

C.A. Groenendijk, Catholic University of Nijmegen, Nijmegen

F. Grondman, Ministry of Finance, The Hague

J.H. Grosheide, Ministry of Justice, The Hague

H. Grotenhuis, Hogeschool Holland, sector HEAO, Diemen

J.C. van Haersolte, T.M.C. Asser Instituut, The Hague

L. Hancher, Erasmus University, Rotterdam

A.J.E. Havermans, Burgomaster The Hague, The Hague

A.W.B.M. Hendriks, Ministry of Finance, The Hague

D. Hoefnagel, Ministry of Education and Science, Zoetermeer

S. Hoedt, Martinus Nijhoff Publishers, Dordrecht

T.P. Hofstee, Ministry of Foreign Affairs, The Hague

F.W. Hondius, Council of Europe, Strasbourg Cedex

R.P. Hoogenboom, Council of State, The Hague

T. Hoogenboom, University of Amsterdam, Amsterdam

J.P. van Iersel, Member of Parliament of the Netherlands, The Hague

F.G. Jacobs, Court of Justice, Luxembourg

I. Jalles, Portuguese Bar, Lisboa

P.E.L. Janssen, University of Heerlen, Heerlen

E. Janssen, Ministry of Finance, The Hague

H.U. Jessurun d'Oliveira, European University Florence, Florence

C.D. de Jong, Ministry of Justice, The Hague

G.A.A. de Jong, Social Security Bank, Amsterdam

J.S. de Jongh, T.M.C. Asser Instituut, The Hague

C. Kann, Belmont Lawyers, Brussels

A.E. Kellermann, T.M.C. Asser Instituut, The Hague

L.A.D. Keus, Pels Rijcken & Droogleever Fortuyn, The Hague

R.A.A. Khan, University of Amsterdam, Amsterdam

P. Klinckhamers, Katholieke Universiteit, Leuven

T. Koopmans, Supreme Court, The Hague

A. Kosto, Ministry of Justice, The Hague

E.D.J. Kruijtbosch, Benelux Economic Union, The Hague

B.H. ter Kuile, De Brauw, Blackstone & Westbroek, The Hague

F. Kuitenbrouwer, NRC Handelsblad, Amsterdam

A. Kuyer, Nederlands Centrum voor Vreemdelingen, Utrecht

C.W. Kuijpers, De Nederlandse Bank, Amsterdam

R.H. Lauwaars, University of Amsterdam, Amsterdam

R. Lawson, Europa Instituut, Leiden

M. Lepoivre, Council of the EC, Brussels

W.M. Levelt-Overmars, Gemeenschappelijk Administratiekantoor, Amsterdam

J.A.H.M. van Lith, Catholic University of Brabant, Tilburg

J. Lonbay, Institute of European Law, Birmingham

J.P. Mead, Lawyer, London

G.W.A. van de Meent, Erasmus University, Rotterdam

A.P. van der Mei, University of Limburg, Maastricht

N.W. Meuter-Dikkers, European Movement, The Hague

P.A. Michael, Registration Chamber, Rijswijk

M.R. Mok, Supreme Court, The Hague

K.J.M. Mortelmans, University of Utrecht, Utrecht

C.E.M. Nispen tot Sevenaer, Barents & Krans, Lawyers, The Hague

D. O'Keeffe, Durham European Law Institute, Durham

Siofra O'Learly, European University of Florence, Dublin

J.H.A.M. Peek, Ministry of Justice, The Hague

G. Peeters, Legal Service Council EC, Brussels

J. Pertek, European Institute of Public Administration, Maastricht

R. Plender, Queens Chamber, Lawyers, London

L. Poffé, Ministry of Justice, The Hague

R.A. van der Pol, Pels Rijcken & Droogleever Fortuyn, The Hague

R. Podsiadlik, Embassy of Poland, The Hague

F. du Pré, Erasmus University, Rotterdam

S. Préchal, University of Amsterdam, Amsterdam

M. Puumalainen, Ministry of Justice, Helsinki

M. Raes, Adamson Associates, Lawyers, Brussels

K.K. Rasmussen, Permanent Representative at the EC for Denmark, Brussels

J.M. Reijntjes, University of Heerlen, Heerlen

M. de Rijke, Pels Rijcken & Droogleever Fortuyn, The Hague

G.J. de Roode, T.M.C. Asser Instituut, The Hague

A.E. Rosenboom, Martinus Nijhoff Publishers, Dordrecht

D. Ruimschotel, European University of Florence, Florence

B. Schattenberg, Bundeskriminalamt, Meckenheim

H.G. Schermers, University of Leiden, Leiden

L.C.J.P. Schillings, Ministry of Foreign Affairs, The Hague

H. Schneider, University of Limburg, Maastricht

A.A.M. Schrauwen, University of Amsterdam, Amsterdam

M. Schreuder-Vlasblom, Council of State, The Hague

E.C.R. Schut, Council of State, The Hague

J.J.E. Schutte, Ministry of Justice, The Hague

H.G. Sevenster, Europa Instituut, Leiden

K. Sevinga, Erasmus University, Rotterdam

W.J.T. Siegers, Heelsum

T. Sleeswijk Visser, Europa 2000, Nuenen

P.J. Slot, Europa Instituut, Leiden

B.W. Smagge, University of Groningen, Groningen

R.J. Smit, Ministry of Economic Affairs, The Hague

R. Smits, De Nederlandsche Bank NV, Amsterdam

J.A.M. Steenbergen, University of Leiden, Leiden

E. Steyger, University of Limburg, Maastricht

S.H. Storey, Howard Cohen & Co Solicitors, Leeds

H. Storey, University of Leeds, Leeds

A. Strootker, Benelux Economical Union, Brussels

A.H.J. Swart, Willem Pompe Instituut, Utrecht

H.C. Taschner, Commission of the EC, Brussels

A.M.M. Teubner, University of Groningen, Groningen

C.W.A. Timmermans, Commission of the EC, Brussels

S. Towle, European University Institute of Florence, Brussels

M. van Traa, Member of Parliament of the Netherlands, The Hague

J.J.M. Tromm, T.M.C. Asser Instituut, The Hague

P. Uiterlinden, Ministry of Foreign Affairs, Zoetermeer

D. Vaughan, Brick Court Chambers, Lawyers, London

R.B. van de Ven, T.M.C. Asser Instituut, The Hague

J. Verraes, Benelux Economic Union, Brussels

J.A.E. Vervaele, University of Utrecht, Utrecht

H. Verschueren, Universitaire Campus, Diepenbeek

C. Vincenzi, Huddersfield Polytechnic, Huddersfield

T. Vis, Education Council, The Hague

H. Visser, Nato Schiphol, Schiphol

T. Wade, T.M.C. Asser Instituut, The Hague

G. van der Wal, Barents & Krans, Lawyers, Brussels

E.M. Waller, KPMG Klijnveld, Amsterdam

J.S. Watson, Council of State, The Hague

J.H.H. Weiler, Michigan Law School, Michigan

H. van der Wel, Registration Chamber, Rijswijk

K.C. Wellens, Catholic University of Nijmegen, Nijmegen

E. Whiteford, Europa Instituut, Leiden

J.A. Winter, Free University of Amsterdam, Amsterdam

B.E.F.M. de Witte, University of Limburg, Maastricht

C.F. Wittebrood, Commission European Communities, Brussels

A. Woltjer, Ned. Centrum voor Vreemdelingen, Utrecht

J.W. de Zwaan, Ministry of Foreign Affairs, The Hague

The first session of the Asser Colloquium on European Law was held in 1972. The following is a list of sessions held since 1972:

23 March 1972	Uitvoering Gemeenschapsrecht in de Nederlandse rechtsorde
7 July 1972	Colloquium of law teachers
7 June 1973	Het onderwijs in het Recht van de Europese Gemeenschappen aan de Nederlandse Universiteiten en Hogescholen
6 September 1974	De verhouding tussen het onderwijs in het Europees Recht en het onderwijs in andere juridische vakken
11 September 1975	Rechten van de mens
9 September 1976	Plaats en taak van een Europees Parlement bij een verdere beleidsintegratie op sociaal-economisch gebied in Europa
9 September 1977	Externe betrekkingen van de Europese Gemeenschappen
7 September 1978	De Europese politieke samenwerking
6 September 1979	EEC-Comecon relations
5 September 1980	Uitvoering van het Gemeenschapsrecht in Nederland
4 September 1981	Europeesrechtelijke aspecten van consumentenbescherming
3 September 1982	De rol van de Europese Gemeenschappen in een Nieuwe Internationale Economische Orde
9 September 1983	EEG-Handelspolitiek en beschermende maatregelen tegen de invoer uit derde landen
7 September 1984	Gedifferentieerde integratie in de Europese Gemeenschappen
5/6 September 1985	Experiences and problems in applying the preliminary procedure of Article 177 EEC
5 September 1986	Legal aspects of technological development and cooperation in Europe
4 September 1987	Europees milieurecht: praktische problemen bij de totstandkoming en uitvoering
9 September 1988	Fraude in de Europese Gemeenschappen
8 September 1989	De economische en sociale samenhang in de EG - de Europese structuurfondsen
7 September 1990	Een Economische en Monetaire Unie (EMU) in Europa - juridische en constitutionele consequenties
12/13 September 1991	Free movement of persons in Europe - legal problems and experiences

MILNROW

BELFIELD

...or aries
books and more...

Please return/renew this item
by the last date shown.
Books may also be renewed by
phone or via the web.

Tel: 0845 121 2976

www.rochdale.gov.uk/libraries